Design Dictionary

Michael Erlhoff
Tim Marshall
(Eds.)

Design
Dictionary

Perspectives on Design Terminology

Birkhäuser
Basel · Boston · Berlin

Foreword BIRD

The understanding of design in general and the structure of scientific research in design inevitably leads to discussions of the central categories for design. Constructive debate and struggles for acceptance fuel such a process—a process that, as a sign of fruitful further refinement, can never be completely finished. It is well known that such a development, especially in design, cannot be addressed without obstacles and indeed dissent. Even within a single cultural or linguistic realm, the positions are supposedly irreconcilable. Any undertaking that attempts to create understanding across cultural and linguistic borders is that much more ambitious.

It is, after all, one of the principles of BIRD's work to promote understanding of important design categories and concepts internationally. The publication of a categorical dictionary thus naturally suggested itself. The members of BIRD agree that there can be different approaches to such a project; no approach, description, or explanation will remain undisputed. And just as there can be no unambiguous and conclusive definition of terms like "design research," for example—because, very much in keeping with the essence of design and by all means indebted to different approaches to explanation, they are constantly transforming—a dictionary of design can be no more, and no less, than the beginning of a process of understanding.

The *Design Dictionary* that Michael Erlhoff and Tim Marshall have compiled, which is being published simultaneously in German and English, is an important step in this context. The editors have managed to attract to their project authors from all over the world who have presented their contributions from a variety of perspectives and with an excellent grasp of their subjects that will enrich the discussion of design terms. We are expecting it to provoke contradiction—and indeed we desire that. Both the members of BIRD and the editors will welcome that in the spirit of enlivening the discussion.

Through its various publications, BIRD presents important positions in the context of design research. The *Design Dictionary* belongs to a series of publications of important reference works in books and anthologies in the original language and/or in translation in order to collect materials and points of reference that can enrich the international discussion of the development of design research. For the members of BIRD the point is to emphasize the diversity and heterogeneity of existing positions, to make the controversial character of a living debate on research clear, and to stimulate and promote further discussion.

Board of International Research in Design, BIRD

A DICTIONARY BEGINS WHEN IT NO LONGER
GIVES THE MEANINGS OF WORDS, BUT THEIR
TASKS.

Georges Bataille

Design in a Dictionary

The Editors' Comments

The idea to publish the *Design Dictionary* was based on our belief that there was a compelling need to more firmly establish a shared design language within, across, and beyond the multiple and disparate design practices. In other words, the book is intended to facilitate communication, discussion, and debate between the various groups that have a stake in the state of design today, whether they identify themselves as designers, manufacturers, managers, marketers, educators, or scholars. It is also intended to assist the general interested public—the users of design—in navigating the complex and varied objectives, methodologies, and technologies that are used to create the products and systems they use in their lives.

We gave serious thought to the linguistic categories and terminology that underpin design discourse today. That said, it became clear while working on the book that we had omitted a number of valuable terms. This fact will undoubtedly be the subject of critique by reviewers and readers alike, and we expect that the project will provoke as many questions as it will answers. We encourage this and only ask that you help us identify these gaps so that we may include worthy suggestions in the next edition.

Language is of course always in flux, and design itself is a highly dynamic domain. Consequently, the language of design can be infuriatingly broad and slippery, often evolving through a highly verbal discourse. This may account for why there have been few attempts to establish a design dictionary to date, and also why this one does not aspire to any definitive or dogmatic "truth." Instead, we have endeavored stylistically to balance a dictionary tone with the individual, uniquely authored voices and perspectives that make design such an exciting and vibrant practice.

The project became even more of an adventure the moment we decided to publish English and German language editions. This not only introduced the arduous task of comparing German and English terminology, but also complicated issues of context based upon what we found to be significant differences between Anglo-Saxon and Germanic philosophical frameworks. It also means—or so we hope—that the readers of the dictionary will approach the book from vastly different cultural outlooks. Consequently, it was essential—also challenging and ultimately inspiring—to invite authors of differing backgrounds and cultures to contribute. As a result, the dictionary is not only heterogeneous in style, but also documents various trends and, in certain cases, contradictions within the global design discourse. The depth and diversity of these perspectives will become evident if you navigate your way through the book as designed, using the indicated cross-references to guide you along certain lexical pathways.

We thank many people for contributing to the *Design Dictionary*. In particular, we express our deep debt of gratitude to the authors, who wrote excellent texts on very complex subjects under considerable time pressure. We thank BIRD publishing consultants and the people at Birkhäuser and Springer-Verlag, who did not always have such an easy task dealing with the editors.

We also must express our very great thanks to the expert and wonderful editorial and production assistants and in particular, Jen Rhee, Dorothea Facchini, Dirk Porten, and Arne Willée.

We hope the readers of this publication will find the following dialogue as exciting and inspiring as we do!

Michael Erlhoff
Tim Marshall

A

ACOUSTICS

→ *Sound Design*

ADDED VALUE

Added value is an implicit idea of worth that extends beyond the functional requirements or basic use of a product or service to satisfy (→) need. Added values communicate essential information about a company or (→) brand's culture, values, and attitude to consumers, and are therefore crucial to how they perceive and respond on an emotional level to branded products.

For example: a luxury sports car's added value may be to build male ego or afford the user particular status within a community; the purchase of certain brands of organic produce may come with the added value of promoting environmental (→) sustainability or animal rights protection; and wearing clothing from sweatshop-labor free fashion labels has the added value of supporting fair trade practices. It is particularly interesting to note how a product's added value might appeal to a consumer's personal values, and inspire him or her to be more environmentally or socially responsible (→ *Ethics*). Because added value not only promotes but encourages consumers to bond with brands, it is highly influential in product differentiation and consumer decision making. As a result, the concept of added value is becoming increasingly important within oversaturated markets in particular. KSP |

→ *Advertisement, Branding, Value*

ADVERTISEMENT

Advertisements are representations designed to affect and inform a market through knowledge of its needs and wants, over a form of mediated channels that result in an exchange of values.

A fifteenth-century definition of "advertisement" as "the turning of the mind to anything: attention, observation, heed" still seems appropriate for the twenty-first century when gaining attention for one's products has become exceedingly difficult with keen competition in most product categories, mature product lifecycles, and little product differentiation.

In the fifteenth century, advertisements were used in the creation of shop signs, the billboards of the time. Since few people were able to read, symbols and signs represented the product, service, skill, or craft within the store. Advertisements were in the form of announcements such as stagecoach schedules or classified ads seeking an exchange of information. Media consisted of outdoor advertisements which were posted in city centers, personal selling from wagons, and crafted signage of the day used by merchants to announce the products they were selling.

At the onset of the twenty-first century, an age bursting with new technologies and almost unlimited choice, products seek differentiation and so (→) branding has become an essential form of signage to connect the product more firmly with the consumer. The difference between products is no longer inherent in the product and its attributes, but in the benefits that accrue for the consumers when they purchase the product. Representations in the form of symbols, signs, icons, and imagery attempt to attract the targeted consumer through a prism of the individual's own culture, and their linguistic, social, and personal identity.

An advertisement is usually developed under the auspices of a marketing department and a creative team. The marketing group investigates and researches the market and develops a statistical and lifestyle profile of the potential target market, of the competition and the product's "unique selling proposition" (→ USP). This is then presented to the members of the creative team in the form of a creative platform. Typically, creative design fosters and maintains the connection between product and (→) brand, and advertisement and consumer. The goal is for the consumer to recall, immediately and in detail, the brand and its perceived attributes when presented with an advertisement.

Members of the creative team, known in the industry as "creatives," will use design methodologies such as (→) semiotics to convey meaning through sign or (→) symbol. However, aspirational styles of advertising lead to new signifiers as the consumer becomes part of the designed experience. Visual imagery with little text is needed for the advertisements in a Corona (→) campaign, for instance, in which the viewer looks through a window to a sun-drenched beach and two beach chairs facing the ocean. The only sign of a product is at one side where two frosted beers await the beachgoers. The brand invites the viewer to step in, pull up a chair, and be part of the experience.

Advertisements are part of the branding process and are seldom designed to stand alone; rather, they are intended to become part of a continuing conversation with the listener, viewer, or reader as they are going about their everyday lives (→ Corporate Identity). The most important aspect of this process is identifying with the target market (→ Target Group) and designing a media network that continues to sustain the consumer experience. With the exponential increase in numbers of people and products over the centuries, new (→) information industries have grown to collect market data that can then be analyzed and used in advertising design. The ability to know "the market" for a product has become complex, requiring research that not only reveals where consumers live, but why and how they live—that is their (→) values and (→) lifestyles. Today, fragmentation of audience and media due to an increasingly technological and mobile society has opened new avenues in (→) market research. Database management, along with other sciences as vast as economics and history and as diverse as anthropology and neuroscience, has emerged and joined the fields of demography, ethnography, and psychology, among others, to help one define target markets and understand their needs and wants. Since the 1990s, companies have been using a new form of brand research, Coolhunting, to seek out emerging (→) trends. The original goal was to make observations and predictions about fashion or design from the street in order to enhance a brand's "coolness" or "buzz." Companies have also begun to employ young undercover scouts from among their target demographics to provide intelligence, test products among selected segments and persuade adoption through peer networks. Most recently, companies have begun data mining blogs and using them as "tuning forks" to analyze the electronic musings and desires of millions. These new hunters are becoming the source, the medium, and the representation of brand communications, all of which can now change in a nanosecond.

Where applicable, advertisers use (→) need or motivational platforms to design and extend appeals and execution techniques in the development of advertisements. Abraham Maslow's "Hierarchy of Needs" is the best known of these platforms. It is depicted as a pyramid consisting of five levels: the four lower levels are grouped together as "deficiency needs" associated with physiological needs, while the top level is termed "growth needs" associated with psychological needs. While deficiency needs must be met, growth needs are continually shaping behavior. The basic concept is that the higher needs in this hierarchy, such as the needs associated with social recognition, self esteem, and actualization, only come into focus once all the needs that are lower down the pyramid, such as physiological and safety needs, are mainly or entirely satisfied. In affluent societies, promotional appeals are mostly based on social and self-esteem needs, which emphasize luxury and recognition by others. The goal of an advertisement is to design persuasive choices that involve either emotional and/or rational approaches.

Creatives use different hierarchical forms to help design the appeals and the structure of an advertisement. The first is the Foote, Cone & Belding (FCB) planning model. This is a four-part grid formed by two intersecting axes that examines product and consumer relationships. From here, creatives try to determine the promotional platform defined by the dimensions of thinking and feeling and the level of involvement required from the consumer in purchase decisions. Cars, new homes, and other complex products are defined as high involvement/thinking products that require an informative strategy compared with lower involvement/emotional products such as food, clothing, and confectionary.

Value attributes given to products are often embedded within the development of a copy platform. People use objects to set themselves apart from others (→ *Added Value*). Examples are luxury fashions or automobiles that promise to confer a special status and class with ownership. The Virgin brand has been endowed with the personality traits of its owner, Richard Branson—adventurous, individualistic, and nonconforming. Volkswagen attempts to humanize and personalize their Rabbit brand with campaigns such as the birds and bees "Multiply" commercial and, of course, the classic Beetle ads. Indeed, personalization is the buzzword of the twenty-first century. Companies often choose celebrities to be their spokespeople—to represent the brand and to imbue the products of that brand with the qualities seen to be intrinsic to that projected character. The two most important determinants of celebrity success are, firstly, the basic promise that the product/brand will benefit from its association with that celebrity, and, secondly, the relevance and credibility of the celebrity.

A second planning model used by designers when converting the strategy and the "unique differential" or "big idea" into an actual advertisement is called the Creative Pyramid. This helps focus on copy and art and its ability to move consumers through cognitive or "thinking" stages to affective or "feeling" stages of advertising. Whether the medium is print or electronic, the same structure is used within the visual and copy field; the advertisement seeks to gain interest, create desire, and close with an action such as a sale.

The creative process is not finished until a medium is chosen to carry the message to the end user or consumer. Advertisements are called commercials on television and radio and are defined by their time—fifteen, thirty, or sixty seconds. Other media such as newspapers and magazines have longer lives but lack the multimedia advantages of broadcast. Billboards and transit advertisements are designed as support media within advertising campaigns and all of the above are considered non-personal media. Direct personal forms are mail, telephone, in-person representation, and forms of digital interaction such as e-mail and rich media channels among others. More recently, a proliferation of advertisements has crossed the editorial boundaries drawn between commercial and factual advertising. They come disguised in editorial formats such as video news releases, infomercials, advertorials, docudramas, and various forms of product placement in television and films. Advertisements designed for one of these informative approaches, usually "how to" or testimonial appeals, may be part of an advertising campaign. Originally processed by viewers as fact or coincidence rather than as part of a persuasive discourse, a brand or product line may arouse negative feelings of incredulity and indignation when the deceit is exposed. Advertainment channels, which are specifically produced, multimedia, product presentations, have become popular to extend a commercial's life onto a corporate web site. These are clearly designed as advertising and do not provoke the ire of consumers to the same extent that formats such as infomercials, video news releases, and product placements do. Truthfulness in brand and advertising messages are of overriding importance in building relationships with and gaining the trust of the consumer market (→ Credibility). Corporate advertisements in the form of cause and advocacy appeals are on the rise to empower consumers to vote for their values in a sustainable brand relationship.

The type of medium selected is not only important within the (→) communications process but in dressing the advertisement in different vestments to suit the occasion. The mood, ambiance, and temporal properties of each medium are given careful attention, as are the reader, viewer, or listener profiles. For instance, the inability to reach a selected market could be the result of using media channels that are too congested. Television runs commercials one after another, with little time to process meaning, and so a potentially award-winning advertisement can fail to be decoded appropriately. Marshall McLuhan held that "the medium is the message"; that is, that content follows form, so the form in which one receives the message affects one's interpretation of it.

In conclusion, the key goals of any advertisement are the transmission of the message from the source to the target market; the identification of that target market with the values attributed to the advertised product, service, or idea; and the purchase or espousal of that product, service, or idea. The successful design of any advertisement, from the initial research stage to the selection and design of the medium, thus depends on how well the marketers understand the values of the communities they are targeting and how well the creatives are able to translate these values into a form that engages them. NS |

→ Corporate Identity, Strategic Design

Belch, G. E., and M. A. Belch. 2005. *Introduction to advertising and promotion: An integrated marketing communications perspective*. 5th ed. New York: McGraw Hill; Chicago: Irwin.
Moeran, B. 1999. *A Japanese advertising agency*. Honolulu: Hawaiian Univ. Press.
Mooij, M. K. de. 2005. *Global marketing and advertising: Understanding cultural paradoxes*. 2nd ed. Thousand Oaks, CA: Sage Publications.
Vakratsas, D., and T. Ambler. 1999. How advertising works: What do we really know? *Journal of Marketing* 63, no. 1: 26–43.

AERODYNAMICS

Aerodynamics analyzes and documents the behavior of air interacting with a solid body, traditionally through empirical research conducted in wind tunnels. It was first applied at the beginning of the twentieth century to study ways of increasing aircraft lift force and establishing the most streamlined forms.

In 1925, Paul Jaray (1889–1974) achieved a milestone in the automobile industry with close-to-the-ground designs inspired by the shape of a water drop, at that time considered the ideal natural streamlined form. These early developments in automobile aerodynamics were later refined by designers such as Wunibald Kamm (1893–1966), who demonstrated that the water drop form was actually relatively ineffective in reducing wind resistance (→ Automobile Design).

American (→) streamline design proved to be more about pseudo-aerodynamic stylistic (→) trends than about actually reducing drag, and its significance receded following the whimsical "rocket" designs of the 1950s. In the postwar era, by contrast, Luigi Colani (born 1928) designed the first vehicles and aircrafts in accordance with an aerodynamic principle inspired by (→) bionics. In the late 1960s, another attempt at creating an ideal streamlined form resulted in the discovery of the "v formation," which remains the most aerodynamically proven form today. PT |

AESTHETICS

The word "aesthetic" when used in a design context is usually loosely understood to be a synonym for "beauty" or "styling." If an aesthetics specific to design was to be developed, it would need to avoid being split into, first, a theory of beautiful objects and, second, a critique of aesthetic judgment, but that process has yet to begin. It would also have to be open to an aesthetic theory that abides by that, which reveals itself to be aesthetic in perception and experience.

The term "aesthetics" has become a catchphrase in almost every area of life since (→) postmodernism. The radical pluralism that followed the reassessment of the modernist movement traced diverse paths leading out of Modernism, with many subsequent political, social, technical, and aesthetic upheavals. In the process, the standard definitions (that had prevailed until the 1970s) of aesthetics as an objective discipline and a branch of philosophy themselves changed. It became essential to reformulate the (→) semantics of the word because of significant changes in the status of differing forms of knowledge, ways of life, and behavioral patterns. Today, aesthetics appears in various contexts with different meanings and emphases; even the plurality and scope of the word has become the subject of prolonged debate. Nevertheless, the most evident thing now about aesthetics is that there is no longer anything self-evident about it.

The recent revisions that attempt to reevaluate the established term are motivated by a focus on removing boundaries: first, by recalling the original Greek word *aisthesis* meaning (→) perception through the senses, and second, by expanding the scope of aesthetics beyond the arts to include fields like design. Yet, because a specifically formulated design aesthetic is lacking, the term is usually used in its colloquial sense in the context of design. That is to say: in advertising, marketing, (→) branding, and even elementary design (→) criticism, aesthetics is a loose synonym for "beautiful," "tasteful," or "inoffensive." Many who use the term "aesthetics" actually mean (→) "styling," or to identify what are assessed as the beautiful or ugly features of a certain object. The word "aesthetics" also implies an important aspect of the product's effect in relation to its material, social, political, ecological, and symbolic contexts.

The two aspects of aesthetics mentioned above are embedded in the historical development of the term. In the eighteenth century, there was a semantic shift from *aesthesis* to aesthetic, from sense perception in general to a focus on the arts in particular. And, thus, the word "aesthetics" gradually came to denote a branch of philosophy that focused on what set the beautiful apart, why we had such a category, and on the arts in general. As a result, products of the arts in European and non-European history, along with their associated theories, became aesthetic objects. Philosophy rejected the notion of aesthetics as a doctrine of sense perception because knowledge derived from the senses was, in the wake of the Enlightenment, largely considered contrary to rational knowledge, which was based on strict terms and definitions. Today, philosophy defines aesthetics as either a theory of sensory perception or a philosophical or sociological theory of art.

Put into simple terms, "aesthetics" deals with the question of whether (and, if so, in what manner) words such as "beautiful" or "ugly" can be applied to specific objects, or whether it is perhaps the sum of our personal and social idiosyncrasies that interprets something as beautiful or ugly. The aesthetic (→) value of an object is determined either by terms and definitions, or its particular sensory quality and what it represents in conjunction with the object's system of (→) symbols. "Aesthetic difference" implies the specific features of an object that qualify as aesthetic. It has also been argued that aesthetics is intrinsic to an (→) object. Empirical sciences such as experimental psychology disagree with this theory, maintaining that aesthetics is the attempt to understand the criteria that humans use to evaluate things as either beautiful or ugly—even those that are not a product of the arts.

Words such as (→) "beauty," however, were being used long before aesthetics was formulated into a philosophy. Homer, for example, who saw artistic creation as a productive, skilled work of God, spoke of beauty and harmony. Heraclitus defined beauty as the tangible, material quality of the real, whereas art, by copying nature, would be just the opposite; and in the Pythagoreans' cosmological and aesthetic philosophy, the theory of numbers and proportions plays a crucial role in beauty and harmony.

Socrates believed that the beautiful and the good coincide, but that stance caused a stir in design, especially after the Second World War, in debates over the good design of everyday objects.

Yet, even if we may have moved beyond the Socratic notion of design, it is still very relevant in current discussions pertaining to the ecological principles of designing industrial manufacturing processes, sustainable sources of energy, and recyclable materials. Plato, by contrast, although he adhered to the notion of the subjective reality of the human senses, attributed an extra-sensory character to beauty, which is why this, as an idea, applies to human understanding or the capacity to reflect. Yet if things are merely a reflection of ideas, then design, as craft and art, merely emulates the reflection of things (→ Form). Consequently, Plato was critical of the contribution made by art or craft to ideas. Any form of conceptual art, from Duchamp to Kosuth, is hence a type of Platonism.

Aristotle, who criticized Plato's notion of aesthetics and developed his own aesthetic views on the basis of the art of his time, also tried to comprehend the relationship between the good and the beautiful. His attempt to define the dialectics of essence and appearance and their relationship to the beauty of artifice has been fundamental to the history of aesthetics. Another of his proposals turned out to be even more influential with regard to the aesthetics of the made in design. Aristotle spoke of art serving to stimulate and purify certain emotions (catharsis), and it is precisely this aspect of aesthetics that has been adopted by marketing and branding. For Aristotle, this was substantiated particularly by the fact that artistic endeavors were supposed to be an acting out of alternatives. If art shows how things could be, rather than being bound to a factual and truthful version of reality, then this notion of aesthetics, even in its orientation toward the possible and exemplary, can be quite relevant to an analysis of design as process.

On the one hand, evaluating an object as beautiful and therefore aesthetic has always been associated with (→) craft skills and with the distinctive qualities that characterize those things produced with such (→) skills. Hence, a notion of aesthetics that considers beauty to be a property of things—attached to things, as it were—is not only closely related to design; it also prevents a reorientation of aesthetic thought to base it on the (→) design process, since the product only exists when the process is completed. On the other hand, the aspect of aesthetics that believes products convey specific material, intellectual, and social qualities is already embedded in the history of aesthetics as a (→) discipline.

Alexander Gottlieb Baumgarten reestablished aesthetics as an independent philosophical discipline in the mid-eighteenth century. Even though the new discipline would compete for a long time with poetics and (→) rhetoric, aesthetics quickly became a fashionable term, leading Jean Paul in his *Vorschule der Ästhetik* (School for Aesthetics) to note that "our age teems with nothing so much as aestheticians" (trans. Margaret R. Hale). By integrating sensory impressions and emotions into the field of philosophy, aesthetics attempts to overcome the conflict between philosophy and art and to reconcile the truth of art and poetry with the truth of thought. Baumgarten's theory claimed that logic and its foundations in rational knowledge forfeit their preeminence, and that humans in their sensory and emotional relationship to the world become the subject for whom personal truth is reproduced as aesthetic truth in humanities and the arts. Criticism at the time opposed the logician (*logicus*) or those who were merely self-taught and compared them unfavorably to the humanity of the aesthetician (*aestheticus*). This turned aesthetics into an art of living and revealed a tendency to attach importance to using sense perception as a guide and to accept its process-based character. From then on, aesthetics would examine the logic of different types of knowledge based on the senses and the possibilities of perfecting that knowledge, including knowledge regarding the beautiful, the sublime, the miraculous, and their production by means of art.

The debate about the real nature of aesthetics and what it is capable of delivering continues today. Whether it is Kant, in his *Critique of Judgment* (1790), separating transcendental aesthetics from the criticism of taste, and defining aesthetics not as an attribute but as a specific reflection elicited by the nature of an object, which as such affects sensations; or Schelling and Hegel restricting the field of aesthetic phenomena to a philosophy of art; or Kierkegaard defining aesthetics as a part of life subject to ethics and religion; or Adorno in his book with the programmatic title *Aesthetic Theory* (1970) exposing aesthetics and its various categories to the movement of history—the concept of aesthetics always encompasses, and focuses on, different areas of knowledge and (→) practice. This includes an aesthetics of change described by Heinz von Foerster, the inventor of second-order cybernetics, as a reflective style of thought and a new mode of perception that plays with ideas involving self-referential logic, circular causality, and other factors of a cybernetics of cybernetics (→ *Constructivism*). Hence, aesthetics must investigate how to deal with the relationships between different areas of life and knowledge.

Nonetheless, aesthetics has still not escaped the flaw of attempting to be apolitical and of specifying an affirmative field of compensation. There is more to aesthetics than merely beautifying an otherwise meaningless world, as is clear from its relationship to the good and from the fact that aestheticizing really means no more than rendering something perceivable and palpable. Lyotard speaks of how aesthetics, "that is, being receptive to the nature of something according to spatial and temporal forms that form the foundations for critical and romantic Modernism, feel it is repressed, weakened, and forced to resist the true predominance of a scientific, technical, and pragmatic reception of time and space." (→) Postmodernism, in an age characterized by emotionalism, renames aesthetics as a "science of aesthesis," in order to defy rational objectivity and the pragmatics of a rationale that is tailored to the logic of making money.

With regard to a specific "design aesthetics," yet to be formulated into a method, this implies that it would have to overcome the split into first, a theory of beautiful objects and second, a reflection based on the power of judgment. It would also have to accept an aesthetic theory that abides by that which appears as aesthetic perception and experience. It has to surrender its fixation on the object, in order to have a broader view of the design process and allow for individual, social, economic, ecological, political, and cultural aspects of production and reception. TW |

→ *Style*

Adorno, T. W. 1997. *Aesthetic Theory*. Trans. Robert Hullot-Kentor. Minneapolis MN: University of Minnesota Press.
Hegel, G. W. F. 1975. *Hegel's Aesthetics: Lectures on Fine Art*. Trans. T. M. Knox. Oxford and New York: Clarendon and Oxford.
Kant, I. 1951. *Critique of Judgment*. Trans. J. H. Bernard. New York: Hafner Publishing.
Welsch, W. 1990. *Ästhetisches Denken*. Stuttgart: Reclam.

AFFORDANCE

Affordances result from the coupling of any feature of the immediate environment (object, space, text) with a receptive subject or subjects. In other words, an affordance is the yield or potential yield of actions, meanings, and affects in the complementary relationship between the world with its objects and the intentions, perceptions, and capabilities of a person or group.

The term "affordance" was first coined by the perceptual psychologist J. J. Gibson in 1966 to describe the latent possibilities for action in features of the immediate environment presented to a sentient subject, or "actor." Gibson conceived of affordances in two seemingly contradictory ways. First, he thought of affordances as possibilities embedded in the environment and its objects, independent of an actor's engagement with them ("real" affordance). He determined these latent "offerings" of the environment to be "invariants"—constant in how they are presented/presenced, but waiting to be mined (drawn out and in some way owned in use). Second, he understood that affordances are constructed in contexts that are subject-specific, and that the actor and the environment are therefore mutually dependent.

For example, a staircase affords—provides or furnishes—an adult human being the means of ascending to another level in a building. It does not necessarily offer the same opportunity for a crawling infant or, indeed, a toddler—the risers being too high.

To them, crawler and toddler, at the top, the staircase is danger-ous and affords the possibility, or risk, of a fall. More positively, the staircase also provides young children (and occasionally adults) the opportunity to play, to toboggan down the flights on trays or jump from step to step. The physical features of the stair-case (incline gradient, height of risers, width of tread, construc-tion material and so on) are the invariants on which the affor-dances are constructed. But the affordances are only determined in the type of actor that ultimately interacts with the stairs. The different action possibilities that the staircase offers—climbing, tobogganing, falling down—are "nested" within a range of pos-sibilities, an "affordance complex," that is actor-contingent.

Gibson's focus was predominantly on connecting the action potentiality of the environment and the action capabilities of the actor. Most of the criticism responding to Gibson's notion of affordance, and his ecological psychology in general, centers on the idea that he did not take internal representations—the ways in which perceptual activity is shaped by the thinking, imaginings, and feelings of the individual subject—into ac-count (→ *Perception*).

In contrast, in translating the idea of affordance into Human Computer Interaction (HCI) and (→) interface design, design theorist Donald A. Norman focused on the way affordances in the actual world are constructed through "perceptual" activity. He states ". . . the term affordance refers to the perceived and actual properties of the thing, primarily those fundamental properties that determine just how the thing could possibly be used" (Norman 1988). One may appreciate that, as a spherical object, a ball may bounce or roll (afford bounceability and roll-ability); however, one would not know that a particular ball af-forded golf, for instance, unless one was of a culture that was familiar with the game of golf. Norman suggests that afford-ances are dependant on foreknowledge and the expectations of the individual, on perceptual schema that are to some extent culturally determined.

In Norman's philosophy, the program for design is highly "moti-vated." He uses "perceptual affordances" as a tool to build an argument for disambiguity in design practice, where design communicates clearly that which it affords and what it affords is somewhat determined (what we might call "motivated afford-ance"). In reality however, the course of design thinking and practice is becoming progressively less motivated—dissonance, ambiguity and openness being desirable features of design. This is sometimes referred to as "open affordance"; what a design affords is open to discovery and not programmed in from the outset (→ *Non Intentional Design*). To a greater or lesser extent, all designs are "open." To illustrate what is meant by "open" and "motivated" affordance, one may consider the design of Lego blocks: the early designs had no specific target for the object to be built and thus afforded the user the opportunity to build any structure of his or her choosing, whereas in contrast, the Bionicle Lego toys were designed so that a very particular object (a car, a building) would be built. The Bionicle legos are thus more motivated in what they afford.

Affordances move across different registers of existence and experience. As with Gibson, one may think of affordances in terms of the physical or biological (Gibson extended the concept of affordance to the body—for example, lungs coupled with air afford us the possibility of breathing). In Norman, affordances are perceptually governed. A taxonomy of affordances would register affective affordance (the emotional yield of an event), cognitive affordance, semiotic affordance, and so on; the taxonomic categories covering the different ways the actor engages the environment.

Gaver, W. W. 1991. Technology affordances. *Human factors in computing systems: CHI '91 conference proceedings.* 79–84.
Gibson, J. J. 1979. *The ecological approach to visual perception.* Boston: Houghton Mifflin.
Norman, D. 1988. *The design of everyday things.* Cambridge, MA: MIT Press.
Norman, D. 1999. Affordances, conventions and design. *Interactions* 6, no. 3 (May 1999): 38–43.

In summation, affordances may be thought of as tolerances or movements in meanings, (→) use, and/or affect. These tolerances play in the connection between objects or environments, and perceiving, acting, receptive subjects. By using the word affordance we index "the possible" existing as tolerances in what we design. The "possible" meaning, use and affect is revealed or produced in the way a user engages with what is designed. TR |

→ *Form, Function, Human Factors, Performance, Theory, Understanding, Usability*

AGIT PROP

Agit Prop is a contracted, or portmanteau, word that has come into the English language from Russian and refers to the promotion of political ideas, particularly those of the Left, through literature, drama, music, or art. In the 1920s, immediately after the Communists came to power in the Soviet Union, the Department of Agitation and Propaganda was established to advance the ideological education of the masses. The word is a contraction of *agitatsiya* and *propaganda* from the ministry's title. Agitation was intended to appeal to the emotions and propaganda to the intellect, and together they formed a powerful ideological tool for "winning hearts and minds." (Ironically the American right wing used this phrase during the Vietnam War to describe their efforts to "win over" the Vietnamese people to pacify the country.) The Constructivist (→ *Constructivism*) designers undertook many agit prop commissions and the word is still used to indicate politically left-wing graphic designs. Initially the term was not derogatory, though in the West it soon acquired negative connotations as it was used to refer to overtly biased and oppressive political persuasion techniques. It is now often used proudly by the Left to indicate resistance to the institutional politics of the Right—as can be seen by the blogs, zines, typefaces, and so on that use the term. ^{TM} |

→ *Design and Politics, Protest Design*

ANIMATION

The word "animation," derived from the Latin word *animare* (to give breath to), is frequently associated with web and entertainment industries such as film, television, and (→) game design. Animations can also be used to instruct and inform, particularly when a process is communicated more easily through (→) visualization than through the written or spoken word (in contexts where language constraints are an issue, for example).

Simply put, an animation is comprised of a sequence of static images, strung together to provide the illusion of movement. Stop-motion animation, one of the simplest forms of animation, typically makes use of puppets, clay figures, photos, cutouts, or drawings. The process involves shooting individual photographs frame-by-frame while making very minimal physical changes to the object or scene after each shot. When viewed, a continuous sequence of 24 of these single images per second creates the illusion of movement.

2-D and 3-D computer animation today uses a variety of different techniques and technologies ranging from flash to motion capture. When compared to stop-motion or traditional hand-drawn cel animation, these modern techniques have the ability to simulate highly complex and far more realistic movement sequences. ^{TG} |

→ *Audiovisual Design, Broadcast Design, Character Design, Presentation, Screen Design, Time-based Design, Virtual Reality, Visual Effects*

ANONYMOUS DESIGN

At first glance, "anonymous" seems like a pejorative: an unknown thing, unrecognized, and therefore impersonal and not associated with any particular individual. In the context of contemporary design's overly fashionable trends, however, the seemingly grey character of the attribute "anonymous" becomes a desirable quality.

It first has to be said that the design virus has slowly infected nearly every activity that is even remotely associated with (→) *Gestaltung*. Even time-honored skilled professions such as metalworking have been spruced up to look cool and refashioned as metal design.

This of course wears thin over time, and leads to the exact opposite. What supposedly ensured a high image factor and hence high prices has long since become an economic depressant;

what was once devised as a pricey symbol of exclusivity might now at most excite chain store consumers.

This is not the case with anonymous design because there are no specifications, categories, or names. It merely indicates that the designer, meaning the author, is unknown or forgotten. This has two implications: first, that the design is the product of a deliberate act of designing and that the external form of the appliance, tool, or piece of furniture is not accidental, but the unique result of someone's specific criteria. Second, that the person who designed this is unknown or unacknowledged, meaning it has existed for long enough to become standard, and in the process has lost its creator's name.

With this in mind, we encounter the label anonymous mostly on objects that have developed over centuries in different cultures and that are more or less dependent on the resources available in that culture. This means the daily (→) tools and appliances that are characterized by an unmistakable functional value and immediately recognizable operating instructions. The resources are not limited to a culture's natural conditions or a region's traditional skills, but also include the materials, technologies, and skills of a global industrial culture. Meaning this category not only consists of handmade appliances or clay, glass, stone, wood, or iron containers, but also industrially produced bottle openers, crown caps, preserving jars, and the everyday basic tools that we would never categorize as design, yet which were in fact, at one point, designed by someone. They were never christened with the name of their author, yet their sustained use has earned them the highest rating available in design: the fact that they have become standard. VA |

→ *Auteur Design, Brand*

ARCHITECTURAL DESIGN

There is an interesting history behind the intertwinement of design and architecture that is predominately related to the design of interiors, lighting, and housewares. Given that architecture has been historically understood as a closely associated but distinct practice to design, this entry deals with architects working in design and not the field of architecture itself.

The reason for architects' interests in design is clear. They usually tried to design more than the enclosed space and be responsible for at least a part of the interior as well and so extended their practice to design furnishings and to commission tradesmen to realize these ambitions. As architecture had existed long before the other design fields, craftwork and trade skills had for a long period been architecture's only true competitors.

This fact in turn established a tradition and influenced the beginnings of the development of design. It also inspired or seduced architects to dabble in design. Mies van der Rohe and Frank Lloyd Wright experimented with design, as well as Walter Gropius (who even designed a car), and later Robert Venturi and Michael Graves, Peter Eisenman, Zaha Hadid, and Norman Foster. Yet in Italy, a special situation characterized the relationship between design and architecture up until the end of the 1980s. It was almost impossible in Italy to study design as a separate (→) discipline; moreover, all Italian designers were obliged to study architecture.

Which is why it is still very normal in Italy that those who became famous in the design context, such as Sottsass, Mendini, Marco Piva and Branzi, all developed architecture practices alongside large-scale (→) product design.

Several questions arise from the historical and empirical connections between design and architecture. First, can (→) design competence be found in architecture at all? Does an inherent relationship between architecture and design truly exist? And even: if an architect had been dabbling in design, is this immediately recognizable? This has led to discussions about scale, and questions about whether objects are not really in effect miniature examples of architecture and whether buildings, in their turn, are enlarged objects—which would in fact point to an inherent connection between the two.

This has been debated in many publications, including Alessandro Mendini's "Alessi," which for example has initiated projects in which architects were invited to design coffee sets and these designs clearly betray an architectural influence.

The question became even more interesting when prominent designers (such as those mentioned above as well as Philippe Starck, among others) began designing large buildings.

Yet all of these discussions about architectural design quickly become redundant when contemplating design's true complexity (with components like service, communication, corporate, engineering, or interface design, as well as design research). It still remains an issue because the borders between the two disciplines do occasionally blur, or practitioners of one stray into the other's territory, and the outlook from that standpoint often presumes affinity. In this respect, an end to the discussion is not yet in sight. BL |

→ *Design, Furniture Design, Interior Design, Lighting Design*

ART DECO

"Art Deco" is the term used for a design movement that was highly influential in architecture, interior and industrial design, fashion, and the visual arts.

Art Deco was somewhat disparate in that it encompassed a wide range of stylistic criteria and did not have a truly unified theoretical or ideological foundation. Nevertheless, there were some common features: a general propensity for surface (→) ornamentation, stereometric and geometric forms, an emphasis on quality craftsmanship (→ Craft), and the use of expensive, rare, or novel (→) materials like precious metals and stones, ivory, ebony, exotic woods, fine leather, bakelite, and aluminum. Examples of Art Deco consisted mostly of individually commissioned, customized designs, and demonstrated the sophisticated and luxurious taste of a new urban class (→ Luxury).

Art Deco is an abbreviation of the French *arts décoratifs*, a phrase first used in 1925 when a collective of French artists, La Société des Artistes Décorateurs, founded at the beginning of the century, held an "Exposition Internationale des Art Décoratifs et Industriels Moderne." It wasn't until the mid-1960s that the term became well-known, with large retrospective exhibitions of the style held in Paris (1966) and Minneapolis (1971). The style was characterized by an adventurous eclecticism that drew on cubism, fauvism, and futurism, but it is primarily acknowledged as a search for an elegant and functional new modernism. Its proponents were equally fascinated by the "primitive" arts of Ancient Egypt, Africa, Mexican Aztecs, and the absolutely contemporary (→) modernity of electricity, aviation, radio communication, and skyscrapers.

Geographically, Art Deco was most influential in France, where it strived to develop a unified art form that merged architecture, interior, furniture, and product design with poster and book art, small sculpture and painting. The movement had little influence in central Europe and, in particular, Germany because a more functionalist philosophy of design had become firmly established in these countries (→ Functionalism). American galleries and museums, on the other hand, were relatively quick to pick up on the trend, largely due to the efforts of then Secretary of Commerce Herbert Hoover. Consequently, the late 1920s saw a boom in Art Deco styling in the United States, particularly in fields of architectural and interior design. Some excellent examples from this period include the Chrysler Building and Rockefeller Center in New York. After a slight time lag, Art Deco emerged in England around 1930, and remained influential there until the 1940s. The English variant was noted for its geometric and abstract formal visual language, evident in numerous product and interior designs of cinemas, hotels, and theaters of the time. PE |

→ *Art Nouveau, Ornament, Streamline Design*

ART DIRECTION

In essence, art direction is the articulation of guidelines for a specific creative outcome. Historically, the term has most often been applied to a set of skills or job role associated with a project's visual or graphic components. However, art direction is intentionally and essentially a collaborative experience, with the art director generally making the final decisions based on the advice and input of a larger team of diverse talents.

That said, the term "art direction" can be misleading. Somewhat counter intuitively, the phrase is generally not associated with the fine arts or standard curatorial practice. Another commonly held misconception is that art direction relates exclusively to the advertising industry. Although it may have been popularized within this field—the job title of "art director" made its debut around the turn of the twentieth century and gained prominence in the 1950s through advertising and magazine design in particular—the phrase is used in most creative endeavors that require the collaboration of multiple players: graphic design, illustration, film, photography, and so on.

Indeed, the title of art director may be becoming somewhat dated within the advertising industry. Historically, this role made up one half of the traditional creative team model: the art director (directed the use of images) and the copywriter (directed the use of words). However, this model is changing dramatically due to developments in technology, globalization, market shifts, and integrated servicing, and the traditional job titles, including art director, have steadily been swept aside to be replaced by the general term—"creative."

An art director's talent lies in seeing the big picture, knowing how, when, where, and why to make final creative decisions, and guiding experts in their own creative fields in a collaborative process to produce an appropriate outcome. Directing a creative project to its greatest potential is a difficult balancing act; in this sense, an art director functions like a kind of visual curator of sorts, albeit in a different kind of curatorial capacity from the standard fine-arts practice. And it must be said, there is definitely an art to directing people—particularly creative ones. KF |
→ *Advertisement, Collaborative Design, Creativity*

ARTIFACT

Quite literally, an artifact is an object that is the product of human (→) skill and ingenuity. The term derives from the Latin *ars* (art or skill) and *factum* (made or done), and thus is a pivotal term to describe almost any designed entity. All products of design are artifacts of one kind or another, and a common definition of design is the organization of the interface between humans and the "made world," that is, the interaction between people and our artifacts. For instance, a typographer designs the readers' interaction with the artifact of a book and the architect designs the interaction between the residents, users, or passersby with the artifact of a building.

Although usually understood to refer to a material (→) object, artifact can also refer to designed spaces, images, software, systems, or environments where these act as coherent units. The artifacts of a scholar's research can include books, lectures, Internet postings, and e-mails. Cultural and religious (→) values, beliefs, and systems of thought are expressed through the artifacts they produce.

In archaeology, an artifact is anything that is not part of the "natural" earth surrounding it, and in medicine and astronomy, artifacts are observational anomalies—visual errors on a film plate or the by-products of the observing technology itself. ᵀᴹ ǀ
→ *Industrial Design, Product, Product Design, Tools*

ART NOUVEAU

Art Nouveau, as it is known in France, England, and the United States, was an international movement that dominated design and aesthetics from the 1880s to 1914. In Germany, the equivalent art movement was called Jugendstil; in Austria it was Secessionsstil, and there were strong movements throughout Europe, particularly in Poland, Scandinavia, Scotland, Belgium, and the Netherlands, all with specific and defining national characteristics. Although Art Nouveau had its foundations in Europe, its effects were significant across the globe.

Art Nouveau artists and designers embraced a new approach to design that broke away from recycling existing stylistic forms. They often adopted nature as a theme, but came at it from two fundamentally different approaches. The first approach involved reinterpreting the surface of an object—for example the body of a vase, the surface of a book cover or the facade of a building—with stylized, organic, and curvilinear forms referencing foliage and flora. Despite their use of an ornamental and organic visual vocabulary, Art Nouveau artists and designers of this ilk rejected traditional notions of (→) ornamentation as mere surface decoration and instead regarded it as intrinsic to the overall design. The second approach produced a more scientific view and engaged a deeper investigation into basic organic principles. This somewhat Constructivist-oriented (→ *Constructivism*) analysis resulted in a simpler, more formal visual language that can be seen as anticipating functionalist approaches to design (→ *Functionalism*).

Art Nouveau celebrated and endorsed the (→) integration of multiple art forms and a reciprocal discourse between the arts and (→) crafts (known in German as *Gesamtkunstwerk).* Art Nouveau artists and designers included architects, interior designers, painters, graphic designers, jewelry, fashion, and product designers (then called artisans). They sought to synthesize all of the art and design disciplines, irrespective of categories such as "high" or "low," "fine", or "applied." Accordingly, they were dedicated to elevating "craftwork" not only by designing everyday ordinary objects as practiced in the (→) Arts & Crafts movement, but by applying the same aesthetic rigor to the posters, small advertisements and logos that they designed.

In Germany, the term "Jugendstil" was first introduced to describe a style adopted by the Munich publication *Jugend* (youth) which was first published in 1896. Looking for new forms of expression, *Jugend* endorsed an open approach to design. It did not use consistent (→) typography or uniform (→) layouts, and the magazine's appearance varied with each issue. It was a platform for a new form of (→) aesthetics and inspired artists, designers, and architects such as Otto Eckmann, Richard Riemerschmid, Julius Diez, Bruno Paul, and Peter Behrens who began incorporating more floral, flowing forms in their work.

Berlin, Munich, Darmstadt, and Weimar were the centers of German Jugendstil. Emerging artists' associations, the "secessionists," private printing presses, and artisan workshops embraced and developed the new aesthetic. The first secessions were established in 1892 in Munich and Berlin as a protest against the official art of the academy. In 1898, Hermann Obrist, Bernhard Pankok, Bruno Paul, August Endell, Richard Riemerschmid, and Peter Behrens founded the Vereinigte Werkstätten für Kunst und Handwerk (United Workshops for the Arts and Crafts) in Munich, which produced high-quality, handcrafted household products. They merged with the Dresdner Werkstätten für Handwerkskunst (The Dresden Artisan Workshops) in 1907 to become the Deutsche Werkstätten (German Workshops) and were able to mass-produce high-quality work (→ *Deutscher Werkbund*).

In Darmstadt in 1899, Grand Duke Ernst Ludwig of Hesse invited Joseph Maria Olbrich and Peter Behrens to establish an artist colony at Mathildenhöhe. Its artists designed and furnished Mathildenhöhe's apartment houses, studios, and a large exhibition hall, making it one of Jugendstil's most important centers. In 1902, the Belgian Henry van de Velde, became the consultant to the craft industries in Weimar. The building he designed for the School of Arts and Crafts, later the (→) Bauhaus, set the foundations for a more functional version of Jugendstil. Other centers of Art Nouveau, in addition to those in Germany, arose in France, Belgium, England, Scotland, Austria, and America.

In France, the term "Art Nouveau" derived from the name of the gallery of art dealer Siegfried Bing. In Paris, Art Nouveau developed largely in opposition to the École des Beaux-Arts. There, Hector Guimard designed the entrances to the Paris Métro (still one of the best examples of Art Nouveau); Henri de Toulouse-Lautrec, Alphonse Mucha, Théophile-Alexandre Steinlen, and

Jules Chéret developed new directions for poster design; and René Lalique designed perfume bottles, lamps, vases, and jewelry with dragonfly and Cicada motifs. Nancy, a small provincial city where glass artists Auguste and Antonin Daum and Émile Gallé developed a strong symbolic expression of Art Nouveau, also became important center for the movement in France.

With artists' groups such as Le Vingt and La Liberté Esthétique, Belgium was already a progressive hub of art and design activity as early as the 1880s. Victor Horta was one of the first and most significant Art Nouveau architects, combining new materials of the industrial revolution (like iron girders and glass) with organic ornamentation in large constructions that appeared to rise like plants from the ground. By designing the furniture and murals as well, Horta created a unity of structural design and ornament so that the building, its facade, and its interior décor were fully synthesized and resolved.

A very different direction developed in the United Kingdom. A new formal language in English print and book design began emerging in the 1880s. Drawing on the Arts & Crafts tradition and inspired by Japanese wood cuts, Aubrey Beardsley developed a graphic style that looked to nature for its flowing, organic, curvilinear forms. At the same time, a group of architects and artists in Glasgow, Scotland were developing a new functionalist formal language characterized by predominantly neutral tones like black and white and little ornamentation. Led by designer Charles Rennie Mackintosh, they formed the Glasgow School of Art, best known for its geometric forms and planar areas with graceful horizontal and vertical lines.

In 1897, Gustav Klimt, Koloman Moser, and Otto Wagner established a new artists' association called Secession in Vienna, which became the center for Art Nouveau in Austria. They used a formal visual vocabulary characterized by strong angles and lines that was partially influenced by Mackintosh's work in Glasgow. In 1903, the Wiener Werkstätte (Viennese Workshop) emerged from the Vienna Secession.

In America, Art Nouveau was exemplified by the stained and blown glass, ceramics, and jewelry designs of Louis Comfort Tiffany. PE |

→ Ornament

Eschmann, K. 1991. *Jugendstil: Ursprünge, Parallelen, Folgen*. Göttingen: Muster-Schmidt.
Greenhalgh, P. 2000. *Art Nouveau, 1890–1914*. New York: Harry N. Abrams.
Sembach, K.-J. 1990. *Jugendstil: Die Utopie der Versöhnung*. Cologne: Taschen.

ARTS & CRAFTS

Industrialization, which, as is well known, first appeared and was most intense in England, led to the eradication of the once direct relationship that existed between product and consumer—along with increasing urbanization, market expansion, the creation of a class of industrial workers, that is the proletariat, and the alienation and division of labor. In preindustrial times, a carpenter built a table after direct discussions with the customers and designed it specifically according to their wishes; the same applied to shoemakers, furriers, and so on. Industrialization turned customers and producers into anonymous participants in an open market.

Moreover, the responsibility for design also changed radically and in some instances completely disappeared; no one person in production was accountable for it. This only intensified the miserable state of production and the abject (→) quality of its products.

English authors of the Romantic age (Percy Bysshe Shelley, 1792–1822, and William Wordsworth, 1770–1850, for example) or even the belatedly Romantic philosopher and political economist, Karl Marx, 1818–83, were already vehemently condemning this, yet it took another few decades for this dire state of affairs to be really understood and to be addressed. However, although many people analyzed the problem well and with the best of intentions, in retrospect—as is true of most initial, general reactions—their efforts to address the problems ended up either ineffectual or quixotic.

Some of the figures active in England at this time were John Ruskin and William Morris, and later, although in a somewhat different manner, Charles Rennie Macintosh from Scotland. The philosopher and author John Ruskin was working on reproducing an integrated culture and on a return to notions of high quality and individual workmanship. William Morris—inspired by an 1836 British government report on design and industry and by the London World Expo in 1851—founded the firm Morris, Marshall and Faulkner, which produced textiles, wallpaper, and furniture (and later lettering under Morris' name) in the best traditions of craftsmanship. In 1888, he founded the Arts & Crafts Society—which eventually developed into a major art and design movement.

Like the German Romantics several decades before them, the proponents of the Arts & Crafts movement categorically and with a degree of revulsion rejected industrialization in favor of traditional preindustrial forms. A good example for this in German Romanticism can be found in letters exchanged between the writers Ludwig Tieck and Wilhelm Heinrich Wackenroder. One had recently spent some time (in the first half of the nineteenth century) in Fürth, then the most industrialized town in Germany, and described to his friend his fury over the factories, noise, smog, poverty, and pace of life that he observed there. They agreed that they should leave this town immediately and meet in nearby Nuremberg, a town that still looked and impressed them as being medieval and unspoiled.

John Ruskin did the same by condemning, among other cities, Manchester and Liverpool, both enormously successful centers of industry, and praising the countryside and the very traditional country house style, even when this was already sentimentally nostalgic (→ Nostalgia). This definitely found supporters, for example in early work of the Italian Futurist architect Sant'Elia or in the Garden City Movement.

William Morris explained his program in his novel *News from Nowhere* (1890), a mixture of absurdly simplified socialist concepts (advocating the abolition of money, the partial dissolution of the family and the end of the division of labor) with a jubilant abolition of any and all industrialization, and a complete return to medieval ideals of craftsmanship and the simple life.

The practical effect of this was that the Arts & Crafts movement returned to individual production but in truth, could only serve the nouveau-riche middleclass who had the means to afford its products. This prompted renowned German philosopher Ernst Bloch to describe the followers of the Arts & Crafts movement as petit-bourgeois socialists. Considering their philosophical championing of the rights of workers, it was very strong criticism indeed.

Nevertheless, the Arts & Crafts movement became very popular and created a markedly increased awareness in England of product and communication design. It also influenced the (→) Art Nouveau, (→) Deutscher Werkbund, and even (→) Bauhaus movements. For this reason, many now claim the Arts & Crafts movement was the true beginning of a separate discipline of (→) design. ME |

→ *Craft, Industrial Design*

Cumming, E., and W. Kaplan. 1991. *The Arts and Crafts movement*. World of Art. New York: Thames & Hudson.
Kaplan, W. 2004. *The Arts and Crafts movement in Europe and America: Design for the modern world, 1880–1920*. New York: Thames & Hudson.
Morris, W. 2003. *News from nowhere*. Oxford, United Kingdom: Oxford Univ. Press. (Orig. pub. 1890.)
Naylor, G. 1980. *The Arts and Crafts movement: A study of its sources, ideals, and influence on design theory*. Cambridge, MA: MIT Press.

ASPEN

Once a year, design professionals and enthusiasts meet at the International Design Conference in Aspen, Colorado where approximately 300 international participants discuss design, architecture, art, science, and technology. The conference aims to achieve a global appreciation of social and cultural concerns and to exert influence by implementing the results and conclusions that emerge from its workshops and seminars.

Chicago industrialist Walter Paepcke and his wife Elizabeth founded the design conference in 1951. Their idea of bringing together diverse skills to approach problems from different perspectives was reflected in the diversity of the participants invited to the conference. As a result, author Max Frisch (1956), composer John Cage (1966), and video artist Nam June Paik (1971) have all contributed to the development of design philosophy. Choosing Aspen as the conference's venue was also significant. Paepcke believed that the natural beauty of the Rocky Mountains, a wholesome diet, and the distance from the distractions of everyday concerns was necessary for the participants' peace of mind and ability to focus on ideas during the conference. These opportunities plus the knowledge gained at Aspen would "renew their spirit and rejuvenate their minds." Thus, the Aspen idea was born.

The fact that the International Design Conference at Aspen has attracted professionals from different disciplines for over fifty years is evidence of design's influence on international sociopolitical issues. In 2006, the name was changed to Aspen Design Summit—analogous to the (→) St. Moritz Design Summit, thus emphasizing a shift of focus from enlightenment to the newly defined objectives of commitment and action and thereby also marking a modernization of the Summit's philosophical foundations. ^{DPO} |

AUDIOVISUAL DESIGN

Audiovisual design or AV design, also known in various contexts as (→) time-based design or motion design, is a relatively new (→) discipline that integrates sound with moving images. Generally speaking, the practice of AV design typically falls under one of three broad subcategories that often overlap: film design, TV design, and (→) animation. The process also draws upon a number of associated disciplines including (→) typography, (→) illustration, (→) sound design, and (→) branding.

Despite the fact that the film industry has always relied upon the expertise of designers, it was traditionally considered to be a separate category, distinct from design. This changed with the specialized disciplinary profession of "production designer," which first emerged in 1939 to ensure that the overall look and style of a film was coherent. Today, production designers are charged with overseeing everything from storyboards to special effects to supervising the entire art department of a film or television production. The responsibilities of the "TV designer" are similar to those of a production designer (→ *Broadcast Design*). This role emerged after the television broadcast boom of the 1980s, and had a significant effect on making audiovisual design a highly profitable field of practice.

Since animation is so often categorized as a sub-genre of film or television, the practice of AV design in this context is not often addressed. However, in the course of the media industry's economic development, there have been many advances in animation techniques and technologies that should not be overlooked. The possibilities inherent in 2-D and 3-D animation technologies in particular have deep implications for the future of TV and film production and its related professions. It is clear that audiovisual design is also becoming increasingly important in relation to (→) interface and (→) web design. These days, the development of the World Wide Web and mobile telecommunication devices have to be taken seriously when discussing audiovisual design, especially as their significance will only intensify in the years to come.

Until the 1980s, audiovisual technologies relied on analog image manipulation using the classic rostrum stand and camera to construct frame by frame pictorial compositions and animations of varying complexity. The tedious processes involved in monitoring the results (developing, editing, scoring the film, and so on) often resulted in simplistic or inconsistent design concepts. The introduction of electronic media marked the beginning of a broader approach to audiovisual design that took place in the 1980s, and was quickly followed by the introduction of (→) hardware and (→) software systems that further facilitated designers' abilities to work with image and sound. The effect that these innovations had on animation in particular was clear from the outset. When open desktop computer systems began replacing black boxes (computers used solely for video production) in the late 1990s, yet another realm of possibilities became available. In the course of the digitalization of all design-relevant production phases, audiovisual designers have claimed increasingly central positions in almost all of the media-based entertainment industries. [BB] |

→ *Screen Design*

AUTEUR DESIGN

The auteur designer (sometimes referred to as a "signature designer") can be seen as analogous to the auteur filmmaker in that both are both motivated by their own unique personal vision. Both are typically not commissioned by nor obliged to answer to anyone other than themselves. Because they are responsible for defining their own project briefs, securing their own funds, and promoting their own designs, auteur designers can act more independently than other designers in formulating and expressing their particular philosophies of design.

Although independent design projects may at times be very risky endeavors, there are many benefits to being a single designer with complete control over an entire project. For example, since they do not need to answer to anyone for their mistakes and failures, they can treat them as valuable learning experiences. Furthermore, the acclaim that accompanies a successful design is generally intensified when it is created by an individual designer. When auteur designs are well received by the public, other designers, and critics, their creators receive all of the financial rewards as well as all of the credit—which is crucial in ensuring the possibility of continued designs.

Realizing an auteur design not only indicates that the designer had the confidence to put him or herself on the line, to be exposed to both praise and censure alike, but also proves that his or her unique perspective is attractive or interesting to the general public. The designer is thereby conferred with the status of an artisan or master, and all future works will be judged on the basis of this one success. Moreover, an auteur design typically will have a significant enough impact on the field that the work of other designers will be compared to it as well. VA |

→ *Anonymous Design, Collaborative Design, Credibility*

AUTOMOBILE DESIGN

Once the work of talented stylists and multi-talented engineers, today automobile design is a discipline whose complexity is often underappreciated. It is the product of team-work and involves conceiving, planning, and designing all the elements and functions of the entire automobile and of its various parts.

In the strictest sense, automobile design is a field of (→) industrial design and is divided into exterior design and interior design. It is an interdisciplinary process involving the manufacturer, components supplier, and feedback from consumers, and consists of numerous subdivisions. This is due to the complexity of the automobile business, which requires large-scale, long-term investment before a new model can be introduced to the market, in order to minimize financial risk.

The design process starts with a (→) brief that defines the technical package. The industry's term for a package that consists of an adaptable base for a family of models is a platform, and this can be used by different manufacturers or brands. The characteristics of a package or platform (meaning dimensions, weight, type of construction, chassis, and engine) together with the specifics of the brief (the desired vehicle type, market position, and production costs) determine the amount of freedom given to the designer. Usually, designers working from competing studios begin by developing two-dimensional (→) sketches and (→) renderings during what is called the (→) brainstorming stage. Since the 1990s, this process has been almost fully replaced by computer-aided styling (CAS), which allows three-dimensional (→) models to be generated at very early stages. The models can be displayed on a monitor or virtual wall and can be analyzed true to scale and detail.

To assist the final decision process, modelers using Computer Numerically Controlled (CNC) milling machines produce clay models that are practically identical to the finished product (→ *CAD/CAM/CIM/CNC*). The modelers' role in the design process is more significant than typically assumed, because they translate the designer's ideas into tangible, three-dimensional objects and thus make an independent contribution to the final result. Internal and external tests are then carried out based on a painted clay model and, if necessary, modifications are made before arriving at the final design—during the so-called "design freeze." At the same time, in accordance with the simultaneous engineering processes, the design solutions undergo feasibility tests (→ *Feasibility Studies*). After the design freeze, the industrialization phase begins and initially focuses on producing an operational (→) prototype.

The automobile industry is concerned with reducing the time-to-market phase, meaning the duration between the start of the planning stage and the release of a new model on the market. In the 1990s, this took about four to seven years. It was reduced to twenty-four months by 2005, and now takes about eighteen months. The acceleration and intensification of the design process is a significant creative challenge to designers and makes teamwork indispensable.

Our understanding of the phrase "automobile design" needs to be critically reexamined, despite the fact that the term is well-known and readily understood. From the beginning of the age of the automobile until the 1930s, automobile manufacturers produced only the motorized chassis, or the rolling chassis, which was then custom fitted for the customer by coachwork builders. An illustrator was responsible for depicting the manufacturer's expertise and interpreting the taste of the client, but also strived to develop innovative ideas and set new trends. The client was presented with a selection of artistic color drawings, called *figurini* in Italian, from which to choose. His or her selection was then formed directly from tin, creating a unique object that rarely resembled the original drawing. If the "line" was successful, it was reproduced in a limited series or used on different chassis. Leading firms at the time included Fleetwood (United States), Farina (Italy), Erdmann & Rossi (Germany), Saoutchik (France), and H. J. Mulliner & Co. (United Kingdom). The illustrators, also called stylists, had little knowledge of automobile construction or engineering and were rarely involved in other phases of the process. Their artistic abilities were all that was required, which is one reason why automobile design was long considered inferior to architecture or other design-based disciplines.

The trend toward mass motorization made it necessary for the industry to produce more efficient designs and to develop a holistic approach to the automobile as a product. Henry Ford (1863–1947) set a new modern standard with the Model T in 1908, yet was surpassed in the 1920s by General Motors under the management of Alfred P. Sloan (1875–1966). Sloan's theory of planned obsolescence was that the consumer should want and be able to afford to buy a new car every year. Sales and marketing structures should adapt to market patterns and brands be strategically positioned. With this, the significance of (→) strategic design was born.

In 1927, Hollywood-born Harley Earl (1893–1969) became the first director of an in-house automobile design department: the General Motors Art and Color Department. The phrase "art and color" reveals quite a bit about the status of automobile design at the time—a stylist's job was simply to design a colorful shell and stylish interiors and nothing more.

Unlike the vehicle industry in the United States, automobile design in Europe developed in line with modernist theories in architecture and applied breakthrough findings in (→) aerodynamics. Brilliant engineers rejected the fashion for (→) styling and focused on refining the functional and economic aspects of automobiles. Following this strict, self-imposed dogma, automotive engineers such as Ferdinand Porsche (1875–1951), Dante Giacosa (1905–1996), and Alec Issigonis (1906–1988) working in small teams produced modern design benchmarks in a relatively short time (these were respectively: the VW Typ 1, 1938; FIAT 500 Topolino, 1936 and FIAT 600, 1956; and the Austin Seven/Morris Mini Minor 1959). After the Second World War, Italian coachbuilders—in particular Bertone, Ghia, Pininfarina, Touring and Vignale—and stylists such as Giovanni Michelotti (1921–1980) and Mario Felice Boano (1903–?) continued to play an important role in automobile design and influenced the whole discipline worldwide. Nonetheless, the status of the profession remained essentially unchanged, and terms like stylist and styling and, hence, styling department or *centri stile*, continued to be used.

In the early 1970s, the oil crisis had a substantial impact on automobile design—although this was virtually ignored by American manufacturers, whose only response was to shorten their rather exaggerated chassis. The resulting emergency economic measures caused the European industry to understand automobile design as a rational process that should result in a rationally optimized product—a utopian, perfect world car. Giorgetto Giugiaro (born 1938), founder of the design studio Italdesign, contributed greatly to establishing automobile design as a fully-fledged (→) discipline that would plan the entire architecture of the exterior and interior of an automobile both aesthetically and technologically. His Lancia Megagamma (1978) and Lancia Medusa (1980) prototypes are milestones in automobile design.

Strong competition from Japanese car manufacturers forced the international automobile industry to restructure in the 1980s. In order to satisfy the need for precisely defined (→) brand management, it became increasingly important to develop and integrate

Molineri, G., S. Pininfarina, and P. Tumminelli. 2006. *Mitomacchina: Il design dell'automobile; Storia, tecnologia e futuro*. Exh.
cat. Milan: Skira.
Norbye, J. P. 1984. *Car design: Structure
and architecture*. Blue Ridge Summit, PA:
TAB Books.
Sparke, P. 2002. *A century of car design*.
London: Mitchell Beazley.
Tumminelli, P. 2004. *Car design*. New York:
teNeues.

different individual automobile design skills. Hundreds of employees are now responsible for designing and building a car. Simultaneous engineering and computer-aided design (→ *CAD/CAM/CIM/CNC*) became the catchphrases of the 1990s. New areas of specialization were discovered, new categories such as the (→) "crossover" were developed, and more models were released on the market. The automobile design discipline has been experiencing a rather euphoric phase since 2000. (→) Sound, smell (→ *Olfactory Design*), (→) lighting and multimedia design are all being integrated into automobile design and safety aspects are being reemphasized. However, true automobile design has not developed much further in the age of brands and branding. (→) Retro design is and will remain fashionable, classic designs are being reinterpreted, and a flamboyant, pimp aesthetic is on the rise. This might be due to the teamwork aspect as even while the public spotlight is directed at the chief designer, products are no longer the work of an individual mind (→ *Collaborative Design*). PT |

→ *Engineering Design, Transportation Design*

B

BAUHAUS

The Bauhaus (1919–1933) was the most influential art school of the modernist period. It consolidated the various avant-garde trends of its time, developing them into an aesthetic functionalist philosophy that fused art and production.

The Bauhaus was founded in 1919 by Walter Gropius as the Staatliches Bauhaus in Weimar (State Bauhaus in Weimar), after a merger of the Weimar School of Arts and Crafts (Grossherzogliche Kunstgewerbeschule) and the Weimar Academy of Fine Arts (Grossherzogliche Hochschule für Bildende Kunst). It moved to Dessau in 1925, where it opened as the Academy of Design (Hochschule für Gestaltung) in a building designed by Gropius. In 1928, Gropius left the Bauhaus. Swiss architect Hannes Meyer succeeded him, but was forced to step down in 1930 under pressure from the National Socialists. Meyer's successor, Ludwig Mies van der Rohe, attempted to depoliticize the school—albeit, with little success. In 1932, again under National Socialist pressure, the Bauhaus was forced to leave Dessau and move to Berlin, where it closed its doors in 1933.

The Bauhaus was influential in developing a new pedagogical concept for educating designers. In 1919, Johannes Itten introduced a one-year preliminary course that was meant to free students from the ballast of traditional rules and ideas and introduce them to the fundamental artistic elements of design. After this stage, students chose a Bauhaus workshop in specific area of interest. Here, they were further educated in workmanship techniques by a "master craftsman" and by an artist, or a "master of form." Lyonel Feininger, Walter Gropius, Johannes Itten, Wassily Kandinsky, Gerhard Marcks, Paul Klee, Georg Muche, Lothar Schreyer, Oskar Schlemmer, and László Moholy-Nagy number among the well-known designers and artists who taught at the Bauhaus.

The Bauhaus produced a significant alumni body, and several of its talented graduates—such as Marcel Breuer, Josef Albers, Herbert Bayer, Joost Schmidt, Hinnerk Scheper, Gunta Stölzl, and Marianne Brandt—remained there to teach as "young masters." The historical influences of the Bauhaus on the theory and practice of design can be broken down into five broad phases as follows:

1. The Expressionist workmanship phase (1919–1922). A manifesto was published at the founding of the Bauhaus in 1919 that called for consolidating the arts under the authority of architecture. Following the English (→) Arts & Crafts movement, it promoted work reform ideas that propagated a return to the medieval idea of the *Bauhütte* (stonemasons' lodge). One characteristic at this time was an Expressionist-inspired formal language that was reflected in handcrafted, individual pieces. Johannes Itten was particularly successful in fusing the enthusiastic mood of

new beginnings with experiments in design, and gradually became one of the Bauhaus' central foundational influences. The school's Weimar beginnings were also influenced by the religious philosophy of Mazdaznan, a modern version of ancient Persian Zoroastrianism that advocated breathing exercises and a vegetarian diet, as well as by eurhythmics, lantern festivals, and collective work in the Bauhaus vegetable garden, which helped to improve the meal plan at the Bauhaus in the difficult years after the war.

2. A shift to aesthetic functionalism (1922–1923). The years 1922 and 1923 were marked by a deliberate shift to industry. After the Thuringian local government asked Gropius in 1922 to account for the Bauhaus' achievements, he organized an exhibition he called "Kunst und Technik: Eine neue Einheit" (Art and technology: a new unity). This motto not only described the exhibited works, but was indicative of a coming shift in the Bauhaus' focus from design as a form of expressive experimentalism to design at the service of industrial production. This ideological shift was met by bitter opposition by Itten, and came to a head when Gropius proposed using the furniture workshop (then led by Itten) to fulfill a large work order for an industrial company. The "Gropius/Itten" clash, which ultimately became a fundamental debate about the Bauhaus' new direction, ended in Itten's resignation. He was replaced by Gropius' "personal discovery," László Moholy-Nagy, whose enthusiasm for light and clarity greatly impressed the director. Moholy-Nagy took over Itten's preliminary course and replaced it with a foundational one in which three-dimensional objects were developed in line with Constructivist principles (→ Constructivism). He also took over the metal workshop and, together with Joost Schmidt and Herbert Bayer, designed the clear and unadorned (→) typography for the advertising graphics that were used to promote the Bauhaus' 1923 exhibition. These developments resulted in more and increasingly intensified collaborations with industry.

3. Exemplary manifestations of a new aesthetic for the industry and media (1924–1927). Despite all its successes, reactionary groups forced the Weimar Bauhaus to close in 1924. The period between its closing and its 1926 reopening in Dessau saw yet another shift in focus, to organizational issues and the creative planning of new buildings designed by Gropius. The cubelike forms typical of Bauhaus architecture were clear and simple, the use of large reflective windows a symbol of transparency and dematerialization. This industrial aesthetic was also reflected in the steel-tube furniture and metal lighting designs from the period.

During this time, the Bauhaus increased and professionalized its media presence by producing publications such as the *bauhaus* journal and the Bauhaus series of books, nearly all of which were designed by Moholy-Nagy in keeping with the principles of his "New Typography." The increasing significance of print media was also reflected in the curriculum. When the Bauhaus moved to Dessau, it added lettering, typography, and advertising to its academic program; in 1927, architecture was added as an independent course of study taught by Hannes Meyer.

4. Programmatic focus on economic efficiency and technical and academic methodology (1928–1930). Hannes Meyer became director after Walter Gropius resigned, a shift that represented more than a mere personnel change; with Meyers at the helm, the Gropius era's understated aesthetics were replaced by the era of "functionality." Unpretentious furniture made of plywood that could be self-assembled was to reduce the price of Bauhaus products and, in line with Meyer's socialist slogan "popular requirements instead of luxury requirements," make them affordable for the working class. This emphasized the economic and commercial value of Bauhaus products even more. Rationality and technical and academic methodology dominated the curriculum's philosophy. The architecture department for instance began producing "functional analyses" that depicted in diagram form a wide range of factors and scenarios relating to a building's use, including lighting, noise, and sequences of movement (with examples given even for postmen and thieves). Typographical graphic design for printed materials was dominated by photographs with clearly defined motifs, mostly close-up views, in order to achieve the highest level of clarity possible.

5. The Bauhaus as depoliticized School of Architecture (1930–1933). Mies van der Rohe replaced Meyer as director after the radical right-wing party forced him to abandon his position. Because of the difficult political situation, Mies van der Rohe concentrated on depoliticizing the Bauhaus. He restricted students' rights, shortened the program to six semesters, and changed the objectives and structure of the workshops. In-house production was stopped, and building models were created to deliver to the industry. He also merged the metal and woodworking/furniture workshops with the architecture department's technical workshops to form a "building and assembly workshop." This act not only damaged the thriving production in the workshops that helped finance the Bauhaus, but also essentially turned it into a school of architecture with some affiliated, subordinate workshops. Nonetheless, these efforts were ignored after the National Socialists won the election in Dessau in 1932. The school moved into an abandoned telephone factory in Berlin-Steglitz.

Directed by Mies van der Rohe as a Freies Lehr- und Forschungs-institut (Free teaching and research institute), the Bauhaus was dissolved in 1933 after the Gestapo searched and sealed off the premises.

But there is also a postscript: while other members of the Bauhaus were displaying a more or less ambivalent attitude toward the new power structure, Hannes Meyer turned up in the Soviet Union with a red Bauhaus brigade in 1930. Gropius and Wilhelm Wagenfeld were also vocal in their opposition to Hitler's seizure of power, particular with regards to the enforced political conformity of the (→) Deutscher Werkbund in 1934. Yet, at the same time, Gropius and other advocates of modernism hoped to establish it as specifically "German art." These ambitions were realized in the sense that many members of the Bauhaus were given positions in fields like industrial engineering, advertising, and exhibition design that suited the interests of the new Nazi government. In 1934, Gropius and Mies van der Rohe designed sections of the propaganda exhibition "Deutsches Volk—Deutsche Arbeit" (German people and German work), and Mies van der Rohe designed a section in Speer's pavilion at the Paris Expo in 1937. Of the early Bauhaus masters, Herbert Bayer was perhaps most influential in forming the "look" of important Nazi propaganda, at least until his work—and that of almost every other Bauhaus painter—was defamed in the Munich exhibition "Entartete Kunst" (Degenerate Art).

Eventually, Bayer permanently emigrated to the United States along with Gropius, Mies van der Rohe, and many other members of the Bauhaus. Josef and Anni Albers were awarded professorships at (→) Black Mountain College in Aspen, Colorado; Gropius was called to Harvard University in Cambridge, Massachusetts, where he taught together with Marcel Breuer; Mies van der Rohe went to Chicago in 1938 to become director of architecture at the Amour Institute, later the Illinois Institute of Technology (IIT), where he was supported by former Bauhaus professors Ludwig Hilberseimer and Walter Peterhans. László Moholy-Nagy founded the New Bauhaus in Chicago and Herbert Bayer became a successful advertising, graphics, and exhibition designer.

Yet, many other former members of the Bauhaus continued to work until the end of the Third Reich in Germany—in Hamburg, for example, for Büro Speer, or in other fields in the service of the Nazi government. A few years before the end of the war, Mies van der Rohe wrote to the Reichsarchitekten-Kammer (Guild of German Architects) to express how happy he would be to return to Germany to help rebuild the country. PE |

→ *Design and Politics, Education, Functionalism, History, Industrial Design, International Style, Modernity*

Droste, M. 2006. *Bauhaus, 1919–1933*. Cologne: DuMont.

Haus, A., ed. 1994. *Bauhaus-Ideen, 1919–1994: Bibliografie und Beiträge zur Rezeption des Bauhausgedankens*. Berlin: Reimer.

Wick, R. K. 2000. *Teaching at the Bauhaus*. Trans. S. Mason and S. Lebe. Ostfildern-Ruit: Hatje Cantz.

Wingler, H. M. 1978: *The Bauhaus, 1919–1933: Weimar, Dessau, Berlin, Chicago*. Cambridge, MA: MIT Press.

BEAUTY

It is striking to note that the adjective "beautiful" (as well as its opposite "ugly") occurs quite frequently in public discussions of design, whereas professional and academic reports on the subject scarcely mention the word. Clearly, the latter is a reflection of the fear that the use of the term will reduce design to the status of decoration, and thus fall prey to superficial chat about taste. Consequently, reflecting on beauty has been left out of most design discourse to date.

Certainly some of what should be considered and written about beauty in the context of design is already formulated in the category of (→) aesthetics. Nevertheless, it is worth at least recalling the possibility of reflecting on beauty in and of itself. It is all the more important to do so given that design necessarily moves within a network of ideas that use appeals to rationality to bolster its legitimacy, and thus risks sacrificing its unique identity. Precisely because of this, designers should not be surprised when their work is dismissed as ideological and merely decorative.

More than that, one should perhaps consider whether beauty will represent a key category for the future observation and understanding of design. After all, the idea of beauty demands so many questions about thinking and action and judging that it opens up very complex territory to be explored by design practitioners and theorists. This becomes even clearer if not only beauty but also "the beautiful" are to be defined and described.

That is because "the beautiful" is distinct from, say, taste (which, according to Immanuel Kant, is not open to dispute since it is merely a private matter) and even from the simply attractive, which is usually dependent on the specific contexts of a time period or culture. It would be just as mistaken to reduce the beautiful to harmonies—that is, purely to what can be calculated. Linking the beautiful firmly to the zeitgeist or a lifestyle or simply with some notion of perfection would also be inappropriate or contentious; the former is too random and manipulative, while the latter dismisses the quite realistic possibility of considering the imperfect beautiful. It would also be too simplistic merely to view the empirically pleasing as a perception of the beautiful, since such pleasure would have to be examined under specific conditions and would therefore be subject to ongoing criticism. For example, the human apparatus of (→) perception is apparently at times so enthusiastic about serial structures like parallel lines or right angles that, as the German scientist Hermann Helmholtz demonstrated back in the nineteenth century, the brain constructs them itself, since all its neural networks are presumably stimulated by, for reasons of efficiency, things that remain the same and are efficient at comparing similar things.

Moreover, it is not especially surprising to note that some things have been called beautiful in different historical periods, whereas others have continued to be considered beautiful throughout the ages. The question of whether the description of the beautiful, as that which is perceived with "disinterested pleasure" (Immanuel Kant), can apply to design as well is inherently challenging—and even perhaps describes its subversive core. Of course, we are also still left with the question of whether the beautiful exists at all, even though empirically we often seem to have it at our disposal. BL |

BEL DESIGN

Bel Design, which translates to "beautiful design" in English, was the Italian equivalent to (→) Good Design in Germany. Bel Design had its heyday in the 1960s and early 1970s, beginning with the onset of Italy's economic boom and ending when the oil crisis and industry-critical antidesign movements resulted in widespread cynicism about design's role in progress. The typical characteristics of Bel Design were elegant form, experimentation, and collaborations with industries interested in and open to innovation. Collaborations with the plastics industry proved to be especially productive. Bel Design produced many modern classics such as Plia, Giancarlo Piretti's Plexiglas folding chair for Castelli (1968), 4867, Joe Colombo's chair for Kartell (1968), Selene, Vico Magistretti's plastic chair for Artemide (1969), and the Divisumme 18, Mario Bellini's calculator for Olivetti (1972). CN |

→ *Industrial Design*

BENCHMARKING

The term "benchmarking" refers to the processes of comparing a specific product, process or program with other successful products, processes, or programs; assessing any weaknesses; and establishing strategies or measures to improve performance, practice, user response, competitiveness, productivity, and so on. In other words, the goal of benchmarking is to identify and implement "best practices" within a company or organization. The term is used most often in the fields of information technology (IT) and business management, though anything from computer programs to forms of government can be benchmarked.

Regardless of what is being evaluated, the principles of benchmarking remain the same: 1) compare, 2) assess weaknesses, 3) establish strategies for improvement, 4) implement the strategies, 5) reevaluate. For designers, the information obtained through benchmarking could lead to significant improvements to the design of a product or, via a better understanding of marketing potential, innovative new strategies and services. TG |

→ *Design Management, Globalization, Information Design, Quality, Research, Service Design, Strategic Design, Trend*

BIONICS

Bionics is a field that analyzes biological principles and systems in order to apply this knowledge to the creation of engineering systems.

The etymology of the word "bionics" stems from the confluence of two words: the "bio" of biology and "onics" of electronics. The "Six Million Dollar Man" is a popular icon from the 1970s who represents this convergence: a human electronically rewired to possess superhuman strength and speed.

A large focus of this field is on human bionics: the creation of electromechanical devices that interact with the human body to replace or restore bodily functions through engineering (→ *Mechatronic Design, Engineering Design*). The idea is to create a seamless integration between human thought, generated in the brain, and movement, generated by an externally created mechanical device.

The design of these devices relies upon electronic feedback mechanisms that measure the real-time behavior and performance of body parts in order to determine their level of functionality, and to improve upon it. For example, cochlear implants restore hearing function by bypassing damaged portions of the ear and sending electronic signals directly to the auditory nerve. Retinal implants stimulate retinal cells electrically to create the sensation of seeing light.

The design of artificial limbs for amputees has evolved due to the influence of bionics: instead of relying upon movement of the residual limb (the portion of the limb remaining after amputation) to generate movement in the prosthetic, bionic prosthetics move via control generated by the central nervous system. The general idea behind these types of devices is to allow human thought to stimulate mechanical movement, in the same way that natural biological systems currently function.

In this field of design, there are several different methodologies currently used to achieve communication with the brain: some researchers focus on implanting electrodes in the brain or scalp, while others experiment with detectors outside of the body. In essence, the brain generates a command signal that is transmitted through the nerves to sensors that measure the electric impulses, and then to a computer that analyzes these impulses. This data is then transmitted to mechanical prostheses—hands, arms, and legs—that move according to the impulses generated by the brain. An example of the use of this technology is a prosthetic arm that sends electronic signals directly to the nerve endings of the residual limb to restore mechanical functions of above-elbow amputees.

Other useful applications of this kind of bionic technology are targeted toward helping those who have been paralyzed. Electrical impulses from the paralyzed user's brain can stimulate the motion of a wheelchair, or a mouse, enabling the user to move and to communicate in a way that would have been impossible even in the very recent past.

The present trends in bionic devices seem to focus mainly on restoring human function. However, the potential to attempt to enhance human powers beyond natural human abilities certainly exists. Some evidence of this controversial stance can be found in the field of running prosthetics: the prosthetic legs of Aimee Mullins, a double amputee and US Paralympian, are based upon the biomechanics of a cheetah. Constructed from carbon fiber, with a shock absorber and spring, these legs give their wearer the ability to mimic the running motion of the world's fastest land mammal (clocked at seventy miles per hour). By means of this external prosthetic, the wearer is able to store energy in a manner that is much more efficient than human locomotion. Though humans who wear such prosthesis may not attain the same speeds, their enhanced ability to run like swift animals instead of humans has been debated.

Another manifestation of bionics is robotic applications based upon animal motion and behaviors. Physiology and robotics researchers at Stanford, U.C. Berkeley, Harvard, and Johns Hopkins universities recently collaborated to mechanically model the joint and leg structure of the cockroach. Their intention was to develop a running robot with six legs that could run on uneven terrain, and be used in applications like bomb diffusion and military reconnaissance. NASA has also considered robots based on insect motion for its missions to explore Mars, known for its irregular landscape. Researchers in the Leg Lab, within the Media Lab at MIT, have created robots that walk and hop based on the biomechanics of kangaroos (called the "Uniroo") and dinosaurs (called "Troody"). Mechanically modeling these kinds of animal motions can lead to advances in prosthetic development.

Bionics is also sometimes referred to as "biomimicry," the study of biological systems, patterns, behaviors, and forms to create innovative new products. This often involves examining the evolutionarily optimized behaviors of animals and plants to glean information that could be applicable to the creation of products. Some common applications of "biomimicry" include Velcro (based on the grappling hooks of seeds) and the airplane wing designs of the Wright brothers (based on the wings of birds). The applications of "biomimicry" stretch beyond consumer (→)

products and tangible objects to the design of systems based upon the principles of ecological systems, in fields such as agriculture, architecture, and computing (→ *System*).

The field of biomaterials represents another manifestation of "biomimicry": high-performing natural (→) materials are analyzed in order to develop synthetic versions with similar properties. These materials, though synthetic, are often biodegradable. An example of this is spider silk, an incredibly light material that, due to its unusual molecular structure, possesses three times the strength of steel. Scientists have researched spider silk's molecular structure in order to produce a human-made version; potential applications of this new material include biodegradable sutures for surgery, and artificial tendons and ligaments. In another example, in order to create a very strong, waterproof glue, scientists have studied the way that the blue mussel generates a waterproof adhesive to attach itself to surfaces in rough waters. Many of the ideas behind bionics were once only expressed within the realm of science fiction. This fictional genre, which expresses humans' fascination with artificial life, has created imaginary creatures that represent the melding of human and other species' characteristics. As technology and the field of bionics continue to advance, the merging of the science fiction world and the real world seems an increasingly possible reality. AR |

→ *Futuristic Design*

Benyus, J. M. 1997. *Biomimicry: Innovation inspired by nature*. pp. 4–7, 118–125. New York: Morrow.
Kennedy, S. 2006. Biomimicry/bimimetics: General principles and practical examples. *The Science Creative Quarterly* 2: 321. http://www.scq.ubc.ca/biomimicrybimimetics-general-principles-and-practical-examples/
Vogel, S. 2003. *Comparative biomechanics: Life's physical world*. pp. 3–5. Princeton, NJ: Princeton Univ. Press.

BLACK MOUNTAIN COLLEGE

Black Mountain College was founded by Andrew Rice, a Professor of Classics, in 1933. Located in the mountains of North Carolina, close to the city of Asheville, the school became a hotbed for experimental art and design during its twenty-three years of operation. While scholars often associate Black Mountain with important fine artists, such as Cy Twombly and Robert Rauschenberg, and musicians, such as John Cage, design was also integral to the school's curriculum. Joseph and Anni Albers, Walter Gropius, and Buckminster Fuller all spent time teaching and shaping the history of twentieth-century design while at Black Mountain.

After losing his teaching position at Rollins College in Florida, Rice vowed that Black Mountain would be an oasis of academic freedom. He mandated that his new school would be based on the principles of Athenian democracy, where faculty had complete say over academic policies. Deans, trustees, provosts, chancellors, and other mainstays of university life, were not included in Rice's plan, and in place of this hierarchical structure a board of fellows, run by the faculty, was implemented. This board would hire, fire, and work on financing Rice's new endeavor. From the outset, Black Mountain positioned the arts as important as traditional subject matter. The arts were not pigeonholed as an extracurricular folly; they were integral to every student's course of study. No requirements, and an unusually flexible idea about what constituted good (→) education, provided an environment where the arts and design flourished.

To ensure the strength of its design courses, Black Mountain's founders hired Joseph Albers to run its art program. After spending years teaching at the German (→) Bauhaus, arguably the most important art and design school of the twentieth century, Albers came to the United States with his wife, Anni, in 1933. Albers made certain that many of the leading names in early twentieth art and design, such as Walter Gropius, Marcel Breuer, and Ferdinand Leger, came to teach and lecture at Black Mountain. Focusing on color theory, geometry, textile design, materials, graphic design, and other issues related to the design process, the Alberses brought their experimental vision to American students. When the campus of the school moved, in 1941, Marcel Breuer and Walter Gropius were asked to design a master plan. While magnificent in conception, fiscal prudence meant that Black Mountain had to go with another plan by architect A. Lawrence Kocher.

One of the most celebrated designers to spend time at Black Mountain College was Buckminster Fuller. Joseph Albers asked Fuller to come to Black Mountain in the summer of 1948. At the school, Fuller experimented with Geodesic Domes—a form of architecture that utilized what he termed an Octet Truss, a support structure that relied on Fuller's obsession with geometry. He worked closely with students trying to assess how issues related to tensile strength and affordable design could help revolutionize architecture.

In a special issue of *Design* magazine, which celebrated Black Mountain's 1945 Summer Art Institute, there are short articles about the utopian ideals that the school attempted to uphold. Walter Gropius, Joseph and Anni Albers, Julia and Lyonel Feininger, and others reported on how their work at Black Mountain brought forth a democratizing sense of art education that would, they contended, change the face of what it means to live with art and design. The most powerful words are those by Jane Slater, a student who had recently finished her course of study at the school. Slater ends her description of her fellow students by explaining that the Black Mountain educational process helps "to prepare the student to meet the indiscriminately crowded world." Through a revolutionary conceptualization of art and design education, Black Mountain incited novel ways of thinking about design in the twentieth century. DB |

Duberman, M. 1972. *Black Mountain: An exploration in community*. New York: E. P. Dutton & Co.

Harris, M. E. 1987. *The arts at Black Mountain College*. Cambridge, MA: MIT Press.

Katz, V., ed. 2002. *Black Mountain College: Experiment in art*. Cambridge, MA: MIT Press.

BLUEPRINT

The blueprint process is a photographic printing process (using light exposure) that was first developed in 1842. Blueprints are also known as cyanotypes due to their typical cyan color. They are negative images because it is the blue areas between the lines that are printed, rather than the white lines themselves. The blueprint's precision has long made it a reliable method of reproducing technical engineering diagrams. Blueprint is also a more general term used to indicate any plan, (→) prototype, or (→) model in design—for instance, the proof pages reviewed before the final approval of a (→) layout. ^{TK} |

BRAINSTORMING

Brainstorming describes a problem-solving technique by a group of people in any field and involves the spontaneous and uncensored contribution of ideas from all members of the group. It is a popular method for generating ideas in the design field. It was devised by the advertising industry in the 1950s and remains popular in this sector. Typically, it would be a facilitated, though loosely organized, session in which group members are licensed to propose any idea without censure, in order to increase the likelihood of innovative and original ideas emerging (→ Innovation). It is also linked to such approaches as "blue-sky thinking" and has received growing criticism. Empirical research on the effectiveness of brainstorming suggests that it is a better technique for team building than it is for generating useful ideas. Due to this research, a number of new methods of brainstorming have evolved which seek to strike a better balance between an individual's ability to generate original ideas and the brainstorming potential of having those individual ideas receive a range of inputs from other team members. The Post-it note and the whiteboard are favored recording media for such sessions. ^{TM} |

→ Collaborative Design, Participatory Design

BRAND

A brand is a name, design, or symbol that distinguishes the goods or services of one seller from those of competitors through (→) added value. The brand's added value is a modern construct of negotiated relations at the center of all exchanges and interactions among consumers, businesses, and marketing climates.

The term "brand" is broadly applied to goods, services, and even people in the fields of marketing, advertising, sales, promotions, public relations, design studies, and design implementation, among others. Here, the meaning of the brand is discussed from two different perspectives: the brand as it applies particular meaning for marketing and advertising purposes; and the brand as it assumes new meaning for social scientists and designers. When we speak of a brand, we may think of an objectified product or service that can be bought, sold, traded, aspired to, and so on, by consumers; yet the brand is also a highly interactive process that is never static. This text regards the central marketing concept of the brand from a critical perspective, moving from popular applied views to a more current critique in recent scholarship. In this, the notion of a brand is treated as a modern construct of negotiated relations at the center of all business and marketing interactions in economic systems of exchange. From a functional perspective, a brand is a name, design, symbol, or any other feature that distinguishes the goods or services of one seller or group of sellers from those of its competitors. A leading US marketing theorist, David Aaker (1996), adds that brand identity is a set of associations that represent what the brand stands for and implies a promise to customers from the organization's members. This identity helps establish a relationship between the brand and the customer by generating a value proposition that involves functional, emotional, or self-expressive benefits. For instance, a popular brand name such as McDonald's carries many associations for people: hamburgers, enjoyment, children, fast food, and the golden arches. These associations collectively make up the brand image, and the brand, in return, promises to deliver on these associations and expectations. All companies, therefore, strive to build a strong favorable brand image for their consumers.

The brand obtains meaning and relevance for consumers through repeated use of designs, advertising, sales, and promotions. Successful and well-known brands like Nike, for instance, acquire meaning and (→) value through frequent associations with other culturally relevant symbols, such as associations with basketball star Michael Jordan. Through repeated association, the social relevance, fame, success, popularity, and sex appeal of Michael Jordan (himself a brand) transfers associated meaning to the Nike product, thus giving it meaning. Eventually even the designed (→) logo of the Swoosh is instantly identifiable without the Nike name, and becomes an object of aspiration and devotion for consumers. To be sure, a brand can acquire negative associations as well as positive ones, such as health concerns about obesity for McDonald's, or exploitive labor practices for Nike. This requires the brand to respond proactively, such as providing healthy menu options, or codes of conduct for factories. In other cases, brands can act as political vehicles for corporations to mitigate negative images or further public goodwill. For instance, the Starbucks Corporation now promotes fair-trade practices with its local coffee growers to lessen hegemonic images and create more favorable consumer impressions, and Barbara's Bakery—makers of Puffins cereal—donates funds to the Maine coast Audubon society for care of puffins.

At the core of the brand is the marketers' and designers' task of creating a sense of difference for their product, and then maintaining this difference in the face of competition from other brands. Developing a sense of difference for a product or service is variously expressed in business vernacular as the (→) USP (unique selling proposition), the brand equity, and point of differentiation, and is thought to add value and differentiate the product as unique in the eyes of the consumer. Brands are thus more than products in how the added value persuades consumers to buy and use the product based on perceived differences. From this perspective, a brand is mainly distinguished from a commodity by the user's perceptions and feelings toward the branded product and how it performs. This means, for some theorists, that the brand ultimately resides in the psyche of the consumer.

Still other theorists define the brand as a complex (→) symbol that carries various meanings for an individual, conveying up to six levels of significance. These levels include brand attributes (its tangible features), brand benefits (the physical or emotional advantage of using the brand), brand values (linking user and producer in a shared belief system), brand culture (a reflection of the manufacturer's association), brand personality (characteristics that the user projects onto the brand), and finally the user him/herself (the type of consumer who actually buys or uses this product). Brands have also been discussed as conceptual entities that live at the center of contemporary marketing discourse. Like (→) trademarks of earlier times, brands can function as "virtual worlds" which attempt to establish intimacy with consumers through anonymous and abstract advertising messages, creating sort of a prosthetic personality.

The difficulty with these understandings of the brand is that they do not articulate the interconnected cultural, social, and economic factors that shape the brand along with the individual consumer's own sentiments and attachments. People's attachments to brands aren't merely virtual or symbolic, but real, creating functional roles in people's lives that are meaningful. For the designer, a brand not only resides as a symbol in the mind of the consumer, but is also a material (→) artifact put to various intended and unintended uses by the consumer. Some anthropologists note, for instance, how gift cloth used in Indonesian weddings changes meaning as it is used, modified, and passed to others; or how a car in Africa alters meaning as it is passed on to different owners and transforms from a status symbol, to a less desirable used car, to a taxi, and then to a cart for mules (sans engine). Material objects and the brands they support are subject to multiple uses and interpretations. Brands are not merely arbitrary signs, but as their material condition changes, their meaning and use changes, since they are subject to shifting physical, economic, and semiotic conditions (→ Semiotics).

Thus designers must incorporate the transient nature of material artifacts into the brands they design and the designs they brand. In the network of relations that surround them, brands are also the means to calculate and strategize corporate agendas for marketing managers. For instance, brands are used by ad agencies as a means to further their personal and professional liaisons with corporate clients (Malefyt and Moeran 2003). In addition, brands are used as tools for creating, modifying, and adapting new insights by vendors, suppliers, and the whole network of individuals and groups who are strategically committed to making a brand "live." The brand thus exists as an imagined and real relationship from which value is constructed in a process of continual adjustment and modification by internal and external inputs of individuals, corporate initiatives, and cultural forces.

Even an apparently stable brand is subject to cultural forces and adaptive inputs by consumers and market conditions. For instance, Volvo is a brand that famously stands for safety. Yet safety is a fluid concept that is continuously negotiated in the consumers' lived experience. Ideas and practices around safety change with consumers' experience with injury or avoidance, with life stages and situations, with memories and recollections, as well as with how product (→) quality and (→) performance are perceived through factory recalls, new models, and so forth. Thus the essential brand meaning of safety for Volvo is really a constantly negotiated and challenged social construct that must be continuously readjusted and reevaluated by the corporation, advertising agency, media channels, and automobile designers, with newer styles, images, and shifting ideas of what safety is and the role it plays in consumers' lives.

From this perspective of fluidity, brands are created in relation to multiple systems of constantly shifting meaning. Indeed, brand value derives its meaning from the exchange, interaction, modification, adaptation, and contestation of all its relational aspects: consumers are in motion, constantly buying more, so that the percentage of market share grows; advertising is in motion so that ad campaigns never become stale; (→) trends are in motion, against which brands identify; corporations are in motion as employees shift positions within and among companies; and especially advertising agencies are in motion since thirty-five to forty percent turnover per annum promises a constant refreshment of new people, new ideas.

What this means is that brands are about continuously shifting relationships and positions among people, things, contexts, and subjective and objective conditions. From this perspective, the primary characteristic of a brand—that of differentiating its position from other brands while remaining unique for consumers—is about sustaining change. Differentiating a brand through constant improvement and ($\rightarrow$) innovation is not only about brand positioning, but may indeed be the most relevant expression of the brand as change. Change creates ($\rightarrow$) value. This means that brand change, which occurs as a result of constant realignment (or positioning) relative to market shifts and other brands, is not merely a byproduct of branding, but rather, change is central to the brand, in and of itself. The fact that companies hire new branding groups and designers, marketing teams constantly field new studies, and new insights continuously challenge, build on, and replace old studies, attests to the notion of change as a constant in the business world. In other words, brands are about sustaining difference for the sake of adding value, and value is created through perpetual change.

We can also take the notion of change in terms of exchange value to distinguish a brand from a commodity. When we examine brands within the systems of economic exchange in which they belong, brands stand at the opposite end of a spectrum from commodities. A commodity has practical use value that can be exchanged in a transaction for money or something else of more or less equivalent value. A brand, in contrast, is decommoditized and its value is achieved from being singular, exclusive, and unique. For a brand to be differentiated from a commodity through added value, it must ultimately be unexchangeable or inalienable. This presents a paradox for the brand. For what marketers vehemently guard from competitors as the brand's most cherished possession—its unchanging core essence—is also what is strongly promoted for its functional use value in commodity-type exchanges. In this sense, a brand might be viewed as a specialized form of "guarded" exchange, or what anthropologist Annette Weiner (1992) has termed a process of "keeping-while-giving."

Weiner addresses this paradox of economic exchange among the Trobriand Islanders as a central issue of all social life: how to keep some things out of circulation in the face of pressure to exchange and give other things away. She notes that while some things are easy to give away, like Trobriand Kula shells, other things are closely guarded and never given away, such as Trobriand heirlooms. Along these lines, we can apply this idea to the brand as a uniquely constructed, special type of commodity relation that creates an exclusive exchange of keeping-while-giving. The brand's special type of relation of keeping-while-giving between corporation and consumer allows the corporation a certain legitimizing and even sacred authority over what is essentially a functional commodity. Thus, while what the brand means in all its intangible symbolic value is kept, what the brand does as a tangible product is given away in commodity-market exchange with consumers.

Since a brand is both physical and tangible as a commodity product, and yet, imbued with great symbolic and intangible meaning, it becomes highly ambiguous and therefore powerful. Indeed, it is this source of ambiguity in brands—an immutable symbol that is also a malleable product—which lets individuals and groups use material resources and social practices to gain authority and legitimate control over it. The brand thus achieves value in its ambiguous mutability. It shifts between a physical commodity of exchange where it is modified, altered, adapted to particular changing consumer needs, and a highly symbolic, unchanging icon that supports a corporation's values, beliefs, and practices.

It is brand's paradoxical mutability, in fact, which allows it to secure an enduring and permanent position in a world where loss and decay normally deteriorate material possessions. The brand acts as a stabilizing force against market place changes since its transcendent symbolic presence authenticates the corporation, its history, origins, and mission as symbolically unchanging. In this way, the inalienability of the brand through its unchanging essence and corporate history becomes a representation of how (→) corporate identities are maintained through time, even while the physical features of the brand allow it to change, adapt, and modify to new contingencies of markets and consumer use (→ Continuity). For example, Ford looks to its founder Henry Ford for the corporation's unchanging values of success, inventiveness, and capability, even though its cars today are completely different from what Henry Ford envisioned.

It is precisely this ambiguity that is central to the brand paradox which gives the brand its power, value, and social extendibility. The use-value of the brand as product, performing functions in certain social settings for the consumer, converges and diverges with the image-value of the brand as symbolic carrier of corporate identity in settings of the board room and marketing meetings. The brand, thus as a social force reflective of permanence and change, brings together actors from the corporate, design, and consumer sides, in the continuous negotiation of its meaning.

Finally, the brand as a modern construct of negotiated relations in design, business and marketing interactions can be treated as a special field or space of charged engagement. According to Brian Moeran, every social world has a primary frame of interaction or social drama in which that social world is legitimized and sustained (Moeran 2005). In the world of corporate marketing, the brand becomes the social drama that sustains and gives legitimacy to the many actions of marketers, corporations, advertising agencies, media suppliers, designers, and so forth. The brand, therefore, is not an actual objectified thing or symbol for individuals as commonly treated by marketers and designers, but rather represents a dynamic space for strategic interactions. The brand is more like a social drama, since it is through the notion of a field that is never stable or static in which agents are always making their moves; it is a space of possibilities. In this regard, the brand shifts its status as an object (trademark, (→) logo, corporate color) to that of an entire set of agents engaged in the field that constantly create, shape, and re-create the brand's meaning. In other words, brand meaning and value are not produced by a corporation, ad agency, or even consumer, but by the entire set of agents engaged in the field. Thus as an expression and outcome of many types of interactions, the brand acquires a certain social value and acceptance, which allows all these interactions between agents to be legitimate.

To summarize, the brand is both an exchangeable and commoditized object as well as the symbolic subject of calculated and contested relationships among consumers, manufacturers, advertising agencies, distributors, designers, and the myriad vendors who come in contact with it. Brands, thus, are as much a perpetual process of sustaining difference to maintain uniqueness and added value as they are the tangible service or product of which consumers functionally use and enjoy everyday. TWM |

→ *Advertisement, Branding, Campaign, Market Research, Product, Social, Strategic Design*

Aaker, D. 1996. *Building strong brands*. New York: Free Press.

Malefyt, T., and B. Moeran, eds. 2003. *Advertising cultures*. Oxford, United Kingdom: Berg Publishers.

Moeran, B. 2005. *The business of ethnography: Strategic exchanges, people and organizations*. Oxford, United Kingdom: Berg Publishers.

Weiner, A. 1992. *Inalienable possessions: The paradox of keeping-while-giving*. Berkeley: Univ. of California Press.

BRANDING

Brands generate pictures in the minds of consumers. For instance, an apple with a bite taken out of it represents not only the functional products of Apple computers, but also comes with a host of associated brand characteristics such as simplicity, uniqueness, and aesthetics. As Apple has expanded its product line to include mobile audio devices and phones, these too have been branded with the same characteristics.

This example reveals a general and essential dimension to the development of brands (that is the process of branding). Although the attribution of certain brand characteristics to the product is ultimately dependent on consumer interpretations, the process of branding is always entrepreneurial, that is, purposefully initiated and guided.

Around the turn of the twentieth century, the direct, personal contact that had previously existed between buyer and seller at the local market level was largely displaced by the rise of anonymous, transregional mass markets. As local businesses were supplanted by major commercial companies, entrepreneurs who had spent lifetimes struggling to establish their visions, ideas, and comprehensive business philosophies became the first brand creators. Isolated examples of local entrepeneurship in the branding process still exist today in small or new businesses, even on the global level. However, the creators of brands today are generally acknowledged as temporary employees with a dedicated purpose within a company's marketing division.

The organizational conditions under which brands have developed over the last century may have changed, but the fundamental conditions behind successful marketing development have remained largely the same. The starting point of any potentially successful brand construction is, of course, the development and subsequent differentiation of its products. Since the functional aspects of products are becoming more and more similar, other features are needed to distinguish a product from its competitors. This is where the process of value-adding in brand development becomes important (→ *Added Value*). Once the branded characteristics of the product are developed and defined, they provide the basis with which the brand communicates its (→) values to the consumer, effecting all aspects of the product's appearance, packaging, marketing, and so on. The consistent use of these brand characteristics across a variety of medium for a sustained period of time ultimately serves to develop and establish a constructed image of the brand in the mind of the consumer.

In today's oversaturated and increasingly complex markets, with their endless cycles of new (→) product development, consumers can often feel overwhelmed or spoiled for choice. By providing consumers with a consistent point of reference with which to identify, brands can come with significant consumer benefits.

Commercially, brands are important because they ensure that specific businesses stand out amidst the mass of complex, dynamic, and globalized markets; that their core promises are conveyed; and, ultimately, that they remain anchored in the minds of their target groups. They also profit businesses by facilitating efficiency and effectiveness in (→) communications, presenting opportunities to capture new markets, and creating a loyal clientele base.

Internationally standardized processes are currently being developed to assess the ways in which brands accrue profit for its owners. Activating brand value in business financial reports is imminent, and finding ways to utilize it profitably for a company's many financial interests is no longer only an issue for communication experts, but also for investors and financial groups.

After more than two hundred years of existence, brands are more important than ever before, and encompass an everwidening field of applications. Branding is now attracting the non-profit and public sectors, and is even beginning to penetrate the very personal realm of the "me brand." Of course, it is important to acknowledge that the rise of the brand has also been accompanied by some serious, sometimes criminal, consequences.

Those seeking to profit from the power of brands have begun to produce, distribute, and sell (→) fake products at an alarming rate—today, counterfeit goods comprise over ten percent of the global market. This does not only pertain to (→) luxury goods; spare parts, medicines, and other products that can potentially effect the safety and well-being of its users are also counterfeited regularly. The danger that these contraband items pose to the economy and to society has prompted repeated calls for government intervention.

The fact that brands have become so ubiquitous in day-to-day culture and society has naturally stirred broader resistance. In recent years, brands have also been widely and loudly criticized for using politically, environmentally, and socially irresponsible means to achieve profit. In other words, the process of "branding" has come to be generally regarded as carrying more weight—and more connotations of unscrupulous behavior—than the related process of advertising, which is, at worst, condemned for being "subliminal." Brands have in fact become powerful (→) social institutions, and their creators and owners should be aware of this and act responsibly (→ *Ethics*). Attentive observers of contemporary society should also investigate the phenomenon of brands more closely, as constitutive aspects of modern society at the beginning of the twenty-first century. JH |

→ *Advertisement, Brand, Consumption, Corporate Identity*

BRIEF

The term "brief" has its origins in the notion of design as a (→) problem-solving activity. After a client identifies a problem, he or she prepares a suggested solution in the form of a "brief" to the designer, who decides how this idea is best realized. Pierre Boulanger, the CEO of Citroën, prepared a very simple and famous brief in 1938 as the basis of the popular 2CV design: "the car had to be an umbrella on four wheels with seats and capable of carrying fifty kilos of luggage, at a speed of 60 km. Its suspension must enable it to cross a field with a basket of eggs on the seat without breaking them with a maximum fuel consumption of 3 liters per 100 km." The task was defined by market research carried out by Citroën's principle stockholder, the Michelin company.

Today, a brief can consist of several hundred pages describing in detail the situation and (→) target group, the results of quantitative and qualitative (→) market research, the required service aspects (the quantitative and qualitative objectives of the project), as well as the available resources and schedule. The briefing—that is, the process in which both client and designer analyze and agree on the project's scope, aim, and budget—is therefore an important element of the (→) design process.

The complexity inherent to such negotiations makes it all the more surprising that a brief's structure and form can now be subject to standardization regulations, in Europe in accordance with DIN 69905 (→ *Quality Assurance*). Regardless of the quantitative specifications for project objectives and resources, the question arises as to whether it is at all possible to standardize and a priori "tie down" the design process. Indeed, practice has proven that knowledge gained by an integrative (→) heuristic design process can and should enhance the content of the brief at any given stage of the project. At the same time, practitioners of design are becoming more aware of both the growing need for and potential benefits of so-called "blue sky" projects for which, by definition, no briefs are prepared. PT |

→ *Design Planning, Problem Setting*

BROADCAST DESIGN

Broadcast design refers to the creation of (→) audiovisual designs for the screen. The term is closely—but not exclusively—associated with the television industry. Broadcast designers have a range of skills and are called upon to use graphics, (→) visual effects, live action, and (→) animation in their work.

Broadcast designers are involved in an very extensive range of on-air designs; title and end credits for TV shows and films, commercials, (→) trailers, music videos, and scrolling news tickers are just a few examples of the various forms their work can take. If live action is involved, they will often collaborate with other set, sound, and lighting designers to achieve the final product.

They may also be hired to create entire television or film network identities. This involves the design of all screened (→) logos, image clips, and commercials that are presented to strengthen and support the network's (→) brand identification. Broadcast designs of this nature will need to align with the designs of other print and off-air promotional products like packaging and stationery.

It was not until the 1970s in North America and the 1980s in Europe that broadcast design began to emerge as a discrete field in the television industry. This development intensified with the rising popularity of televisions, the resultant increase in the number of networks, and the development of broadcast technologies. In particular, the replacement of analog tools by digital technologies had a substantial effect on facilitating the efficient processing of screen images.

The first design studios specializing in audiovisual design products appeared on the expanding television market during the 1980s, and were largely dominated by American companies. This changed, however, when affordable (→) hardware and (→) software became available in the 1990s, triggering a dynamic boom in small and midsized design agencies in and outside the United States. Eventually, television networks began to address their broadcast design needs within their own graphic design departments. Although freelancers are often called in to work on complex projects, most networks continue to handle the bulk of their broadcast promotions needs in-house.

Well into the 1970s, title sequences and other audiovisual design elements were created on an editing table or using a rostrum camera that would record the material. In the 1970s, the company Quantel revolutionized broadcast design by introducing Paintbox®, a computer program that allowed designers to use a graphics tray and pen with traditional methods to develop still images and later moving images. Paintbox® became synonymous with broadcast design until the 1990s, when it was superseded by industry standard desktop systems. BB |

→ *Screen Design, Time-based Design*

C

CAD / CAM / CIM / CNC

The field of computer-aided design (or CAD) originated during the late 1950s and early 1960s with the development of several computer programs including Sketchpad, a rudimentary graphics interaction program developed by Ivan Sutherland at the Massachusetts Institute of Technology in 1963. Since then, computer-based tools have offered designers, engineers, architects, and other constructors newer, faster, and more precise possibilities for realizing their ideas at a rapidly evolving pace. Shifting the means of design from the traditional manual methods of drawing and model building to the digital process of materializing by way of a CNC (Computer Numerical Control) milling machine has had a significant impact on both the design process and its products. These processes present drawbacks as well as new opportunities. On the one hand, the digitalization of (→) product development processes has resulted in designs that rely almost exclusively on computers for every stage of development, and consequently neglect the important (→) haptic experiences that inform the process of object creation. In these cases, it is often difficult to test the product's functionality until very late in the production stages (→ *Testing*). On the other hand, mastering software can save time and resources, and make it easier and faster to carry out changes and corrections. The consolidation of work stages can also result directly in the broadening of the designer's responsibilities.

A CAD system model can be converted into production data for machines using CAM (Computer-Aided Manufacturing) software. The method of conversion depends on the desired product and the procedure it requires. Other production methods in addition to CNC include stereo lithography, Selective Laser Sintering (SLS), fused deposition modeling, laminated object modeling, and 3-D printing. These (→) rapid prototyping methods not only guarantee fast production, but are also economically sound alternatives to mass production or the creation of complex individual items.

In addition to the production of (→) prototypes and (→) models, companies use computers for a variety of purposes including computer-aided quality control (CAQ), computer-aided planning (CAP), and job costing. Consequently, all computer-aided processes and databases in the industrial sector are grouped under the phrase CIM (Computer-Integrated Manufacturing). DPO |

CAMPAIGN

The term "campaign" is most commonly used in the context of the military, politics, or advertising, and refers to a series of connected activities intended to produce a desired result. It can also refer to money-raising (capital or charitable campaigns) and public-awareness strategies (public health campaigns). Campaigns are most relevant to communication and media-based designers as they are almost all information-based (→ *Information Design, Visual Communication*). Campaign designs can last for weeks or years, and are frequently highly collaborative activities that utilize multiple modes of communication.

Political campaigns (→ *Design and Politics*) generate a great deal of work for graphic, image, and web-based designers as well as filmmakers, writers, (→) set designers, (→) event designers, and, increasingly (→) service designers. Politics is becoming more about packaging an image and less about debating the substance of policies and so has much in common with the strategies of (→) branding. Consequently, advertising and branding agencies are commissioned to manage political campaigns. They concentrate on presenting the candidate in an appropriate and convincing manner using a broad range of direct and indirect forms of (→) communication.

Public-awareness campaigns are most commonly taxpayer-funded communication strategies intended to create general awareness (of a new tax regime or the amalgamation of government offices, for instance), and/or to modify behavior (such as to reduce drunkdriving or prevent violence against women). There is a growing body of research into these very complex issues that can be used to help design effective campaign strategies. Behavior modification is, without question, the most difficult and unpredictable of campaigns. For example, the filmic shock tactics that are used in a bid to influence driving behavior and thus reduce car accidents will not necessarily modify the behavior of the age group at greatest risk—those that often find visual images of high-risk behavior exciting. An alternative approach could see a campaign designed to appeal to a sense of personal responsibility and shame by creating a scenario that anticipates the sense of overwhelming remorse experienced by a driver who has killed someone. Or peer and "hero" pressure might be used (having young girls express a lack of interest in boys who smoke or famous football players in anti-homophobia campaigns) to appeal to the aspirational goals of the viewer.

Essentially all advertising campaigns now use the same multi-platform approaches to promote products and services, and therefore go to great lengths to integrate their campaign messages across an everincreasing variety of media and communication channels. Because of this, the idea of a campaign (that is, an integrated series of operations) becomes even more relevant as the advertisers have to try harder to reach an audience across many media and contexts. Marketing often attempts to camouflage the promotion of a product by using strategies such as product placement in the film and TV industries. Within this diffuse "mediascape," advertisers are attempting to both "find" the audience for the product and to advertise to them in ways that are hard to avoid or resist or even to identify.

The rapid rise of the Internet, the dispersion of communication channels, and the general public skepticism about the ability of charities and politicians to "make a difference" has put traditional campaign approaches under pressure to adapt. In the 1990s, "viral marketing" was pioneered by campaigns trying to find forms of communication and context that were more likely either to find the desired viewer and/or to be passed along through social networks by way of web links, blogs, and so on. Political campaigns have also adapted to this social networking phenomenon with candidate web sites that enable voters to view messages and speeches, make suggestions, get involved in linked blogs discussing various issues, link these into other blogs, and so on. This approach has been concurrent with a rapid rise in portable image and video capture, particularly in the case of new cell-phone technology, that has resulted in almost every moment of a political campaign potentially being "on the record" and able to be distributed through web-based social (→) networking (now being referred to as the democratization of the campaign itself). In this context, the "image managers" struggle with the inherent contradiction of controlling every dimension of a campaign while fully utilizing the potential of these anarchic information distribution networks. TM |

→ *Advertisement, Brand, Branding, Strategic Design*

CAPITAL GOODS

In the (→) industrial design sector, capital goods design is a specialization that focuses on the conception, design, and construction of standard machine products. In the (→) suppy chain, capital goods are complex technological products that are implemented to manufacture commodities and build capital using technical services.

Capital goods design is sometimes reduced to nothing more than designing a stylish shell around the complex machinery the closely related discipline of (→) engineering design produces for the interior mechanisms (→ *Coating, Styling*). It is important to note, however, that capital goods products are also pieces of engineered equipment and thus subject to strict, prescribed (→) ergonomic and constructive rules. Occupational safety, achievability, maintenance, process cycles, (→) usability, and the reduction of product complexity to the most essential recognizable features are only some of the parameters that need to be considered when designing capital goods. Design's social responsibility in relation to capital goods is mainly to create industrial equipment that is easy for the user to operate.

Aesthetic formal expression and the application of corporate industrial design to capital goods is important because it helps capital goods manufacturers to stand out in a highly competitive market through the recall factor of a (→) brand and the development of (→) product families. Here, introducing and integrating design into every (→) product development phase and every product level (from (→) components to (→) packaging) plays an essential role.

Capital goods design is not one of the "loud" design disciplines, yet it is one of the most complex and diverse, and involves and integrates the many skills of design. SAB |

CAR DESIGN

→ Automobile Design

CHARACTER DESIGN

The term "character design" is mainly used in the context of animated films, comics, and games in which there are one or more fictionalized characters with whom the audience is meant to identify. In addition to determining the character's physical appearance, the process may involve fashioning his or her patterns of speech, body language, actions, and so on. Fully developed character designs are an important part of the production process in these contexts, and may ultimately determine whether or not the final product is successful on the market.

Character designers utilize a variety of techniques, most of which are dedicated to figurative representation. In 3D (→) animation, characters are designed using three-dimensional methods such as maquettes, character models, and motion tracking. In recent years, as the rise of Internet has increased interest in the field, the definition of character design has expanded to include character-driven designs outside of the film, comic, and game industries. The Pictoplasma Conference (www.pictoplasma.com) was recently established to discuss new developments and contributions in character design. BB |

→ Audiovisual Design, Broadcast Design, Game Design, Illustration, Screen Design

COATING

The increasing demand for functionality and appearance has made a product's "coating"—the application of a specifically designed surface layer—an important element of the design and production process. Coatings add functional and/or aesthetic value (→ Aesthetics) to a variety of products ranging from cars to pharmaceuticals. They are primarily used to insulate or provide protection against environmental influences such as heat, corrosion, or mechanical strain. They can also be used to change an object's surface-material properties such as electrical conductivity, elasticity, or water and air permeability.

There is a range of processes available for applying seamless and permanently adhesive surface layers to an object. These include various chemical, mechanical, thermal, or thermo-mechanical processes like vaporizing and spraying, or immersion in electro-plating baths. Coatings are often quite complex in and of themselves, consisting of several separate cohesive layers that perform different yet coordinating functions.

In addition to defining the particular physical and chemical properties of an object's surface, coatings play an important role in the interface between consumer and product. By determining the outward presentation (color, (→) haptic features) of any given product, coatings are often key factors in determining its market success of failure. In a world where the functions and attributes of designed products are increasingly difficult to distinguish from one another, coatings have also become critical to the process of product differentiation and (→) branding.

In recent years, as developers have come to fully recognize the significance of coatings in brand recognition, sales, and functionality, advances in design technologies have made it possible to provide an increasing number of products with sophisticated and function-specific designable coatings. A growing number of products today are designed with coatings intended to address specific (→) target groups through the use of aesthetic (→) styling. In this way, coatings are also significant at the semiotic level (→ Semiotics), reflecting the general socio-cultural (→) trends of the market at any given moment. In an age where production cycles are getting shorter and product differentiation is key, coatings are taking on a new degree of significance for designers today. AAU + MF |

→ Customization, Interface Design, Materials

Goldschmidt, A., and H. J. Streitberger. 2003. *BASF handbook on basics of coating technology*. Hannover: Vincentz Verlag. Nanetti, P. 2006. *Coatings from A to Z*. Hannover: Vincentz Verlag.

COLLABORATIVE DESIGN

Until relatively recently, design was commonly perceived as a predominantly individual activity; the designer, trained in his or her (→) craft, was expected to identify, frame, and solve a design problem more or less in isolation from others. In the twenty-first century, however, this perception of the (→) design process is becoming increasingly removed from actual practice. Designers today routinely work in teams, collaborating to create processes and products that reflect the different kinds of expertise amongst the team members—and designers who are not skilled as collaborators are increasingly unlikely to be successful.

Even in the most prototypically individualistic ventures, designers have always worked with others, whether directly or indirectly. The needs and desires of clients and endusers for instance affect both the processes and products that designers create. At a very broad level, the consuming public's embrace or disdain of a designer's work is a large-scale collaboration with the designer, noticeably influencing what the designer does next. All design always has been and always will be collaborative in the sense that multiple parties commission, influence, and require iterative change in what any given designer does.

Design as a process is akin to other activities that have often been conceptualized as isolated practices but in reality require collaborative and dialogic contexts (as argued by multiple social scientists and theorists). For instance, design is collaborative in the same sense that the tennis player's ace depends not only of the tennis player's own efforts, but also on the opponent's not returning it—or in the sense that in conversation, a speaker shifts and molds her utterances based on her partner's ongoing mm-hm's and what's. Whenever a designer changes a ($\rightarrow$) prototype based on a client or user's real or even anticipated feedback, a form of collaborative design has taken place. Therefore, even in situations where there is a single credited designer, there are multiple collaborators involved, whether imagined (the product's eventual users) or real (the client or consumers who provide iterative feedback at various points in the design process).

Despite the fact that all design can be said to be inherently collaborative, the term "collaborative design" most typically refers to design activities carried out within design teams. These teams consist of various collaborators (team members) who are active in the creative process. Some teams have a single leader who is ultimately responsible for the process and outcome, while others involve a more distributed and consensual process with no one party in charge. They may be composed of individuals with drastically different areas of expertise, or similar backgrounds and fields of practice. The process of design differs according to the composition and structure of the team. When team members come from similar fields of expertise, they generally approach the design problem from a similar working methodology. On the other hand, when there is a wide and disparate range of expertise involved, the process is as much about coordinating the activity of design as well as it is about producing the outcome. Collaborative design of this sort is quintessentially interdisciplinary ($\rightarrow$ Discipline), and requires a breadth of understanding beyond what solo or discipline-specific collaborative designs require.

No matter the structure or nature of the team, methods of clear communication are central to collaborative design. The process involves the same human dynamics that are present in any other group effort, with dimensions of power, politeness, social distance, and cross-cultural differences clearly at work. Although many design teams still utilize group ($\rightarrow$) brainstorming sessions around a table (as embodied in the studio model), the rise of cross-global design projects ($\rightarrow$ *Cross-cultural Design, Globalization*) has necessitated members of the same team communicating solely via remote media. This shift has resulted in a growing need to understand the elements of collaborative skill, and how those skills differ in the context of different communication media (face to face vs. via asynchronous blogs vs. instant messaging vs. desktop video-conferencing, and so on) and in a variety of languages.

($\rightarrow$) Research is currently being conducted into the dynamics of design teams, and although it is unlikely that definitive outcomes outlining successful collaborations will be reached, it is clear that understanding collaborative skill will become an increasingly important element of putting together teams, facilitating their work, and training the next generations of designers. MS |

$\rightarrow$ *Communications, Integration, Participatory Design, Problem Solving*

COLLECTIONS

$\rightarrow$ *Design Museums, Fashion Design*

COMMERCIAL

$\rightarrow$ *Advertisement*

COMMUNICATION DESIGN

$\rightarrow$ *Graphic Design, Visual Communication*

COMMUNICATIONS

The word "communication" means "to impart, share," literally "to make common." It is derived from the Latin: communicare *or* communis. Communis *is a combination of* com *(meaning "together," "common") and* moenia *("defensive walls") which is related to* murus *("wall"). As a literal translation from the Latin, "communication" can thus be described as something along the lines of "walking around within the same walls." This description of the word leads to a curious and, ultimately, plausible contradiction: it indicates that communication basically describes a process that is bounded. In other words, it suggests that communication is based on exclusiveness and not open-ended ($\rightarrow$) integration.*

On reflection, the paradox inherent in a universally accepted definition of communication is appropriate, because those who participate in communication are privy to a shared language and congruent knowledge of all the relevant signs (including gestures, body language, fashion), which excludes all those not familiar with the foreign national language or regional cultural system. This reality is problematic because, historically as well as today, communication is ardently (even ideologically) presented as an enthusiastic promoter of openness and integration—and design in particular often professes to develop communicative methods for as many as possible, ideally for everyone.

This problem has become even more aggravated over the past few decades. Increasing migration has led to more drastic national linguistic and regional cultural barriers, fueling social segregation and partially dissolving communicative bonds. On the other hand, this complexity has generated hybrid forms of language and spawned other means of communication, making the task of defining communication media all the more difficult.

These parallel languages, each with their own communicative secrets, develop even within the same broad linguistic community. Young people for instance are constantly creating their own secret languages and signs that simultaneously identify them as an integrated group (or subgroup) and distinguish them from the rest of the community. A similar phenomenon occurs when specific professional groups use technical language and idiomatic phrasings and, in so doing, ignore any possibility of general communication, or even defy it, in order to demonstrate singularity.

It is important to recognize that the phrases and expressions that, at least partially, abdicate any motivation for universal communication, are also responsible for the dynamic properties of language and other forms of articulation—in other words for the development of (→) social communication. This is all the more true in the globalized world of today, as many people learn to adjust, depending on situation or mood, to different linguistic worlds and to even intelligently play with them (→ Globalization).

These changes and shifts in communication have significant consequences for design, as communication design has strived to create and provide universally understood means of communication. At the same time, it is important to remember that design does not exist in a vacuum—just like any other language, it has developed its own particular signs and markers that identify its objects and systems to its users. Any and all designed things will evoke impressions through their forms (meaning also their color, sound, haptic quality, or scent) that themselves communicate value, functionality, means of interaction, possible emotional or intellectual relationships (product semantics), and so on. Services, when carefully designed, will do the same, as the gestures, dealings, and procedures typical of the service industry are constantly creating meaning through signs and (→) symbols (for example the folded end of the toilet paper roll, indicating that the toilet has been cleaned).

It is not only products and services that attempt to communicate with people, of course, as, very importantly, people talk to each other via products, such as their cars, clothing, watches, eyeglasses, apartment furnishings, or with the food and drink they enjoy. Communication is never reduced to the purely visual, as it is increasingly common to communicate via the connotations of acoustics (→ Sound Design) and (→) haptic signals, even via smells and taste (→ Synesthetic). Some meals are prepared so as to encourage conversation, or to evoke enthusiasm or wonder, and wine is proffered to quicken the spirits of its drinkers and encourage social intercourse (also about the wine), or shared dreams—the same holds true for the communal rituals for drinking tea and coffee. Scents and perfumes have been created to produce joy and have an effect on others. There is a sense behind the German saying "Ich kann ihn nicht riechen (I can't stand how he/she smells)," meaning, "I don't like this person." Medical science established long ago that the sense of touch conveys information about surface, volume, and form and that the sense of hearing is not only empirically the most important source of sensing danger, but also fundamentally establishes substantive communication (which took most designers many decades to fully apprehend). People who have lost partial or complete use of one or more of their senses recognize this in particular.

Despite the importance of all the senses, the preeminent communicative impression is commonly attributed to sight. This is due to diverse historical and psychological reasons that have been explained often in literature (and as evidenced by the expression "I see" meaning "I understand"). It is no coincidence that optical verification is always referred to as a faithful and objective proof of truth. Accordingly, design, when creating communication structures, almost always engages the visible dimension first and foremost (→ *Visualization*).

Yet, designing the visible requires great effort, given the diversity of artifacts requiring designing and the available material—take for example the graphic lettering used to document language (→ *Typography*). A virtually infinite palette of fonts and symbols has been created, each given a variety of particular features in a variety of languages, and each endowed with designed advertency (such as bold, lightface, larger or smaller, italics). Once a font has been chosen, the designer has the choice of arranging these fonts in an infinite number of ways (→ *Layout*), then of designing the pages that contain these fonts as an integrated visual field, or ordering the sequences of pages in a characteristic manner. All these design decisions have a drastic effect on readers' advertency and their aptitude for reading and understanding. In the design process, a range of different texts can be produced even when they are composed of identical letters and words. The written word does not exist in and of itself, but is always designed, with the design conveying and deciding the nature of its legibility and comprehension.

Other fundamental means of (→) visual communication are the (→) logos, (→) trademarks, icons, and (→) symbols that can be seen everywhere and constantly demand our attention. (→) Pictograms that are used to instruct, warn, or draw attention are an important medium to consider as well—they can be found in airports, train stations, and department stores, on signposts and notices, in instruction booklets and on machines. Pictograms are used when the communication of essential information and orders need to be linguistically as concise as possible. It is also clear that these forms of communication, as helpful and useful as they may be, can very often be authoritarian and bossy, as well. A controversial topic in the realm of (→) visual communications is whether or not the meanings behind these kinds of signs always need to be learned, or whether they could be so fundamentally communicative that they communicate as quasi-substantive signs within a learnable discourse and beyond linguistic singularities. The question then, is whether there is within the communicative process a potential universal validity for design. This question points back to the problem mentioned at the beginning of this text about a basic multilingualism that on the one hand calls for communicative means and articulation within the relevant language, yet on the other hand is partially supported by a longing for the universal and shared, for communication that "breaks down walls." Communication design is at the heart of this contradiction and double requirement, and is actively working on designing new methods, aware of the continuity of communicative experiential processes. ME |

COMPLEXITY

From bent wire paper clips to cathedrals, design practice has always located itself on a continuum from the simple to the complex. In the twenty-first century, however, the meaning of the term "complexity" has gained new significance due to the influence of scientific theories about (→) systems, (→) organization, and order.

Complexity science asks the question of how randomly organized masses of elements come to exhibit seemingly conscious, surprising, and even adaptive behavior. Complexity, in this sense, is a system state that is neither ordered nor chaotic, but at the "edge of chaos." That is, the whole manifests coherent properties that emerge out of a tangle of interconnected, unpredictable variables. A swarm of bees has no leader and no organizing intelligence. And yet, as a swarm, it is able to maneuver and direct itself as a collective toward its goal. One cannot infer the global intelligence of the swarm from any single bee's directive, and yet the totality shows striking, coordinated, global behavior. The swarm can even react to unpredictable interruptions and still maintain its goal-seeking, coordinated behavior. The whole is not reducible to its parts; the sum is greater than its parts. Complex systems are, therefore, nonlinear. In opposition to reductionist theories of system change, complexity science proposes that one can understand more about the nature of a system's change and development from the behavior of the totality rather than from the reduction of that totality down to determinative parts. Complexity science also proposes that a complex adaptive system can learn and adapt as a whole, as illustrated by the examples of birds flocking and bees swarming. It took the computing capacity of the modern computer to allow researchers to ($\rightarrow$) model the complex interactions of multi-variable environments in order for the study of complexity to begin to yield striking analyses.

The idea of complexity entered into the design lexicon in the 1960s, principally through the works of two authors—Jane Jacobs and Robert Venturi. Each inveighed against the predominant ideology of ($\rightarrow$) simplicity, reductionism, and ($\rightarrow$) functionalism often associated with the European modernist movement ($\rightarrow$ *Modernity*) and particularly with the work of Mies van der Rohe and Le Corbusier. In *The Death and Life of Great American Cities,* Jane Jacobs argued that city planners could learn more from and plan better cities by observing the messy, street-level interactions of people and the built environment. At this level, she contended, there was a form of embodied intelligence and adaptability that functionalist planning doctrine ignored. Her focus on organized complexity was in stark contrast to the prevailing methodology of modern city planning ($\rightarrow$ *Urban Planning*), which reduced the complexity of a city down to smaller, elemental building blocks that could be rationally built up to create orderly, predictable outcomes. Robert Venturi was also reacting to the reduction of architecture ($\rightarrow$ *Architectural Design*) down to first-order principles of simplicity, rationality, and ($\rightarrow$) function, though his embrace of complexity was more at the level of building composition and ($\rightarrow$) aesthetics. In *Complexity and Contradiction in Architecture,* Venturi argued that architecture that prioritized simplicity and functionalism ignored the rich diversity of human experience. In program, structure, meaning, and function, Venturi argued for an architectural complexity that eschewed mannerism but reflected the increasing scale and complexity of modern life. While Mies van der Rohe proclaimed, "Less is more," Robert Venturi echoed back, "Less is a bore."

The impact that these modernist discourses had on architectural, industrial, and urban design fields is clear. More recently, the principles of complexity have been integral to the conceptualization and production of interactive designs as well. In particular, several computer and video games (including Will Wright's *SimCity* and Eric Zimmerman's *Gearheads)* have harnessed these principles to powerful effect, eliciting higher-order phenomena from the complex interactions of simple order behaviors ($\rightarrow$ *Game Design*).

With the advent of ($\rightarrow$) globalization, the continued migration to urban centers, and growing concerns with ($\rightarrow$) sustainability, accessibility, and safety, designers today are increasingly required to respond to complex issues that lie beyond the capacity of a single ($\rightarrow$) discipline—much less a single designer—to address

Jacobs, J. 1961. *The death and life of great American cities.* New York: Random House.
Johnson, S. 2001. *Emergence: The connected lives of ants, brains, cities, and software.* New York: Scribner.
Taylor, M. 2001. *The moment of complexity: Emerging network culture.* Chicago: Univ. of Chicago Press.
Venturi, R. 1966. *Complexity and contradiction in architecture.* New York: Museum of Modern Art.

comprehensively (→ *Wicked Problems*). At the same time, the explanatory power of complexity has taken on new relevance with the rise of electronic communications networks (→ *Networking*) and decentralized Internet collaboration. These technological developments have empowered vast numbers of social actors to collaborate and create—without necessarily relying upon a centralized, organizing leader. As a result, decentralized, complex, large-scale experiments in technological, social, and political self-organization are challenging dominant modernist orthodoxies of everything from vertically integrated corporations to centralized command structures and the designer as author. JHU |
→ *Deconstruction, Integration, Postmodernism*

COMPONENTS

Components are the parts and elements of a whole and are connected according to set rules and laws. The sum of all the components coordinates the function and form of a workable system or product, and determines its (→) quality, efficiency, and (→) usability.

In (→) product design, the term typically describes the parts of a construction unit in the form of (→) hardware (as for example in computer electronics). In music, components are a part of the composition as a whole, or in other words, the artistic sequencing and arranging of the elements of a musical piece. Components also complement one another in design to form a completed work. SAB |
→ *Construction*

COMPOSITING

Compositing means combining several visual (→) components to create a new image. It can include different design areas, such as photography, graphic elements, 3-D images, and typography. The term "compositing" is used in both still image (print, web, and so on) and moving image contexts. In the past, rostrum cameras were the customary analog means of creating collages. These days computers and special software programs are common. BB |
→ *Audiovisual Design, CAD/CAM/CIM/CNC, Photographic Design*

CONCEPTUAL DESIGN

Conceptual design is not so much a specific category of design as an approach to design that exists across a spectrum of activities. Conceptual designs speculate with (→) form in ways that "push the boundaries" of what is understood to be acceptable in design.

In some ways, conceptual designs are philosophically close to conceptual art in that both are motivated primarily by ideas over other material considerations (form, functionality, aesthetics, or marketability, for instance). As such, they are generally not intended to be mass-produced but rather, to circulate through exhibitions or publications. However, the categorization of conceptual designs as art instead of design assumes a very narrow interpretation of what design entails. Indeed, the very purpose of conceptual design is to use design as a medium to provoke discussion and debate, and to challenge assumptions regarding what it means to be a designer, a user, and a consumer. Furthermore, conceptual designs do not address the concept or the idea in complete isolation from principles of functionality, something that applied arts can afford to do. In other words, expectations of everyday (→) use are always important to conceptual design, whether the designer is defying them (unusable furniture, unwearable jewelry), challenging them (barely legible grunge graphics), or creating alternative or future scenarios of fictional or hypothetical use.

This latter category of conceptual design typically considers the speculative psychological, social, and ethical relationships between people and objects as much as (or parallel to) their functional relationships. The ostensible (→) "function" of these designs may or may not ultimately be feasible or even rational; in fact, conceptual design proposals of this sort are often intentionally made to be unrealizable in order to highlight the (economic, social, cultural, philosphical, and so on) forces that limit their potential. As designers, we need to develop ways of speculating about future scenarios and emerging technologies that are grounded in fact, yet engage the imagination and allow us to debate different possibilities.

The danger of course is that these designs will become mere fantasies, and therefore the designer's challenge often lies in maintaining a sense of realism. In this capacity, conceptual designs could be said to engage the same suspension of disbelief that filmmakers and writers use. In other words, interactions with these products should generate complex narratives related to use; by emphasizing alternative scenarios and future interactions before they happen, conceptual designs of this type exist somewhere between fiction and reality, and are nearer to the intentions and processes of cinema and literature than those of art. They can be approached as props for nonexistent films, for example, or as prompts for playing back imaginary films in our own minds.

As with (→) critical design, the conceptual design process is therefore not about (→) problem-solving so much as setting up a situation that facilitates public engagement, discussion, and debate. In one way or another, the main subjects of conceptual design are questions about the future of society, technology, (→) aesthetics, and (→) social behavior—questions about the future of design itself. It is a process that provides a space where ideas can be tested, presented, and communicated, a parallel design channel or genre dedicated to conceptual exploration.

As mentioned above, most conceptual designs are not intended to be mass-produced, but rather to make users reflect, ask questions, and think about the impact of the design in their lives. There are many forms of speculative design approaches that are ultimately market-driven: concept cars shown at automotive shows to test the market's openness to new ideas, for example, or future-vision projects undertaken by large corporations to speculate on new product possibilities and applications. Haute couture is also often considered to be quite conceptual (but is somewhat idealistic and utopian in aspiring to something beyond "the now" that you can buy, own, and wear today). These forms of design are clearly related to conceptual design in that they are speculative and future-oriented, but the objectives behind the processes differ considerably.

The act of conceptualizing design—the process of (→) prototyping various possible solutions in search of an optimum final design—is also distinct from conceptual design as described in this text. Any formal (→) design process clearly requires stages of idea generation and conceptual analysis. The difference lies in whether or not these ideas and concepts challenge or take precedence over the expected material or commercial considerations. FR |

CONSTRUCTION

Construction (Latin: *con* = together, *struere* = to build) describes both the process and the result of the methodical and targeted production of a material or immaterial (→) artifact. Construction also establishes a definite relationship between (→) form and (→) function. The term is often, and sometimes misleadingly, used as a synonym for (→) design.

Material constructions include devices, machines, production plants, and buildings; immaterial or mental constructions include mathematical theories, philosophical systems, and bodies of law. Construction processes describe the sequences of steps, procedures, calculation rules, and standards implemented to produce a construction efficiently, and are often the focus of construction sciences / (→) engineering design (Pahl and Beitz 2006).

Nonreflexive, scientific, first-order observation is concerned with "objective" facts, functions, calculations, and procedures. Here, constructions are (→) systems consisting of elements and correlations that accomplish a well-defined purpose and can be clearly described in syntactic, geometric, topological, and structural terms. These constructions are often complicated in structure and function, yet it is always possible to describe them causally. The relationship "function–form" is asymmetric, meaning form follows function.

If observing the construction is the issue, then we are dealing with second-order observation. This means observing differences with regard to their bilateral form, in other words, their implicit inclusion of what they exclude. Consequently, second-order observation is also the observation of observers, since differences can only exist if established by a viewer. Flexibility and a certain degree of freedom then become possible for the construction (→ Constructivism). This freedom is determined only temporarily via communication, in that second order observers agree on first order observations (Baecker 2005). This applies to both immaterial and material construction.

The shift to second-order observation also indicates an essential difference between construction and design. In design, form and function exist in a symmetric relationship. In the design process, they are brought into playful dialogue in such a way that form informs function and vice versa. Consequently, the form of a design can be varied with regard to possible functions and, conversely, with regard to form, new and different functions can be discovered. These constructions create momentary, observer-dependent "fits" for the interfaces between body / consciousness / communication and artifacts (Alexander 1964, Baecker 2005); they are complex.

Construction views artifacts as "trivial machines" (von Foerster 1981) and design, in contrast, as "nontrivial machines" that can behave in a context and history-dependent manner. Construction solves "well-defined" problems; design tackles "ill-defined" problems. In other words, construction operates within the technical-scientific paradigm; design's paradigm is yet to be formulated. WJ |

→ *Observational Research*

Alexander, C. 1964. *Notes on the synthesis of form*. Cambridge: MA: Harvard Univ. Press.

Baecker, D. 2005. *Form und Formen der Kommunikation*. Frankfurt am Main: Suhrkamp.

Foerster, H. von. 1981. *Observing systems*. Seaside, CA.

Pahl, G., and W. Beitz, 2007. *Engineering design: A systematic approach*. Trans. K. Wallace and L. Blessing London: Springer.

CONSTRUCTIVISM

Constructivism is the general term used to describe various philosophies concerned with the concept of (→) construction that emerged in scientific and academic areas during the twentieth century. Constructivism was particularly influential in the context of the visual arts at the beginning of the twentieth century, the new grounding of mathematics during the foundational crisis, the theory of science developed in the Erlangen and Constance schools, and the development of operative epistemology in the tradition of second-order cybernetics.

In general terms, constructivism (re)constructs a method of human action and discourse in complex areas of scientific, technological, and political practice that is methodically sound, comprehensible, and based on an indisputable relationship to society and life. The following essay focuses on the epistemological concept of "radical constructivism."

Radical Constructivism, (*Radikaler Konstruktivismus* in German, a phrase coined by Ernst von Glasersfeld) describes the complex of theories that emerged in the 1970s as "operative epistemology" or "second-order cybernetics." These theories were largely formulated at the Biological Computer Laboratory of the University of Illinois at Urbana, under the direction of Heinz von Foerster. Radical Constructivism is not one unified (→) theory, but a loosely related combination of theories. The most significant component is Maturana and Varela's biological epistemology ("autopoiesis").

The basic assumption of these theories is the existence of operative, informational, self-contained, cognitive, and (as per Niklas Luhmann) social (→) systems—meaning, systems whose operative processes are recursive and impermeable to instructive information from the outside. One characteristic of a self-contained system is that (→) communication is modeled as the interactive production of meaning, rather than the conveyance of (→) information. The most significant implication of this assumption, according to S. J. Schmidt (1992), exists in the fact "that we construct the world in which we live by our 'living together' . . . that observers and observing produce, primarily through strict self-referentiality, those constellations which become conscious and communicable to us as world."

Some characteristics of radical constructivism include the rejection of any epistemologies rooted in the metaphysical or transcendental, and the denial of ontological depictions of reality. Because system operations are always dependent on previous operations, there is an inclination to support a genetic or evolutionary theory of the construction of meaning. Truth becomes an *Eigenwert* (semantic marker or stable variant) of the social process.

Linguistic communication occurs when structurally coupled organisms operate in a conceptual area, initially without content. The operation of observing operations facilitates a construction of meta-descriptive areas relating to the current act of operating. Consequently, an observer can act as an external element. It is then possible to ascribe meaning to the communicative act.

It may be popular knowledge that "objective" world descriptions are not even viable in the natural sciences and that, instead, every observation is perspective and that this influences what is observed. Nevertheless, the implications of this understanding are rarely taken seriously. The "normal" sciences still maintain that concepts and theories may not reoccur within the scope of their own object. Von Foerster coined the term "autological conclusion" to describe functions, observations, or theories that are self-applicable. For example, a theory of human cognition should be able to explain how it was derived. In studies of sociology, psychoanalysis, political economics, and even (→) design, it is equally necessary to adopt a considered and productive approach in order to avoid dogmatism and ideology. Designing establishes the framework in which further action and thinking will take place, and this goes on and on in an endless cycle. We need mindsets that permit self-reference.

This begins with the formal concept of observation as an operation of distinguishing and defining.

Von Glasersfeld (1987) drew a distinction between external-observation and self-observation. Referencing Piaget's genetic epistemology, he noticed that there was no real reason to assume that our experience begins with ready-made objects, life forms, or people. The object, its environment, and the regularities of its behavior are created only after there has been an active excising of the perceptual and conceptual elements of experience. He illustrated this notion by referencing the perceptual capacities of the element "frog"—something about which we can say it is able to perceive things. When we offer "explanations" for a frog's behavior and for its interactions with its environment, we are really establishing relations between elements of our own experience, and so it makes sense to make statements about the frog's ($\rightarrow$) perception. However, it is fundamentally different when making statements about one's own perception. We have the ability to observe ourselves and our environment from a position external to our own experience. There is no autonomous access to one thing or another that we (like the frog) can hold responsible as the cause of our perception. Nonetheless, it is "useful" for us to attribute the causes of our perceptive experience to a preexisting world.

Our acquired "knowledge" is always the knowledge of the invariants and regularities that we derive from our own experience, and which are thus part of this experience. The constant effort it takes to construct stable invariants in our experience ultimately leads to attributing cognitive abilities, meaning the abilities to construct a world, to the organisms we call "fellow people."

In *Laws of Form* (1969) ($\rightarrow$ *Form*), George Spencer Brown provided essential elements for formalizing the theory of observation. He interpreted observation as an operation of "drawing a distinction" between one thing and another. This distinction is the contingent starting point for the knowledge-seeking subject to structure the unobserved, or the "unmarked state." Separating the two sides is important because it forces observation to originate from one side (and not the other). It has to use language to describe what is being observed. Yet this description also implies the other side, the side that is not in question. The "unmarked state" could be, simply, the rest of the world. Yet for the most part, the side not in question is already restricted by the manner in which the distinction is drawn. In other words: observing = distinguishing + defining (identifying + linguistically marking).

Gregory Bateson (1979) defined observation (information) a bit more succinctly as "any difference which makes a difference in some later event." The operation of drawing a distinction itself remains unobserved at the moment it is implemented, because it cannot be referred to as belonging to one or the other side of the difference. The difference is the "blind spot" that is presumed, in every observation, to be the condition of its very possibility.

Systems theory sociology understands observation as the "base operation" of psychological and social systems. The only things that can be described are those things that can be observed and shaped into a semantic figure (→ Semantics). When communicating, individuals produce descriptions of their observations in the medium of a common language. Observation itself is the first (shaping) difference that is associated with a stipulation. It is practiced naively when implemented and can only be distinguished by another observation (that of a different observer, or the same observer at a later point in time).

The world sets the conditions of observation; observation, however, necessarily changes the world in which it occurs. Which means that observation is not a passive gateway to an external world, but rather the empirical operation of distinguishing and defining. The search for absolutely certain foundations of empirical knowledge is thus replaced by the observation of observing. Luhmann (1990) stated it more precisely: the observation of an operation, even that of observing, is initially a simple registering of changes in physical symbols or signs (first-order cybernetics). The observation of observing, that is, an operation as observation, calls for a second-order level to solve the fundamental paradox (second-order cybernetics). Otherwise, some "blurring" might occur, but no real observable differences.

Conceptually separating operation and observation allows for a distinction to be drawn between the reality and the objectivity of observation. Reality is assumed when the operation is performed; yet this does not suggest objectivity. On the other hand, the convergence of observations from more than one observer, which would generally imply "objectivity," does not allow any inference to be made about the reality of its object—or, at most, the inference that communication has taken place. The difference between objective and subjective now becomes insubstantial and can be replaced by the difference between external reference and self-reference, which is, again, only a structural moment of observation itself.

The structure (knowledge) directs the operation (identification), which in turn confirms or modifies the structure. According to Luhmann, this cycle can be broken by chronological sequence and not by a metaphysically determined variation in the character of the subjective and objective. Observation, as the act of distinguishing and defining, cannot differentiate between "true" and "not true." It understands its own biological, historical, and socially conditional difference as its "blind spot," which means all observation (even the observation of observation [of the observation]) proceeds uncritically on an operational level relating to its own reference. That is why there are no reflexive hierarchies of increasing levels of "objectivity," no external positions, and no observations that do not reveal information about the observer. The world—whatever it may be as an "unmarked state" open for observation as per Spencer Brown—is, according to Luhmann, "a paradox that can be made temporal" for the observer, an "observable unobservability." This excludes definitive representations and only allows stable *Eigenwerte* or semantic markers to be created in a recursive process of observing observations that fix indications for further observation and communication. Both language and (design) objects are examples of this (von Foerster 1981).

Processes such as these determine system boundaries. The difference of system/environment, which results from the initially isolated operative act of observing, can be addressed linguistically and reentered into the system (Spencer Brown 1969). This enables the system to describe itself as a unit (unlike the environment). It becomes capable of self-observation and, thus, of a productive handling of the "blind spot" problem. Von Foerster's axiom, "We cannot see that we cannot see" presumes the "blind spot" as a condition of the possibility of seeing.

Linguistic metalevels of world description can be constructed by observations of observations of observations. Knowledge, identification, and science are based purely on the communicative produced stability of these levels, not on external, objective points of reference. Each level is afflicted with the blind spot of the differences it utilizes.

An epistemology that claims to be universal recognizes that it is itself part of its subject and is thus based on a cyclical process. Constructivism is a valuable contribution to the development of a naturalized cognitive science, of a (→) theory that can explain its existence. Constructivism does not solve the problem of constructing all knowledge, yet it is capable of focusing precisely on this as a central point. The neurological foundation of cognition should not be exaggerated; giving it the status of "true" origin would discredit ambitions to be understood as a complex structure. The focus should be on communication and operation; they alone constitute reality (even that of biological theory!). WJ |

→ *Design Process, Observational Research, Understanding*

Bateson, G. 1979. *Mind and nature: A necessary unity*. New York: E. P. Dutton.
Foerster, H. von. 1981. *Observing systems*. Seaside, CA: Intersystems Publications.
Schmidt, S. J., ed. 1987. *Der Diskurs des Radikalen Konstruktivismus*, pp. 7–23. Frankfurt am Main: Suhrkamp.
Spencer Brown, G. 1979. *Laws of form*. 3rd ed. New York: Dutton.

CONSUMPTION

Consumption refers to the active meanings that people attribute to various goods and services as they are designed, circulated, and used in a society. Consumption was once negatively defined in terms of conspicuous display and frivolous spending by those persons expressing a desire for social mobility. However, more recently consumption has taken on a broader significance, beyond popular and commercial culture, in terms of expressing national identity, local politics, foreign policy, race, ethnicity, gender history, and even (→) modernity.

The idea of consumption is still polemical. It has been described as central to capitalism and growth for nations like Trinidad; justified in countries like India as a necessary road to democracy and collective economic growth; and vital to American national identity from early European exploration to the present. Still, debates about the moral, economic, environmental, and political consequences of consumption and its effect on society continue.

Above all, the consumption of goods is considered a (→) social, rather than purely individual phenomenon. Consumption is no longer viewed as the passive end of production; rather, it offers an active and creative means for people to interact, express their attitudes, beliefs and values, to self and others. People find (→) value in the things they buy and give because things provide meaning to interpersonal relationships. This means that we can understand consumption beyond self-serving purposes and locate its meaning as central to social systems of exchange. As such, consumption is integral to social structure and articulating relationships, and is not simply the end result of work.

Indeed, modern views of consumption have turned the old production-consumption formula on its head. No longer do manufacturers simply produce goods to sell in markets; rather, retailers and consumers inform manufacturers of what they want through consumer demand. This means that consumers are the active players in the construction of commodities and consumption, and manufacturers must respond accordingly by creating well-designed products. The Apple Corporation's recent approach to design exemplifies an emphasis on (→) aesthetics and functionality that consumers appreciate.

So rather than viewing consumption as the end of the road for goods and services, it can be seen as the very means of sending and receiving social messages, expressing identity, cementing relationships, and even modernizing our rituals. For instance, consumption often builds upon social rhythms and repetitions in culture, such as seasonal cycles of Christmas, summer vacation, or back-to-school, which invite people to strategize and calculate how they buy and spend on goods and services for the

perceived benefit and payoff it will bring. Consumption thus emerges not as a result of vague and indeterminable human (→) needs, but rather as a function of a variety of social practices that marketers and designers can attend to. ^{TWM} |
→ *Product, Use*

CONTINUITY

Continuity describes the primarily time-based relationship between self-developing processes. Continuity occurs when any tangible or analytical event appears as a linearly developing movement in time.

Defining the category of "continuity" with regards to erratic or even chance historical developments is not only difficult historically and theoretically, but also particularly within the context of design. To begin with, design is always bound to something that exists and needs to be further developed, yet design also promises new, innovative, or fashionable developments and a design-related reference to current social, economical, technical, and cultural conditions. This paradoxical relationship is also apparent in the seemingly contradictory activities of corporations, which seek to both increase profitability through the regular introduction of new products to the market, yet have an equally powerful interest in maintaining continuity in the realm of (→) brand recognition—not to mention costs and facilities. Consequently, the design process is deeply influenced by the continuity paradox. ^{BL} |
→ *Convention, Corporate Identity, Innovation, Product Family*

CONVENTION

Convention is a general agreement on an issue, behavior, way of thinking, belief, object, principle, criteria, social form of interaction, application, expectation, aesthetic, value, or attitude. Conventions were either decided on at a given point or developed, and became established over time through the legitimization of power structures, habit, or socialization. Thus, conventions are afforded a more or less stable and unrivaled position; they become important points of reference, orientation, and history.

At the same time, however, the definition of convention as a general agreement automatically implies that a conventional position or perspective can be redefined, restructured, or even replaced by the gradual acceptance of another agreement. Consequently, it is possible to deal playfully and subversively with conventions.

Design plays a fundamental role in both the development and establishment, and the (→) critique and (→) transformation of conventions, and has always reacted creatively to their ambiguity. By inventing and designing new objects, alternative visual worlds, relevant arguments, convincing visuals, formal expressions, and enlightening associations, design develops and introduces references that allow conventions to be perceived, communicated, and practiced across multiple individuals and groups. At the same time, design increasingly draws on established conventions to make creative concepts, innovative solutions, and unconventional ideas as directly negotiable, conceivable, and communicable as possible. In the process, design exploits the paradoxical structure of conventions in order to infiltrate, criticize, change, transform, reassess, and reinterpret them. SG |

→ *Critical Design, Innovation, Social*

CONVERGENCE

Convergence is when two or more topics, areas, cultures, technologies, or ways of thinking come together. The resulting combinations are dynamic and open, and make way for new combinations, hybrid formations, mixtures, displacements, and innovations to take place. Design enables, restructures, visualizes, and confirms the creation of alternative visual worlds, relevant designs, concrete artifacts, material areas of negotiation, and conceivable references through the dynamics of convergence. SG |

→ *Coordination, Cross-cultural Design, Crossover, Innovation, Synthesis, System*

CONVERSATION PIECE

A conversation piece is a designed (→) artifact that is intended to stimulate conversation. Although it may come with other functions, it is typically purchased and prominently displayed in the home for this express purpose. It is important to address in the context of design because it demonstrates how design can help people to socialize. ME |

→ *Social*

COORDINATION

As a category, design could be defined as a fundamental coordinating force, because diverse and diverging contents are cast into a (→) form or emerge always as formulated, or, in other words, as a perspective or view.

For this reason, questions are vital that address which form actually achieves coordination without breaking in the process, destroying the contents, or rendering them unrecognizable; and: which forms correspond best to their contents and can these contents communicate, improve, or animate via their coordination. Inasmuch, form as an expression of coordination is always also bound to the content that needs to be coordinated—which again must lead to the question of whether the contents demand a certain specific coordination, and of whether noncoordinated contents exist at all.

Design, as a means of structuring form, acts and thinks essentially amid this relationship as a coordinating energy and communicative force. To put it another way: it coordinates the social, economic, psychological, and cultural dimensions of its content. Design consequently is coordination, and the quality of design is based on the coordinative competency of the respective form. BL |

→ *Convergence, Organization, System*

COPY

The Latin word *copia* means "supply" or "abundance." Over time, the word "copy" evolved to mean the reproduction of an original object, rather than the accumulation of things. In order to secure data or distribute information, copies are usually produced using paper printing methods (such as photocopying [blueprint], xerography [electrophotography], and [book] printing processes) or electronically writable disks (such as DVDs, CDs, external hard drives, and USB sticks, etc.). Abusing the availability of duplication technologies by copying money is considered counterfeiting and is punishable by law. Unauthorized reproductions of paintings or other works of art are also prohibited.

Despite these proscriptions, a trend called "copy art" emerged at the end of the 1960s, led by artists like Emmet Williams, Martin Kippenberger, and Joseph Beuys. By elevating the status of the copy to that of art, these artists sparked an interesting theoretical debate on the nature of reproducibility (copying) versus the creation of new and unique works (art). The complex and contradictory human relationship to the idea of the copy is also reflected in the fear and fascination people express when confronted with the possibility that they themselves could be copied into clones. DPO |

→ *Copyright, Fake, Intellectual Property, Plagiarism*

COPYRIGHT

Copyright, a type of (→) intellectual property, is a set of exclusive rights proscribed by national or international law for original works of authorship fixed in a tangible form of expression. These works of authorship can include literary works such as poems, novels, and plays; movies; choreographic works; musical compositions; audio recordings; works of visual art such as drawings, paintings, photographs, and sculptures; software; radio and television broadcasts of live or taped performances; and in some jurisdictions, notably those in Europe, databases.

Most copyright statutes provide protection for a range of rights, which can include the right to reproduce, distribute, make derivative works (works that adapt the original work such as creating a screenplay from a book or creating a painting from a photograph), publicly display, or perform the work. These rights generally can be independently sold or licensed on an exclusive or non-exclusive basis. Violating these rights, that is, using work without the copyright holder's permission, is infringement and a copyright holder may seek remedies including damages and an injunction to stop the unauthorized use.

Copyright protection attaches the moment a work has been expressed in a tangible form and it applies only to the expression; it does not protect ideas, concepts, facts, styles, or techniques that may be included in the work. To be eligible for protection, a copyrighted work generally must meet minimal standards of originality and exhibit a modicum of creativity. The internationally recognized symbol for copyright is ©, but copyright notice can also be written as "copr." or by spelling out "copyright" followed by the date and the creator's name.

Taken literally, copyright is the right to make copies of a work and to stop others from making copies without permission (→ *Copy*). Copyright protection is not a natural right; it is a form of monopoly granted by the state. Because it is a monopoly, all copyright systems attempt to balance owner's rights and user's rights by limiting the duration of copyright protection. In 2007, copyright protection lasts for the life of the author and, depending on the jurisdiction, continues for a minimum of fifty years and a maximum of seventy years after the author's death. When copyright protection ends, the work becomes public domain and anyone can use the work without permission.

The idea of copyright did not exist prior to the invention of the printing press because copying a manuscript was a laborious manual process. Copyright, as the literal right to make copies, began as a publisher's right in England in 1586 as a way for the government to maintain order among members of the book trade, organized as the Stationer's Company. England codified copyright in 1710 when it enacted the Statute of Anne, generally considered to be the first copyright law. The Statute of Anne shifted protection from publishers to authors, granting them a fourteen-year original term and a fourteen-year renewable term. The United States passed copyright legislation in 1790, modeling its law after the Statute of Anne. The US law included the general idea that the government should promote knowledge by encouraging authors to create and disseminate work, but that neither the creator nor the public should be able to retain or appropriate all the benefits that flow from an original work of authorship.

In most common law systems, copyright laws do not include moral rights or *droit moral*. Those rights are provided separately, if at all, and generally provide weak protection. However, in France, Germany, and most other civil-law countries, copyright laws have two components: economic rights (copyright) and moral rights. Economic rights grant to the author the right to sell and license an original work of authorship and the rights can be ceded. Moral rights grant the author the right of attribution, the right to share in the profit if the work increases in value, and the right to prevent the work from being altered or destroyed. Moral rights usually cannot be ceded. China's copyright laws, codified as the Chinese Copyright Act (CCA) in 1990, generally follow common-law principles, but include stronger moral rights provisions.

The balance between owner's rights and the need for the general public to be able to freely share ideas has always been difficult to maintain in copyright law. If owners could stop all unauthorized use, they could stifle commentary and criticism. To maintain the balance, copyright laws recognize that some unauthorized use must be permissible, particularly if the unauthorized use is for commentary or criticism, or for educational purposes.

Civil-law countries deal with the concept of permissible but unauthorized use through statutory provisions that codify the permitted conduct. If the use is not listed, then it is usually not permissible. Common-law jurisdictions achieve the balance through the concepts of fair use or fair dealing. The idea underlying fair use or fair dealing is that some use of copyrighted material must be allowed even if the copyright holder doesn't agree. Otherwise a copyright holder could close down the free exchange of ideas by preventing any use, however small, of a copyrighted work. Fair use allows someone to copy, publish, or distribute parts of a copyrighted work without permission, generally only for commentary, criticism, education, news reporting, or scholarship. In a fair-use analysis in the US, courts consider four factors: 1) the purpose and character of the use 2) the nature of the copyrighted work 3) the amount and substantiality of the portion used 4) the effect on the market for or value of the original work. Because these factors are "fact-specific" and thus have to be judged case-by-case, fair-use disputes must be litigated, which can be costly.

International copyright has always been complicated but is now significantly more complex due to rapid expansion of communication technology and the globalized economy. In response to the global trade in intellectual property, almost all countries who are signatories to the World Trade Organization (WTO) have tried to harmonize copyright and related laws through various treaties and agreements, chief among these being the Berne Convention for the Protection of Literary and Artistic Works, first adopted in 1886, and most recently amended in 1979. The Berne Convention established several principles of international copyright, including the key notion that a country must extend the same copyright protection to foreigners that it accords to its own authors. The Berne Convention also established minimum standards that all signatories must meet. Countries who meet the Berne minimal standards may provide their own specialized form of protection, so international copyright laws still remain less than uniform.

Copyright laws adapt to cultural and technological changes. They have been continually expanded in duration and extended to protect works not originally protected, such as software programs and databases. Today, however, copyright systems are threatened by the digital revolution. Some critics wonder if copyright can adapt to the twenty-first century.

The Internet and related technology devices have created new modes of expression, peer-to-peer (P2P) networks, instantaneous communication, and the ability to create an unlimited number of perfect copies, all of which challenge the monopoly structure of copyright. To stem unauthorized copies, content providers of music and movies developed copyright protection technology embedded directly onto a CD or DVD. Hackers responded with software programs to crack the encryption code and distributed the programs on the Internet. Industry cried foul, and most legislatures worldwide passed laws to criminalize the dissemination of technology or computer programs created to allow users to circumvent copyright protection methods embedded in a CD or DVD. The US version, the Digital Millennium Copyright Act (DMCA) passed in 1998. Most European countries have amended national laws to implement the 2001 European Directive on copyright, which conforms to a 1996 World Intellectual Property Organization (WIPO) treaty that addresses the same issues as the DMCA.

Critics contend that these laws tilt the balance too far in favor of the copyright holder because they shift the traditional focus of copyright from protection toward criminalizing the creation and use of devices and software programs designed to circumvent copyright protection measures, whether or not the circumvention technology was employed by anyone and whether or not the use of the copyrighted material made possible by the circumvention would have been a copyright violation. For the first time, copyright violation isn't the crime; creating technological tools that can violate copyright is the crime. These laws have no fair use or fair dealing provisions so there is no instance in which breaking encryption code is legal, even for research or education.

Given the economic stakes, the debate surrounding copyright is impassioned. Proponents defend the need to create economic incentives to encourage artists and authors to continue creating and to protect copyright holders from rampant piracy made possible by digital technology. Others believe that the idea of copyright protection is fundamentally sound, but that protection lasts too long. They bemoan the loss of the intellectual "public

Lessig, L. 2004. *Free culture: How big media uses technology and the law to lock down culture and control creativity.* New York: Penguin.
Litman, J. 2001. *Digital copyright.* Amherst, NY: Prometheus Books.
Patterson, L. 1968. *Copyright in historical perspective.* Nashville, TN: Vanderbilt Univ. Press.
Thierer, A., and C. W. Crews Jr. 2003. *Copy fights: The future of intellectual property in the information age.* Washington, DC: Cato Institute.

commons." Other critics call for abolishing all copyright because it is an industrial age notion and has no place in the technological world of P2P networks that could enable a virtually limitless number of international participants to have access to high-quality digital media and entertainment, on demand 24/7 from nearly any place. They believe that the expansive trend in copyright law will hamper the very potential of the digital revolution and that eventually all culture will be controlled by a few people or a few mega corporations. It is fair to say that both sides of the debate need to be heard and copyright laws will be revised once again. MB |

→ *Intellectual Property, Plagiarism, Publications, Trademark*

CORPORATE CULTURE

→ *Corporate Identity*

CORPORATE DESIGN

→ *Corporate Identity*

CORPORATE FASHION

Corporate fashion is rooted in the production of garments for work. These have a long tradition in crafts, public service, and the service industry, where they fulfill a variety of functions that are now being taken up and further developed by corporate fashion.

Corporate fashion supports the recall factor of a (→) brand by helping customers associate an employee with a specific company or corporation. It also facilitates customer access by giving transparency to various roles and functions, and differentiating service personnel from other employees. In addition to contributing to the development of a (→) corporate identity in the eyes of both customers and employees alike, corporate fashion also works on a smaller scale, by developing the employee's role identity. Literally and figuratively speaking, wearing a garment that reflects one's professional identity adds a new, sometimes protective layer or dimension to their personal identity. Not only does the garment help characterize the employee's professional identity, it also—at best—works to support it. This is because, like any accessory, clothing helps model its wearer's behavior (posture, gait, stance, and so on), which in turn serves to shape self-image. Ultimately, garments associated with a specific role (like security) also have to support certain essential functions— in the process, well-designed work garments can make the work itself easier in many respects.

Corporate fashion thus demonstrates that work clothes in the corporate context can be about more than depersonalized uniforms and strict dress codes—they can also address and influ-

ence the adoption of a collective professional philosophy, where an overarching corporate style allows for greater freedom and actively contributes to the wellbeing of its employees. BM |
→ *Fashion Design, Service Design*

CORPORATE IDENTITY

There are many questions pertaining to corporate identity that are either difficult or impossible to address sufficiently. Consequently, attempts to define the term often result in empty phrases. The most common formulation, however, is that corporate identity is the harmony of the internal and external image of a company.

Despite the fact that the nature and significance of corporate identity has been discussed at length over the past two decades, a definitive, universally accepted definition of the term is still wanting. This is because some consider the concept of corporate identity too young to be defined, while others have already declared it obsolete.

Notwithstanding the debate about the concept's popular relevance, it can be argued that the real potential for corporate identity is only just beginning to be explored. This perspective is based on studying familiar and observable (→) trends in both the competitive corporate world and the everyday life of consumers, which have been irrevocably altered by changes in industrial culture, market (→) globalization and restructuring, and the increasing complexity of products. From an industrial and economic perspective, these developments substantiate the belief that clearly, credibly, and convincingly communicated corporate identities will become increasingly significant in the years to come.

Others argue, on the other hand, that the conceptual distinction between "corporate identity" and "brand identity" (→ *Brand*) has become increasingly ambiguous, and that the latter term has in effect made the former obsolete.

Nonetheless, at least three aspects appear fundamental to defining the term "corporate identity." First, corporate identity is the sum of all forms of corporate outward show. In other words: in addition to the visual image a company provides (corporate design), it also involves all the verbal expressions, behaviors, and structures that a company uses when interacting both within its own corporate structure and with the public. Second, corporate identity requires that all of the above forms of expression are adequately consistent. This consistency does not have to be absolute. Conflict and ambivalence is not necessarily at odds with an attractive and identifiable corporate identity. Third, a successful or competitive corporate identity must refer to an essential core in all its forms of expression. In other words, corporate identity has to revolve around a core set of (→) values.

It is helpful when facing these ambiguities to progress beyond questions like: "What is corporate identity?" "How relevant is corporate identity?" and "How does corporate identity differ from branding?" and instead examine the issue from a more procedural perspective. For example, the question of how a corporate identity is created helps us recognize it not as a defined result, but as a process of development. Likewise, investigating the various ways in which corporations form their identities illustrates that the process is both nonlinear and complex. Even the simple breakdown of one corporation's day-to-day process of identity development reveals it as a creative task.

It is important to abandon any notion of a linearly developed corporate identity and instead conceptually envisage the process as a cyclical one. The origin and course of a corporate identity can almost never be located definitively in that it is too dependent on a variety of contextual and cultural factors. The process is highly politicized; that is, always contingent upon the results of conflicts, the powers of self-assertion, and on forming consensus and reaching compromise. The politics of corporate identity development are not particularly surprising because, of course, corporations are themselves political institutions that must contend with the realities of power struggles and conflicts of interests. The development of a corporate identity is a continual, cyclical, and often contested process. In other words, dead ends and detours are an inevitable part of a journey for which there is no specified destination.

The process of corporate identity development is ultimately about translating a company's core values into concrete procedures that describe the desired interaction between the company and the consumer or general public. These procedures are ultimately intended to form a consistent chain of experience for the consumer. Once its core values have been established, the three main steps to creating and sustaining a successful corporate identity can be broadly described as follows:

· Creative and strategic conveyance of core values through all text-based and visual materials and interactions.

· Deeper establishment of corporate identity in consumer consciousness through professional and consistent management.

· Regular evaluations and assessments to ensure consistency and identify weaknesses.

In successful cases, this cycle of identity development can eventually come to achieve a certain synergistic energy (→ Synergy). Individual elements between separate fields intersect, individual activities optimize each other, the process accelerates, and the company's internal and external operations come into greater alignment. Initiating and maintaining an ambitious and complex identity program of this sort requires vision, courage, power, perseverance, as well as charisma, confidence and, above all, (→) creativity.

Creative thinking and action therefore are required of all aspects of corporate identity development, not just those that specifically involve the activity of design. Creative solutions are always needed to find innovative outcomes, facilitate communication across multiple networks, develop flexible product systems, and invent new processes. Overseeing vested rights and reevaluating proven solutions and strategies in critical situations are not necessarily sufficient ways of developing a comprehensive program of corporate identity. The synergistic relationships mentioned above must be constantly reevaluated, as otherwise it could turn into a vicious cycle.

Using the term "creativity" within this context also helps clarify what is not meant here, that is, the creativity of an independent artist or an autonomous genius (→ *Auteur Design*). Creativity in developing identity programs for companies means constantly searching for originality and (→) innovation for all communicative problems. Yet, while developing specific corporate identities, creativity also has to display a reasonable and recognizable relationship to the given situation—that is, it must serve and adapt to the relevant cycle.

Even if what follows seems initially like a contradictory list, creative identity development must, above all, be focused. The broadest possible variety of creative ideas is not what is needed. It is important to reduce the universe of creative possibilities down to only those ideas, activities, and things that most convincingly relate to the defined features of the corporate personality in question. In other words, it is necessary to creatively narrow this search in such a way that the results are not banal, but rather, distinctive and convincing. Secondly, the designs have to be made stylistically consistent. To maintain this consistency, it is important to narrow the variety of possible responses, and focus on a consistent (→) integration of all the corporate identity's forms of expression, so that each contains a recall factor while avoiding monotonous homogeneity. Thirdly, the designs should be striking and memorable. This is not to say that solutions that are consistently new and unique are always best; it is necessary to remain faithful to the corporate personality's core message, while exploring the possibility for fresh interpretations. The result should be a constant reiteration of its central message in a way that does not become tedious, but always stimulates attention. ^{JH} |

→ *Branding, Continuity*

CRAFT

The term "craft" in this definition refers to the skill and mastery of working with materials and/or processes. Craft is associated with the applied or "low" arts and it is often suggestive of (→) ornamentation, decoration, the handmade, and folk art.

The etymology and meaning of the word "craft" in the English language was virtually synonymous with that of art up to the late eighteenth century. Up until this time, art and craft both referred to the skill and mastery of a particular method, trade, applied art, or discipline, and included such activities as writing, woodturning, shoemaking, and scientific experimentation. The meaning of the terms art and craft diverged in more recent times, starting with the Industrial Revolution and more particularly after the First World War. Art took on a stronger philosophic, poetic, and critical mission as design emerged and became strongly associated with the material-based crafts. The (→) Bauhaus, and many other design schools since, based their pedagogy on the crafting of old and new (→) materials and media.

Design thus became associated with a more industrial version of craft and both domains had a certain second-class status in relation to the art of high culture, due to their connection with utility. By the later part of the twentieth century, design progressively sought to develop both an intellectual and strategic legitimacy and to free itself from the traditional associations with handmade craft. At this point, schools and associations began dropping the word craft from their names in order to appear up-to-date with the dramatically shifting technological landscape of the digital revolution. This may have been a little hasty as, just as the (→) Arts & Crafts movements were a backlash against the Industrial Revolution, so has there been a rapid resurgence of serious interest in craft in the late twentieth and early twenty-first centuries. This resurgence is in response, in part, to the ubiquity of digital processing and the widespread feeling that it has produced a facile homogeneity of both process and aesthetic. Craft, with its associations with the handmade and ornamental, has thus emerged as a pursuit for authenticity in what is seen as an increasingly inauthentic world—and despite the fact that it is still sometimes viewed with cynicism as an outmoded or naive concept, growing numbers of designers and artists are reinvesting in it as a critical design sensibility. The works of Petra Blaise, Hella Jongerius, and Denise Gonzalez Crisp are indicative of this influence.

Though the reemergence of craft as a design sensibility can be seen as a reaction against digitization, these two approaches to design are not mutually exclusive; indeed, designers have begun investing a sophisticated craft sensibility into digital processes as well as utilizing technology masterfully in order to create distinctive and unique products. This confluence of craft sensibilities with digital processes can be seen throughout design from cars to clothing to graphic design and architecture. Craft is the topic of a growing number of serious conferences and publications indicating that this resurgence may have a lasting impact on both art and design. [TM] |

→ *Ornament, Skills*

CREATIVITY

Creativity is a complex and much debated term referring to the process of undertaking creative work. Generally it is a word that distinguishes a method or an activity from one that is overtly intellectual, formulaic, methodological, or critical. Terms such as creative arts and creative writing generally describe work that is understood to issue as much from the imagination as from analysis and that is inventive and original rather than derivative.

While creativity is commonly used to describe the activity of artists, novelists, performers, and so on, this can be narrow and misleading. Creativity is a quality that is in evidence in all aspects of human endeavor. Scientific, engineering, agricultural, and entrepreneurial breakthroughs can all involve genuine creativity. It is equally misleading to suggest that those in the creative arts are operating in some kind of intellectual or methodological vacuum relying only on "unteachable" intuitions, talent, and reflexes. Many of the greatest creative artists utilize highly analytic and systematic processes.

Understood this way, creativity becomes a quality evidenced in work. It is present when a person or people undertaking an activity can employ understanding, skill, fluency, and capabilities to gain a new and different perspective on this activity and, through the combination of their imagination and their preexisting understanding, are able to arrive at a genuinely unique and original perception. Terms such as "inspired," "genius," "aha moments," "eureka," and so on are often used to identify precisely those moments of creative breakthrough and new insight that can happen in every and any activity.

"Creativity" has been an ambiguous term for designers and design academics and, since the 1980s, has been increasingly viewed as problematic. It is used to "explain away" what non-designers do not understand about the (→) design process, such as the development of visuals or shapes in products, architecture, or clothing that are often described as being the result of "creativity." The problem here is that the analytic, theoretical, and scientific underpinnings that do, or should, inform design decisions are avoided or dismissed or remain unexamined when creativity is used to gloss over that process.

Should a company or government agency pay large sums of money for a design service that can only be explained on the basis of the creative urges of the individual designer? What will be the connotation of this or that color choice or this or that product form? How will users respond and react? How can this be known before large sums of money are spent? If it cannot be explained, then design is seen as a frivolous activity that will only be indulged when profits are sufficiently large and will be the first input cut when times are bad (which indeed has been the case in many companies).

In the search for respectability and the trust of clients and of the traditional science-based disciplines, many designers, design firms, and design academics have attempted to distance design from its historical relationship to the visual and creative arts. Increasingly, designers in many specialisms, with fashion being a notable exception, are avoiding using terms such as "creative," "imaginative," or "inspired" to describe their processes. Ironically, there has been a simultaneous and growing interest in "creative" business leaders. There is an emerging appreciation of the value of creative processes in business settings. Companies often fail to innovate in ways that deliver them competitive advantage even, or especially, when they are run in strict adherence to the accounting efficiency logic taught in standard M.B.A. graduate programs.

There is a reconciliation emerging between the attitudes within, and of, design in regard to creativity. It is now more properly seen as indispensable to design-based (→) innovation. Creativity when understood in this way is built on a deep knowledge of and thorough immersion in the issues and concerns being addressed. It builds on analysis and objective reasoning rather than being an alternative process. The iPod would be the best example of this in the early twenty-first century. The technology and the user behaviors that underpinned its development had existed for some time, as shown by the popularity of Walkmans and the growing ubiquity of memory sticks and other micro digital-memory storage devices. The possibility of converging these technologies and human desires was exploited in a creative moment in a design process in which these preexisting capacities and conditions were "cross-appropriated," infused with high-level design values, and the iPod was born.

There is a growing business and social literature which evokes design as the critical "aha moment" that moves behaviors and practices into new social and cultural spaces. TM |

→ *Design Methods, Heuristics, Intuition, Skills*

CREDIBILITY

In many developed industrial countries, it is quite apparent that people are no longer as fascinated with goods and their novelty as they used to be, and that they are no longer as willing to trust (→) advertisements and banal promotion strategies. Consumers today make their purchases with more circumspection, with a heightened awareness of both cost and environmental consciousness. This could mean that the capitalist-orientated system would lose its legitimacy partially or even completely by reason of unemployment, problematic social policies, environmental problems, and so on, as capitalism is based on the opposite: success and progress.

It is precisely when people begin to lose faith, however, that the credibility of corporations and the products they produce gets called into question—and, simultaneously, that design can work to establish and sustain it. This is because design promises—and guarantees, if necessary—to consistently provide the public with innovation, quality, safety, security, individuality. Design can also reinforce and communicate other measures of credibility such as promoting culture, sciences, and environmental strategies. ME |

→ *Branding, Corporate Identity, Service Design*

CRITICAL DESIGN

Critical design uses speculative design proposals to challenge narrow assumptions, preconceptions, and givens about the role products play in everyday life. The opposite of critical design is affirmative design—a design that reinforces the status quo. Critical design is an attitude and an approach to design rather than a definitive method; indeed, many people who practice it have either never heard of the term, or describe what they do in any number of alternative ways. The act of naming this activity as critical design is useful, however, in that it makes its outcomes more visible and therefore more open to discussion. It is essential that critical designs be able to provoke discussion because, as the name suggests, the primary intention is to make us think: to raise awareness, expose assumptions, provoke action, spark debate, and even entertain in an intellectual way like literature or film.

The discourse of design as critique has existed for decades if not centuries under several guises. Most notably, the Italian (→) Radical Design movement of the 1970s took a highly critical attitude regarding the prevailing social values and design ideologies of the time. During the 1990s there was a general move toward (→) conceptual design that, while not identical to critical design, did make it easier for noncommercial practices like critical design to exist. These movements took place mainly in the furniture world.

The current critical design approach to some extent builds upon the attitude of the 1970s radical design movement that questioned the traditional values of the time. The world we live in today is incredibly and increasingly complex: our (→) social relations, desires, fantasies, hopes, and fears are very different from those at the beginning of the twentieth century, yet many of the key ideas informing mainstream design still reflect the issues from that period. Society has moved on but design has not—and critical design is one of many mutations design is undergoing in an effort to remain relevant to the complex technological, political, economic, and social changes we are experiencing at the beginning of the twenty-first century. Toward that end, critical design shares some of the attitudes and perspectives that inform various forms of activism. Cautionary tales, contestable futures, design fiction, interrogative design, radical design, social fiction, and speculative design are some of the activities and practices that are informed by critical perspectives today for instance.

Critical designers often use irony (in the way of political romanticism) or humor to introduce a critical perspective. In these types of critical designs, the viewer is meant to experience a dilemma and carry something of a burden of interpretation: Is this serious? Is it supposed to be ironic? Is it real? As such, satire is the goal (as opposed to parody and pastiche, which tend to be intellectually lazy and borrow from existing formats). As with the best political comedians, the critical designer's intention is to engage the audience's imagination and intellect to convey a message.

Critical design is a response to the fact that design views its users and consumers as obedient, largely uniform, and predictable whereas nearly every other area of culture acknowledges people as complicated, contradictory and even neurotic. One of the main functions of critical design is to question the limited range of experiences offered through designed products and to expand how design might not only respond to complex problems but also acknowledge the complex emotional and psychological landscape of people. It is assumed that design is always intended to make things nicer—as if designers have taken a silent Hippocratic oath to limit their engagement with the darker sides of human nature. A critical designer, on the other hand, takes account of these complexities of living, and can even use negativity constructively to draw attention to scary possibilities (as in the case of cautionary design tales). Critical design recognizes and draws attention to the ways in which we are designing our world, whether they be benign or insidious.

The criticisms of critical design itself and the misconceptions it suffers are numerous and varied: that it is negative and antieverything; that it is only commentary and cannot change anything; that it is jokey and full of one-liners; that it is not concerned with aesthetics; that it is against massproduction; that it is pessimistic; that it is not real-world; and that it is not design at all, but rather a form of art. While critical design might heavily borrow some of its methods and approaches, it definitively is not art. We expect art to explore extremes, but critical design needs to be close to the everyday and the ordinary as that is where it derives its power to disturb and question assumptions. Too weird and it will be dismissed as quasi-art; too normal and it will be effortlessly and unquestiongly assimilated. It is only when read as design that critical designs can suggest that the everyday as we know it could be different—that things could change.

A danger for critical design is the possibility of ending up as a form of sophisticated design entertainment enjoyed more for its humor or novelty than its insights. Critical design needs to avoid this situation by identifying and engaging with complex and challenging issues. The increasing reliance on future forecasting for instance would benefit from a more gritty view of human nature and the ability to make abstract issues tangible. It could also play a role in public debates about the social, cultural, and ethical impact on everyday life of emerging and future technologies. FR |

→ *Communications, Criticism, Critique, Design and Politics, Ethics*

Dunne, A., and F. Raby. 2001. *Design noir: The secret life of electronic objects*. Basel: Birkhäuser.
Lasn, K. 1999. *Culture jam: How to reverse America's suicidal consumer binge—and why we must*. New York: Quill.

CRITICISM

Criticism is a genre of reflective writing on design generally characterized by a detailed description and comparative assessment of a product or system in relation to like products, function, stated intentions(s), or the process/realization in relation to a specific social context. The dissemination of design criticism in diverse (→) publications such as newspapers, popular magazines, design, and art magazines, online reviews, professional publications, academic journals, blogs, and other print, media and online outlets is indicative of its present scope, varied modes of writing, and unpredictable standards. One of the primary missions of criticism—informing and shaping public views and opinions—has been broadened as this traditionally journalistic form of writing has been transformed into a hybrid of popular, poetic, promotional, and academic discourses. This development within criticism has opened up the field to disciplinary perspectives such as history, sociology, philosophy, visual and popular culture studies, urban studies, film studies, gender studies, and others fields beyond art, design, social sciences, and humanities. Design criticism must also take into account an even broader context since the role of design work and process is integrated into technological, business, and economic systems that rely on (→) innovation and (→) transformation. Because of its breadth, design criticism is an expanding and emergent field of reflective writing, one that is indicative of the current understanding of the design mission and process itself. Design criticism often requires specific expertise about the systems, organizations, and spaces within which designed work functions, and it must take into consideration strategies of (→) communication and relationships with the intended users. This combination of disciplinary expertise and trans-disciplinary flexibility has enabled new ways of thinking about the role and significance of design in contemporary debates (→ *Discipline*).

Criticism published in specialist journals is most often geared to an academic or professional audience with dissemination of current design issues limited as a result. Newspaper criticism, by contrast, is often written as a means to educate and influence the public about specific design projects. One of its central goals is to generate debate with a public audience conversant with the issues raised by the design work.

Beginning in the 1990s, the relevance of criticism and its mission became the subject of debate among critics themselves. Some fundamentals of these arguments are the all-inclusiveness of contemporary criticism, allowing both cursory descriptive reviews and academic writing to inhabit the terrain; and the shift in criticism away from opinion or judgment as one of its primary ends. Increasingly, criticism is written by designers, artists, and curators who are themselves, at times, the subject of criticism. This interchangeability of roles has further challenged any residual suggestion of objectivity or critical distance from the subject. Criticism is often aligned with the mission and audience of the newspaper, magazine, journal, or online sites where the writing is published. But generally, criticism about design draws, at least in part, on the methodologies of the disciplines themselves; this may include formalist writing, iconographic analysis, contextual analysis, and postmodern perspectives on identity, gender, and postcolonial theory, for example.

Criticism as a distinct form of writing has taken shape within Western cosmopolitan cultures, often written by generalists who surveyed art and design within the broad cultural milieu. As a developing form of writing, it emerged from the intellectual inquiries of Enlightenment, the culture of urban centers, the development and growth of cultural venues and markets, and the availability of print and other media outlets. With the expansion of interest in contemporary design globally, criticism outside the West has tended to follow a similar trajectory with academic criticism often informed by sociology, anthropology, and contemporary social theory. RO |

→ *Critique, Research, Theory*

Buchanan, R. 1989. Declaration by Design: Rhetoric, argument, and demonstration in design practice. In V. Margolin, ed. *Design Discourse: History, theory, criticism*. Chicago: Univ. of Chicago Press.
Margolin, V. 2002. *The politics of the artificial*. Chicago: Univ. of Chicago Press.
Rubenstein, R., ed. 2006. *Critical mess: Art critics on the state of their practice*. Lenox, MA: Hard Press Editions.

CRITIQUE

"Critique" is a term derived from critic and (→) criticism. In an educational design setting, the term is used to describe the process of evaluating and assessing students' work. The intention is not necessarily to be critical in a pejorative sense but rather to provide the student with expert judgments and insight into their designs. As such, most critiques will highlight aspects that are successful as well as those that are ineffective.

Usually the critique is undertaken by a panel of representatives with relevant disciplinary proficiencies and can also include representatives of potential clients and users—that is those with a stake in the actual or potential design outcome. Typically, the critique will inquire into the proposal and provide a range of reactions and responses to the resulting design. Frequently, the critique will not consist of a single set of coherent (→) values, so the student designer is required to interpret the divergent opinions and weigh up how to respond appropriately. Given the intrinsic subjectivity of the critique format, the feedback can be explicitly contradictory, compelling the students to sort and evaluate the insights that they feel are most relevant to their intention.

The critique can be an emotionally difficult situation for a student and learning how to receive and benefit from this form of criticism is an important aspect of a young designer's education. Adopting an open and enthusiastic approach to the critique process, rather than being defensive and dismissive, leads to much better learning outcomes as the student can engage flexibly and productively with the responses. Designers must function with and manage a wide range of agendas, requirements, reactions, attitudes, and approaches. The designer is rarely present when people interact with their designs, so they must develop a strong understanding of how to interpret and respond to the range of reactions to their designs.

The skills learned through critique sessions are invaluable in preparing a novice designer for the realities of the profession. While the formal critiques experienced in school may not be encountered in quite the same form once the student has graduated, pitching ideas to clients, responding to user-centered research and so on are the unstructured forms of critique that every designer must learn to work with. The challenge is to use these encounters in ways that both extend the designer's continuing education while also using them as opportunities to communicate the thinking that has informed the design outcome. TM I

→ *Critical Design, Education, Evaluation*

CROSS-CULTURAL DESIGN

Cross-cultural design speaks to the ability of design (→) products, designers, or design-producing entities to traverse cultural boundaries. Either the products themselves physically and literally traverse cultural boundaries, or designers and design entities cross the boundaries and operate within the domain of another culture. The cultural boundaries can be aligned according to broad national, ethnic, or geographic categories, but they can also be defined according to smaller-scale, socioeconomic divisions within a culture.

Cross-cultural design raises a number of issues. Among them is the question of hegemony, wherein one culture is thought to have greater cultural power than another, whether because of economics, politics, social standing, or other reasons. As such, discussion of cross-cultural design relies heavily on the theoretical discourse of colonial or postcolonial (→) criticism, which in turn finds its roots in the work of structuralism, poststructuralism, phenomenology, and Marxism, each of which raise questions of epistemology and of connections to underlying power structures. Within these approaches, design is seen to be the carrier of cultural (→) values that cross borders, so any particular act of design can be the site of contestation between one set of values and another. As an embodiment or carrier of cultural values, design can be mined for information on the dynamic interactions between the central or dominant culture and the marginalized or peripheral culture. Within this dynamic, design is also seen as a means by which a subjected culture regains its independence.

Viewed in less polemical ways, cross-cultural design relates to the concept of trans-cultural design, or the ability of design to transcend the limitations of a specific context and speak to universal or common contemporary values shared by other cultures. As such, design moves out of the realm of culturally bound language and text and becomes an easily translatable language of (→) communication based on (→) aesthetics, formal qualities, or (→) function. From this perspective, design constitutes a flexible universal language and a powerful medium of cultural exchange that is rapidly being appropriated for business, politics, and other purposes. Taken another step further, cross-cultural design moves into the territory of globalism and global culture (→ *Globalization*) in which culture separates from traditional political or geographic boundaries and establishes new global territories of operation. These new territories, or "scapes" as some theorists have called them, denote new relationships between and among design objects, users, institutions, and systems of commerce that span the globe and connect people in radically new ways unprecedented in history. ᴱᵀ |

→ *Collaborative Design, International Style*

CROSSOVER

Crossover is the (mainly intentional) overlapping of procedures, practices, or styles from two or more disciplines. During the crossover process, certain characteristics and influences from disciplines like architecture, design, art, literature, media, fashion, or music are adapted and coordinated for the generation of new or modified products, services, strategies, or statements. The resulting designs often create new target groups and markets because they reflect a blend of influences from multiple areas rather than one isolated (→) discipline. The creation of these new markets can in turn increase the potential for development, sales, and (→) innovation—but it also means that the expertise and (→) skills associated with traditional disciplinary categories could eventually become overtaxed, diluted, or even lose their significance entirely.

Crossover has become an established strategy in companies and institutions seeking to expand the scope of their reach. Multimedia communication channels are now considered a requirement for successful (→) brand promotion and the holistic integration of on- and off-line identities (→ *Corporate Identity*). In today's globalized word, the expansion of markets through the use of crossover elements from other markets has become a regular activity, albeit one that still needs to be studied in detail. [SIB] |
→ *Strategic Design, Synergy*

CUSTOMIZATION

Customization is the act of adapting design (→) artifacts to particular needs or preferences. The term did not hold any significance until the late eighteenth century, when industrialization put an end to the traditional process of developing, designing, and producing goods on a regional scale and in close collaboration with the customer. The newfound variety of choice offered by industrially manufactured goods directed at a larger, national market could not cater to individual needs and wishes, nor was it intended to. As standardized processes and products became the norm, variations in (→) components or end products were largely eliminated because they raised the cost of production. In turn, manufacturers who continued to adapt designs to meet customer (→) needs turned customization into a high-end industrial production option, available to the select consumers who could afford the steep costs. Modern communication and production technologies have paved the way for mass customization techniques to be integrated into industrial manufacturing processes. [BM] |
→ *Production Technology*

D

DADA AND DESIGN

Design at its simplest is not usually associated with philosophical movements like Dada, but rather with (→) craft movements, such as the (→) Deutscher Werkbund, the (→) Bauhaus, or with the Constructivist (→ Constructivism) art movements of Russia, the Netherlands and other countries. It is as if design is, inescapably, part of a mode of production that is both craft-related and direct, quite removed from all ambiguous or chaotic artistic and creative activity.

Dada began in Zurich in 1916 during the First World War and involved literature, fine arts, theater and music, and was influenced by antiwar and anarchist philosophies—an aspect that was particularly important to Hugo Ball, the Club Voltaire's protagonist from Munich. Dada never propagated arbitrary disorder but questioned the existing concepts and dominant systems of order and government in a profound and radical manner. Having experienced the social and cultural poverty and the violent chaos of the First World War that resulted from the existing social and cultural bourgeois good order, Dada confronted it with new, radical forms of organization and logic.

The ideas, concept, and practice behind Dada had major effects on poetry, fine arts, and music, but also on architecture and, above all, on design. The latter particularly applies to Dada's development after 1918 in Berlin (George Grosz), Hannover (Kurt Schwitters), and Cologne (Max Ernst and Johannes Bargeld), and was assisted by the fact that postwar Germany, with its chaotic economy and the resumption and redefinition of politics, open debates, advertising, and propaganda greatly influenced day-to-day life. Moreover, the ordinary and the "everyday," as opposed to highculture, itself gained major relevance in (→) theory and art. Flyers and pamphlets also popped up everywhere, touting or criticizing political programs and parties; at the same time, trade and industry were exploiting advertising in order to rekindle consumerism. There was also a need, typical after the breakdown of any regime, to reorganize and redesign the forms of mass communication such as ordinances and bulletins.

This is where Dada came in and Raoul Hausmann, one of the most important protagonists and theoretical founders of the Berlin Dada movement and publisher of the magazine *Der Dada*, was able to pinpoint profound and thoughtful ways to communicate and deal with the public. As a consequence, Hannah Höch and Raoul Hausmann, and later John Heartfield among others, designed photomontages and collages as a contemporary medium to understand, visualize, and communicate the nature of a fragmented existence. Collage and other media were also developed by Dada to address the enormous escalation in speed and noise, the jumbled worlds of experience, and to design forms of work and publications appropriate to this incoherent and confusing world.

Dada published ($\rightarrow$) flyers and magazines with totally new lay-outs and typographical formations including overprinting; they experimented with phonetic writing, like graphically screaming characters and simultaneous writing (text that can be started or ended at any point) or simultaneous poems (collaborative per-formance poems in which two or more voices speak or sing si-multaneously). They also organized actions—not only to confuse people, but as a way to publicize and to digest all these new im-pressions, experiences, and philosophies. Dada regarded experi-ence as the essential starting point of design, and the ($\rightarrow$) social dimension of experience was a fundamental aspect of this; hence the design practice was always directed at the general pub-lic and sought popular acceptance.

As one expression of a radical new order, Dada publications chose collage and photomontage as media and played with typo-graphical symbols and scale. Question and exclamation marks, slashes, dashes, and periods were systematically scaled up and pushed to the fore—giving individual letters, as the smallest components of texts, a completely different presence. This set up some revolutionary principles for a new approach to graphic images that no longer followed traditional rules or conformed to a simple sequential compendium of design and thought (as fre-quently found in Constructivism). Dada (quasi-romantically) im-plemented these principles to make a radical attack on a linear sense of logic, and, in the process, exploded the encoded gram-mar of the relationship between subject and object.

Kurt Schwitters was particularly influential in this progressive prehistory of design. He lived mainly in the northern German city of Hannover, once worked as a technical draftsman, and called his form of Dada "Merz." He painted, created collages, assemblages, and sculptures, wrote poetry, polemic, and critical and theoretical texts. He also suggested a way of entering a movie cinema for free (that is, backward through the exit, in other words, with negative energy), opened the Werbezentrale Merz (an advertising agency), and later founded the Ring Neue Werbegestalter (the Circle of New Advertising Designers) with members such as Vordemberge-Gildewart and Max Burchartz.

Schwitters drew a strong line between his artistic (even poetic) work and his other design activities; however, his visual and action-based experiences (he gave action readings and wrote theater plays) were equally important in developing his general design practice.

He designed a new font (and gave detailed and precise explana-tions for this), as well as an ad for the ink and fountain pen company Pelikan, advertising slogans for the Hannover streetcar company, and from 1927 onward, he even designed stationery (including the logo) for the City of Hannover and its public authorities, such as the school system. In addition, Schwitters worked with architect Otto Haesler on the Celler Volks-Möbel (Celle is a small town near Hannover), creating affordable tables and chairs and a very concise and attractive advertising brochure. Kurt Schwitters also cooperated with Walter Gropius (the founder of the Bauhaus) and designed the plans and publications for the Dammerstock-Siedlung, an architectural project designed by Gropius that was built near the city of Karlsruhe. Moreover, Schwitters conceived new design forms for the theater stage and for spatial arrangements that adapted to human beings by continually changing in response to human movement and behavior.

The obvious basis for all of his design work was a constant questioning of the concept of order, which he would not accept as an abstract mechanism, but always viewed as use-oriented, even empirical, always fluctuating and concrete. Schwitter's radical critique of the Bauhaus and the formulations from similar institutions or movements is symptomatic of his evercritical view of order (and is thus symptomatic of Dada's reflection on and practice of design in general). Since these architects and institutions, he once wrote, aspired to design harmonious spaces and objects, and that this, by definition, is inhumane, as then any person entering such a space or using one of these objects fundamentally and empirically destroys this harmony. ME |

DECONSTRUCTION

Since Friedrich Nietzsche introduced (→) aesthetic parameters into the Western discourse on rationality, the concept of deconstruction has been focused on questioning Platonic and Aristotelian notions of logic, particularly as manifested in linguistics, philosophy, ontology, and scientific positivism. The principle of deconstruction attempts to free thought from bivalence and directs it instead at polyvalence. This principle challenges the belief in naive forms of illustrative and descriptive representation, as it replaces traditional notions of metaphysics with complex models of disidentification, analogy, decontextualization, and iterative intricacy. The philosopher Gilles Deleuze and writers such as George Spencer Brown introduced, through deconstruction, the category of temporality into logic itself. A break was made from previously popular notions of finality, (→) continuity, and purpose-orientation.

The impact that the general concept of deconstruction had on the practices of architecture and design was largely formulated on the basis of ideas developed by the philosopher Jacques Derrida. Similar to Niklas Luhman and Jean-François Lyotard, who negated the societal, central standpoint of the observer and the potential of common great narratives, Derrida overrode the structuralist discourse in favor of one that privileged difference and decentralization.

Applying deconstructivist methodology enables architects and designers to distance themselves from the (→) conventions of traditional formal language and style guidelines. In Peter Eisenman's and Frank Gehry's architectural designs, for example, (→) form and (→) function engage in a loosely joined relationship: lines are broken, styles are combined, and the qualities of chance and imperfection are taken into account in the transformation of buildings into architectural sculptures. In David Carson's graphic design work, conventional typographical rules and formats dissolve and flow into creative text and image collages. SA |

→ *Construction, Constructivism, Functionalism, Postmodernism*

Collins, M., and A. Papadakis. 1990. *Postmodern design*. New York: Rizzoli.
Deleuze, G. 1994. *Difference and repetition*. Trans. Paul Patton. New York: Columbia Univ. Press.
Derrida, J. 1978. *Writing and difference*. Trans. Alan Bass. London: Routledge.

DECORATION

→ *Ornament, Ornamentation*

DESIGN

At the risk of disappointing you, dear reader, it is impossible to offer a single and authoritative definition of the central term of this dictionary—design. Design's historical beginnings are complex and the nature of design, what it is and what it isn't, is the subject of diverse and ongoing arguments as can be seen from the perspectives offered in this dictionary. Indeed, even in the two languages used in this dictionary there are two related but distinct definitions. In German, design primarily relates to the creation of (→) form while in English the term is more broadly applied to include the conception—the mental plan—of an object, action, or project (→ *Gestaltung*). It can be assumed then that the general sense of the word exists in most languages and cultures with the exact meaning reflecting specific cultural characteristics and biases. Therefore, in this text the reader will be offered several, principally "western," definitions from which to construct a sense of what design has been, is, and might possibly become.

Design comes from the Latin word *designare* meaning to define, to describe, or to mark out. At a certain point in history, design shifted from a term that generally described a great number of human activities, toward its current status as a defined and professional (→) practice. Not surprisingly, it was Leonardo da Vinci who first founded an academy dedicated to design. At the time, the concept of design was implicitly linked to both art making and the construction of objects and spaces, but it could also be argued that this was the first step toward identifying a particular professional person as a designer. It proved to be something of a false start, however, as this Renaissance understanding of design shifted soon after and, until the Industrial Revolution during the later half of the eighteenth century, the term designer remained wedded to the idea of craftsmanship and the graduated and sequential learning required to master the (→) skills of a (→) craft. Up until the period of the Industrial Revolution, the designer/craftsperson was in direct contact with the client. Customers approached a specialized craftsperson to have their needs met directly, and often exclusively, by the specialist's skill. The necessity of this direct, individual contact and the reassurance of the master's "hand" in the final product became the limiting factor for these craft-based designers, even as transport and communication systems in the early colonial period opened new markets, needs, and opportunities. In other words, it was precisely the nature of craftsmanship and the individual craftsperson that became the limiting factor in relation to these new markets with their mediated and anonymous business dealings. The growing markets that accompanied colonialism and the attendant rise of the mercantile classes can now be seen as the first significant step toward what we now understand as (→) globalization.

New global markets demanded new forms of production and the direct personal service of the crafts became increasingly irrelevant. The guild organizations established around craft practices were steadily forced to make way for the engineering-based process of industrialization and semimechanized mass production and marketing. The surge of industrial production marginalized craftsmanship together with its interpersonal consulting style. This early period of mass production developed in response to the invention of new tools, the reorganization of human labor's relationship to production and by new methods of transport, distribution, and marketing (→ *Advertisement*).

The last quarter of the nineteenth century saw mass movements of labor from the agrarian sector to urban manufacturing. This dislocation resulted in a lack of social justice for these new workers and a rapid decline in the quality of products. The emergence of the labor union movement in England, in particular, as well as in France was in response to these issues, while the new and older wealthy mercantile and ruling classes harbored a deep discontent regarding the decline in the quality of industrial products and the lack of adequate service structures in these now distant and anonymous processes.

This historic period of profound change was the context within which the (→) Arts & Crafts movement, initiated by William Morris and John Ruskin, arose in Great Britain. The movement attempted to reinstate the craft-based notions of product (→) quality and personalized service relationships. The Arts & Crafts movement was influential in the second half of the nineteenth century and was fundamentally driven by a desire to return to the roots of craft-based production and products and, for Ruskin, to restore the importance of pastoral life and architecture and a rejection of machine-made objects as "dishonest" and, for Morris, to reinstate the accompanying medieval structure organizing the craftsman's direct relation to the clients. It is important for this discussion to understand that, although this movement tried to reform society and its products through a nostalgic imperative (→ Nostalgia) (the philosopher Ernst Bloch criticized them at the time as "petit-bourgeois socialists"), the Arts & Crafts movement became so influential that it is very often cited as the beginning of design as the term came to be understood through the twentieth century. (This tension between craft and industrial production and different definitions of design dominated the common understandings of design throughout the twentieth century.) The influence of the Arts & Crafts movement's approach spread through the (→) Art Nouveau aesthetic movement in France and the craft-based (→) Deutscher Werkbund and the (→) Bauhaus in Germany. (The Bauhaus School, 1919 to 1933, despite its strong association with the aesthetics and philosophy of modernism, organized its teaching curriculum around the traditional handcrafting of materials and defined its pedagogy through master classes.)

Design developed in the modern era through the actions of key individuals responding to the new potentials and fears associated with developments in technology, and to changing socioeconomic and political conditions and contexts. In the first quarter of the twentieth century there are two designers in the development of European and American design whose respective practices illustrate the broader trend away from the Arts & Crafts movement. The first, a former Art Nouveau artist and founding member of the Deutscher Werkbund (founded in 1907 as an association of architects, designers, and industrialists for the improvement of German manufactured goods) is Peter Behrens. Behrens attempted to position the Deutscher Werkbund as an organization dedicated to industrial development—in clear contrast to the Arts & Crafts movement. Behrens became the exclusive designer for one of the largest German companies of the time, AEG (General Electrics, Germany) and was the first designer to work across the previous demarcations of the material crafts—in other words, he could be considered one of the first general designers. Behrens created what we would now call a (→) corporate identity for AEG and worked on (→) branding, designed the (→) logo and all published communications of the company (including designing several new fonts), together with many of the actual products, including a wide variety of lamps, ventilators, electric heaters, kettles, clocks, and so on, and even designed aspects of the corporate architecture. This approach represents a significant step away from the notion of the designer as the originator of a handmade original that makes clear its relationship with the hand of the master, and toward designing as the conception of a system or family of artifacts for production and identity.

This period can be seen as a fertile time for the ongoing debate about these ideas of design and production. The Bauhaus definitely heralded the infiltration of modernism into everyday life, combining both a socialist agenda committed to improving the quality of life for the masses, while at the same time positioning design as a powerful servant of the new capitalists. In this sense the Bauhaus could be seen as an advanced form of Arts & Crafts that tapped into many areas of creativity (fine arts, film, photography, architecture, graphic design, and handcraft production) then connecting these to new forms of design based on industrial processes (such a standardized components) and using media such as tubular steel and other new materials.

The continuing departure of design from its craft origins is evident in the work of Raymond Loewy, a French-born US immigrant who had studied fashion then moved to product and graphic design and was one of the initiators of (→) streamline design. In assessing Loewy's contribution you cannot ignore his individual designs for particular products (for Coca-Cola, the car industry, boats, locomotives, and so on), but as innovative and influential as these have been, his main contribution, it could be argued, was through radicalizing Peter Behrens' approach to design. Loewy, like Behrens before him, took the notion of design as a comprehensive system for designing interrelated products and identities and fully launched what we now understand to be corporate design.

Loewy gave up the artistic as well as the craftsman's attitude to generate this original approach to design—for him design was the discipline that endeavors to continually improve existing systems and products. This approach became possible once it was understood that all our interactions with the "made" world are designed—from the logos that represent the manufacturer to every aspect of the human interface with say, a car or any other machine, to the packaging and communication and through to a product's soundscape (→ *Sound Design*). From this perspective, design can be understood as an immensely complex undertaking, as it attempts to optimize the psychological, social, cultural, and ergonomic aspects of people's interaction with the designed world.

To this end, design requires a precise awareness of both reality ("what is") and the tendencies explicit or latent in a society that can be understood through economics, science, culture, and technical developments. Design, by its very nature, is involved in all the social processes and when these are ignored the outcome will be compromised and unsatisfactory and, thus, it has to be grounded in high quality research across many fields. Indeed the notion of design (→) research, that is now seen as essential, can be seen beginning to emerge at during the late modernist period of the 1960s and 70s. It also marks the start of understanding design as a process as well as a product—a process that is, due to the growing complexity of the issues, increasingly collaborative (→ *Collaborative Design*).

This description implies that design does not exist as an exclusive (→) discipline but rather acts to integrate a range of academic, economic, environmental, scientific and artistic insights, knowledge, and opinions together with the everyday process of lived experience into the artifacts, systems, and processes of our constructed lives. Design crosses the borders of disciplines and coordinates and transforms activities while attempting to synchronize multiple understandings of a project. From this viewpoint, design is precisely opposed to the traditional academic logic that defines a discipline. Rather than needing to know all that there is to know in a discrete field, design needs to know "just enough" of the multiple perspectives that frame and shape any project.

Design established itself as a distinct profession, because its specific practices aligned with the material and economic processes associated with housing, manufacturing, media, technology, clothing, and so on. These fields further subdivided through the later part of the twentieth century with the emergence of fields such as (→) service design, (→) strategic design, (→) event design, (→) branding, and so on. In parallel with this increasing specialization and splintering of the design profession has been a counter trend that attempts to harness design's intrinsic interdisciplinary qualities as a process. Problems and issues requiring a diversity of design and nondesign proficiencies—such as complex or (→) "wicked problems"—are increasingly addressed by expanding our understanding of design. This gives the design process, and the conceptual and strategic planning that arises from it, increased authority over the more limited understanding of specific design authorship of a particular artifact. This is most clearly evident when dealing with multidisciplinary issues such as sustainable systems (→ *Sustainability*), (→) urban design, and other areas of (→) environmental design.

Design is seriously implicated in environmental issues, as so many of the critical decision points that influence the environmental impact of products and environments are part of the (→)

design process. However, working toward a sustainable society requires the coordination of scientific, social, cultural, economic, technological, and political tendencies and realities— and of the various intellectual disciplines that attempt to understand, and act through, these specialties. Indeed, it could be argued that these complex issues, including globalization, complex media systems, and the like, lie beyond the scope of any single traditional discipline to understand, much less improve.

Today these two dimensions of design remain evident. There are professional designers who operate within companies, design studios, and agencies as highly specialized workers improving and finessing particular aspects of artifacts and systems for the paying client. On the other hand, many design teams assemble a range of competencies, both general and specialist, to enable complex project work to be undertaken that cannot successfully be undertaken by any design or non-design expertise in isolation.

Either way, as Herbert Simon outlined in the 1960s, design can still be said to be about transforming existing situations into preferred ones. The ever increasing complexity of identifying what that preferred situation might be requires designing our ability to know our own designed world—how it came to be and how it really acts. ME + TM |

DESIGN AGAINST CRIME

The Design against Crime initiative was formalized in 1999 as a (→) research program at Sheffield Hallam University and the University of Salford in the United Kingdom. Through research into the reasons as to why people commit crime as well as methods in which they do, the program has developed a knowledge base that helps designers to better integrate measures to reduce criminal activity in the initial stages of design development.

Since its inception, the program has developed a number of projects aimed at creating safer urban environments and products to deter potential criminal behavior, promote social inclusion, and improve business performance, both in the United Kingdom and abroad. RL |

→ Design and Politics, Safety Design, Urban Planning

DESIGN AND POLITICS

Design has a complex relationship with the practice of politics and is affected by policy in a myriad of ways. This brief overview will discuss a number of ways in which design and politics interact.

The role designers take in the service of political ideologies is complex and varied. All political forces in democratic and non-democratic states make significant use of the persuasive potential of communication design and the power of the visual image to persuade populations of a particular political idea and a vision of the future, and to encourage them to identify themselves as members belonging to a particular communal project.

The classic examples of this are the right and left wing graphics of the Soviet era (→ *Agit Prop*), the Maoist Cultural Revolution in China, the Italian Fascists and—the most notorious and comprehensive political design and branding campaign in history—that of the German Nazi party through the 1930s and 40s.

In all political (→) campaigns the assessment of color schemes, typography, graphic icons, and TV presentations, through to the hairstyles, glasses, and clothes worn by the politicians, the tone of a politician's voice and so on has become a quasi-science, employing psychologists and designers in the quest to present a perfectly packaged message. In postindustrial democracies, political campaigns are almost entirely designed events with less and less left to chance. The intense scrutiny applied by the media and the rise of gossip-reporting has fuelled this development in Western (and Western-style) democracies.

Increasingly, governments in many countries have promoted design as an integral dimension of economic growth and social policy. In emerging economies such as India and China, and before them Japan and Korea, design has been identified as an essential means for economies to emerge from their positions as sources of cheap goods, designed by and manufactured for foreign companies, to one where they develop indigenous brands competing in global markets. Design has proved critical in this endeavor, integrating products, visual identities, and marketing, and exporting this local design and production to world markets. As a consequence, an increasing number of countries are investing vigorously and enthusiastically in design education, because design is seen as such a critical dimension of economic competitiveness.

In the economies that emerged as world powers through the dominance of their heavy industries, this shift to manufacturing offshore has seen their great industrial heartlands decline and become "rust belts." Increasingly, the technological innovations of these countries—media technology and integrated global transportation systems primarily—have resulted in companies being able to exploit cheaper workforces in poorer countries. The resultant impact on the working class areas in these now "postindustrial" countries has seen a number of governments try to revitalize old manufacturing communities and sites with the essential ingredients of this new postindustrial economy.

The promotion and introduction of "culture industries" into these locations is one dimension of this and recognizes that culture and creativity are essential components of an innovative society. Global competition itself has placed a very great emphasis on a company's and a country's ability to innovate. Art, design, and culture have been promoted and at times relocated to the old ship-building, steel-working, and textile manufacturing cities, such as Manchester and Glasgow in the United Kingdom and in various parts of Europe and Australia, precisely to address both the consequences of the decline of the old manufacturing era, and the need for different capabilities in the "new" economic structures emerging in the late twentieth and early twenty-first centuries.

Singapore is a good case study of this trend. It made its wealth from being extremely efficient, and an economically and politically safe gateway into and from Asia. The Singapore government realized that both in order for corporations to establish headquarters in the country and to safeguard Singapore's own economic future, culture and (→) innovation had to be consciously fostered and developed through an integrated government initiative. They have invested heavily in art and design education, galleries, museums and performing arts centers have been built, and design research and development partnerships with brands such as BMW have been secured. This is probably one of the most instrumental examples of a broader worldwide trend.

In a similar vein the "design icon" has also seen certain industrial centers revitalized. Commonly, this is through architectural icons with the clearest example being the economic revitalization through tourism of the industrial town of Bilbao in Spain since the opening of the Frank Gehry designed Guggenheim Museum. The overwhelming attention and (→) branding that this radical and (importantly) photogenic building form has provided for this otherwise relatively overlooked town is mimicked in other cities tempted to use architecture as a form of civic branding.

The practice of design is shaped directly and indirectly by government policies in many ways. While traditionally the only designer that required accreditation in order to be licensed and practice has been the architect, there is a steady increase in the "legislation" of the other design practices. This is usually in the form of registration rather than accreditation—meaning that anyone can practice in the field, but registration provides a form of legitimacy to those educated in "approved" programs as a means to help clients discern the standing of designers and thus to choose from among them.

Government shifts in policy, from laws determining city zoning or regulating environmental impacts, to laws designed to protect people from an almost limitless range of potential dangers, to policies governing written-language usage (such as the requirement for all communication to be in multiple languages), immediately affect and provide new opportunities for designers. A new environmental law, for instance, that requires manufacturers to be responsible for the packaging material of their products, will immediately alter the incentives around the way products are presented and marketed. Designers then have to shift their designs to take account and advantage of such changes. Indeed, changing government policy is directly responsible for generating a great deal of designers' work.

Lastly, it could be argued that design and politics share a certain conceptual approach to their respective activities. While there are very obvious differences between design and politics (politics being principally for the creation and amendment of policy and law, and design the production of artifacts and systems) they do operate under similar constraints. Both these practices are essentially about the future: they both "make and shape" the world and they have to make decisions about this future within a predetermined configuration of what is possible. Both design and politics structure and posit possible (→) lifestyles, in the larger sense of this term, and, in so doing, both practices have to negotiate a range of seemingly irreconcilable cultural, social, environmental, technological, and economic forces (→ *Wicked Problems*). In different ways, these practices have to negotiate this complexity and make decisions on a very small and seemingly banal and local level, as well as ones of significant complexity, consequence, and reach. TM |

→ *Cross-cultural Design, Globalization, Outsourcing, Protest Design, Strategic Design*

Nelson, H. G., and E. Stolterman. 2002. *The design way: Intentional change in an unpredictable world*. Englewood Cliffs, NJ: Educational Technology Publications.
Spinosa, C., F. Flores, and H. L. Dreyfus. 1997. *Disclosing new worlds: Entrepreneurship, democratic action, and the cultivation of solidarity*. Cambridge, MA: MIT Press.

DESIGN ASSOCIATIONS

Design associations are coalitions that enable designers to promote their work through a variety of means. They provide platforms for the exchange of experience and information, help members manage their economic and political interests, and provide information about design protection by means of (→) trademark registrations, utility models, and patent (→ *Intellectual Property*). Design associations also post recommended rates of pay in order to give designers (and clients) a point of reference while negotiating contracts. Despite these efforts, they have been unable to successfully legalize or even codify rates of pay in the field of design. Furthermore, designers' interests are only partially represented in comparison to other professional fields. Other professional associations can be traced back to trade guilds of the Middle Ages, and have evolved into highly organized and effective institutions that charge membership fees to finance their lobbying activities. Professional associations of architects and advertisers have also proven to be more effective than those for designers.

Yet designers are still less willing to join associations and prefer to invest in self-marketing, because it seems more efficient. This may be because designers—even those who claim to embrace collaborative methods—still view the prospect of sharing information and support with potential or real competitors with skepticism. Nevertheless, enhanced communications between designers could do much to strengthen design's economic and social significance, and also improve communications between designers and the public.

The first design associations were founded directly after the Second World War, mainly by artists and artisans who wanted to professionalize the practice. Their collaboration with interested clients had a significant impact on the design profession, as well as the organization and content of design (→) education. They wanted to popularize a pragmatic approach to design and establish the designer as a natural partner in the development and production process. In order to achieve this, designers cooperated with (→) design centers to organize exhibitions, lectures, and design prizes (→ *Design Awards*).

Although it would appear that design is popularly acknowledged today as a legitimate practice, it is still uncertain as to whether it will ever achieve the same professional standing as other more established practices. The impact that design associations will have on clarifying the profession's evolving status also remains to be seen. Changes in the design profession mean that designers today have to be general practitioners as well as specialists.

The mid-1960s saw a surge in the number of active design associations, after large corporations began establishing design departments and employing large numbers of designers. As a result, design associations became very popular as quasi-trade unions that also provided a platform to discuss issues relating to the profession. Design associations experienced another boom in the 1980s, when the concept of "design" began being discussed and researched in earnest by sociologists, psychologists, philosophers, and linguists. This resulted in the professional practice of design expanding far beyond the then standard fields of (→) industrial design and (→) visual communication. Although some older design associations viewed this development with skepticism, the broadened definition and discourse on design opened up new possibilities for many individual designers. Small and midsize design firms began replacing large design departments, and independent entrepreneurs without corporate interests began shaping the design scene. Nonetheless, design associations have still not met the challenge of establishing a binding and comprehensible definition of the profession. TE |

DESIGN AWARDS

Design awards are sponsored competitions intended to support a variety of different design activities. They are generally distinct from awards presented for life achievement, individual work phases, preexisting works, or visionary concepts and designs—though organizers sometimes take these factors into account. In addition to raising valuable publicity for the award winners, design awards also reflect positively on the sponsor organization.

The market success or failure of a designed object often depends on factors that the designer can only partly influence. As a result, (→) design centers and (→) design associations developed the design award as a platform to highlight extraordinary examples of design. A jury consisting of designers, company representatives, and sometimes journalists typically conducts the process of selecting the award winner. Under the pretenses of professionalizing design, jurors were sometimes selected from other fields such as psychology, philosophy, or sociology, but this became less standard after the 1980s. The jury assesses the submitted designs (including user interfaces, a company look, or a product or product series) against criteria such as longevity, functionality, sustainability, or any other previously discussed (often ambiguous) criteria. The jury's decision is ultimately subjective, and the attempts made in the 1970s to reduce the jury-decision process to a formula failed—as did attempts to objectify or standardize design. The quality of a jury can be measured by its power to make its decisions plausible and convincing.

Design awards have become an important public relations tool in a market environment where professionally designed products have become the norm. They are particularly important for emerging designers and firms, as they offer the opportunity to have the (→) quality of their work judged and endorsed by a neutral authority. (Asian manufacturers even pay bonuses to their designers for winning awards.) In the 1950s, design awards were predominantly associated with the sponsorship of (→) public designs. Since then, they have evolved into large, international competitions that charge fees for everything from registration to catalog and Internet publication, or even for using the award's logo—making the organizers interested in offering as many awards as possible. Yet, these awards provide a level of publicity otherwise unavailable to the individual designer or manufacturer, which gives rise to the question as to whether design awards are ultimately "bought" by the winner. It is also problematic that many sponsor organizations allow designers and manufacturers to participate in the competition and also act as members of the jury. Even if these individuals are asked not to take part in discussions or voting, this is a situation that obviously needs reconsideration.

The thematic focus of design awards is changing as quickly and dynamically as the areas of design themselves are developing but compared to architecture, however, there are still very few open design competitions. Competitions have proven complicated when they result in the sponsoring company proceeding to manufacture the award-winning design. Misunderstandings can only be avoided if the sponsor makes a clear distinction between the competition, award, and fee, and the design execution. Designers should never participate in a competition that requires the designer to transfer the (→) copyright and rights of use to the sponsor (→ *Intellectual Property*).

"Emerging designer" awards represent a relatively new and important category. Compared to established designers who generally receive a certificate or trophy for their award winning work, up-and-coming designers are usually presented with a cash prize and the respected design awards publicize the event to other professionals in the field. Yet the recent exaggerated level of publicity given to "emerging" designers has created irrelevant designs that merely assimilate or repeat market (→) conventions. This is resulting in young designers on the whole beginning to conform to market demands due to the number of design awards offered, yet, at the same time, design awards have an equalizing effect because they offer the same extensive publicity to corporations, design departments, and new designers alike. TE |
→ *Evaluation*

DESIGN CENTERS

The term "design center" is used to describe three different environments: regional institutions that promote design, upscale shopping malls, and centralized design departments within large companies.

Since the 1950s, the term "design center" has been typically used to refer to state-sponsored (and occasionally industry-sponsored) organizations dedicated to the promotion of design (→ *Design Associations*). Their task in a national or regional context has been to convince small- and mid-sized businesses of design's cultural relevance. The centers also organize exhibitions, seminars, workshops, and lectures for the public as informational platforms on particular aspects of design. Design centers are supposed to bring various strengths together. They are based on an educational philosophy, as was the case with their pioneer models in handicrafts (→ *Craft*) and industry at the beginning of the Industrial Revolution. Today, the idea behind these model institutions, which were meant to have a direct, positive effect on businesses and consumers, seems both idealistic and outdated. Nonetheless, after the Second World War they were considered internationally *the* model for success in state support of design, as first instituted by the

Design Council in England in 1946. The idea of the design center—as a neutral meeting place for designers, industry, and scientists of different disciplines—also met with great interest in Germany for a while.

In line with Germany's federal structure, decentralized design centers were established, each with a different objective. The Rat für Formgebung, or the German Design Council (founded in 1953), the Industrie Forum Design Hannover (also in 1953), and the Design Zentrum Nordrhein Westfalen (in 1954) all achieved international recognition. Since the 1990s, however, any attempts to establish design centers in former East Germany have failed. Institutions that promote design began redefining themselves in the mid-1990s. In the course of this strategic professionalization, the parties involved began seeing design mainly as an economic factor and, after state funding was largely stopped, most design centers turned into service enterprises. They organize competing design competitions (→ Design Awards) that primarily serve to boost designers' and companies' egos and to market those products that win awards. Commercial design centers are shedding unnecessary baggage and, in the process, design itself is losing the authority of insight. A designer's intentions also play a role in this case and are often as short-term as their clients' expected rate of returns.

This transformation is taking place all over the world. The Design Council in London has become a design business center that supports the economic renewal and export of British design services and goods. The Netherlands closed its new design center as early as the late 1990s. Dutch design is now far more influenced by experimental design academies and design groups than conventional design sponsorship. In Italy, institutional support is rare because there has always been a close collaboration between business management and external designers.

In the 1980s, America introduced an entirely new definition of design center. Now the term can also mean a shopping mall, where furnishings, (→) lifestyle products, and interesting products or brands can be purchased in various shops located under one roof. Germany adopted this term, translating it as *Stilwerk* (style factory). There are now four different shopping malls located in major German cities, whose suppliers network in order to enrich commerce with culture. Yet it is difficult for a design center-cum-marketplace to develop and maintain a genuinely interesting profile.

A third use of the phrase design center is found within the corporate context, whereby (→) design management consolidates the design department under one roof in order to understand the particularities of regional markets and brands faster and convert this knowledge into new products and services. Design departments of car manufacturers are concentrated at company headquarters or in attractive cities or regions such as Barcelona, London, or California. Unlike institutions that sponsor design, design departments attempt to scout out decentralized cultural differences.

Some German design centers are financially very successful, yet their influence on national exports is marginal. A sociology dissertation written in 2000 recommends that German design centers should overcome their divisions and start being more aggressive at marketing.

All three uses of the phrase share one common objective: focusing on design. In the age of global (→) networking, new forms of organization are being created that will no longer rely on a geographical concentration and location of design skills. TE |

DESIGN COMPETENCE

The design profession itself has become as complex as the various aspects of life that call for design solutions. It obviously requires a high level of competence; reducing design to a mere mastery of (→) form and (→) function would be far too simple.

Designers are expected to process design tasks analytically, find creative solutions, be informed about the newest technologies and materials, and be able to use them strategically in their work. They are expected to create designs for the future, know target groups and manufacturing processes, and of course, to develop aesthetic, sensible forms. In short, they are expected to inhabit the roles of artist, structural designer, visionary, sociologist, and marketing expert, all at the same time.

Every designer possesses various levels of expertise for each of the above (→) skills. Yet in order to successfully create products for the market, designers also need "material literacy," which is an additional ability that consolidates their know-how. Material literacy is at its core a communicative competence, whereby designers implement the effect of color, form, material, and surfaces in such a way that gives new designed products a (→) semantic (meaning a nonverbal) significance. The reason there are so many watches on the market, from the techno pilot watch to the nostalgic chronometer with moon phases and various gadgets, is that they all reflect an array of (→) semiotic needs. Good designers are able to play the entire range of symbols like a virtuoso pianist, to anticipate and respond to the expectations of both the client and the seller. Design competence would be meaningless if companies and consumers did not respond to it. The design of a product first has to be "read," appreciated, produced, and bought.

Design competence is an important market factor today, as scientific research has confirmed. The British Design Council recently published a study that examined 1,500 small, mid-sized, and large companies. Alarmingly, the results showed that regardless of size, those companies that had not invested in design were in gradual decline. Many companies have long recognized that an investment in design has a significant impact on attracting market attention. Increasingly decision-makers today are beginning to understand the (→) value of investing in an aesthetic that is suited to a brand—informative and distinctive packaging and user-friendly product designs, for instance. The impact on the industry is far-reaching: car manufacturers sell their products primarily on the basis of their surface designs (→ *Styling*); tool manufacturers and plastics companies advertise using design competence as a catch-phrase; advertisements for design firms list design prizes as significant accomplishments. A brand with a high level of design competence invested in its products, messages and services implies high (→) quality and will distinguish the brand from others.

Although consumers are at the center of the efforts made by companies and designers, they have always been the least calculable factor. Despite rational arguments, shopping—discovering, deciding, and paying—is still a very emotional act, whether browsing or focused. With a combination of impulse and calculation, consumers orchestrate themselves and their everyday world more or less consciously (→ *Consumption*). The need for individual expression uses the codes in the culture for a highly differentiated nonverbal communication. No-name computers, brand watches, and IKEA shelving units are all part of an orchestra of symbols. Consumers' design competence is demonstrated by their deployment of product associations. Designers create the "correct" differentiation of products and this is their essential competence for businesses.

Futurologists, trend agents, and business consultants are speaking of a change in the traditional distribution of roles between designers, companies, and consumers. With the growing significance of e-commerce and the availability of new technologies like 3-D printing, the borders between these three roles are becoming more and more blurred. As "prosumers," former consumers have in effect become their own producers in that they "design" product (→) prototypes according to their own needs, and can even produce them at home with a 3-D printer. The designer's role here is to consult, to make design suggestions to would-be prosumers, or to equip the printer with the appropriate print data. In this way, ordinary consumers influence the market during production, and not simply afterwards with their selections of existing goods.

According to this theory, designers' competence will increasingly be directed at customers, whose own design competence in turn will be increasingly challenged as the possibilities of their influence increase. ^{MG} |

→ *Design Management, Strategic Design*

Bourdieu, P. 1984. *Distinction: A social critique of the judgement of taste.* Trans. Richard Nice. London: Routledge.
Eco, U. 1971. *Il segno.* Milan: Isedi.

DESIGN CRITICISM

→ *Criticism*

DESIGN EDUCATION

→ *Education*

DESIGN HISTORY

→ *History*

DESIGNING

→ *Gestaltung*

DESIGN MANAGEMENT

The term "design management" has been used to describe a range of micro and macro-level practices for planning and implementing design processes within the context of business performance.

At the micro level, design management encompasses tasks relevant to the completion of individual projects. Spanning the life cycle of a project, these tasks can include proposal writing, design briefing, contracting, budgeting, staffing, scheduling, sketching, prototyping, day-to-day workflow management, production oversight, quality control, documentation, and archiving. At the macro level, design management encompasses tasks relevant to the utilization of design for competitive advantage and the fulfillment of business objectives (→ *Strategic Design*). These tasks can include strategic planning, organizational design, (→) branding and identity, marketing communications, standards and policies, initiatives (sustainability), and various forms of (→) research (customer, competitor, materials, and technologies). Some tasks pertain to both levels (budgeting, staffing) but differ in scale and degree of authority.

Given this spectrum of tasks, the distinction between "management" and "design management" might seem indistinguishable. A critical distinction is the disciplinary heritage of design, which embraces values, practices, and legacies unique to it (as with all disciplines). Design is poised between humanism and technology, between art and (→) craft, and between customers and businesses. As a peculiarly intermediary practice, design synthesizes inputs from many sources to fulfill the technical, (→) ergonomic, financial, and (→) aesthetic criteria that comprise a proposed solution. The combination of creativity, collaboration, advocacy, and humanism that is at the heart of design (→) education and (→) practice distinguishes it from management education and practice, which emphasizes financial performance and operational efficiency.

The significance of design management is also underscored by the prominence of the visual in contemporary life, particularly within the context of business and commerce. The scenario of (→) consumption typically includes many visual aspects: the product itself, its packaging, logo, associated advertising, an adjunct web site, point of purchase displays, the surrounding retail environment, and so on. Thus, visual literacy becomes essential in (→) product development, (→) brand identity, and marketing communications. Designers are trained as visual experts and, acting as "cultural barometers," sense the cultural climate in order to inscribe artifacts and processes with symbolic as well as pragmatic significance. The visual expertise required to undertake this process of cultural inscription is necessary for businesses to communicate successfully within the increasingly competitive visual landscape. This is yet another distinguishing feature of design management—visual literacy and its role in supporting business performance. Design literally helps companies stay visible in the marketplace to both customers and competitors.

Advocates of design management generally propose the integration of "design awareness" into all aspects of the business and at every organizational level, whether the company delivers goods or services. While this can present cultural challenges due to differences in language, priorities, and values between those trained as "designers" and those trained as "businesspeople," cultivation of design awareness can help senior decision-makers recognize and make use of design's potential to enhance business performance along many dimensions—innovation, strengthened brand identity, and increased product ease-of-use among them. For planning purposes, design strategies are often mapped against business strategies in order to coordinate, integrate, and align design activities with core objectives. Discrete design tasks are specified to fulfill top level design and business strategies (for example "research and develop new typographic and color standards suitable for a target customer segment").

Whether design activities are undertaken internally by a large firm or outsourced to smaller studios, knowledge of design values, methods, and genres is necessary to successfully contract and manage these resources (→ Knowledge Management). Companies who have chosen to prioritize design activities internally have benefited from increased innovation and creativity. Such design-driven companies select organizational structures and procedures that ensure advocacy at senior management levels and multidisciplinary (interdepartmental) collaboration (→ Discipline).

Recent concepts in design management have included a focus on "customer experience," a term which describes the complete orchestration of the interaction between a consumer, product (or service), and manufacturer (or provider). Multi-media, multi-modal design strategies are typically employed to direct the prospective customer through immersive sales and media environments both persuasive and comprehensive in their "theatrical" totality. An outgrowth of the widespread adoption of digital technology in business, design, and culture during the 1990s, experience design acknowledges consumption itself as a pervasive "site," and exploits virtual and physical channels (retail stores, the World Wide Web) to strengthen brand presence and loyalty (→ Retail Design).

While the discipline of design management remains formally under-represented in educational institutions, undergraduate, graduate, and certificate programs and courses exist, typically within design schools and business schools. Training is also available through professional organizations and through independent consultants.

As competition increases in the global marketplace, and as electronic communications provide ever greater opportunities for sales and marketing (e-commerce), design becomes an increasingly critical component for achieving competitive differentiation and advantage. Design management provides the concepts, tools, and values necessary for stewarding creative activities in the business arena. LS |

→ Design Planning, Design Process, Innovation, Logistics, Quality Assurance

Bruce, M., and J. Bessant. 2002. *Design in business: Strategic innovation through design*. New York: Financial Times/Prentice Hall.
Cooper, R., and M. Press. 1995. *The design agenda: A guide to successful design management*. Chichester: John Wiley & Sons.
Design Management Institute. Boston, MA. www.dmi.org.
du Gay, P., et al. 1997. *Doing cultural studies: The story of the Sony Walkman*. Thousand Oaks, CA: Sage Publications.

DESIGN METHODS

Designers use a broad range of methods in the course of their work, many of which are also employed by practitioners in other disciplines. It is the generative manner in which designers press such methods into service that is distinctive.

For the purposes of this definition, it is useful to examine design methods in relation to scientific methods. In both scientific and design practices, methods serve as an infrastructure through which (→) information is conveyed and knowledge is codified, and are thus used to delineate legitimate forms of engagement. In other words, they are the rules and routines with which practitioners develop common perspectives and build upon lessons learned by others.

Although scientific and design methods can be seen as sharing the same overall (→) function, the processes through which they are employed differ. In descriptive pursuits such as the sciences, accurate depictions of reality are of primary concern; as such, practitioners must adhere to reliable protocols and apply methods in a uniform, consistent manner in order to calibrate their work against external criteria. Such calibrations have less significance in the course of design, which is oriented toward the conception of that which is new. Design practitioners have more latitude to employ methods in an improvisational manner, and are able to adopt, discard, and tailor methods to address the specific circumstances in which they are used. Designers often define their methods on the basis of project (→) briefs, for example, while scientists must contend with universal laws and previously established principles. It is in the terms that are used to assess (→) quality, however, that the differences between these approaches to methods are most salient. Scientific findings are evaluated on the basis of validity and reliability, whereas the work of designers is judged on the basis of ingenuity.

Since designers do not need to produce accurate depictions of reality, they are thus free to experiment with methods in a manner that other disciplines do not tolerate. Methods are often applied with little regard to the parameters for which they were developed, for example, and immediate feedback is generally valued over procedural competence. Such practices can obscure lessons that are embedded in methods in ways that appear to be at odds with (→) convention, but this cannot be decoupled from design's own disciplinary expectations concerning (→) creativity—improvisation is often the only way to proceed when (→) innovation is the objective. RR |

→ *Design Competence, Design Process, Heuristics*

Alexander, C. 1964. *Notes on the synthesis of form*. Cambridge, MA: Harvard Univ. Press.

Jones, J. C. 1970. *Design methods*. New York: John Wiley and Sons.

Lawson, B. 1997. *How designers think*. 3rd ed. Oxford, United Kingdom: Architectural Press.

Rowe, P. G. 1987. *Design thinking*. Cambridge, MA: MIT Press.

DESIGN MUSEUMS

Design museums chart the history of design movements and influence design principles and contemporary taste because the objects that make up their collections are considered to be exemplary works. They not only exhibit the history of design by displaying objects, they are also a public forum for the dissemination and discussion of new design developments. Design museums function as educational establishments, as technology museums, and as a driving force for local business development.

"Museum" originally referred to a temple or shrine erected in antiquity to honor the muses, the female personifications of literature, music, and dance. However, the most famous of these, the Museum of Alexandria, was more acclaimed for its legendary library than its collection of objects. This storehouse of knowledge was a meeting place for scholars and the center of a social and intellectual community. Besides collecting, preserving, and procuring objects, one of a museum's priorities is stimulating a collective production of knowledge, whether in the form of talks, research projects, or (→) publications. Yet ancient and contemporary museums have something else in common: both were created to preserve objects that are so treasured they need to be removed from daily use and economic circulation. Initially, these objects were sacrificial offerings to the gods; now it is the evidence of past cultures, artworks and design objects considered exemplary by experts, or simply those things accumulated by an obsessive collector who has then founded a museum, hoping to defy the passing of time and to leave a record for posterity.

Critics have always made an issue of the fact that museums transform things into aesthetic cult objects by removing them from their social, functional, religious, and economic contexts.

Theodor W. Adorno polemicized against the "family sepulchers of works of art" and Karl Hillebrand, Heinrich Heine's secretary in Paris, called for the abolition of museums as early as 1874 in his anonymously published *Twelve Letters of an Aesthetic Heretic,* because they wrench artworks from their true contexts, robbing them of much of their significance. This was quite a risky assertion especially in Paris, where the royal collection was opened to the public in 1793 as part of a "revolutionary celebration of unity and fraternity." On the other hand, the history of the Louvre shows that museums in fact are quite capable of creating new contexts. Napoleon Bonaparte cleverly used the Louvre as a political instrument by declaring it a national museum and also a "school for patriots." Napoleon increased his (and the museum's) fame by packing the Louvre with art looted from European estates during his military campaigns. Napoleon let it be known that he appropriated these trophies from the ancien regime for the purpose of social enlightenment. For the first time, (→) luxury goods, previously reserved for a privileged few, fulfilled a service for the public at large: they became material for the education of a nation.

Applied and decorative arts museums also owe their existence to the quest for national supremacy, as demonstrated by the history of the Victoria and Albert Museum (V&A) in London. It was founded in 1852 to improve the quality of consumer goods and make them more attractive to the international market. Great Britain became a free-trade area in the 1840s, which allowed it to compete economically with other countries, in particular with France. In this context, Prince Albert of Saxe-Coburg, the consort of Queen Victoria, advocated a reform of British Arts & Crafts. Guided by consultants, he was a driving force behind the first world fair, the "Great Exhibition of 1851," held in Hyde Park at the Crystal Palace designed by Joseph Paxton. The profit generated by this event flowed into collecting applied arts, especially for the Museum of Manufacturers that was affiliated with the Government School of Design. The museum was moved to its present location in South Kensington in 1857 and was renamed the Victoria and Albert Museum in 1899. Henry Cole, as its first director, was responsible for the museum's collection policies. As he had also been a joint organizer of the Great Exhibition, it is not surprising that some of the museum's first acquisitions were products shown at the Great Exhibition that proved to be particularly innovative and cutting-edge (→) artifacts.

Henry Cole believed that the aim of a decorative arts museum was not only to display the (→) skills of the designer, but also to educate all the social classes and to establish a new criterion of taste. With this in mind he introduced Sunday and evening opening hours, so that the working classes would be able to visit the museum. For rest and relaxation, Cole introduced museum cafés (refreshment rooms) in 1866, one of which was designed by William Morris (→ *Arts & Crafts*). Cole's ambition was to improve the (→) quality of British products by showing students, designers, manufacturers, and users the physical reality, functionality, and production technology of British craftwork using historical examples. He also integrated new products into the collection that he thought continued these traditions.

Cole's initiative soon found emulators around the globe—from the Museum für angewandte Kunst (Museum of Applied Arts) in Vienna (1864), to the Deutsches Gewerbemuseum (German Museum of Applied and Industrial Art) in Berlin (1867), the Leipziger Kunstgewerbemuseum (Leipzig Museum of Decorative Arts) (1874), the Nasjonalmuseet for Kunst, Arkitektur og Design (Museum of Decorative Arts and Design) in Oslo (1876), and the Metropolitan Museum of Art in New York (1870). After Cole retired in 1873, his followers lost sight of the role that a museum could play as a bridge between the past and the present, and resorted to expanding their inventories of historic works. It was not until the 1960s that the V&A remembered its wonderful history and, by researching cutting-edge examples from the past, inspired contemporary production. Retrospective exhibitions featuring Alfons Mucha (1963) and Aubrey Beardsley (1964) had a significant influence on Pop Art, especially on the graphic design used for Beatles album covers, and provided many of the motifs and inspired the design practice that surrounded psychedelic art.

By this time the Museum of Modern Art (MoMA) in New York had long become the epitome of a culturally, politically, and economically influential design museum. MoMA was founded in 1929 for "encouraging and developing the study of modern arts and the application of such arts to manufacture and practical life, and furnishing popular instruction," as stated in its founding charter. Its first director, Alfred H. Barr, justified his focus on mass-produced articles of daily use with an argument similar to that behind the establishment of the nineteenth-century decorative arts museum in Europe, namely, that of developing new markets. Consequently, attempts were also made in the United States to campaign against the "miserable mediocrity" of products designed and produced in America. Modern art was given the task of making designers and users more aware of an aesthetic sensitivity to form that should be present in every facet of life, including typography, clothing, furniture, kitchen utensils, tableware, and architecture. Everything designed in the twentieth century was to serve the beauty of mathematics, mechanics, and purpose.

After studying art history and philosophy at Harvard, Alfred H. Barr traveled to Europe in 1927 and became an enthusiastic advocate of ($\rightarrow$) Bauhaus principles. Like Walter Gropius, Barr was convinced that the Bauhaus program precluded placing modern design in a decorative arts museum. The desired unity of the arts and, in particular, the orientation toward the requirements of industrial production, represented too radical a break from the applied and decorative arts tradition. When admiration for individual creativity and esteem for the skills required for individual handiwork with challenging materials was replaced by respect for the inventive spirit and the elevation of machine aesthetics, Arts & Crafts and design were seen as incompatible opposites whose products could never be placed under one roof. ($\rightarrow$) Modernity—which made fetishizing the original and bourgeois conventions things of the past—needed its own home, one that was dedicated to future visions of "new men" and not to relics of the past.

New York's MoMA, a model institution for the entire world, happily took on this challenge. Right up to the 1940s, European modernity was accepted as mainstream culture, especially as it was possible to point out that the United States was willing to guarantee this modernity, particularly when it could be shown that it was supported by migrants like Mies van der Rohe or Herbert Bayer who had been persecuted and exiled by fascism. With clear, didactical concepts, Alfred H. Barr and curator Philip Johnson campaigned against the conservative tastes of the "uneducated" masses and directed them toward an interest in contemporary design. With exhibitions such as "Objects: 1900 and Today" (1933), Barr and Johnson unapologetically showed the public what objects should be removed from the modern home because they were "decorative," and thus aesthetically repetitive (for instance any imitations of natural forms and any objects by Guimard and Tiffany), and what could be shown to be "useful" ($\rightarrow$ Functionalism). Labeled in this way, an object was venerated when its ($\rightarrow$) form was motivated by ($\rightarrow$) function and that identified and celebrated its practical purpose. This included an anonymously designed welders' protective mask, a watering can by Christopher Dresser, and a table clock by Marianne Brandt. Embracing modernity had more to do with a mental attitude than bulging moneybags, a fact demonstrated by MoMA in 1938 with exhibitions such as "Useful Household Objects under $5," a selection of inexpensive, well-designed kitchen articles and travel implements.

Educating the public in aesthetically correct consumerism remained a chief objective for MoMA well into the 1950s. Edgar Kaufmann, the son of a Pittsburgh department-store magnate and curator at MoMA from 1946, managed to encourage greater involvement from the retail trade sector. Kaufmann was inspired by the (→) Deutscher Werkbund's activities in the 1920s to organize a series of exhibitions called (→) "Good Design." This allowed mass-produced furniture by Herman Miller and Knoll Associates not only to take over museum spaces from 1950 to 1955 but also to tour schools, universities, and department stores. In a time of growing prosperity, "Good Design," accompanied by symposia, advertising campaigns, and questionnaires, proved to be a credible buyers' guide, arranged by apparently impartial experts.

Yet Philip Johnson's exhibition "Machine Art" in 1934 demonstrated just how radically a collection of functional objects could challenge the perceptual conventions of visitors and the authority of the museum. Johnson based his concept on something Marcel Duchamp apparently said to his friend, the sculptor Constantin Brancusi, in 1912 while visiting an exhibition of aviation technology at the Grand Palais in Paris: "Painting is washed up. Who will ever do anything better than that propeller?" With the help of manufactured items from MoMA's permanent collection, Philip Johnson exposed the beauty of propellers, coils, and laboratory equipment to public admiration with these objects, minutely and accurately labeled, in front of gleaming white walls, on top of white pedestals and protected under glass vitrines. It showed the public how to view common objects from an aesthetic perspective. Even if a designer's name was occasionally highlighted, as in the case of Sven Wingquist's ball bearing, the exhibition presented anonymous mechanical engineers or manufacturers' brands as the ingenious creators of startlingly beautiful objects (→ *Anonymous Design*). MoMA remained consistent to this paradigm shift by starting to organize exhibitions about company histories in the 1960s. In 1964, it was the design philosophy of Braun und Chemex on show and, in 1971, the Olivetti company. Besides the principles of modernity that Philip Johnson had always highly respected—machine-like simplicity, smooth surfaces, lack of ornamentation—issues gradually surfaced involving the economy of means, the cost/performance ratio, a company's social commitment, and an object's associative and emotional content. Yet it was still form that remained the decisive criterion.

Arthur Drexler, curator at MoMA for thirty-five years, summarized his experience as follows: "An object is chosen on the basis of its quality, because it intends to attain, or has created a foundation for the ideals of beauty which has been established as important in our time." Only the most impressive examples from design (→) history—an equivalent of a masterpiece in art—found their way into MoMA's design collection, which now contains more than 3,000 objects. Significantly, it is a collection of unique pieces. There are no bodies of work or clothing articles integrated into the collection that might be considered fashionable items, because MoMA adheres to a further principle of traditional museums: the objects must possess a timeless quality, both in terms of rising above the influences of fashion, and being made from materials that do not easily decay or decompose. Weapons are routinely and automatically excluded from the collection. The museum claims to draw a clear distinction between the aesthetic and the political, yet this has opened the institution to attack. The following appeared in the *New York Times* in 1984: "A helicopter, suspended from the ceiling, hovers over an escalator in the Museum of Modern Art ... The chopper is bright green, bug-eyed and beautiful. We know that it is beautiful because MoMA showed us the way to look at the twentieth century." But the museum failed to state that the helicopter was manufactured by arms manufacturer Textron in Fort Worth, and was used against civilians in El Salvador, Honduras, Nicaragua, and Guatemala.

Every design museum in the world has to position itself in relation to MoMA's powerfully effective template regarding both the rationale behind its collection and its approach to presentation. The Design Museum in London describes itself as a research institute primarily devoted to contemporary European design tendencies. To distinguish itself from MoMA, the Fonds national d'art contemporain (Fnac) in Paris focuses on production processes, and the Museu de les Arts Decoratives in Barcelona has been concentrating on ecological design ($\rightarrow$ *Environmental Design*) since 2001. Other museums focus on computer culture, system development, or automotive design. Many new design museums have been registered since the 1980s. They are often either the result of a close connection with local companies that have design ambitions (MARTa Herford), or they are directly linked to initiatives by a company (Vitra Design Museum). Even though these kinds of design museums are sometimes treated with suspicion as subtle yet effective marketing ploys, they are still sociopolitically relevant in that they illustrate the invisible connections between aesthetic preference, technological innovation, material developments, and economic factors, by means of a collection and display of objects. ANT |

$\rightarrow$ *Exhibition Design, History*

Antonelli, P. 2003. *Objects of design: The Museum of Modern Art*. New York: Museum of Modern Art.
Crimp, D. 1993. *On the museum's ruins*. Cambridge, MA: MIT Press.
Hufnagl, F., ed. 2004. *Design museums of the world*. Basel: Birkhäuser.
Mundt, B. 1974. *Die deutschen Kunstgewerbemuseen im 19. Jahrhundert*. Munich: Prestel.

DESIGN PLANNING

Generically used in reference to the allocation and management of design-related resources, design planning denotes the conceptualization, specification, and articulation of goals and processes that are used to organize design efforts. Typically, design planning is most salient in the early stages of projects, when strategies and tactics are addressed in a formal manner. It is not unusual, however, for designers to adjust such structural frameworks throughout the course of a project in response to unforeseen developments. For this reason, design planning is best viewed as an ongoing activity that addresses organizational aspects of design at multiple levels of granularity in formal as well as informal ways. ^{RR} |

→ *Brief, Coordination, Design Management, Design Process,*
     Product Development, Strategic Design

DESIGN PROCESS

Regardless of whether the generation of form is considered from an evolutionary perspective or from that of the practice-oriented disciplines, richly nuanced definitions of the design process can be derived from the interaction between actors and their environments.

At a basic level, most descriptions of the design process concern ways in which (→) form is derived from interactions between actors and their environments. In practice-oriented disciplines, such as architecture, product design, or engineering, the design process is generally viewed as the means by which people shape their surroundings. Designers are expected to define problems that can be solved in a step-wise manner (→ *Problem Setting, Problem Solving*). They are trained to conceptualize the process of design as a series of activities that unfold over time, and to view the completion of each activity as a step toward some predefined goal. In other words, designers are expected to model futures that can be realized through strategic engagements with their environments. Implicit in this formulation is the assumption that designers are rational actors. Moreover, it is assumed that environments are stable enough to be modeled, yet pliable enough to be shaped. While such situations may arise, they are far from common. In practice, the process of design only approaches this ideal when rationality is tightly bounded. Architecture, for example, may be an efficient way for people to solve some problems that are tightly coupled to the built environment, but such efficiencies soon dissipate when these problems are located in broader social or economic contexts.

In other disciplines, such as the natural sciences, the agency of the actor is rarely so privileged. Instead of addressing the design process as a means of solving problems, the process is usually described in terms of the structural relationships that exist between actors and their equally instrumental environments. It is the alignments and misalignments of these two factors that give rise to form. In Darwinist theories of evolution through natural selection, for example, there is no need for rational actors because the process of design is motivated solely by environmental "fitness." There is no need for rational actors because form develops in the absence of predefined goals. It is precisely this designer-less conception of design that distinguishes evolutionary approaches to the process from those of most practice-oriented disciplines. The fact that design occurs in the absence of rational actors and their strategic plans does not mean, however, that the two approaches are at odds. Everyday experience clearly suggests that both processes coexist. What is required is a perspective from which the two approaches to design can be viewed on a continuum—a definition that addresses the process of acting on an environment as well as that of acting in an environment.

Every design initiative is situated in its own complex environment of dynamic and interrelated requirements. One of the ways in which designers deal with the difficulty of working in such situations is by employing higher-order frameworks such as rules and (→) heuristics. These frameworks codify lessons gained from prior experience in ways that enable designers to model and stabilize dynamics that are at play in unfamiliar environments. The effectiveness of this practice is severely compromised, however, when the environments in which lessons are applied differ significantly from those in which they were learned. It is useful, therefore, to articulate the nature of relationships between dynamic environments and, in particular, to address such relationships in the form of "hierarchically-nested systems." Such hierarchies enable designers to focus on "niches" that are characterized by the features of local situations (such as their particular social, economic, or political dynamics). By identifying common conditions in which such features are expressed, designers can consider the viability of deploying practices across niches in advance, and thereby generate estimates of potential fitness.

Clearly, such forethought can be advantageous in that it permits strategic planning. Designers need not plan in advance, however, in order to engage complex environments effectively. Parallel and complementary approaches can be used that allow problems and solutions to emerge without such rational analysis. This is particularly relevant in the pursuit of (→) innovation, where the end goal is not explicitly defined at the outset of the process. For instance, many elegant designs are the result of tacit lessons that designers have learned by continually (→) testing their (→) intuitions and aptitudes as they experiment with alternate solutions. This approach to design is significant in that it echoes the concept of "local optimization" that scientists use to explain the development of form in the natural environment. In both cases, the design process may appear to be random and open-ended, but it is still path-dependent in that each step of the process inherently limits the range of possible subsequent steps.

The goal-oriented practice that informs many approaches to design can be at odds with the systemic focus that is inherent in evolutionary perspectives on the design process, but this need not be the case. While the desire to downplay the importance of individual-level initiative can be compelling when addressing the design from an evolutionary perspective—perhaps because this stance is often taken in the context of scientific disciplines—there is no need to view the design process in a dichotomous manner. As a human activity, the process of design can be goal-oriented as well as fitness-driven, it can be motivated by rational choice as well as intuition, and it can occur in environments that are stable as well as dynamic. Regardless of whether the generation of form is considered from an evolutionary perspective or from that of the practice-oriented disciplines, richly nuanced definitions of the design process can be derived from the interaction between actors and their environments. CTE + RR |

→ Design Methods, Product Development

Certeau, M. de. 1984. *The practice of everyday life*. Trans. Steven Rendall. Berkeley: Univ. of California Press.
Kauffman, S. A. 1993. *The origins of order*. New York: Oxford Univ. Press.
Schon, D. A. 1983. *The reflective practitioner*. New York: Basic Books.
Simon, H. A. 2001. *The sciences of the artificial*. 4th ed. Cambridge, MA: MIT Press.

DESIGN PUBLICATIONS

→ Publications

DESIGN RESEARCH

→ Research

DESIGN SOLUTIONS

→ Problem Solving

DESIGN STRATEGY

→ Strategic Design

DESIGN THEORY

→ Theory

DEUTSCHER WERKBUND

The Deutscher Werkbund (German Work Federation), founded in 1907 in Munich, was a state-initiated professional association of artists, architects, craftsmen and women, industrialists, and critics dedicated to improving the quality of German design and manufacture. It marked the highpoint of the applied arts movement that had begun in Germany in the 1890s. It was concerned with giving a consistent, symbolic form of expression to a society that had come to be dominated by industrialization, and with developing and propagating high (→) quality design.

The Deutscher Werkbund's focus on good design was basically democratic and socially conscious in nature, and initially articulated at the level of a national folk culture. Since the question of form had significant economic and cultural connotations, the Deutscher Werkbund remained valid as a design movement well into the second half of the twentieth century.

The Werkbund's activities were always characterized in part by the different political philosophies of its members. These ranged from socialist or social democratic oriented architecture and town planning as evidenced in housing projects in Frankfurt, Stuttgart, Dessau, Breslau, and Berlin such as *Existenzminimum* apartments (dwellings for low-wage earners) to matters involving the affluent domestic culture of the liberalized bourgeoisie, as seen for example in villas designed by Hermann Muthesius. They were also directed at improving the quality of products and even the work process itself, especially in workshops established in accordance with the English (→) Arts & Crafts movement. Although the members specifically repudiated a nostalgic return to handicrafts, their objectives included the integration of art, (→) craft and industry. A general concern of the Werkbund was the consistent appearance of the material culture: from a company's (→) brand and (→) corporate design to a housing estate and town planning.

Classic Werkbund leaned toward "form without ornament" (Pfleiderer 1924) as a symbolic expression of contemporary design: functional form in product design, *Neues Bauen* (new building) in architecture and city planning, *Neue Sachlichkeit* (new objectivity), initially a counter movement to Expressionism in painting, to some extent *Neues Sehen* (new vision) in photography, and the provision of non-persuasive, factual information in (→) advertisement design.

The key events in the Werkbund's early history were the "Werkbund Exhibition" in 1914 in Cologne, the Weissenhof Estate (an estate designed for working class tenants by sixteen architects supervised by Mies van der Rohe) in Stuttgart in 1927, the architecture exhibition "Wohnung und Werkraum" (Dwellings and Workspaces) in Breslau in 1929, and the exhibition "Film und Fotografie" (FiFo) in 1929 in Stuttgart.

In 1934, the National Socialists who were in power disbanded the Deutscher Werkbund, yet many of its members continued to work for the Third Reich.

After the war, the Werkbund reestablished itself first in regional alliances, then as an umbrella organization with Hans Schwippert as its chairman between 1950 and 1963. Some highlights of the postwar Werkbund include participating in the international architectural exhibition "Interbau" in 1957 in the Hansaviertel area of West Berlin, building the German pavilion for the World Fair in Brussels in 1958, publishing *Deutsche Warenkunde* (Understanding German Products), and establishing the Rat für Formgebung (German Design Council) in 1953. Many of its members were directors or teachers at art academies or other relevant schools of design and architecture.

The Werkbund was soon accused of being a *Tassenwerkbund* (Tea Cup Confederation) because of its form- and object-focused love of detail, but in 1959 it took a position that was critical of both society and business with the Werkbund-organized conference "Die große Landzerstörung" (The great landscape destruction).

(→) Publications were a particular strength of the Werkbund. Many of its members discussed the relevant issues at length in the various applied arts movement trade journals or in the Werkbund's own periodicals *Die Form* (1922–1934), and *werk und zeit* (from 1952). One focus of the institution's philosophy was

Breuer, G., ed. 2007. *Das gute Leben: Der Werkbund nach 1945*. Tübingen: Ernst Wasmuth.
Durth, W., and W. Nerdinger. 2007. *100 Jahre Deutscher Werkbund, 1907–2007*. Munich: Prestel.

DIGITAL DESIGN

→ *Interface Design, Web Design*

DISCIPLINE

"Discipline" is a difficult word to define in relation to design. The term is used with a variety of meanings, but most commonly to define design as an area relative to other fields of study, principally the sciences and the humanities, and to differentiate the specializations in design—industrial design, fashion design, graphic design, and so on—from each other. Defining this broad term is made more complex by the fact that at different moments and in different contexts the word "design" will refer to a particular designed thing, for example an (→) artifact, or to a process or to a system.

educating the consumer—enlightening and sensitizing him or her to make good (meaning rational) purchases—by means of information centers, competitions, and, after 1953, with design prizes awarded by the "Rat für Formgebung." [GB] |
→ *Industrial Design*

According to the *Oxford English Dictionary*, the word "discipline," as derived from the work of a scholar or disciple, is etymologically antithetical to the word "doctrine," which pertains to the work of a doctor or teacher. As this etymology suggests, "discipline" describes the manner in which a belief and/or knowledge system is practiced or exercised, whereas "doctrine" is more closely associated with the development of abstract theories. The word "discipline" thus carries with it a sense that the way in which someone practices—such as the daily routines of worship and symbolic sacrifice in various religions—is as important as the ideas and philosophy that are the "content" of this behavior. Indeed, both the theory and the manner in which this theory is practiced (the disciplinary method) substantiate and express each other.

This notion of discipline as practice and ritual method has developed from the scholarship of religion and has been continued in the scholarship of emerging fields of knowledge and inquiry throughout history. The discipline of science which emerged from Christian and Islamic religions in the Middle Ages took as its mandate the disclosing of "God's hand" at work in the universe and this disclosure was understood to be another form of honor and acknowledgement. The development of the scholarly disciplines from religion can be seen in this seventeenth-century list of the four "objective disciplines": theology, jurisprudence, medicine, and philosophy.

As these knowledge disciplines developed, they became synonymous with the exercise of particular methodologies, evidence of the importance of the manner in which knowledge is gained to verify its "truth-value." Science progressively distanced itself from religion to take a relatively autonomous and powerful position by asserting, through its investigative and verifiable methodology, its authority over truth. These disciplinary methods stressed objectivity through the use of empirical evidence to support hypotheses as to how the world worked. This scientific disciplinary method was designed to "protect" knowledge by attempting to isolate it from the personal and cultural bias of the researcher and, thereby, to claim for science the power that had until then been exclusive to belief systems. The authority of this scientific approach led other disciplines to adopt scientific methods in the pursuit of evidence-based knowledge in the social and cultural spheres, hence the development of the social sciences.

History is, of course, not entirely linear, as can be appreciated by the fact that even after several centuries, the contest between science and religion in the West over authority and ownership of the ultimate truths continues. Design itself has been called in on the side of belief through the "intelligent design" proposition in the United States. The intention of this (→) rhetoric is to ascribe the ultimate "authorship" of the world to a higher power by designating none other than God as the intelligent designer of the universe.

The professional fields—business, architecture, design, and so on—operated for many years with a different logic as they emerged from the mercantile trades and the craft guilds. These practices dealt with the pragmatic actualities of life where disciplinary scholarship had less of an influence than did specific training and skills learnt through apprenticeships and professionalized through experience. As education in these fields became progressively more complex, professionalization increasingly became the product of (→) education rather than experience alone, and responsibility progressively shifted to institutions of higher learning including universities. This has led to a pressure and a desire, from within and outside the professional fields, to legitimize their fields as scholarly. This has also been true for design as a community of professionals and academics increasingly sought to draw to themselves some of the authority afforded by the scientific disciplinary method. Critical to this effort was the establishment of distinct and evidence-based methods—by exercising particular design methodologies the outcomes would be legitimized. In other words, they would be "free" of the perceived idiosyncrasies of individual designers because these outcomes would be based on objective, quantifiable, and comparable methods. In this context, an idea such as (→) creativity became deeply problematic as it implied personal bias and hence invited perceptions of illegitimacy due to a lack of quantifiable proof supporting one proposal or outcome over another.

The (→) design method and design science movements emerged in the latter half of the twentieth century as attempts to lay down a methodology in order to establish the "discipline" in the practice of design. It was presumed that what would then emerge would be the basis of the abstract theories exclusive to design that would become the doctrine of the field. Inversely, the doctrine would then be proven through the exercise of discipline (methodologies) in the process of designing. This move was both intended to gain intellectual legitimacy for design and to demarcate clearly a disciplinary "space" alongside other fields of study.

While the effort to establish design science is ongoing, there has also been a parallel and somewhat competing attempt to be better able to articulate and account for the intrinsic, particular, and peculiar manner in which design operates and the reason for its existence, rather than simply adopting the modus of traditional scholarship. The development of design scholarship in the academy and, increasingly, in business can be seen, in part, as the debate and dialogue between these two positions, with each modifying and learning from the other through both contest and collaboration.

This effort to articulate and legitimize the intrinsic disciplinary qualities of design has coincided with traditional disciplines questioning and debating their own disciplinary logics. The knowledge boundaries that the disciplinary methodologies had established have been seriously critiqued, in particular by feminist, postmodernist, and postcolonial cultural and scientific complexity theories (→ *Gender Design, Postmodernism, Cross-cultural Design, Complexity*). Rather than representing the highways to truth, the disciplines were seen as expressions of the inevitable bias that results from specific gendered and cultural worldviews. This questioning has also been influenced by the fact that the traditional disciplinary methods were increasingly proving to be partial and incomplete when dealing with, and accounting for, the world in its interrelated, complex, and highly contingent state. The impact of (→) globalization, emancipatory movements, ecological crises, and new media technologies dramatically shifted the perception of the traditional disciplinary paradigms and their ability both to know fully and, more importantly, to engage with these issues. These (→) "wicked problems" have brought the disciplines and the professional fields into a new alignment evidenced by the increasing influence design is having on business, politics, social sciences, science, and so on. The emergence of the field of sustainable design has more fully exposed what was previously the largely tacit and nascent quality of design as an organizing engagement with overwhelmingly complex issues (→ *Sustainability*). Rather than operating as one discipline among others, this understanding of design references its unique ability to operate across disciplines and access the knowledge and methods particular to each and harness them for the task at hand. Design here is not defined by the rigor of its acquisition of knowledge so much as the ability of a designer to deploy knowledge on an "as needed basis" for the situation at hand. The designers' expertise, in this sense, is better understood as locating, organizing, and integrating the knowledge or information that is required to make a particular intervention effective.

The traditional disciplinary methods in isolation are not equipped to tackle extremely complex issues and problems that are resistant to abstraction. A disciplinary methodology necessarily excludes ways of understanding a situation in its multiplicity—it gains its insights by identifying and focusing on one aspect of the existing dynamic. Ultimately, design is not about the study of existing phenomena but rather it proposes, intervenes, changes, and restructures the future of the designed world.

Confronted with these complex situations, there has been an increased awareness that for the different fields of knowledge to act on the world and for the professional fields to better understand the implications and impacts of their interventions, new collaborative and integrated forms of practice and scholarship will be required. Consequently, there has been a growing emphasis in universities and business on interdisciplinary, multidisciplinary, and transdisciplinary modes of working, studying, and knowing. This demand for both (→) education and (→) research that crosses traditional disciplinary boundaries has grown to the point where universities are restructuring themselves to make this a central and defining characteristic of, rather than peripheral to, their defining logic.

It is worth outlining the definitions of these now commonly used terms that have grown out of the new disciplinary structure. "Multidisciplinary" typically describes either a team of people, each with their distinct disciplines, working together on a research or applied project, an individual who is expert in more than one discipline, or a course of study requiring mastery of more than one discipline. In design, the term would usually refer to multidisciplinary design teams—consisting, for instance, of a media designer, anthropologist, psychologist, and engineer—assembled to develop the designed artifact or system and to better understand the people or situation that will be affected by the design (→ *Collaborative Design*).

A multidisciplinary education in design would normally mean studying two or more of the design specialisms. It may also suggest an education that, for example, combines industrial design with mechanical engineering and management, or graphic design with information systems and communication studies.

"Interdisciplinary" usually describes a process, project, or research rather than a person or people. An interdisciplinary project attempts to work between and draw from a range of disciplinary methods, occasionally needing to redraw or dissolve the boundaries between them. (→) Design management will often entail devising the means and methods to execute interdisciplinary processes. Design, when used to denote a process, is often described as being interdisciplinary. The term may also be used more loosely to describe projects that involve multiple design specialisms.

An interdisciplinary education is one that stresses the integrative and strategic aspects of the designing process.

"Transdisciplinary" generally describes an actual issue or problem. It suggests an issue that by its very nature cannot be meaningfully addressed by any one discipline, or even by a disciplinary approach. One good example is the issue of ecological sustainability and how to achieve this goal. No single discipline can understand the issues comprehensively nor can it propose solutions in isolation. It can only be properly understood as a matrix of cultural, social, economic, political, technological, and behavioral issues as well as an environmental issue and it is, therefore, transdisciplinary. Issues and dynamics such as globalization, community, or aging and health are other examples of transdisciplinary concerns. Design processes are particularly suited to addressing transdisciplinary problems precisely because of design's potential to integrate the understanding of many disciplines and to deploy the necessary knowledge and understanding they can yield to tackle transdisciplinary problems meaningfully.

To illustrate these distinctions, we can describe them operating in direct relation with one another: people with expertise in specific disciplines work together in multidisciplinary teams in an interdisciplinary process, in order to better address the complexities of a transdisciplinary issue or problem (bearing in mind that one of the people on the multidisciplinary team is a designer, whose expertise is the management of the interdisciplinary process).

In conclusion, the traditional disciplines of the sciences and the humanities predominantly rely on evidence as the basis for their hypotheses. Their methods are designed to disclose the truth about what is, and why things are or act as they do, and the primary metric by which they are judged is how accurate a hypothesis proves to be when tested by others in the discipline or as history unfolds.

The professional fields such as design, management, politics, and so on, take this knowledge as well as their own indigenous expertise and experience to make proposals regarding how things might be done differently or anew. This work tends to be judged by how effective and advantageous the proposal proves to be over time. Intrinsically, these fields are oriented to the future rather than on understanding existing or historical factors. So in order for disciplinary knowledge to be able to act on rather than reflect on the world they need the professional fields. Similarly, for the professional fields to make meaningful and effective proposals that at least come close to understanding the consequences of an intervention, the disciplinary knowledge of how and why people and situations act and interact as they do is essential. All disciplines are currently rethinking their disciplinary boundaries and origins in the light of an awareness of the everincreasing complexity of the world's problems. The future of design as a discipline is probably defined by its lack of respect for the boundaries of other disciplines, which can offer fresh perspectives on the research and insights of other fields. Hence, as the issues become more complex, that is, increasingly transdisciplinary, so the need for multidisciplinary approaches and interdisciplinary methods increases. [TM] |

DISPLAY

The meaning of the term "display" has broadened from its original meaning—to show something or put something in view. It can now also be used to describe any monitor that processes electrical signals in a computer, mobile telephone, or other electronic device. The different technical methods of data conversion have produced different categories of displays including LCD (liquid crystal display), MFD (multifunction display), and VRD (virtual retinal display) among others.

The term "display" is also used in association with sales-related methods such as posters, product stands, or packaging. [DPO] |

→ *Retail Design, Screen Design*

E

ECO DESIGN

→ Environmental Design, Sustainability

EDUCATION

Design courses in general and academic design courses in particular are not only extremely complex and varied, but also differ greatly from country to country. Furthermore, the professional title of "designer" is hardly protected in any way, so that anyone is entitled, in principle, to call him- or herself a designer. The completion of a design course is therefore very important as evidence of genuine professionalism.

Design education is offered at many levels, from preuniversity courses held at high schools and evening schools, to training organizations that prepare students primarily in the field of graphic design, to Ph.D. level study at competitive universities. It is important to note that the place where a designer receives a recognized professional education is generally in the higher education of universities and colleges.

Design-degree courses typically run at technical colleges, art colleges or academies, universities of all types, and at colleges of design. (These institutions have different names in different countries; the names themselves say little about the quality of the courses.) The use of design-degree terminology is confusing and there are specific variations country-to-country and even within countries. Course-entry requirements, structure, and duration together with the relative emphasis a program places on conceptual, strategic, theoretical, skill-based, managerial, and general education are the best guide to the general tendency of a program. Following is a basic and broad overview of the major degree types.

A great variety of degree names and levels exists particularly in Australia, most Asian countries, Canada, Hong Kong, New Zealand, Latin America, and the United Kingdom. In these countries, low-level skill-based courses have such titles as "Certificate," "Advanced Certificate," "Diploma," and "Advanced Diploma." Typically these qualifications lead to either further study or trade-level positions. In the United States there are "Associate Degrees," often taught in technical and community colleges for four semesters, that are also generally skill-based programs. We will not discuss these degrees, as they do not meet the professional and conceptual level a designer needs to be a "full designer."

The bachelor's degree in most countries is the degree that offers the beginnings of a genuine, rounded education in design. It should be noted that progressively the basic configuration of a bachelor undergraduate degree and a master's graduate degree is becoming the norm around the world. Continental European design degrees have traditionally been based on the eight- to ten-semester diplom—roughly equivalent to the M.A. (Master of Arts) or something in between the B.A. (Bachelor of Arts) and M.A.)—offered by art academies, universities of applied sciences, as well as by polytechnic and by general universities. Although the traditional diplom is still in evidence, the European Union is increasingly requiring the standardization of degrees to reflect the Anglo-Saxon system of bachelor and master's degrees as a result of the Bologne agreement.

Although many different types of educational programs have entrance examinations and special aptitude tests, the nature of such tests, the number of applicants, and the applicants' chances of success differ considerably. At an academy of art and design in southern China, for instance, some 60,000 people apply each year to study design (with about 1,000 places available). This situation demands a very formal entrance examination. At other colleges with fewer applicants, the applicants are called upon to submit portfolios showing examples of their work (drawings, sketches of their ideas, and so on). These are supposed to show whether they possess a "talent" for studying design. Those considered to be the best are sometimes invited by a commission, usually composed of professors, to complete further tasks, such as drawing a technical object, representing it in a different manner, or undertaking collaborative work. Some colleges no longer expect candidates to submit portfolios and give applicants home tests instead, in which they are expected to work conceptually and display a wealth of ideas. The best candidates are then invited, in a procedure resembling that adopted by companies and agencies, to a carefully planned interview.

Procedures and selection processes vary from college to college and from country to country, and depend on the college's or teacher's conceptions of how a design course ought to be: whether it ought to have a more practical, commercial, or theoretical bias. The number of places available will also be affected by the relevant financial and policy situation: private colleges, whose financing may be more heavily dependent on student fees, may grow more aggressively than government-funded schools which typically have a specified quota.

The master's degree is the most common graduate design degree internationally (Europe and Australia, much of Asia, Canada, Hong Kong, New Zealand, South America, and the United Kingdom). A key difference in master's degrees is the relative weighting of research training to advanced coursework. In some countries there is a separate master's degree for research and for coursework while in others they tend to be variously combined in the one degree. Again the naming standards vary so it is best to look closely at the content to determine the relative weighting of the research thesis to determine the true nature of the program.

Note: The use of the term "honors" varies in English-speaking countries. In the United Kingdom a Bachelors with Honors suggests the requirement to complete a major project and written piece for graduation in the third year. In Australia and New Zealand a Bachelor of Design (Honors) indicates the completion of an additional year or alternative fourth year that one has to apply for entry to and is specifically research orientated. In the United States "honors" tends to suggest a program of study or track within the B.F.A. (Bachelor of Fine Arts) that emphasizes a greater degree of theory and concept-based studio work. Typically it would be available only to students with a high grade-point average.

Traditional thesis-based Ph.D.s are progressively being modified in some countries to allow for research-based studio work to be incorporated within the academic research based program. The outcome will typically be a major theoretical or historical thesis that is either entirely text-based—or a combination of written and studio-based evidence of the research undertaken.

What are known as "professional doctorates" grew in popularity in a number of fields such as education and increasingly design from the 1980s on in many countries. Typically these are doctorates that allow for multiple components (such as published articles, curriculum design, design artifacts, and so on) to be examined as an advanced portfolio with an exegesis for this award. In this case the practical work of an experienced designer can be recognized as a main part of the Doctorate of Design (D.Des.).

Different procedures and criteria generally apply for entry to master's and doctoral degrees. Research-based programs will usually consider both the academic achievements and the research proposal of the applicant. Coursework or "taught" masters will generally consider prior study and professional experience. These courses generally accept fewer applicants than undergraduate programs.

The differences are even more marked with respect to the content of courses taught at the various colleges. Although most colleges around the world offer a one or two-year course on the "foundations" of design, there are huge differences in opinion as to what constitutes the "foundations." Some argue that it lies primarily in developing drawing or other graphic skills, whilst others attach great importance to technical media skills. Some attach more value to (→) craft and design (→) skills, and others prioritize conceptual, strategic, and integrative abilities. Here, however, a distinction still has to be made between whether such a foundation course is obligatory (as is the case at some colleges) for all new design students, or whether courses are divided according to subjects from the very beginning.

Some colleges do without foundation courses completely, arguing that everything they offer is fundamental to design and to studying design, and that studies should by no means be limited to certain skills. In such cases, students are compelled to dive in at the deep end, with the colleges relying on students being taught and learning skills as integral elements in complex design processes. Hence, one side neatly divides up students and puts its faith in successive learning processes, whilst the other combines the different years and views learning and studying as erratic rather than as linear processes.

The situation is even more bewildering when one looks at specific courses, especially as many colleges used to, and continue to, clearly distinguish them from one another as separate ($\rightarrow$) disciplines.

It becomes easier to understand this if one considers how design courses originated in the teaching of craft skills. At the ($\rightarrow$) Bauhaus, for instance, a distinction was made between the old trades, which were themselves subdivided according to materials. Hence, students studied either in the ceramics course, the metal course, or the courses for textiles, wood, and so on. Then there were subjects that were either studied on an interdisciplinary basis or as separate disciplines such as drawing, painting, and other graphic techniques. ($\rightarrow$) Typography as well as printing and other aspects of graphic designs formed a separate field. This is the most basic template of early design to which various cultures added their own specialties, such as calligraphy in Asia and in the Middle East. This began to change after 1945 at the latest. Some educational establishments continued—and continue—to instruct students in the traditional manner, especially in those countries where the national economy was—and remains—very reliant on craft skills for various reasons. Other colleges restructured their curricula, occasionally retaining some of their arts and crafts departments in the process, and supplementing or replacing others with disciplines such as industrial design and graphic design. Depending on the size of the colleges or their main specialized areas, there were also departments such as textile design, fashion design, furniture design, and interior design. In addition, many colleges started offering courses in art, design history, and cultural studies.

Later, the discipline of graphic design (which often retained an artistic aura) was replaced by the far broader fields of visual communication and communication design, to which were subsequently added new fields such as transportation design, and public design. Such divisions clearly testify to the general and the historically specific state and conception of design on the one hand, and to its conception at particular colleges on the other. Design now existed as a process of working and as an economic driver that had broken with craftsmanship.

Design colleges today generally tend to develop in two exemplary directions: on the one hand, they try to do justice to the professional reality of design and, on the other, address the social and explicitly economic requirements of design by offering a complex and integrative design curriculum. Colleges addressing design as a strategic process will typically offer courses with a strong research and methods basis (that is, in "design management," "interface design," "service design," "design theory and history," "ecology and design," "production technology," and so on). The aim of a curriculum that integrates the professional, skill-based and strategic aspects of design is to encourage students to study design as a whole, so that they can experience and grasp its full complexity, and pursue their careers as designers professionally trained in various aspects of design. This educational model presupposes a student studying extremely intensively for at least four or five years. It is based on the notion that design, in all its cultural, social, and economic ramifications and in its professional reality genuinely needs graduates with an integrative and conceptual approach to thinking and planning.

Design degrees that attach more importance on specialization do so either because they believe that the demands placed on designers reflect these specializations, or because they consider it impossible to train individual students for the full complexity of design. This approach is becoming ever more closely linked with another reality facing design colleges of this type: marketing and branding. For design colleges, as well as higher education institutions in general, it is becoming increasingly important to identify unique characteristics that they can use in the competitive international struggle to create appealing images as well as attract sponsors, research funds, and students. Hence, these colleges are continuously developing new courses and specialize in niche curricula.

Both sides have their share of successes. There is still considerable potential for development here, as the tendency for design colleges to offer ever more advanced training shows. A growing number of students from other disciplines are now taking continuation courses or "career-changing" degrees (which include master's courses in some cases). They will have completed courses in other subjects and now want to deepen their knowledge of—or specialize in—design. This option may be attractive to people with prior degrees in economics, engineering, cultural studies, and so on. This is also reflective of an increasing awareness of the importance of "life-long learning."

There continues to be much debate and experimentation regarding the optimum approach to design learning but, generally speaking, the more advanced degrees are moving away from narrowly defined (→) problem solving. Pioneered in the United Kingdom, an increasing number of governments are imposing

(→) quality assurance mechanisms on education and accreditation measures with mixed results. This is considered as an attempt to more systematically account for the progressive and systematic learning that students achieve in their studies.

In certain institutions, particularly in Europe, the open-structured school model has been introduced to design. In these schools, project-based learning, rather than linear and progressive learning, defines the actual structure of the degree. In these cases, design is taught through theme-based projects with students from across the years enrolling in a project team run by a professor rather than the project being inside a particular studio unit. In either model the learning is often structured around clearly defined tasks and challenges, (→) brainstorming sessions, discussions, drafts, and designing, then criticism and presentations in studio and seminar settings.

Many degrees will include both professional placements (internships) with design companies and projects undertaken with outside companies, agencies, and institutions. These adaptations of the apprenticeship model of education are intended to provide direct experience of the profession prior to graduation.

Forward-looking design education generally has a complex blend of multidisciplinary approaches intended to develop both broadly educated and professionally viable designers. Increasingly the core skills and knowledge of the design graduates are being identified around such qualities as collaboration and communication skills and the ability to think and act strategically while being responsive to complex issues such as the impact of globalization on designing and an active recognition of the impact of design decisions on the environment. ME + TM |

→ *Black Mountain College, Critique, Discipline, Not-for-Profit, Practice, Research, Skills, Theory, Ulm School of Design, Understanding*

Davis, M., et al. 1997. *Design as a catalyst for learning*. Adria, VA: Association for Supervision and Curriculum Development.
Lave, J., and E. Wenger. 1991. *Situated learning: Legitimate peripheral participation*. Cambridge, United Kingdom: Cambridge Univ. Press.
Schön, D.A. 1987. *Educating the reflective practitioner*. San Francisco: Jossey-Bass.

ENGINEERING DESIGN

Engineering design departs from the arena of (→) style in that its content focuses on scientific methods while taking into account aspects of sustainability, as well as environmental, material, and production technologies that play an important role in innovative (→) product development processes.

The activity of designing began long before the phrase "engineering design" was coined and for as long as people have existed (→) form has been a decisive factor when selecting objects. This applies to objects found in nature, *objets trouvés*, as well as (→) artifacts. Defining design as art with a (→) function means that there would be another interface between the applied and fine arts at the point when the primary functional use that prompted the particular choice of form becomes secondary, transforming the once purpose-specific object into an object that is now observed, appraised, admired, or even worshiped for its (→) aesthetics. As none of the variations of the aphorism "form follows x" (where x = function, emotion, and so on) are adequate definitions of design, it is important to remember that even Louis Henry Sullivan, the man behind the three-word declaration, adorned his own modern high-rise architecture with ornaments and decorations, and that even today (→) ornament is still not a crime. One example of a piece of contemporary (→) high tech ornamentation is the rubber knobs on the handle of Braun electric shavers, which have no real (→) haptic or ergonomic (→) function.

In fact, there are many examples of design elements that are independent of functional rationalization, even in areas that at first glance would appear to be outside the scope of styling. An example of this phenomenon from the nineteenth century is the vertical form of steam engines that was a deliberate reference to ancient Greek and Roman architecture and not a technical or functional necessity.

In the twentieth and twenty-first centuries, the appearance of machines and equipment is reinforced by stylistic elements that are there to convey technological supremacy visually. Car styling (→ *Automobile Design*) has had an enormous influence on the sector that constructs machinery, where a curved and graceful line is evident in a vast range of equipment, including static objects like Heidelberg printing presses. Consumer goods manufacturers, dedicated as a rule to minimalism and reduction, also employ design details that are not entirely based on function. (→) Coating technologies simulate luxury finishes in car interiors or on cell phones, where special laminations can simulate carbon fiber or galvanized plastic can imitate metal. This is called mimicry design. The technologically-inspired decoration serves subconsciously to convey ideas of beauty and technological innovation. Of course, stylistic elements also have a cultural context and are implemented accordingly by global companies to support product-marketing strategies.

Something akin to engineering design probably already existed in the Stone Age or at the moment a suitable, natural object became scarce and needed to be replaced by an artificially made, easily reproducible version. Even in the Stone Age it was necessary for form, materials, and production methods to focus on optimizing function. If more than one material is required, then construction and assembly methods play additional roles in constructing the artifact with regard to its intended functions. This function could be a secondary one based on adornment or display, as commonly seen on hatchets and axes. The intended primary purpose of an object greatly influences its shape via design, material, and production method if the aim is to make it function better.

Engineering design cannot freely invent a purpose-related form, because this is determined by function—which, again, largely determines the choice of the most appropriate material and production method. Optimizing purpose-related form requires clear, causal relationships. Perhaps this is why general designers do not design airplanes, wing sections, rockets, satellites, internal combustion engines, or cardiac pacemakers. Engineering design's progress is attributable to the development of mathematical models that determine the manufacturing process and the associated virtual simulations (→ *Virtual Reality*) that allow one to analyze many more variations than would be possible without a computer (→ *CAD/CAM/CIM/CNC*). (→) Materials research and further development in amalgamation and (→) production technologies are making it possible to create completely new and innovative forms (→ *Rapid Prototyping*).

All this feeds into the purpose-related form. The memoirs of French-born American industrial designer Raymond Loewy were called "Never Leave Well Enough Alone." Striving for optimal outcomes is a never-ending task—and yet, the world economy is growing despite the fact that most of the goods, capital or consumer, available today are not professionally designed. From this it can be deduced that design is obviously not the most important factor in this burgeoning consumerism. Design has always been a niche concern of the intellectual bourgeoisie in mainly Western, industrial countries. Design can also mean that something might look better, but function less well, cost more, and be less durable than other similar products. Engineering design counters this with scientific methods for finding the optimal form coupled with (→) intuition and aesthetics. This might be why engineering design seldom concerns itself with furniture, household accessories, or things that are not actually essential—making it fundamentally different from the field of design in general.

In the second half of the twentieth century, (→) bionics began to influence artifacts. Bionics is based on examples taken from nature, but does not merely duplicate these in the technical, manmade world. Bionic architecture (a building for cognitive science modeled on the workings of the brain) and objects (a car whose shape is derived from a trunkfish so that it can accommodate equipment) are based on direct, phenomenological counterparts of natural models mostly borrowed ad hoc from biology. The study of bionics, also called "biomimicry," could become the somewhat fantastical technological metaphor for the next phase of modernity.

Charles Darwin was and continues to be misunderstood as if the survival of the fittest meant the fastest, strongest, or best survive. In reality, the fittest means the solution that best fits the situation at hand. From this it follows that the minimal use of resources and energy for maximum results, coupled with a perfect economic loop, becomes an essential part of the equation for success. Regarding material, combination, and (→) production technologies, this implies a shift from isotropic (uniform) to anisotropic (composite) materials, from linear to non-linear, and from mono- to multi-functional integrated properties. In the future, environmental technology will play an ever-increasing role in the sustainable development of the human race (→ *Environmental Design, Sustainability*), especially where the production of its artifacts are concerned. Engineering design is geared to this development.

The fact that the terminology of design has become so compartmentalized reveals how highly fragmented our understanding of the discipline is, a discipline that requires a series of specialists rather than a unified approach. The unity of art, science, and technology was standard when Leonardo da Vinci was working during the Renaissance without a need for the term "engineering design"—despite the fact that so many inventions, even those that derived from direct observation of nature, were made at that time. This compartmentalization is reflected in our educational strategy—even in the two-phase bachelor/master's progression at university—and in the specificity of the academic degree, Graduate Engineer in (→) Industrial Design. Maybe in the future, the latter could be replaced by the invented word "scionics," a composite of science and bionics. AT |

→ *Capital Goods, Mechatronic Design*

Herwig, O., and A. Thallemer. 2005. *Air: Unity of art and science*. Stuttgart: Arnoldsche.

Reese, J., ed. 2005. *Der Ingenieur und seine Designer: Entwurf technischer Produkte im Spannungsfeld zwischen Konstruktion und Design*. Berlin: Springer.

Thallemer, A. 2004. Die Zukunft des Design. In K. Buchholz and K. Wolbert, eds. *Im Designerpark*, pp. 206–10. Darmstadt: Institut Mathildenhöhe.

ENVIRONMENTAL DESIGN

Environmental design is a framework that situates the planning, production, and evaluation of objects of every scale, including products, buildings, parks, human settlements, and infrastructure, in a reciprocal relationship with the functioning and resilience of natural systems. By explicitly extending the ethical (→ *Ethics*) and temporal considerations of design across generations and beyond the bounds of solely anthropocentric concerns, environmental design has significantly altered certain design practices. It has inspired environmentally reflexive landscape architects, urban designers, architects, interior designers, and industrial designers to consider the environmental cost of their work as a core metric in evaluating success. As a result those practices are introducing the conservation of energy, natural resources, and (→) materials into the design process and producing objects, spaces, and landscapes of increasing durability and long-term social flexibility.

Environmental design had a history long before it had a name. In the broadest sense all design is a (→) transformation of the natural environment. Nature provides the raw material of design in the form of energy, chemicals, metals, wood, silica, water, and so on. Natural landscapes are rearranged by the (→) pattern and (→) function of human settlements and natural systems are mimicked, altered, supported or obliterated by human activity.

The degree to which nature is explicitly a part of the (→) design process is largely a function of the particular cultural significance of the term "environmental" or other synonyms such as "natural," "sustainable" or "ecological." As the meaning of these adjectives changes over time, the meaning of environmental design changes too. Thus environmental design acquires meaning and relevance in relation to the social and temporal significance of nature within a given culture at a given time. As a result, environmental design is integrally linked to the ethical and philosophical zeitgeist.

Throughout history people have defined themselves as made of, part of, outside of, and interconnected with nature. Each perspective influences how the objects and processes of design are mediated in relation to the level of human understanding and concern for the environment.

With the formal introduction of the term "ecology" in 1866 the German biologist Ernst Haeckel gave name to a set of emerging theories on the structure and functioning of living organisms in relationship to their surrounding natural context. Distinct from the more mechanistic and fragmentary view of nature that preceded it, ecology provided the basis from which to think more systemically and holistically about the environment. Ebenezer Howard's idealized Garden City movement (1898), blending nature and the city into an integrated whole, can be seen as a design response to the emerging field of ecology.

Similarly, the American naturalist tradition (of the mid-nineteenth through early twentieth century, that is: Emerson, Thoreau, Leopold) found expression in conservation movements and ethical frameworks that led to policy designs as well as landscape and wildlife preservation in the form of National Parks and the Forest Service. Leopold's "land ethic" formed the basis of the modern environmental movement, which was born in 1945 at the dawn of the nuclear age. The new realities of the cold war, coupled with an emerging realization that humanity possessed the capacity to irrevocably alter the planet, led scientists (Rachel Carson and Barry Commoner), designers (Buckminster Fuller), and writers (Stewart Brand) toward political action, on the one hand, and project-driven solutions on the other. Fuller's *Spaceship Earth* and Brand's *Whole Earth Catalog* evidence the new global scale of environmental design.

In 1987 the Bruntland Commission codified the term "sustainable development," joining the use of natural resources and environmental protection to human need over time. Like ecology before it, ($\rightarrow$) sustainability presents a holistic view of the function and value of natural systems, but establishes human ($\rightarrow$) need as the baseline metric to evaluate success. Sustainable design strategies consider the full life cycle of products and measure the embodied energy of processes or building ($\rightarrow$) components. This allows for an accounting of energy and material ($\rightarrow$) consumption and a measure of environmental cost. Environmental design within the paradigm of sustainability includes the use of nontoxic, renewable raw materials, product recycling, and natural resource preservation.

Today ecosystems are seen as non-linear and dynamic. Best captured under the rubric of "patch dynamics," this theory sees ecosystems as spatially heterogeneous flow structures (Pickett and White 1986). Environmental design in this context is a deeply cross-disciplinary ($\rightarrow$ Discipline) activity engaging in ($\rightarrow$) research, public policy, and outreach in addition to design solutions at the scale of landscapes ($\rightarrow$ Landscape Design), watersheds, infrastructure, and human settlements. The Baltimore Long-Term Ecological research project provides a model for the role of environmental design today. JT + MK |

$\rightarrow$ Sustainability

Brand, S., ed. 1968–98. *The whole earth catalogue.* Menlo Park, CA: Portola Institute.

Haeckel, E. H. P. A. 1866. *Generelle Morphologie der Organismen: Allgemeine Grundzüge der organischen Formen-Wissenschaft, mechanisch begründet durch die von Charles Darwin reformirte Descendenz-Theorie.* G. Reimer, Berlin.

Howard, E. 1965. *Garden cities of tomorrow.* Rev. ed. Cambridge, MA: MIT Press. (Orig. pub. 1898.)

Pickett, S. T. A., and P. S. White. 1986. *The ecology of natural disturbance and patch dynamics.* San Diego: Academic Press.

Worster, D. 1996. *Nature's economy: A history of ecological ideas.* 2nd. ed. Cambridge, United Kingdom: Cambridge Univ. Press.

ERGONOMICS

The discipline of ergonomics is based upon an examination of the physical requirements of the human body, and a desire on the part of designers and engineers to address these needs through design. Much of the work in this field is motivated by attempts to improve human interactions with ($\rightarrow$) products, environments, and ($\rightarrow$) systems.

The derivation of the term "ergonomics" stems from two Greek words: *ergon,* meaning work and *nomoi,* meaning natural laws. The science of ergonomics has touched many fields from pens that fit well in the hand and facilitate smooth writing, to chairs for computer workstations that improve posture and reduce backache, to assembly plans for line workers that reduce repetitive-motion injuries.

The birth of ergonomics occurred during the Industrial Revolution. As the assembly line developed as the means to create mass-produced objects, workplace injuries increased as a result of tasks that required repeated motions. The ($\rightarrow$) discipline grew during the Second World War, when it was recognized that optimizing the ergonomics of airplane cockpits was crucial to preserving the lives of pilots and to the success of bombing missions. The position of the buttons, controls, and displays of planes, as well as other aspects of their user interface were analyzed and designed by early practitioners in this field ($\rightarrow$ Usability, Interface Design).

In 1959, using military data to compile a list of anthropometric standards, Henry Dreyfuss' book *The Measure of Man* (now renamed *The Measure of Man and Woman*) created conventions of human body dimensions and stances that are used to this day to design products and environments. The updated version of this book features anthropometric diagrams that detail the average dimensions of the human body, and illustrate typical bodily positions while engaged in such activities as typing at computer workstations, driving automobiles, and working in factories. The information in this book has exerted great influence over the years on the design of furniture (→ *Furniture Design*) and products (→ *Product Design, Industrial Design*).

Much of the current research in ergonomics has been motivated by problems in the workplace that cause injury or discomfort. Recognition of the link between designing a safe work environment, increasing productivity, and profit potential has also led to the expansion this field. Greater efficiency through ergonomic optimization has been shown to manifest itself both in the workers' ability to complete tasks more quickly, and in the reduced amount of time off for injury, two very attractive factors for employers (→ *Safety Design*).

As injury rates have risen, governmental organizations have become involved in the field of ergonomics, developing lists of criteria intended to reduce workplace discomfort. These sets of criteria exist for the benefit of both employer and employee, often requiring by law that the employer comply with certain standards to avoid being fined. This, in turn, has led to an increased interest in this field. In the United States, the Occupational Health and Safety Administration (OSHA) produces guidelines for multiple industries that are intended to minimize workplace discomfort and injury. In Europe, the European Agency for Safety and Health at Work produces similar guidelines. These kinds of organizations have focused on work environments as disparate as laboratories, farms, and assembly lines, in order to develop ergonomic recommendations for both employers and employees. They also identify ergonomic hazards, most often characterized by the following conditions: extreme temperatures (hot or cold), vibration, repetitive motions, motions that involve expending a great deal of force, and awkward postures that compromise the natural stance and motion of the body.

The advent of the personal computer and its increasingly seamless integration into people's lives has been responsible for another growth spurt in the field of ergonomics. A sector of this field now exists to prevent and attend to the injuries that arise from extended use of computer workstations, maladies that include carpal tunnel syndrome, lower back pain, and eye strain. By examining the posture and limb positions of heavy computer users, practitioners can recommend methods of combating injury through application of ergonomic principles. This has led to design (→) innovations in computer chairs, desks, keyboards, and mice, objects that have been specifically designed to prevent repetitive-strain injuries in the workplace.

The term (→) "human factors" is often used interchangeably with "ergonomics." Historically, these two fields have differed in that ergonomics has been perceived as focusing on the measurement and motion of human body parts and their effect on interactions with products, furniture, and machines, whereas human factors has typically focused on the psychological factors that influence human behavior (→ Need). As studies into human conduct and decision-making have brought to light the complex interrelationships between physiology and psychology, however, the distinctions between ergonomics and human factors have become increasingly blurred. As a result, the pool of practitioners in ergonomics has expanded beyond designers and engineers to include psychologists, anthropologists, computer scientists, and biologists.

Beginning with the Industrial Revolution and stretching to the present, the field of ergonomics has examined the body measurements and limb positions of humans in order to optimize people's physical relationships with products, machines and systems. Practitioners in the field have used the results of ergonomic analyses to design safer, more comfortable products and work environments, with the goal of improving both the leisure and professional lives of humans. AR |

→ Universal Design

Tilley, A. R., and Henry Dreyfuss Associates. 2002. *The measure of man and woman: Human factors in design*, p. 10. New York: Wiley.

ETHICS

Ethics is the domain in which judgments are made about how humans should behave toward one another and those creatures and things around them. Given that design also involves making judgments about how humans should be helped with products, environments, and communications to interact with those around them, there is a sense in which the phrase "design ethics" is redundant: all designing involves ethical judgments, whether the designer knows it or not.

Ethics is distinct from ontology (questions about what exists) and epistemology (questions about how we know about what exists) by being action-oriented; ethics concerns what ought to be made the case, rather than what is the case. Ethics is also distinct from politics (the social processes and institutions through which ethical determinations are enforced) and morality (legislated codes of ethical behavior) in that it involves deliberations about what is most appropriate rather than addressing systems that remove the need for deliberation.

Western philosophers have attempted to develop frameworks in which such considerations can be made. There are at least four such frameworks: universalism, utilitarianism, alterity, and virtue. Universalism is primarily associated with Immanuel Kant's rationalization of the maxim common to most religions: do unto others as you would have them do unto you. Kant saw ethics as the imperative to apply reasoning to the question: can my action be a rule that everyone can follow? Utilitarianism, on the other hand, is associated with British empiricists like John Stuart Mills, who had a more pragmatic version of Kant's question: does my action maximize the happiness of the most number of people? Utilitarianism lends itself to more economic forms of reasoning, such as cost-benefit analysis. Whilst universalism and utilitarianism are explicitly rational approaches to ethics, they have an emotive foundation, empathy, in that they assume that all people are fundamentally the same (an assumption that is enshrined today in the principles of human rights). By contrast, alterity begins with the assumption that "others" are absolutely different from "me," and that ethical actions must therefore be subjected to a respect for the other person's "otherness." This is a more recent framework associated with the renegotiation of Hebraic morality by Emmanuel Levinas and Jacques Derrida. Virtue is a contemporary revival, primarily by Alasdair MacIntyre, of Aristotlean ethics. Aristotle called ethical judgment "phronesis," or case-by-case practical reason or prudence. As a virtue, phronesis is something that one becomes good at, an ability to discern the best balance between what is necessary and what is desirable, the individual and the whole. An excellent ethical judgment allows all involved to flourish as best they can (as opposed to just being happy).

In contrast with these more or less cognitive accounts of ethics, non-western traditions often lie closer to the etymological meaning of the term "ethos," a harmonious way of living that does not need consideration, a habit in keeping with the others that make up a habitat. In this sense, there is nothing more unethical than the person who has to think about, let alone calculate, what to do in a certain situation; an ethical person is instead the one that acts without thinking, immediately doing what best helps a situation (see Dreyfus & Dreyfus 1990 and Varela 1999).

Design ethics often refers to professional codes of conduct, which according to what has been said so far, are better defined as design morality. Less deterministic design ethics comprise case studies of ethical judgments on the basis of some or other version of the frameworks mentioned above. Included within design ethics are moral and legal obligations to make designs universally accessible or "inclusive" (→ *Universal Design*), the undertaking of pro bono work for communities that could not otherwise afford design services that would nonetheless improve their lives (→ *Not-for-Profit*), and contributions to political activism (→ *Design and Politics*).

It should be apparent though that there is a stronger overlap between designing and ethics in excess of conventional "design ethics." All designing involves decisions about what ought to be made the case. Such decisions are made on consideration of maximized benefit (utilitarianism); but also, in the context of mass production, consideration of what it would mean for everyone to use this or that designed artifact (universalism). And yet, the decisions made will always be particular to a specific design context, and never merely the formal application of an established rule (virtue); as such, design will engage a range of "user-centered" research methods (→ *Participatory Design*) to access the otherness of those it aims to service (alterity). The inherent link between design and ethics has been brought to the fore by Bruno Latour's technology studies, which argue that design is a process of "moral delegation" or "the ethical made durable" (Latour 1992). In other words, products exist to permanently enact ethical intentions—for example, automatic doors unthinkingly opening to all that might need them, no longer discriminating like conventionally handled doors against those too old, too young, or too burdened to push them open. To this extent, all designs are more or less ethical gifts to others (Dilnot 1995). CT |

→ *Sustainability, Usability*

Dilnot, C. 1995. The gift. In V. Margolin and R. Buchanan, eds. *The idea of design*. Cambridge, MA: MIT Press.

Dreyfus, H., and S. Dreyfus. 1990. What is morality? A phenomenological account of the development of ethical expertise. In D. Rasmussen, ed. *Universalism vs. Communitarianism*. Cambridge, MA: MIT Press.

Latour, B. 1992. Where are the missing masses? The sociology of a few mundane artifacts. In W. Bijker, and J. Law, eds. *Shaping technology/building society: Studies in sociotechnical change*. Cambridge, MA: MIT Press.

Varela, F. 1999. *Ethical know-how, wisdom, and cognition*. Stanford, CA: Stanford Univ. Press.

EVALUATION

Evaluation is the systematic and ordered process required to determine the effectiveness (or effect) of something so as to assess its worth, (→) quality, or utility. Essential to the process are criteria that articulate the values that are to be assessed. Evaluation can only be undertaken after establishing this (→) value system and, importantly, this may or may not be related to the intention of the designer. The measure of success, impact, consequence, and so on, is in relation to the criteria of the evaluation process.

Evaluation can be undertaken from any number of perspectives. The designer may have one understanding of worth, the marketer another, and a social researcher assessing the impact of a design yet another. As a consequence, evaluation is a highly contextual and relational process, as it requires the determination of what constitutes success or failure.

The evaluative process is related to but distinct from (→) testing. Testing determines whether the design succeeds in relation to its intended (→) use, while evaluation assesses whether the design is successful relative to the articulation of a particular value system. This could be an improved experience, greater sales, reduced environmental impact, or changed behavior, and so on. These criteria will at times be at odds with one another and at others be complementary. In other words, a manufacturer may determine that using a particular material is the cheapest way to achieve high sales of a product, but this may have deleterious environmental effects. Once this evaluation is put into the public domain it may then become an issue related to the marketability of the product.

These shifting perspectives on a product are most commonly evident in relation to health and environmental issues and often disclose a conflict of different agendas that can be accounted for by their using discrete evaluation processes. (Mechanisms such as the introduction of triple bottom-line accounting—social, financial and environmental—are an attempt to integrate these otherwise incompatible perspectives). Often the (→) design process is called on in an attempt to reconcile conflicting criteria for the inscribed value of the designed artifact. Consequently, understanding how to evaluate design is a critical competency for designers and a failure to better account for the full range of critical perspectives in the evaluation process can lead to short-term gains and long-term problems. TM |

EVENT DESIGN

For centuries, churches have held religious services to draw people together and convey religious ideas. The building, designed setting, dramaturgy, and rituals all combine to attract and sustain many people.

Today the success of religion, political parties, initiatives, brands, and products relies just as heavily on the contexts in which their ideas are communicated, because the need for innovative products and services is not always immediately apparent and information or advertising is not always enough to generate the human desire to participate or purchase what is on offer. There are so many similar products of equal quality on the global market today that it is now even more important to be culturally and socially relevant, to identify and communicate the mind-sets and values represented by corporations, initiatives, associations, and cities.

What do World Youth Day, the World Economic Summit, a Soccer World Championship, Art Basel, Miami Beach, Mac World, and even furniture trade fairs in Milan have in common? They are successful, temporary events, the perfect medium to attract attention and create an experience from the spirit of a (→) brand—whether it is the Catholic Church, international economics, the World Soccer Association, or the computer and furniture industries. Above all, they gather people together at one site where initiators, supporters, and purveyors of ideas and products can mingle with clients and consumers as well as each other.

Hence, events can be considered extended markets. Events and their design have become so important that event design is now a commodity itself that focuses on the creation of happenings ranging from exclusive one-off events in small locations to continuing series of large international occasions.

The need to create cultural and emotional effectiveness has grown so much that different fields of industry have staged events that have become permanent institutions. For several years now, the automobile industry has promoted a mix of museums and adventure parks. VW Autostadt in Wolfsburg and BMW World in Munich are examples of brand productions that have become permanent operations by constantly orchestrating new events. The obvious objective here is to develop an emotional connection between the public, the product, and its brand.

However, most are temporary, multimedia, and multisensory events, which makes designing an event a multidisciplinary task that involves architects, (→) communication, (→) product, (→) lighting, and (→) sound designers, copywriters, project managers, and public relations experts. Events have precisely orchestrated dramaturgies, based on a program with a motto or statement that conveys the desired corporate communications clearly and distinctly. Most events need a messenger—a star like the pope, Steve Jobs, a star athlete, or top designer who can communicate this idea and attract the public—and a design with a simple, understandable, and effective symbolism.

Content determines the choice of staging which begins, according to the size of the event, with designing different forms of communication, such as invitations, press kits, newsletters, web sites, event documentation, and special give-aways (→ Gimmick) that all have a unified appearance. The unifying element of event design used at the venue plays an important role. This could be the brand color, fonts and materials, as well as the interior, the style of clothing, language, and imagery. It can also include scent (→ Olfactory Design), and sound, light, and video projections that together create a brand-specific image for corporate or national events. The example of a religious service can again be a useful illustration here: according to the occasion, the feel of a religious event includes everything from the church building itself (corporate architecture), the symbolism of the cross, the appearance of the church ornaments, numbers of candles, lights (event look), and priests' robes on to the theatre of the liturgy and mass and the choice of songs and texts. For global corporations to be able to hold events in different countries and cities at the same time, it is necessary to have highly precise, sustainable planning and design programming that is accessible to people from various cultures. Event guidelines that secure a globally unified brand identity are an important tool in achieving this. KSP |

→ Branding, Corporate Identity, Service Design

EXHIBITION DESIGN

*The diversity of media—art, world exposi-
tions, thematic museums or collections, trade
shows, and department stores—that must be
dealt with by an exhibition designer makes
exhibition design a complex field. It requires
a wide range of skills encompassing pedagogy,
marketing, the technical expertise needed to
install exhibitions (museography), and the design skills involved in making and painting
theatre sets. (→ Set Design).*

As a rule, exhibition design is an anonymous profession. The
exhibited works and facts must be the focus of attention and
take priority over the designer's own ideas or design ambitions.
After salon exhibitions were replaced by gallery exhibitions, and
along with the growing autonomy of art in the twentieth century
(that may yet prove illusory), this attitude crystallized with the
emergence of the "white cube"—the term coined by Brian
O'Doherty in 1976 for an unadorned, pure white exhibition
space. However, in *The Power of Display* (1998), a critical examination of exhibition practice at the Museum of Modern Art
(MoMA) in New York, Mary Anne Staniszewski describes the
white cube as only one specific development of exhibition design. Nonetheless, the white cube managed to become so closely
linked with the paradigm of art's autonomy that it developed
into a fundamental component of the twentieth-century art system—a fact that made it difficult to recognize the white cube as
a construct, and gave rise to Staniszewski's justifiable theory of
the "unconscious of an exhibition." Much earlier, however, as
the object emerged as a commodity, exhibitions had already become a generally accepted and widespread phenomenon. Consequently, the unfamiliar history of exhibition design refers to a
mechanism for producing and transforming the popular (→)
consumption of objects and information that is both driven
and shaped by a multitude of social forces. Today, the "black
box" and new media pose additional challenges to exhibition
design, and the shifting varieties of tourism and the "blockbuster" phenomenon are changing the conditions under which
exhibition designs are perceived.

Tracing the theory and practice of exhibition design reveals historical examples such as the cabinet of curiosities, dioramas, the
theater and film stage, parks and panoramas, market squares
and department stores, propaganda, and advertising. This variety reflects different forms of appropriation of data and facts
and different ways for the public to access these; that is, there
are many avenues for collecting and structuring, observing and
differentiating, imagining and looking, constructing and strol-
ling, and finally offering, negotiating, and consuming. Every degree of perception and reflection—from being involved to being
deeply moved, from illusion to persuasion—can be a consequence of these forms and practices. All exhibitions are based
on a specific procedure and relationship of exchange that is
made effective by the exhibition, and this unites the exhibited
objects and facts with the curators and viewers by means of its
unique mixture of agreements, (→) conventions, and techniques.
Exhibition design merges the displayed, spoken, and viewed elements on a primary universal level. On a secondary and reflective

level, exhibition design is responsible for rendering the events recognizable, logical, and publicly accessible.

The term (→) "display" requires an explanation: in the context of exhibition design, it describes an ensemble of spaces and objects that, through the process of exhibiting, communicating, and perceiving, becomes effective and functional. A display is thus an effective system that adopts very different dimensions: from the museum itself—and not just the building, but also its context (the Guggenheim, the Louvre, museums of natural history, museums of local history, and so on)—to structuring space and systems of orientation (using backdrops, color, pedestals, vitrines) or the graphic design used in wall texts and signs that convey information about the exhibition. Moreover, the contexts in which the exhibits are seen vary according to the exhibition environment—meaning that a sign provides not only scientific, historic, or artistic details of an object but also the "house style." In this broad sense, the display implies the sum of conditions in which (→) artifacts are presented.

The relationship between the exhibition and the exhibited works is defined by two categories of objects: firstly, those produced for the art system and thus considered artworks, and secondly, those from other contexts, such as historical or technical objects, facts, substances, and everyday objects that are placed in a display environment. The artist Marcel Duchamp completely and deliberately blurred the border between these two strictly defined areas by signing a pissoir in 1917 and presenting it as an artwork for exhibition. This single gesture marked the beginnings of the "ready-made." Duchamp had already worked as an exhibition designer, and the famous opinion that an artwork is incomplete without an observer is attributed to him. Friedrich Kiesler, a friend and contemporary of Duchamp, conducted groundbreaking research on the relationship between an artwork and the viewer. He developed his Correalismus theory and, as early as the 1920s, spoke of art being conveyed electronically in the future. He mastered the white cube for Peggy Guggenheim in 1942 with the extraordinary and seminal exhibition *Art of this Century*, before the term "white cube" even existed. Kiesler, like Duchamp, considered the viewer to be more than a spectator, but an active element in each individual, open collection. A fundamental phenomenon of this collection is that the viewer experiences the exhibition by moving through it rather than looking at it from a static position, meaning that the viewer, the exhibits, and the context are in constant motion in space and time, with continually shifting points of reference and perception. Hence, the exhibition space—even if it is unusually concentrated or illusionistic—is always part of a public, complex, and urban space, and it will become increasingly evident that exhibition design, besides designing context and spaces, also designs time.

In the 1920s and 1930s, (→) Constructivists and Futurists adopted the emerging forms of mass media, advertising, photography, and moving image that constituted a new and urban mode of "living between words, images, and commodities" (Jacques Rancière). El Lissitzky and Rodchenko's Constructivist spatial environments are as legendary in Soviet art history as Libera, Terragni, and Persico's Futuristic constructs are for Italian fascism. The unconditional drive of exhibition design with a propagandizing agenda exploited the urban facade, yet also overemphasized the fragmentation of urban life to make a clear ideological statement. How susceptible the design, the desire to inform, and the constructed environment configuration are to idéology and propaganda can be examined through historical exhibitions in the (→) Bauhaus tradition: for instance, those by Mies van der Rohe and Lilly Reich ("Samt und Seide," 1927; "Deutsches Volk / Deutsche Arbeit," 1934) or Herbert Bayer, who applied his theories of perception on all fronts from the Bauhaus to Nazi propaganda ("Road to Victory," 1942, MoMA).

Urban displays of propaganda became just as important as points of reference for exhibition design as Kiesler's constructions and viewing apparatuses. Of course, these had less an art context than a context of elaborate theme and science exhibitions, dedicated largely to the above-mentioned second category of exhibits. World expositions made these scenographies famous on a massive worldwide scale but even company presentations at, for instance, automotive trade shows were organized by event managers. The relationship between display, artifact, and viewer varies greatly in the course of fully synchronized and spatially orchestrated scenographic events. Kiesler saw the display as a constructed third party which, along with the artifact and the viewer, was involved in an open, moving spatial design and thus, as an area, was open for reflection. In contrast, the display of scenography exists completely within the technical setting of an orchestrated production to ensure the illusion's effect (→ *Set Design*).

Scenographers use the term "worlds" to describe the spaces into which they lure viewers. They borrow from film and stage design, work with narrative and suspense, are concerned with precise timing, and creating a virtual, skillful continuum, which the visitor experiences like a traveler following a prescribed route. Visitors are encouraged to interact with the orchestrated worlds, which increases their participation in the scene. This demonstrates that scenography's contribution to exhibition design satisfies its desire for a supposedly attractive and contemporary marriage of experience and education via a one-sided, predefined delivery of content and emotions. Yet this position and its strict regime of time and media continuum becomes problematic as soon as exhibitions claim to be discourses and constructions in public, social, and urban space. At the same time, the viewer sees his or her role differently, which also affects exhibition design as a whole. Spectators who enter the scene as a consumer and pay an entrance fee in exchange for the experience, now supplant viewers, once guided by intentions and the spontaneity of an open environment. Adopting the film industry term "blockbuster" and applying it to exhibitions is indicative of a marked shift and is, moreover, a paradoxical development, in which an apparently effective marketing strategy damages and destroys precisely those cultural events and products it set out to market successfully in the first place.

As video and media art increasingly incorporate the "black box" into the "white cube," the traditional spatial regime of a museum is linked in a new way with the dimension of time. Its underlying mission of delivering a time-based experience makes viewers morph into spectators of projected apparitions who are now bound to linear temporal duration and emotional intensity (→ Time-based Design). They are no longer moved between suspended indifference and simultaneity or by artworks with which they can decide to be engaged at a time of their choosing; spectators oscillate between feeling they arrived too late or left too early. Timed attention has now been added to undivided attention as a requirement of serious viewing. The same applies, of course, to all forms of time-based performance art. Perhaps spectators see art fundamentally as a (→) performance practice. Ultimately, there is a significant difference between spectatorship and observation. The spectator's role is one of witness, consumer, and participant. Yet observation, as a leisurely practice of the social negotiation of facts, is also a form of art (comparable with the art of speech). As such, it appeals to its own power of imagination to visualize a fact internally, in other words, to place something somewhere in order to assess and (in the Duchampian sense) to complete it. This incidentally is the fundamental form of interaction required in any exhibition situation, meaning that the spectator still has to activate their internal viewer, in order to become a partner in their own perceptions.

A new parallelism is developing today between the transformation of social and urban space and the notion that exhibitions offer interest in or explanations of reality. Once observers became time-based spectators, exhibition organizers and designers began examining how visitors to an exhibition might become

Bredekamp, H. 1995. *The lure of antiquity and the cult of the machine*. Trans. Allison Brown. Princeton, NJ: Markus Wiener Publishers.

O'Doherty, B. 1986. *Inside the white cube*. Berkeley: Univ. of California Press. (Orig. pub. 1976.)

Schwarz, U., and P. Teufel, eds. 2001. *Museografie und Ausstellungsgestaltung*. Ludwigsburg: avedition.

Staniszewski, M. A. 1998. *The power of display*. Cambridge, MA: MIT Press.

leading characters in their own experience and environment, if exhibitions primarily address global tourists rather than local citizens. This has less to do with general problems concerning the communication of, for example, content and knowledge in different language and codes; rather it is about cooperative skills, which are required for negotiating conditions and instances of social reality and which of course includes the venues and practice of exhibiting. Just as urban space is being transformed from a bourgeois to a tourist society, the museum will also change the view it has of itself and its method of operation. It will go through a process of (→) branding in order to compete in the market for attention, and, like universities, will offer its educational product online to an international public. Alliances will form—and the museum will learn from those places that long ago mastered how to drive and steer engrossed masses: department stores and emporia. The patchwork of exhibition design's new tasks and skills will continue to develop during this process of transformation. MV |

→ *Design Museums, Event Design*

F

FAKE

A fake—also referred to as a counterfeit item or knockoff—is a deliberate attempt to (→) copy an original. Money, documents, art, literature, votes, medicine—even identities—can be faked. In a design context, fakes may claim a false history or resemble expensive designer (→) brands. Since they are often made with very sophisticated technology, it can be difficult to distinguish the fake from the original.

People who attempt to sell fakes as original designs for profit can be charged with committing (→) trademark infringement or fraud. Because it is a tax-free business, counterfeiting (the process of distributing and selling fakes) results in significant monetary losses not only for the companies but also for the country in which the fraud takes place; when customs officials in Hamburg, Germany, made a counterfeiting arrest in November 2006, the fakes were valued at 383 million euros. Fakes can also be used for purposes more serious than monetary gain. For instance, photographs are regularly manipulated to intentionally mislead viewers and disguise the truth—as demonstrated by Stalin's removal of Trotsky's image from all photographic evidence. The distinctions between the "fake" and the "authentic" have been debated for centuries in the realms of art and design (→) theory as well as those of philosophy and science. Although the term "fake" connotes certain elements of deception, this is not always the case—fakes and replicas can also be used to question, to amuse, or to educate. Some fakes are, in fact, reproductions that strive to be more than mere copies—deliberately recognizable, exaggerated versions of the original. SIB |

→ Copyright, Intellectual Property, Plagiarism, Postmodernism

FASHION DESIGN

Fashion design is a relatively new category, marking the shift from the dominance of French haute couture in the 1950s to new fashion centers in the United States, Europe, and Japan. Youth, street styles, and pop culture have become increasingly central to fashion design, economics, and media presence.

As early as the fifteenth century, *la mode* (Latin: *modus* = rule; manner, mode, way, method) in France implied the "custom, fashion, manner, and way in which one dresses or makes oneself beautiful; in short, everything to do with attire and splendor" (Diderot 1713–1784). Yet the word fashion was not integrated into the English language until the mid-sixteenth century. It derives from the French *façon* (workmanship, way of doing something, mannerisms) but took on connotations of "the made" in addition to "custom" or "disposition." *Façon* is etymologically related to "fetish" and also to "faction" (political party, or section) as a symbolic representation of a political ethos. In France, "à la mode" meant someone who wore courtly, worldly clothing, signifying the imperial authority to exercise absolute power. Louis XIV, as a ruler *à la mode*, established France as the European center of fashion, and by the second half of the seventeenth century, monthly shipments of the latest, greatest, stately fashions were being sent to the grande and not quite so grande dames of London, and later to those in Germany, Italy, and Russia. Magazines as a means of distributing descriptions and pictures of fashionable clothing and accessories began with the *Mercure* in 1692. This was available in France, England, and Germany, and the *Journal des Luxus und der Moden* (The journal of luxury and fashion) began publishing everything related to intellectual, social, and domestic fashions in 1786. Nevertheless, from the 1620s onward there was an active critique of fashion and the fashionable. German semantics combined the French phrase *à la mode* with social criticism in the phrase *a-la modische Kleiderteufel* (fashionable little devil) (Grimm, *Deutsches Wörterbuch*, 1854). This was directed not only against the French hegemony of absolute aristocracy and the prevalence of French attire in German lands; it also mocked the frenchified "clothes devil" to assert the moral (and nationalist) superiority of the world of (German) bourgeois reality over (French) aristocratic appearances. The French Revolution started a lively dialectical relationship between fashion and anti-fashion or even protest fashion as an attempt to negotiate the antagonism of modern class, race, and gender systems. The relationship between fashion and (→) modernity formed part of the new era—it created a dynamic relationship with time, because the French word *moderne* meant "consistent with contemporary fashion, *façon*, attire, mannerisms" (Grimm 1854). As an indicator of this, fashion became an aesthetic imperative: "whoever and whatever does not comply with fashion should be ashamed" (Grimm 1854). In fact, the more articulately the political anatomy of nineteenth-century modernity clothed the male body and its economics with the uniform of the suit—helping of course to separate the men from the dandies—the more fashion became a symbol of the elite, of the superficial, and a synonym for the feminine.

The discourse on fashion's naturalness or artificiality is still a part of the biopolitical debate. The "aesthetic movement" and those who identified with the artistic and intellectual avant-garde at the end of the nineteenth century opposed fashion and advocated naturalism, "rational" clothing and the removal of corsets. Clothing in support of this position was designed by feminists such as Amelia Bloomer, doctors like Heinrich Pudor, artists such as William Morris (→ *Arts &*

Crafts), Edward Burne-Jones, and Henry van de Velde
(→ *Deutscher Werkbund*), stage actress Anna Muthesius, and
writer Oscar Wilde.

The idea that the body should no longer conform to the artificial
and unhealthy demands of fashion but should be allowed its
own natural shape formed the basis for the twentieth-century
biopolitical movement that placed the body at the center of fashion, in turn paving the way for body fashion, which became the
heart of a global economic sector embracing nutrition, sport,
cosmetics, and more recently, cosmetic surgery. Around 1900,
this created a new synthesis of art and fashion, the first that approached the category of design, in the form of a modern, industrially manufactured clothing industry. Educational institutions
were established in London, Vienna, Berlin, and New York where
the Chase School (now Parsons The New School for Design) in
1906 was the first to offer a course in fashion design.

However, Parisian haute couture continued to dominate fashion
well into the first half of the twentieth century, as *prêt-à-porter,* or
ready to wear, clothing became popular. Charles Frederick
Worth's (1825–1895) annual collection was the first to earn its
designer the title of "couturier," which had previously only existed in the feminine form, meaning seamstress. Because he
signed his creations, Worth awarded himself the status of artist.
He succeeded in turning his name into a product, similar to the
modern concept of (→) branding, and clothed queens, ladies of
the bourgeoisie, famous actresses, and other grande dames of
modern haute couture. Yet, it was Paul Poiret (1879–1944) who
first picked up on the clothing reform with his "La Vague" and
culottes creations. Haute couture at that time drew inspiration
from art, theater, the opera, and ballet. Poiret designed clothing
for the stage as well, and worked with professional models. In
1914, Jeanne Paquin (1869–1936) held the first fashion show in
London, presenting her line of tango dresses. Poiret developed a
range of products including his own perfume, accessories, and
interior furnishings. In the 1920s and 1930s, women such as
Coco Chanel (1883–1971), Madeleine Vionnet (1876–1956), Alix
Grés (1899–1993), and Maggy Rouff (1876–1971) dominated
haute couture. Popular culture also focused on women in motion: in the workforce, playing sports, doing the Charleston, at
dance revues, in films, and shopping. A broad spectrum of gender subversions, from the *garçon* or flapper style to the vamp or
diva look, was typical of women's fashion at the time. Cross-
dressing by wearing pants or suits shifted gender borders even
further. Elsa Schiaparelli (1890–1973) experimented with ready-
mades and, along with Marcel Duchamp, worked closely with
the art and intellectual avant-garde scene. Her styling helped

make stars out of Zsa Zsa Gabor and Mae West, and her other customers included Katherine Hepburn and Greta Garbo.

Fashion and cosmetics have always been essential in the film industry and the making of stars and, accordingly, its influence on daily fashion is immense. Yet Hollywood fashion trends, which were sold in American department stores after the release of films, evoked costume directors and cosmetic companies. French couturiers, like Louis Féraud or Hubert de Givenchy, who designed for Audrey Hepburn, first began to work consistently in the film industry during the 1950s.

America took on the leading role in fashion during the Second World War. A distinctively American fashion style developed in the 1940s, dominated by sportswear that was exported to Europe after the war, as well as blue jeans and the image of the American teenager.

Christian Dior's "New Look" in 1947 was a new beginning for haute couture and marked a transition to a more accelerated turnover of fashion lines, the end of the French era—and the beginnings of "fashion design" as we understand the term today. London's new academies began educating young fashion designers who ignored established couturiers such as Hardy Amies (1909–2003) or Norman Hartwell (1901–1979). In the 1950s, a new structure of fashion started to emerge from the interplay of sub-cultural street styles, pop culture, art, and design. During this period, fashion became part of the creative industries and sub-culture styles—like those of the mid-1950s Teddy Boys who mixed retro-Edwardian detailing like velvet and ruffles with American rock and roll attitude—were absorbed by mass-produced, mainstream prêt-à-porter clothing. Street styles from different cultures ranging from the Teddy Boys, Rockers, Mods, Hippies, Punks, and Skins to the New Romantics became closely identified with designers such as Mary Quant, Vivienne Westwood, John Galliano, and Alexander McQueen. Quant's miniskirt adapted and shortened a creation by couturier André Courrèges, who originally designed it in 1964 in line with (→) Bauhaus principles.

In (→) style, as a medium of symbolic communication, the postproduction boundaries between wearer and designer start to blur because both the designer and the wearer create fashion by selecting, sampling, and reinterpreting historical, social, cultural, and gender images and/or objects. Street styles are also hybrids since they create a mix of white, black, Asian, Indian, or Caribbean youth cultures. The flower power generation of the 1960s not only made a (→) trend out of second-hand clothing; it also challenged bourgeois sexuality and its representation of masculinity. Punk fetish clothing by Westwood and McLaren offered a queer statement about the deconstruction of bourgeois heterosexuality. Camp extravagance has been popular in the club scene since the 1970s. Stars like Freddie Mercury were styled by glam-rock designer Zandra Rhodes, and David Bowie became Ziggy Stardust with the help of stylist Freddie Burretti. Queer (→) aesthetics pervade fashion from Jean Paul Gaultier to the Antwerp Six, and were introduced to the mainstream in the 1990s with the style of the "metrosexual" man. This is part of a particular economy beginning in the 1980s where (→) brands dominated the fashion scene and the focus was not only on stars, but also on minorities and youth rebels. The post-subculture styles of the 1990s are characterized by their close commercial involvement with different historical youth culture styles, and by the New Tribalism body modifications of tattoos and piercings. Hip-hop, as a black style that was characterized by the subversive appropriation of (→) luxury items and brands (bling) associated with the white middle classes, generated further youth cultures that deliberately styled themselves using replica luxury brands. Italian and American designers are mainly responsible for jeans and sportswear and have established most of today's brand corporations: Gucci, Prada, Armani, Versace, D&G, CK, Hilfiger, Ralph Lauren, and Donna Karan. Since the late 1970s, Japanese fashion designers have increasingly won recognition on the fashion scene: Kenzo, Issey Miyake, and Yoshi Yamamoto. The founder of Comme des Garçons, Rei Kawakubo, clearly challenged the architecture of the Western body in 1997 with her "body meets dress" collection.

Digital media technology has enabled new possibilities for designing wearable computing and, in the form of body scans and virtual try-ons, has provided new means of presenting and producing fashion. For example, mass (→) customization has enabled clothing to be custom tailored and fitted using individualized (→) blueprint techniques. Even gene technology and life sciences have altered the materiality of fashion. Nanofibers, bacteria, and stem-cell cultures are beginning to define innovative structures for future fashion design. EG |

→ Brand, Textile Design, Trend

Breward, C., and C. Evans, eds. 2005. *Fashion and modernity*. Oxford, United Kingdom: Berg Publishers.
Jones, T., and S. Rushton, eds. 2005. *Fashion Now 2: i-D selects 160 of its favourite fashion designers from around the world*. Cologne: Taschen.
Vinken, B., and M. Hewson. 2004. *Fashion zeitgeist: Trends and cycles in the fashion system*. Oxford, United Kingdom: Berg Publishers.

FEASIBILITY STUDIES

Feasibility studies are investigations undertaken to determine whether a certain design is viable for a company. They are based on precise and detailed analyses of the company's financial, logistical, and sales-related capacity. Some important factors to establish include the company's access to the necessary finances; the product's relationship to the existing image of the company (including its systems of symbols, services, and so on); the availability and condition of the machines and technology required for production; the need for specialists in the production process, communications or sales; and the ($\rightarrow$) logistics capacity to control the full cycle.

Feasibility studies also investigate the specific design elements in relation to the company's resources. This requires researching whether the design's chosen material is adequate, if the work plan and energy costs are reasonable, whether installing the necessary production means and work force is sustainable, and whether every detail is really necessary—in other words, whether the cost, effort, and strategy of implementing the design will ultimately prove lucrative for the company.

In order to determine the answers to all of these questions, various systematic methods are used. In that the process of conducting a feasibility study requires both foresight and imagination in order to predict potential possibilities, problems, and complications, it is at times similar to the process of design itself. BL |

$\rightarrow$ *Benchmarking, Design Management, Quality Assurance, Strategic Design*

FLOP

"Flop" is the term used to imply a disappointment or failure and usually refers to the commercial aspect of a product. "Flop" is often used as the opposite of success and can be applied in different contexts. A personal flop, failing a test or a job interview for instance, refers only to one's private life. Of greater consequence is the flop of a product or service that was unsuccessful on the market and can have lasting negative consequences for the company or person responsible. A flop can also involve a loss of money and a damaged image. The former can be compensated for by subsequent good performance, but if the flop is a flawed item, the loss of customers' trust in the ($\rightarrow$) brand can have long-lasting consequences. A company's bad planning can also produce a flop. If facts derived from ($\rightarrow$) market research and analysis are based on incorrect or irrelevant questions and conclusions, then a flop, in this case measured by a lack of sales, is inevitable. The production or service industries can also produce flops if the ($\rightarrow$) quality of individual components, employees, or other contributing factors is inconsistent.

In most cases, companies keep quiet about their flops; they are not advertised or announced. Flops can be the result of minor carelessness, such as the name of a product or a culturally inauspicious color, and occur almost daily on the global market. For example when the Pajero, a Mitsubishi SUV, was introduced to the Americas and Spain, the name needed to be changed, as *pajero* was Spanish slang for "masturbator." In France, the laundry detergent Persil has a problem because *persil* means parsley, which is difficult to associate with clean, white clothing. Introducing brand names to the market in Asian countries is also very complicated because of pronunciation or naming issues. The name of the oil corporation Esso has a Japanese homonym that means broken-down car.

A flop does not always lead to the demise of a company. Usually a company can learn and recover from a flop and the blunder can sometimes end up strengthening it. A predicted flop can even turn out to be a surprise success. In 1976, who, other than Steve Jobs and the designers working in computer graphics, believed that Apple Inc. computers would become a global success when the first Macintosh 128K was launched? SIB |

→ *Design Competence, Design Management, Strategic Design*

FLYER

Flyers are leaflets that advertise mainly local services and upcoming events. They are usually distributed to people on the street, placed in mailboxes or on car windshields. Computers and the Internet now make it possible to also send flyers cost-efficiently via e-mail. Their designs have to be eye-catching, attractive, and immediately understood. Since flyers are usually designed to be stylish and reflect current notions of attractiveness, they are an excellent source of discovering new (→) trends. CH |

→ *Advertisement, Poster Design*

FOOD DESIGN

Food design is a vast subject. It covers the many and varied services involving food and nutrition including the subject of designer food, in other words, artificial food. (→) Industrial design (kitchen appliances and all things involved in food preparation and presentation both domestically and industrially), (→) packaging design, and advertising all add to and influence the form and function of food; they whet the appetite and simplify or complicate preparation and handling. Moreover, food technology goes beyond simple food production; it also involves technical, chemical and genetic modifications.

The category of food design is, of course, always about food and about design, but that connection still permits quite distinct activities to be included. There are food stylists who implement their talents and use various ploys so that the ingredients and dishes in photographs make your mouth water. Food design is not only important when illustrating recipes or creating good product advertising; images in supermarkets also function as consumer support. The old-fashioned corner grocery store used to give customers tips for the kitchen for cooking, storing, and preparing food while selling its familiar goods. Today this information is often either missing, or it is conveyed by packaging and other visual and text-based promotional material. This also applies to menus or the layout of a restaurant, especially for visitors in foreign countries.

Cooks can also be food designers. The most important design prize, the Lucky Strike Designer Award, was awarded in 2006 to the Spanish chef Ferran Adrià, who creates dishes in new, completely unexpected forms and specializes in culinary foams. In Asia, the arrangement of a meal according to form and color is a highly regarded practice with a long tradition. Much skill and attention is given to carving fruit and vegetables into decorative shapes. Food design is not just a concern for haute cuisine; it is very much an everyday matter. Moreover, with increased industrial production, almost all food today is the result of a deliberate design process.

There are a variety of reasons for designing food, some of which are very old. For example, bread in the shape of a braid once symbolized the sacrifice of hair. Even when the knowledge of a specific form's origins is lost, it often continues to be used. Besides the symbolic or emotional connotations, there are more mundane reasons behind particular shapes. These reasons can involve simulation (gummy bears), production technology (cone-shaped pralines dissolve better), making portioning easier (segments in chocolate bars), convenience (cheese slices the size and shape of bread), shelf life and perishability (a glaze keeps cake fresh and attractive), brand identity (such as (→) logos on cookies, examples of (→) branding in the literal sense of the word), and advertising (extra coloring gives yogurt its desirable fruity appearance). Sensual factors such as the sound, feel, and color of food are important in all food design, regardless of the target group.

Besides being purely nutritional, food is a significant part of religious, cultural, and social identity. Ways of eating, the type of food and how it is presented are important to identity and cultural difference (forbidden or required by religion; traditional or regional specialties; chopsticks or fork; fast food or haute cuisine). These factors are rarely static, as social shifts also affect food culture and introduce new products to the market. A mobile society loves take-away coffee, and as more women enter the workforce, supermarkets will increasingly fill their shelves with convenience foods that can be prepared quickly. The style of an era is reflected not only in literature, art, and architecture, but also in day-to-day objects—and in the most day-to-day thing of all: our food. KWE |

→ Olfactory Design, Packaging Design, Sensuality

Catterall, C. 1999. *Food, design and culture.* London: Laurence King.
Stummerer, S., and M. Hablesreiter. 2005. *Food Design: Von der Funktion zum Genuss.* Vienna: Springer.

FORM

Form is shape organized in the service of content. It is a term with a long and contentious history in the theory of aesthetics, for the issues of whether form is a materia or a mental construct, whether form serves specific or a universal content, and whether organization is a natural or an artificial order, are fundamental to the very definition of how works of art, architecture, and design become meaningful entities. The concept of form encompasses the immutable entities of Plato's metaphysics, the structural substrate of Aristotle's theory of tragedy, the material-based practices celebrated by Henri Focillon, Clive Bell's ahistorical, abstract, compositional relationships, and the organic morphologies of D'Arcy Thompson and his successors. In this sense, the definition of form is as variable as the epochs that have struggled to define it.

Rudolf Arnheim, the renowned professor of the psychology of art, tells a story of how he learned to write. In Berlin during the Weimar Republic, the young scholar was the film critic for the *Weltbühne* cultural review. He would watch, for example, a performance by Chaplin, walk back to the *Weltbühne* offices, and, in the span of a few hours have to write out a complete review, fully polished, for the next morning's edition. How did he produce what have since become legendary critical essays? The compositions were forged—not actually written but given definite shape, like a piece of sculpture—during the nightly walks. Arnheim formed a mental image of the final piece. He did not imagine actual textual fragments or key words, but rather he sculpted his narrative, gave it mental-visual structure. The structure was the content; it was sufficiently complete to offer a comprehensive image of the finished work—how it would begin, how it would develop, and how it would end. The form determined whether an essay would be linear or curve back on itself, whether it would have discrete divisions or flow seamlessly, whether it would balance along a central spine, or reach out precipitously with occasional counter-gestures to reestablish balance, and so on. This sculptural shape, with its fine-grained articulations, this precise "form," was the essential essay; typing it was transcription or decoding.

"Form is the visual shape of content." This is the definition (originally by the painter Ben Shahn) Arnheim cites for the concept that figured so productively in his own creative practice. And this position is widely held. In this view, form is a very particular class of configurations, namely those that are visualized thought (→ *Visualization*). As such, form is a kind of cognition rendered as a precisely shaped entity. If such an entity sounds abstract, it is because abstraction is a key attribute of form. Form is precisely not the actual concretization—that is, materialization—of a concept or notion, but rather its dematerialized conceptual sibling (→ *Virtuality*). Form is not the cast bronze figure, the molded plastic cup, the wooden bed, or the written text. Form is a mental, not physical, construct.

The historical roots of this particular conception of form are found in Plato's metaphysics. Plato evokes two distinct worlds, the World of Becoming and the World of Being. The former is the world as we experience it, a collection of individual objects fabricated by craftsmen and made of physical material with its attendant transitory nature and association with the "unreliable" nature of sense impressions. In the World of Becoming colors change in different light conditions, perspective foreshortens apparent length, hot and cold are context-specific sensations, dimension is only as fixed as the unit measure, objects degrade over time, and so on. The World of Becoming, as the name suggests, is ever changing. In contrast, the World of Being is immutable. Whereas the World of Becoming is accessed through the senses, the World of Being is accessed through reason; it alone contains the laws of mathematics, the five Euclidean solids, and the universal abstract constructs—the so-called Platonic forms—that underlie the actual things that comprise the inferior material world. For example, when a craftsman makes a wooden bed he is modeling his design on some essential configuration that is common to all beds. This configuration is the bed's "form," and this unwavering bed-form is a permanent element in the eternal World of Being. For Plato, who privileged reason over sensation, our material world was in fact less real, and certainly less perfect, than the very abstract world of forms. Plato's world of forms was the product of a craftsman-like demigod; subsequent neo-Platonic thinkers would come to associate the unchanging order of the World of Being with God, the Christian craftsman of the heavens.

Despite the strangeness of Plato's conception to our contemporary sense of the real, the notion of a world of universal abstract forms that somehow exists outside of material specificity is resurrected whenever the argument is made for universal perceptional constants (→ *Perception*). The primary geometric forms (particularly the circle and the square)—famously described by the Roman architect Vitruvius, and even more famously depicted by Leonardo da Vinci, as the geometric constants inherent in the human body itself—were used late into the Renaissance to plan churches and other sacred structures, precisely because these geometries were thought to resonate with the eternal forms of the heavenly orbs. At the dawn of twentieth-century Modernism (→ *Modernity*), the architect Le Corbusier offered a thoroughly neo-Platonic argument for a formal vocabulary of Euclidean primary solids by suggesting that if he showed a white billiard ball to anyone on earth, the immediate sensation that would be awakened would be unmediated "sphericalness." The presumed lack of intervening cultural considerations, the universality and timelessness of this Platonic sensation, was precisely the ground that modernism sought on which to erect a timeless, universal formal language. Many modernist designers, artists, and architects spent their design talents minimizing any expression of material, gravity, and assembly (for example, the preference for smooth surface treatments, the lack of the classical tripartite composition with a clear top, middle, and bottom, and the general distain for overt signs of craftsmanship); this can be understood as a strategy for nudging an actual material artifact as close as possible to a presumed universal, immaterial, and eternal language of pure form.

A significant consequence of imagining form as existing outside, or just behind, or hovering above, the world of concrete things is the tenuous relationship that results between form and content. If form is universal and abstract it cannot easily be the carrier of individualized and concrete meanings. Aristotle, Plato's student, initiated this distinction between form and content in describing the role of form in the crafting of a dramatic work. In his *Poetics,* Aristotle described form as the shape of the plot or structure of a dramatic work rather than the actual specific narrative material. That is, all (good) tragedies shared common formal/ structural attributes, even though the actual narrative content of any two (good) tragedies varied significantly. The integrity and unity of the formal structure of a given dramatic work was the basis for critical valuation. Such an (→) aesthetic doctrine that places primary value on the formal attributes of a work of art or design is known as "formalism." Formalism attempts to peel away (or "see through" or "dig below": the metaphors vary) the layers of meaning, connotation, association, referentiality, and instrumentality—layers that collectively might be called "content." Formalism is not typically interested in the "billiard-ness" of the billiard ball.

A good example of privileging form over (explicit) content is the work of the English art critic and theorist Clive Bell. In 1914, Bell published his influential book *Art,* which opened with a chapter titled "The Aesthetic Hypothesis." The hypothesis in question is that all art—and Bell includes works of architecture and design as art—has one, and only one, common attribute. This attribute is "significant form." Significant form is not the idiosyncratic, medium-specific, representational content of an artwork. Rather it is the architectonic arrangement of line and color, shape and proportion, so that a certain sensation is evoked in the beholder, the sensation that Bell calls "aesthetic emotion." It would take us quite far afield to unpack Bell's notion of aesthetic emotion; suffice it to say that it is the experience that sensitive souls have in front of artworks, and since it is caused by materially disparate things made by disparate individuals with individual motivations and for disparate purposes (ranging, in Bell's text, from Sumerian sculpture, to Gothic cathedrals, to paintings by Cézanne), the aesthetic emotion must necessarily have its cause in some non-material, non-biographical, non-representational attribute. This attribute is form.

It is ironic and revealing that Bell's formalist theory can not be fully appreciated without understanding the milieu in which he was writing (the last thing a committed formalist would accept is that formalism is the product of historical circumstances). Bell's generation of art critics were trying to make sense of a number of late-nineteenth-century artists (most notably Cézanne, but also Gauguin, Picasso, and Matisse) who themselves were confronting a crisis of representation triggered by the rise of photography. Formalism established a new agenda for art and design, in which the evocation of significant form trumped the replication of nature's figures. Bell's aesthetic hypothesis paved the way for approaching and appreciating the "non-objective" compositions of Vasily Kandinsky and Paul Klee, the "neo-plastic" abstractions of Piet Mondrian and Gerrit Rietveld, the purist paintings of Amédée Ozenfant, and the geometric formalism legible in products designed by the (→) Bauhaus masters including the chairs by Marcel Breuer, the lamps by Wilhelm Wagenfeld, and the table products by Marianne Brandt.

By the mid-1920s, in an impressive art-theoretical rear-garde assault, formalist precepts even came to dominate photography and film, the two media that, because of their marriage to the overwhelming texture and detail of uncomposed reality, initially seemed impervious to formalist design strategies. A seminal text in this assault was undoubtedly Rudolf Arnheim's *Film as Art* (1932), in which the then new medium of the moving image was theoretically liberated from being a mere mirror of reality, and reintroduced as a fully temporal artform, subject to many of the same formal compositional rules as music and dance. The avant-garde films of Hans Richter, in which patches of light on a dark field were choreographed in a non-narrative temporal dance, are celebrated by Arnheim as vital experiments in formalist cinema.

Formalism's strength was its weakness: as form expanded to become the dominant aesthetic criteria for myriad art-and-design practices, its interpretive and generative capacity became proportionally diluted. Formalism became paired with—and is still frequently paired with—unflattering adjectives such as "empty," "meaningless," "imposed," "unmotivated," and so on, reflecting the high cost that formalism seemed to impose on design work in terms of shunning any kind of contextual, cultural, and material specificity.

A remarkable attempt to redeem form from imposed empty meaninglessness was *The Life of Forms in Art (La vie des formes)* written in 1934 by the French art historian Henri Focillon. Focillon's project was to return to form a (→) material as well as a (→) craft basis, to reunite form and content, and to preserve an autonomous history for form. Form never exists without its material body, wrote Focillon. Without material, form is "little better than a vista in the mind, a mere speculation." Physical material and its associated techniques constitutes the life force of the world of forms. To use Focillon's terminology, form is always "incarnated." Material is transmuted in the process of becoming artistic form; the wood of the statue is no longer the wood of the tree, marble no longer belongs to the cliffs, bricks are divorced from the clay pit. Technique is the transformative agent, and technique is specific to a material condition (Focillon goes so far as to distinguish between an engraved line and an etched line; they are two different forms, with two genealogies.) Creative activity in any material medium immediately partakes in that medium's unique formal history, and these histories can be mapped and described in much the same way as any economic, political, or social history. But history, Focillon points out, is not unilinear; the lives of forms plot their own graphs that may or may not coincide with the lifelines of, say, political upheaval or scientific discovery. It is in this sense that the life of form retains a degree of autonomy and avoids becoming merely a by-product of social and cultural practices, that is, all billiards, no ball.

Focillon's use in his title of a biological metaphor to describe the evolution of form is largely rhetorical; he does not subscribe to an actual organic or biological model as the basis of form. But there is a powerful trend in the theory of form that posits precisely this: that form is the organic result of forces acting on a given situation. The landmark text in this vein (although certainly not the first instance of this conception) is the often glossed, albeit less read, exhaustive tome by the English zoologist and mathematician D'Arcy Wentworth Thompson entitled *On Growth and Form* (written in 1917 and revised in 1942). Thompson was broadly and deeply interested in the morphology of organisms, how "the forms of living things can be explained by physical considerations ... and to realize that in general no organic forms exist save such as are in conformity with physical and mathematical laws." All forms in nature, and all changes in natural forms, are the product of forces acting on matter and therefore the form of organic matter can be described (if not actually explained, since this is a metaphysical, not scientific, problem) in the language of natural science. Thompson's reach and research were breathtaking. It included the morphology of cells, the structure of tissue, the geometry of falling drops of liquid, the construction of bee hives, and behavior of thin film membranes. For designers, the chapters on form and the strength of materials offered the clearest demonstration of the logic of organic form by showing how animal forms are structurally optimized with regard to gravity and dynamic loads. For Thompson, form is unveiled as the result of an organism's accommodation to the force vectors of the immediate natural environment. For each set of vectors there is only one optimal form that nature unfailingly selects.

It is, of course, ontologically tricky to transfer Thompson's lessons from the realm of nature to the work of human agents, but faulty ontology has not prevented the concept of "organic form" from entering the designer's vocabulary. The architect Louis Sullivan's dictum "form follows function" was intended to advance his belief in an organic ornamentalism (→ Ornamentation) that echoed the integrity of natural systems. Frank Lloyd Wright famously coined the term "organic architecture" to describe the assumed "natural" fit between his architectural forms and the American cultural and geological landscape. Structural determinism, in which the loads acting on a structure "dictate" the resultant form, has historically been a privileged design methodology, precisely because form appears to be organically mandated, rather than arbitrarily chosen, by the combined action of the forces of nature and the nature of materials. The large-span concrete structures by Italian engineer Pier Luigi Nervi, the bridges by Swiss structural engineer Robert Maillart, and, most spectacularly, the inverted hanging tensile study models invented by Spanish architect Antonio Gaudí to help determine the form of his buildings, fall into this taxonomy of a near-sacred methodology.

But the profound potential of D'Arcy Thompson's conflation of mathematics and biology can only be fully appreciated with current extraordinary advances in computational and mathematical modeling, developmental biology, artificial intelligence, and computer-numerically-controlled fabrication technologies. These apparently diverse fields have found common cause in an area of study termed "Emergence." "Emergence" investigates morphogenesis (the genesis of form) from an evolutionary perspective (→ Design Process). It investigates structures that typically involve relatively large numbers of simple actors following rule-bound behavior to construct highly complex systems with attributes that cannot be reduced backwards to the component parts (→ Complexity, System). For example, ants and termites produce massively complex artifacts without anything like a building plan; birds form flocks and fish form schools with obvious coherent formal properties, but without any centralized design; when we run across a busy street our entire physiological system recalibrates itself without any conscious agency. Such forms "emerge" from iterative, rule-bound entities acting in and on a given environment. These entities and environments can be modeled mathematically, feed-back loops can be scripted, and the iterative process can be enacted and visualized in a digital environment (→ Heuristics). If fabrication parameters are incorporated as part of the system's generative logic, the resulting forms can be output in material using computer-guided machinery (laser cutters, routers, mills, three-dimensional printers, and so on). Morphogenetic models can be used to study the behaviors of large metropolitan regions to simulate the ecological consequences of urban policies; they can be used to optimize structural and mechanical systems in buildings and to rethink the form of business organizations.

The biomorphic forms and complex geometries associated with the most sophisticated emergence (→) research are showing up in contemporary design with remarkable frequency. Yet this author is quite certain that the biomorphic shapes of certain contemporary couches, tennis shoes, cars, shampoo bottles, watches, briefcases, water bottles, backpacks, and baby carriages are best treated under a term other than "form" (→ Gimmick). KK |

→ Complexity, Construction, Function

Arnheim, R. 1954. *Art and visual perception*. Berkeley: Univ. of California Press.
Bell, C. 1914. *Art*. London: Chatto and Windus.
Focillon, H. 1934. *La vie des formes*. Paris: Presses Universitaires de France.
Hensel, M., A. Menges, and M. Weinstock. 2004. *Emergence; Morphogenetic design strategies*. Special issue of *Architectural Design* 74, no. 3 (2004).
Lee, D. trans. 1977. *Plato: Timaeus and Critias*. London: Penguin.
Thompson, D. 1948. *On growth and form*. Cambridge, United Kingdom: Cambridge Univ. Press.

FUNCTION

Function comes from the Latin functio, *meaning performance or execution. Webster's dictionary defines function in a design context as: "a philosophy of design (as in architecture) holding that form should be adapted to use, material, and structure." This definition extends the (→) semantic field to include purpose, defined as to propose, that is something set up as an object or end to be attained. With regard to design, we can assume that function represents the goal of an objective's intended result: function is the goal of an action.*

Function is a central component of design, involving not only the technical and practical performance of a product but also aspects of (→) aesthetics, communication, politics, and economy amongst others. To understand the history of design as a discipline, it is necessary to address the various ways in which the status of function has been discussed and debated. Each design practitioner will have an explicit or implicit personal stance regarding function.

For a long time, architectural theory influenced, indeed dominated, how the concept of function was used in the design context (→ Architectural Design). From the Renaissance to the nineteenth century, architectural discourse drew on the ancient Roman pronouncement—as passed down in Vitruvius' *De architectura libri decem (The Ten Books of Architecture)*, from the first century BC—that a building should be robust, useful and beautiful. Vitruvius differentiated between *firmitas, utilitas* and *venustas*, which respectively describe the technical side of architecture, the purpose of the building, and its aesthetic appearance. Leon Battista Alberti codified these three objectives of good architecture into a norm that persisted far into the nineteenth century. Design theories since the (→) Arts & Crafts movement have analyzed and developed this notion further, studying the relationship between (→) beauty and technical functionality, the contribution of art and real (→) usability.

It is tempting to speculate that the word function would probably never have acquired such centrality and privilege in the theory of design if the phrase "form follows function" had not become one of design's most famous sayings. The phrase was first coined by the American architect Louis Henry Sullivan in his essay "The Tall Office Building Artistically Considered," and quickly acquired the status of axiom.

In fact, it is and has always been intrinsic to how designers understand their role that function is inherent to design. Design is a means of fulfilling an intention. Drawing a distinction between the formal and commercial aspects of function challenges the basic notion of their unity. Pronouncements such as these distinguish between design and function in a way that suggests an increase in (→) value or prestige if an object is not only aesthetically pleasing (as in the sense of a stylish surface), but also functional (as in the fulfillment of a practical purpose).

The "form follows function" aphorism is problematic here. Linguistic and even intellectual distinctions are frequently made between (→) form and function—yet in reality, they are inextricably linked, two sides of the same coin. An object's form cannot be peeled off like a sticky label to reveal the naked function; any changes to an object's form are usually accompanied by changes to its function. Take for instance the Phonosuper SK 4, the combined radio and record player designed by Hans Gugelot, Otl Aicher, and Dieter Rams in 1955 for Braun. This record player went beyond the standard formal criteria of that time, consequently changing the function of the object. It not only provided a means of playing records or listening to the radio, but also became a decorative element that contributed to the overall interior design of a room. In other words, it became an object with which consumers could make a statement about how they perceived themselves and how they wanted to be perceived.

The word "follows" seems to be the source of some of the confusion surrounding the phrase "form follows function." It implies that there is a strict and logical sequence: B emerges after A is defined. Yet (→) beauty is not a consequence; it is something that is perceived. Nor is form a consequence; it is not inevitable and does not arise automatically after function has been achieved. It is the product of a sequence of active procedures and conscious decisions, and not the inevitable result of that which remains after all unnecessary elements have been removed—just as a sculpture is more than what remains after an artist has chiseled away bits of superfluous stone. Form cannot follow function because function is not a constant; it is a variable contingent on a user's observation and application. In fact, the reverse can often apply—that function follows form. The back of a chair is a perfect place to hang a coat, and a juicer can be used as a decorative element to impress guests (→ *Non Intentional Design*).

(→) Functionalism is function's pragmatic escalation from practicality to something absolute—an ideology that attempts to keep function as unadulterated as possible. Phrases such as "pure function" refer to the belief that the nature of an object is its function; objects that do not express their essential functions as clearly as possible are therefore "corrupt," distortions of reality.

This view becomes highly questionable when not only the functional object's beauty, but also its truth or authenticity, is attributed solely to its perfect fulfillment of function. When judged entirely against functionality, design is accorded an absolute—the harshest critics even call it polemic—total claim to being "right," and prioritizes general methods over responding to particular contexts and problems. This is one of the central critiques regarding the legitimacy of twentieth-century Modernism (→ Modernity). High Modernism maintained that it was able to address individual cases without relying on preexisting solutions; however, in actual practice, modernist techniques often resulted in recurring examples of formulaic mediocrity. Critics of functionalism trumpeted these kinds of failures untiringly, particularly after Adorno's lecture on "Functionalism Today" and Alexander Mitscherlich's *Die Unwirtlichkeit unserer Städte* (The Inhospitality of the Modern City). In the 1970s, architects and designers in Italy and the US began abandoning the sober formalism of modernism and embracing ironic reactions to the fetish of functionality (→ Postmodernism).

This all boils down to the fact that a universally accepted definition of function will never be achieved. Any object will come with multiple functions and function potentials (→ Affordance) and design has to determine how to prioritize these. In other words, the concept of function is an abstraction—*functions* are the reality. When used by consumers, an object often acquires more functions than the designer originally intended. Most chairs in reality serve as stepladders or as places to hang clothing. The quality of a design is evident in how clearly it distinguishes between practical, aesthetic, communicative, marketing, business management, or even corporate strategic functions, and how well it establishes and develops the importance of particular aspects of these functions. [RS] |

→ *Non Intentional Design, Use*

Adorno, T. W. 1979. Functionalism today. Trans. Jane Newman and John Smith. *Oppositions* 17:31–41.

Mitscherlich, A. 1965. *Die Unwirtlichkeit unserer Städte*. Frankfurt am Main: Suhrkamp.

Sullivan, L. H. 1896. The tall office building artistically considered. *Lippincott's Magazine* (March).

Venturi, R, D. Scott Brown D., and S. Izenour. 1972. *Learning from Las Vegas: The forgotten symbolism of architectural form*. Cambridge, MA: MIT Press.

Vitruvius, P. M. 1960. *The Ten Books on Architecture*. Trans. M. H. Morgan. New York: Dover Publications.

FUNCTIONALISM

Functionalism played a very important role in the development of design as a practice, process, and academic discipline. There are at

As immortalized by the famous statement "form follows function," functionalism dictated that function was to define the logic of design and, more specifically, of (→) form. This statement necessarily implies that function is an element that can be clearly defined or at the very least, can be represented as a *least three plausible reasons for this. Firstly, in attempting to describe function objectively, it was possible to view design itself as objective and thereby avoid a sometimes arbitrary or accidental subjectivity, something that would continue to be attributed to art. Secondly, by celebrating function as the fulfillment of a particular (→) need, design could liberate itself from the merely decorative aspect of the arts, and thus demonstrate its alliance with industry and the world of commodities and production. Thirdly, design (like any form of thinking or acting, at least on a superficial level) needed a frame of reference in order to stake out and shape the territory in which it operated and to avoid fizzling out in formlessness. In other words, it needed to develop a focus, a central perspective, or conceptual vocabulary that clearly integrated the (→) theory of design with the (→) practice of design.*

basic consensus in the perception of designed artifacts. Initially this implication seems quite plausible within the framework of the physical world. For example, a pair of glasses is supposed to improve vision; a car, to be driven; a cigarette lighter, to light cigarettes; a lamp, to shed light; a cup, to hold liquid; a chair, to be sat on; a sign, to be recognizable; writing, to be legible, and so on.

On closer inspection, however, it becomes clear that considering say, the function of a car as simply a means of providing transport, overlooks the (arguably secondary but nonetheless important) practical requirements of the car as related to safety, comfort, speed, lighting, and so on. To put it another way, designating legibility as the sole function of writing is incorrect in many cases, since it can also be designed to facilitate or prolong comprehension, to evoke certain emotions, connections, and reactions from the reader. A definition that took into account the layered multiplicity of function would considerably expand the semantic framework of the term, and rightly so; consequently, a discourse on design that appealed to this broader definition of function would rapidly become much more complex.

One could, on the one hand, find and explain countless examples of how historical and contemporary design has mastered such functions, fundamentally qualified functionality, and even developed and designed new functions within this narrow framework of functionalism. On the other hand, it is also evident that very many different formal solutions have been found for the same technical functions. There are thousands of different chairs on which one can sit almost equally well, and innumerable models of cars that can all be driven, and perhaps even equally quickly, comfortably, and safely. Countless forms of writing and their variants enable one to read and communicate. We all know this, and so the question arises what differences in functions could justify such a variety of forms.

This question, however, opens up entirely new areas within the territory mapped out for function. For example, one function of a market is that it caters to people living in a specific era—but markets also enable companies to make profits, and thus develop their own logistical structures and criteria for evaluating the relative function of their products. In other words, the functional design of a product, if it is to prosper on the market, has to submit to the function of that market. Although the technical functions of the product and those of the market are not necessarily mutually exclusive, neither do they always coincide or reinforce each other. Consequently, a new, highly functional safety feature for a car may not be introduced by a company for reasons of cost, or the introduction of a more powerful engine capable of higher speeds may be contraindicated for a certain segment of the market, and so on. Moreover, in the competition between (→) brands, it occasionally happens that functions are invented simply as a feature to differentiate a company and its product from its competitors, if only temporarily, and thereby ensure market success and increased profits.

Design has demonstrably done much to satisfy this expanded definition of (→) function. More than that, design has integrated another large aspect of functionalism: a heightened understanding about the circumstances of our physical environment. In particular, design has addressed the need to develop durable products that can be repaired, reused, and recycled; responsible energy uses; and biodegradable materials (→ *Sustainability*). It is clear, however, that there are considerable contradictions that may arise from this new aspect of function—for example, a specific material that is ecologically friendly may prove itself to be too costly or ergonomically unsound.

Thus it becomes clear that the representation of function as neutral—which is, after all, necessary for "form follows function" to define itself as a clear guiding principle—is an illusion; the logical consistency it was supposed to provide for design is no longer tenable.

This is particularly true today, as the replacement of mechanical tools by digital technologies has made even the simple justification of sequences and volumes largely obsolete. A typewriter, for example, had a minimum volume that was determined by the demands of the structure and mechanism; there was a certain pressure that had to be applied to the keys, and it was required to accommodate standard paper sizes and adult fingers. With the advent of the word processor, these requirements suddenly disappeared, and it became possible to imagine a typing device too small for human fingers to manipulate. These developments changed the direction of design so that it had to focus even more emphatically on the conditions of use and human limitations.

With all these expansions to the category of the functional, however, something else becomes clear—that functionalism, for ideological reasons, neglects to fully address the (→) complexity of function within the context of human living. In other words, functionalism ignores the idea that a pair of glasses should be designed to flatter the face; that cars are regarded as status symbols; that lamps are treated in many homes like sculptures; that texts stimulate emotional responses and represent forms of play. The wishes, fears, dreams, and needs of people should never be overlooked when considering in the world of function, for it is precisely these emotional attributes that will be stimu-lated or alleviated by the use and possession of functional prod-ucts. The current practice of design does indeed sometimes op-erate within such a degree of complexity that many argue that the notion of function has become too vague and diffuse—some even question whether the concept of function is still suit-able as a primary focus of design today.

The question of functionalism is made still more complex when it is discussed in relation to the realm of (→) ethics. As far back as the late 1950s, the German philosopher and sociologist The-odor W. Adorno persuasively attacked the formalism of design based on function as a form of ideology by arguing that National Socialism in Germany and Fascism in Italy could, according to the dictates of functionalism, be considered as having func-tioned "well." Fred Leuchter, a recently deceased designer of electric chairs in the United States, said himself that he always designed these lethal machines to be functional and ergo-nomic.

In the light of such considerations, it is clear that the category of function as an overarching organizing principle might initially have been overestimated in the early discussions of design, and that it is now necessary to discuss function using very different criteria. At the same time, the contradictions inherent to a dis-course on function in the field of design—just like those in which technology, architecture, and human beings themselves operate—have not yet been resolved. On the one hand, design should always be subject to the dictates of function because there will always be needs that require solutions in the form of designs. We still need lamps to give light, vehicles to transport us from place to place, signs to be understandable and provide information. On the other hand, it should be acknowledged that designers can sometimes best express their creativity and achieve (→) innovation precisely when something fails to func-tion. All of this suggests that the category of function will always be interpreted in various (and at times ambiguous and contra-dictory) ways. HS |

→ *Modernity, Use*

FUNCTIONAL MODEL

A functional model is a true-to-scale (→) copy of an existing piece of equipment or a concrete example of a planned device. In con-trast to a design model, a functional model is specifically pro-duced to either demonstrate an existing device's technical prin-ciples or test functional performance during the design process. The (→) model's external appearance is secondary at this stage. DPO |

→ *Product Development, Prototype, Testing*

FURNITURE DESIGN

Furniture design encompasses the micro-architectures of seating, reclining, storage, and display. Its products include chairs, benches, couches, stools, beds, cabinets, shelving, desks, and tables.

In the West, the history of furniture is strongly rooted in temporal functionality; bureaus evolved from stacked wooden crates carted from residence to residence by nomadic rulers, and even as late as the seventeenth century, chairs were placed around the perimeter to be pulled into social groupings as needed. In the East, the practice of privileging space over furniture largely endured until the integration of Western conventions in the years after the Second World War.

In tandem with the practical forces behind the evolution of furniture (the affordance of temporary comfort), hierarchical distinctions between pieces of status and pieces of service became manifest in typologies (state bed vs. sleeping pallet) and craftsmanship (→ *Craft*). The self-conscious succession of styles began in the Renaissance with references to antiquity, and received added momentum with the discoveries at Herculaneum and Pompeii in the eighteenth century. By the nineteenth century, the notion of attaching cultural and political values to furnishings was common practice, yielding a series of vogues ranging from Neo-Renaissance to Egyptian and Gothic revival. Another motivation for the accelerated rate of stylistic shifts was the introduction of mass production with the Industrial Revolution. Both anxiety about the loss of handwork and enthusiasm for the potential of a more democratic means of manufacture and distribution were evident at cusp of the twentieth century, with (→) Art Nouveau resisting rationalization, Mission style taking a more equivocal stance toward the machine, and (→) Art Deco enthusiastically embracing it. More socially ambitious were the early modernists (→ *Modernity*) who actively referenced the changes wrought on daily life by mass production. Populist innovations associated with the (→) Bauhaus, such as Marcel Breuer's 1926 Wassily Chair (said to be inspired by tubular steel used for bicycles) radically changed the material landscape of furniture design. Over the course of the twentieth century, the overt industrial character of these early experiments was gradually tempered, notably by the Scandinavian predilection for natural materials and organic lines.

In the nascent twenty-first century, furniture is in a state that might be best described as one of extrapolation, clearly profiting from the late twentieth-century's art furniture movements, themselves built on the foundations of 1960s Pop Art. The biggest influences on contemporary furniture, however, can be traced to the 1980s. This was the decade that saw the emergence of postmodern (→ *Postmodernism*) historicist styles, forays into the field by prominent architects (Michael Graves, Robert Venturi, and Denise Scott Brown), increased experimentation with irregular mass and materiality (Gaetano Pesce's poured-resin

furniture), and the acceptance of furniture as functional sculpture (Scott Burton's bluntly carved stone seating and the Memphis group's iconoclastic furnishings). Collectively, this diverse
group of architects, artists, and designers created important
precedents for liberties increasingly normative in the design industry today.

Recent work by furniture designers exhibits a deliberately tenuous relationship to the qualities of stability and solidity once
requisite of tables, chairs, beds, wall screens, and shelves. No
longer are precious woods and rare metals considered to be the
only appropriate ($\rightarrow$) materials for furniture. Today, materials are
exploited not only for their practicality—a Bauhaus concern—
but also for their narrative and their structural capacities, be
they cut felt in the case of Toord Boontje, stiffened rope in the
case of Marcel Wanders, wood and fabric scraps derived from
the *favelas* of São Paolo, as per Fernando and Humberto Cam-
pana, or the "twig" screens of extruded plastic used by Erwan
and Ronan Bouroullec.

Today, subtlety and singular purpose have given way to multiple
readings, reflecting the larger social experience of plurality and
simultaneity fostered by the proliferation of communication media, from the World Wide Web to television to satellite radio.
There is evidence that designers are responding to the non-linear behaviors of these media by collapsing historical references
into modern materials such as clear plastic, exemplified in the
Louis Ghost Chair (1996) by Philippe Starck, the French designer
known for his Swiftian games of scale. More overtly critical are
works such as Dutch designer Maarten Baas' series of charred,
blackened furniture entitled Smoke (2004) that comments on
destruction and memory.

Distinctions are also blurring in the programmatic applications of
furniture. There is a weakening of the segregation of furnishings
produced for institutions and offices and those produced for the
residence: the contract furniture industry is taking its cues from
the home as the work week grows longer; and it is increasingly
common to find office furniture (such as Bill Stumpf's iconic
1994 Aeron Chair) in the home, now that the computer has become
a domestic appliance. This process has been aided and abetted
with the rise of companies that allow consumers to purchase furniture formerly only available through professional decorators and
designers. Even firms that specialize in contract furnishing fabrics
offer select lines of their upholstery to the general public. In addition, the emergence of online retail has accelerated the practice
of marketing directly to the customer.

The proliferation of print ($\rightarrow$) publications devoted to design can
also be credited with engendering widespread popular interest

in mid-century modern furniture, once considered a rarified taste. In some cases, this was done by plumbing historical archives and in others by marking anniversaries with special sales promotions, as with the Eames lounge chair in 2006. Furthermore, mass-market commercial chains have begun to commission designers, normally showcased at boutiques, to create affordable versions of their work for the mass market.

Furniture has always served as a laboratory for ideas about living. Today, however, the rapid absorption of those ideas into the marketplace as (→) social brand marks of taste has accelerated both the pace of experiment and the frequency of stylistic revivals. Unique to this moment is the conflation of both. SY |

→ Interior Design, Product Design, Retail Design

Antonelli, P., ed. 2001. *Workspheres: Design and contemporary work styles.* New York: Museum of Modern Art.
Schouwenberg, L. 2004. *Hella Jongerius.* London: Phaidon.
Yelavich, S. 2007. *Contemporary world interiors.* London: Phaidon.

FUTURISTIC DESIGN

The term "futurism" was coined by the Italian poet Filippo Tommaso Marinetti, who published the "Manifesto of Futurism" in 1909 in the French newspaper *Le Figaro*. With this, a name was given to a movement that attracted artists such as Balla, Boccioni, Carrà, and Sant'Elia. These artists called for a radical rejection of social and artistic traditions, an unconditional respect for the new and modern, and a closer relationship between art, architecture, technology, and everyday objects—ideas that gained popularity in Russia and other countries in the following years.

After the Second World War, design theorist Reyner Banham took up the term "futurism" once again, but applied it to the designs of his time rather than the Italian avant-garde. Since then, futuristic design has been used to specify the designs of any period that make prominent reference to a vision of the future. The stylistic characteristics of futuristic designs have been greatly inspired by the emergence of modern technological innovations in the fields of space travel, bioscience, and automobile technology, as well as the growing popularity of the science fiction genre. Unlike the concept of (→) innovation however, futuristic design, at least as an aesthetic category, is related to form, surface, and display, but not necessarily to design that is technically or artistically innovative.

Examples of the genre can be found in the (→) aerodynamic designs of early modernists like Gerrit Rietveld and Jean Prouvé, as well the streamlined forms (→ *Streamline Design*) of the 1930s and 1950s. Yet the most significant period for futuristic design by far was the decade between 1960 and 1970. During this time, designs that looked like they came "from the future" were inspired by the race to land on the moon, as well as by new plastics designers like Joe Colombo, Pierre Paulin, and Olivier Mourgue in the product industry, and Paco Rabanne and Pierre Cardin in fashion. Another inspiration for designers was the flourishing

Banham, R. 1960. *Theory and design in the first machine age.* New York: Praeger.

Kries, M., and A. von Vegesack, eds. 2005. *Joe Colombo: Inventing the Future.* Weil am Rhein: Vitra Design Museum.

Schmidt-Bergemann, H. 1993. *Futurismus: Geschichte, Ästhetik, Dokumente.* Reinbek: Rowohlt.

Topham, S. 2003. *Where's my space age.* Munich: Prestel.

genre of science-fiction films. The ($\rightarrow$) set designs for the early James Bond films and Stanley Kubrick's *2001–A Space Odyssey* were some of the most prominent examples. The following decades saw futuristic-looking designs by Shiro Kuramata, Philippe Stark, and Marc Newson, but these were relatively less fashionable in the future-critical 1970s and 1980s. The genre experienced a revival in the 1990s when the miniaturization of technical components, especially in the consumer electronics sector, opened up a new range of possibilities in product-casing design. The decade also saw the introduction of numerous new plastics into the industry. These developments gave the economy new faith in the future-altering power of innovative technologies. Some recent examples of this new form of futuristic design include the Apple computers by Jonathan Ive, furniture designs by Werner Aisslinger and Karim Rashid, and the numerous aerodynamic ($\rightarrow$) redesigns of the automobile industry.

Today, futuristic designs in consumer industries ranging from sports equipment to game consoles are typically directed at young, techno-savvy target audiences. These industries are often as concerned with achieving aesthetic differentiation through futuristic ($\rightarrow$) styling as they are with making actual innovations in technology.

In order to differentiate the uses of the term "futuristic design" in the contemporary context from historical stylistic trends, the term retrofuturism is sometimes used to describe futuristic aesthetics from the past. [MKR]

$\rightarrow$ *Bionics, High Tech, Retro Design*

G

GAME DESIGN

Game design is a complex, multilayered design activity, whereby systems of meaning (games) are created through the design of rule sets resulting in play. As products of human culture, games fulfill a range of needs, desires, pleasures, and uses. As products of design culture, games reflect a host of technological, social, material, formal, and economic concerns. Because rules, when enacted by players, are embodied as the experience of play, game design can be considered a second-order design problem. A game designer only indirectly designs the player's experience by directly designing the rules of play.

The real domain of game design is the (→) aesthetics of interactive systems (→ *Interface Design, System*). As dynamic systems, games produce contexts for interaction with strategic and quantifiable outcomes. This interaction is often digitally mediated (video games are played on computers, consoles, or other digital platforms) but not always, as much of the knowledge basic to the practice of game design applies to the design of nondigital games as well. Long before computers existed, designing games meant creating dynamic systems for players to inhabit. All games, from *Chess* or *Go* to *The Sims* and beyond, are spaces of possibility for players to explore. Designing this space is the focus of game design. Game designers design gameplay, conceiving and designing systems of rules that result in meaningful experiences for players.

While it would be very challenging to describe the fundamental principles of game design, an abbreviated list can help establish the groundwork for an understanding of this highly interdisciplinary practice. Fundamentals include understanding design, systems, and interactivity, as well as player choice, action, and outcome. They include (→) complexity and emergence, game experience, procedural systems, and social game interaction. Finally, they include the powerful connection between the rules of a game and the play the rules create, the pleasures games invoke, the ideologies they embody, and the stories they tell.

If one were to write the rules of the game for game design itself it might read as follows:

· Rules are a fundamental part of any game. Defining the rules of a game and the myriad ways the rules fit together is a key part of a game designer's practice. When rules are combined in specific ways, they create forms of activity for players, called "play." Play is an emergent property of rules: rules combine to create behaviors that are more complex than their individual parts.

· Because games are dynamic systems, they react and change in response to decisions made by players. The design of the rules that guide how, when, and why a player interacts with the system, as well as the kinds of relationships that exist between its parts, forms the basis of a game-design practice.

· Game design is the design of systems of meaning. Objects within games derive meaning from the system of which they are part. Like letters in the alphabet, objects, and actions within a game gain meaning through rules that determine how all of the parts relate. A game designer is responsible for designing the rules that gives these objects meaning.

· Games are made up of game (→) components, which include all of the objects that make up a game world. Components include game characters or markers, the game board, the scoring system, and other objects defined as part of the game system. Game designers must choose which components make up the game, and assign behaviors and relationships to each of these components. Behaviors are simply kinds of rules that describe how an object can act. A game character might be able to run or jump, which are two different kinds of behavior. A door might be assigned an "invisible" behavior, which means that it cannot be seen on screen.

· Game design—when done well—results in the design of meaningful play. Meaningful play in a game emerges from the relationship between player action and system outcome; it is the process by which a player takes action within the designed system of a game and the system responds to the action. The meaning of an action in a game resides in the relationship between action and outcome. The relationship between actions and outcomes in a game are both discernable and integrated into the larger context of the game. Discernability means that a player can perceive the immediate outcome of an action. Integration means that the outcome of an action is woven into the game system as a whole.

· Players want to feel like the choices they make in the game are strategic and integrated. Game designers must design the rules of a game in such a way that each decision a player makes feels connected to previous decisions, as well as to future decisions encountered in the course of play. Degrees of randomness and chance are two tools that game designers have at their disposal to balance the amount of strategic choice a player has in a game. Choice is related to the goal of a game, which is often composed of smaller subgoals a player must meet to win the game. All games have a win-or-loss condition, which indicates what must be achieved in order to end the game. Because all games must have some kind of quantifiable outcome to be considered a game by traditional definitions, defining the win-and-loss states for a game is critical feature of a game's design.

· Game design models player interaction on several levels: human-to-human interaction, human-to-technology interaction, human-to-game interaction, and defines the interface between all three. A game designer must address different types of interaction in a game.

· The core mechanics are the experiential building blocks of player interactivity, which represent the essential moment-to-moment activity of the player, something that is repeated over and over throughout the game. During a game, core mechanics create (→) patterns of behavior, and is the mechanism through which players make meaningful choices. Mechanics include activities like trading, shooting, running, collecting, talking, capturing territory, and so on. Game design relies on the design of compelling, interactive core mechanics.

· Interaction between the player and an input device allows the player to control elements within the game space. Design of the input device is connected to the design of the game interface, which organizes information and allows a player to play the game. A game interface can be simple or complex, but should always provide a player with access to the elements and activities of the game.

· Interaction between different game components is defined by rules that describe what happens when these components interact. Does the ball (component) bounce (rule) off the wall (component), or smash (rule) a hole (object) in it?

· Game design uses an iterative (→) design process: a game is designed through an iterative sequence of modifications to the rules and to the behaviors of game components. Game design follows a cycle of design—playtest—evaluate—modify—playtest—evaluate—modify. It is through iteration that game designers achieve the right balance between challenge, choice, and fun.

· Game designers tune or balance their game, so that it is not too easy or too hard for players to play, and work to create just the right amount of challenge. All games are made up of challenges or obstacles a player must overcome in order to reach the goal's set forth by the game rules.

· Game design involves the design of resources, or game components used by players during the game. Resources can include things like money, health, land, items, knowledge, or ammunition, for example. In some games, resources are parts of systems known as game economies, which determine how resources are managed and circulated, and how many of each resource might exist within a game. The word "economy" does not necessarily refer to currency, but to any collection of pieces, points, cards, creatures, or other items that form the system of a game. A game economy is a set of parts that are won or lost, traded or brokered, hidden and revealed, hoarded or stolen away. In defining economies, game designers must consider both the formal make-up of the economy and how players interact with it.

Games reward players in many different ways, which is one way that a game communicates, or gives feedback to a player about their performance. Game designers have to make decisions about the kinds of rewards they want in their game, on both a moment-to-moment level (did the players know that they killed the monster?) and on a game level (did the players know they won? Or that they raced faster than the last time they played?).

A highly interdisciplinary (→ *Discipline*) endeavor, game design involves collaboration between experts in (→) graphic design (visual design, interface design, information architecture), (→) product design (input and output devices), programming, (→) animation, interactive design (human computer interaction), writing, and audio design (→ *Sound Design*), as well as experts in content areas specific to a game. Game designers must know how to speak the "language" of each of these fields, in order to see the possibilities and constraints of their design. The intersection of constraints from each area with the rules of play shape the game in innumerable ways and drive the design process forward.

Game design requires the design of a possibility space, exemplified through the design of both a system of rules, and a space in which the game is played. The design and organization of space is of central concern to game designers. What kinds of activities and interactions does the game space encourage or discourage? Do players hang out, trade goods, or race through at breakneck speed? What strategic and storytelling opportunities does the space afford, and what forms of navigation does it support? Game spaces allow for and restrict player action, whether the wide-open cityscapes of *Grand Theft Auto*, or the grooved tracks of *Frequency and Amplitude*. As representational systems with spatial dimensions, games give players a chance to build meaning through spatialized interaction. Pass Go, collect $200. Type "N" to move North. Use the D-Pad to control the camera. B-7, hit: You sunk my battleship!

Technology plays a large role in determining the nature and qualities of game spaces. From text-based adventure games and vector-drawn space fields to real-time rendered, physics-enabled 3-D, the (→) affordances and limitations of technology determine a great deal about how game spaces are depicted and inhabited. Technology informs space informs design. KS |

→ *Audiovisual Design, Character Design, Collaborative Design, Complexity, Prototype, Social, Virtual Reality, Virtuality*

Fullerton T., S. Hoffman, and C. Swain. 2004. *Game design workshop: Designing, prototyping, & playtesting games*. San Francisco: CMP Books.
Koster, R. 2004. *A theory of fun for game design*. Scottsdale, AZ: Paraglyph Press.
Raessens, J., and J. Goldstein. 2005. *Handbook of computer game studies*. Cambridge, MA: MIT Press.
Salen, K., and E. Zimmerman. 2003. *Rules of play: Game design fundamentals*. Cambridge, MA: MIT Press.

GARDEN DESIGN

→ *Landscape Design*

GENDER DESIGN

Design has only recently become aware of gender as an issue that influences not only the form and practice of design, but also the effects on the application, use, and purchase of design by women and men. This has long been a point of focus in marketing and (→) market research especially in relation to (→) target groups, but now designers and companies are also gradually beginning to understand that design is incomplete if it does not consider gender.

Gender design is dedicated to the analysis of objects (object here being the general term for all designed products, signs, concepts, and processes) and the relationship between subject and object with regard to their genderization. Not only do design professionals—consciously or unconsciously—design as socially and culturally conditioned gendered beings, but the everyday use of designed objects also involves gender-specific modes of action and behavior. Moreover, projections and desires always possess a gendered subtext. This perspective systematically reveals some more or less hidden or negated gender phenomena, and their effects on design can be explored in order to make them a self-evident element of design research and practice.

The impact of gender in the design context must be considered in its historical, socio-cultural, economical, ecological, and technical dimensions. Students, designers, and marketers in virtually every area of design are all urged to recognize the theoretical, conceptual, empirical, design-related, and practical implications of gender, and to actively address them in their theoretical and practical work. This applies to any kind of design as there is no specific design area that governs the form of communication or of appropriating the methods, theories, and procedures that incorporate gender as an essential category and gender mainstreaming as a standard element into the design process.

The social imbalance of gender roles is evident in design on all levels. Design on both the academic and professional level is still very gender-segregated, and aptly demonstrates the persistence of "special talents" that society has attributed to male and female roles. Thus, there are hardly any female designers in the automobile or capital-goods industries. The few that do work in these fields are largely employed in positions that call for "female talents"—and needless to say, they are not in the technical design department. Men dominate the fields of product and industrial design, while female designers tend to be more successful (though not, generally, as successful as men) in the fields of fashion, accessories, and increasingly, visual communications (at least at the academic level). The influence of constructed gender norms continues to be relevant to the ways in which designs are marketed, purchased, and used, as well.

For the above reasons, it is essential in design education to closely analyze the issue of gender relations on all three levels. These relate to (→) theory, (→) research and the relevant methods, (→) observation, as well as the (→) design process. The following represents some examples for integrating gender issues more thoroughly into the design process:

· Integrate (inter)cultural theories regarding women's and gender studies, but also sociology, psychology, and ethnology into the current discourse on design. This is particularly important to a basic understanding of the gender-constructed subject-object relationship and the interface between people (man/woman) and things, which in turn can help to illuminate the emotional, cultural, and economic requirements necessary for the design process.

· Consider the artifacts and contexts of everyday culture with regards to their gendered implications: private and public space; domestic worlds; the culture of objects; symbol and sign systems; body language and the body politic: designing the body via posture, motor activity; clothing as "second skin"; body design (control, identification, branding); virtual body worlds (cyborgs, "characters," and so on); sexual body images: androgyny, unisex, macho, "girlie."

· Systematically analyze the history of design developments, design movements, and design institutions in relation to gender.

What is a unique to the design discipline (and otherwise only to architecture) is the necessity to associate theoretical and empirical work with one's own creative process. Design practice must consider gender-relevant requirements because it is environments, products, signs, as well as (→) "skills" that possess different varieties and intensities of experience according to gender. Gender is a part of our culture. A gender-free or gender-neutral reality does not exist, everybody is "doing gender" (Judith Butler) every day. For this reason, any design development has to consider a range of different gendered identities, experiences, and interests on the level of design and use.

The question then follows as to whether design contributes to maintaining gender constructions that adhere to the two-gender paradigm, or whether it serves to balance or marginalize them. To date, the creative process of design has ignored the category of gender to an appalling extent. The few exceptions here are products oriented explicitly and intentionally toward a female or male target group. Products that are not marketed towards a gender-specific user group, on the other hand, are rarely examined with regards to their gendered implications, whether they attempt a gender "neutrality," or even look to transcend traditional gender models. UB |

→ Critical Design, Social

Attfield, J., and P. Kirkham, eds. 1995. *A view from the interior: Women & design.* London: Women's Press. (Reprint with new material.)

Butler, J. 1990. *Gender trouble: Feminism and the subversion of identity.* New York: Routledge.

Feuerstein, G. 1997. *Androgynous.* Stuttgart: Axel Menges.

Kirkham, P., ed. 1996. *The gendered object.* Manchester: Manchester Univ. Press.

GESTALTUNG

Gestaltung primarily describes an intervention in an environment that deliberately transforms it. The (→) transformation can occur in concrete, perceivable objects such as spaces,

The German word Gestaltung *(English = de-sign) generally means a purpose-oriented process of transformation. Internationally, the term is associated with Gestalt psychology (German* Gestalt = *form), a branch of psychology founded in Germany at the beginning of the twentieth century.*

objects, or processes, or in theoretical constructions such as ($\rightarrow$) lifestyle, or politically designed social structures.

Gestaltung is mainly the conscious modification of the visual ($\rightarrow$) aesthetics of objects, information, and so on, or the means of giving something an abstract, two- or three-dimensional form.

The term refers to a strategic sequence of actions (the act of or process of designing) or its result (the product, plan, model, presentation, look, or overall design).

The relationship between the English word "design" and the German word *Gestaltung* is ambiguous. They are often used as synonyms in German, yet there is an important difference.

With the onset of factory production in the nineteenth century and the ensuing design of industrially manufactured bulk commodities, the word *Gestaltung* became a job title, as did the German phrases *industrielle Formgebung, Industrie-Entwurf,* or *Werkkunst,* which are all variations on the English phrase "industrial design." These terms were developed to emphasize the difference between ($\rightarrow$) industrial design and the ($\rightarrow$) Arts & Crafts.

The English word ($\rightarrow$) design was rejected increasingly until the 1970s in non-English speaking countries, because of its associations with banal, superficial product cosmetics ($\rightarrow$ *Styling*). Yet, over the last few decades in Europe, the term has become internationally established as the name of a profession as well as its object and/or results. The word "design" has since become a fashionable term that is used and abused in many different areas: designer carpets, designer kitchens, nail design, and so on. Design is a marketing instrument and is implemented as such in every thinkable way, which is why an alternative tendency developed in Germany leading studios and agencies to begin again using the German word *Gestaltung* to distinguish themselves from pure styling and to refer to the complexity of their profession. Yet in international contexts "design" is still used as an equivalent to *Gestaltung.*

The term *Gestalt* found its way into the English due to its associations with the branch of psychology known as Gestalt theory. Gestalt theory is a branch of Gestalt psychology, which is concerned with creating order in psychologically perceptible events. Gestalt psychology is based on theories developed by the philosopher Christian von Ehrenfels in 1890. He questioned, contrary to the popular atomist trend in psychology, whether breaking up a phenomenon into individual parts would actually lead to scientific conclusions concerning the test subject. He documented the qualities of ($\rightarrow$) perception that can be gained by observing the whole. Von Ehrenfels called these "Gestalt qualities" and propagated holistic observation techniques.

At the onset of the twentieth century, Max Wertheimer, Wolfgang Köhler, Kurt Koffka, and Kurt Lewin of the Berlin School further developed this theory and performed extensive experimental research in perception. Their research resulted in the following core hypotheses:

· The whole differs from the sum of its parts.

· Observing the whole differs from the combined perception of the individual parts.

· Elements are interrelated and influence the perception of the whole, regardless of the respective structure of this relationship.

· Belonging to the whole also changes the characteristics of the individual elements.

This theory is called Gestalt theory, partly in order to point out its relevance to scientific areas outside the field of psychology. Theories regarding Gestalt qualities have influenced researchers in different disciplines who were searching for alternative methods to the analyzing of test subjects by means of dividing them into individual elements.

On this basis, Max Wertheimer established the "Gestalt laws," which outline what is visually considered a unit versus what is visually considered a group of separate entities. Borders form, according to Wertheimer, where "qualities intersect" or places where two different qualities come together as seamlessly as possible, with the ensuing whole being as unified as possible.

The law of *Prägnanz* (concision), also called the Law of Good Gestalt, has priority over the other Gestalt laws. The individual visual elements of a figure are joined to form figures *(Gestalten)*, because precise, defined features allow perception systems to connect optical impressions. If the figure is ambiguous, elements are recorded which possess certain distinguishing characteristics, which allows the image to be interpreted as simple and complete, rather than complex and incomplete.

· The Law of Proximity: Elements in spatial proximity are perceived as belonging together.

· The Law of Similarity: Elements that are similar are perceived as belonging together more than elements that are dissimilar.

· The Law of Continuity: Stimuli that appear to be a continuation of previous stimuli are perceived as belonging together. Objects are linked in time, creating an impression of movement.

· The Law of Closure: Single elements that enclose a surface are understood as a unit or pattern. If necessary, gaps are filled or missing information is added in order to complete the figure.

· The Law of Common Fate: Two or more elements are perceived as a figure if they are moving in the same direction.

· The Law of the Continuing Line: Lines are always perceived as following the simplest path. If two lines cross, the viewer does not assume there is a break in the course of the line.

In the 1990s, Stephen E. Palmer defined the following Gestalt laws:

· The Law of a Mutual Region: Elements in enclosed areas are seen as belonging together.

· The Law of Simultaneity: Elements that change simultaneously are seen as belonging together.

· The Law of Connected Elements: Connected elements are perceived as an object.

To date, over one hundred laws have been established, and some have found a direct use in design within the field of (→) interface design.

To escape the National Socialists in Germany, many researchers in Gestalt psychology emigrated during the 1930s and 1940s to the United States, where they continued their work. This resulted in Gestalt theory spreading to and developing in America, Italy, and Japan. Wolfgang Metzger, who was a student of Köhler and Wertheimer, continued to develop Gestalt theory in Germany.

Gestalt theory has been rediscovered and reinterpreted recently by designers, philosophers, and sociologists concerned with the interdisciplinary task of designing complex intellectual, communicative, and social process. Bernhard von Mutius, the German social scientist, philosopher and management consultant, supports establishing an educational program in "Gestalt skills," which would enable designers to handle the complex intellectual challenges of the information society. As the design of knowledge, processes, and systems continue to dominate the profession more and more, the word *Gestaltung* will increasingly be used in the context of immaterial objects. AD |

→ *Complexity, Design, Form*

Lidwell, W., K. Holden, and J. Butler. 2003. *Universal principles of design*. Gloucester, MA: Rockport Publishers.
Metzger, W. 1975. Was ist Gestalttheorie? In Kurt Guss, ed. *Gestalttheorie und Erziehung*. Darmstadt: Dr. Dietrich Steinkopff Verlag.
Palmer, S. E. 1999. *Vision science*. Cambridge, MA: Bradford Book.
Wertheimer, M. 1924. Über Gestalttheorie: Vortrag vor der Kant-Gesellschaft, Berlin am 17. Dezember 1924. Verlag der Philosophischen Akademie Erlangen, 1925. Reprinted in *Gestalt Theory* 7 (1985).

GIMMICK

Gimmick, which is derived from the vernacular expression "gimme," or "give me," is the term used for an inexpensively produced and often eye-catching object that is distributed in order to advertise a product, service, or company. DPO |

→ *Advertisement, Brand*

GLOBALIZATION

Globalization is the most recent phase in a long history in which humans and their (→) artifacts have moved to localities outside their original homes.

Humans have always moved, and in so doing, have also long invented new technologies, lifestyles, languages, and (→) patterns of conduct. Starting in the early Christian era, with even older precursors, the great figures of such movement were traders, warriors, scribes, saints, and their families and followings. These large, though relatively slow movements were often connected with important (→) innovations, such as writing, the domestication of the horse, epic narrative, and kingship. In the last thousand years of our history, these movements created enduring links in money, trade, and scholarship, that led scholars to speak of world systems, some Western in origin, others associated with the world of Islam, the oceanic worlds of Asia and the Pacific, and with the long-distance movement of commodities and ideas across the Sahara to and from the African subcontinent.

What we now call the era of globalization has its immediate roots in the period of the Industrial Revolution of England and the Continent, starting in the eighteenth century, and their associated connections with world conquest, commodity capitalism, and major innovations in maritime technologies and technologies of war more generally.

Globalization proper belongs to the period after 1970, when a series of events occurred that caused corporations to accelerate their search for global markets and triggered an uneven and volatile flow of finance capital across national borders in new forms. In the 1980s and 1990s, this process became even more extensive due to the fall of the Soviet Empire and the concomitant spread of cyber-technologies to many parts of the world. The Internet and the ideology of democracy were in many ways the structural markers of the period of high globalization, which may be dated to about 1990. After this time, the movement of people, messages, and goods across national boundaries leaves no human society outside its integrative reach.

Although the worldwide ($\rightarrow$) integration of economies is the primary marker and driving force of globalization, it would be a mistake to lose sight of its deep cultural consequences and concomitants. Though cultural similarity has been the result of some aspects of the globalization of mass media and the aspirations of global corporations, the production of cultural difference, which has also been referred to as "cultural heterogenization," has been even faster. This is due to the fact that as cultural material reaches new shores, new audiences, and new users, it never lands on a blank slate. It invariably encounters local purposes, constraints, and patterns of thought, which both shape and are shaped by what arrives over the political transom.

The most important of these political transoms are the territorial boundaries of the nation-state, which are now simultaneously more rigid and more open than they have ever been in the past. This paradox is virtually a defining hallmark of globalization. As goods, ideas, and people move across national boundaries, they do so today in a bewildering array of circuits, some legal, some illegal, and others in a gray zone, which exist outside the law and beneath the screen of official prohibition or interdiction. All sovereign nations have to design their borders so that they keep out what is undesirable while encouraging cross-border flows that are deemed to be desirable. Since the same machineries, ultimately arms of the state, are charged with both responsibilities, most nation-states find themselves torn about what constitutes the right sort of membrane, equipped to sort out the black from the white kind of money, the right from the wrong trade in arms, the good from the bad kind of drugs, and the virtuous from the evil among people.

Thus, a central political fact about globalization is that it has changed the very nature of sovereignty, by forcing societies, including the very wealthiest, such as the United States, to rethink their ideas about citizenship, fair trade, immigration, and diplomacy. The poorest as well as the richest nations now depend on the decisions of political elites in other countries, and they all suffer from the mistakes of other nations near and far. Global warming is perhaps the most dramatic example of the contradiction between national political sovereignty and planetary-resource management.

Globalization has also created a new set of challenges surrounding identity, citizenship, and human rights. Due to the close links between the reigning ideologies of democracy and the ascendancy of the idea of universal human rights, all sorts of previously "weak" citizens—women, refugees, prisoners, children, migrants—are now able to contest individual states in the name of a legally recognized humanity. This leads to a blurring of the lines between cultural and political identity, with cultural claims now bursting out of the confines of home and family and political entitlements increasingly claimed in the name of cultural identities.

We must resist the temptation to see the cultural flows that characterize the era of globalization as being entirely benign. Globalization, especially in the realm of culture, has given rise to powerful cultural and religious mobilizations that, as in the case of radical Islam, have changed the face of war and security in the last decade. The circuits of globalization also make it easier to move children, sex workers, illegal arms, drugs, and a variety of other quasi-commodities across national boundaries.

Above all, there is mounting evidence that globalization increases wealth across the world but that it does not have salutary effects on equity and equality, within or between nations. Free trade, foreign direct investment, cross-border financial flows, and rapid sharing of technological innovations have not created a "flat" world except insofar as the world's managerial classes are concerned. For the world's poor, globalization is still substantially an unkept promise, and in some cases, a broken contract. This is a good part of the reason for the single most important trend of the twenty-first century, which is the massive movement of people into very large cities, many of which are already characterized by deep inequality, serious disrepair in systems of governance and infrastructure, and high potential for crime and violence. Such megacities could contain more than sixty percent of the world's population by the year 2050, many of them in cities with populations in the range of 30 million.

For designers, therefore, globalization presents both unprecedented opportunities and unprecedented challenges. On the one hand, the global traffic in taste, styles, technologies, and images of the good life, creates dramatic new opportunities for designing new goods and services (→ Service Design) as well as new arenas for retailing and merchandizing and new technologies for creating the raw (→) materials of design, such as fabrics, fonts, colors, shapes, and structures. The global growth in shopping malls, credit cards, public advertising, and media images of style, has created a global, interactive class of consumers who demand superior design in every aspect of their everyday lives.

On the other hand, as many people in the world move into the underbelly of the world's cities, as rural populations grow increasingly disenfranchised and desperate, and as the world's poor struggle with disease, poor housing, and economic exclusion, they are not likely to look at the world of high-end (→) consumption with indifference. This could be a recipe for increased violence and mass social breakdown.

Thus, all designers must also begin to think like planners. In other words, as designers ride the euphoria of the global present, they need to pay heed to the trusteeship of the global future. While planners need to recognize the desires that globalization produces in the present, designers need to think about (→) social and environmental (→) sustainability, as our planet hovers on the edge of social crisis and environmental Armageddon. While designers need to be more responsible, planners need to be more modest. A world that is poorly designed is not just a boring world. It might also turn into an uninhabitable world. AAP |

→ Communication, Cross-cultural Design, Mobility

Appadurai, A. 1996. *Modernity at large: Cultural dimensions of globalization*. Minneapolis: Univ. of Minnesota Press.
Easterling, K. 2005. *Enduring innocence: Global architecture and its political masquerades*. Cambridge, MA: MIT Press.
Rosaldo, R., and J. X. Inda, eds. 2001. *Anthropology of globalization: A reader*. Oxford, United Kingdom: Blackwell Publishing.
Sassen, S. 1999. *Globalization and its discontents: Essays on the new mobility of people and money*. New York: New Press.

GOOD DESIGN

Good design was a 1960s movement that aimed to replace subjective opinion based on taste with strict objective criteria and promote the international competitive ability of German companies and their products.

Design developments such as the one called *Gute Form* (Good Design) in the Federal Republic of Germany were symptomatic of the approach to evaluating design in design-oriented countries in Europe during the 1960s. Their different names, for example (→) Bel Design in Italy, point to the different ways they processed this still new development and to what degree they were involved with it. In the Federal Republic of Germany, the 1960s were characterized by the *Wirtschaftswunder* (economic boom) that swept away the postwar era's economic, political, and social chaos. Even design had found its place. The post-style era that saw the heterogeneous mixing of old (→) Bauhaus virtues with the search for new forms, the long with short-lived, the dignified with (→) kitsch and the peculiar was to be consigned to the past. Taste alone was no longer enough.

Good design was to be anchored in the minds of the people. Max Bill (→ *Ulm School of Design*) coined the term in 1949 for a traveling exhibition by the Schweizerischer Werkbund (Swiss Work Federation). It became established and, equipped with additional features, reached its peak in the 1960s. Subjective taste was replaced by strict, supposedly objective criteria. Design was now more closely associated with industry. Industrial mass production dominated the rapidly accelerating complexity of the goods and products maze. There was a need for (→) evaluation criteria and this was something that every designer and company could agree on—even if their motives differed. Industry was looking for objective arguments in order to give (→) credibility to their products despite arbitrariness and similarity (→ *USP*) and to improve their marketability, and saw design evaluation as a possibly decisive factor (→ *Design Management*). The designers, on the other hand, once again saw an opportunity to establish their ideas about the true definition of good design.

Three interrelated forces shaped design in the 1960s: the increasing mechanization of production, the evaluation of design using universally accepted criteria, and education. The motives were of course not only social or cultural but there were also real economic considerations. The goal was to improve the image and international competitiveness of German companies by utilizing good design. This awareness of design led to significant government-backed schemes for funding design. Academies of design were established or expanded and, in addition to the Rat für Formgebung (German Design Council) established in 1953, other regional (→) design centers were opened. Consumer organizations were formed that promoted good product design and contributed to the increasing number of design competitions established both by government institutions and private enterprise.

The unstoppable belief in general objective evaluation criteria for good design soon grew to become a strict design codex. Products, whose design was evaluated by various juries, had to prove themselves using this evaluation structure and eventually a distinctly German, good product design formula was established. An identifiably German style (even if German designers vehemently rejected this concept) could be recognized and was characterized by being reserved in appearance, functional in use, serious, reliable, rectangular, gray, black, or white, reduced to precise, technically necessary details—that was the ideal look of the products that matched the good design charter.

Products by Braun AG were seen as a byword for good design (which was also the title of the most prestigious German design competition established in 1969) and consistently won awards (→ *Design Awards*). The design brief for the radio and phonograph combination (especially the radio and record player combo SK 4, dubbed Snow White's Coffin), which had been initiated in 1955 by Hans Gugelot, a teacher at the Ulm School, was taken up and continued by Dieter Rams, the next Head Designer at Braun, and he expanded it to apply to the design of other products. Objects like the first all-wavelength portable radio, the World Receiver T 1000 (1963), the electric dry shaver, the sixtant (1962), the electric food processor, KM 32 (1964), or the tabletop cigarette lighter, TFZ 1 (1966)—note the technical and ambiguous product names based on the German—are legendary and have long since become costly cult and collector's items.

In other words, what happened was exactly what the advocates of objective, universal criteria for good design wanted to avoid. Good design is just as timeless, subjective, and emotional as any other movement. Ultimately, it is a (→) trend and, at best, eventually becomes a (→) retro design classic. [UB]

→ *Design Methods*

GRAPHIC DESIGN

In the broadest sense, graphic design describes the conscious organization of text and/or images to communicate a specific message. The term refers to both the process (a verb: to design) by which the communication is generated, as well as the product of this process (a noun: a design). It is used to inform, advertise, or decorate, and typically embodies a combination of these functions. The more (→) aesthetic and sensory latitude involved or allowed, the closer graphic design veers toward art (poetics); the less, the closer toward science (functionality). Today the term encompasses a notoriously wide range of activities, from the design of traditional print media (books and posters) to location-specific media (signs and signage systems), and electronic media (CD/DVD-ROMs and web sites).

Graphic design emerged as an autonomous (→) discipline in the first half of the twentieth century, encompassing both long-standing and emerging activities such as (→) typography, book design, and advertising. After a few decades marked by avant-garde experimentation in the first half of the twentieth century, the discipline acquired a degree of professional acumen during the decades immediately before and after the Second World War. Toward the end of the millennium this status was destabilized through the so-called democratization of publishing ("desktop publishing").

During the shift from the mechanical to digital, the tools of graphic design production—page makeup and imaging software, typefaces, and so on—became freely available and relatively cheap. This demystified the notion of graphic design and, by extension, questioned both the professional standing and relevance of the graphic designer. Like many media roles, graphic design is now characterized by this uncertain identity.

Rather than the way things work, graphic design is still largely (popularly) perceived as referring to the way things look: surface, style, and increasingly, spin. It is written about and documented largely in terms of its representation of the zeitgeist. In recent decades, graphic design has become associated foremost with commerce, becoming virtually synonymous with (→) corporate identity and advertising (→ Advertisement), while its role in more intellectual pursuits is increasingly marginalized. Furthermore, through a complex of factors characteristic of late capitalism, many of the more strategic aspects of graphic design are undertaken by those working in "middle-management" positions, typically within public relations or marketing departments. Under these conditions, those working under the title graphic designer fulfill only the production (typesetting, page makeup, programming) at the tail-end of this system.

On the other hand, in line with the ubiquitous fragmentation of postindustrial society into ever smaller coteries, there exists an international scene of graphic designers who typically make work independent of the traditional external commission, in self-directed or collaborative projects with colleagues in neighboring disciplines. Such work is typically marked by its experimental and personal nature, generally well-documented, and circulated in a wide range of media.

As these two aspects of graphic design—the overtly commercial and the overtly marginal—grow increasingly distinct, this schizophrenia renders the term increasingly vague and useless. At best, this implies that the term ought always to be distinctly qualified by the context of its use. SBA |

→ Layout, Packaging Design, Photographic Design, Poster Design, Publications, Visual Communication, Web Design

Hollis, R. 2002. *Graphic design: A concise history*. London: Thames & Hudson.
Meggs, P. 1983. *A history of graphic design*. New York: Van Nostrand Reinhold.
Potter, N. 2002. *What is a designer: Things, places, messages*. London: Hyphen Press.
Poynor, R. 2001. *Obey the giant: Life in the image world*. Basel: Birkhäuser; London: August.

GREEN DESIGN

→ Environmental Design, Sustainability

H

HANDICRAFT

→ Craft

HAPTICS

Haptics, the science of the sense of touch, comes from the Greek, haptikós, *to grasp. There is a difference between the stricter definition of haptics, that is, tactile perception (from the Latin,* tangere, *to touch), which refers to the touching of surfaces, and the broader definition of haptics that includes kinesthesia (from the Greek,* kinēsis, *movement and* aesthesis, *perception), or the sensing of movement in the body. To date, design has largely used the stricter definition of the term.*

The sense of touch is understood as a specific and autonomous sense related to external (→) perception. Haptics, the science of touch, is therefore concerned with the transmission of such sensations as pressure, vibration, pain, and temperature.

Design is concerned with how significant touch is when operating and controlling technical machinery and equipment. For this purpose, different forms of levers, switches, knobs, and buttons are tested for their operational reliability. What is important is the distinct feedback the user experiences through touch or other senses. This allows the user to determine, by the amount of haptic resistance on a push-button switch for instance, whether pressing it has activated the electric system or not. This is also conveyed acoustically by a clicking sound and visually by a small light next to the button. The light by the button is important, because while the button usually returns to its original position after being pushed, the light remains on as long as the electric system continues to be activated. The surplus feedback involving three senses makes it highly unlikely that the machine will be operated incorrectly. The same applies for flip switches and levers. Because these, unlike a push button switch, allow the user to see immediately if the switch has turned a system on or off, in this case, one can forgo the small light even if the redundant three-way feedback system is retained.

These examples show how important haptic feedback is, because blind or deaf users can safely operate mechanical equipment equipped with these switches. This is only partly feasible with a push-button switch. Another advantage of this now rather old-fashioned switch control system is the protruding position of a control panel switch. Users who are blind or working in the dark can examine the control panel and its switches by touch and, once briefed, can also operate it.

An example of an inadequate form of tactile control is the touch screen. It may well allow the user to control it by touch, but it lacks any haptic feedback, making the user totally dependent on visual and acoustic feedback. Blind users cannot identify different activation fields, because they only feel smooth, cold glass, and they do not receive any haptic feedback that confirms that the field has been activated. Today's demand for designs suited for the disabled could actually trigger a revival in the design of control panel switches and buttons (→ *Screen Design, Universal Design*).

Another example of the relevance of haptic feedback can be found in the automobile industry. Drivers lose their sense of speed in quiet luxury cars. For safety reasons, this has led to the idea of actually creating a deliberate vibration, activated when the car reaches a certain speed, so that the haptic sense can assist the driver to recognize the speed at which he or she is driving (→ *Safety Design*).

The most comprehensive definition of haptics was developed by Edmund Husserl (1859–1938), in the context of the philosophy of physical phenomenology, giving weight to individual subjective experience as the source of our understanding of objective phenomena. This includes a general theory of people's kinesthesia. The body and its haptic sense play a central role in this philosophy of perception. Husserl defines the body in relation to the constitution of an object and space as:

1. a medium of all perception
2. a free-moving entity of the sensory organs and
3. a center of orientation.

As a free-moving entity, the body expresses the function of spontaneity, the "I can." "I" decide whether I want to go left or right in a room, straight ahead, or backward. "I" decide whether I want to run my hand along the surface of a table to feel whether a shiny mark on it is sticky or not. "I" tilt and turn my head to be able to better hear if the cat is meowing. In addition to the function of spontaneity, there are also two correlating classes of sensations that belong to the constitution of space and object: first, the sensations that constitute the characteristics of things, for example, color sensations and sensations of surface properties, and second, the kinesthetic sensations, meaning the physical sensations of the different body parts, like the sensation of eye movement when looking or the sensation of the arm moving when reaching out to touch something. In fact, it is impossible to imagine a perception, regardless of which sense is activated, without a corresponding physical sensation. The body is in almost constant movement; even while you are sitting down, your eyes blink, your head turns, you cross your legs, you even feel your inner organs: your heart beats, your belly rumbles. Of course, people are usually less focused on their kinesthetic bodily sensations and more on the sensation of perceiving the characteristics of a thing. But adjusting the settings, so to speak, makes it easier to shift the focus to bodily sensations. When hiking through the woods, most people's senses are focused on the landscape and the plant and animal life there; they become aware of their own body only if they stumble. Marathon runners, however, exert their bodies so much that their own physical sensations necessarily become the point of focus.

Perception always entails activating more than one sense at a time. If I look at a black, polished table surface, my haptic sense anticipates that the surface of the table will have a sensation characteristic of smoothness. Acoustically, I also expect a squeaky sound if I rub my finger along its surface. For the rational understanding of the external world, our consciousness provides a constant organization of the simultaneous stimulation of the individual senses *(Deckungssynthese)*. Ultimately, sensory perception is the product of a system of different physical senses that is constantly balancing the information it assimilates and processes. Conscious acoustic, visual, haptic, or olfactory experiences form an interactive system of anticipations that are either fulfilled or disappointed in the process of perception. The fact that several senses exist allows even the abstract, isolated "I" to develop an initial form of objectivity, as Husserl shows in *Ideen II*. This initial partial objectivity develops when the "I" recognizes haptically when one of the senses is inaccurate or contradictory (for instance, if you have a wart on a fingertip), because the other senses, and the *Deckungssynthese* they provide, help the unity and coherence of the perception process to remain intact. This admittedly is not genuine objectivity. Objectivity is only generated from intersubjective association.

Maurice Merleau-Ponty was the first to further develop Husserl's phenomenology of the body into an intersensory theory, when he more precisely analyzed sensorial interaction.

Whereas in architectural theory the broad definition of haptics has long been established and successfully applied in research and doctrine, its experiential, trial and error quality has only recently been recognized in design research. TF |

→ *Olfactory Design, Synesthetic, Texture*

Friedrich, T. 2001. Phänomenologie für Künstler und Designer: Grundlegendes zum Verständnis der Wahrnehmungstheorie Edmund Husserls. *Visuelle Sprache: Jahrbuch der Fakultät Gestaltung der Bauhaus-Universität Weimar* 1.

Husserl, E. 1952. *Ideen zu einer reinen Phänomenologie und phänomenologischen Philosophie.* Vol. 2. *Phänomenologische Untersuchungen zur Konstitution.* The Hague: Ernst Biemel.

Hughes, F. 2005. Multimedia-Kultur und das "Intersensorische." In T. Friedrich and R. Dommaschk, eds. *Bildklangwort: Grundlagenwissen Gestaltung* 1. Munster.

Merleau-Ponty, M. 1945. *Phénoménologie de la perception.* Paris: Gallimard. English trans. by C. Smith as *Phenomenology of perception.* London: Routledge, 1989.

HARDWARE

Science describes "hardware" as a body consisting of solid material, the "solid goods," or the mechanical thing. In English, "hardware" also describes (→) tools and implements. In computing and electronics, the term is used to differentiate the material elements of the technology (that is, processors, monitors, and controllers) from the immaterial (→) software programs and code. SAB |

→ *Components*

HEURISTICS

Heuristics are guides that designers use to generate or evaluate ideas.

Design (→) research has borrowed the term "heuristics" from cognitive science (via Herbert Simon), where it refers to the pre-existing values that decision-makers use to negotiate a problem. An individual may exercise "bounded rationality" to restrict the scope or complexity of a problem for instance (looking for fair-trade coffee, but not for local fair-trade organic coffee in recycled-content packaging), or "satisficing" to predetermine what would count as a "good enough" rather than a definitive solution to the problem (accepting organic coffee over local coffee if organic local coffee cannot be found). In this context, heuristics help decision-makers to weigh various possibilities in order to calculate the optimum course of action. In the absence of explicitly defined problems with explicitly defined solutions, decisions made using heuristic processes are never entirely rational, but always contingent on the decision-maker's individual abilities and prejudices. In this sense, heuristics involve aspects of human cognition that are not-readily-computational (that is, "hunches," "emotional intelligence," and "intuition") in the search for optimum solutions.

The term "heuristics" derives from same ancient Greek root as *eureka,* Archimedes' famous exclamation "I have found it." Because searching involves looking for things whose location, nature, and even existence you can never be sure about, all searching involves heuristics, that is, determinations as to where and what to look for that are hopefully informed guesses, but never sure things. This is particularly true of the (→) design process. There is no single abstractable theory or method of designing that can be taught and then applied to a wide range of problems. Designing is not a rule-bound activity, but a situated one, constrained by the particular problem context in which it is being conducted, the decisions the client, designer, and prospective user make, and/or the historical and cultural specifics of the society in which it exists. Because most design problems are complex and "wicked" (→ Wicked Problems), that is, without any definitive or objective form, it is difficult, if not impossible, to automate any design process.

However, close observation and analysis indicate that the design process is not random; rather, designing unfolds in more or less similar ways in the context of problems that are judged by the designer to be more or less similar. What differentiates novice designers from expert designers tends to be the ability of the latter to discern quickly what kind of problem a particular design (→) brief is, and consequently determine the most promising ways of tackling such a brief. In contrast, novices often do not know where to begin, or tackle all briefs in the same way. Whilst this perceptive ability that comes with the course of expert practice tends to be discussed in terms of (→) "intuition," it is nevertheless articulatable, that is, part of an expert's procedural knowledge-base (which includes the "know-how," but also "know when"). When asked to rationalize aloud how they are designing, experts can usually explain the (→) pattern of design problem and design process that they are working with—in other words, the rules they are consciously following. These patterns are usually explained as a combination of extrapolated precedents, explicit learned principles, procedures modeled from mentors or peers, or personal habits and tastes (Lawson 2004). However, these patterns are not guarantors of success, nor are they entirely validated on past experience or authority, nor are they methodically applied in each circumstance where they could be—in other words, they are not justified and normative rules. For all these reasons they are known as heuristics, "rules-of-thumb" for discovering inventive design solutions.

User-centered design research is emerging as strongly heuristic because user research is a form of searching where users cannot easily articulate what they want, particularly in regard to designs that do not yet exist (→ Usability). Design researchers are therefore developing a wide range of "generative research" techniques that elicit consumer habits, expectations and desires through creative exercises that customers undertake (for example Elizabeth Sanders' Generative Design Research tools, Bill Gaver's cultural probes, and Zeisel 2006) and allow designers to creatively empathize with what is thereby elicited.

Heuristics is also the technical name for the type of programming that results in "expert systems" (→ CAD/CAM/CIM/CNC). These are matrices of predetermined values and relations that either check for conflicts (an important tool, for instance, in large-team, time-poor concurrent designing) or generate a comprehensive set of product form variations. CT |

→ Design Methods, Innovation, Problem Setting, Problem Solving

Lawson, B. 2004. *What designers know.* Oxford, United Kingdom: Architectural Press.
Zeisel, J. 2006. *Inquiry by design.* Rev. ed. New York: Norton.

HIGH TECH

The term "high tech" is both an evaluation and a general description. It describes the grade of technological input into a product or system in relation to similar products or systems. It is also used to distinguish something from technology-free products or systems (low tech), or as a synonym to "modern" in certain cultural contexts.

High tech is always the result of a complex scientific process of research and development that aims to expand the current potential of materials and techniques. This process can be contingent on a defined requirement or an experiment. High tech products are often developed in the fields of air travel, space travel and in the military, and subsequently adapted and altered for general use. Today, there are a number of diverse fields that fall within the category of high tech design including nanotechnology, biotechnology, computer technology, and a large sector of (→) materials research.

The practices of design, engineering, and architecture often form the interface between the process of scientific research and development and the industrial application of high tech materials and processes. Over the last hundred years, architecture in particular has been influential in developing a distinctly high tech style that is typically characterized by the use of industrial materials, exposed building elements, and a functionalist approach (→ *Functionalism*). Prominent examples of high tech architecture include Paxton's Crystal Palace (1851), the Centre National d'Art et de Culture Georges Pompidou (1976), and Foster's building for the Hong Kong and Shanghai Bank in Hong Kong (1979).

The term "high tech" is becoming increasing relevant to design practice due to the progressive integration of innovative materials and production means into the product world of day-to-day life. Examples of high tech technologies that enable the production of faster, lighter, stronger, and more intelligent designs include nano (→) coatings for surfaces, super-elastic carbon-fiber composites for prosthesis manufacture, bio-ceramic bone replacements, and clothing that compensates for a wearer's mineral deficiencies through his or her skin.

High tech processes and technologies are very desirable in today's market because they help a product stand out in the eyes of consumers. High tech products also represent some of the most fascinating and radical (→) innovations in design, innovations that shape future vision and push the limits of conventional design expression. Consequently, high tech advances are often the starting point for designers seeking to improve the quality of day-to-day life today. SAB |

→ *Bionics, Engineering Design, Futuristic Design, Mechatronic Design, Modernity, Production Technology, Smart Materials*

HISTORY

When compared to the more established neighboring disciplines of art and architectural history, the study of design history is still comparatively young. It is closely connected with other branches of the humanities and social sciences including sociology, cultural and media sciences, and at times depending on the specific country, with anthropology, industrial archeology, philosophy, economics, linguistics, and psychoanalysis. Despite its comparatively short history as a discrete field of study, subdisciplines have already emerged, including design semiotics during the 1970s in France, Germany, and the United States; industrial culture during the 1980s in Germany; and design-based cultural studies and visual studies, popularized in the 1990s in English-speaking countries. The later subdisciplines diverge from the study of traditional design history by utilizing an interdisciplinary approach that bridges the subject of design with other aspects of popular culture like advertising, photography, gender studies, and so on.

The development of design history varies considerably from country to country. Nonetheless, the practice of design as an independent (→) discipline is most commonly traced back to the Industrial Revolution that took place during the mid-nineteenth century. At the early stages of the period, the subject of design was largely conceptualized as an alternative to the "art industry," particularly with regards to the (→) Arts & Crafts movement in England. At the beginning of the twentieth century, however, design began to align itself more closely with the realities of industrial mass production, making it possible to study it as a discrete field of practice. The fundamentally normative canon of modernism's (→ *Modernity*) practical, purpose-built forms opened up the *via regia* for design history until the 1970s, when (→) postmodernism emerged as a critique of modernism. Since then, there has been a greater emphasis on the pluralization of design directions and a separation from a classification in style and "isms."

Because the study of design history is still not supported at most universities, it is often dependent on trade, journalism, and exhibition markets that are ultimately driven by trends, fashions, and a constant search for the next "big name." This is also why attempts to illuminate design history are so often reduced to mere chronological listings of achievements by notable designers, groups, or schools. It is clear that a more sustained approach to design history that also addresses less prominent works would illuminate key movements through the course of its history. Publications that address the anonymous histories of things—like Sigfried Giedion's *Mechanization Takes Command* (1948) that criticized the consequences of technology in the Second World War and the growing American influence on Europe—stand out as isolated works, but they as yet have not had any lasting impact on developing design history as an academic subject (→ *Anonymous Design*).

Traditional design history has focused almost exclusively on the design object (see Lucius Burckhardt's criticism in *Design = unsichtbar [Design = Invisible]*, 1995). It does not typically integrate the fields of commercial art or (→) visual communications, and other approaches that examine aspects of consumer behavior (like reception history and theory, the culture

Burckhardt, Lucius. 1995. *Design = unsichtbar*. Ed. H. Höger. Ostfildern: Cantz.
Schepers, W., and P. Schmidt, eds. 2000. *Das Jahrhundert des Design: Geschichte und Zukunft der Dinge*. Frankfurt am Main: Anabas.
Selle, G. 1983. *Die Geschichte des Design in Deutschland von 1870 bis heute: Entwicklung der industriellen Produktkultur*. 3rd ed. Cologne: DuMont. (Orig. pub. 1978.)
Walker, J. A. 1989. *Design history and the history of design*. London: Pluto Press.

of taste, psychology, and shifts in cultural values) remain sporadic.

Companies sometimes make an effort to document their own design histories (Thonet, Olivetti), or even to document more general design histories if their interests are served by the process (Designmuseum Vitra, Weil am Rhein). Some countries have their own associations of design historians who work together to have their work published (like Great Britain's *Journal of Design History*, founded in 1977). GB |

→ *Agit Prop, Art Deco, Art Nouveau, Bauhaus, Bel Design, Black Mountain College, Constructivism, Dada and Design, Design Museums, Deutscher Werkbund, Exhibition Design, Functionalism, International Style, Good Design, Memphis, Radical Design, Razionalismo, Retro Design, Ulm School of Design*

HUMAN COMPUTER INTERACTION (HCI)

→ *Interface Design*

HUMAN FACTORS

Human factors is a field of design practice that directly interfaces with the social sciences to better understand the experiential contexts in which products of design processes are used and circulated. Observational techniques are deployed in the design discovery process to create experiences and products responsive to the individual, social, or psychological contexts of interaction and (→) use. From its origins in (→) research investigations into the effectiveness and safety of human-machine interaction within aviation and maritime systems in the Second World War period, human factors techniques have been used in many other design and engineering areas from product design to interactive design, architecture to environmental systems and organizational design. Specialists in the field include anthropologists, psychologists, and other social scientists. Human factors act as much more than evaluative techniques for assessing a product's functionality and (→) usability; they are critical to understanding the broader contexts of (→) perception and experience through design interventions. CM + VR |

→ *Engineering Design, Ergonomics, Interface Design, Needs Assessment, Social*

HYPERTEXT

In 1945, Vannevar Bush introduced the concept of what he called the memex (memory extender), a groundbreaking method of organizing of information that formed the basis of today's hypertext system. The means of cross-referencing linked texts allowed users to view (→) information non-sequentially, which is similar to the way humans think—that is, by association rather than in a linear sequence. To produce these "associative" links, individual elements (chunks) are marked with catchwords (tags) that enable dynamic links to open systems. Designers have the task of structuring the content, determining the links, and making navigation via the nonlinear organization of information easily identifiable and intuitive. Today, hypermedia uses audiovisuals to enhance text. PH |

→ *Information Design, Web Design*

I

ILLUSTRATION

The verb "to illustrate" comes from the Latin *lustrare*, "to shed light on." Illustration is the art of communicating concise ideas with images in a variety of media. It can both illuminate the meaning of a subject and also create a new context in which to view the world.

An illustration tells a story, in one or a sequence of images, often in relation to text. Whether created for a page, screen, or wall, a successful illustration is both an expression of the illustrator's point of view and personal approach to his or her medium and techniques, as well as a cogent elucidation of narrative. It is, in a sense, writing with images.

Illustration relies on three crucial skills that are applicable to many fields: conceptualizing ideas (how the world is seen), creative problem solving (how the vision is conveyed), and precise, evocative (→) rendering skills (how it can be accurately depicted). These three skills, in their emphasis on pragmatic approaches to creative production, help define illustration as a medium reliant on a high level of (→) craft in order to facilitate its most basic function: the (→) communication of ideas.

Illustration is mostly (but not exclusively) a commercial practice, and frequently acts as a part of a larger commerce-based, mass-produced enterprise. It exists at the intersection of graphic design, fine art, and interactive design, and encompasses a wide range of creative activities: illustration for newspapers and magazines, advertisements and product packaging, books for adults and children, short and long-form moving images in motion graphics and animation, and imagery for comics and graphic novels. More recently, illustrators have embraced non-traditional (that is, nonprint media) activities such as toy and (→) textile design, imagery for large and small screens (animated film, web-toons, cell-phone graphics) as well as street-derived forms such as skateboard, sticker, and graffiti imagery. Though illustration has historically existed most often in the context of words, as accompaniment to a text, it has taken on a more autonomous role in recent years as the culture becomes increasingly visual.

Illustrators have employed every medium the history of art has offered, including, but not limited to, oil paint, watercolor, tempera, etching, silkscreen, engraving, collage, scratchboard, pen and ink, sculpture in wood, paper, and moldable mediums, and digital tools such as Illustrator, Photoshop, Flash, and Dreamweaver. And while historically illustration has been indifferent to the original (→) artifact, even employing ephemeral and non-archival mediums to achieve its effects, increasingly illustrators approach their work as objects to be displayed in gallery settings. There they create work very much of the same sensibility that is employed in commissioned work, but it is instead generated from the illustrator's own imagination and responsive to the illustrator's own inner needs.

Whatever medium, motive, or idea is employed, at its best, illustration allows the viewer to see the world in a new light or enter an entirely new world. DN + SGU |

→ *Animation, Graphic Design, Poster Design, Storyboard, Visual Communication, Visualization*

IMITATION

→ *Fake, Plagiarism*

INDUSTRIAL DESIGN

Industrial design aims to improve the functional, interactive, and aesthetic qualities of industrially manufactured (→) products for human use.

As a field of practice, the parameters of industrial design are broadly and somewhat loosely defined, and often overlap with other fields like (→) engineering and (→) interface design. Many industrial designers work in subfields related to the production of specific products ranging from cars to electronics to furniture. (→) Product design is often categorized as a subfield under the umbrella of industrial design as well, although these terms are used interchangeably in practice.

Historically, industrial design has been understood largely in opposition to craft-based production techniques. This apparent dichotomy between the pursuit of handcrafted aesthetics and methods of mass-production can be traced back to the Industrial Revolution and the emergence of counter-industrial production movements such as (→) Arts & Crafts and (→) Art Nouveau. Subsequent movements such as the (→) Deutscher Werkbund and the (→) Bauhaus attempted to reconcile the complexities of modern industry with artistic, cultural, and social (→) ethics. These attempts to improve the quality of mechanically manufactured products for common human use are widely considered to be the starting point of modern industrial design.

Despite their significant contributions to design, however, these movements nevertheless failed to entirely eliminate the anti-craft connotations associated with everything "industrial." As a result, the contemporary practice of industrial design is still often regarded as privileging the technical elements of design over the more creative ones. Nonetheless, aspects of aesthetics, creativity, and quality are critical to the process; successful industrial designers must not only exhibit technical proficiency, but imbue their products with the distinctive social values and visual characteristics that compel consumers to purchase them.

Due to the broad parameters of the field, industrial designers rarely work in isolation, but in collaboration with other designers, engineers, psychologists, and scientists. As a consumer-oriented (→) discipline, aspects of manufacturing cost and market value are also increasingly important; as a result, final designs often hinge upon other non-design professions such as business and marketing. The design process itself engages levels of (→) research and development that continually test and refine design (→) prototypes until they meet predetermined performative and aesthetic criteria. Typically, analog processes of form finding and analysis include modeling in clay, wax, or plastic, vacuum forming, steam bending, foam cutting, and many other tactile techniques for modeling and researching in three dimensions. These analog processes tend to be articulated in the context of product design, but as product design and industrial design are often practiced by one-and-the-same person, they inevitably share techniques and methods.

The past few decades have seen incredible advancements in the fields of industrial manufacturing with techniques of production linked to computer (→) software. Today, designers often use three-dimensional digital software to visualize, model, and analyze products in virtual space prior to manufacturing. This process helps designers move from conceptualization to production in a time and cost effective way. In addition, improved techniques of CNC (computer numerically controlled) (→ *CAD/CAM/CIM/CNC*) fabrication have made the physical output of products and product components speedier and more precise, and in consequence, more economical. Digital fabrication and (→) rapid prototyping have vastly broadened the formal palette of the industrially manufactured object and made it possible to explore formal complexity without sacrificing the precise efficiency of machine mass-production.

Although the emergence of new manufacturing technologies has undoubtedly had a significant commercial impact on industrial design, currently there is strong momentum pushing the discipline toward taking ecology into as much account as economy. The constant and ever increasing production of new objects has resulted in a growing awareness regarding the production of waste and the excessive use of carbon-emitting energy resources in both manufacturing processes and final use. These concerns have encouraged many industrial designers to seek

Banham, R. 1967. *Theory and design in the first machine age*. New York: Praeger.
Benevolo, L. 1992. *History of modern architecture*. Cambridge, MA: MIT Press.
Schwartz, F. 1996. *The Werkbund: Design theory and mass culture before the First World War*. New Haven: Yale Univ. Press.

alternative solutions to ecologically harmful industrial processes, a development that has become an important aspect of the practice. Recent innovations along these lines have included the integration of new sustainable materials (→ *Materials, Sustainability*), the adoption of renewable energy resources, and an emphasis on the reuse or responsible disposal of consumer products. EPV |

→ *Craft, Ergonomics, Function, Product Development, Styling, Use*

INFORMATION

Design's role in developing ways to facilitate the autonomy of information systems when dealing with super-complex databases is growing in importance. The goal is to support diverse styles and types of knowledge. In the process, design's functions have been extended from producing (→) form to creating meaning. The appropriate theoretical foundations have yet to be formulated to underpin these additional functions.

As information is not made up of matter or energy, it cannot be designed in a direct sense. It needs to be translated into something perceptible and tangible, as demonstrated in phrases such as "information architecture," "information flow," and "information landscape."

Design when applied to information becomes effective as a catalyst for the production of artifacts (mainly objects concerned with media) that can improve the probability of the recipient processing information in the intended and appropriate ways.

Besides this, there is the research issue of whether (→) information design is able to justify an independent epistemology that integrates diverse styles and types of knowledge, and uses experiments to investigate the functions of sensory knowledge. Unlike scientists, designers tend to believe that the global effort to improve universal welfare is restrained not by a lack of data and the information it helps to shape, but more by a lack of ability and an unwillingness to create the appropriate information from the available data, and, hence, to justify relevant action. This is how the democratically chartered rights of informational self-determination become a politically effective factor, via practical data management and information access.

Design's descriptive methods are sometimes considered inferior to scientific methods and, therefore, as the last step in the process of creating knowledge (→ *Design Methods*). Yet these digital representations of actions and ideas, in the context of vastly complex databases, are first positioned as catalysts for actions and knowledge. The actual machinery for information processing then takes center stage, and design's potential contribution to envisaging the technologies necessary for future information processing becomes the primary focus of (→) research. Today, information designers who create socio-technical systems according to this philosophy are part of an established approach, leading from Otto Neurath (visual systems), Wilhelm Ostwald (Die Brücke) and Herbert Bayer (Globoscope) to Charles Eames (films, exhibitions), Buckminster Fuller (the Dymaxion world map, synergetics), the Department of Information at the (→) Ulm School of Design, and groups like Superstudio (→ *Radical Design*).

Digital media has paved the way for new and diverse possibilities for effective, design-related information systems, but the theoretical basis necessary for its development has still not been determined. In the process, information aesthetics in the 1960s tried to formulate a common description for scientific and artistic productivity, technical function, and aesthetic information that would unite all these concepts—a project that now seems even more necessary considering the ubiquity of today's digital systems.

There are many information design projects being completed at the moment that can be summed up as "info-aesthetics" (Manovich 2006). It is vital to recognize this field of practice and research as cutting edge, but claiming that it is new indicates a lack of historical perspective about design and leads to a theoretical deficit.

The term "information" is fundamental in postindustrial societies, giving rise to phrases like "information society" or "the age of information." But there is still no consistent theory of information able to integrate the necessary aspects of the psychology of (→) perception and cognitive sciences with the scope of communication theory and technology and social and political perspectives.

Essentially, there are two identifiable positions in information theory: the scientific-technical position, in which information is mathematically determined as a degree of improbability, and a system-theoretical/Constructivist position that assumes that there is a disparity between a (→) system and its environment and postulates that the viewer is a self-contained system where information is concerned (→ *Constructivism*). Both positions believe that information cannot be understood as matter or as energy, despite the reality that compressing atoms and energy into bits (that is the smallest possible units of information able to be stored in a computer as 0 or 1) is one of today's most essential research issues, for example in quantum computers, biological information, or cellular machines.

Information does not exist as an absolute; it can only claim to be the "difference that makes a difference" from an observer's perspective (Gregory Bates). Perceivable differences that materialize as matter or energy enter the full range of human senses as jumbled signals. Only a fraction of these can be processed consciously, whereas selecting where to direct attention is subject to anthropological patterns of perception as well as cultural, individual, and situational filters. The perception system is structurally linked to its environment and develops expectations in relation to the nature of the future of that environment that are based on past experiences and consequent anticipations. Disparities in the environment that do not correspond to these experiences acquire additional value as information because they are events that need to be interpreted—the less probable the event, the higher the informational value. Therefore information cannot exist in the environment per se; it has to be created by a structurally linked, self-contained information system. This version of the term "information" corresponds to positions of system theory guided by the philosophy of radical (→) constructivism. Accordingly, (→) understanding is perceived as a process of selection that constantly updates the difference between (→) communication and information, because the same sensory stimulus, that is communication, can construct a range of credible information forms. The sentence "I go" could be understood as "I go on foot" (not by car) or as "I am going to the door" (while you remain seated) or "I go away" (and you stay here). The difference between communication and information is particularly evident in intercultural communication, where the same gesture can have different or even opposite meanings.

If design is to be understood as a producer of cognitively and emotionally effective interfaces (→ Interface Design) between system and environment, then an effective and functional definition of information is absolutely vital. Because in the selective process of understanding, even meaning, which is a definitive criterion for design, appears as a point of difference between the development of potentially plausible information and that of actual, realized information. Seen in this light, the difference between (→) form and content is not an issue, and the designer (as in the one who creates form) strives to develop new interpretations that can communicate a selection of meanings.

This definition demonstrates that information is a commonly misused term. Data, not information, can be transmitted, recorded, and stored. The Internet contains data, not information, and certainly not knowledge. This inadequate, conceptual separation often comes from carelessly applying technical scientific models to human information and communication systems. Hence, despite its confusing title, Claude Shannon's *A Mathematical Theory of Communication* (1948) focuses exclusively on technical problems in signal transmission. Even here, maximal unpredictability corresponds to maximal information value: the less predictable a system's behavior is and, thus, the higher the number of possible, equally probable interpretations there are, the higher is its information content that can then be mathematically calculated as a statistical factor. Yet, if no (→) human factor were to be introduced into this model, the white noise that results from the simultaneous jumble of every single frequency on an audio channel would provide more information than could be obtained from a poorly tuned modulated frequency, or a dead radio channel. It is obvious that a statistical definition such as this is not transferable to the field of human information. A comprehensive and functional definition of information must always assume there is an interpreting observer—a theory developed in (→) semiotics, which, besides syntax, is also concerned with (→) semantics and pragmatics. The sphere of information consists, firstly, of the fact that information is based on data that is in turn based on signals and, secondly, that information is required for knowledge. This builds an ascending sequence of signals, data, information, and knowledge, whereas the processes of selection, (→) pattern, and contextualization come into effect when proceeding from one level to the next. Knowledge is not only the apex of this process; it also forms its context, which allows for self-reference and, hence, (→) complexity. Using available knowledge, signals are filtered and data is structured that, by way of interpretation, becomes information and, by being used in context, generates new knowledge.

The expression "information society" is based on a definition formulated in the 1950s stating that symbolic and tele-media processes would have higher economic value than the development of other resources such as capital, labor, and land in post-industrial societies. Cultivating information, in the possible guise of "information management" and its resulting (→) "knowledge management," presents a particular challenge. This became clear when the exponential propagation of data, fueled by the expansion of digital technology, did not lead to an equivalent growth in information, but in many situations actually led to its reverse (info overload, disinformation, (→) misinformation). The quality of information and a potential ecology of information then became very contemporary issues, and produced a boom in new disciplines such as informatics, derived from library studies, that is concerned with the consequences of information agents working on the digital market as intermediaries between human clients and technical systems among other issues.

The further development of design's contribution to the quality of information is driven by the technical need for a more robust structuring of data (information modeling) and also determined by aspects of the psychology of perception that

Bense, M. 1969. *Einführung in die informationstheoretische Ästhetik.* Reinbek: Rowohlt.

Coyne, R. 1995. *Designing information technology in the postmodern age: From method to metaphor.* Cambridge, MA: MIT Press.

Moles, A. A. 1958. *Théorie de l'information et perception esthétique.* Paris: Flammarion. English trans. by J. E. Cohen as *Information theory and esthetic perception.* Urbana: Univ. of Illinois Press, 1966.

Nardi, B. A. 1999. *Information ecologies.* Cambridge, MA: MIT Press.

INFORMATION DESIGN

Despite the fact that "information design" describes a broad and increasingly important field of design, it has proven difficult to arrive at a universally accepted definition. Generally speaking, information design involves the process of translating complex, disorganized, or unstructured data into accessible, useful, comprehensible information. The term is somewhat misleading in that it is not necessarily the content of (→) information that is designed, but rather, the form of its delivery.

will allow complex databases to be understood and developed more efficiently.

Both aspects come together in the concept of (→) information design. This integrates semantics (by understanding how meaning is determined by the arrangement and relationships between units of information and determining the limits on their combination and recombination of info-chunks), syntax (by selecting and developing suitable data structures and audio-visual presentation), and pragmatic aspects (by integrating socio-technical systems and processes into existing environments). PS |

Although information design typically involves visualizing data using graphic or interactive means, it would be incorrect to simply classify it as a subcategory of graphic or communication design (→ *Graphic Design, Visualization*). Information design is a (→) discipline in its own right, comprising a multidisciplinary and intermedial spectrum of activities that combine scientific and (→) design methods in unique ways. For example, information designers in the analysis and planning phases will utilize (→) research methodologies derived from the social and applied sciences (specifically cognitive psychology, ergonomics, and environmental psychology) as well as from the practices of scientific illustration, communication design, interface design, and graphic design. The process also may require specific professional expertise in writing, databases, (→) web design, signage design, even product or industrial design.

Regardless of what specific techniques are used in the process, the focus of information design is always the end user. Because people receive information in very different ways, information design has to consider not only the users' (→) needs, but also their perceptual capabilities and motivations (→ *Perception*). When designing information for large user groups, the designer has to either find the largest common denominator or allow for a system with different access points in order to ensure unhindered use by as many people as possible (→ *Universal Design*).

The designer must also consider the context in which the users will receive the information, as environmental factors will necessarily have an effect on how the data is translated and understood. The goal is to convey the information as clearly and unambiguously as possible, but also to create a (→) design that is tailored to the recipient.

It is difficult to map out a linear history of information design, but it is appears as though the first professionally-driven attempts to convey information and knowledge were established sometime around the start of the nineteenth century. One of the first (and still most impressive) works from this time was Charles Joseph Minard's diagram depicting Napoleon's Russian campaign from 1812 to 1813. In the 1920s, the Viennese sociologist Otto Neurath created a system to convey information using a standardized visual language. Based on this method, he developed the *Wiener Methode der Bildstatistik* (Vienna Method of Pictorial Statistics), together with the Düsseldorf graphic artist Gerd Arntz, and later further developed it into the "ISOTYPE" or "International System of Typographic Picture Education," which continues to used today.

At the moment, the field of information design is experiencing an upsurge in development, as evidenced by its canonization as a discrete program of academic study. This development is not surprising; in today's complex postindustrial societies, designers are critical to the process of decoding, organizing, and communicating knowledge for the information age. AD |

→ *Communications, Crossover, Interface Design, Transformation, Visual Communication*

Brückner, H. 2004. *Informationen gestalten—Designing Information*. Bremen: Verlag H. M. Hauschild.
Institute for Information Design Japan, ed. 2005. *Information Design source book*. Basel: Birkhäuser.
Jacobson, R., ed. 1999. *Information design*. Cambridge, MA: MIT Press.
Petterson, R. 2002. *Information design: An introduction*. Amsterdam: John Benjamins Publishing.

INNOVATION

Innovation in design is a change in the development, production, distribution, or use of an artifact, environment, or system that is perceived as being different from its precedents by its proposed users or target audience (→ *Target Group*). In this context, innovation is distinguished from "invention," in that it can only be truly understood by examining a contribution's precedents as well as the consequences it creates. In other words, an innovation can only exist in a continuum, defined not only by what comes before it, but how it is received. For instance—regardless of how strongly a product or process breaks with (→) convention, it can only be described as innovative if the public responds to it as such. Indeed, many of the most innovative designs of the twenty-first century were made possible not by radical breakthroughs in technology, but by the cross appropriation or reapplication of existing technologies and methods across markets (→ *Crossover, Redesign*). Innovation necessitates the contribution of a new definition, perspective, or set of circumstances to a community; therefore, issues of diffusion and adoption are critical when labeling anything as "innovative."

Design innovation is the result of a heuristic process (→ *Heuristics*). Rather than simply responding to a given problem, designers identify a number of possible solutions as well as inconsistencies, alternatives, and consequences to those solutions. In doing so, the process of design innovation illuminates the relationships and adjacencies that typically occur within a complex problem or set of problems. Although difficult to evaluate quantifiably during the design and production processes, innovation is nonetheless a key factor in determining the continued success of a company today. As this fact has come to light, managers who previously privileged efficiency-based approaches (ROI, IRR, and so on) at the expense of less quantifiable heuristic approaches (collaboration, independence, creativity, user-centric design, and so on) have begun to appreciate and engage both in order to establish a culture of innovation within studios and companies. It is exactly at this intersection of "management thinking" and "design thinking" from which "real" innovation is borne.

Generally, innovations can be organized according to their type and their dynamic. The type of innovation (incremental or radical) describes the degree of change that the innovation represents; the dynamic of innovation (sustaining or disruptive) describes the effect that an innovation has on a given market and its targets.

Incremental innovations take their form from an emphasis on "trajectory-based thinking." They are defined as much by the kinds of innovation that contributed to their earlier development as by the independent contributions a particular iteration makes. An example of incremental innovation is the conversion of photography from a silver-halide-based medium to a digital medium. Radical innovations may derive their function from other preceding innovations as well, but the effects of their introduction completely change the grounds on which other similar innovations are defined. An example of radical innovation occurred when the emergence of nuclear weapons changed the context of war from a conflict involving groups using conventional weaponry to that of a "global conflict." (It is important to note that with so much positive emphasis being placed on innovation today, the determination of an innovation's overall contribution to humanity always requires ethical judgment (→ Ethics)).

Within these two types of innovation, incremental and radical, one can derive two dynamics of the innovation process. The first, "sustaining innovation," is an innovation that is primarily based on performance along a timeline, and does not drastically affect the design of other components on which its function relies. For example, the design of the paths on a piece of silicon that raised the speed of microprocessors from 286 megahertz to 386 megahertz was a sustaining innovation that improved the speed of "computing" without significantly altering the experience.

The second kind of innovation dynamic is known as "disruptive innovation." This dynamic is based on its impact on fellow (→) components rather than any performance metric. This dynamic might not denote a significant improvement in the function of a system or larger design, but does signify a break from established methods, materials, and/or functions. Therefore, a disruptive innovation provides an opportunity for change and often makes some methods, materials, and functions obsolete in doing so. For example, the introduction of the laptop significantly changed the way in which computers were designed, used, distributed, manufactured, and marketed, signifying a change that would drive an entirely new realm of computing known as "personal" and "portable" computing.

In short, design innovation is a complex process that relates to the development, application, and reception of a new solution to a relevant problem and therefore can be distinguished from simply generating ideas. HW + SP |

→ *Design Process, Problem Setting, Problem Solving, Product Development*

INTEGRATION

Integration is an intentional and deliberate process of bringing together people, organizations, media, bodies of knowledge, methodologies, or professional practices that are otherwise separate. Integration can be either process-oriented or outcome-oriented: it can occur either through the processes of designing and production, or through the processes of experiencing and using a designed object, system, or service. As a practice, integration is commonly triggered by the escalation of (→) complexity and is simultaneously driven by a desire for rationalization, a need for increased efficiency, improved cognitive comfort, and a more holistic understanding. In the design of systems and organizations, integration can bring together different organizational units and subunits in order to maximize communication and production, whereas in the design of products, integration brings together different platforms or individual product-features in order to improve experiential outcomes at the user end.

In the design industry, integration is commonly conceptualized and performed either as vertical integration or horizontal integration. Vertical integration is hierarchical, occurs intra-organizationally, and is commonly internally driven (→ *Strategic Design*). Through such a process, organizational units are assigned specific tasks in relation to the vision of the organization as a whole. One of the best examples of a vertically integrated business in the computer industry is Apple, a company that directly manufactured its own hardware, accessories, operating system, and most of its software through the late 1990s. Investments in design, as well as in (→) Research and Development (R&D), are customarily greater in vertically integrated companies.

In contrast, horizontal integration occurs inter-organizationally and is externally driven. A good example of horizontal integration is Dell Computers, a company that controls the process of assembly but not production: the design is outsourced to a few local firms in Austin, Texas, and individual units and platforms are manufactured by a worldwide network of suppliers (→ *Outsourcing*). A variation on horizontal integration occurs when a company establishes subsidiaries in a variety of local markets; such subsidiary companies customize, design, and sometimes produce those product features that cater to the local cultural milieu.

The conceptualization of vertical and horizontal integration can be applied to design (→) education as well. In design education, vertical integration can be thought of as an intra-disciplinary activity in relation to the overarching curriculum (→ *Discipline*). A good example of vertical integration in this context occurred in the 1980s, when design schools worldwide began to offer disciplinary-bound design history and theory courses instead of relying exclusively on art history departments. In contrast, horizontal integration in design education arises out of the recognition that all contemporary issues are "inherently interdisciplinary." Unlike vertical integration, horizontal curriculum integration aims at increasing student understanding by establishing connections between and across the design disciplines (such as product design, graphic design, architectural design, or fashion design), as well as design and other disciplines (such are engineering, business, ethnography, or sociology). Whether such integrative curricula are truly multidisciplinary or have a strong disciplinary bias, they are commonly topically or thematically organized in order to facilitate integrative approaches, teamwork, and collaboration (→ *Collaborative Design*). With the ever increasing complexity of daily life, a globalizing economy and the need for a sustained human-centered focus, integrative design thinking has found applications in fields as diverse as healthcare, public policy, law enforcement, crime prevention, and community planning. MM |

→ *Convergence, Synthesis*

INTELLECTUAL PROPERTY

Intellectual property, often referred to as IP, is an umbrella term for various legal exclusive rights or entitlements that attach to certain types of commercially viable intangible products of the human mind. Intellectual property laws, conferred by jurisdictions and countries, enable owners, inventors, and creators to protect their intellectual property from unauthorized uses.

Intellectual property laws encompass a variety of traditional legal fields: patents, design patents, utility patents, copyrights, moral rights, trademarks, trade dress, trade secrets, and rights of publicity.

·   Patents are exclusive rights that protect, for a limited time, devices, methods, processes, or inventions that are novel and useful and that prevent anyone else from making, using, selling, or importing what is patented.

·   Design patents specifically refer to the appearance of designed objects, specifically ornamental configuration and surface decoration that are new, original to the inventor, and not obvious.

- Utility patents apply to an apparatus, process, product, or a composition of matter.
- ($\rightarrow$) Copyrights protect original works of authorship such as literature, movies, art, choreographic works, software, and musical compositions.
- Moral rights, or *droit moral,* either exists as a separate law or as part of copyright law, depending on the country. Moral rights grant authors the right of attribution, the right to share in the profit if the work increases in value, and the right to prevent the work from being altered or destroyed.
- A ($\rightarrow$) trademark is a distinctive word, name, symbol, device, or other designation that identifies and distinguishes a company's goods or services.
- Trade dress refers to the total image of a company's goods or services and consists of distinctive, nonfunctional features such as the color or design of the packaging.
- Trade secrets protect a business or company's confidential information and can include formulas, practices, processes, designs, instruments, or patterns that are generally not known to the public and confer an economic benefit.

Protecting property of the mind is not new. The Romans used a form of trademarks and patents were first protected in the Middle Ages with the Venetian Patent Act of 1474. However, the modern and widespread use of the phrase "intellectual property" can be traced to 1967 when the United Nations World Intellectual Property Organization (WIPO) was formed and WIPO began actively promoting the phrase.

Intellectual property laws in general are based on the legal concept that a person can own real property and tangible objects and that property is an asset to be bought, sold, licensed, or even given away at no cost. Intellectual property laws confer those same rights onto intangible products of the mind. The move from owning real property to owning property of the mind is philosophically complex and continually controversial. The common-law rationale owes its origin to John Locke's notion in *Two Treatises on Government* (1690) that the labor from a person's hands belongs to him or her. These economically based intellectual property systems assume that if creators cannot own what they create, they will have no economic incentive to work, and that once an intellectual property right is sold, the creator forfeits ongoing interest. Civil law systems draw from Georg Wilhelm Friedrich Hegel's concepts in *Philosophy of Right* that human beings imbue objects with their soul and will. These types of intellectual property systems provide both economic protection and inalienable *droit moral* laws that give creators some ongoing control over the work they create and the right to profit when the work increases in value regardless of who owns the actual object.

Attempts to harmonize intellectual property laws date to the late 1800s, but no comprehensive international agreement existed until 1994 when the World Trade Organization (WTO) Agreement on Trade-Related Aspects of Intellectual Property Rights (TRIPS) was signed. TRIPS established minimum standards of protection for several forms of intellectual property with mandated enforcement provisions and an enforceable mechanism for dispute settlement.

In the past forty years, in response to the rise of the Internet and technological innovations that allow instantaneous communication and perfect copies, intellectual property protection has been continually extended in duration and expanded to cover new products not previously protected such as biotechnology, databases, new plant varieties, computer chips, and boat hull designs. These changes generate strong support and serious criticism. The debate over IP protection is more contentious today than ever before.

Proponents of expanded protection insist that most advances in communications, agriculture, transportation, and health care would not exist without strong intellectual property laws. They maintain that intellectual property rights boost cultural development and standards of living, as well as promote public health and safety. They point to the role that intellectual property laws have played in the rising standards of living in developing countries such as China and India. For example, in 1999 India passed its first intellectual property specific law to protect the intellectual creations of its computer scientists. Proponents insist that this law supports the now burgeoning hightech industry in India, which would otherwise not have developed.

Criticism of the idea of "intellectual" property is almost as old as the protection itself. Thomas Jefferson questioned whether copyright was a natural right and did not believe that inventions could be property. Modern critics consider the phrase misleading. They suggest that the word "property" implies scarcity and ideas and inventions are not scarce. They argue that using analogies to real property is flawed and that intellectual property protection is a form of government subsidy, that is, a legally enforceable monopoly power protecting the creator while preventing all others from using a valuable cultural resource. As more cultural property is controlled by a few people or a few corporations, the general public suffers because strong IP control hinders the free exchange of ideas and products vital to a strong economy and culture. MB |

→ Copy, Fake, Plagiarism

Himma, K., The justification of intellectual property: Contemporary philosophical disputes. Available at http://ssrn.com/abstract=904264. Accessed May 22, 2006.
Landes, W., and R. Posner. 2003. The economic structure of intellectual property law. Cambridge, MA: Belknap Press.
Lessig, L. 2001. The future of ideas. New York: Random House.
Thierer, A., and C. W. Crews Jr. 2003. Copy fights: The future of intellectual property in the information age. Washington, DC: Cato Institute.

INTERACTION DESIGN

→ *Interface Design*

INTERDISCIPLINARY

→ *Discipline*

INTERFACE DESIGN

Over the past ten to twenty years, the domain of the interface together with rapidly advancing technology has led to fundamental changes in the field of interface design.

Understanding the interface as a common boundary at which a user wishing to fulfill a certain task meets the product or artifact that is to perform that task, has increased the user's involvement in the design process. This can be a passive involvement by means of observation or the growing attention given to cognitive or ergonomic aspects, or active in the sense of co-authorship, determining content, or personalizing and (→) customizing products. Such an understanding of the interface inevitably leads to a fundamentally different concept of design in relation to developing hard- or software products.

Interface design goes far beyond the simple layout of external appearance, even if the full design is not evident to the viewer or user at the surface.

One main area of interface design is creating interfaces as access points to digital (→) information. It is important that the link created between the user and the digital application contains a level of feedback—in other words, a system that can respond to a user's command, communication, or selection. Interaction design, a significant part of interface design, is responsible for designing the performance of these processes in relation to the user over time. Interaction between humans and artifacts is the subject of research in man-machine interaction (MMI) and human-computer interaction (HCI). This results in a product having a multitude of operability or (→) usability requirements. The domain of operability touches upon diverse aspects such as perception, cognition, semantics, usability, ergonomics, and quality experience, which are significant to interface design and need to be integrated into the design process. Large projects contain important interfaces with other disciplines. Successful interface design is a key factor in how increasingly complex, system-integrated products such as cellular phones, web sites, cars, and computers are accepted by the user (→ *Convergence, System*).

Interface design develops and designs user situations in different user contexts, so as to achieve an optimal user interface. Today, this usually involves touch sensitive monitor (screen)-based communication and information systems. Involving user context is done via a monitor as a graphical user interface (GUI); it tries to determine which software the user interacts with and under which circumstances, how different media can be used in combination to increase effectiveness and the quality of an experience, into which system individual media are integrated, and how this can be made comprehensible and easy for a user to operate (→ *Screen Design*).

When Vannevar Bush in 1945 laid the foundations for (→) hypertext with his memory extender (memex), he also introduced a major interface design metaphor by using an ordinary desk as a document administration device (the desktop). A good twenty years later, Douglas Engelbart devised the now standard, indispensable computer mouse as a way to intuitively and directly access abstract information beyond the monitor. When Alan Kay in the 1970s at Xerox Parc developed a method to transform the abstract command line interface into a graphical user interface, consisting of layers of windows based on real-world metaphors, the WIMP paradigm (windows, icons, menu, pointer) was born. This created many different areas of application for interface design which involve every machine or application that is used to operate or control media.

(→) Information design is the structuring and formal design of information (meaning sensorial coding) in order to transform data into clear and accessible information. The objective is to discover new aspects and perspectives of content, to reduce (→) complexity by avoiding intricate forms of presentation, and to display a clearer, simplified understanding of the situation to be presented. The interaction with this information integrates information design with interface design. In this way, information systems for public spaces are created, as well as for the Internet (→ *Web Design*), portable terminals, or exhibitions.

An increase in digitalization and media developments will make (→) information the most important resource for interface design. When Richard Saul Wurman coined the term "information architect" at the end of the 1970s, he was imagining a designer who structured inherent (→) patterns into data so as to display complex information in the clearest way possible. Today, information architects are responsible for structuring complex information, and developing sitemaps for web sites or the menu structure for cellular phones, electronic program manuals, or software applications. Since information is no longer only structured statically, but reacts dynamically as a structure to patterns of (→) use (making context-related suggestions for content or functions), developing an interface "backbone" requires a dialog between interface designers, interaction designers, engineers, and users. As a rule, usage cases are formulated and modeled that describe sections or fragments of utilization processes, which are then displayed in usage scenarios that anticipate and demonstrate the needs of individual users. These scenarios and personal developments form an interface with the field of (→) service design.

Interfaces enable information to be provided, accessed, and applied. At the end of the 1990s, however, the ever increasing mass of information led to (→) complexity, which (→) knowledge management systems had to untangle and make accessible and comprehensible again. Content-management systems were developed for the digital administration of information. They separate and store information structurally, independent of formal aspects of presentation. Today, integrating context is becoming more important, making context management using metadata (keywords, prioritization, use information, and so on) an essential aspect of structuring and accessing information.

Given that the underlying structures are rarely apparent to the user, interface design develops visual and audiovisual means of presentation that make it easier to apprehend the information clearly—and in the future may use other senses as well.

The first and most important metaphor used by interfaces is the desktop. Real-world metaphors were applied to the computer to make it seem less abstract: the layers of documents in windows, deleting data by dropping it in the trash, or archiving documents in files. The exponential increase in storage capacity and, with that, stored data, causes these metaphors to lose their transferability—because in the real world, files do not contain more and more subfiles, and CDs or storage media are not dropped into the trash.

Consequently a variety of graphic interfaces were created, such as tree maps or the hyperbolic tree, which represent data and certain qualities (metadata) and make them accessible. At the University of Maryland, computer scientist Ben Shneiderman worked on developing innovative forms of presentation that went beyond metaphors based in reality.

The computer's surge in popularity made accessibility a crucial success factor for applications—from web applications to expert systems and operating systems. Mapping data allowed systems to be structured clearly and to make data intuitively accessible and operable—independent of real world metaphors. Cognitive psychology and real world experiences transferred to digital applications (gravity, surround sound, using blue for spatial depth) contributed to this development. Today mapping, especially when displaying complex data such as stock-market information, is vital for articulating an overview and making informed comments, without having to go into too much detail.

This was necessary because, regarding the maze of interconnected content, users had to make several selections before arriving at the information they wanted. A well-designed interface allows users to go directly to the information they need, without navigating through many levels. Hypertext or hypermedia navigation can be used to allow users to go to a conclusive level of content that can be augmented by links at any point.

This procedure requires strategic orchestration to overcome the conventional, sequential narrative structure. A useful comparison can be made with literature where, much earlier, some writers like James Joyce had experimented with and even abandoned linear narrative techniques.

With this in mind, discourses developed concerning "flow" (formulated by Mihaly Csikszentmihalyi) or "experience design" (by Brenda Laurel and Nathan Shedroff) that had a major effect on interface design.

An interface first becomes real and operable once a user interacts with it. Interaction design describes the use and makes it possible to navigate via content, to restructure content (via a choice of appearances and adaptive interfaces that can be tailored to a user and his or her interests or level of knowledge), and to manipulate audiovisual elements. Interaction design focuses on the time aspect of an interface. Feedback, control, productivity, creativity, communication, learning capability, and adaptability are central aspects of interactivity. Interaction design is primarily about designing spatial experience rather than technologies.

An interface's interaction behavior refers to the design of the performance of individual elements of the interface. How does an interface react to a user's actions? Are these forced? Selecting the right audiovisuals is a major factor in how users experience, understand, and interact with an interface.

Interaction flow implies the structure, or navigation, using the linked elements of a digital application or hypermedium. Information architects define the options for possible structures of different information spaces. One decision to be made when planning dramaturgies and dialogue sequences is how information content can be conveyed at the initial navigation metalevel, so that the navigation itself already contains previously chosen content.

This implies that operability is much more than the basic ergonomic level of (→) usability that is focused on the physiological and psychological level of perception and response. This level of understanding respects the cognitive aspects, yet interface design is mainly interested in reducing cognitive work as much as possible. This excludes experimental work being done in research and development, which is looking to devise a new language of media presentation and interaction principles. These require more cognitive effort from the user, so that he or she can navigate through new structures, metaphors, and interaction principles.

Every interaction presents the user with options for action (Gui Bonsiepe called this the area of action). Action also means providing orientation knowledge for decisions. In this way, navigation systems in cars decide on a certain direction, estimate whether the duration of the journey requires a rest stop, or whether the expected volume of traffic might require a different route. Every time the user makes a decision, the system offers new criteria for any new decision the user might make. It is important to communicate the right balance between the source of decisions and the decisions made by the system—because interactive systems and application have to be intelligible and should not fatigue the user. There are no objective criteria available to help ascertain the necessary balance between system decisions and system-decision-relevant information for the user—but this is precisely where interface design comes in, which is constantly developing and formulating this aspect in anticipation of future possible uses. This shows how vital interface design is in relation to user acceptance of a product (or a system, application, and so on).

Increasingly, space itself is becoming the domain of experience, as a result of new technology, and interactive systems are being developed accordingly. In mediatecture, media-related aspects of architecture are developed which function as membranes between the inside and outside (and vice versa) and form interactions with systems and products. The areas of application range from trade fairs, exhibitions, and museums to buildings that present processes and, consequently, become interfaces themselves. The interaction can take place using portable equipment (such as cellular phones), or via a person's movement through a room (their position and articulation in space). The future possibilities are endless, particularly when (→) display technology advances beyond conventional monitors and displays (which are still often used as synonyms) and when almost any surface can function as a projection surface for information. Interaction design will define the design of interaction with complex systems that, from the user's point of view, will probably present little more than simple and less complex objects—especially regarding site-specific systems that possess the knowledge of the user's coordinates in a room. These location-based services show how important the role of context is (in this case, a spatial context, but also the time context of the user) when developing interfaces. These services will only show the user, dependent on place and time, certain data or place it in a higher position in the hierarchy. Basic technological conditions have a major and crucial effect on the potential of interface design. In research and development, new technological requirements are being developed as well as new areas of application for existing technologies. Examples here are display technology (for example an organic light-emitting diode—OLED), identification technology (such as radio frequency identification—RFID), and global positioning technology (such as global positioning system—GPS). The last two concentrate on developing systems—identification technology needs networked identification systems and global positioning needs satellites. RFID chips allow non-contact objects to be identified, which are then assigned data in a databank. This could be an item such as yogurt that someone bought in a supermarket that shows information, such as recipes, ingredients and even ecological credentials on a display. It could also be a credit card that automatically draws money directly from a bank account to pay a parking fee as soon as you enter a parking lot. Technologically, it is irrelevant whether this is done by credit card or a chip built directly into the car—but in terms of design, the difference is vital.

Services such as these deliver convenience and comfort, but also require handing over a certain amount of autonomy and having faith in a society that increasingly monitors its citizens. What is done with the data is not transparent and demands a high level of trust which is difficult to attain. Convenience has overruled people's right to choose who accesses information about their actions.

Assertive participation in the development of scenarios is an important task for interface design, even if the parking-lot example proves that that interface can at times completely disappear—it is a system, an articulation of people in spatial environments (→ Scenario Planning).

This creates new areas of responsibility for designers who increasingly will deal with integrating products into systems and processes. From the users' perspective, the resulting complexity of systems will be separated at certain moments (such as when parking or bringing home the shopping) from the complexity of the interactive system. Designers will play a greater role in developing the action and use scenarios that are aimed at integrating products into systems, and in defining the interaction between user, product, and system. PH |

→ Ergonomics, Information, Information Design, Perception. Service Design

Bergman, E. 2000. Information appliances and beyond. San Francisco: Morgan Kaufmann.
Bonsiepe, G. 1996. Interface: Design neu begreifen. Mannheim: Bollmann.
Johnson, S. 1997. Interface culture: How new technology transforms the way we create and communicate. San Francisco: HarperEdge.
Shedroff, N. 2001. Experience design. Indianapolis, IN: New Riders Publishing.

INTERIOR DESIGN

Interior design embraces not only the decoration and furnishing of space, but also considerations of space planning, lighting, and programmatic issues pertaining to user behaviors, ranging from specific issues of acces-

Interior design encompasses both the programmatic planning and physical treatment of interior space: the projection of its use and the nature of its furnishings and surfaces, that is, walls, floors, and ceilings. Interior design is distinguished from interior decoration in the scope of its purview. Decorators are primarily concerned with the selection of furnishings, while designers integrate the discrete elements of décor into programmatic

*sibility to the nature of the activities to be con-
ducted in the space. The hallmark of interior
design today is a new elasticity in typologies,
seen most dramatically in the domestication
of commercial and public spaces.*

concerns of space and use. Interior designers generally practice collaboratively with architects on the interiors of spaces built from the ground up, but they also work independently, particularly in the case of renovations. There is also a strong history of architect-designed interiors, rooted in the concept of *Gesamtkunstwerk*, the total work of art, that came out of the (→) Arts & Crafts movement of the late nineteenth and early twentieth century. It is no accident that its strongest proponents (from Frank Lloyd Wright to Mies van der Rohe) extended their practices to include the realm of interiors during the nascency of the interior-design profession. Indeed, it was a defensive measure taken by architects who viewed formal intervention by an interior decorator or designer as a threat to the integrity of their aesthetic (→ *Architectural Design*).

Today, apart from strict modernists like Richard Meier who place a premium on homogeneity, architects who take on the role of interior designer (and their numbers are growing) are more likely to be eclectic in philosophy and practice, paralleling the twenty-first century's valorization of plurality. Nonetheless, the bias against interior designers and the realm of the interior itself continues to persist. Critical discussions of the interior have been hampered by its popular perception as a container of ephemera. Furthermore, conventional views of the interior have been fraught with biases: class biases related to centuries-old associations with tradesmen and gender biases related to the depiction of the decorating profession as primarily the domain of women and gay men. As a result, the credibility of the interior as an expression of cultural values has been seriously impaired.

However, the conditions and the light in which culture-at-large is understood are changing under the impact of (→) globalization. The distinctions between "high" culture and "low" culture are dissipating in a more tolerant climate that encourages the cross-fertilization between the two poles. Likewise, there are more frequent instances of productive borrowings among architecture, design, and decoration, once considered exclusive domains. And while the fields of architecture, interior design, and interior decoration still have different educational protocols and different concentrations of emphasis, they are showing a greater mutuality of interest.

Another way to think of this emergent (→) synthesis is to substitute the triad of "architecture, interior design, and decoration" with "modernity, technology, and history." One of the hallmarks of the postmodern era is a heightened awareness of the role of the past in shaping the present (→ *Postmodernism*). In the interior, this manifests itself in a renewed interest in (→) ornament, in evidence of (→) craft and materiality, and in spatial complexities, all running parallel to the ongoing project of (→) modernity.

Even more significantly, there is a new elasticity in typologies. Today, the traditional typologies of the interior—house, loft, office, restaurant, and so on—strain to control their borders. Evidence of programmatic (→) convergences can clearly be seen in public and commercial spaces that aspire to be both more user-friendly and consumer-conscious. Growing numbers of private hospitals (in competition for patients) employ amenities and form languages inspired by luxury spas; at the same time, many gyms and health clubs are adopting the clinical mien of medical facilities to convince their clients of the value of their services. The same relaxation of interior protocols can be seen in offices that co-opt the informal, live-work ethic of the artist's loft, and in hotels that use the language (and contents) of galleries. Similarly, increasing numbers of grocery stores and bookstores include spaces and furniture for eating and socializing.

Likewise, there is a new comfort with stylistic convergences in interiors that appropriate and recombine disparate quotations from design (→) history. These are exemplified in spaces such as Rem Koolhaas' Casa da Musica (2005) in Porto, Portugal (with its inventive use of traditional Portuguese tiles), and Herzog & de Meuron's Walker Art Center (2005) in Minneapolis, Minnesota (where stylized acanthus-leaf patterns are used to mark gallery entrances). These interiors make an art out of hybridism. They do not simply mix and match period furnishings and styles, but refilter them through a contemporary lens.

Another hallmark of the contemporary interior is the overt incorporation of narrative. Tightly themed environments persist in retail spaces such as Ralph Lauren's clothing stores and in entertainment spaces like Las Vegas casinos (→ *Retail Design*). However, a more playful and less linear approach to narrative is increasingly common. For example, in Akita, Japan, AZB, the partnership of Etto Francisco Ohashi and Takamaro Kouji Ohashi, designed two stores—x-Compiler and x-Assembler—that reference Japanese transformer toys and robots. Narratives are now drawn not just from cultural icons but from design typologies themselves. (For the Claska Hotel in Tokyo, Torafu Architects cut silhouettes of appliances—lamps, hairdryers—into hotel room walls in a playful homage to product design, while also providing economical storage for the selfsame items.)

Of all the typologies of the interior, the residence has been least affected by change, apart from ephemeral trends such as outdoor kitchens and palatial bathrooms. However, the narrative of the residence dominates interior design at large. It has become the catalyst for rethinking a host of spaces once firmly isolated from it, ranging from the secretary's cubicle, to the nurse's station, to the librarian's reading room. Considerations such as the accommodation of personal accessories in the work space, the use of color in hospitals, and the provision of couches in libraries are increasingly common, to cite just three examples. The domestication of such environments (with curtains and wallpaper, among other residential elements) provides more comfort, more reassurance, and more pleasure to domains formerly defined by institutional prohibitions and social exclusions. Unquestionably, these changes in public and commercial spaces are indebted to the liberation movements of the late 1960s. The battles fought against barriers of race, class, gender, and physical ability laid the groundwork for a larger climate of hospitality and accommodation.

It is also possible to detect a wholly other agenda in the popularity of the residential model. The introduction of domestic amenities into commercial spaces, such as recreation spaces in office interiors, can also be construed as part of a wider attempt to put a more acceptable face on the workings of free-market capitalism. In this view, interior design dons the mask of entertainment. There is nothing new about the charade. Every interior is fundamentally a stage set. Nor is it particularly insidious—as long as the conceit is transparent. Danger surfaces, however, when illusion becomes delusion—when design overcompensates for the realities of illness with patronizing sentiment, or when offices become surrogate apartments because of the relentless demands of a round-the-clock economy. In these instances, design relinquishes its potential to transform daily life in favor of what amounts to little more than a facile rebranding of space.

Another force is driving the domestication of the interior and that is the enlarged public awareness of design and designers. There is a growing popular demand for design as amenity and status symbol, stimulated by the proliferation of shelter magazines, television shows devoted to home decorating, and the advertising campaigns of commercial entities such as Target and Ikea. In the Western world, prosperity, combined with the appetite of the media, has all but fetishized the interior, yielding yet another reflection of the narcissism of a consumer-driven society. On the one hand, there are positive, democratic outcomes of the growing public profile of design that can be seen in the rise of do-it-yourself web sites and enterprises like Home Depot that emphasize self-reliance. It can also be argued, more generally, that the reconsideration of (→) beauty implicit in the valorization of design is an ameliorating social phenomenon by virtue of its propensity to inspire improvement. On the other hand, the popularization of interior design through personas such as Philippe Starck, Martha Stewart, and Barbara Barry has encouraged a superficial understanding of the interior that is more focused on objects than it is on behaviors and interactions among objects.

For all the recent explosion of interest in interior design, it remains, however, a fundamentally conservative arena of design, rooted as it is in notions of enclosure, security, and comfort. This perception has been exacerbated by the growth of specialized practices focused, for example, on healthcare and hospitality. While such firms offer deep knowledge of the psychology, mechanics, and economies of particular environments, they also perpetuate distinctions that hinder a more integral approach to the interior as an extension of architecture and even the landscape outside. One notable exception is the growth of design and architecture firms accruing expertise in sustainable materials and their applications to the interior. At the same time that design firms are identifying themselves with (→) sustainability and promoting themselves as environmentalists, a movement is building to incorporate environmental responsibility within normative practice (→ *Environmental Design*).

Over the past four decades, efforts have intensified to professionalize the field of interior design and to accord it a status equal to that of architecture. In the US and Canada the Council for Interior Design Accreditation, formerly known as FIDER, reviews interior design education programs at colleges and universities to regulate standards of practice. Furthermore, the International Council of Societies of Industrial Design (ICSID) embraces interior design within its purview, defining it as part of "intellectual profession, and not simply a trade or a service for enterprises." Yet, the education of interior designers remains tremendously variable, with no uniformity of pedagogy. Hence, interior design continues to be perceived as an arena open to the specialist and the amateur. This perception is indicative of both the relatively short history of the profession itself and the broader cultural forces of inclusion and interactivity that mark a global society. SY |

→ *Furniture Design, Lighting Design, Ornament*

Praz, M. 1982. *An illustrated history of interior decoration from Pompeii to Art Nouveau.* London: Thames & Hudson.
Sanders, J. 2002. Curtain wars. *Harvard Design Magazine* (Winter/Spring 2002).
Yelavich, S. 2007. *Contemporary world interiors.* London: Phaidon.

INTERNATIONAL STYLE

"International Style" was the title of an architecture and design exhibition that opened at the Museum of Modern Art in New York in 1932 (→ *Design Museums*). Henry-Russell Hitchcock and Philip Johnson began preparing it as early as 1930 and this show presented American designers with European design developments that had started in 1916 (open plan designs, ribbon glazing, flat roofs, spatial economy, integrated heating, ventilation, and air conditioning, and built-in or tubular steel furniture) and presented an overview ranging from De Stijl to Czech (→) functionalism. It also paved the way for the increasing influence of the Swiss architect, Le Corbusier, and German architects and designers (such as Walter Gropius, Ludwig Mies van der Rohe, Marcel Breuer) on American design from 1933. The exhibition included an interestingly high percentage of social housing projects (residential estates, rooming houses), still a new field for most American architects. It even led to the American popular opinion at the time that held that Europeans might have the right idea about (→) style but the wrong political philosophy. The open-minded American designers' apolitical ideology, in contrast, may have been more contemporary, yet they lacked the right (meaning, European) vocabulary of style. So the stylistic elements were absorbed without their social connotations and were integrated into the American design practice (for example curtain walls, recessed glass facades, functional rather than spacious family kitchens, cantilever chairs). Conflicts in Europe such as the conflict between organic and geometric designs (Hans Scharoun and Hugo Häring versus Mies van der Rohe) were ignored and consequently solved by integrating them (for example in the work of Charles and Ray Eames). Architects born in Europe but who migrated to and worked in the United States (among them Richard Neutra and William Lescaze) joined forces in 1945 to establish the contemporary style, for example, with Case Study Houses.

Despite the fact that Johnson and Hitchcock considered International Style apolitical, it nonetheless triggered massive political hostility. The National Socialists in Germany denounced it as Jewish, racially impure, and unheroic. In Stalin's Soviet Union, it was denounced as cosmopolitan and plutocratic. However, International Style prevailed in the West, and from the 1960s became the catchphrase for straight-edged (→) modernity.

The black-and-white photographic documentation of buildings that were often quite colorful played a significant role in how International Style was received. The black-and-white reproductions evoked a white modernism that has persevered (as in the work of Richard Meier). Richard Buckminster Fuller was an early critic of European formalism that rarely or, at best only partly, considered issues such as (→) mobility, prefabrication, or centralizing maintenance facilities. Tom Wolfe's *From Bauhaus to Our House* of 1981 is ultimately a polemic that essentially focuses on the American reception of International Style, and could be interpreted as an anti-European analysis of (→) postmodernism. The English magazine *Wallpaper* presents a contemporary interpretation of International Style. It combines International Style with postwar modernism and views it as a consistent element in contemporary design. JS |

→ *Design and Politics*

Perella, S., and T. Riley. 1992. *The international style: Exhibition 15 and the Museum of Modern Art*. Columbia Books of Architecture 3. New York: Rizzoli/CBA.
Wolfe, T. 1981. From Bauhaus to our house. *Harper's Magazine* (July).

INTUITION

Intuition (from Latin *intueri*, or "to look upon," "gaze at," also "consider") is the power to make decisions based on previous experience and quick and ready insight. Colloquially, intuition also means a special "feeling" that often goes against reason: an instinct or impulse to make a critical change that, if not followed, will (in retrospect) turn out to be a mistake.

Intuition describes the relationship between a person's various thinking and learning processes. It can also mean a spontaneous and (supposedly) extemporaneous decision-making process. In design, it implies a "feel" for possible future (→) trends, necessities, and behavioral (→) patterns that will influence a product's current design. Intuitive designers venture away from logical market analyses and conclusions and instead follow an internal conviction founded on nothing other than a "certain feeling." Many important design works are the result of designers acting on sudden inspirations, as well as intuitive decisions made by manufacturers when selecting products to be serially produced. Intuition is an essential element of communications and (→) interface design, especially with regards to the navigation of web sites, cellular phones, and other technical devices. Operating such products should not be too challenging or too easy for the average user, because this could result in unnecessary frustrations or lack of interest, and thus hinder (→) usability and the successful communication of information. User navigation also needs to be intuitive—that is, understandable without the use of instructions, and designed in either an informative, linear, or a playful manner according to the target group. Products with intuitive operating systems tailored to individual behavioral patterns are currently inundating the market and proving to be very successful. The iPod's "click wheel," a user-friendly interface that can be operated intuitively by users across many levels of technical ability, is becoming the standard by which the usability of other designs are measured.

Despite the proliferation of the term "intuition" in current design discourse, it is clear from the designs of most user navigations that many of our presumptions about intuition are incorrect, and that we still know very little about how it works. In this area in particular, (design) (→) research is essential, as without it, the context and use of the term "intuition" might simply come to imply a mere legitimization of thoughtlessness. [SIB]

→ *Creativity, Design Process, Design Methods, Heuristics*

J

JEWELRY DESIGN

Jewelry design involves the creation of wearable adornment. There is a large market for jewelry in which not only small workshops and individuals participate, but also design studios with their own distribution channels, specialized jewelry companies, and fashion, perfume, or accessory firms that successfully market jewelry under their labels. Some jewelry makers strive to be artists, others consider themselves craftsmen, and yet others identify as designers. Even among the latter category there are usually further distinctions made between those who produce small series (even limited and/or signed editions) and those who design for mass production by companies.

In defining jewelry design, it is useful to review the etymology of the word "jewelry." The German word for jewelry, *Schmuck*, is related to the English verb "to smuggle." This root indicates that the definition of the term "jewelry" may have evolved gradually over time, from something to be guarded as treasure to an exhibition piece intended to lend its wearer status and poise. The English word is of course tied closely to "jewels" (very much in the spirit of Marilyn Monroe's song "Diamonds Are a Girl's Best Friend")—though the way we understand jewelry today is by no means limited to the use of jewels or even precious metals, but includes nearly every conceivable (→) material including plastics, paper, rubber bands, and cardboard.

The increasingly open-ended definition of the product has enabled the design to develop new standards of (→) value for jewelry. From the Middle Ages until the (→) Art Nouveau era of the late nineteenth and early twentieth centuries, jewelry's central value was identified almost exclusively by the costliness of its materials. Today, composition, originality, innovation, and distinctiveness are increasingly important in the determining value. This shift has at times led to conflicts between traditional jewelry makers and their markets.

A consideration of jewelry's significance also opens up divergent perspectives. Jewelry can be valued quite simply as a financial investment (especially when jewels, gold, silver, and platinum are used), a playful form of dressing up, or a symbolic artifact reinforcing aspect and respect. This latter application is striking in monarchic, political, and military contexts in particular, with their use of crowns, scepters, and medals as insignia of power and influence. These symbolic applications are evident within the context of everyday use, as well. As with clothing, jewelry may represent its wearer as rich, fashionable, and striking; lend poise and form to the body; create equilibrium or deliberate asymmetry. At the same time, jewelry can serve to draw attention to whatever one wants to emphasize: the ears, neck, décolletage, wrists, and in rare cases feet and toes (with the increased popularity of piercing extending the spectrum of possibilities even further). ME |

→ *Fashion Design, Symbol, Trend*

JUST IN TIME

"Just in time" is a strategic method, introduced in 1950 by the Japanese automobile manufacturer Toyota, to minimize the space and time required to store materials or spare parts needed for production processes. Delivering (→) components exactly when they were needed optimized operational procedures and saved on human labor. What is now known as an intersectoral (→) logistics strategy was then able to shift a large part of the responsibility for guaranteeing smooth production in the manufacturing shop onto the suppliers. DPO |

K

KITSCH

Kitsch is part of everyday culture. Whether and when an object is considered kitsch is defined by its cultural origin, social context and is largely a matter of personal taste. Some regard Bavarian Baroque churches or brightly painted Mexican altars as kitsch, whereas these structures are obviously regarded very differently by those who consider them essential to the perpetuation of their belief systems. The perception of something as kitsch depends on context, individual culture, education, and the zeitgeist. An object that was once considered kitsch could become a highly desirable cult or art object years later because of its rarity. Conversely, pieces of art or design can become banal kitsch once derarified by the processes of mass production and sales.

Kitsch has triggered many impassioned debates in the realm of (→) aesthetics. Even the origin of the word is a subject of debate. It first appeared on the Munich art scene around the end of the nineteenth century. Some believe it is derived from the German word *kitschen* (which means to sweep up dirt from the street), while others believe it is derived from the English word (→) "sketch" (a then-common request by American and English tourists at German art markets). As puzzling as the origin of the term may be, its meaning was very clear by the twentieth century. Kitsch was bad taste; art was good taste. In other words: kitsch represented the social divide between the educated upper classes and the "kitschy" lower classes.

Today, the superficial distinctions between art and kitsch have blurred, in large part due to the influence of artists like Jeff Koons or Pierre et Gilles during the 1980s. Once criticism of kitsch itself became conventional, it could then be used as a means of challenging and questioning (→) convention. The strategy of contextualization or even decontextualization is used to turn kitsch into art.

There are many examples of kitsch today: the architecture of Las Vegas, where casinos do not simply mimic but exaggerate the vibrant, shrill qualities of famous cities; television country-music shows featuring lip-synching stars who reconstruct the (→) nostalgia of down home and small town; the countless romantic novels and gossip magazines; souvenirs sold at museums, famous churches, or places of pilgrimage; crystal and Hummel figurines; garden gnomes; Japanese waving cats, and so on and so forth.

In a globalized world, kitsch can also represent regional origin, hometown, and roots: the interior of an Italian restaurant located in the United States, Germany, or Japan will often be decorated with paintings of the Madonna, romantic harbor photos, and miniature gondolas with the intention of making the restaurant supposedly look more Italian than Italy. Excessive decorations often set the tone in private homes as well—faux-painting techniques on the wall, accessories and knickknacks collected from foreign countries on display.

Kitsch is fascinating regardless of one's personal taste—for Jeff Koons, for instance, kitsch represents "banality as savior" in a society defined by rationality and achievement. KSP |

→ *Dada and Design, Postmodernism*

KNOWLEDGE MANAGEMENT

Knowledge management is the general practice within an organization of collecting, preserving, organizing, and disseminating intellectual assets deemed critical for the success of the organization. The main tenet of knowledge management is that internal (→) information in any particular organization has business (→) value.

From a knowledge management perspective, knowledge can be separated into explicit and tacit forms. Explicit knowledge refers to knowledge that is already codified, such as that appearing in reports or patents, for example. Tacit knowledge refers to knowledge that is not so easily captured and preserved—the processes, methods, relationships, and structures that employees learn through time. One of the significant challenges for any knowledge management effort is identifying and capturing this tacit information.

There are different approaches to effective knowledge management. Some are technology-based, some seek to create a knowledge-sharing culture within the organization, and some are dependent on the development of organizational processes to directly effect transfer of knowledge between workers. Tools used to support knowledge management efforts are typically comprised of applications suites designed to collect and organize knowledge assets and then permit accurate searching and retrieval. These tools are often intranet-based and frequently support collaborative group work.

Changes in the marketplace and workplace are driving the adoption of knowledge management practices in a growing number of organizations. Increasing competition based on information and intellectual assets, greater worker mobility, impending baby-boomer retirements and staff reductions have all forced organizations to attempt to preserve key knowledge assets to maintain competitiveness. MDR |

→ *Design Management, Intellectual Property, Strategic Design*

Davenport, T. H., and L. Prusak. 2002. *Information ecology: Mastering the information and knowledge environment.* New York: Oxford Univ. Press.
Prusak, L. 1997. *Knowledge in organizations.* Newton, MA: Butterworth-Heinemann.

L

LANDSCAPE DESIGN

Landscape design is the practice that makes an idea of landscape manifest as a material project. By transforming the land and determining the distribution of activities in space and time, it functions as a symbolic intermediary between natural systems and the humans who inhabit them. Landscape design is therefore both the activity of design and the reception of that design. It is a shared "commons" as well as a performative space in which various actors and natural systems engage in the unfolding of new landscapes. The landscape designer works in the midst of this feedback loop.

The material work of landscape design traditionally involves processes such as surfacing, cutting, filling, planting, draining, flooding, retaining, illuminating, and sheltering. These processes are worked towards the production of design elements that strategically affect the actor's relationship to ground, horizon, and enclosure. These elements are always understood to be experienced in continuous or discontinuous movement, for example ritual, stroll, or ramble. The unfolding and transformation of materials through this movement in time allows for the shifting (→) perceptions of users.

The ways in which landscape design engages the site is the choice of the designer. One approach is a clear condition where the ground is assumed to be a neutral container that is overlaid with the designer's proposition. Another is to assume that the site is latent with processes and precious life and to attempt to respectfully intervene with minimal interruption. A more middle-ground approach is to recognize the performance and appearance of a site and transform those parts into new ecological relations that are resilient and remarkable.

All of these approaches are based on an imagination of site as a bounded territory or a building lot. However, the understanding of what constitutes a site is also within the designer's control. Any territory is embedded with nested and interconnected scales of organization, process, and value. Nesting and interconnection of scales also refer to the way cities have developed; that is, the local was nested in the regional, or the urban was nested in the agricultural hinterland. Contemporary (→) patterns of city growth are now strongly linked to global processes creating a more patchy landscape oriented around airports, transportation networks, tourist destinations, and centers of knowledge.

This shift in the conception of scales is reflected in the various methods of drawing that inform and define ideas of landscape today. Contemporary drawing tools such as satellite imagery, geographical information systems (GIS), scripting software, movies, and handheld devices are now used in a sophisticated dialogue with the more traditional tools of mapping, scenic painting, and Euclidean geometry. This results in multi-perspective depictions of the contemporary landscape that are able to reference connecting geometries as well as those forces that separate and create borders.

One territory in which contemporary landscape design projects are emerging is the postindustrial. These are grounds that demand clean up and reprogramming. Another is the post-agricultural, where rapid development erases critical eco-social networks and processes. These grounds demand the cultivation of meaningful morphologies informed by existing traces of habitation. Landfill transformation, shoreline stabilization, wetland restoration, new energy systems, and water management are all examples of contemporary landscape design project elements that have been invented in response to new ecosystems.

Yet another territory in which contemporary landscape design projects are emerging is infrastructure. The infrastructure of the city—that is, the network that underlies and informs other urban systems—has recently been reexamined as a landscape design element in itself (→ *Urban Design*). In this context, landscape design is informed by technological efficiency and standardization as well as the manipulation of natural processes. It is within infrastructure projects, often called "landscape urbanism," that the transformative effect of landscape is most clearly explored with determination through experimentation, monitoring, and reconstruction. In addition to city and regional parks, urban waterfronts, public plazas, and transit interchanges are all examples of this newly expanded field of professional practice. These projects are often public or public-private partnership-sponsored (→ *Public Design*).

As well as a professional design field, the activity of landscaping and gardening can be understood as a process to create knowledge, a form of therapy, a way to build (→) social ties, or an indication of (→) luxury and status. Multiple and dispersed, these collective individual actions alter the urban grain in often unintentional ways. Estate planning, yard design, community gardens, memorials, and neighborhood-organized landscape restoration and preservation projects are examples of this often unrecognized landscape design project.

The ecological theory of equilibrium and the idea that humans are separate from nature holds true for many people. This is reflected in the difficult goal of sustainable landscape design (→ *Sustainability, Environmental Design*). More recent ecological theory and non-western conceptions of landscape acknowledge that humans and nature are interconnected and that change is a healthy ecosystem process. As this collective understanding of landscape is one that engages complex human dynamics as an inseparable aspect of the natural world, landscape design as a productive paradigm is enjoying a resurgence over other design fields such as architecture and planning. VM |

→ *Architectural Design, System, Urban Planning*

Corner, J., ed. 1999. *Recovering landscape.* New York: Princeton Architectural Press.
Hunt, J. D. 1992. *Gardens and the picturesque: Studies in the history of landscape architecture.* Cambridge, MA: MIT Press.
Shane, D. G. 2005. *Recombinant urbanism: Conceptual modeling in architecture, urban design and city theory.* London: Wiley.
White, P. S., and S. T. A. Pickett. 1985. *The ecology of natural disturbance and patch dynamics.* New York: Academic Press.

LAYOUT

A layout is a graphic design in which a designer establishes the arrangement, proportions, and relationship between the individual elements on the page to be designed, that is: the images, body copy, headings, captions, and other graphic elements. This is often based on a design grid. The challenge is to visually structure content and to create graphically exciting references. The format depends on the requirements (poster, flyer, brochure). The medium is usually print, yet the graphic structure of a web site can also be called a layout.

Etymologically, "layout" refers to its history as a manual skill, when design elements were laid by hand on an assembling surface and manually placed on the page. Today, all stages of a layout, from design to print, are created virtually on a computer using software. CH |

→ *Flyer, Graphic Design, Organization, Poster Design, Prepress, Typography, Web Design*

LIFE CYCLE

→ *Sustainability*

LIFESTYLE

Since the 1990s, the word "design" has come to be used almost synonymously with "lifestyle" or even "style." Today, almost all printed media, magazines, newspapers, brochures, and mail order catalogs contain the words "lifestyle" or "style" at least once, and increasingly in the title ("Life & Style," "Lifestyle," "Style," "Japanese Style," "The International Magazine of Style," etc.).

Entering "lifestyle" into Google results in 372,000 hits; writing it as two words, life style, results in another 249,000. The number of results received after entering only the word "style" is extraordinarily large:1,130,000,000 (October 4, 2006).

Click on the site for the open-source, free encyclopedia Wikipedia and you find the following: "In sociology, a lifestyle is the way a person (or a group) lives. This includes patterns of social relations, consumption, entertainment, and dress. A lifestyle typically also reflects an individual's attitudes, values or worldview." Yet immediately there is an interpretive error contained here; lifestyle, or way of life, is also commonly applied to people who cultivate the art of living in the conceptual translation of the French phrase *savoir-vivre*: Oscar Wilde, or the Duke of Windsor, or Soraya to name a few. The life led by a well-known music producer and ladies' man from Hamburg or a squeaky-voiced TV icon may well be a way to live, but it would not be designated a lifestyle according to this definition.

Let us look at the term "lifestyle" in the context of sociology, in particular the theories by the Frenchman Pierre Bourdieu (1930–2002). He wrote that the ruling elite establishes its position of power through espousing the values of a superior culture and the nuanced differences of a sophisticated and refined lifestyle. The other social classes on the other hand will develop a habitat, even down to the smallest details of their living-room furnishings, that makes it seem as though their given social status is a consciously chosen lifestyle. "You have what you love because you love what you have."

The Wikipedia entry in German for *Lebensstil* (lifestyle) contains references to the medical subset healthy lifestyle. It is mentioned that "in medical terms, the word denotes the health aspects of a lifestyle." Wikipedia proceeds to note that the data that supports the efficacy of a so-called healthy lifestyle is poorer than those underpinning wholly medical treatments. It can be assumed that the health industry is not committed to clarifying matters, as there is less money to be earned from a healthy lifestyle than from the pharmaceutical industry. But it must be remembered that the money earned by the spa department of international five-star hotels or health clubs, or by Tai Chi and yoga teachers, can be quite considerable. The same applies, of course, to the cosmetics industry, the textile industry (for stylish sports clothing), and for any number of glossy magazines *(Vital, Wellfit,* and *Balance* among others). The electronics corporation Philips recently announced that they had sold their semi-conductor branch and were becoming a "lifestyle brand." That is something very different from their original intention. It puts the company in the same arena as the LVMH group for example, a French holding company known for their ($\rightarrow$) luxury goods including Louis Vuitton bags, Moët champagne and Hennessy brandy and companies such as Hermès, Prada, and Gucci. The ($\rightarrow$) brands that are part of this conglomerate speak of a lifestyle association that signals wealth. On the other hand, clothing by Hennes & Mauritz (H&M), the Swedish fashion company, demonstrates a cost-conscious youthfulness along with high-end design. Nonetheless, cult figures like Madonna, Karl Lagerfeld, or Stella McCartney (daughter of Paul McCartney of the Beatles) create designs for the successful Swedish company, whose brand, along with that of another Swedish design and housewares company, Ikea, has influenced the taste (and style) of an entire generation. Clearly there is a lot of business to be made from lifestyling. The styles promoted by Ikea and H&M have indisputably awakened the design consciousness of a large proportion of the population and this has obviously been beneficial for increasing the standard of formal taste worldwide.

Is the difference between the English word "style" and the German word *Stil* important or useful? The latter receives only 69,500,000 results, and some of those are for topics as diverse as "Stil und Imageberatung" (style and image consultancy) or

"Urananreicherung im grossen Stil" (big-style, as in large scale, uranium enrichment—an article in *Focus* news magazine about Iran). Reading this instead of an issue of *Der Spiegel* magazine led to sociological musings that possibly support Bourdieu's lifestyle theories. But this might be going too far. In any case, Wikipedia, the encyclopedia freely open to anyone to read or expand on, add to or edit, informs us in the German version that the term "lifestyle" differs in its hues of meaning from the German word *Lebensstil* in the same way that style differs from *Stil*. BF |

LIGHTING DESIGN

Human factors, technical evaluation, aesthetics, and environmental impact are some of the most important aspects to keep in mind during the lighting design process. Although the formal profession of lighting design is still relatively young, advances in technology and human factors research have allowed the discipline to evolve in recent years to offer a more comprehensive contextual understanding of the medium.

The term "lighting design" applies to a variety of related professional practices that involve the applications and performance characteristics of light:

Architectural lighting design refers to the design of natural and manmade lighting systems for function and/or effect within or related to an architectural construct, exterior site, or urban context.

Theatrical lighting design refers to the temporary installation of portable electric lighting devices for stage and theater productions.

Daylighting design refers to the evaluation of a building site location, building orientation, shape, configuration, and physical design in order to maximize the functional performance characteristics of sunlight.

Lighting product design refers to the aesthetic and technological development of lighting system components for decorative or architectural application within built environments.

Specialty lighting design refers to the technical study of signage, signal, or display lighting as part of a unique industry such as manufacturing, automotive, airport, or transportation systems.

Although lighting design can refer to the design of a discrete physical device (as in lighting product design or specialty lighting design), it usually involves the interaction of light with other architectural materials and surfaces. Light is almost always integral to our sensory experience of any built environment. For this reason, architectural lighting design is the most broadly recognized category within the field, and often encompasses aspects of the other categories (for example, daylighting design is often an important component of architectural lighting design). Thus, for the sake of this definition, architectural lighting design will be the primary point of reference.

(→) Human factors, technical (→) evaluation, (→) aesthetics, and environmental impact are some of the most important aspects to keep in mind in the lighting design process. Arguably the most important consideration to keep in mind when designing with light is human interaction: the perceptual, physiological, and psychological impacts on the user. Our anatomy is wired to respond chemically to specific environmental conditions that include daily cycles and seasonal transitions associated with light. These biological responses are a cumulative result of cultural experiences learned through the course of our individual lives, as well as universally shared characteristics that go back thousands of years to early evolution. For example, exposure to sunlight triggers specific chemical changes essential to normal biological functions including sleep patterns. The relatively recent evolution of man-made light has significantly altered these biologically established patterns, which could have a noticeable impact on long-term health issues. In recent years, as scientific research has revealed the direct impact of light on our health and psychological well-being, human factors has become an increasingly important consideration in lighting design.

Most definitions associated with lighting design acknowledge the duality between the technical/scientific and the creative/artistic. There is often a distinction made in architectural lighting between lighting design and illumination engineering; lighting design is thought to favor aesthetics while illumination engineering is thought to favor the technical. It should be noted that the authors believe this professional distinction to be somewhat artificial and unfortunate. A creative solution that does not meet technical needs fails, as does a solution that merely solves technical problems yet offers no aesthetic spatial enhancement. An emphasis on technical evaluation frequently results in project types being lumped together into common categories based upon quantifiable task-driven standards and code regulations which make little to no allowance for any deviation based upon unique characteristics. Several organizations—the International Commission on Illumination (CIE), the Illumination Engineering Society of North America (IESNA), and the Deutsches Institut für Normung (DIN) for instance—publish categorical "recommended standards" which are intended to be used as reference for designers and engineers. Unfortunately, these generalized technical standards are frequently misinterpreted and used as a unilateral minimum requirement. When such a literal translation is made as the first order of magnitude, the common result is a solution that meets task requirements but does not extend beyond this statistical problem solving.

The programmatic (→) needs, specific task requirements, client profile, and site conditions of any lighting project need to be considered in each design solution. However, the act of designing implies an application of creative artistic practice in conjunction with planning. In lighting design, this may include aspects of composition, organization, finish, tone, and scale of the luminaires themselves, as well as the resulting spatial illumination. These aesthetic choices are bound to directly impact considerations associated with human factors and technical criteria as well. Each designer is bound to make different aesthetic decisions which will result in unique design solutions. It is critical for the design process to embrace diversity and challenge historical conventions in order to reveal new opportunities for future practitioners to reference.

In addition to the physiological, technical, and aesthetic aspects of lighting design, there has been considerable emphasis more recently on (→) sustainability. In this context, sustainability encompasses more traditional concerns for energy efficiency, but also the impact of light and lighting components/hardware on the environment. Lighting systems constitute a large portion of the overall energy consumption of a building, and are often inefficient. They can also have a negative environmental impact through light trespass and light pollution, as well as the disposal of lighting products, mercury-containing lamps in particular. These environmental factors need to be integrated and balanced with all of the other considerations noted above in the design process.

Architectural lighting design may be executed by a lighting designer, independent specialist, or any individual practicing in related occupations such as electrical engineering, architecture, interior design, and manufacturing. It is not so much the label, but rather the capabilities that define the practitioner. Having said this, however, it should be understood that while many of the individuals practicing in related occupations may possess a basic knowledge of conventional applications and/or aesthetics, they frequently lack an awareness of the most current technologies. Additionally, the specifics of the practitioner's professional origin commonly results in a particular bias toward their primary area of practice. For example, engineers that practice lighting design and have the basis of their design process founded within parallel confines of structural, mechanical, and hydraulic systems training are accustomed to viewing referenced standards as "minimum" criteria based upon life safety or critical load factors. In many cases, their projects are "over-engineered" by a significant margin. These kinds of biases may yield an unbalanced design result that leans too heavily toward a focus on aesthetics, technical study, or product sales, rather than a complex attentiveness to the human, technical, and compositional considerations associated with light. The lighting design profession has evolved in part to offer a more comprehensive contextual understanding of the medium.

The formal profession of lighting design is relatively young (originating approximately seventy-five years ago but only reaching a critical mass in the last thirty to forty years), so there has been no consistent method of education. Most practitioners evolve their knowledge base through a combination of personal experience, research, and professional practice. Even today there are very few academic institutions offering full-time programs dedicated to the study of lighting design. More frequently, lighting education takes place in programs of related study such as architecture, interior design, product design, theater, or engineering, where limited courses are offered. Similar to the professional limitations noted above, lighting design courses oftentimes have a pedagogical bias toward the program of origin. In architectural lighting design courses, for example, a heavy emphasis is often placed on quantifiable evaluation. Lighting is frequently studied in parallel to heating, ventilation, air-conditioning, and plumbing, essentially reduced to the status of a technical evaluation within building systems.

As with most design disciplines, there are no formal educational, professional, or testing requirements associated with the title of lighting designer. In the United States, a lighting certification process is available to demonstrate a reasonable level of competency in lighting design. This is not to be confused with a formal credential or registration, such as a Registered Architect or Professional Engineer, but the process nevertheless is useful in acknowledging basic professional qualifications in a fairly undereducated discipline. The process is established by the National Council on the Certification of the Lighting Professions (NCQLP), an independent organization whose sole purpose is the certification of lighting professionals. As this discipline progresses, technologies advance, and more complexities with human factors are revealed, a specific need may be warranted for a more formal testing regulation. CB + DP |

→ *Architectural Design, Human Factors, Interior Design, Set Design*

Boyce, P. R. 2003. *Human factors in lighting*. 2nd ed. London: CEC Press.
Köster, H. 2004. *Dynamic daylighting architecture: Basics, systems, projects*. Basel: Birkhäuser.
Rea, M. S., ed. 2000. *IESNA lighting handbook*. New York: Illuminating Engineering Society of North America.

LOGISTICS

In general, logistics can be described as the planning and implementation of complex production processes, including the transportation and distribution of goods and people.

Logistics has become increasingly important, particularly in the field of industrial production. In this context, it deals mainly with the sequence of production phases, the correct placement and use of machinery, the provision of materials and components, the duration of a particular production phase, the networking system connecting machines, and the process by which all these elements, including packaging and distribution, interact and ultimately work together.

If the process of logistics design can be described as an advanced form of (→) coordination, two complementary aspects rapidly become clear: first, logistics need to be carefully designed, and second, design can be especially innovative when addressing logistics. This becomes even more important when considering the increasing digitization and automation of production processes, since it highlights the responsibility that design assumes in the process of manufacturing itself. In the design departments of large modern companies (for example in the car industry), both the design and the complete instructions for production are digitally loaded into machines, and the production process from start to finish is preset according to this data. Thus, in this case, logistics is an intrinsic part of design.

It also has to be acknowledged that all machines and automatons, as well as the system that interconnects them, will already be precisely designed—and that design is responsible for both product quality control and the supplier company's own logistics. Some industrial firms have transformed into simple assembly or sales and distribution businesses and need to be given the exact place, time, and quality specifics by a larger corporation in order to integrate and intervene in the production process most efficiently. A significant level of skill is needed to design this very complex interconnection—remembering that logistics extends well into sales and distribution and determines materials inventory, designates contents and shipping addresses, arranges loading, and coordinates pallets.

Incidentally, the word "logistics" comes from the Greek *logos*, meaning "word", and biblically this implies the starting point or central perspective, since the *Book of John* begins with the sentence, "In the beginning was the Word." As a result, logistics is the active direction of activities from one focus, or the design and calculation of the causal chain from the beginning to the diverse ends of a process. BL |

→ *Design Management, Design Planning, Product Development, Production Technology, Strategic Design*

LOGO

The somewhat inaccurate yet common term "logo" stands for the word and/or (→) symbol that represents a company or a material or immaterial product. It is inaccurate because the Greek word *logos* actually means "word" or "speech," thus a more precise derivative would be "word sign."

A logo typically consists of text, graphic image, or a combination of both. It is an important element of corporate design in that it formulates the visual identity of the entity or institution it represents. Some consider the logo to be the foundation upon which the design of a (→) corporate identity is based, while others see it as more of a finishing touch, believing that good corporate designs should ultimately be identifiable without the use of a logo. Due to the growing complexity of global corporate structures, it has gradually become necessary to develop an entire system of signs and symbols for purposes of identification.

Designing a logo is a challenge for many designers. A good logo is quickly understood, enduring, can be reproduced in a variety of media, and is "eye-catching." The ultimate test of a logo's technical reproducibility is often conducted using the fax machine. It is generally the case that if it remains recognizable after several faxes, it will prove successful in any medium. Other factors and methods of application need to be considered, as well: the length of the print run, its translation across a variety of media, and the contexts in which it will ultimately be used all play an important role in determining the designer's final choices about the logo's color and form.

A logo design should communicate the identity of the entity or institution it represents in a clear and insightful way. A logo's function includes social identification (how it is perceived by others), copyright identification (how it differentiates itself from its competitors), and owner identification (how it conveys information about proprietary rights). Some historical examples of how the logo's predecessors exhibited these various functions include the coat of arms (social identification); the branding of cattle dating as far back as ancient Egypt (owner identification); and signatures on ceramic products such as oil lamps in ancient Rome. The technical requirements of a logo have become more complex over time: in the new media of today, the growing use of (→) synesthetic factors like sound and movement in logo design has required designers to expand their range of skills to include aspects like audiobranding and logoanimation (→ Branding, Animation). CH |

→ Advertisement, Graphic Design, Layout, Sound Design, Trademark, Visual Communication

Leu, C. 2005. *Index logo*. Bonn: mitp-Verlag.
Mischler, M., N. Bourquin, and R. Klanten, eds. 2002. *Los Logos*. Berlin: Die Gestalten Verlag.
Mollerup, P. 1997. *Marks of Excellence*. London: Phaidon.
Plass, J. 2001. *Lingua grafica*. Ed. R. Klanten. Berlin: Die Gestalten Verlag.

LOOK AND FEEL

The look and feel of an object, graphic work, or package results from the subjective perception of design. "Look and feel" means the impression that the object makes on the viewer, the effect it produces, the character it seems to possess, or the expression that its exterior forms.

Look and feel can thus be perceived as positive or negative; the feelings that result from perception are subjective. Something can look or feel hard or soft, technical or fanciful, classically elegant or modern, and so on.

The look and feel of the object results from the design process that created it: the materials and colors selected, the forms constructed, the proportions created. The atmosphere thus produced, the (→) aesthetic expressed, the harmony of all the design elements developed, strikes the eye of the viewer and is compared to their expectations, (→) needs, and experiences. If the atmosphere largely tallies with the expectation, it is perceived as harmonious, comfortable, and appropriate. KW |

LUXURY

The word "luxury" comes from the Latin word *luxus* (meaning "rankness," "excess," "debauchery," also "lush fertility") and describes ways of behavior, expenditures, and products considered to exceed what society holds to be necessary or sensible. German sociologist and political economist Werner Sombart defines luxury as the mother of capitalism in *Luxus und Kapitalismus*, his book about the modern world as a product of the spirit of excess. Notions of luxury—in the sense of the physical commodities together with the act of owning them—differ according to culture, social class, and economic status, and have been one of the most important drivers in a society's economic and cultural development. The members of the affluent or ruling classes who have the sufficient time and resources to fund and enjoy luxurious services and products have largely driven luxury culture. Their ongoing drive to outdo one another with ever bolder or more innovative commissions ultimately promoted art, architecture, and handicrafts.

The luxury phenomenon is as old as the history of mankind itself and the conventions surrounding the commodities and services that society categorizes as luxury are constantly revised. The rich have always coveted expensive (→) materials, so products made from gemstones, ivory, and precious metals like gold or silver have always been regarded as luxurious. In Europe, the Age of Absolutism (1648–1789) made especially extravagant use of luxury materials, with tailors making luxury clothing from brocade, velvet, silk, and other precious materials, and commodities such as exotic spices and rare foodstuffs also defining luxury. Cocoa, which was brought back to Europe by the conquistadores, was drunk for the first time in 1544 at the Spanish royal court, and by the eighteenth century it had transmuted into a luxury drink for the European nobility. Products such as coffee, tea, pepper, and other spices were important trade goods and, as sought-after luxury commodities, formed the base of wealth in many European cities. At the beginning of the seventeenth century, the tulip became a status (→) symbol in the Netherlands and its price skyrocketed in the 1630s until, on February 6, 1637, the bubble burst and with it, tulip mania.

There is a long history of criticism surrounding the extravagance and pomposity of luxury. Since the beginning of antiquity, philosophers, lawmakers, preachers, and demagogues have denounced luxury as damaging to society. Its positive role in the development of society was not appreciated until the eighteenth century, when French political philosophers like Montesquieu and Voltaire took up the subject. As Montesquieu remarked: "Were the rich not to be lavish, the poor would starve." Indeed the Swiss clockwork industry was born as a direct response to the Calvinist's religious rejection of bric-a-brac and trinkets. In 1705, jewelers specializing in constructing complex and precise clockwork began settling in the French-speaking Swiss centers of La Chaux-de-Fonds and Le Locle (→ Jewelry Design). Since then, the diamonds have been replaced by ever smaller and more brilliant technical constructions with increasingly elaborate and complicated mechanisms. (Wristwatches are still one of the few opportunities for men to wear luxurious jewelry in public).

In today's day and age, the idea of luxury is almost always associated with exclusive and expensive (→) brands. The pricing strategies for luxury brand goods have laws of their own which are often confusing in the eyes of consumers. Yet brands are essential in helping consumers navigate the near infinite array of choices in today's global marketplace, because consumers no longer need to develop their own evaluation criteria (regarding design, workmanship, and quality, for example). The point being that knowing the most important brand names and then being able to afford them signifies a certain social status.

Even the luxury industry is subjected to aesthetic and economic structures. Luxury brands can lose their status if consumer conventions change. What is seen as luxury today could be "out" tomorrow.

Pricing in the luxury goods industry can depend on a variety of factors:

·   The use of precious and expensive raw materials (a gold watch with diamonds).

·   The value and historical (→) credibility of the brand: this association alone can justify a high price or the value of the materials used as the brand is carefully developed and cultivated by history (heritage) and design.

·   Elaborately designed packaging and international marketing (luxury perfume)

·   The number and complexity of a product's components and the level of engineering skill and labor required in production (the "Grande Complication" mechanical wristwatch).

Similar (→) value attributes can be applied to the luxury hotel industry, where excellent location, extravagant use of space, and

Elias, N. 1939. *Über den Prozess der Zivili-sation*. Frankfurt am Main: Suhrkamp.
Sombart, W. 1921. *Luxus und Kapitalismus*. Munich: Duncker & Humblot.
Veblen, T. 1998. *The theory of the leisure class: An economic study in the evolution of institutions*. New York: Macmillan. (Orig. pub. 1899.)

opulent service can make the customer feel special and pampered—or to the luxury car industry, where value is determined by engine performance, the use of elaborate materials, lavish accessories, technical refinement, and spacious interiors. Craftsmanship, manufacturing techniques, and limiting a series can create luxury.

Semiotically, the luxury phenomenon is not an isolated phenomenon—as is the case with any other aesthetic symbol it is a product of the context of its use. A sports car is a luxury commodity loaded with prestige for a businessman, but for a Formula 1 driver, it is a work vehicle. Exclusive golf courses are not a luxury for professional golfers; they are where they earn their livelihood—and the fishermen on the Volga River eat caviar for breakfast.

The value of luxury items makes their manufacturers vulnerable to product piracy and (→) plagiarism. It is particularly easy to copy products in the fashion and accessories industries, since for the most part they are not elaborate or technically complex. Yet highly complex items, such as mechanical wristwatches, can also be copied very precisely with modern methods of production. Sometimes they are even manufactured secretly in the same factory as the originals. Replicas can have a tempering influence on the idea of luxury (→ *Fake*). They are an anarchical challenge to the price politics of luxury brands, and open up a public debate about the function of luxury.

Luxury goes beyond the world of commodities. Time may be the most important luxury for society's functional elite; peace and quiet for the overworked manager; and space and clean air for the inhabitants of densely populated Asian cities. Access to educational institutions is still the ultimate luxury for many people in the third world and culture itself can be a luxury. Design is always an active part of these conditions and processes. [MBO]

→ *Quality, Social, Value*

M

MARKET RESEARCH

When market structures changed from being driven by issues of supply to those of demand, taking the initiative by acquiring knowledge of market requirements and preferences became increasingly important to industry. Originally, objective quantifying processes were used to gauge people's wishes and demands. Gender, age, income, family status, and consumer habits were compiled and processed using complex statistics and then formed the basis for the development of products and marketing concepts. Even today, market research based on studies of consumer behavior are the standard in many marketing departments. Sociometry, or the gauging of human emotions, desires, and behavior, has long been associated with the belief that directing and controlling human wishes and behavior was actually possible.

Motivational research and quality-oriented research first appeared in the mid-twentieth century. Motivational research, headed at the time by Ernest Dichter, was based on a criticism of consumerism and advocated consumer protection. Vance Packard's 1957 book, *The Hidden Persuaders,* expressed the popular fear that consumers would become the unwilling victims of psychologically manipulative sales and entrapment strategies. Growing knowledge about the psychological effects of colors and shapes, products and packaging, of different (→) point of sale design strategies, of the potential emotional effect of scents and sounds, and of the theatrics of advertisements triggered fears about manipulative practices in the world of consumer goods and marketing.

The tremors have long since settled down and qualitative psychological market and motivational research has become an established element of market research and marketing departments. In-depth interviews, focus groups, panel discussions, projective research design, and anthropological observation are basic methods of qualitative psychological marketing and motivational research. The analysis of social milieus has made the focus-group approach popularly used today by designers and marketers as a point of orientation and means that an emphasis is put on studying consumers' lives and lifestyles.

So-called (→) trend research is also highly regarded in market research, because it is important to try to guess which future developments will influence consumer behavior. Futurology is of course a difficult field, as encapsulated in Niels Bohr's aphorism: "Prediction is very difficult, especially if it's about the future." Nevertheless, future and trend research became important aspects of market research. Trend scouting, collective oracles, scanning, and screening are some of the routine approaches in trend research.

Market research needs to be reevaluated in the light of ($\rightarrow$) globalization, individualization, and the spread of comprehensive communication ($\rightarrow$) networking—which is giving consumers the opportunity to participate in the design of products, while making their behavior less predictable. Interestingly, this predicament has made ($\rightarrow$) intuition an unexpectedly respectable option and clarifying model, precisely where and when the calculations of motivations and behavior elude research. Progress in neurological research is being used to locate intuition and determine the role it plays with the help of magnetic resonance imaging (MRI), in order to contribute to the newly established field of neuro-marketing. BM |

$\rightarrow$ *Participatory Design, Observational Research, Research, Target Group*

MATERIALS

The term "materials" refers to the physical matter used to produce an ($\rightarrow$) object or ($\rightarrow$) product. Materials not only comprise the products we use in our everyday lives, but define the environment in which we live.

The selection of materials is one of the most important decisions that any designer must make, as the implications of that choice will necessarily impact all the processes and decisions that follow. Of course, an almost unlimited number of materials exist, and new materials are evolving and being discovered at an incredibly rapid pace. A broad understanding of existing and new materials is essential for practitioners working in a range of design disciplines, from industrial to architectural to textile design. Designers have to consider and weigh all of the implications before choosing one particular material over other materials: how it feels, looks, smells, moves, how heavy or light it is, its durability, cost, aesthetic or cultural resonance, ecological impact, and so on. Designers also have to consider that every material will evoke different ($\rightarrow$) value assumptions and reactions across users, as well. Successful designs are therefore dependent on the strategic selection of the best materials, coupled with the incorporation of those materials into a design that takes full advantage of their unique properties and characteristics.

Although all materials are derived from the earth, most products today are comprised of materials whose properties are far removed from those of their natural sources. In other words, most products are the result of a series of processes that transform naturally occuring substances into processed goods. Raw materials—unprocessed matter extracted directly from the earth—may be comprised of inorganic matter (iron ore, clay) or organic living matter (wood, cotton, silk). Materials comprised of organic matter are referred to as natural or biotic materials, and are for the most part easily biodegradable. Raw materials are then treated or combined with other materials to become semi-finished or processed materials (metal alloys, composites, paper, cloth). Today, these processed materials are often synthetic or man-made—that is, materials that require a series of extrusion or chemical reaction processes not found in nature (synthetic plastics, rubbers, resins, and fibers such as polyester and nylon).

The proliferation of synthetic materials and processes since their relatively recent invention in the nineteenth century has led to a new field of research and engineering referred to as materials science. Practitioners in this field have opened up a range of new possibilities and techniques by extensive research into existing material capabilities, as well as the creation of new materials with specific properties (in the areas of heat resistance, elasticity, or conductivity for instance). These developments have enabled designers to both improve the performance of existing products and to generate the development of new products and technologies. (→) Smart materials, for example, involve materials that respond to thermodynamic energy transfers. Nanotechnology, as another example, involves the manipulation of materials on an atomic or molecular level. These new technologies and processes have the potential to alter the way designers approach the materiality of their products moving forward.

As we move further into the twenty-first century, the responsibility of material developers and designers to employ materials in a conscientious manner is becoming ever more apparent. Ongoing research into materials allows us to design our lives to be not only more convenient, but also safer and more sustainable. From an engineering-design standpoint, the importance of materials in securing the safety and reliability of products in an increasingly technological and mechanized society is clear. From an ecological standpoint, the environmental impact of designed products depends on the materials designers choose and how they are utilized (→ Sustainability, Environmental Design). As such, recent decades have seen an emphasis on material-output reduction, emissions research, recyclability, and biodegradability. At the same time, advances in nanotechnology and materials science, the proliferation of digital networks, and even innovations in space travel have changed the ways in which we think of design as the manipulation of physical space. A deepening awareness of our impact on natural resources, coupled with our

increasingly complex relationship to our environment as both built and virtual, are changing the ways in which we understand materiality as a concept in and of itself. ^{JR |}
→ *Look and Feel, Virtuality*

MECHATRONIC DESIGN

The term "mechatronics," sometimes called "electromechanical design," represents the symbiosis between electronics, mechanical engineering, and (→) software. The term was first coined in 1969 by a senior engineer of a Japanese company: it combines "mecha" of mechanisms and "tronics" of electronics. The design and (→) product development process brings these elements together, resulting in a collaboration that produces smarter, more responsive products and systems.

The field of robotics, the creation of autonomous objects powered by software and controlled by mechanics and electronics, is one well-known manifestation of mechatronic design. Mechatronics also comprises the design of control systems, which are means of regulating systems through engineering. Other areas of mechatronics include microelectromechanical systems (MEMS), sensors/actuators, and human-machine interface. Examples of commonly used objects that rely upon mechatronics include touchless faucets/soap dispensers and anti-lock brakes. ^{AR |}
→ *Engineering Design, Hardware, High Tech, Interface Design, System*

MEDIA DESIGN

→ *Audiovisual Design, Broadcast Design, Interface Design*

MEMPHIS

The Memphis group, established by a group of postmodernist designers in Italy during the early 1980s, had liberating effects on design far beyond the Italian context. The name of the group refers to the song "Memphis Blues" by Bob Dylan, and was selected more or less randomly by its founders. Membership included Ettore Sottsass, founder and *spiritus rector* of the group, Michele De Lucchi, Andrea Branzi, Masanori Umeda, Aldo Cibic, George J. Sowden, Marco Zanini, Nathalie Du Pasquier, and a number of other young international designers.

The first Memphis exhibition was held in 1981 in Milan, and created quite a stir at the time. The furniture and product designs exhibited represented far more than a selection of postmodern, stylistic trends. The designs made frequent use of collage and protrusions, as well as opulent colors and patterns on large surface areas. Most importantly, Memphis designers distinguished themselves by breaking with accepted (→) conventions of the time. They favored artisanship and the production of limited series over processes of industrial mass production, and deliberately designed objects that were apparently nonfunctional rather than adhering too strongly to the tenets of rationalism (→ *Razionalismo*) or (→) functionalism. This is not to say, however, that Memphis was solely defined by its critique of prior design movements; as Barbara Radice, the group's chronicler and art director, writes: "Memphis does not design utopias and, unlike the radical avant-garde, does not assume a critical position toward the design process... Memphis sees design as a means of direct... communication, contemporizes its content and perfects the potential of a dynamic semantics."

Memphis designers cultivated an open, flexible design culture, and considered the designed (→) artifact to hold important symbolic and cultural significance regardless of its origins. They did not reject commercialism but believed consumer behavior to be an important indication of individual (→) social identity. Herein lies the main difference between Memphis and earlier, more radical or avant-garde movements such as (→) Radical Design or even Alchimia, which was regarded as the forerunner to Memphis. In this respect, Memphis marked the beginnings of a true "new design" (Nuovo Design).

The Memphis phenomenon was eventually picked up by the furniture industry, commercialized, and ultimately turned into a (→) "style." Memphis also triggered another important development in Italian design by placing it in the international context. CN |

→ *Postmodernism*

Radice, B. 1984. *Memphis: Research, experiences, failures, and successes of new design*. London, New York: Rizzoli.

MISINFORMATION

As the word suggests, misinformation describes the deliberate distribution of incorrect information usually through media and what are known as "whispering campaigns." The distribution through the established media or directly from the body politic provides false information with sufficient authority for it to have the desired effect, which is to deceive the targeted audience. Advertising sometimes uses subtle forms of misinformation to trivial or, at times, devastating effect. The advertising (→) campaign for powdered milk in India in the 1970s and the tobacco companies' health claims are some of the best-documented examples of designed misinformation. TM |

→ *Advertisement, Information*

MOBILITY

In a design context, mobility (Latin: *mobilitas)* refers to developing the objects and systems that make movement and transportation possible. The word "mobility" is often used in colloquial speech to imply the availability of the appropriate transport facilities. Yet this disregards the systemic aspect of mobility: that of individual, physical, or mental movability or of the connections between various individual and public systems of transport. In other words, mobility in the design context is not only about designing physical means of transport, such as cars, trains, airplanes, and ships (→ *Automobile Design, Transportation Design*). It also implies designing the networks these vessels traverse, as well as corporate services in visible or non-visible segments of transportation, traffic, and (→) logistics. Design has contributed to democratizing transportation and travel by making it available to a greater number of people, while the digitalizing of transportation network systems allows multiple transportation modes to be comprehensively inter-linked.

"I have discovered," wrote Blaise Pascal in 1670, "that the sole cause of man's unhappiness is that he does not know how to stay quietly in his room... Our nature consists in movement; absolute rest is death." (Pascal 1995). In the modern world, completely abstaining from mobility seems as inconceivable as abstaining from (→) communication—a notion that can be at turns exhilarating and frustrating. On the one hand, the proliferation of mobile phones, laptops, and other wireless telecommunications equipment make it possible to lead both an increasingly stationary and nomadic working life largely independent of geographical location; on the other, the ever spreading skeins of traffic, growing mobile networks, and other structures designed to facilitate mobility also make it difficult for people in most parts of the world to escape the sound of an engine or the ringing of a mobile telephone. In other words, the idea of being mobile in many cases can be much more attractive than the attempt to comply with this possibility. When the flow of traffic swells too much, it jams. Mobility is thwarted and turns stagnant.

In order to make mobility a satisfying opportunity rather than a frustrating necessity, different means and objects of transportation are given emotional perks. Playful and sometimes fairly irrational features are added to basic means of mobility. This applies to cars, but also to furniture that is equipped with wheels not for reasons of practicality, but to show that even home furnishings are mobile, that furniture itself is a movable object.

Transport technologies have had a fundamental effect on our relationship to space and power. Architect, urbanist, and cultural theorist Paul Virilio made this the subject of his study of dromology (the study of the logic of speed that underpins modern technological societies). Virilio claims that modern high-speed technology dissolves space by expansion and duration, and speaks of the "raging standstill" of a society that appears to control space and time but is ultimately designing its own extinction. Sociologist Zygmunt Bauman's popular book *Liquid Modernity* (2000) addresses the transition from heavy to light modernity: "Durability is a burden as well as anything voluminous, stable, or heavy, or anything else that restricts mobility."

Human mobility is undeniably subject to a great variety of constraints and restrictions and this, together with the fact that it is a mass phenomenon, makes it all the more exciting and precarious. As transportation systems are linked together systematically into larger and larger networks, the more vulnerable they are to delays or acts of terror. Designers and engineers have traditionally developed forms of transportation infrastructure that involve tubes and hollow spaces into which great numbers of people are stuffed for short periods of time so that they can travel at high speed and uninterrupted along or under streets, through the air, or along tracks. There is far more attention paid to the quality of the vehicle, train, or airplane, than to the quality of points of interchange—the places where passengers wait, spend time, or are passing through (→ *Public Design*). In the future, these also need to be designed with as much care, empathy and intelligence as the vehicles of movement. Likewise, few graphic user interfaces are optimally integrated into the design processes of new, increasingly complex mobility systems and networks.

Baumann, Z. 2000. *Liquid modernity*. Cambridge, United Kingdom: Polity Press.
Pascal, B. 1995. *Pensées*. Trans. A. J. Krailsheimer. New York: Penguin.
Virilio, P. 1999. *Polar Inertia (Theory, Culture and Society Series)*. Trans. Patrick Camiller. London: Sage. (Originally published as *L'inertie polaire*. Paris: Christian Bourgois, 1990.)

Research into alternative forms of mobility is essential in the face of dwindling energy reserves. The question of mobility entails much more than how to get from point A to point B. Moving forward, design practitioners need to begin considering the implications of their decisions regarding mobility in more nuanced and differentiated ways that take the full range of environmental, economic, and social factors into account. TE |

MODEL

The ability to project an idea and make it tangible has made the model an indispensable planning tool (for example of artifacts) since the beginnings of human inventions. Moreover, its didactic-communicative value makes it an effective teaching means.

Etymologically, "model" is related to the word "mold." It first developed in the fields of architecture and the object crafts, but has gradually been adopted in everyday and scientific terminologies. By the second half of the twentieth century, the term was no longer used primarily to describe the purely handmade, three-dimensional structure, but applied more broadly to describe an extensive variety of objects, systems, and processes. Today, "model" can mean a diagram, chart, site plan, drawing, pictogram, technical test setup (like an automobile model in a wind canal), sound model, globe, or mannequin. It can also refer to conceptual models like theories and analogies. The range of its semantic scope makes it almost impossible to arrive at a comprehensive, universal, yet clear definition. This inspired Klaus Dieter Wüsteneck (1963) and Herbert Stachowiak (1973) to formulate an Allgemeine Modelltheorie (AMT), or universal model theory, that defines what all models have in common. The theory asserts that a model only exists in relation to an original on the one hand, and a subject on the other. The most important element of this triad is man (subject), who, as catalyst, forms the necessary channel between the model and its (existing or nonexistent) original.

Models are used in virtually every aspect of the design process: in the (→) visualization of form, the development of function, the communication of processes, the evaluation of alternatives, and so on. They come in a wide variety of forms: twodimensional sketches, three-dimensional objects (scale model, functional model) and virtual representations (3-D computer rendering).

Different ways of using models need different content-related and formal expressive means. Advances in new media (virtual visualizations) and innovative model-building techniques (→ *Rapid Prototyping*) are expanding this range of possibilities even further. They provide design with new methods and are effecting a partial shift in the widespread perception of model production from a skill-based (→) craft to a computer-generated technology (→ *CAD/CAM/CIM/CNC*). MKU |

→ *Design Process, Functional Model, Presentation, Pattern, Project, Prototype, Rendering, Sketch, Tools*

Arnheim, R. 1969. *Visual thinking*. Berkeley: Univ. of California Press.
Bernal, J. D. 1954. *Science in history*. London: Watts.
Stachowiak, H. 1973. *Allgemeine Modelltheorie*. Vienna: Springer.

MODERNITY

It is not modernism that explains the development of awareness of design but rather the entire history of the different phases of modernity.

One reason why the category of modernity is so important for design is that the practice of design originated in precisely the period most commonly described as the modern era. However, the classification of that era, usually shortened to modernism, was applied to the period between 1880 to the 1920s, or even up to the 1950s when one begins to speak of (→) postmodernism.

The dates cannot be determined exactly. It is, in any case, more important that design, with the aspiration of designability and with the fact that, viewed from today's perspective, more and more things appear to have been designed, actually emerges like an incarnation of an evolved modern era.

In order to better illustrate and understand this context, it is worth looking at the history or, better, at the histories of the modern era. For some time now, there has been a faction of historians that sets the beginnings of the modern period as far back as the early Middle Ages or, more precisely, at the end of the era of judgment based on the proof of the existence of God. Once there was little debate about whether someone had committed a crime or not—the person in question was simply submitted to God's judgment or mercy. The accused had to face a trial, they were thrown into water, had to roll down a mountain, or jump off a cliff. Then everyone waited to see whether he or she survived and thus God or the gods made judgments about guilt or innocence. It cannot be stated precisely when society stopped holding a supernatural being responsible and all-powerful, but historical transitions are rarely sharply defined. When this method was, for various reasons, no longer observed or tolerated, society was faced with many challenges. First of all, it became necessary for guilt to be defined, justified, and proven—which placed entirely new demands on those passing judgment and on society as a whole, and called for a completely new concept of verdict. Secondly, suspects began to be held liable for their actions, in other words, to possess autonomy and responsibility and qualities of individuality—since you can only be guilty if you act according to your own free will and are no longer a passive instrument of God or the gods. Consequently, it was the shift in the notion of criminal liability that made it possible and, indeed, essential to regard people as active subjects, or to begin to reflect on subjectivity at all—which is essential to the concept of design.

The process of this first modernity is familiar. The need for rationality of thought and action prevailed, in fact rationality seemed to be the central perspective of life and societies; feudalism and religion were criticized (in part by revolutionary acts as well as manifestos), and a reasonable *Dasein* (being there) and individualism *Sosein* (being thus) became plausible, possible, and desirable.

Some centuries after the beginning of this first modernity, what some historians have termed a second modernity dawned over the Enlightenment, described by Kant as "emancipation from self-inflicted immaturity." This second modernity was associated with the theories and poetry of Romanticism, and later with the visual arts, music, and architecture. It vehemently asserted that life and thinking are often influenced by things that are deeply irrational. It is empirically evident that there are other, completely different forces that affect or shape human existence and actions and that struggle against and prevail over purely rational thoughts and attitudes—for example, strong emotions like fear, horror, and longing, feelings of guilt and awe, as well as desire, libidinal lust, and even the products of dreams and hallucinations.

Consequently, Romanticism challenged the theories of deductive reason and scientific objectivity and their side effects. It contradicted the notions of inevitability and a designed world, and proposed a roaming, gypsy life, passionate and in tune with nature, contrary to the idea of an organized, existence able to be planned. Romanticism also formulated (which is the basis of all design) that "things artificial," that is, human artifacts, could be authentic and opposed a neatly linear and deductive concept of logic with a logic that proceeds by association. In addition (and this is still fundamental to analyzing design even if it did not exist then as such), Romanticism reacted to the beginnings of industrialization by sharply criticizing some of its effects: urbanization, the exploitation and gradual destruction of nature, the increasing importance of capital and all things mercantile (with money as metasymbol—an overarching symbol for worth and value), and the division of labor and the almost taxonomic classification of the human body and skills. Even though, or precisely because, Romanticism was so much a product of its time, some of its criticisms turned out to be contradictory or paradoxical and some, even more radical.

It is also very important to the debate about design in modern times to note that Romantic antidesign is never simply irrational; rather, it replaces one version of rational with a different concept of rationality. It is not insignificant that the first binary language, the basic requirement for the later development of computers, was created and applied by Ada King, Countess of Lovelace (1815–1852), in cooperation with Charles Babbage (1791–1871). Lovelace was Lord Byron's daughter, and a close friend of Mary Shelley, the author of *Frankenstein*, a novel about the construction of an artificial human being. Karl Marx could also very well be called a late Romantic, since he disillusioned the enlightened hopes of a society that based itself on rational discourse among reasonable subjects (also important as an insight for design) with analytical proof of the entirely different rationality of the market (which at first seemed irrational).

This advent of a second modernity—that is, Romanticism and its effects—had major consequences for thought and action, in culture, society, business, industrial production, and notions of designability. Consequently, Richard Wagner's concept of a complete and unified artwork *(Gesamtkunstwerk)* was developed, as well as the English and French early socialist utopias that aimed to reinstate the dignity of work and completely reorganize the distribution of its products and, with that, reorganize the social order. In addition, the role of women in society was being reevaluated and reassessed, and the nature of supposed irrationality was becoming an object of serious research. On the other hand (or perhaps even related to it), melancholy and irony now seemed to be important forces for thought and action, which allowed the Austrian writer Robert Musil (1880–1942) to develop the idea of a sense of possibilities *(Möglichkeitssinn)* making the world both genuinely complex but still designable.

Charles Darwin's or Sigmund Freud's research and theories would be inconceivable without Romanticism or, for that matter, any of the other myriad debates on a new definition of Enlightenment and, along with that, of society and subjects. Moreover, it was already being suggested in this era that the principal concept of modernity, the avant-garde, was another intentional, radical break from a particular prehistory (although sadly, owing to a lack of imagination, many resorted to patterns from distant historical times, particularly the Middle Ages).

The (→) Arts & Crafts movement and the (→) Bauhaus are testimony to this singularly odd second modernity, at least in the contradictions inherent in their ambivalence of regression, modernity, and utopian thinking. Which leads us to the social period commonly called "modernism" and presented as "modernity." The particular quality of this modernity is best described as the recognizable or obvious amalgamation of a new (or sometimes merely sequential) rationality in architecture and other design activities, often in the context of economics. It can also describe the occasionally radical efforts to devise utopian forms of new societies, concepts of order, and designability. This third modernity apparently dreamed of and struggled to conquer the world—as if a better, more beautiful, more humane, faster or more efficient future could be calculated and engineered.

Certainly, the historical events around and after 1900 fed these notions, yet they were also encouraged by a newly established bourgeoisie, by colonialism and colonial wars, then by the First World War, its end in Germany together with revolutionary ambitions, and above all by the Russian Revolution and its consequences. As a result, in political thought, in politics itself, and in business and culture, the concept of a fundamental designability of every aspect and perspective of social existence and individualism was born—which, as we know, also produced some very sorry spectacles and had terrible consequences. Consequently, the history of modernity describes the history of the contradictions to history, as well as the history of the contradictions themselves. Modernity would then arguably be the new manifestation of enthusiastic concepts, work, and design amidst contradictory developments—being equipped with the awareness of these contradictions and yet sometimes boldly defying them.

This is exactly where and when design emerged: as essentially optimistic, a rebellious dream of complex designability, a machine for progressive ventures, collateral for industrial profit, a guarantee of individual qualities and private property, an active context for the aspirations of individualization and subjectivity, the basis for mass industrial production, a negotiator between thought and action, an ironic and banal agitator—and precisely as an expression and incarnation of modernity. ME |

→ *Craft, Design, Form, Functionalism, Postmodernism*

MOOD BOARD

A mood board is a collage implemented to introduce a certain mood, theme, or consumer world. Mood boards can be created with cutouts from various print products, or put together from sketches and photos. They are used in (→) presentations to display as optimally as possible the designs that are to be presented. Creating mood boards at the beginning of a project can also help designers get in the right frame of mind for the task at hand, especially if the project requirements lie outside the designer's own experience.

Despite the fact that complex presentation technologies are currently available, the sketchy, evocative quality of cut-and-paste mood boards are often the most effective means of conveying a certain mood to an audience. TG |

→ *Look and Feel, Sketch, Style*

MULTIDISCIPLINARY   → *Discipline*

N

NEED

The word "need" describes a feeling of lack and the longing to satisfy it. One influential theoretical investigation into the psychology of need was conducted by psychologist Abraham Maslow. Maslow's "needs pyramid" classifies human needs according to the following levels: 1) physiological needs (breathing, sleeping, food, procreation), 2) safety needs (housing, employment, life plans), 3) the need for social relationships (communication, friendship, love), 4) the need for social acceptance (status, prosperity, career, awards), and 5) the need for self-actualization (individuality, art, philosophy).

Although Maslow's pyramid can be addressed as a kind of general priority list when considering the needs of a group (for example, after a catastrophe), most individuals do not follow the hierarchy of needs satisfaction in as sequential and definitive a manner as one might expect. In certain situations, for example, an individual might prioritize the needs of self-actualization over safety and social acceptance. Indeed, it can be argued that the relative importance of Maslow's five levels of need depend on a multitude of contextual factors. Take for example the ways in which needs are valued within a tribal social structure. If the fulfillment of physiological and safety needs are largely dependent on an individual's functioning within a group, the well-being of the tribe would take precedence over the needs of individuality and self-actualization.

In other words, all needs are at once individually subjective and culturally specific. As another example, the ways in which people define their basic needs for sleep differ considerably from country to country and from person to person: how long someone sleeps, whether they sleep alone or with others in the room, whether they sleep on a bed, on a mat, or outside—all of these factors differ depending on the specifics of their cultural context, gender, age, social status, and so on—as well as individual differences in ability, experience, and motivation.

Design is understood as a means of responding to human need, and recent research into the qualities and benefits of user-centered design has shed new light on the subject (→ *Usability*). However, it is important to also remember that all designs (and designers) are grounded in specific social and cultural frameworks, and that every (→) design process will necessarily require certain assumptions about the needs of users. For that reason, the notion of a "universal design" may be inherently flawed—

even presumptuous or a bit naive—in that it does not fully address the pluralism inherent across individuals, cultures, and populations. In an effort to appeal to everyone in general and no one in particular, designs purporting to appeal to a universal audience can be formulaic and nondescript, thereby inspiring users to individualize and appropriate them either via the personal adaptation of a design (→ Non Intentional Design) or through the aesthetics of wearing and aging (→ Patina).

This individuality of need also explains why there will always be a market for new designs of simple everyday objects that respond to basic needs (such as a piece of furniture). The issues that remain relevant for the contemporary designer are improvements upon the designs that already exist, or researching needs that have not yet been articulated (in other words, the needs that evolve from further social developments). Design today has to consider several need levels simultaneously and, in this way, create radically new developments. CH |

→ *Needs Assessment, Problem Solving, Social*

NEEDS ASSESSMENT

A needs assessment is the process of conducting an inquiry to an end-user or customer population with the purpose of determining their (→) needs and goals related to a particular design project. The inquiry is typically conducted using (→) research techniques designed to illuminate the front-end objectives of a user-centered design process. Most often, qualitative research techniques such as observation or interview are used. However, quantitative techniques such as large-scale questionnaire studies may also be employed to query larger target populations. The derived needs assessment is used in the design process to ensure that the product or service being designed will successfully meet these end-user needs. MDR |

→ *Market Research, Observational Research, Participatory Design, Research, Target Group, Use, Usability*

NETWORKING

A network is an accumulation of nodes with connectors that link them together. As new nodes are added, new connectors may join them to an existing network, and that is how networks grow in size. This simple description, however, does not begin to represent the increasing relevance of network (→) theory for understanding an increasingly diverse range of phenomena in our contemporary world.

Network theory, generally, has come to prominence only in the late twentieth century, and its rise parallels the growth of the World Wide Web—one of the most visible examples of a network. From terrorist organizations to brain functions, from community building to business models, researchers are discovering powerful new explanatory possibilities for network theory across diverse social and organizational enterprises. Whether orchestrated or self-organizing, the powerful collaborative potential that networked practices embody hold the possibility to reframe every step of how things are created, from their conception, design, and evaluation through to their production, distribution, and eventual consumption.

Research into networks has also shed light on the commonly understood meaning of "networking," the use of one's connections to further professional advancement. For example, if one's (→) social network is comprised of "strong ties" (close companions) and "weak ties" (more distant acquaintances), then research that Mark Granovetter conducted showed that it is the "weak" ties that are the more critical links in securing new jobs. It is these weak ties, also, that serve as the key to understanding the "small-worlds" phenomenon, a dramatic illustration of the power of networks to link efficiently two distant nodes. "Small worlds" describes the common experience of meeting someone you don't know but finding out that you have a random acquaintance in common. Stanley Milgram's research in the 1960s showed that through the surprising effectiveness of weak links one could connect together any two people in the United States by 5.5 intermediate steps, spawning the popular notion of "six degrees of separation."

A network, however, is not just a simple accumulation of links. It must be distinguished from other, hierarchically organized structures with dramatically different properties. Hierarchical structures, such as those in the military or in vertically integrated corporations, place greater emphasis and give priority to the decision making of those at or nearer to the top of the pyramid (→ Integration). The chain of command is centralized at the apex and works its way down to the lowest-level producers, who are often unaware of the rationale for decisions made elsewhere. In a network (→) organization, however, there is no centralized command structure, and input comes from and moves to anywhere in the network. Decentralized networks do exhibit clustering, however, which is the tendency for some nodes to gather more connections than other nodes, and to emerge as centers of intense activity. For certain kinds of tasks, though, researchers are showing that networks can be both more efficient and more effective in circulating information and producing collaboratively.

The ability to collaborate virtually on projects in parallel—aided by electronic file sharing—has significant ramifications for the (→) design process. It means that rather than having a single designer author a project, multiple and possibly thousands of designers, users, and consumers can potentially contribute meaningfully as well (→ Collaborative Design). While seemingly unrealistic, it is this model that produced Linux, an Open Source operating system that has captured substantial market share in business and industry. The Open Source model is a novel, collaborative way of designing computer code. Rather than dividing up the code into rational subcomponents and hierarchically

Barabási, A.-L. 2002. *Linked: The new science of networks*. Cambridge, MA: Perseus Books Group.
Benkler, Y. 2006. *The wealth of networks: How social production transforms markets and freedom*. New Haven: Yale Univ. Press.
Granovetter, M. 1973. The strength of weak ties. *American Journal of Sociology* 78:1360–80.
Lewin, R. 1992. *Complexity: Life at the edge of chaos*. Chicago: Univ. of Chicago Press.

NON INTENTIONAL DESIGN

Non Intentional Design describes the everyday redesign of designed objects by the user. It does not create a new design, but through use, creates something new or replaces the old.

assigning the lower-order tasks to entry-level code writers (as was typically done in the computer business), the Open Source model distributes authoring potential to anyone anywhere in a network who is invested enough to work on whatever problems they choose. By circulating and versioning the written code through recursive and iterative cycles, the code begins to take on the best characteristics of its thousands of co-creators' contributions. While not always pure examples of networking, Open Source is emerging as a viable alternative to traditional, hierarchically organized ways of designing (→) software. The potential of networks to empower users to create and produce—as exemplified in phenomena such as the online encyclopedia Wikipedia—represents a radical shift from centralized, Fordist production to networked, user-driven innovation. JHU |
→ *Complexity, Component, Organization, Virtuality*

Non Intentional Design (NID) is a phrase that originated at the end of the 1990s in design (→) research. It describes the everyday, unprofessional (→) redesign of professionally designed objects. NID results when an object is used in a manner different from the prescribed (and therefore restricted) functional intention or when the prescribed application is not honored in the new use. NID is the conversion of norm into ab-norm—everyday, everywhere, and by everyone. NID examines the generation of function and the meaning of objects in and through (→) use. It describes all the applications, processes, treatments, or interventions, great and small, that change people's lives or work environments. People have been using things in ways that were not originally envisaged since they began appropriating objects. This phenomenon goes far back in history—back to the beginnings of (→) object culture. At least as early as the Stone Age, people began using material found in nature with the strategic goal of improving their chances of survival. Stones to make fire, to sharpen as knives to shave, split, cut, and stab, branches to use as spears, arrows, or skewers. In this respect, the impetus to solve problems joins the primordial human ability to make found or given objects serve the user's purposes. However these phases of human history do not fall into the category of Non Intentional Design. NID can only exist within a product culture that has been progressing since industrialization saw the mass production of designed objects.

Non Intentional Design resists normalization, gives diversity to those things that appear to be most straightforward, and entails transformation combined with clever new functionality. NID is a reaction to temporary shortages, responds to convenience, or optimizes (→) function. It can also be the result of play or instinct. It reduces costs and helps cut back on surplus in a world awash with products.

To better define this complex phenomenon, it is important to clarify what is not Non Intentional Design. The products of do-it-yourself, self-promoting handymen or women are not in this category. Because the do-it-yourselfers (most of whom are men) and others who creatively work and build, consciously make ingenious but often useless objects, where the psychological rewards outweigh the practical. Economies like those of postwar Germany, the GDR, or underdeveloped countries that are characterized by shortages also create clever, resourceful, useful things, but not necessarily Non Intentional Design. In these cases, material and social (→) needs are the driving forces behind satisfying one's personal needs or securing one's survival through sales. In the case of the GDR, homemade objects or products assembled according to instruction booklets were the only way of replicating the inaccessible glamour of the West.

Non Intentional Design, however, is not a (→) design process; nothing is designed, as such. The adjective, non intentional, is an indispensable reference to the self-acting subject, who proceeds actively and inventively in his or her reuse of an artifact, but the motivation does not amount to amateur design because there is no incentive to consciously create anything. Thus NID is neither influenced nor informed by the will to design. However non intentional should not be confused with coincidence, the lack of good sense, or being without a goal or strategy because the reuse is very much the result of a desire to solve a problem. The desire to problem solve (→ *Problem Solving*) can spring from different motives and situations, more or less spontaneously, more or less consciously. In NID, the users' motives lie more in wanting to use a thing differently from the professionally determined aim, in order to balance a deficit—either momentary (emergency solution, provisional, improvisational: for instance saucers as ashtrays) or systematic (no product suited to the specific purpose: like beer coasters under a leg to steady a wobbling table). And it always involves using a previously designed product. The chair is used as a place to hang clothes or as a shelf or a ladder, a refrigerator door becomes a notice board, paper clips are good for cleaning finger nails and for removing a CD from the computer, stairs serve as benches or ramps for skateboarders, stockings wait for December 25 to be filled by Santa Claus—the list goes on and on.

The most important principles of non intentional design can be summarized as follows:

· Reversible reuse: an object is temporarily or permanently used in a new context, without altering the original condition and function (a jam jar as a pencil holder).

· Irreversible use: the new use leaves permanent traces (bottles as candle holders) or the object has to be permanently changed to suit the new application (a jar with small holes jabbed in the lid to make it a sugar sprinkler).

· Change of location: things are removed from their original location (pallets as bed frames) or, the opposite, a location is given a new function (parties under bridges).

Reuse via NID is so natural with so many objects that the people who do this every day hardly notice their own actions. This shows, depending on how the basic forms are used, that not only is the object's original application being evaluated, but also its potential for reuse, taking into account the product's inherent features. People become curious or interested only when objects are reused in an unusual or unfamiliar way.

Products and places that are considered strange, misunderstood, or misused according to professional design criteria (and its prerequisite of functional and sensible use) possess great potential for innovation, imagination, and spontaneity. Analyzing use is so enlightening because, despite globalization, the way people use products displays cultural diversity and difference. It is high time to take NID's everyday yet unique new inventions and added functions seriously. UB |

→ *Affordance*

Baudrillard, J. 1996. *The system of objects*. Trans. J. Benedict. London: Verso Books. (Orig. pub. in French 1968.)
Jencks, C., and N. Silver. 1972. *Adhocism: The case for improvisation*. New York: Doubleday.
Rudofsky, B. 1964. *Architecture without architects*. New York: Doubleday.
Selle, G., and J. Boehe. 1986. *Leben mit den schönen Dingen*. Reinbek: Rowohlt.

NOSTALGIA

The word "nostalgia" was originally coined to describe a pathological illness, the symptom of which was an unbearable anguish and pain *(algia)* caused by a longing for home *(nostos)*. Curiously, over time the medical condition diminished and the term moved into common language to refer to a general longing for times past—usually for a time from one's own past but increasingly, due to media representations of history, a past that one was not part of. The closest phenomena today to this sense of the term is probably the intense nostalgia felt by many Soviet bloc people for the old days of the communist regime when life was perceived as predictable and stable. "Yugo-nostalgia," for instance, is the term used in relation to the desire of some members of the population of the old Yugoslavia to return to the "golden days" of the Tito regime.

Nostalgia (and simply evoking the past) is a prevalent theme and source for designers and is very powerfully and manipulatively used in marketing. As technological change advances at disorienting speed so does the recycling of past trends, lifestyles, and aesthetics often in order to introduce the new in a reassuring manner. The use and manipulation of nostalgia is most commonly seen in advertising and fashion though it can be a feature of all design fields. The contemporary use of stone in buildings, for instance, is rarely for structural reasons but rather to convey, through nostalgia, the concept of solidity, reliability, and prestige. Streamlining reappears at regular intervals, as do the color schemes and graphic icons and fashion styles of the 1960s and 70s as a nostalgia for a real or imagined past ($\rightarrow$) lifestyle. TM |

$\rightarrow$ *Retro Design, Trend, Styling*

NOT-FOR-PROFIT

As the term suggests, "not-for-profit" (NFP) describes organizations and institutions whose sole purpose is to generate income exclusively for ($\rightarrow$) social, cultural, and environmental advancement. Legally, there can be no financial profit motive, otherwise NFPs will contravene the "favored tax" status they work under in most countries and in most instances corporations can only make donations to NFP organizations. Many private design schools are operated as not-for-profit enterprises ($\rightarrow$ *Education*). A "for-profit" school is required to return a financial dividend to owners and shareholders, but any money made by a design school that operates on a not-for-profit basis must be returned to the institution's core mission. Many designers, design companies, and design schools work for not-for-profit organizations, such as Non-Government Organizations (NGOs), at a reduced fee or for free, with some dedicating a specific amount of time to such activities. It is also common for students to undertake educational projects serving the needs of NFP agencies' charitable programs. TM |

$\rightarrow$ *Design Management*

O

OBJECT

Although the term has a myriad of possible meanings according to the philosophical, scientific, or (→) semiotic context in which it is being discussed, an object in everyday vernacular generally refers to one of two definitions: a specific concern, problem, issue, challenge, purpose, or goal (as in "the object of this brief"), or a discrete thing with tangible (→) material qualities that are perceptible to human senses.

According to the latter definition, an object may be designed by humans, manufactured by machines, or found in nature; it may be functional, decorative, ritual, aesthetic, customizable, recyclable, or any combination thereof; it may be inanimate and consist of a single indivisible member or possess multiple moving or mechanized (→) components (a compound or composite object). Regardless of its origin, physical characteristics, or (→) function, an object is defined by the fact that it exists more or less independently of the subject that perceives it. Very simply put, design can be thought of as the act of articulating the relationship between subjects (users) and the material objects they perceive. TWH |

→ *Artifact, Form, Perception, Product, Tools*

OBSERVATIONAL RESEARCH

Observational research is the most appropriate empirical procedure for the design process and the objects and functions it researches serve design most effectively.

To behold, stare at, gaze, catch sight of, or even to follow and watch are all pleasant or unpleasant connotations of the word "observation." Observing is a (→) social day-to-day activity, done by everyone in almost every situation (at leisure, when shopping, at work, waiting for something or someone), at different places (the window, on the street, at a bus stop, in a private or public form of transport, at the doctor's rooms), and for different reasons that can range from curiosity, boredom, control, surveillance and fear to desire. A rush of visual stimuli meets the eye at the moment of observation, yet the brain is capable of filtering out the most important stream of visual information according to its importance or appeal. Seeing, along with other modes of perception, is a faculty that has a major role in understanding non-verbal forms of communication. Ordinary, day-to-day observation can be coincidental or random. It occurs spontaneously, subjectively, and without reflection. In contrast, scientific observation is concentrated, goal-oriented, and chooses its subject systematically and consciously.

Observational research is certainly not an empirical method that is exclusive to design (→) research, but it can be said to be one of the empirical research procedures that follows the (→) design process most closely and whose objects of research serve it most effectively.

There have been three significant phases in the history of design research that need to be understood before focusing on observation as it pertains to design.

Observation, even systematic observation, can be traced far back through the course of human history: to accounts of the foreign, to mythology, and later to historiography and literature. There are three stages to be distinguished in the emergence of observational research. Its scientific roots, and the first phase, can be traced back to the nineteenth century when the first ethnological boom triggered by European exploration and colonization. It was the writings of missionaries and later of social anthropologists, such as Bronislaw Malinowski, whose work formed the basis of participant observation. The second phase stems from the growing significance of sociology and its discovery of social questions in industrialized cities, at first in England, then since the 1920s by the Chicago School and Robert Ezra Park, who regarded the city as a social research laboratory. The third and final phase of observational research developed later with the psychoanalytic approach to ethnology (this was pioneered by Hans-Jürgen Heinrichs, Georges Devereux, Maya Nadig, and Mario Erdheim among others). This qualitative, and not yet sufficiently acknowledged, branch of research transforms the necessity of subjectivity into a scientific virtue by way of the researcher's self-reflection, as expressed so well by the German philosopher and sociologist Jürgen Habermas.

The risk of "going native" is higher in scientific observation than in other more standard and apparently more objective methods, because observational researchers—if fully committed and active in their field of research—can gradually assume social roles that compromise their objectivity, resulting in excessive involvement, empathy, or identification with a certain group. Observational research, in contrast, has the great advantage of allowing social behavior, interaction, and emotional gestures to be perceived and recorded at the instant they occur and, hopefully, the behavior and actions of those observed occur spontaneously, unreflectively, and uncontrolled by verbal communication or interference by the observer.

Sociologically or psychologically oriented observational research is concerned with examining and interpreting the social behavior of certain groups or the interactions between subjects. Design is also interested in the fascinating yet complicated relationship between subject and object—for example, in how people communicate or interact in certain situations with products, symbols, and services.

Design practice does not consistently take into account how all of these designed artifacts will ultimately function on a day-to-day basis or how they will actually be used. Ideally, systematic observation would enable the design process to learn more about people's day-to-day needs, their problems with designed objects, and their desires and longings and how these are manifested in emotional ties to objects. Observational studies can provide a more sensitive understanding of people's motives and needs from a social and economic basis, and can also be productive in the critical relationship between users and the world of products, globalization, and cultural differences. Anyone involved in design, marketing, and (→) branding who wants or has to search for and create new (→) trends, will have already discovered observation as a tool and intelligent strategy. Trend scouts or trend watchers comb the world to gather observations that are not necessarily either scientific or analytic, and inspiration for new design ideas for products, services, and campaigns—a process called "spotting," which is more or less a light-weight category of ethnology. In many cases, social interests and strategies will fuse with economic incentives, because ambivalence is an inevitable by-product of all complex and contradictory societies, not only for design (→) theory and (→) research.

Different forms of observation can be adopted according to the situation and aim of design-related, observational research study. First, there is the difference between field and laboratory research. The former carries out its observation in naturally occurring social contexts, that is in the observed group's normal surroundings. Laboratory observation, on the other hand, is undertaken in artificial environments devised for the experiment. For some research purposes, field studies are more conclusive as people are observed in their familiar or natural settings. These are most effective when the researcher nominates specific tasks to be observed in public (on the street or public square) or in semipublic spaces (in the café, streetcar, or shop). However, laboratory observation is more successful if the subjects are unaware of which interaction or activity is actually being observed and their attention is distracted or diverted. Laboratory situations are commonly used in market or user acceptance research to ascertain opinions about products. These methods however, are not classified as observational research, but are simple, abstract (mainly representative) analyses of the status quo.

It has to be differentiated between overt or covert approaches to observational research. In the former, the subject is aware of being observed, making it easier for researchers to be active in the observational environment. However, this approach involves a higher risk of reactivity effects, meaning that the subject's behavior may be affected by the observational situation. Overt observation is subdivided into three categories: active participatory (the observer is an active participant on the same level as the subject), passive participatory (the observer is present but does not participate), and non-participatory (concealed observation from outside, characteristic of laboratory studies).

Secret or covert observation has the marked advantage of having no reactive effects; interaction is natural and the observer is able to study "uncorrupted" subject-object interaction. But there are ethical implications involved because the approach compromises the subjects' privacy unbeknownst to them. This is the case if people are unaware of being observed and do something embarrassing, culturally unacceptable, or if they are doing something surreptitiously or socially undesirable.

Ethically debatable forms of observation are uncommon in design research. It is ridiculous to talk of compromising someone's privacy when trying to establish how a person opens a door, how a door can be designed to signal that it is easy to open, or when consumer behavior or haptic preferences are being observed for (→) gender implications. The meaning of designed objects can also occasionally be analyzed without an active subject—for example, when studying how women and men respectively organize, structure, and individualize their desks or workplaces.

Any form of observation will influence the object of research or the interface between subject and object. That is why it is essential to clearly outline the cognitive interest, goals, activities, time and spatial dimensions and, as a researcher, to take responsibility for the legitimacy and objectives of the research process. Below is a schematic example of the steps and elements that are necessary for an observational research project:

- Establish the cognitive interest and the objectives of the study.
- Formulate a hypothesis.
- Determine the target group or object of observation or relation/interaction.
- Establish the observation field (place, time, social grouping, and the basic conditions).
- Decide on the observation method: field or laboratory, direct or indirect, participatory or non-participatory, overt or covert, structured or unstructured, observation by oneself.
- Prepare a preliminary observation plan and establish the type of documentation that will be required.

· Pretest: free observation without a fixed plan in order to re-examine the approaches regarding completion, feasibility, and categories and adjust accordingly.

· Prepare an observation grid.

· Detailed, precise observation with a fixed plan (test for feasibility and completeness and make any necessary corrections).

· Perform the observational study.

· Evaluate and analyze: quantitative and/or qualitative evaluation.

· Design the presentation and communication of analyses: graphics, diagrams, text, sketches, schematic presentations, sound, (→ Sound Design), photos (→ Photographic Design), (→) film, and/or (→) animation.

· Design approaches to solutions.

· Prepare possible summary of theories, designs, and so on.

Observational research in design, in particular qualitative observational research, is an excellent method that can be applied to unconventional contexts. It allows the designer to better understand the emotional and practical relationship between people and things, to identify usage patterns and wishes, and thus to develop a better understanding of people's motives. It is a good means of challenging conventions and to create genuinely clever, innovative designs. UB |

→ Constructivism, Design Methods, Participatory Design

Abrams, B. 2000. *Observational research handbook: Understanding how consumers live with your product.* Columbus, OH: McGraw Hill.

Jorgensen, D. L. 1989. *Participant observation: A methodology for human studies.* Newbury Park, CA: Sage Publications.

ODM

Original Design Manufacturer (ODM) describes a company that designs and manufactures products that will ultimately be sold under another company's brand name. While ODMs exist in all countries, they are particularly important for those that are seeking to develop economically beyond a reliance on outsourced manufacturing (→ OEM, Outsourcing). ODMs can show how these countries are no longer simply manufacturing products on behalf of developed industrial countries, but are capable of unique research, development and design.

This is one reason why governments and companies in many Asian countries are investing so aggressively and successfully in design. It is a well-founded challenge for traditional industrial countries and their companies. SAB |

OEM

Original Equipment Manufacturer (OEM) typically refers to a contracted company that manufactures products (or components) that are sold under or within the brand of another company. In the context of increasing (→) globalization, OEMs have become important to countries that are seeking economic growth through the development of international manufacturing standards. For these countries, it is priority to demonstrate their capacity to utilize advanced technology and production methods. (Confusingly, OEM is also used in some contexts to refer to the vendor company instead of the contracted manufacturer). SAB |

→ *Logistics, ODM, Outsourcing*

OLFACTORY DESIGN

In literature, Marcel Proust's madeleines immortalized the world of scents and their power to evoke memories. Scent and its extreme ambivalence reached an even broader public with Patrick Süskind's novel *Perfume* and the subsequent film version. In fact, we really cannot escape smells (unless our olfactory organ is damaged or our noses are blocked)—everything has a smell, everywhere, always, whether good or bad.

The sense of smell is located somewhere between the distant senses of sight and hearing and the near senses of touch and taste; subjectively, it is often polarized as scent or stench. The sense of smell is closely associated with breathing and connects us to the world; it also has an evolutionary, biological protective function and is directly related to emotions and particularly to sexuality. The sense of smell also involves innate responses, which makes it a fascinating, and a debatable, attribute to influence. We do not pay much attention to a particular odor (whether a pleasant scent or an unpleasant stench) if it does not stand out among the usual mix of smells. This can be problematic since it can still have a significant, though unconscious, influence on our physical and, even more, on our psychological and social states. In other words, smell can be easily used as a subtle means of manipulation.

In recent years, methods of creating artificial fragrances and flavors have become more sophisticated and as more food in the future will be either genetically manipulated or flavor-altered, -enhanced, -intensified, or -neutralized (→ *Food Design*), olfactory design is also on the rise. Regardless of our cultural differences, society, and its increasing desire to sublimate human instinctive drives, is gradually rejecting natural human and other smells. Sweat, in a controlled everyday public environment, is condemned as being an almost animal stench by a society obsessed with hygiene and removing all evidence of human perspiration. Nonetheless even pleasant smells have cultural and social connotations that result from individual psychological patterns and the personal memories they can trigger.

Hence, studios and businesses are beginning to dedicate themselves to the design aspects of scent and smell as they do to (→) sound design. Their approach to designing smells is usually directed at creating what are considered good and pleasant fragrances, or neutralizing unpleasant smells or stenches.

Chemists, biologists, and designers busy themselves with deactivating odors considered repulsive (for example, in toilets). But it begins to be even more interesting when scent inhibitors can be used for birth control. Recent research has established that sperm uses scent receptors to track egg cells, meaning, metaphorically, that if the sperms' noses are blocked, they will be unable to find the egg cells.

Scent design that is aimed at concealing the human smell, or standardizing it artificially by making it smell good, that is socially acceptable, is even more enlightening. This includes all cosmetic products, especially perfumes or colognes. The famous noses of the perfume business are a highly sophisticated coterie of scent designers. Although perfume is nothing more than a mixture of essential oils or extracts—almost all of which are now synthetic—dissolved in alcohol, there are over two thousand standard substances available to the perfumer. A typical perfume recipe consists of approximately forty, though sometimes as many as a hundred, different essential oils.

But there are areas other than perfume-making where olfactory design is not as obvious and cannot be consciously detected. They range from the real leather fragrance applied to imitation leather in affordable cars to the appetite-stimulating smell of freshly baked bread emanating artificially from the bakery, gas stations that smell of freshly brewed coffee instead of gasoline, travel-agent offices that smell like beaches and the ocean, and finally to the "air care" or "indoor air quality" concepts in department stores, boutiques, and office buildings. These subtly and barely perceptible scents are emitted in shops or offices by air-conditioning systems in order to stimulate, relax, increase attention, or raise the trust of shoppers and office workers, making olfactory design an important part of advanced strategies in (→) branding and establishing (→) corporate identity. UB |

→ *Perception, Sensuality, Synesthetic*

Claassen, J. 1994. *On the scent of taste.* Baarn: Tirion.
Corbin, A. 1986. *The foul and the fragrant.* Cambridge, MA: Harvard Univ. Press.
Kunst- und Ausstellungshalle der Bundesrepublik Deutschland, ed. 1995. *Das Riechen.* Göttingen: Steidl.
Wilson, D., and R. Stevenson. 2006. *Learning to smell: Olfactory perception from neurobiology to behavior.* Baltimore: Johns Hopkins Univ. Press.

ORGANIZATION

In general, organization (from the Greek, *organon*, meaning "tool") is the specific relationship of an entire system to its parts. Whereas "aggregate" means a whole that is the sum of its parts, "organization" refers to a whole that is more than the sum of its parts. The latter can be said of (→) systems as well, yet the word "organization" also implies natural and biological as well as man-made.

First, organization can be process-related, meaning that something is accomplished, such as a design conference. This is about the planning and execution of an event. But organization can also be static and institutional, in the sense of a group of people or institutions with a specific structure of responsibilities, authorities, and relationships. In this sense the Deutsche Gesellschaft für Designtheorie und -forschung (German Association of Design Theory and Research) and the Rat für Formgebung (German Design Council) are examples of organizations.

Forms of self-organization or, synonymously, emergence or autopoiesis, are special cases in this context. Emergence originally meant the surprising appearance of new qualities in the stages of natural evolution. Typical characteristics of emergence are (→) innovation and radical novelty, or features not previously observed in similar systems. Today, phenomena of this kind can be explained using theories of self-organization, also called autopoiesis. The term "autopoiesis" describes the operational self-containment and self-propagation of living systems. A biological cell is such a system as, on a molecular level, it is continually creating the components it needs for its own internal organization. The German sociologist Niklas Luhmann (1927–1998) transferred the original biological theory of autopoiesis to social systems.

In the design context, the concept of autopoiesis is interesting as a possible explanation of the various phenomena of contemporary mass culture that can be seen on the Internet for instance. Design and cultural projects, which are fundamentally open to all, are constantly appearing in the form of stories, videos, and drawings. Anyone can log in, make a comment about the issue at hand, work on a collective drawing, or continue a story by picking up where someone else left off. The terms "author" or "work" do not sufficiently explain phenomena such as this, which have become self-operational and continuously recreate their own order. TF |

→ *Coordination, Design Centers, Design Planning, Gestaltung*

Krohn, W., and G. Küppers, eds. 1990. *Selbstorganisation: Aspekte einer wissenschaftlichen Revolution.* Brunswick: Vieweg.

ORIENTATION SYSTEM

Orientation systems are intended to systematically guide a person from point A to point B in any particular environment. To develop a successful orientation system, the designer must familiarize him or herself with the specifics of that environment, as well as the typical and learned behavioral patterns that occur within it. Orientation systems are implemented though visual and acoustic means, and generally need to be accessible and understandable for as many people as possible. TG |

→ *Audiovisual Design, Information Design, System, Visual Communication*

ORNAMENT

Ornament is by nature diffuse and complex. It can be a singular, like a brooch or an earring, or systemic, like the intricately woven pattern of a jacquard textile. The perception of ornament is also culturally conditioned. For example, Middle Eastern cultures have traditionally understood ornament as intrinsic to a surface or object, while Western cultures have generally seen it as something applied. It is this latter view that led to the disparagement of ornament for the better part of the twentieth century, when it was treated with outright hostility. Outlawed from the modernist (→ Modernity) canon by the Viennese architect Adolf Loos in his seminal 1929 essay "Ornament and Crime," and eschewed by modernist advocates of "less is more," ornament was condemned as superfluous. By the turn of the twenty-first century, however, ornament had found new champions among (→) postmodern designers who embraced a larger view of history and a non-linear aesthetic. Ornament re-entered design and the visual arts as not only a stylistic fashion, driven by cycles of consumption, but also, more significantly, as a potent outgrowth of the flows of (→) globalization. Contemporary designers are developing form languages that use ornament to bridge culture, class, race, gender, as well as the formerly discrete realms of the decorative arts, design, and fine arts.

In a postcolonial era, ornament can be seen as an instrument of cultural "reconciliation," not unlike the way it operated in past moments of globalization, such as in the hybrid visual culture of medieval Andalusia, Spain (→ Cross-cultural Design). Projects like Tramjatra (2001–), led by Mick Douglas in Melbourne, Australia, tap the potential of ornament as a universally recognized mode of speech that can communicate multiple messages to diverse audiences. In the case of Tramjatra, ornament is used to enliven local trams through recognizing the cultural dynamic between Australia and Southeast Asia, offering an alternative to corporate advertising and promoting sustainable public transportation. Here, ornament functions as an advocate for cosmopolitanism.

In addition to being a means of rapprochement in addressing the inherent divisiveness of nationality and ethnicity, ornament is used as a tool of engagement in the conflicts surrounding race, gender, and class. Commenting on contemporary racial tensions, New York graphic designer Melissa Gorman uses gilded barbed wire as an ornamental motif on the *More Mega* CD for the rap artist Lif (2006). Both class and gender inform the work of Swiss artist and graphic designer Sandrine Pelletier, who, in 2002, created a series of embroidered portraits of young backyard wrestlers in northern England. Pelletier literally sews together status symbols of heroism and feminine domesticity.

Ornament is also coming under reconsideration as designers seek to create a more quixotic visual landscape than the specious diversity offered by corporate capitalism. In this context, ornament privileges production, as can be seen in the graphic identity of the Walker Art Center in Minneapolis, Minnesota, designed by Eric Olson and Andrew Blauvelt in 2005, where ornament becomes a network of systems open to manipulation.

The capacity for manipulation is a direct consequence of the new levels of interactivity offered by digital technologies. The same technologies are also yielding new levels of formal complexity and advancing new narratives. American graphic designer Denise Gonzales Crisp has developed a theory of the "decoRational" to articulate the ornamental possibilities offered by advanced computation. Where Gonzales Crisp uses (→) ornamentation to amplify typography and graphic design, British designer Rachel Wingfield uses technology-driven ornament to underscore the dynamic between the human and natural environment. She embeds electroluminescent technology in everyday objects so that their presence (and the user's awareness of them) becomes stronger or weaker in response to changing light levels.

One of the most fertile uses of ornament today is within the culture of design itself, which no longer defines its origins as coterminous with mass production, but has broadened its parameters to include the decorative arts. Two examples from 2005 by designers from the Netherlands illustrate this point: the chain-link fence (titled, *How to Plant a Fence)* woven to look like lace by the collaborative Demakersvan and the series of blankets (titled, *Sampler Blankets)* by Hella Jongerius appliquéd with overblown fragments of decorative motifs taken from embroidery samplers.

As an aspect of visual language that is regaining its voice, ornament finds its relevance in its potential to enlarge the discourse of design. It is at once both formally expansive and socially inclusive. Today, ornament is understood as more than a border or a frame, or a mere sampling of exotica, but rather as a process of integrating systems of form and production that can yield (→) innovation. SY |

→ *Modernism, Ornamentation*

Gombrich, E. H. 1979. *The sense of order: A study in the psychology of decorative art.* Ithaca, NY: Cornell Univ. Press.
Gonzales Crisp, D. 2003. Toward a definition of the decorational. In B. Laurel, ed. *Design Research: Methods and Perspectives.* Cambridge, MA: MIT Press.

ORNAMENTATION

The terms "ornamentation" and "decoration" are frequently used interchangeably. Art historian James Trilling offers that all ornament is decoration, though not all decoration is ornament. Ornamentation fuses inseparably with a host—a wall, a pitcher, a gate, a rug, a book, an alphabet—any physical thing that claims some ostensible (→) use and that otherwise would function sufficiently without so-called embellishment. Such integration presumes a kind of symbiosis: ornamentation relies upon the context and purpose established by the host, and the host relies on its ornamentation to claim its unique identity and cultural function.

Ornamentation takes any form in any (→) material, limited only by the skills and imagination of the craftsman and the technology creating it. Historically, motifs abstracted from nature or constructed from geometry or styled into narratives connect through visual organization such as repetition (→ *Pattern*) or compositional balance. Ornamentation's formal and cultural roles have placed it therefore at the table of Art, under the rubric of "applied art," along side painting, sculpture, and architecture. (→) Aesthetic discourse maintained the integrity of ornament as complement to function and content, variously argued by John Ruskin, A. Welby Pugin, Alois Riegl, and Karl Grosz, to name but a few influential theorists.

The height of the Industrial Revolution brought mass-produced, machine-manufactured ornamentation informed by historical material culture. And while mechanization precipitated unrivaled invention, it also ushered in capricious imitation. Ornamentation was in danger of losing its elevated art-based status. Aiming to educate against facile appropriation, English designer Owen Jones responded in a seminal book *The Grammar of Ornament* (1856). With the expressed aim of awakening "a higher ambition" among manufacturers and craftsmen, Jones sorted motifs of ancient cultures into categories that demonstrated their respective formal logic. Jones and other defenders of ornamentation's traditions then called for reinvention, for utilizing the lessons of history to forge new paths true to the motives of art rather than to commercial profit, a seemingly unstoppable force that picked styles a la carte from the archives of visual history.

The modern charge to invent new ornament was fulfilled in the years surrounding the turn of the century in Europe and the US. The aesthetic ideals promoted in the Glasgow Style, the Viennese Secession, the English (→) Arts & Crafts movement, (→) Art Nouveau, the American Prairie Style, and the work of Antoni Gaudí and Louis Sullivan, forces unto themselves, introduced architectural, graphic, textile, and furniture design that revived the status of ornamentation as an art form of consequence. These theories and practices helped rejuvenate the spirit of (→) innovation for a time, partly as a response to the excesses of industrialization; however, expanding industry with its power to respond to the thrust of progress, as well as to the public's insatiable demand for novelty, trumped such idealistic strains.

At the dawn of the twentieth-century, the influential essay "Ornament and Crime" signaled the beginning of another strain. Viennese architect Adolf Loos voiced the emerging conviction among the vanguard that "a surfeit of ornament is a symptom of vulgarity." Inspired also by the efficiency of the machine—articulated by the architect Le Corbusier in 1925—design practitioners and educators increasingly suppressed ornamentation as antithetical to (→) modernity. Instead a "functional" aesthetic (→ *Functionalism*), defined in major part by a lack of ornamentation, would represent modern life and help mediate its perceived (→) complexity. Meanwhile traditional ornamentation—produced at the hands of craftsmen of every sort as well as mechanized usurpers—descended into second- or third-rate status synonymous with the old guard and popular taste, or relegated to the purview of the dubious art of advertising and worse, bourgeois domesticity.

By the mid-twentieth century the art of ornamentation as a significant (→) craft and as a high design concern seemed to disappear, but in fact was folded into an evolving modern aesthetic. For instance Charles and Ray Eames' plywood, fiberglass, and steel office furniture exploited formally conspicuous surfaces and colors "natural" to those materials and to their manufacture. (→) Artifacts inspired by automated production methods, represented in the ball-and-spindle clocks by George Nelson, advanced arguably "superfluous" yet innovative ideas. In the last third of the twentieth century many designers actively rebelled against the ideological forces of twentieth-century functionalism. Herb Lubalin, Wolfgang Weingart, Ettore Sottsass of the (→) Memphis group, and architects Venturi Scott Brown, among others, imaginatively infused modern visual vocabulary with playful, so-called extraneous form, which initiated ornamentation's return to its artful roots.

Today Owen Jones' call to innovation thrives. Contemporary perspectives embrace ornament as a facet of both function and content. Hella Jongerius, Tord Boontje, and the Dutch collective Droog Design represent a generation of designers around the world who are restoring ornamentation as a vital component of social and intellectual expression. DGC |

→ *Function, Functionalism, Ornament, Style, Styling*

Frank, I., ed. 2000. *The theory of decorative art: An anthology of European and American writings, 1750–1940*. New Haven: Yale Univ. Press.
Snodin, M., and M. Howard. 1996. *Ornament: A social history since 1450*. New Haven: Yale Univ. Press.
Trilling, J. 2003. *Ornament: A modern perspective*. Seattle: Univ. of Washington Press.

OUTSOURCING

Outsourcing describes the practice of contracting external companies to perform a client company's tasks, in order to allow that company to focus on its core business operations. Many modern companies outsource everything from research and development to the entire production, transport, logistics, and packaging of its products. Design is also a common outsourced service. Outsourced tasks are increasingly performed in foreign countries: for instance, design might be done in the United States, production in Asia, data processing in Poland, logistics in Holland and so forth. This allows the outsourcing company to concentrate on defining and securing its (→) brand claim and brand value as the responsibilities for the outsourced services are taken on by third parties. Its concerns are with the planning, controlling, and quality management of all their outsourcing partners. KSP |

→ *Branding, Corporate Identity, Design Management, Strategic Design*

P

PACKAGING DESIGN

A designed product's package fulfills several different functions—it provides a protective shell for transportation and storage, acts as a vital source of information to the product's user in today's heavily manufactured world, and performs an important marketing role to make it stand out amid a flood of similar articles. As such, package designers are required to integrate of range of skills in their work; in addition to an eye for (→) typography and (→) layout, they need to demonstrate expertise in materials (glass, plastic, paper, and other processed raw materials), form, color, and production technologies.

The logistical material functions of a product's packaging are relatively straightforward; packaging should protect the product from the elements (light, heat, dampness, dirt) and make it resistant to damage (through squashing, tearing, and so on) during transportation or storage. Many packages enclose the product entirely, though there are certainly exceptions. Textiles, for example, are often packaged with an exposed opening so that consumers may feel the fabric inside.

In addition to providing a protective cover for the product, packaging also conveys essential information to the intended user. One of the primary functions of the packaging is to accurately depict what is inside, either by revealing the product through plastic or through photographic, illustrative, or text-based means. As consumers today typically buy their products through industrial manufacturers (as opposed to artisans, craftsmen, or specialty stores, as was the case before industrialization), the packaging is often relied upon to provide instructions for use, as well.

The package design will effect how the product inside is valued (→ *Value*). The same product will seem less valuable if presented in a cardboard package with a crooked information label than in a velvet-lined slipcase. The product can be made to seem more valuable if the experience of unpacking it is a special one. Depending on the product, the price of the package can sometimes exceed that of the product itself. This is particularly common with products for which image is more important than use value, such as gift articles or (→) lifestyle products. On the other hand, other products are deliberately packaged to look inexpensive. Generic supermarket brands, for example, are often designed with intentionally plain graphic elements and colors, so as to conform with consumer expectations about pricing. On the basis of appearance alone, the elaborately designed package on the shelf next to it will most likely be passed over by the shopper looking for a bargain. Packaging can also represent an effective form of (→) branding and (→) advertisement; in addition to promoting brand recognition in the usual ways, well-planned packaging can unfold to reveal a "sales item" or other such marketing technique.

Packaging design can have a significant impact on the retail experience (→ *Retail Design*). Packages today are frequently designed to promote ease of sale, with large, scannable barcodes on the sides. The now-common Radio Frequency Identification (RFID) tags are even more convenient: each sticker has a unique number that gives off a radio signal when in the vicinity of a strong electomagnetic field. So-called "smart" shelves can recognize the presence of such tags and pass the information on to an inventory system, and cash registers can immediately assess the contents of shopping carts. Such RFID technology makes it possible to recognize goods automatically at a distance of several meters, even if there is no line of sight.

Opening the package should be difficult enough to discourage shoplifters, and easy enough to enable access to the product without destroying itself or the product inside. This is an issue with self-seal labels in particular, which may leave ugly traces of adhesive or scratches behind after removal.

As is the case in many other design disciplines, the question of (→) sustainability is becoming increasingly important in the field of packaging design. To facilitate the separation of waste for recycling, most packaging designers today try to limit the use of multiple materials (like cardboard and plastic foil) in their designs. In Germany, for example, licensing fees may be incurred if designers and manufacturers do not comply with packaging regulations that require the use of ecologically sound materials. Research is currently being conducted into the development of renewable and biodegradable (→) materials like polylactic acid (or PLA) made from corn, and packaging designers are increasingly asked to balance the needs for durability with the benefits of biodegradability (→ *Environmental Design*) KW + STS |

→ *Brand, Graphic Design, Product*

PARTICIPATORY DESIGN

Participatory design describes a collaborative approach to the design of products, services, spaces, or systems that includes the range of stakeholders in the creative process. People who have a stake in the final design outcome are invited to be part of the design team at points when decisions critical to them are being made. Practitioners of participatory design believe that an approach based in creative collaboration between producers, designers, and end users will inherently lead to results that are more effective, more appropriate, and more desirable.

The historical roots of participatory design lie in Scandinavia, with the introduction of technology into the workplace in the 1970s. The goal was to democratize the process of workspace design, ensuring that trade unions were included in the creation of systems that would affect their members. In order to formulate goals and negotiate implementation strategies in the best interest of the workers, trade union representatives needed to work closely with management and technical designers to understand the implications and possibilities of the new technologies. Formative projects from this period were the NJMF project in Norway (Nygaard 1979), the Swedish DEMOS project (Ehn and Sanberg 1979), and later the Danish DUE project (Kyng and Mathiassen 1982).

In the 1990s, participatory design methods came into wider usage in the United States, and also were applied to a wider range of design challenges. As design teams adopted the methodology to develop products within and for a commercial context, the motives in many cases became de-coupled from the philosophy and political views of earlier practitioners. No longer understood solely as a tool for democratization, participatory design became seen by newer practitioners as a way to more quickly conceive of and refine products, environments or services that were desirable to end users (in some cases workers) and also good fits for the capabilities of the organization. In part, this shift can be attributed to differences between the socio-economic and political contexts of Europe and the United States, but it is also likely related more generally to decreasing levels of union influence in the workplace.

Most recently, the approach has been applied to effect shifts in organizational cultures. With these types of projects, participatory design methods provide a supporting framework for solutions that originate primarily from the members of the organizations, or the "users" themselves, with the participatory design practitioners acting mainly as process support.

Over time, a common set of methods has been developed to facilitate group ideation, communication, and collaboration. The five most common are: collaborative design sessions (also called "future workshops"), scenario prototyping, rapid prototypes, mockups, and contextual inquiry. The "collaborative design session" is a key component of any participatory design project; it is a group work session that brings people involved in the project together to reflect, prioritize, examine, and then collaboratively invent, prototype, and refine solutions. Generally several of these sessions will be held over the course of a project. One technique often used during collaborative design sessions is "scenario design," or enactments by the participants of various possible situations in which a design might be put into play (→ *Scenario Planning*). "Rapid prototypes" or "mockups" allow participants to evaluate rough versions of how a solution might be configured and to discuss implications and refinements (→ *Prototype, Rapid Prototyping*). "Design games" are sometimes employed as a way to frame a discussion or exploratory session: game rules and pieces help keep the context or solution elements in mind, and may include objects, photos, words, or video. "Contextual inquiry" is a method often employed by design team members who are less familiar with the context for which the group is creating solutions. This method helps to sensitize designers to the context, and also to frame or bring to the group's attention to key aspects of the situation that present design challenges and opportunities. FD + GJ |

→ *Collaborative Design, Design Process, Need, Strategic Design, Usability, Use*

Participatory Design Conference Proceedings, 1998–2006. Computer Professionals for Social Responsibility.
Schuler, D., and A. Namioka, eds. 1993. *Participatory design: Principles and practices*. Hillsdale, NJ: Lawrence Erlbaum Associates.

PATENT

→ *Intellectual Property*

PATINA

The term "patina" is derived from Latin and literally means "pan." Figuratively, patina is the residue left on cookware or any surface whose structure is changed by a natural or artificial aging process. In the context of art and architecture, patina means the oxidized surface of bronze objects (also artificially produced by patinating); in design, the term denotes the ways in which the human/object interface can be changed through the process of "wear and tear."

Although initial traces of previous use generally depreciate an object's material (→) value, the intrinsic value it acquires may ultimately appreciate its worth again over time (sometimes to the point of its disintegration). Both an antique dining table with visible blemishes and a pair of frayed, torn, and faded jeans can be valued for the ways in which they evoke the lived past. Patinas also create another level of value-association in that objects exhibiting clear traces of (→) use in certain places betray how often and in which ways they were used. Dog-eared books describe the journeys and habits of readers, while hand-polished doorknobs convey insight into the ways and number of times they have been used. The commercial use of patina, or its anticipation, has by now become an established part of the design process. DPO |

→ *Coating, Styling*

Aigner, C., and U. Marchsteiner, eds. 1999. *Design auf Zeit: Haltbar bis . . . immer schneller*. Die Kunst der Zeit 3. Cologne: DuMont.
Toyka, R. 2000. *Patina*. Hamburg: Junius.

PATTERN

A pattern is a ($\rightarrow$) tool used to create or assemble something else. Guides, stencils, templates, and molds are all examples of patterns in design. Clothing construction for instance relies upon patterns that act as ($\rightarrow$) templates for transferring shapes to fabric; the body is mapped out with these patterns which are then pieced together through a series of notations and diagrams as if constructing a three-dimensional puzzle. Once transferred, the different parts of a garment are sewn together. Diagrams, ($\rightarrow$) models, and ($\rightarrow$) blueprints are also patterns, despite the fact that they may not be scaled to the final product. Architecture relies upon a series of drawings and models that include plan, section, elevation, and detail to convey information that is then translated and constructed into built form.

Although a pattern can be a singular unit as demonstrated above, common usage of the term often connotes multiplicity and repetition. When we speak of patterns in this sense we are referencing repeating or recurring patterns. Recurring patterns may be naturally occurring (a spiral within a shell), specifically designed with an agenda (a grid that organizes text or imagery), even behavioral (patterns of behavior, patterns of human settlement, and so on). What defines them as patterns is that they are organized in a fashion that is not arbitrary; that is, they somehow exhibit a consistent or characteristic uniformity.

Two-dimensional patterns are common to ($\rightarrow$) graphic design, ($\rightarrow$) textiles, and wallpaper. William Morris of the ($\rightarrow$) Arts & Crafts movement helped define this highly patterned style through the design of his organic wallpaper patterns referencing natural forms. The recurring pattern begins with a single unit (the original "pattern") and repeats. The repeat, a term used for multiplying a single unit into a pattern, aims to proportionally balance the units when covering a larger area such as a wall. Taken a step further, the two-dimensional pattern can be translated into a three-dimensional form as can be found in the works of architect Louis Sullivan. Similar to the organic forms of Morris, Sullivan transforms organic imagery into three-dimensional terra-cotta tiles on the interior and exterior of buildings. Sullivan's use of decorative tiles act as ornamental ($\rightarrow$ *Ornamentation*) framing thresholds such as arches and doorways. Depending upon the content and implementation of a pattern, it can act as purely ornamental, functional, or a mixture of both.

The term "pattern" in design most often refers to applied use, that is, the direct application of a pattern to material in order to realize a final product. However, many designers depend on the analysis of recurring patterns within conceptual or behavioral frameworks as well. An urban planner ($\rightarrow$ *Urban Planning*) for instance applies the term "pattern" when analyzing transportation such as pedestrian, mass transit, or vehicle movement. In this example, planners generate diagrams that rely upon time and observation in order to recognize the behavioral patterns being formed. LW |

→ *Copy, Organization, Ornament, Template*

PERCEPTION

"Perception" refers to the ways in which conscious beings sense, interpret, and understand the larger environment in which they exist. In other words, it is the process through which we organize and ascribe meaning to the world around us. Design both responds to and shapes the world as experienced and thus is shaped by and shapes perceptions.

Perception always implies subjective bias. This is evident even in purely physiological contexts that describe perception as the sensory and neurological functions through which we process external stimuli. Our perception of any given object for instance is dependent on a multitude of factors apart from the physical aspects of that object: our biological sensory capabilities, motivations, and emotional state for instance. Another important component of perception is the effect of past experiences. As we see, smell, taste, hear, and touch the world around us, we automatically organize and translate that sensory (→) information into a form (memory) that we can use to interpret and understand new sensory information. Sensations alone are therefore unable to provide us with an (→) understanding of the world around us; we require perception to provide the framework through which we encode, store, and retrieve information about the environment in which we exist. As such, our accumulation of prior experiences necessarily affects the ways in which we perceive everything else that follows.

Most physiological approaches to perception assume that there is an external world outside our bodies that we react to—in other words, that we are inherently separate from the objects we perceive whether we are able to perceive them or not. This assumption of course is one that has been extensively and hotly debated throughout centuries by a myriad of thinkers, philosophers, and even cognitive psychologists, particularly those interested in the realm of epistemology (the nature of knowledge). This debate has generally been framed as the condition of empirical knowledge versus rational knowledge (or direct realism versus indirect realism). Very simply put, the doctrine of empiricism posits that nothing is knowable without reference to sensory experience, while rationalism attests that knowledge can be gained independently from the senses.

The physiological approach to perception thus tends to privilege the ways in which the external world shapes our experiences, while philosophical or even phenomenological approaches to perception tend to privilege the ways in which our experiences shape our perception of the external world. Everyday living demonstrates, however, that both processes occur simultaneously: human beings are not passive observers of the external world, but active, subjective participants in the creation of (→) form. On the other hand, we cannot deny the fact that our accumulated experiences are framed, not only by the physical environment around us, but by the social and cultural contexts in which we live.

The reconciliation of these two approaches can be understood when one approaches the world as explicitly designed. Perception mediates between the senses and the intellect based on experience and a range of subjective and cultural biases. For example, this publication would be perceived differently if it had a leather cover with the title in Gothic script as it would resonate with a different set of sensory (smell, touch, sight) and cultural references (bibles, old reference books, "the classics"). As the act of organizing sensory information in a meaningful fashion, design can be thus defined as the articulation of perception. Design is always an intervention in the world, and the accumulation of our designed actions has utterly altered the physical reality of our material environment and, consequently, our perceptions of it. (The garden changes, through design, our perception of nature). Design therefore simultaneously generates from and responds to the broader context in which it is produced; in other words, design both articulates and changes perceptions of the world. JR |

→ *Affordance, Human Factors, Interface Design, Synesthetic, Understanding, Visualization*

PERFORMANCE

The rhetorical and visual arts have always been interpreted within the context of an advanced differentiation in the relationship between work, authorship, and auditorium. At the end of the 1950s, this development enjoyed a brief peak with the public appearances of different artists involved in (→) agit prop, happenings, and Fluxus movements. The performance itself became the work, the artist or "actor" the content, and the public could enjoy the dramaturgy of personal interactivity. Design in today's day and age can profit from this history.

Widespread product-advertising (→) campaigns, similar to those we know by Apple Computer Inc. and its CEO, Steve Jobs, possess performance characters that do not only enhance the (→) credibility and dignity of the product palette, but also bring commodity aesthetics together with the lived world by dissolving the borders between the performer/manufacturer and the visitor/consumer.

The improvisational integration of the public heightens the experience and triggers visual and acoustic, even tactile stimuli.

These principles also apply on a small scale. Whether pitch, (→) presentation, lecture, or interactive show, the performance ability of the designer contributes decisively to the public reception of the product. It is essential in this respect to create a balance between credibility and showmanship.

We also speak of products' (→) functions as their performance (→) qualities, as if they were animated or independent beings. Their inherent, independent objective existence dissolves into a scenario and animates us to participate. Karl Marx once described this as the deceptive character of commodities; when a table appears to be dancing, it is hiding the fact that it is merely manufactured. SA |

Brock, B. 1977. *Ästhetik als Vermittlung.* Cologne: DuMont.

PERSONA

The word "persona" derives etymologically from *phersu*, meaning actor's mask, though it is more commonly used today as a synonym for "character" or "role." Personas are used in design—usually in the context designing services—in order to apply fictive user perspectives thoroughly and systematically during the designing process. True to its etymological roots, the development of personas in design replaces individual features with typological generalities. Personas may be attributed traits according to the typical demographics of age, gender, class, race, and so on—but often, these are not the focus. In most contexts, the persona's imagined (→) needs, experiences, (→) lifestyles, and capabilities to use certain interfaces or services take precedence. Once the persona's characteristics have been identified and translated into a prototypical client or user profile, they are usually used in the design process to help visualize fictive contexts of use, or scenarios (→ *Scenario Planning*). Persona development was first introduced to interaction and experience design by Alan Cooper (→ *Interface Design*). BM |

→ *Service Design*

Cooper, A., and R. Reimann. 2003. *About face 2.0: The essentials of interaction design.* Indianapolis: Wiley.

PHOTOGRAPHIC DESIGN

Photographic design is a term with a number of related interpretations that stem from, but are not restricted to, a concern with the formal or visual properties of photographic images. The three key meanings of the term are used to describe: the use of photographic imagery as an integral visual component of (→) graphic designs; a type of photographic practice in which photographs are preconceived, preplanned, or art-directed constructions;

The application of the photographic image as an integral graphic component in design was first articulated by Lázló Moholy-Nagy in 1925. Moholy-Nagy coined the term "typophoto" to describe the practice he developed using photographs as graphic elements in graphic and typographic design layouts (→ *Layout, Typography*). In this practice, the photograph itself was not an inviolable object; rather, it was treated as raw material to be cut up, manipulated, or transformed in whatever manner necessary to achieve the communicative and visual objective. Commonly used techniques were collage, montage, and photograms.

Though much of the work produced by Moholy-Nagy using this approach was strongly based on the formal properties of photo-

and a concern with the formal design principles of photographic practice (such as image structure, composition, tone, light, color, visual weight, and so on) that can be applied to any photographic genre or practice.

graphic and graphic elements, a concern with communicating meaning was not absent. Typophoto was developed as a consequence of Moholy-Nagy's concern with the ambiguities of verbal language. In typical modernist (→ Modernity) fashion of the time, he believed that photography, as an objective extension of human sight, was capable of rendering universal truths and meaning. In other words, by virtue of its mechanical nature, photography had the potential to eliminate communicative ambiguities. Such an enterprise was part of a larger interest at the (→) Bauhaus in the idea of a systemized visual language based on universal faculties of (→) perception as opposed to cultural conventions. That this pursuit was itself grounded in the cultural conventions of the day almost goes without saying.

Overlapping this more interventionist approach to photographic design practice was the exploration of the graphic qualities of photographs in and of themselves. This exploration was informed by the medium's complex relationship to other methods of realistic representation, particularly painting. The relationship between photographic and painting composition is as old as the invention of the first camera, the camera obscura, which was used to assist artists in rendering perspective accurately from the Renaissance onward. The invention in the mid-nineteenth century of image fixing techniques sparked a critical dialogue between proponents of painting and photography regarding the nature of realistic representation and the role of the artist in its creation. It was not long before photographers came to understand the medium as manipulable in its own right.

Edward Steichen, originally trained as a painter, was one of the first photographers to see the potential of compositional graphic form in photographic imagery. Employed as a staff photographer for the Condé Naste publishing house in the early 1920s, Steichen produced a body of editorial and advertising photographs that fused early modernist concerns with shape, (→) form, and universal meaning in images that were strongly graphic and clearly contrived, marking a distinct departure from the overwhelmingly realist frame that had dominated the field up until that point. Arguably, these were some of the first art-directed photographic images used for commercial purposes, though contrived artistic photographs were not a new phenomena.

Art-directed photography (→ Art Direction), primarily utilized in advertising and editorial publishing, is a type of visual communication design (→ Visual Communication) practice in which photographs are pre-conceived, often in rough sketch form by non-photographer visual designers, prior to the act of shooting. Though they may depict realistic scenes, be shot on location or in a studio, each component of the image is carefully considered prior to and during the shoot. This type of stage-managed photographic practice is markedly different from photo-documentary practice in which photographers shoot "real" events unfolding in front of them (this is of course a simplistic distinction between notions of the real and the fabricated that does not take account of the common and often controversial practice of staging documentary photographs).

Advertising and editorial photography has changed significantly since the days of Steichen, but the idea of the art-directed photograph being designed still holds sway. Photographic design practice in this sense is concerned with the full range of visual design issues, from identifying the communication objective of the images to be shot, the style of image, the sets or locations to be used, the actors to be cast, the props to be included, the type of lighting and the compositional and graphic features of the image itself. Further consideration is often given to the graphic context in which the photographic image itself will be used, demonstrating the visual legacy of Moholy-Nagy's early experiments.

The concept of photographic design can also be applied to other genres of photography that are not art-directed or constructed, but premised on the notion of documenting an observed phenomenon or object in a real setting. Such genres include, but are not limited to, photo-documentary, architectural, news, and landscape photography. Here the idea of photographic design relates to the conscious use of compositional techniques such as light and shade, cropping, depth of field, shutter speed, visual weight, film type, and the like, to emphasize the visual and communicative aspects of the scene, object, or phenomena being observed and documented.

Finally, with the advent of photo-imaging computer software, seemingly endless possibilities for the manipulation of photographic imagery abound. Once the preserve of specialists, the time-consuming techniques of photographic collage and montage popularized by early modernists such as Moholy-Nagy, El Lissitzky, and John Heartfield have become widely accessible. The range of possibilities made possible by this technology are such that photographers and non-photographic visual designers alike can manipulate the image as required at virtually any stage in the process. Digitally altering the image is now regarded as an integral aspect of photographic design, and though the techniques, practices, and motivations may differ substantially, the continued interest in photographic manipulation demonstrates strong parallels to the work of the early modernists. MR |

→ Advertisement, Aesthetics, Communications, Dada and
    Design, Visual Effects

Hurlburt, A. 1983. *Photo/graphic design: The interaction of design and photography.* New York: Watson-Guptill.
Lupton, E. 1988. Modern design theory: Design research writing. http://www.elupton.com/index.php?id=47. Accessed February 2, 2007.
Moholy-Nagy L. 1973. *Painting, photography, film.* 4th ed. Cambridge, MA: MIT Press.

PICTOGRAM

Pictograms are visual images, usually in the form of abstract graphic (→) symbols, that convey information to viewers. They can often be found in the context of (→) orientation systems or the Internet. Pictograms seldom contain letters, and are thus frequently employed in order to communicate a certain idea, instruction, or process across national and linguistic barriers. That said, it must be noted that even the simplest of visual images are subject to cultural connotations; many pictograms are not automatically understood and need to be learned. TG |

→ *Communications, Information Design, Interface Design, Public Design, Visual Communication*

PLAGIARISM

Plagiarism (Latin *plagium* = kidnapping, abduction), as it relates to design, is the more or less exact (→) copy of an existing (→) artifact which is then released on the market under the plagiarist's name. The plagiarized goods may even come with (→) logos or labels that are similar in appearance to that of another (→) brand or company, thereby causing additional confusion for the consumer. The difference between plagiarism and counterfeiting is at times subtle, but plagiarism involves appropriating aspects of another person's creative work without proper acknowledgement, while counterfeiting attempts to replicate the authenticity of an original in its entirety. In other words, plagiarists pass off the work of others as their own, whereas counterfeiters sell their goods under the name of the original manufacturer or brand.

Design plagiarists typically copy products that have already been introduced onto the market. This saves on the costs of design, construction, and of course, marketing. On top of that, they often use cheaper (→) materials and have lower (→) quality standards for their copies. Consequently, plagiarists are able to offer their products at much lower prices.

Many laws have been enacted in advanced economies to protect individuals against theft of their (→) intellectual property and there has been a strong push to have internationally binding Intellectual Property laws. As a result, the World Trade Organization passed the Agreement on Trade Related Aspects of Intellectual Property Rights in 1994 after intense lobbying, primarily by the pharmaceutical and media companies. (This has led to the ongoing controversy regarding unaffordable AIDS drugs in poor countries, particularly Africa, where the production of generic versions of these medications goes against international law).

Intellectual Property laws cover an extensive range of creative work including literary texts, musical compositions, paintings, sculptures, and architecture (→ *Copyright*). The Patent Law protects engineering inventions as long as they are adequately novel, inventive, and useful. The Utility Model Acts in many countries provide protection for technical objects that are new but do not fulfill the requirements necessary to be patented as inventions. Design Acts protect the formal aesthetic designs of products. In the process of adapting different national European interpretations of the law, it became possible on April 1, 2003 to apply for a Community Designs Bulletin at the European Union Office for Harmonization in Alicante, Spain. This protects a product in all twenty-five states of the European Union. Plagiarists generally violate one or more of the above laws, depending on the nature of the copy, and are punished accordingly. They have their goods confiscated, are required to pay a fine, and may even serve prison sentences.

Counterfeited products not only violate the above-mentioned laws, but also are in violation of (→) trademark registrations (→ Fake). The worldwide financial damage caused by product piracy is estimated at 258 to 387 billion US Dollars. Product piracy is not limited to (→) luxury items, but exists in virtually every product group across a variety of price ranges.

A high percentage of today's plagiarized goods often originate in the Far East. This is often excused with the argument that those countries regard it as a "compliment to the manufacturer" of the original. MBO |

POINT OF SALE

It is at the point of sale that goods are exchanged for payment in the retail environment, and the market success of any given design product determined. As the interface between sale and purchase, the point of sale should be given a well-considered and attractive design. ME |

→ Display, Retail Design, Service Design

POSTER DESIGN

A poster is a piece of paper that is at least 297 x 420 mm or 11½ × 16½ inches (ISO A3) displayed in a public space. It advertises or conveys political messages and information about events. As a communication medium, it has to be eye-catching and able to communicate the what, where, and why of its contents quickly and easily. Posters and placards became more effective and better developed after industrialization, reaching a highpoint at the end of the nineteenth century with the introduction of color lithography and the emergence of poster art. Henri de Toulouse-Lautrec and Alfons Maria Mucha were the first artists to combine art and (→) advertisement.

Music played a major role in the poster's renaissance, especially during the hippie movement of the 1960s and the punk movement of the 1970s. The hippie movement was popularized in San Francisco, strongly influenced by the rise of anti-war demonstrations and student protests. Wes Wilson, Alton Kelley, Stanley Mouse, and Rick Griffin were among the best-known representatives of the resulting Great Poster Wave. Music, dance, and drugs were going to liberate the people from conventional, bourgeois life, and this was made clear in the posters. Colors were bright and wildly mixed and the lettering was sometimes distorted beyond legibility. Using collage techniques, they mixed quotes and images from different cultural eras and combined them with areas of decoration. Poster art at that time often used Art-Nouveau-style lettering (→ Art Nouveau), imagery from the turn of the century, and references to Pop Art.

Hippies wanted to change the system, but the punks did not want a system at all. This anarchistic, even destructive, philosophy could be seen in their poster design. Their posters were designed and produced as cheaply as possible and did not follow any linear structure or formal rules. The best-known poster artist of this era was Jamie Reid, the Sex Pistol's graphic designer. His lettering looked like typical blackmail letters made from cutout bits of newspaper. When this development began, poster art and album cover design were closely related. Over the next few years, artists such as Robert Williams Coop and Frank Kozik set new standards in this tradition, developing visual styles that created a direct association with a specific genre of music.

Today, this is used to relate new bands with a certain musical style using their (→) brand identity, which simplifies marketability. Moreover, by referring to these design elements, advertising can place products within a certain context and attract specific (→) target groups. TG |

→ Communications, Crossover, Flyer, Graphic Design, Illustration, Public Design, Protest Design, Style

Kozik, F. 1999. *Ode to Joy: Posters, prints and other work of Frank Kozik*. San Francisco: Last Gasp.
Weill, A. 2004. *Graphics: A century of poster and advertising design*. London: Thames & Hudson.

POSTMODERNISM

"Postmodernism" is a complex and strenuously debated term that applies to many disciplines including architecture, philosophy, art, literature, music, fashion, film and science. As a movement, postmodernism was based on challenging the prevailing ethos of modernism and the nature of subjectivity.

A composite of the Latin *post*, meaning "after," and "modernism," postmodernism is a polemical, somewhat combative term that refers to a philosophical response to the prevailing ideas and (→) aesthetics of modernism (→ Modernity). In the various disciplines of cultural studies, the term has been used in many, often contradictory, ways. The proclamation of postmodernism was not intended simply as a retrospective diagnosis of the end of modernism; rather, it was supposed to bring about fundamental change. Although the term was first used by Rudolf Pannwitz in 1917 in a discourse on the philosophy of culture in reference to Friedrich Nietzsche, Charles Jencks introduced the term to architectural theory in 1975.

The point of departure was the assumption, in the early 1970s, that modernism found itself in an existential crisis. Modernism had to be humanized, was the cry. Prominent architects and designers, including American Robert Venturi, Italians Ettore Sottsass, Alessandro Mendini, Michele de Lucchi, and Matteo Thun (→ *Radical Design*), and others, all came to realize that the promises of High Modernism—in particular the dominant version of it that Henry-Russel Hitchcock and Philip Johnson called the (→) International Style—had not been fulfilled since the 1920s. Postmodernists argued that the built environment was by no means in a better state than it had been before modern design and architecture began to reform it. Cities had not become paradises characterized by aesthetic harmony and functional quality. In fact, an inhuman, or even anti-human, aspect had become dominant as a consequence of modernism's obsessive pursuit of (→) functionalism, and design outcomes were consistently marked by coldness, impersonality, monotony, and simple-mindedness. (→) Ergonomics had become a clumsy justification for aesthetic sameness, and functionalism a canonization of rationality that increasingly was dictated by the logistics of business.

The response to modernism's failures by postmodernism's early advocates was marked by the use of irony and the re-evaluation of prevailing standards of truth and value. In 1972, Venturi proposed learning from the architecture and (→) urban planning of Las Vegas, Nevada. The (→) Memphis designers posited a direct challenge to the orthodoxy of High Modernism and the formulaic aphorism "form follows function" by focusing on designing surfaces. Instead of an ideal of clarity that laid claim to finality, postmodernism appreciated ambivalence, irony, arbitrariness, polyphony, triviality, and spontaneity as human qualities.

It is characteristic of postmodernism in design that designers were far more interested in stylistic issues than in the technical refinement of objects. The combination of diverse historical forms and styles became one of the most important postmodernist techniques. Designs were made unfamiliar or even unrecognizable by combining stylistic features from antiquity, the Renaissance, the Baroque, Pop Art and Art Deco periods, Hollywood or Biedermeier and by distorting and/or altering proportions, materials, and colors. Classical designs were not only referenced, but also frequently caricatured or "sent up." The aura of the excessively classical that clung to these objects was not necessarily destroyed by this caricature; in fact, when these were placed on pedestals in museums alongside the classics at which they took aim, they reinforced the significance of the classics as originals in the context of the art history discourse.

The use of basic geometric forms like the cylinder, pyramid, sphere, and cube was another typical phenomenon of postmodernism. This was particularly evident in architectonic designs for objects for living rooms and dining tables (like those by Michael Graves for the Italian manufacturer Alessi). The tea kettle was crowned with an equilateral roof; the candleholder looked like a high-rise; the teapot like a temple; the salt and pepper shakers like splinters from the Tower of Pisa; and the table clock like a triumphal arch. The addition of volumes, structures, textures, and surfaces was a translation of a visual vocabulary originally used in architecture to small-scale domestic objects. One combination that became relatively ubiquitous was the cylinder sitting on a cuboid with an enthroned sphere on top and a semicircular arch as a handle attached to its long sides. This popularity of this look, applied to everything from lamps to pitchers to bookends, reflected the realization that external appearances had, to a large extent, become somewhat arbitrary. Modernism, which typically tried to solve every problem based on the qualities inherent to it, had resulted in increasingly monotonous outcomes.

The provocative challenge to the preference (which had begun to be perceived as a dictate) of High Modernism for white, gray and black was also expressed in surfaces that were designed with bold colors and decorative patterns. Ettore Sottsass' wormlike Bacterio pattern, which was used on Abet laminates for furniture and faux terrazzo of all kinds, became a famous (or notorious) example of this trend.

The theorists of postmodernism argued that modernism's disapproval and rejection of the past had resulted in environments antithetical to human values. They argued that, contrary to the tenets of modernism, historical knowledge actually enriched design. This led to a self-consciously eclectic, historicizing style that came to be seen as typical of postmodernism, though it went beyond it as well. The elitist separation of high culture (the idealized projects of modernism) from popular culture also had to be reversed. Consequentially postmodernism elevated (→) kitsch to the status of the avant-garde, and made such aesthetic gestures as placing a lopsided wooden column, distorted to the point of nonsense, at a part of the building where it made no structural sense, to characterize a stairwell.

Such ironic twists were not always appreciated and were sometimes taken at face value. To put it another way, postmodernism's success became its undoing. The success of postmodernist aesthetics as a popular, fashionable trend could not have been possible if the mass media, with its rapidly increasing influence on everyday life, had not embraced it so enthusiastically. The topic of design suddenly attracted broad public attention for the first time; designers became stars, and design objects were

Branzi, A. 1980. *Moderno, postmoderno, millenario*. Milan: Alchymia.

Fischer, V., ed. 1988. *Design today*. Trans. Hans Brill. Munich: Prestel.

Flagge, I., and R. Schneider, eds. 2005. *Revision der Postmoderne / Post-modernism revisited*. Hamburg: Junius.

Jencks, C. 1986. *What is post-modernism?* New York: St. Martin's Press.

Venturi, R., D. Scott Brown, and S. Izenour. 1972. *Learning from Las Vegas*. Cambridge, MA: MIT Press.

incorporated into international art, gallery, and museum markets. Cheap manufacturers quickly caught up with the trend and began taking aims to capitalize on postmodernism's embrace of (→) nostalgia, (→) ornament, and decoration. Manufacturers of promotional items flooded the market with garishly colored pens with spheres or cones as push buttons, marketing them as "designer pens." The joke became serious, the effort to turn the everyday into kitsch succeeded. Despite these pitfalls, many of postmodernism's ideas and methods still remain relevant today, particularly its insistence on regarding design as more than simply a means to fulfill technical ends. RS |

PRACTICE

The word "practice" comes with a number of different yet related meanings. Colloquially, it refers to a professional activity—for example, the practice of graphic designers. Closely related is the definition of practice as an applied (→) discipline, sometimes (but not always) in exchange for monetary compensation. It is important to note here that the term "practice" always carries the implication of action; "discipline" refers to the methods and processes people use to achieve a certain goal, while practice refers to the application of those methods and processes. More generally, the term "practice" is also used to refer to the repetitive or sustained performance of a certain action in order to acquire skill or refine and improve ability—as in the commonly used adage "practice makes perfect."

In addition to these everyday uses, the term "practice" in scholarly or academic contexts is usually linked, either implicitly or explicitly, to the concept of (→) theory. This dichotomy of theory and practice serves to emphasize the distinctions between, on the one hand, the process of reflection and contemplation, and on the other, the process of action. Of course, one can not really exist without the other; performing an action always requires thought, and recent developments in sociology and cultural studies indicate that every thought may ultimately be connected to the performance of a personal action (known as "practice turn").

Taking this into account, any discussion on the nature of practice should be situated within material, physiological, and social contexts. In other words, every action or activity occurs in a specific environment upon which the meaning and relevance of that action or activity is contingent. Of course, this includes material and spatial environments, but also—as actions (that is, practice) are always performed by a subjective being—perceptual and physical capabilities, experiences, and motivations. (→) Social contexts play an essential role, as well, for the sense and meaning of an action is constituted and determined largely through interactions with other people.

Against this backdrop, design can be defined, first, as a practice within all the various semantic dimensions as discussed above. Second, design can fundamentally be understood as a central motivating connection between theory and practice, for it mediates the complex—often contentious—relationship between thinking and acting. Thirdly, design is expected to define itself in response to a specific context for use; as such, it almost always attempts to locate itself materially, physiologically, and socially.

From this perspective, designers are, on the one hand, able in essence to guide action by creating the artifacts, systems, environments, and services that people experience and use in their day to day lives; and on the other, any design's ultimate use, meaning, and relevance can only truly be understood in the context of the environment in which it is used. SG |

PREPRESS

Prepress refers to the last stage in the print design process before it goes to the printing press. Common processes that occur in the prepress stage include scanning, photo retouching, and image imposing, as well as the integration of all of the various elements of content and (→) layout into the final design. TK |
→ *Graphic Design*

PRESENTATION

A presentation is a strategic demonstration in which knowledge, information, ideas, products, or services are communicated and/or delivered to an audience.

Most designers rely on presentations in order to obtain and maintain relationships with potential clients and receive feedback from potential users. Uses include demonstrating expertise or vision, conveying product ideas or concepts, and providing information about the specifics of a particular project at various points in the design process. In the business context, presentations are generally held to plug an idea or review a project's status by communicating research results, data analyses, and user feedback. Companies and designers may also hold presentations at trade fairs and other such events to promote their product lines to specialists, other professionals, and the general public. These kinds of presentations provide opportunities to enhance (→) brand recognition as well, and are thus intended to sustain the audience's continued interest in the company or designer after the presentation is over.

When preparing a presentation, it is always important to keep the target audience (→ *Target Group*) in mind. This includes considering their capabilities and frames of reference, their relationships to one another, political ideologies, backgrounds, and so on. It is also important to clearly define the primary intentions of the presentation at the outset, whether the intent is to educate, sell an idea, obtain support, or to demonstrate or sell a finished product. In addition to organizing content in a clear and comprehensible fashion, presentations should be designed to be visually dynamic. Because the task of preparing a presentation is so complex, multiple parties are often involved in the process.

Presentations are presented two-dimensionally in the form of texts and graphics; three-dimensionally using physical (→) models, (→) prototypes, and products; or—as is increasingly the case—with the help of computers, projectors, and other audio-visual or multimedia tools (→ *Audiovisual Design*). If time or geographic constraints require it, presentations may also be presented entirely online through the use of virtual demonstrations and videoconferences—though it is generally preferable to engage a live audience as it encourages personal exchange. In addition to the more traditional presentation methods of charts, blackboards, and overhead projectors, there are a number of sophisticated computer programs that support the creation of multimedia presentations available today: PowerPoint, MagicPoint, OperaShow, Staroffice, and FotoMagico, to name a few. KSP |

→ *Event Design, Mood Board, Point of Sale*

PROBLEM SETTING

The first phase of the design process is problem setting. During this phase, research is performed in order to analyze the situation, the market, and the target group and its needs. Then a qualification specification (goal construction) is established and, especially in (→) product development, the knowledge is then published in a functional specifications sheet (outlining the technical possibilities, and so on) and a user requirement specifications sheet (outlining the requirements of the product's features, price, (→) USP, and so on). Since these documents are often highly complex, the design-related factors are often summarized in a (→) brief.

The shift in the designer's role from (→) problem solving to problem setting positions the designer to influence the strategic criteria framing a project rather than simply executing the problem setting of others. Problem setting is significant for the subsequent progress of the design work. The more clearly the goal, the criteria and the values are formulated, the more precisely the initial structure is documented, the higher the probability of success. AD |

→ *Design Planning, Design Process, Heuristics*

PROBLEM SOLVING

The (→) design process is a problem-solving process. "Problem" here means an aim to be achieved, when the precise ways and means of accomplishing this are still unknown, especially as it usually implies distinguishing between previous solutions. While the term "solution" refers to the end result of a development process, the term "problem solving" refers to the active system of fulfilling a previously defined requirements specification (→ *Problem Setting*).

Problem solving is a task supported by knowledge, which in design is often combined with learning by trial and error. A successful design process unites the abstraction and restructuring of what has been learned, so that it can generate new or modified solutions to apply to the present situation. This is why it is seldom possible to apply the same design solution to more than one problem. Yet, experiences from similar situations naturally contribute to the process; experiential knowledge is adapted to the specifics of a situation through the application of generalized strategies and problem-specific modifications (→ *Heuristics*). The design process is not only influenced by a rational, analytical work method, but also by an emotional, intuitive process (→ *Intuition*). The two approaches are often coupled together and are mutually reciprocal.

The problem solving process in design is seldom linear because (→) evaluation techniques are an essential feature. The varieties of possible solutions originate for the most part as short-term proposals. The process of evaluating these proposals does not only lead to a design decision, but also often leads to changes and developments to the original problem setting. Dealing with the problem-setting process in a sensible manner is essential here. A requirements specification determines the framework that can provide a point of reference in this process (→ *Brief*). Yet often, distancing oneself from a direct goal-oriented approach by abstracting the problem, searching for analogies, or reversing the question—in other others words, embracing a problem-oriented approach as opposed a product-oriented one—can ultimately result in more innovative solutions.

This is because design problems are so often highly complex, contingent upon multiple interests and influences that cut across often many different fields (→ *Discipline*). The dynamics of a design problem are thus often systemic , and the process of intervening in these systems almost inevitably has unintentional consequences (→ *Wicked Problems*). In psychology, a similar process would be the attempt to find a solution to a poorly structured problem, where the end result is highly unpredictable.

Well-structured problems, on the other hand, are tasks with familiar solutions.

"Creativity methods" have been developed to generate innovative solutions. These methods generally involve heuristic processes that have become quite popular, particularly within the corporate sector. Some of these methods, like ($\rightarrow$) brainstorming and mind mapping, have been adopted in design fields, as well. Ultimately the design process can never be fully automated or documented into anything approaching a manual—while conventional solutions may indeed be reached using established methods, ($\rightarrow$) innovation can only be achieved by breaking the mold. AD |

Funke, J. 2003. *Problemlösendes Denken*. Stuttgart: Verlag W. Kohlhammer.
Heufler, G. 2005. *Design Basics: Von der Idee zum Produkt*. Sulgen, Switzerland: Niggli.
Mayer, R. E. 2004. *Thinking, problem solving, cognition*. 2nd ed. New York: Palgrave Macmillan.

$\rightarrow$ *Design Process*

PROCESS

PRODUCT

A product is the type of ($\rightarrow$) object that human beings produce at any given moment in their history. It can also be examined as a historical process, an economic and technological ($\rightarrow$) artifact, and an ongoing challenge for design professionals.

Human beings have been making products for at least two million years. Indeed, there is a line of argument, stretching from the primatologist Sherwood Washburn to the sociologist of science Bruno Latour, that the very distinction between products and the people who make them is not tenable: Washburn suggested that the common sense truism that "people make things" is actually backward—that the products of human ingenuity so transform our environments that they become factors in our physical evolution. Latour has abandoned the language of objects altogether and prefers to speak of conjoined networks of "human and non-human actants."

Whatever position one takes, one thing is clear: For nearly the whole of human history, the products fashioned by human beings were one-of-a-kind, hand-made objects intended for use, much later for exchange, and more recently (in the grand scheme of things) for sale. Only with the Industrial Revolution was the product abruptly transformed from a singular object "made-by-hand" (the literal meaning of manu-facture) to a machine-made object produced in multiples. The ($\rightarrow$) trends were already apparent to the eighteenth-century authors of the French *Encyclopédie* who depicted the specialized machinery and the resultant division of labor that would be theorized by Adam Smith in *The Wealth of Nations* in 1776. By the end of the nineteenth century the hand-made, one-of-a-kind product was fast becoming a luxury and a curiosity. Its defenders—most famously William Morris—understood themselves to be swimming against the tide of history, while the champions of industrial mass production framed the discourse of twentieth-century modernism (→ *Modernity*).

Modern design discourse can be read as a protracted debate about the nature of the product in an age of universal mass-production: familiar concepts such as "quality" or "craftsmanship" need to be redefined in a manufacturing environment in which a needle, a typewriter, or an iPod may be produced in the millions. Over the course of the twentieth century some designers grappled with this challenge by trying to preserve the element of artistic singularity in their work; the *fin-de-siècle* movement known as (→) Art Nouveau typifies this trend, which continues to the present day. Others embraced the logic and even the aesthetic of the machine and sought to banish all evidence of the hand of the designer; Le Corbusier's demand—"Il faut créer l'esprit de production en série" (We must create the mass-production spirit!) remains their inspiration.

Today it is common (at least in design schools) to speak of the process of creating products as either (→) "industrial design" or (→) "product design." The former usually refers to the application of (→) ergonomics, materials science, and other more or less technical factors to industrial objects in order to make them safer, more comfortable, more efficient, or simply more attractive. Product design more commonly refers to the entire cycle of new (→) product development, which may begin with idea generation and include behavioral analyses, market research, and the creation of a viable business (→) model.

For both product and industrial designers (and they are often one-and-the-same person), the cultural and technological transformations of the last twenty-five years have been staggering: (→) smart materials, (→) rapid prototyping, robotic manufacturing systems, the microprocessor, and of course the Internet—not to mention a growing recognition of environmental limits—have compromised received ideas of what a product is and liberated new dimensions of practice.

Etymologically, the word "product" means "to lead" or "to bring forward," and this ancient root seems appropriate. Whether we are speaking of industrial or consumer products, financial products, software products, Internet-enabled products, or a plethora of others, the human propensity to make things seems to be leading us inexorably forward. BK |

→ *History, Materials, Tools, Virtuality*

Csikszentmihalyi, M. 1981. *The meaning of things*. Cambridge, United Kingdom: Cambridge Univ. Press.
Dormer, P. 1993. *Design since 1945*. London: Thames & Hudson.
Latour, B. 1991. *Nous n'avons jamais été modernes*. Paris: La Découverte.
Sterling, B. 2005. *Shaping things*. Cambridge, MA: MIT Press.

PRODUCT DESIGN

Product design is a practice that involves the creation of objects that are simultaneously functional and (→) aesthetic. These products are not limited to a specific status, but extend from the mundane, everyday (→) artifact to the exotic luxury item.

Toward that end, product designers often need to manage a wide range of expertise including (→) ergonomics, manufacturing techniques, engineering methods, marketing strategies, cultural awareness, environmental issues, and aesthetic judgment.

Although distinctions between product design and (→) industrial design vary greatly depending upon different contexts, the former is often considered to be a subfield of the latter. This categorization may be confusing to many because in practice the terms are used interchangeably—and indeed, they encompass the same spectrum of output possibilities, ranging from domestic artifacts like furniture and tableware to mechanized products like electronics and appliances. However, the two practices do tend to come with different connotations. In particular, product designers are often seen to embody a more customized, craft-based (→ *Craft*) approach to the (→) design process. This is not to say that the products they design are not ultimately manufactured with industrial mass-production techniques; rather, it simply implies that product designs may be geared towards more specialized consumer markets, or be characterized by relatively lower-run productions. In other words, product design is often identified as a subfield of industrial design, not because of a reduced range of possible products, but by a specific perceived approach to the design process itself.

This distinction may have resulted from a number of different factors. Firstly, the term "industrial" can be said to be somewhat outmoded in its historic relationship to the Industrial Revolution. Product design as a professional (→) discipline largely developed in response to this perceived shift in context. Furthermore, the term "industrial" implies an explicit emphasis on manufacturing aspects over other steps in the (→) product development process. Although product designers also frequently collaborate with manufacturers in developing their designs, this relationship is not necessarily a defining characteristic of the practice.

The apparent dichotomy between craft-based approaches versus the more technical elements of design may account for why recent years have seen increasing numbers of practitioners, educators, and managers adopt the phrase "product design" over "industrial design." Whether this perceived distinction is accurate in actual professional practice is of course up for debate; most self-identified practitioners of industrial design pride themselves on their aesthetic abilities, and many product designers privilege engineering concerns over issues of (→) style. Ultimately, both practices share almost all the same objectives, processes, and technologies, and the phrases are still often used interchangeably. EPV |

→ *Form, Function, Materials, Product, Prototype*

PRODUCT DEVELOPMENT

Product development is typically defined as the process by which a new product is brought to market. The development of new products is often used as the means to build a new company, or to increase the market share of an existing company.

Interpretation of the term (→) "product" has changed over time, and now is no longer limited to an object manifested in physical form. It also includes non tangible solutions such as services, interactive experiences, and software packages. Potential end products of the product development cycle include solutions ranging from flyswatters, to chairs, to interactive environments, to hand-held mobile applications.

The process of product development is characterized by work in multidisciplinary teams, in which members from once disparate fields, including industrial design, mechanical engineering, marketing, anthropology, software development, electrical engineering, packaging design, industrial engineering, and interaction design collaborate and play active roles in the phases of development, often exchanging roles as the process unfolds (→ *Collaborative Design*).

A typical product development process is comprised of phases; a broad overview of this cycle includes (but is not limited to): research, conceptual development, design detailing, production, and commercialization. Though this sounds like a linear progression, it is often much more of a zigzag; information gleaned in one phase typically raises questions, and a return to activities in a previous phase is often necessary to answer these questions. Each design practitioner or company conceives of this cycle in a slightly different manner, depending on the nature of the project, the details of the industry being served, and the culture of the organization.

The first phase, (→) research, is an opportunity to develop a deep understanding of the (→) needs (both physical and emotional), motivations, behaviors, and economic/social/ethnic composition of potential users. In recent years, this kind of user-centered approach has also been dubbed "ethnographic research." Procuring this type of early information is intended to help designers create products that are intuitive to use, and that fulfill real human needs (→ *Usability*).

This initial phase of product development is also a chance to evaluate potential areas of opportunity in the market via quantitative (→) market research, and an analysis of this data. If the product involves interaction with the human body, (→) ergonomic research will often be conducted. If the project involves a potential usage of an innovative new (→) material, material research may begin in the early stages of development.

The next phase typically within this cycle, conceptual development, builds upon the findings of the research phase. It involves translating research analysis into initial ideas or frameworks for products or services. This phase tends to be extremely prolific; emphasis is placed on producing a copious range of innovative concepts, rather than quickly selecting a few ideas. (→) Brainstorming is an important activity in the first two phases, and involves clearly articulating problem statements that groups can use as a basis for springboarding their ideas.

After developing a wide range of concepts, the most promising ideas are usually selected, and the parameters of the design development are narrowed down. Specific areas or concepts are chosen for additional, in-depth exploration and development. In the case of client-based work, this funneling process is an interactive one that involves client input and direction, and includes multiple points of review.

As the cycle progresses to the design detailing phase, concepts are increasingly winnowed down, and final technical specifications are determined. The deliverable at the end of this phase is typically a single production-ready product or service (→ *Prototype*).

The production phase involves the actual "build"—the creation of the final product in multiple units that can be sold to, and used by, the end consumer. In the case of tangible products, this involves sourcing and working with manufacturers to manage the production of consumer-ready objects.

Typically, the final phase of the product development cycle involves commercializing the product. This can include advertising the product, setting up distribution chains, building relationships with partners and customers, and so on.

In addition, the idea of (→) sustainability has been progressively inserted into the product development process. For practitioners, this has involved looking at the entire product development cycle in a holistic manner, from the building blocks that create the raw materials used, to the very end of the lifecycle of a product. This trend involves a shift in thinking from "cradle to grave" to "cradle to cradle": Instead of the lifecycle of a product ending in a garbage dump, designers are now thinking about greatly extending the lifespan of the objects they create through such methods as repurposing (→) materials. Heightened awareness of environmental considerations has brought ideas of recycling and reuse to the forefront of the list of designers' considerations.

The goal of the product development cycle is to create a product that resonates with consumers in the market, and helps to boost sales for a company. As such, sales and consumer awareness are methods by which the efficacy of the product development cycle is often evaluated. AR |

→ *Design Methods, Design Process*

Kelley, T. 2001. *The art of innovation: Lessons in creativity from IDEO, America's leading design firm*, pp. 53–66, 69–76. New York: Random House.
Norman, D. 2002. *The design of everyday things*, pp. 1–4. New York: Basic Books.

PRODUCT FAMILY

Equivalent to a biological relationship between people, animals, or plants, (biological systematics), a group of products can also be called a product family as long as there is a "genetic" congruence. Genetic congruence implies similarities in the formal, aesthetic, constructive, and semantic characteristics among products. A product family consists of several individual, closely related products with the same "gene code." Genetic congruence can continue to develop in an evolutionary process and thus remain recognizable for several subsequent product generations. The grouping of products into families can help them stand out from similar products in form and content, and contribute to increasing their recall value. SAB |

→ *Brand, Continuity, Corporate Identity, Semantics*

PRODUCTION TECHNOLOGY

An understanding of the different kinds of production technologies available is one of the most important factors in field of (→) product design. Although industrialization revolutionized the form and function of our world of products by relegating hand crafts to a niche market, innovations in three-dimensional printing and (→) rapid prototyping techniques have the capacity to fundamentally change the field yet again by putting the production of individually customizable products within reach.

Starting from the beginning of the twentieth century, industrial means of production have gradually replaced hand (→) crafts, and consequently strengthened a product's direct dependency on the production process. Since then, the possibilities and limitations of industrial production have proven both restrictive and inspiring. Not unlike the ways in which the laws of gravity dictate the needs and demands of architecture, design moves within tight boundaries determined by the methods of production. Designers both provoke (→) innovation by pushing the limits of production technologies and design novel applications for newly invented production processes.

A good example for understanding the limitations imposed by production technologies is the undercut. Most products made from plastic and metal today are manufactured using various molding (or prototype molding) processes. At the simplest level, molding involves creating depressions in two blocks of metal, pouring a heated fluid material into the depressions, and later separating the blocks to remove the solidified, molded mass. An undercut is a formal element that makes it difficult (if not impossible) to open the casting mold, since the cured mass joins the two blocks together. Undercuts can be safely removed from the casting molding if it is made of more than two parts or has additional movable parts. In this way, more complex shapes can be created to make it possible, for example, for two molded components to snap into one another.

Products may also be made using "lost mold" or extrusion molding techniques.

In the prior process, the mold is destroyed after casting to separate the cast component from the mold. This process is often used for casting hollow objects that require absolute precision such as bells or complex sculptures. In extrusion molding, a material (usually a plastic or metal) in a warm, viscous state is pushed through a pattern. An "endless" profile, corresponding in cross section to the pattern, comes out of the pattern's other end. Everyday example of such "endless profiles" include plastic window frames, or steel H- or I-beams.

Material can also be formed without first constructing a mold using material removal processes like sawing, filing, grinding, drilling, turning, milling, planning, shearing, cutting, and thermal separation, as for example by laser or cutting torch. The relatively new processes of laser and jet cutting use streams of high-energy light or water to cut contours into the surfaces or out of three-dimensional bodies of almost any material.

A commonly used toolless technology is "recasting," which changes the form, but not the volume, of an object. The recasting process can include forging and bending metals, and milling sheet metal. Sometimes semi-finished plastic products are subjected to bending in production. For plastic, however, the most frequently applied recasting technique is "deep drawing," a process that requires a one-sided tool. A frame-mounted plastic plate is heated and placed in a mold in a softened state. Before the plastic hardens, air is removed from between the mold and the plastic plate. This vacuum sucks the soft plastic skin into the mold, where it cools. This technique is used to produce many familiar items such as yogurt cups, bicycle helmets, and interior panels for car doors.

Drink bottles are made by a similar process. A heated blank (resembling a particularly thick-walled plastic test tube) is inflated inside a mold. The plastic is forced out to line the exterior walls, where it cools. The mold is separated and the plastic maintains the desired bottle shape.

In addition to molding processes, (→) coating techniques can also be used to improve the function and appearance of manufactured components. Besides paint and powder coatings, galvanization (chroming) is a particularly effective surface treatment for increasing durability and stability. For metals, hot-dip galvanization is another option. Metal is often used in designing products because it is particularly subject to changes to its material qualities—that is, the inner structure of the material itself. For instance, the hardened blade of a knife is created by carefully reheating and rapidly cooling (tempering) the metal to reach the desired mix of rigidity and durability required for the object's intended use.

In most cases, it takes more than one of the aforementioned processes to create a finished product. In the manufacturing process that follows, the (→) components produced by these methods are assembled. Molded synthetic shells are screwed together to become tool casings, curved metal parts are welded or riveted together to form automobiles, and aluminum-foil lids are glued onto deep-drawn yogurt cups, and so on. Any given product must go through many stages of development before it can be presented to consumers (→ Product Development). Coordinating these multiple processes and guaranteeing a sustained, uniform, and extremely high level of (→) quality at a competitive price always represents significant challenges for the product-development staff, designers and manufacturers involved, particularly when the product is intended for a global market.

Modern (→) rapid prototyping techniques, through which products can be three-dimensionally "printed" directly from a data set, will undoubtedly bring about major advances in production technology over the next thirty years. By implementing production processes that do not require the preliminary construction of molding tools for individual components or even entire units, factories may be able to meet demand more consistently than ever before. Issues related to the economies of scale in production will also change. What is more, these new technologies will abolish design limitations like the undercut discussed above, or the need for final assembly, since it will become possible to produce all of the components in a unit directly at their appointed usage site. The years to come will show us the full extent to which our design strategies will change, both technically and aesthetically, as a consequence of these developments.

The significance of these developments will become even more apparent if three-dimensional printers become affordable for individuals. Since industrialization, the demand for mass-produced products intended to appeal to broad consumer demographics has largely relegated the creation of individualized handcrafted products to a niche luxury market. However, just as the mainstream availability of ink-jet and laser printers have had a profound impact on the democratization of production in the media fields, widespread access to three-dimensional printing and rapid prototyping technologies could, in theory, put the production of individually customizable products at a mass scale within reach (→ Customization). Such developments will also raise a range of questions including the ownership of (→) intellectual property rights. STS |

→ Industrial Design, Materials, Product Design, Tools

Bleicher, S., and J. Stamm, eds. 1988. *Fabrik der Zukunft: Flexible Fertigung, neue Produktionskonzepte und gewerkschaftliche Gestaltung.* Hamburg: VSA.
Deutsches Institut für Normung, ed. 2003. *Fertigungsverfahren: Begriffe, Einteilung (DIN Norm 8580).* Berlin: Beuth.
Peters, S. et al. 2006. *Handbuch für technisches Produktdesign.* Berlin: Springer.
Westkämper, E., and H. J. Warnecke. 2006. *Einführung in die Fertigungstechnik.* Stuttgart: Teubner.

PRODUCT SEMANTICS

→ Semantics

PROJECT

The word "project," derived from the Latin verb *proiacere* (*pro* = forward, for; *iacere* = to throw), refers to a specific, often unique plan, similar in nature to that of an experiment. The term implies the achievement of a certain goal within a defined period of time. Design projects may involve a high risk of failure, and are therefore often monitored and controlled through processes like (→) product development (for industrial manufacturing projects), EDP planning (for educational design projects), and project organization or project management (for complex projects like the design of buildings or transportation systems). TK |

→ *Design Methods, Design Planning, Design Process, Problem Setting, Strategic Design*

PROTEST DESIGN

Protest design is not a design direction in itself. It is a relatively new term that describes a stream of mainly younger designers, who reflect and comment on current social and political developments and events in their theoretical and practical work (→ *Critical Design*).

These designers primarily react to specific political actions taken by countries and governments that cause protest. For example, especially in New York but also in other American states, designers employed genuinely intelligent design methods to participate actively in protest actions in the run-up to the reelection of American president George W. Bush in November 2004. In Germany, various designs for posters, flyers, texts, and sound objects were created when student fees were introduced at government colleges and universities. There was also the establishment of the anti-DRM (digital rights management) group Defectivebydesign that campaigns for free access to software and, thus, against Bill Gates and Microsoft. There are thousands of protest initiatives, and many use the Internet not only as an advertising platform, but as an instrument by which and through which protests can become a global, even virtual, open phenomenon. Clever, eye-catching design will be more in demand as the forms and actions of protest increase that need to be internationally and collectively monitored or designed on the World Wide Web. Every social and political protest needs its own intelligent design strategy. The protest's aim and purpose should be clear at first glance if the goal is to inform and involve new people. Short and succinct text, mottos, slogans, and how these are best conveyed typographically need to be considered, along with an image (eye-catcher), or (→) sound design (a scansion of phrases, song, and "instruments.")

Protest design can contribute to making the reception and result of a protest more effective. It can make people pay attention, laugh, wake them up, it can provoke the opposed party, or spotlight different situations of concern in general. UB |

→ *Design and Politics, Ethics*

Steffen, A., ed. 2006. *Worldchanging: A user's guide for the 21st century*. New York: Harry N. Abrams.

PROTOTYPE

Prototypes (Greek *protos* = first) are intended to test the (→) function and (→) performance of a new design before it goes into production. Generally speaking, prototypes represent one of the last stages of the (→) product development process before the product is industrially manufactured. In rare cases, a prototype can also be devised as a unique piece (that is, not intended for mass production), meant to simulate a product analysis as realistically as possible. Despite the complexity and costliness involved, prototyping is integral to the design of most products by monitoring construction, enabling user feedback about diverse (→) model types, and highlighting weaknesses or flaws in the product before it goes into serial production.

The prototype is often fabricated by hand or with (→) rapid prototyping technologies, and is differentiated from the final products manufactured as part of a mass produced series. Nevertheless, prototypes can often be indistinguishable from the final manufactured products, especially in the eyes of everyday users. A product will typically go through the following stages as part of the product development cycle before the final prototype is constructed:

· Drawings and (→) renderings: preliminary two-dimensional representations of the future product, intended to help product management steer the direction of the design.

· Proportional models: rough renderings of the outer shape and three-dimensional measurements of the product.

· Design model: three-dimensional, realistic presentations of the future product that may not be fully functional.

· (→) Functional models: models that demonstrate a product's function, or particular product functions (for example, the closing device for the roof of a convertible car.)

The last stage before introducing the product to the market is the preseries model, which is typically built using the latest tools and equipment, and serves as the trial or field test prototype. New prototyping technology now allows for up to 500 pieces to be made and trialed during this phase. Once the trial has proven successful, the final tools and equipment are installed for serial production of the product to begin. MBÖ |

→ *Testing*

PROTOTYPING

→ *Rapid Prototyping*

PUBLICATIONS

Publications on design are widespread and vary greatly in both form and content. Designer monographs, exhibition catalogs, design magazines, and (→) design award books are some of the more obvious examples, though virtually every publication deals with the subject of design in one way or another. One look at a newspaper will aptly demonstrate the ubiquity of design in modern culture, as articles on the subject can be found in almost all of the sections: arts and leisure, business, politics, technology, real estate, and so on.

Publications dedicated to design and (→) visual communication may deal with the subject in a broad and integrative fashion, or specialize in discrete fields such as (→) architectural, (→) automobile, media, (→) interior, (→) product, or (→) industrial design. They may be relatively straightforward image compilations or heavily text-based. Increasingly, many are designed, written, and self-published by the designers themselves, particularly in the field of architecture. Monographs—scholarly books that focus on a single designer, design approach or period—are typically comprised of images and critical essays, and are often connected to exhibitions. They have a long tradition in English-speaking countries and to a lesser extent Italy, but are still relatively new in Germany, where they first appeared in the 1980s. On the other hand, Germany began publishing extensive documentation on the subject of design awards much earlier.

While magazines and books with diverse approaches to design research and theory have emerged relatively recently there is also a boom in the sale of publications that that are ostensibly dedicated to design, yet deal with the topic on a relatively superficial level—(→) lifestyle, home, and garden magazines, and thick highly visual "coffee-table" books. Public interest in design-related publications has grown so significantly over the past decade that bookstore sections dedicated to design and independent specialist design bookstores have grown in size and number. HS |

→ Criticism, History

PUBLIC DESIGN

Useful public designs in the form of park benches, trash cans, or street signs are a ubiquitous part of our day-to-day life. Yet these elements of our designed streets are far less overtly influential than the public's use of media and technology, which in effect dissolve the borders between private and public space.

Public design is evident in any product, system, or environment created for public use. The term "public design" is most often used to describe discrete furnishings and signs such as park benches, lamps, crowd barriers, bollards, trash cans, concourses, street signs, and so on—products designed to be weatherproof, wear-resistant, easy to clean, easily secured, uncomplicated to use, and in general aesthetically pleasant. However, the term also encompasses the design of larger spatial, navigational, and orientation systems intended for public engagement. The layouts and infrastructures of our city streets, parks, gardens—even entire city neighborhoods—are all examples of public design, as are the processes and networks of information we use to navigate them. Marketing (→) campaigns that turn private interests into public opinion represent another form of public design that is equally ubiquitous today, apparent in the pervasive

Habermas, J. 1989. *The structural transformation of the public sphere.* Trans. T. Burger and F. Lawrence. Cambridge, MA: MIT Press.

Hosokawa, S. 1984. The Walkman effect in popular music. *Popular Music* 4:171–73. (Orig. pub. 1981.)

Sennett, R. 1977. *The fall of the public man.* New York: Knopf.

Wimmer, M. 1994. Zur Anatomie des "dritten" Ohrs. In Kunst- und Ausstellungshalle der Bundesrepublik Deutschland, ed. *Welt auf tönernen Füssen.* Göttingen: Steidl Verlag.

presence of (→) advertisements in our communal spaces—on billboards, bicycles, taxis, buses, kiosks, shopping bags, window displays, and so on.

To define public design, one must necessary give some thought not only to what constitutes "private design," but also to changing conceptions of public and private space. Changes in our global social and economic structures have had marked effects on the ways we think about ownership, privacy, and the function of public space today. In ancient Rome, for instance, public space was used as a meeting place to discuss social, political, or cultural issues; today we use the telephone or the Internet in order to make contact and exchange with other people. People at the beginning of the nineteenth century took on the role of actors in public space (as described by Sennett) so as to meet strangers yet maintain the necessary (→) social distance; today we expect to be left in peace by strangers on the street.

By blurring the distinctions between public and private space, innovations through design—mobile technologies, communication channels, and transportation systems in particular—have also radically changed the way we consider the environmental typologies of the domestic interior (the home) and the public exterior. Take for example two icons of contemporary design culture that have had a noticeable effect on the ways in which we both perceive and move through public space: the car and the iPod. These products are ostensibly designed for individual use, yet introduce private space into the public realm in very telling ways: cars act as steel-and-glass enclosures to protect us as we move through the environment, while iPods and other portable audio devices provide us with a mask of acoustic privacy, transporting us to a completely different sensory world. "With the Walkman effect the body is opened; it is put into the process of the aestheticization, the theatricalization of the urban—but in secret." (Hosokawa 1984). This effect is perhaps best described as the phenomenon of "cocooning"—the user is able to in effect bring his or her private space into the public realm.

Public design thus encompasses far more than the park benches, street lanterns, and advertisements that take up our communal spaces, and can be defined broadly as any design that assists and facilitates a functioning (that is, discursive and discerning) public. However, in that all design is both socially communicative and interactive, the term "public design" can be thought of as somewhat redundant. Indeed, changing conceptions of what constitutes "the public," together with the increasingly indistinct boundaries between public and private space, will no doubt have an effect on the definition of the term moving forward. MSI |

→ *Mobility, Orientation System, Urban Design, Urban Planning*

Q

QUALITY

Like art, design is an endeavor that aims at high quality. Because both the path to that destination and the reception of such effort are highly dependent on subjective factors, any appeal to indisputable facts has to be replaced by a reference to relationships, differences, and (→) semantics. Quality cannot be measured empirically and cannot be revealed by logical analysis. Quality calls for detours, devotion, Kairos (the god of the fortunate moment), and Philia (love). A world without quality is possible, but it would be sterile and desolate. Quality is an approach to improving things, commencing the process of giving things (→) value without clinging to structures.

Quality is obviously, therefore, a complex concept. It should be distinguished from both quantity and rationality, from which it has been distancing itself ever since Aristotle's formulation of bivalent logic. The concept of quality can be applied to the world of material and intellectual products and services, to the nature of both the processes and events intrinsic in these procedures, to the sensory and epistemological abilities of recipients, and to the relationships among these dimensions.

Quality is the dimension that connects "what questions" to "why questions." In the material world, quality describes the inherent composition of a specific item as distinct from other items and in relation to predetermined requirements. Mahogany certainly falls into the category of fine woods, but is it therefore of better quality per se than fir or cedar? Not necessarily. Its use in making musical instruments, for example, shows that mahogany's inherent properties, such as torsion resistance, density, sensitivity to temperature, surface qualities, and so on, make it a distinctive material. When a material is used appropriately with respect to preexisting parameters such as longevity, robustness and comprehensive functionality as well as aesthetic pleasure, then it is said to do justice to the work. However, the relativity of such parameters is evident, for example, in the fact that longevity (→ Sustainability) implies an entirely different length of time in the field of digital media than it does in instrument making.

If a finished or designed product is broken down into components and manufacturing steps, then the degree of (→) complexity thus created is already an indication of whether doing justice to the work has been achieved, and the specific form of the latter is in turn an indication of quality. The example of instrument making shows that using the correct combination of heterogeneous materials ensures a product's overall quality. What use are the finest woods if the instrument's strings cannot be adjusted precisely because of the dimensions of the pegs or fingerboard? The overall interaction of all the components determines the ultimate quality of the object.

The situation with intellectual products and services is similar. The quality of a process is determined by the subtly differentiated and harmonized approach measured against a requirement. At this point, particularly when conceiving a design, another methodological dimension comes into play: namely, the relationship of reality and possibility, of rejected and implemented possibility. Designers live in a world of possibilities, moving through it both laterally and associatively. Every valuable design concept derives its quality from analysis and research that opens up a world of possibilities and then condenses this range of possibilities again in a continuous, goal-oriented process to the point where what remains is what is best suited to the intended (→) use. The context of that use thus points beyond itself to other things that have not yet been realized and communicates its capabilities, its advantages, and its significance to the user. The selectivity thus obtained is the basic parameter of every design, which clearly demonstrates the relevance of the feedback loop of reflection built into the (→) design process. The chain of the design process extends from (→) research and analysis about the concept and design to realization and then to (→) testing for suitability. Building in a feedback loop of reflection early on—in the form of documentation, records, and the communication of objectives—optimizes the processes of (→) communication at their points of intersection. This shows how different professional design services are from the provision of mere decorative surface treatments, and how valuable these types of constitutive design services are when quality is an issue.

This presumes that users have been taught to differentiate between design products and services. What use is the best product, the most plausible service, if the user or consumer is unable to distinguish it from a lesser solution? Here, as always, it is tough for design. The demand for high quality is time-consuming, complicated and correspondingly expensive. Because the sophistication of professional services required to conceive a superior product leaves only a trace in the finished product and is not the primary focus of attention, the user tends not to value these hidden services. For that reason too, the value of development services, research, documentation and other efforts at reflection is often still underestimated today and

Aicher, O. 1994. *Analogous and digital.* Trans. Michael Robinson. Berlin: Ernst & Sohn.

Burckhardt, L. 1985. *Die Kinder fressen ihre Revolution.* Cologne: DuMont.

Pirsig, R. M. 1974. *Zen and the Art of Motorcycle Maintenance: An Inquiry into Values.* New York: Morrow.

QUALITY ASSURANCE

consequently is paid for reluctantly. It is necessary to teach users that the overall product will not be of high quality if these aspects are overlooked. It is thus increasingly important in the modern design process that customers be made aware of the necessity for reflection in the process of design and manufacture. Design has to be the path that modern quality management follows, though without succumbing to a normative canon of rules. SA |

→ *Product Development, Quality Assurance*

Quality assurance refers to the planned processes that are used to ensure that designed products, services, or systems, meet prescribed standards. In design contexts, (→) "quality" is often determined by the degree to which the design is successful in meeting or exceeding user expectations; however, it can also encompass characteristics such as freedom from defect, safety, reliability, maintainability, and adherence to requirements. Quality assurance procedures are typically implemented to provide confidence via some form of objective measurement that these standards of quality have, in fact, been met (→ *Evaluation*).

The modern conception of quality assurance can be traced back to industrial manufacturing processes established in Japan during the post-World War II era. With the assistance of advocates such as W. Edwards Deming, the Japanese were able to raise demand for their industrial output by focusing on management processes leading to quality rather than simple postproduction inspection methods. These successes evolved into quality management strategies known as Total Quality Management (TQM). The basic principle of TQM is that a focus on quality must be present at all levels in an organization and during all stages of (→) product development. The idea is that these efforts to reduce defects and improve customer satisfaction will lead, in turn, to a more successful business.

Deming, W. E. 1982. *Out of the crisis.* Cambridge, MA: MIT Press.

Feigenbaum, A. V. 2004. *Total quality control.* 4th ed. New York: McGraw-Hill Professional.

Hoyle, D. 2005. *ISO 9000 Quality Systems Handbook.* Oxford: Butterworth-Heinemann.

Pyzdek, T. 2003. *The six sigma handbook: The complete guide for greenbelts, blackbelts, and managers at all levels.* New York: McGraw-Hill.

A number of quality assurance certifications are available for organizations seeking to apply quality management principles. Among them are the International Organization for Standardization (ISO) 9000 family of standards and Six Sigma (developed by Motorola). Companies attaining certifications in these standards must demonstrate adherence to their respective quality management best practices. MDR |

→ *Design Management, Strategic Design*

R

RADICAL DESIGN

Italy's Radical Design (Italian: *Disegno Radicale*) movement emerged in the late 1960s and was influential until the late 1970s with three major centers of activity: Milan, Florence, and Turin. Radical Design was influenced by a number of earlier movements and collectives, particularly Archigram, a group of architects and designers that was active in England during the early 1960s.

Advocates of Radical Design included, among others, the members of the Archizoom, Superstudio, and Strum groups, as well as the architect and designer Ettore Sottsass, the filmmaker Ugo La Pietra, the artist Gaetano Pesce, and the theorist Andrea Branzi. Radical Design (or "Architettura Radicale" as it was then called, a term coined by Germano Celant) first emerged in 1966 during a period of widespread (→) social transformation. The young architects and theorists involved formulated a critique of dehumanized modernism (→ *Modernity*) and rigid (→) functionalism. Politicized and discontent with the working conditions of the time, the direction that (→) architectural design was taking, and the consumption-oriented (→) Bel Design of most industrial products, they dedicated themselves to developing alternative social and cultural understandings of architecture and design.

Process was reexamined, especially in design. Their critique of industrial products led to a revitalized emphasis on (→) craft, drawing, and photomontage, the production of small series, and the formulation of ideas for future residential worlds (including urban utopias). Examples of Radical Design include the Mobili Grigi designed by Ettore Sottsass for Poltronova in 1970; the artificial turf Pratone by the Gruppo Strum for Gufram in 1971; the Mies chair by Archizoom for Poltronova in 1969; and the Il Monumento Continuo project by Superstudio in 1969. By the mid-1970s, many of the architectural and design studios that had exemplified Radical Design's ideologies had broken up. Subsequent movements and initiatives like Alchimia and (→) Memphis reflected many of the same interests and concerns of Radical Design, but for the most part were less politically motivated. CN |

→ *Postmodernism*

RAPID PROTOTYPING

Also known as "solid freeform fabrication," rapid prototyping is a term used to describe a range of fabrication processes where three-dimensional CAD (→ *CAD/CAM/CIM/CNC*) data is used directly in the construction of components or objects. The data from the CAD model is broken down into a number of thin layers which are then reconstituted by the cutting, fusing, or depositing of physical material, layer upon layer until a physical representation of the data exists. The main advantage of rapid prototyping is that it allows for the construction of highly complex geometry without the need for costly and time-consuming tooling. For this reason, it is particularly important for designers.

There are several different methods of rapid prototyping. In stereolithography (SLA), the CAD data is sent to an ultraviolet laser which scans the surface of a tank containing a liquid photopolymer which is hardened where the two make contact. After the scan is completed, a platform on which the model sits is lowered into the tank by approximately 0.1 mm and the laser repeats the process with the next layer until the model has been completed. The platform is then raised to reveal the finished object, which must then be cured in an oven before any final finishing can take place. Stereolithography is the most widely used form of rapid prototyping. It is considered to have the best surface finish and there is a wide range of materials available that can mimic commercially used plastics such as ABS. Ceramic materials are also currently in development for the process.

Fused deposition modeling (FDM) is the second most popular method of rapid prototyping after stereolithography. It extrudes a heated filament of thermoplastic or wax through a heated nozzle attached to a mechanism which can move both horizontally and vertically. The material is layered in a similar fashion to cake icing onto a bed below and successive layers are bonded by thermal fusion. The machinery is capable of producing support structures for overhanging elements which can be removed at the end of fabrication. While the surface finish has improved greatly over recent years, it does not have the resolution of stereolithography.

Selective laser sintering (SLS) works in a similar way to stereolithography, but here the laser scans a bed of highly compacted, heat-fusible thermoplastic or wax powder. The surface finish and accuracy of objects created using SLS are inferior to those achieved through stereolithography and finished objects need to be left to cool for a considerable time before removal from the machine. However, objects created by SLS do not require support for any overhangs or undercuts due to the fact that they are supported by the surrounding compacted powder in the bed. Sinter metals and ceramics have also been recently introduced to this process.

Laminated object manufacturing (LOM) cuts profiles into paper or another type of web material and then laminates another layer on top of the previous one until an object is created. This process is less accurate than other methods of rapid prototyping but has lower production costs and the final objects can be finished like wood.

Three-dimensional printing (3DP) works in a similar fashion to selective laser sintering, except where SLS uses a laser to fuse a thermoplastic or wax powder, 3DP uses a liquid adhesive to create and bond the layers of powder together. The objects must then be treated with a hardener before they can be handled. Materials that can be used in this process include powder metals and ceramics. Although the resolution and surface finish of the objects created using 3DP are limited when compared to other technologies, it is the fastest and cheapest form of rapid prototyping currently available.

Photopolymer phase change inkjets (PPCI) works in a similar way to normal inkjet printers. A print head containing a photopolymer is used to lay down a single layer of the object which is then cured using a UV light before depositing the next layer. A second print head is filled with a support material to deal with overhang and undercuts within the object. The support material can be washed away with pressurized water at the end of the build. PPCI technology is able to produce very high resolution models as layers can be no more than sixteen microns thick and the finished objects do not require any curing or cooling. However, it cannot currently produce large-scale objects and the properties of materials used in the process are limited when compared to other rapid prototyping technologies.

The limited physical properties and surface finish of materials used in rapid prototyping, as well as the relative expense and slow speeds of the technologies involved, currently make these technologies unsuitable for the mass production of (→) components or objects. These drawbacks have limited its use to the fields of (→) product design (for concept development and product testing) and engineering (for tool production). However, increased commercial availability of the machinery coupled with improvements in material properties and resolutions have seen a number of designers and artists experimenting with the processes as a means of creating objects in their own right. There have also been developments in the field of medicine where they are being used to create bone replacements for reconstructive surgery. The University of Manchester's School of Materials in the United Kingdom has produced a three-dimensional printer that can produce layers of skin using cells taken directly from a patient which can then be directly applied to wounds. RL |

→ *Engineering Design, Industrial Design, Materials, Product Development, Production Technology, Prototype, Testing*

RAZIONALISMO

Whereas the concept of rationalism in the discipline of philosophy is generally associated with theories developed by René Descartes, the term came to be used in the design context to refer to an architectural movement that arose in Italy during the 1920s and 1930s.

Inspired by the Modern Movement that was developing throughout Europe at the same time, Razionalismo was oriented around both modern principles of composition and classical forms founded in Roman antiquity. In 1926, the Gruppo Sette (Group Seven) was founded and included Luigi Figini, Gino Pollino, and Giuseppe Terragni, among others. Two organizations firmly committed to the philosophies of modern architecture emerged from this core: the Movimento Architettura Razionale, or MAR, in 1928, and the Movimento Italiano per l'Architettura Razionale, or MIAR, in 1930. The young architects involved were sympathetic with Fascism at first, openly supporting Mussolini and in some cases becoming party members. The Casa del Fascio in Como, a clear steel-and-glass construction built by Giuseppe Terragni between 1932 and 1936, became renowned for reflecting the ideals of Razionalismo architecture. The Olivetti factory in Ivrea by Luigi Figini and Gino Pollini, completed in 1937, also took its lead from this architectural style.

From the outset, the movement competed with a style more closely tied to neoclassicism. During the mid-1930s, Mussolini turned away from Razionalismo and began favoring monumental neoclassicism, elevating the latter to the status of the party's "official" style. Razionalismo was suppressed and the magazine *Casabella*, an important forum for the movement, was banned in 1943.

Despite the fact that the industrial development and manufacture of products was still relatively underdeveloped in Italy during the 1920s and 1930s, the influence of Razionalismo ideas on the design of furnishings was evident from the outset. For example, the modern, industrial material of tubular steel was employed—influenced by developments at the (→) Bauhaus—by architects such as Luciano Baldessari, Piero Bottoni, Giuseppe Terragni, Giuseppe Pagano, Gabriele Mucchi, and Gino Levi Montalcini. Most of these designs, however, were merely (→) prototypes and never became mass-produced industrial products.

The end of the Second World War saw a strong resurgence of Razionalismo principles, both in architecture and in the design of everyday objects. In Italy's flourishing industrial sector, the legacy of Razionalismo continued to be influential in the work of the Studio BBPR and of Franco Albini, Alberto Rosselli, Marco Zanuso, Anna Castelli Ferrieri, and many others. Razionalismo appealed to young architects in the postwar period, in part because of the dearth of architectural commissions, and in part because they were moved by the idea of creating a democratic Italy where simple and inexpensive products were provided for everyone. They employed its modern, functional formal idiom and refined it in the context of increasing industrialization. Razionalismo became the measuring stick and point of reference for several generations before more radical movements such as Antidesign, Alchimia, and (→) Memphis began questioning the doctrine of pure (→) functionalism in earnest.

It must be said that the theoretical and historical debate about Razionalismo in architecture and design in Italy is marked by considerable ambivalence. The movement's approaches to modernism have always been lauded as visionary, but the relationship between Razionalismo and Fascism is almost always avoided in discussions of the prewar period, even, or especially, by the architects and designers of the younger generation who usually view themselves as leftist or liberal. CN |

→ Architectural Design, Design and Politics, Function, Modernity

REDESIGN

The practice of redesign involves refining, improving, or reinterpreting an already existing functional design.

Until the late nineteenth century, it was common in the then craft-based industry to work from "pattern catalogs," which resulted in product models varying only slightly from case to case. This canonization of product models continued through the early twentieth century, as well, during which designers continued to repeatedly reference prior designs in their work. For example, in his theory of *objets-types,* the Swiss-born French architect Le Corbusier described a set of product models to be used as the basis for modern reinterpretation. His interest in stylistic revivalism was also evident in his designs, as demonstrated by the *fauteuil à dossier basculant* (sling chair), which was based on the classic colonial chair. Seminal design works by other designers like the *Sitzmaschine* (seating machine) by Josef Hoffmann and the Barcelona chair by Ludwig Mies van der Rohe were also based on refining existing models.

Such explicit references to the history of design became the exception rather than the norm in the days of early modernism (→ Modernity), however, when designers began considering radical breaks with the past a prerequisite for true (→) innovation. Only in the postwar period did an understanding of design prevail that sought to reconcile modernism's pursuit for innovation with the realities of industrial production, in which introducing completely new models is often associated with complicated and expensive technical adjustments. Designers such as Gio Ponti of Italy and Hans Wegener of Denmark made designing from historic models acceptable again, and scholars such as Enzo Paci and Umberto Eco offered important fundamentals for design (→) theory on themes such as mass production, the genesis of (→) form, and individuality that contributed to the concept of redesign from the 1960s onward (though were rarely employed in practice). The concept of redesign experienced some controversy in 1978, when the Italian design, and theorist Alessandro Mendini created a furniture series that playfully altered the applications of modern classics, and called them "redesigns." Since then, "redesign" has become a generic term for all designs that, for economic, technical, or artistic reasons, refer to a clearly defined precursor design.

It is important to distinguish redesign both from (→) retro designs, where the references are less to specific designs than to general stylistic (→) trends, and from (→) fakes, which violate the legal or moral rules of authorship that a redesign must always respect.

Redesigns are not only implemented by industrial manufacturers, but also by designers who produce smaller series and embrace a more conceptual approach (→ Conceptual Design). In such cases, designers often address redesign through the notion of the "ready-made"—as exemplified by Italian designer Achille Castiglioni, who used functional everyday objects as the basis of his new designs during the postwar period. In many (→) postmodernist examples of redesign, there is a perplexing effect of reinterpretation—for example, Shiro Kuramata's Homage to Josef Hoffmann chair, Ron Arad's adaptation of a Rover automobile seat, or many of the products by Droog Design.

Redesigns in the industrial sectors are often intended to reference the established (→) semantics of a familiar design, as well, but usually for more pragmatic reasons of economy and efficiency. For example, redesigns can be used to ensure continued demand for certain model types in saturated markets, or in response to changing cycles in fashion. As the technical attributes of products are becoming increasingly similar, redesigns can also be used to differentiate a product from its competitors through aesthetic means. Conversely, technical innovations can necessitate a redesign in which the product's "shell" is adapted to its modernized interior. And finally, the modernization or restructuring of production processes can make a redesign necessary, as well (when the production process itself is redesigned, it is known as "reengineering"). In all of these cases, redesigns reflect a desire to profit from the successes of the precursor design, to build upon the market's familiarity with the precursor design (thus strengthening brand recognition), and to make use of existing investments in development and production.

One sector that has a decades-old, almost ritualized tradition of redesign is the automobile industry (→ *Automobile Design*). Here, the redesign of entire series has become a central element in a policy of innovation and customer loyalty. Elaborate relaunches at regular intervals introduce new models to the market that have adapted the features of earlier models in such a way that stimulates consumption without undermining the (→) brand's (→) continuity. Depending on the degree to which such changes are met with success, manufacturers may follow a more conservative or more aggressive policy for subsequent redesigns. Other industry strategies of redesigns are evident as well. The "upgrade" of a model that becomes increasingly elaborate and expensive over the course of several redesigns creates room for less expensive models in the product line. Redesigns are also used to maintain continued interest in a successful product line, in which a single base model evolves into several different successors over time, all based on the same "platform." When the redesign of a model is not based on an immediate precursor but on a model with historical significance it can adopt some of the qualities of retro design: for example, the redesign of VW's Beetle.

The modernization and "rejuvenation" of (→) corporate identities has always relied on redesigns, as well. The spectrum of successful examples extends from Peter Behrens' corporate identity for AEG to the decades-long evolution of corporate (→) logos for Nivea or Lucky Strike. Along the same lines, new typefaces are often developed to adapt to changes in technology, habits of perception, and market requirements. In the contemporary marketplace, the redesign of product lines and corporate identities is treated in hand in hand with the process of (→) branding. As such, a company's ability to successfully redesign its product and image is considered to have a direct effect on its ultimate success or failure, and requires strategic coordination through (→) design management.

Redesign has taken on a new importance in light of the technical possibilities afforded by advances in digital media. In the case of (→) web designs in particular, redesigns are no longer necessarily reliant on designer interventions, but made through a continual updates that increasingly involve user participation. Similarly, new production methods in the area of (→) rapid prototyping have made it easier to get from the design stage to the production stage more quickly, more efficiently, and with increasingly accessible resources at hand. In the context of these advancing technologies, the meaning of redesign is transforming, from a definition that involves the elaborate reshaping of entire processes to one that allows for more continual and gradual updates to an existing design. MKR |

Bickmann, R. 2002. *Corporate Identity— Best Practice: Das Management von Komplexität*. Munich: DVA.

Sambonet, G. 1986. *Alchimia, 1977–1987*. Turin: Umberto Allemandi.

Wassermann, M. 1992. *Rethink, redesign, reconstruct: How top designers create bold new work by reinterpreting original designs*. Cincinnati: How Design Books.

REGISTERED
DESIGN

→ *Copyright, Intellectual Property*

RENDERING

"Rendering" refers to a (→) sketch produced by hand to illustrate textures and properties of materials in three dimensions, especially in (→) automobile design. "Rendering" is also used for the computer-aided conversion of individual graphics into a simulated 3-D drawing such as an (→) animation. SIB |
→ *Model*

RESEARCH

Design research is vaguely defined; it includes theory and practice, process and drafting. There are various concepts of research manifested in different communities.

For several years the discussion in and around design research has grown enormously in importance: international symposia are organized where trends, methodical approaches and relevant research content are wrestled with and sometimes hotly debated. Design research is not pursued solely in academic environments and their communities but is gaining the attention of other institutions and companies as well. Now design research has prevailed in the wider world as a necessary and self-evident component of the whole broad field of design.

In contrast to the role of research in better-established academic disciplines, however, the concept of research in design is not clearly defined. It is increasingly evident how closely reflection and investigation about the profession are enmeshed with the concept and the (→) design process. There are few other well-established academic disciplines that question whether they can be justified as a field of scholarship—which always logically implies research. Art, possibly, would be the other exception, but because of the separation of art history and theory as an independent discipline, it can still justify itself through scholarship and research.

The way design is viewed in the English-speaking world seems to deal most straightforwardly with the concept of research—though one could also say that that is partly as a result of being largely unaware of its problems. The question of the specifics of design research and other possible forms and approaches this research might take does not play an especially large role in this debate. The reasons for this are to be found in the tradition of the concept of design and the nature of educational and research institutions in the English-speaking world. The debate about design has a longer history in Britain than in other countries. It must, however, be recalled that the English definition and use of the word "design" is much broader than its equivalent in German, where from about the mid-1970s it began to be used side by side with the German word (→) *Gestaltung* (which has the meaning of shape and organization implicit in it) which was the common expression until that time.

The original sense of "design" in English covers numerous meanings, only a few of which relate explicitly to the German concept of *Gestaltung*. That is both an opportunity and a problem—on the one hand, this breadth per se suggests multidisciplinary processes. On the other hand, this reduces and obscures the precision of what is meant in each case. Sometimes imparting information about design is closer to the approach used in cultural studies—that is to say, it does not seek to link competence in design theory or history with practical skills. In that sense design research remains too closely bound to cultural or social studies for a new concept of design research to emerge. This is also true in general of research and teaching at the university level in the English-speaking world, where their roles are often articulated differently than other countries, especially within continental Europe.

Hence, although the meaning of design in English is, on the one hand, broader than in any other language, the field is then divided into many subdisciplines or perceived too narrowly. Another reason for this perhaps too clearly defined concept of design in regard to research in the English-speaking world, lies in the long and enduring tradition of, on the one hand, mentioning design and art in the same phrase ($\rightarrow$ *Arts & Crafts*), while also integrating engineering, computer science, psychology, and other disciplines into the canon of design theory and research. As little as there is to object about a multidisciplinary approach in a world that is already networked, it is nonetheless dubious to fuse all these things uncritically into a form of research dominated, or so it seems, by opinions about research from the hard sciences versus cultural or social studies. This makes it more difficult for the young discipline of design to develop its own particular understanding of research.

The productive ambiguity mentioned at the outset is a favorable outcome in other contexts of research (for example, in German-speaking countries). The concept of research in design is vague, and this vagueness has its correspondence in several areas: between theory, practice and *Entwurf*; between artifacts and their contexts; between the visible world and the world of ideas of traditional scholarship. This lack of specificity is not always a disadvantage; on the contrary, the possibility of making the concept of research more fluid represents an opportunity to distinguish design from other forms of study. Where the latter can be seen to be burdened by their long history in the form of ossified norms and standards of scholarship, design studies and research can formulate a concept of research that can in its turn also stimulate other sciences. This fluid definition of research is, of course, by no means undisputed.

It should be reiterated that in terms of the quantity of discussion about design research, the dominant theoretical views are influenced by the English-speaking world. What is published and said in English can be understood in many parts of the world, since English is the established world language. Discourses, journals and books in French, German, Italian, Japanese, and so on, have a much harder time being noticed at all. Moreover, these linguistically diverse communities for design research are only now starting to come together.

Three networks on design research will be presented briefly here as examples of different approaches:

·   The Design Research Society (DRS), founded in the United Kingdom in 1966, sees itself as a multidisciplinary, international society whose members come from about forty countries. With just a few exceptions, the chair and other posts are all filled with English-speaking designer researchers. The DRS declares its common denominator to be supporting and communicating about "design in all its many fields."

·   The European Academy of Design (EAD) was founded in 1994 as a loose association of various university and other educational institutions teaching design to support design research by linking of theory and practice, to improve international cooperation, and to issue publications and newsletters. Every year an international conference is organized by one of the universities and, thus far, there have been meetings in England, Sweden, Portugal, Spain, and Germany.

·   The Deutsche Gesellschaft für Designtheorie und -forschung (German Society of Design Theory and Research, or DGTF) has existed since 2002. It should more accurately be called the German-speaking Society, since it includes Swiss and Austrian design researchers. The DGTF sees itself as committed to an open, deliberately vague concept of design research and considers itself neither subject to previously developed scholarly standards (a risk inherent in the concept of design in the English-speaking world) nor subsumed by scholarship in design but rather as exploring something in-between that is as provocative as it is productive.

These initiatives make it clear that, with the exception of the DRS, an awareness of the relevance of design research as a separate discipline is relatively new, but it is making itself heard through the committed work of individuals and a growing number of associations.

Whatever concept of design is favored by these various research communities and conferences, all of them refer back—however different their interpretations, adaptations, and critiques—to the criteria formulated by Christopher Frayling in 1993 (then professor at the Royal College of Art in London and since 1996 its rector), which continue to define the debate. He distinguished between three types of design research: research into, for, and through design.

Research into (or about) design is the easiest one to explain, since it corresponds to the conventional concept of research. Design becomes the thematic object of analysis—from the perspectives of history, sociology, cultural studies, philosophy, or technology. It is viewed retrospectively, from outside, from a distance and with the declared intention of not altering the object of analysis. (It must be said, however, that the conviction that this approach does not influence the object of research is at best illusory and at worst simply ideological. At least since Immanuel Kant, it has been known that even so-called disinterested, objective viewing of an object will influence it as research represents an intervention and hence has an effect.) Research into or about design is the oldest and most widespread form of research, and the one most like research in other disciplines.

Research for design supports in specific ways the (practical, active) process of design whose product is an artifact; market and consumer research but also product semantics are examples of this form of research. It can be identified as a kind of preparatory empiricism or ancillary science for the practical process of design. It is a form of research that need not be manifested solely in written or oral forms of communication but also incorporates visual and analogous representations.

Finally, research through design is perhaps the most original and distinctive approach to research in design, since it is characterized by a high degree of similarity between the process of design and that of design research. It is a research method unique to design that demands the direct involvement of design researchers in the very object of their research. In this approach, theory and research do not pursue the verification or falsification of preformulated hypotheses with the goal of consistency— an approach better suited to positivist approaches. Rather researchers feel their way into the field of research, interact with it and, if necessary, alter it through considered and deliberate interventions. Immediacy is desirable and areas of ambiguity are deliberately explored. Research through design presumes a hermeneutic understanding of design and this works when the design process is open to taking into account an interactive dialogue with the design situation. The particular situation should be perceived, even anticipated, in order to better acknowledge the object of research appropriately. That requires openness in the research process and readiness to engage in new, surprising situations in the course of research.

The different cultural understandings of design are manifested most clearly when considering "research through design." Critics in English-speaking countries tend to doubt that this kind of research exists at all, instead simply equating research in general with design. Or they reduce the "through" to the trivial statement that it is a "vehicle" of research that merely serves as a means of communicating the results of research. The continued insistence by the proponents of research who claim that they can observe in a disinterested and non interfering manner from the outside has been explained by Jonas as a "flight to allegedly safe ground, but away from the questions that are really interesting.... You escape the paradoxes and swamps, but you abandon the familiar tools of the craft. That might be justified politically over the short-term, but over the long-term it hurts design."

Design research and theory at their most intelligent could perhaps best be described as "experience-based" judgment. UB |

→ *Discipline, Practice, Theory*

Alexander, C. 1964. *Notes on the synthesis of form*. Cambridge, MA: Harvard Univ. Press.
Frayling, C. 1993–94. Research in art and design. In *Royal College of Art Research Papers* 1, no. 1.
Friedmann, K. 2002. Towards an integrative design discipline. In B. Byrne and S. Squires, eds. *Creating breakthrough ideas*. Westport, CT.: Greenwood Publishing Group.
Jonas, W. 2004. http//www.dgtf.de/fileadmin/TheorieUndDesign/Jonas.pdf.

RESPONSIBILITY

The word "responsibility" derives from the Latin verb *respondere* meaning to "reply" or "respond." Responsibility places human action in causal contexts of temporal, social, religious, and other meaning. Morally it is regarded as a positive (→) value.

In order to derive a concept of responsibility relevant to design, it makes sense first to differentiate the meanings of the term. Two categorizations can help with that. The first is seeing responsibility as a multilayered phenomenon, whereby the primary responsibility is that of the particular task and deed, the secondary responsibility is that of accountability or jurisdiction, and the tertiary responsibility is liability as compensation and punishment. The second is the ethic of responsibility according to Max Weber, in which estimating the cosequences for possible actions of politicians is contrasted with the (→) ethics of conviction.

For design, as a primarily active (→) practice that intervenes in real-world circumstances, the responsibility of action proves to be a useful means of orientation. Systematic and time parameters are relevant to responsibility in the design process. Invention, (→) innovation, economy, production, reception, (→) function, and (→) form all serve as systematic parameters. The past, present, and future serve as time parameters. Ideally, design takes responsibility for (→) creativity, historical reflection, and orientation for the future. How these aspects are to be apportioned, valued, and accounted for is, however, largely subject to the designer's conviction. Thus in the view of many designers, design's responsibility is reactive and demand-oriented as it is based on economic success. Others, in turn, see design's responsibility as being in the field of proactive and world-changing modernizations and improvements in the culture of communication and objects.

The question of whether design should actively change the world, or whether conversely the living world should generate design, is the polarizing fundamental question designers are asking themselves today. Ultimately it is also the question determining action and thus relevant when assigning responsibility. From it we can derive a descriptive concept of responsibility for design. Whereas the designer oriented toward demand simply acts on the basis of economic success, the proactive concept of responsibility in design is more complex. The latter considers not only the economic consequences but also and above all the (→) social, political, ecological, and ethical consequences of that design. Nevertheless, neither of these convictions precludes integrative action. This results in a complex ethics of responsibility for design that can be described as a variable for designer action and thus as a free responsibility analogous to Max Weber's ethics of responsibility in the following ways: first, the necessary differentiation and ideally reconciliation between design's objective (success) and vision (social responsibility); second, the analysis of the actions of designers in the historical discourse (learning from history); third, identifying parameters relevant to production and sales; and fourth (as a proxy for design's truthfulness), the generation of creative, new, usable, and original solutions avoiding repetitions. Nevertheless design must be subjected to the shifting nature of responsibility through discourse with reality. In particular, the great significance of the delimitation and recreation of contexts in design sometimes calls for a type of responsibility that is project-specific. According to Aristotle, coercion, necessity, error, and mental illness can partly or completely relieve one of responsibility. ᴱˢᶜ |

Aristotle. 2000. *Nichomachean Ethics*. Trans. Roger Crisp. Cambridge, United Kingdom: Cambridge Univ. Press.
Eickhoff, H., and J. Teunen. 2005. *Forum/Ethik: Ein Brevier für Gestalter*. Ludwigsburg: avedition.
Weber, M. 1958. Politik als Beruf. In *Gesammelte politische Schriften*. Trans. R. Livingstone as "Politics as a Vocation." In M. Weber, *The vocation lectures*. Indianapolis: Hackett, 2004.
Weischedel, W. 1958. *Das Wesen der Verantwortung*. 2nd ed. Frankfurt am Main: Klostermann.

RETAIL DESIGN

To define retail design we must start with the definition of retail itself: a culminating link in a supply chain that results in the sale of goods for (→) consumption. Retail design, as the design of the environment that displays and purveys these goods, thus has "the sale" as one of its functional goals, and is dictated by short, middle, and long-term goals of profit making. Although the term usually refers to the act of designing the physical retail environment—the storefront, entrance, window display, interior display, point of purchase, and storage—it almost always involves less tangible aspects of (→) branding, advertising, sales, and post sales services (→ *Service Design*) as well. Each element in the physical design performs an integral function:

· The storefront and window ($\rightarrow$) display provide public visibility and attract consumers into the interior sales area; as such, they are considered of paramount importance.

· The entrance acts as the initial threshold or portal that controls access to the interior retail space. It also often provides a taste of the brand identity (for example the hidden entrance for L'Eclaireur, Paris indicating the brand's exclusivity).

· The interior display is composed of fixtures—that is, items that are intended to support sales but not intended for sale themselves. Common retail fixtures include items such as shelves, platforms, lighting, vitrines, niches, hanging racks, face-outs, and mannequins. Visual merchandising is the term for interior or window display placement and styling.

· The ($\rightarrow$) point of sale or cash wrap is the point of transaction where the goods and payment are transacted. Examples include serviced and self-service checkout stations.

· Storage or stock rooms are often needed to carry inventory reflected in the displayed merchandise. Since this area is typically not trafficked by the consumer public, the design generally emphasizes ease of access as opposed to the consumer perspective.

Various other interior components will be integrated as needed, depending on the goods sold, the typical duration of the retail experience, and the target consumer demographics ($\rightarrow$ *Target Group*). Bathrooms, waiting areas, fitting rooms, daycare facilities and so on, will ideally reflect the design elements of the main retail area, even while providing their own specific functions.

While the goods may vary, the experience of purchasing with the intent of consumption has several common typologies, and within those typologies, common design components. These typologies include monobrand stores, multibrand stores, and temporary markets.

Monobrand retail design involves the display and sale of goods that are of a single ($\rightarrow$) brand. Since a singular brand identity informs the design of monobrand retail environments, stores in the same brand chain or franchise will typically look very similar. However, differences certainly exist. For instance, "shop-in-shops" located within department stores or malls typically are smaller than freestanding stores, and the retail design usually requires reconciling the department store's overall design standards and rules with those of the brand. On the other hand, the main purpose of freestanding flagships stores is to create a high impact brand environment that increases visibility, a long-term goal that takes priority over immediate or short-term sales quotas. These flagships are typically located in highly trafficked and visible urban environments, with large expanses of expensive real estate devoted to intensifying the brand image. Merchandise is therefore carefully displayed in order to highlight the iconic character of each product as opposed to the volume of stock. A related sub-category, the showroom, is a sales environment that displays goods (furniture, automobiles, audiovisual equipment) primarily for demonstration purposes. (→) Models are available for customers to experience, yet the actual product to be purchased is picked up or shipped separately. Since the function and eventual sale of the product takes priority in these environments, an emphasis is often placed on sales and service staff.

Multibrand retail design involves the display and sale of goods from multiple brands. Most modern-day retail experiences can be traced back the first multibrand department stores in late-nineteenth-century Paris and London, an innovation that changed the culture of consumption and made the activity of shopping into a performative and branded experience. Typical department stores today sell a wide range of merchandise and organize their goods according to broad categories of use, such as menswear, appliances, tableware, and so on. Within each category, products may be further grouped according to brand, use, morphology, or combined in a (→) "lifestyle" format. Since the appeal of the department store is the convenience of "one-stop-shopping," a clearly defined and easily navigable retail space is key. Of course, different multibrand retail environments emphasize different display priorities depending on their targeted audience; upscale department stores like Printemps in Paris, Harvey Nicols in London, and Barney's in NYC generally highlight a select number of high-end brand-name items in product display, while "big box" stores (or superstores) like Home Depot, Costco, and Walmart tend to use volume as a key factor in sales. Indeed, the display-to-stock ratio is usually directly related to the value of the goods to be sold: rarer, more expensive goods are often displayed more iconically, while goods intended for mass consumption are often displayed in large quantities, with ease of access in mind. Big box store displays and fixturing therefore often prioritize the efficiency of stocking and purchasing over display and service. An interesting phenomenon occurs when multibrand department stores become powerful brands unto themselves, with an umbrella brand identity that supercedes the identities of the individual brands that comprise it. Target in the United States and Colette in Paris are two examples of multibrand companies that have developed their own lifestyle visual merchandising.

Most permanent retail environments are monobrand, multibrand, or a complex combination of both. However, retail design can also happen on a more individual ad hoc basis. For instance, temporary flea markets, craft fairs, and bazaars, constructed around circulation routes and dismantled after a set duration, often highlight the goods of a single producer, artist, or artisan over those of any corporate brand. The design of these spaces is typically limited to fixtures that are easily assembled and disassembled (in mobile retail, a related category, retail spaces are either self-propelled or towed vehicles). Another prominent contemporary example of temporary retail design is the art fair, where booths or stands are set up by individual galleries to showcase their artists and shows. In contrast to galleries (which may be categorized as freestanding retail stores) and auction houses (which are similar to showrooms), art fairs allow collectors and museums to view a great variety of works at one time. The contemporary art fair is an interesting example since it presents a marked departure from the norm in terms of display/supply ratios in the conscious effort to create more affordable, accessible art (→ *Exhibition Design*).

Guerilla and street retail are the most temporal forms of retail. Because they are not sanctioned by the government, the speed with which the goods may be installed and de-installed for display is prioritized. These forms of retail therefore often reuse an environment's existing features or involve an intentionally minimal number of easily disassembled fixtures brought in specifically for the sale. DL |

→ *Advertisement, Event Design*

RETRO DESIGN

Designers have always made deliberate references to earlier styles in their work. The popularity of stylistic revivalism reached a peak during the influential (→) Arts & Crafts movement of the nineteenth century, and a low point during the early modern (→ *Modernity*) era, when designers began rejecting these references as reactionary and sentimental. It was not until the 1950s and 1960s that older designs were rediscovered and repopularized as stylish and potentially inspiring for designers of the new age. During these decades, the numerous reeditions of prewar modernist works demonstrated their canonization as "design classics," and the term "retro" was used for the first time to refer to designs that deliberately referenced a particular stylistic direction from the history of design. Nevertheless, in English-speaking countries, it remained far less common than the synonymous term "revivalist" for several decades.

In the 1960s and 1970s, theorists such as Charles Jencks and Robert Venturi defined the term "retro" in such a way that made stronger parallels and distinctions between traditional and stylistic design methods for the twentieth century. In their wake, advocates of (→) postmodernism like Alessandro Mendini and Michael Graves began to use references from earlier stylistic periods in a self-conscious and playful manner, often employing an ironic undertone, or referencing a number of different historical stylistic periods simultaneously. Only from the 1990s onward, then, when the history of design ceased to be discussed so exclusively within the framework of postmodernism's critique of modernism's ahistorical outlook, did the term "retro" come to take on any real significance and traction in the world of design.

These days, designers regularly draw inspiration for new works from virtually every historical design period. Examples from the world of (→) industrial and (→) product design include Jasper Morrison's references to the simple wood furnishings of the 1950s, André Dubreuil's interest in nineteenth-century metal furniture, and Karim Rashid's use of shapes and materials from the 1960s. Household items from the 1990s on have also attempted to evoke nostalgic associations in users by mimicking the forms and chrome and wood veneers that were so popular in the 1950s. In the automobile industry, recent examples include the (→) redesigns of the Beetle by Volkswagon, BMW's new Mini, and the PT Cruiser by Chrysler. Recent years have also seen an emerging trend of retro futurism, which refers to a futuristic style of the past (→ *Futuristic Design*).

The appeal of retro design can be examined in light of theoretical insights that were contributed by scholars such as Vilém Flusser, Umberto Eco, Jean Baudrillard, and Marshall McLuhan, who as early as the 1960s pointed to the significance of semantic and mythological aspects of our commodity culture. Thanks in large part to the influence of these key thinkers, the 1980s and 1990s saw a marked rise of interest in the socio-cultural implications inherent to the design of everyday objects. Against this backdrop, particularly in industrial contexts, retro design was seen as an opportunity to charge everyday objects with historical, emotional, and cultural (→) value through the use of (→) nostalgia, thus ensuring unique selling propositions (→ *USP*) that distinguished them from competitors.

It is important to distinguish retro design from processes that draw from different stylistic periods and trends indiscriminately, and without an overarching point of historical reference. It should also be noted that there are numerous attempts to replicate design classics from earlier periods to look as close

Bingham, N., and A. Weaving. 2000. *Modern Retro: "Living with Mid-Century Modern Style."* New York: Ryland, Peters & Small.
Breuer, G. 2001. *Die Erfindung des modernen Klassikers: Avantgarde und ewige Aktualität?* Ostfildern-Ruit: Hatje Cantz.
Heller, S., and L. Lasky. 1993. *Borrowed design: Use and abuse of historical form.* New York: Van Nostrand Reinhold.
Venturi, R., D. Scott Brown, and S. Izenour. 1977. *Learning from Las Vegas.* Cambridge, MA: MIT Press.

to the originals as possible. These designs are more aptly described as replicas (→ *Fake*), and when unauthorized, can be found in violation of (→) copyright and (→) intellectual property laws. Likewise, re-editions of unaltered design classics, which have become popular in recent years, are not legitimate examples of retro design because they are not appropriated into a new design but rather are simply re-issued. Redesigns, on the other hand, can sometimes be considered retro design if the original is old enough to be perceived as a historical artifact. MKR |

RHETORIC

Since the middle of the twentieth century, design has been referring to rhetoric, the ancient theory of communication, to derive from it both ideas for design theory and techniques for design practice.

Since antiquity, rhetoric has been the name for the *ars bene dicendi* (art of speaking well), as Quintilian called it: the art of well-formed and persuasive verbal (→) communication. Until the end of the eighteenth century it was a core element of education in Europe, particularly for liberal arts or humanities scholars. Throughout its 2,500-year-old tradition, words were not rhetoric's only medium; rhetorical criteria were also applied to images, buildings, and pieces of music. Its (→) theory is fundamentally multidisciplinary. It is an interdisciplinary association of sub disciplines including, for example, the effect of body language, questions of presentation and how to stimulate the audience emotionally—all issues that are still significant for art and media theory today. These sub disciplines continue to be applied and refined in rhetorical practice today with the goal of strategically effective communication. Rhetoric still retains this status of an area of knowledge that stretches across disciplines, and its theory can be transferred to other fields. On that structural basis, design too can follow rhetoric's template.

There is a break in the historical tradition of rhetorical theory in the eighteenth century, which initially caused the significance of the discipline to decline. Only in the middle of the twentieth century did interest in its theories reawaken: in the English-speaking world, there was talk of the New Rhetoric, which went hand in hand with a resurgence of interest in the topics of the ancient discipline. This movement provided the theoretical basis for opening up rhetoric to include the mass media also. In the German-speaking world, the phrase *Allgemeine Rhetorik* (general rhetoric) is used to describe a new reconstruction and expansion of rhetorical theory and practice. Both these movements refer to the ancient foundations of the discipline, especially as represented by Aristotle, Cicero, and Quintilian, and apply them to today's media. Thus the historical developments have prepared the ground for transferring the theory of rhetoric to design.

In addition to examples of direct adoption of existing rhetorical rules—examples include the adoption of musical rhetorical tropes by practitioners of sound design—the transfer from rhetoric to design takes place on two levels. First, rhetoric's sub disciplines offer practical information and competencies. On this level, for example, we can derive knowledge about inventing ideas, structuring and shaping communication, rhetorical tropes, and the art of memorizing. Second, rhetoric systematizes its subdisciplines, from which it is possible to derive higher-order models. These models describe the relationship between theory and practice, between production and analysis, as well as the process of rhetorical communication and all its constituents.

Design can both transfer knowledge directly from the subdisciplines and also refer to rhetoric's models. Both forms of transfer require three working steps: abstraction, contextualization, and continuation.

In the first step, the (→) information has to be abstracted in order to separate it from the original context of its use. For example, the theme or topic (topos), as part of inventing ideas, can be abstracted from its use in speech-making to be useful for design. Topos applied to advertising include the look books and photo catalogs that designers use in the first stage of design. The abstract conception behind it is that designers use topoi to find ideas, compare motifs, and test their potential for argument and arousing emotions.

The point of the second step is to place this knowledge in a new context. That means determining the context of the use and validity of rhetorical knowledge in relation to design. What fields of rhetoric can be transferred and for which aspects of the design process are they valid? Applied to the example of the topos, this means contextualizing it in the field of advertising. Here the rhetorical knowledge of the effective use of topoi to persuade a recipient can be used to design advertising messages in both print media and film.

In the third step this procedure necessarily leads to a (media-specific) expansion of rhetoric and its original store of knowledge. By being transferred to other disciplines, classical rhetoric itself is continued—a process that continually ensures its competence for description and its practical effectiveness. In the example given, the topos of speech is supplemented by the specific topoi of advertising graphics, of film, of product design, and of the design of services.

There have already been fruitful results for design theory from both these levels of transfer (that of applied knowledge and that of systematics). On the first level, for example, there is the theory of tropes used in advertising graphics (Bonsiepe, Ehses) and for film (Clifton) as well as works on patterns in interface design (Tidwell). On the second level, for example, there is the description of the activity of design as rhetorical argument (Buchanan), audiovisual systems for analyzing cinematic tropes and patterns (Joost), and the conception of unmediated affective techniques in design (Scheuermann). These works underscore the fact that the (→) design process is not as a rule based on the inspiration of genius, so to speak—the designer is not an artist—but is rather an example of the rhetorical process. The plan is a product of a working process that aims to integrate its constituents—such as requirements regarding (→) target group, function, material and context—into both the concept and design. The goal is to trigger in the recipient an appropriate and desired effect from the interplay of the constituents.

Have the means of design been chosen appropriately for the product (what would be known as *aptum* in classical rhetorical analysis)? Is the target group suitably addressed in terms of its abilities and needs—specifically on the rational-logical level of logos, the entertaining level of ethos, and the highly emotional level of pathos? Are the design and its presentation clear in the sense of the rhetorical call for distinctness *(perspicuitas)* and clarity *(claritas),* and is its external form designed to be congruent with its content *(ornatus)*? A product or service thus becomes persuasive in the rhetorical sense when these factors of influence are carefully harmonized with one another and the right techniques are employed to present an idea effectively to a target group. Rhetoric, in contrast to idealistic aesthetics, provides the appropriate categories for describing and evaluating. It defines not only the strategic decisions in this process along the stages of production of finding ideas *(inventio)*, conception *(dispositio)*, design *(elocutio)*, and presentation *(actio)* but also the connection between partners of communication and interaction.

The theory transfer as a whole results in a new perspective on design: designing effectively and successfully becomes a rule-based skill *(ars)*. The result of a rhetoric of design—as the theoretical works thus far have concluded—is not only a body of tropes and patterns of design and rules for their application but also a descriptive model for the phases of the design process and its associated instruments. These results are quite concretely applicable to design practice—specifically, for structuring design processes, adapting techniques, and using the tropes for successful design. However, so far comprehensive rhetorics for various media such as film, games, radio, the Internet, products, and services have not been written. That is a subject and an approach for research that needs to be addressed.

Barthes, R. 1977. Rhetoric of the Image. In *Image, music, text.* Ed. and trans. Stephen Heath, pp. 32–51. New York: Hill and Wang. (Orig. pub. as Rhétorique de l'image. *Communications* 4 [1964]: 40–51.)

Bonsiepe, G. 1989. *Interface—Design neu begreifen.* Mannheim: Bollmann. Also: www.guibonsiepe.com/pdffiles/rhetorik.pdf.

Buchanan, R. 1985. Declaration by design: Rhetoric, argument, and demonstration in design practice. *Design Issues* 2, no. 1:4–23. Reprint in V. Margolin, ed. *Design discourse, history, theory, criticism*, pp. 91–109. Chicago: University of Chicago Press, 1989.

Scheuermann, A., and G. Joost. 2006. Design als Rhetorik. Eine Grundlegung für die Designforschung. In *Drawing New Territories: Publication on the 3rd Design Research Symposium of the Swiss Design Network.* Basel: Swiss Design Network.

Overall, rhetoric, as one theory among others, is particularly suited to naming, analyzing, and systematizing the design process with an eye to the relationship between the designer, the design process, the artifact, and the recipient. Knowledge about design and its (often implicit) structures is extended by the rhetorical perspective on these relationships. Design practice, in turn, can derive knowledge for its daily tasks from rhetorical case studies and analysis, since rhetorical theory is closely aligned with practice. If a rhetorical design theory and practice is used for training in design, it produces a coherent theoretical structure that communicates a comprehensive understanding of the instruments and processes of design. Theory and practice are interlocked in that structure because theory is derived from practice and can in turn influence it. The designer who sees himself as a rhetorician is aware of the tools at his disposal for influencing the recipient via product, service, and medium and can calculate the resulting effects logically. GJO |

→ *Communications, Discipline, Practice*

S

SAFETY DESIGN

Safety Design is a continuous process by which designers and other individuals, groups, and communities contribute solutions in an effort to reduce risk and avoid or ameliorate the impact of hazardous situations. Its aim is to ensure the security of physical surroundings and natural environments, to alleviate pain and damage, and to enhance local material, social, and psychological conditions. In addition to protecting us from the potential dangers of day to day living, safety design can also be thought of as a specialist area that responds to urgent needs arising in emergency situations. In this context, safety design is a discipline that offers design solutions for particular circumstances to save, support, and rebuild people's lives when natural or man-made disasters occur.

Formulated a different way, safety design encompasses both designs developed in order to prevent potentially hazardous situations (safety measures), and those produced during or after crisis situations (emergency responses).

Designs in the former category, often referred to as "safety measures," are intended to address a wide range of potential yet unforeseen misuses, malfunctions, and environmental factors, and thus require continual attention and development. They also generally require clarity in the transmission of (→) information about (→) use. In addition to their preventative functions, some designs in this category are ultimately intended to be used in the event of sudden disasters that have not yet come to pass. In the field of medicine, for example, it is essential that designs of first-aid kits, tools, and medical equipment, as well as the planning and interior layouts of ambulances and emergency departments of hospitals, respond well to various kinds of critical conditions. The latter category of safety designs, typically referred to as "emergency responses," requires action during the course of disasters like famines, tropical cyclones and floods. A time factor is usually involved in these instances, and may demand strategic and well-executed design decisions. Actions are generally prioritized on the basis of perceptions of risk to those exposed. In large-scale natural disasters, effective design relies on the thorough integration of other emergency plans at all levels, both governmental and non-governmental. In some situations, such as earthquakes, basic needs surface immediately, like the priority of protection from severe weather conditions. For this, emergency shelter solutions in the form of easily-built temporary structures can provide substantial support and improve living conditions for those affected.

It is important to note that the practice of safety design in this context is by no means limited to the context of natural disasters—it also serves the needs of people who have, for instance, been injured, traumatized, or forced to leave their residences due to war, terrorism, epidemics, famine or other such catastrophes. Safety designs may also at times encompass conditions of socioeconomic distress; today, temporary shelters provide aid and support to homeless people, refugees, and victims of violence, abuse, or drug addiction. Such shelters typically include services and advice concerning education, health, and employment to help reestablish economic and emotional stability.

The concept of safety has taken on a new degree of urgency in contemporary society. Surfacing economic, political, and social problems resulting from (→) globalization and increased urbanization, together with the realities of war and terrorism, have radically changed the ways in which we think about and discuss the needs of both individual and national security. This has, in turn, led to new demands on the practice of design, which has traditionally been thought of as responding to conditions of (→) need. As a result of this changing climactic and political environment, safety design has found itself in a period of development as a concept as well as design action, and will most likely continue to redefine itself over the coming years. ᵀᴮ |

SCENARIO PLANNING

Scenario planning in design practice refers to the creation of a hypothetical narrative illustrating a usage event or series of events. In user-centered design, (→) personas are frequently used by design teams to represent archetypal users of the product or service being designed. Whereas a persona characterizes a user's needs, goals, and motivations, scenarios are used to animate the persona through a realistic though fictional event crafted to ground the designers in the world inhabited by the user. In other words, personas portray motivation, while scenarios portray context. Scenario planning may be used in a variety of disciplines ranging from architectural design to software design, but the goal is the same: to represent veridical users doing veridical tasks.

Scenarios help the design team anticipate concrete interactions rather than potentially idiosyncratic, non-representative abstractions. For example, in an airport terminal redesign project, the team might create a story about a business person named Susan, traveling with a garment bag and a laptop bag, whose goals are to check in with minimal effort, grab a quick, healthy meal, and check her e-mail messages before boarding. Susan's scenario

Hackos, J. T., and J. C. Redish. 1998. *User and task analysis for interface design*. New York: John Wiley & Sons, Inc.

Pruitt, J., and T. Adlin. 2006. *The persona lifecycle: Keeping people in mind throughout product design*. San Francisco: Morgan Kaufmann.

Rosson, M. B., and J. M. Carroll. 2002. *Usability engineering: Scenario-based development of human computer interaction*. San Francisco: Morgan Kaufmann.

would be constructed to walk her through the steps and obstacles associated with reaching these goals. The designers can refer to Susan, among the other personas and travel scenarios constructed, when planning the redesign.

Scenario planning is most often performed early in the design process to help orient the design team. It provides a powerful (→) heuristic device and facilitates (→) brainstorming focused on end users. Scenarios can be captured using a variety of techniques including (→) storyboards, high or low fidelity (→) prototypes, or simple text-based narrative. MDR |

→ *Problem Setting, Usability*

SCENOGRAPHY

→ *Broadcast Design, Set Design*

SCIENCE OF DESIGN

→ *Research*

SCREEN DESIGN

"Screen design" is a term used to describe the organization of informational and interactive elements on screen-based interfaces. Screen design has close ties to (→) interface design and interaction design, and also to (→) time-based design practices such as (→) animation and motion graphics that rely on the dynamic characteristics of screens. Unlike static images and text, screens may represent multiple temporal and spatial modes and symbols as well as different functionalities depending on the situated nature of their use.

Screens are present in our lives in a wide variety of contexts. At work, millions of people manipulate information through computer screen-based graphical user interfaces (GUIs); at home, broadcast narratives and live world events unfold on televisions; and in between, the intimacy of miniature screens on mobile phones and digital cameras compete for our attention with large-scale public screens on buildings and billboards (→ *Web Design, Broadcast Design, Audiovisual Design*). From cathode ray tubes to liquid crystal (→) displays (LCD) and plasma technology, screens are increasingly mobile, portable, and pervasive. Screens are also a part of a larger system of interactions, symbols, and messages exhibiting different functionalities, intentions, and goals. From entertainment to communication to monitoring and interacting with complex systems, screen design is increasingly inherent in the design of our interactions with the worlds of information, people and things.

Screen design considers these contexts and the different ways we interact with tools and technologies in the architecture of screen elements and content. With emphasis on an understanding of (→) human factors, human computer interaction (HCI), and interaction design principles, screen design aims to make (→)

information accessible to users and audiences through the visual and informational hierarchy of display, the development of metaphorical or symbolic interface elements, and the integration of motion and dynamic feedback.

Interacting with screen elements may entail different forms of input, and often screen designers must modify their designs depending not only on where and why, but also how users will engage with screen content. The design of interfaces for touch screens, mouse and keyboard driven input, video game controllers, remote controls, and other physical input methods such as motion sensing must be responsive to the (→) ergonomics of each form as an integral aspect of the interaction. In addition to different physical modes of input, interfaces on screens often consist of metaphorical (→) symbols referencing the physical world. Icons like buttons, handles, shopping carts, and trash bins are common screen design metaphors exhibiting behaviors similar to their "real-world" counterparts. These icons are considered part of a graphical user interface (GUI) and often mimic physicality. However, as interactive media and screen design mature, new icons without physical references are beginning to appear.

In addition to the design of screen appearances and functionality, screen designers are also often involved in the design of the non-visual, whether it's through the architecture of information and navigation systems, the programming of code-based interactions or the design and manipulation of sound and other forms of feedback (→ *Information Design, Sound Design*). Screen design adopts traditions from the fields of (→) graphic design for the organization of visual systems, human computer interaction (HCI) and ergonomics for an understanding of the cognitive processes involved in the manipulation of interfaces, and motion graphics and animation to be able to bring screen elements to life through motion and gesture. CM |

→ *Visualization*

Laurel, B., ed. 1990. *The art of human-computer interface design*. New York: Addison-Wesley.

Moggrige, B. 2007. *Designing interactions*. Cambridge, MA: MIT Press.

Raskin, J. 2000. *The human interface*. Reading, Mass.: Addison-Wesley.

Thissen, F., and J. G. Rager. 2003. *Screen design manual: Communicating effectively through multimedia*. Berlin: Springer.

SEMANTICS

Semantics is concerned with the content of signs, that is, their meaning and reference. A designed object can be analyzed on three different levels: autonomous (as relating exclusively to its form), semantic (as relating to its symbolic meaning), and pragmatic (as relating to its (→) function).

An object's semantic meaning relies on the cultural context in which it is observed and understood. Whereas an object's autonomous (→) form does not evoke any formal associations (for example, a polished stone that is not reminiscent of anything else) and its pragmatic form comes with inherent instructions for use so to speak (for example, the form of a spiral that inspires a user to press it together like a spring), its semantic form is a purely symbolic allusion. It cannot be observed without associations, but neither does it require any action to be effective.

Take for example the semantic meaning of the Christian cross. When two lines of equal length cross at their centers, we see an intersection. As soon as the horizontal line is significantly shorter than the vertical one and crosses the latter in its upper half, however, an eye influenced by Christian culture will perceive it as a ($\rightarrow$) symbol of Christ's cross.

The concept of semantics originally derived from linguistics; design theory has adapted it to its own purposes. Linguistics, too, speaks of both meaning (the aspects of content that result from the relations of signs, words, sentences, and so on, to one another within the system of language) and reference (the aspects of content that result from the relations between the signs and the world). This distinction goes back to a 1892 essay by the philosopher of language and mathematician Gottlieb Frege: "Über Sinn und Bedeutung" (On Sense and Reference).

Semantics is one of the three subdisciplines of ($\rightarrow$) semiotics, the general theory of signs, its systems, and its processes. The other two of the subfields, which overlap somewhat, are syntax and pragmatics. These fields are defined in terms of their relationships between signs, the reference of signs, and the users of signs in a specific situation. The syntax corresponds to sign $\longleftrightarrow$ sign; semantics corresponds to sign $\longleftrightarrow$ reference; and pragmatics to sign $\longleftrightarrow$ user and situation. KW |

$\rightarrow$ *Communications, Rhetoric*

SEMIOTICS

Semiotics is the study of signs. A sign can be any form of representation, object, or practice that evokes a referent distinct from itself. Most current applications of the term come from extensions of the work of American philosopher Charles Sanders Peirce (1839–1914) and of the Swiss linguist Ferdinand de Saussure (1857–1913). Peirce identified three essential modes of signification possible in any sign: iconic, symbolic, and indexical. The icon relates to its referent by means of resemblance; it looks, sounds, smells, feels, or tastes like what it represents. ($\rightarrow$) Symbols are arbitrary signs; they relate to their referent only because an interpretive community agrees on the relationship. Language is largely a symbolic system. The index evokes its referent by a physical trace. A footprint, for example, signifies a person's presence indexically. Most signs relate to their referent by some combination of these three modes.

Peirce also described the functioning of signs in terms of a three-part system. The ($\rightarrow$) form of representation (or representamen) functions in relationship with, on the one hand, its referent, and, on the other, an interpretant, someone who reads, sees, hears the sign. Iconic, indexical, or symbolic representations are understood as different interactions among these three elements.

Saussure described the workings of the linguistic sign, roughly equivalent to Peirce's symbol. The Saussurean sign is composed of two parts: its material form, the signifier, and its representational aspect, the signified, which is the concept of the referent that the signifier designates. Saussure noted that a sign system can only work if one signifier can be differentiated from another; the sign is thus defined by difference.

Applying Saussure's terms to visual material, Roland Barthes (1915–1980) described how culturally based (→) conventions could become languages in which to read design. Barthes made a distinction between direct, denoted meaning in objects and their connoted meanings, the symbolic resonance of some aspect of the object within a system of cultural conventions, or codes. He noted that an image or object can imply an array of connoted messages depending on which codes the observer invokes. Later authors have analyzed (→) typography in a similar manner: the linguistic meaning of the words is the denoted message, and their graphic features—the allusions implied by the typeface, layout, and so on—is the connoted, or coded, message. Barthes also proposed that fields of design, such as fashion, could be conceived of as languages, adapting a Saussurean distinction between language as purely a system and speech as the creation of signs within it. Combinations of individual items, such as a suit of clothes, could thus be discussed as utterances within the sign system of fashion.

Many authors have also used Peirce's categories of signs as models for interpreting design objects (→ *Semantics*). The iconic meaning of an (→) object relates to its formal or stylistic similarity to other objects—natural or man-made—or its metaphoric properties. The physical properties of the object can be considered indexical signs of the materials and conditions of its production, and the object's function, or any of its formal qualities, can also have symbolic meaning, inasmuch as these qualities possess arbitrary meanings defined by convention among the object's audiences. Another line of inquiry further breaks down the symbolic valuation of objects into denoted meanings, based on recognition of the object's (→) function, and connoted meanings, based on affective (→) values associated with both the object itself and its formal qualities.

Max Bense (1910–1990) (→ *Ulm School of Design*) developed a semiotics of the (→) design process itself, which he characterized as the realization of a (→) function (the synthetic dimension of

Barthes, R. 1977. *Image, music, text*. New York: Hill and Wang.
Bense, M. 1971. *Zeichen und Design*. Baden-Baden: Agis Verlag.
Peirce, C. S. 1931–1966. *Collected papers of Charles Sanders Peirce*. Cambridge, MA: Harvard Univ. Press.
Saussure, F. de. 1974. *Course in General Linguistics*. London: Peter Owen.

an object) in materials (the hyletic dimension) resulting in a form (the morphetic dimension) that serves a (→) use (the pragmatic dimension). In other analyses of the design process, the conception and planning of the object are understood as a form of representation, as they involve a series of substitutes for the actual thing, and are thus related to Peirce's representamen. The production process itself reifies the plan into material form, becoming the referent of the sign. Users of the design object, the interpretants, then realize its proposed functions and attach to it symbolic meanings. ER |

→ *Product, Visual Communication*

SENSUALITY

Sensuality can be defined as the refined human capability to perceive and enjoy environmental stimuli with all the senses. We enjoy the look of a beautiful landscape and its particular smell, taste a delicately spiced meal, appreciate the presence of someone we love, and are pleased by his or her familiar voice and unique scent.

Our senses encounter thousands of products every day. From the breakfast table to the office chair and on to the bed, from the car to the airplane, we see, hear, smell, and feel. Sensuality is also one of the core competencies of designers. Products are supposed to be designed to function perfectly and unobtrusively and at the same time to create a sensory experience that is as pleasant as possible. Designers thus make an important contribution to encouraging consumers and increasing sales.

We experience the world of commodities principally with our eyes (→ *Visualization*). In shop windows, in advertisements, and in most places, we take in visual information first. If we do not like the (→) aesthetics of the product, we are hardly likely to give it a second chance. If we like its appearance, however, then its (→) haptic qualities come to the fore. We touch the object to feel whether the temperature and surface are pleasant on the skin and its weight is comfortable in the hand, testing its functioning and (→) ergonomics—often unconsciously. Acoustic stimuli (→ *Sound Design*) such as the pop when a seal is opened or the quiet clicking of a switch are other relevant sensory experiences. With a few exceptions, taste does not play much of a role in the design of objects. Smell is generally avoided (→ *Olfactory Design*).

Just as musicians train their musicality, designers train and sensitize their sensuality. This training enables them to guide consumers' often-unconscious responses to an object. Good design can ensure that the on-off switch is immediately visible, for example, or that it is clear whether a handle needs to be pulled or turned. Functionality alone will rarely stimulate a purchase therefore designers strive to impart a sensual, and ultimately emotional, charge to products. The exciting and flattering form of a pair of glasses, the velvety surface of a pen, or the rich sound of a car door closing often turns these everyday objects into objects of desire.

This requires, however, that the object's messages are communicated to the consumer as subject. Neuroscientists like Francisco J. Varela and Gerhard Roth have shown that human (→) perception is a immensely complex process of (→) construction by the brain. When we construct sensuality, we determine which of the many thousands of sense impressions find their way into our individual reality. This also determines the intersection that will result from the sense perception of consumers and designers. When a designer creates a product he or she considers sensual and sensible or of high quality and durability, it does not by any means guarantee that the product will find a buyer. Success or failure depends on the realities of designers, producers, and consumers corresponding. MG |

→ *Food Design, Synesthetic, Value*

SERVICE DESIGN

The economic basis of Western industrial nations has changed dramatically in the last three decades from manufacturing to the provision of (→) information and services. Services now typically represent between sixty and seventy percent of the gross domestic product of developed nations and almost all new companies being founded and jobs created are in this so-called tertiary sector.

New challenges have emerged as this once minor sector has expanded rapidly. In the past, manufacturing was the main source of investment in research and development. This meant that research and development concentrated on the optimization of the means and processes of production and the invention of products; and investments in (→) market research and product design were taken for granted (→ *Product Development*). By contrast, no objective methods were established for the development, research, and creation of services. Moreover, marketing of services was first identified and addressed as an independent topic in the United States in the 1970s, and service design did not exist as a concept until the early 1990s.

Under pressure from a rapidly changing market, however, there have now been noteworthy developments. While service engineering is still trying to establish itself as a discipline at universities and in practice, service management is no longer unusual as a path of study in business administration courses. Service marketing has established itself internationally, and service design, mocked when first introduced as an academic field in design ($\rightarrow$) education at the beginning of the 1990s, now has credibility in teaching, research, and practice around the world. What exactly is service design? Service design addresses the functionality and form of services from the perspective of clients. It aims to ensure that service interfaces are useful, usable, and desirable from the client's point of view and effective, efficient, and distinctive from the supplier's point of view.

Service designers visualize, formulate, and choreograph solutions to problems that do not necessarily exist today; they observe and interpret requirements and behavioral patterns and transform them into possible future services. This process applies explorative, generative, and evaluative design approaches, and the restructuring of existing services is as much a challenge in service design as the development of innovative new services. When seen from this angle, service design stands in the tradition of product and interface design, enabling the transfer of proven analytical and creative ($\rightarrow$) design methods to the world of service provision. In particular, there are close ties to the dimensions of interaction and experience that originated in ($\rightarrow$) interface design. Even if these fields of study are still primarily oriented around designing human-machine interfaces, parallels have emerged in theoretical and methodological development, in the search for factors to be noted and influenced when designing an experience, though experience cannot really be designed, only the conditions that lead to experience.

The development of a formal language for services is one of the exciting new fields in development and practice, because a formal language of services just might become the basis for systematically creating conditions that would make it possible to design the experiences of services. A formal language for services empowers service designers to create interactions, spaces, and processes on the basis of a solid knowledge of causal relationships.

The use-oriented approach that came to the fore in interaction design in the 1990s and channeled creativity in the development of methods such as ($\rightarrow$) persona creation is one of the approaches refined and rigorously applied in the creation of human-human and human-artifact interactions in service design. Taking the perspective of clients as the starting point reverses many customary approaches by service companies and raises questions about truly innovative and user-centered, flexible, and dynamic organizational structures and processes.

The understanding of product-service elements that has since become well established in service provision research has been an especially important factor in giving the interdisciplinary ($\rightarrow$) networking of competencies (which is, in itself, characteristic of design processes) a central role in the service sector. There is still debate about whether service design is primarily about the simultaneous definition of virtual and material aspects of the service, the coordination of human-human and human-machine interfaces, or the design of experiences where functionality and emotionality are equally accounted for in the (→) integration of new technologies for intelligent and client-oriented standardization. This debate can ultimately only be resolved by interdisciplinary design teams (→ *Collaborative Design*).

On the one hand, service design can make use of theoretical and methodological competencies in established design capabilities; on the other, it opens up new questions. Can service-specific methods—for example blueprinting that was developed in service marketing—be further developed and optimized as a creative tool? The creation of service (→) blueprints was certainly an important first step in making virtual services an actual and visible object of design. Nonetheless, this method remained very much anchored in the presentation of processes in the form of flow diagrams and left open the question of how the emotional dimension of client interaction with these processes could be integrated systematically into the design process.

That question led to the development of the client journey as a schema by which service design can capture and illustrate the complete process of a service with its emotional, material and procedural components from a client's perspective—thus making it possible to model it (→ *Scenario Planning*).

"Touch points" are essential to understanding the client journey. The analysis of existing services examines whether touch points are correctly positioned. Is the concrete, visual, olfactory, acoustic, and tactile evidence suitable for making the service comprehensible and able to be experienced by clients? Hence the development of service evidence is an autonomous focus in service design concerned with making it possible to observe the virtual and assign dimensions to it.

All approaches to (→) redesign and to the innovation of services are extremely well served by design competencies in prototyping (→ *Prototype*), because service prototypes are vital aids in the whole process of developing ideas and making decisions. (→) Storyboards illustrate the newly created service process from the perspective of the clients and help to visualize the full observation of scripts, roles, scenery, and props. With little effort, mock-ups can clarify where design interventions are possible in service provision. Service enacting—role-playing service interactions—is a method for designing services that amounts to a new form of (→) rapid prototyping: acting out service situations very quickly clarifies the direction the service design process should take.

The performing arts are one field being explored by current service design research projects to tap into their potential for concept transfer and provide inspiration for innovative forms of organization, notation, and communication. Perceptions and procedures derived from the performing arts have proved useful when embarking on the service design process. Hence the metaphor of front and back stage is a very helpful model for creativity, because it reveals the necessity for a comprehensive view of the whole system and the necessity to cast processes, locations, props, and actors from one mold. Storyboarding provides a comprehensive system for thinking about and visualizing the procedural narrative structure from the perspective of clients. There may be many more such impulses concealed within the theatrical process of ideas to (→) performance that would be valuable and fruitful for the autonomous design of services.

Service design is a rapidly growing field that has since been given a thorough theoretical and methodological basis and has established itself internationally in research, teaching, and consulting. However, it is still a very young discipline that contains many exciting, undiscovered lines of research and continues to invite us to explore the unknown and pursue exciting experiments. BM |

→ *Event Design*

Erlhoff, M., B. Mager, and E. Manzini. 1997. *Dienstleistung braucht Design*. Neuwied: Luchterhand.
Mager, B. 2004. *Service design review*. Cologne: Köln International School of Design.
Mager, B. 2006. *Service design basics*. Cologne: Köln International School of Design.
Parker, S., and J. Heapy. 2006. *The journey to the interface: How public service design can connect users to reform*. London: Demos.

SET DESIGN

Set design is the creation of the physical space in which the action of a performed event takes place. Primarily used to describe theater productions, it constitutes all the scenery, furniture, props, appearance, and overall look of the stage. Set design is also known as scenic design, theater design, theatrical design, and stage design. Although these terms are used interchangeably in most instances, set design or scenic design have become more popular in current terminology because they can be applied to television and film as well as theater. A related and more recent term, scenography, encompasses the sound, costume, lighting, and all other technical designs of a theatrical production. Production design is the term used for the comparable craft in cinema or television (→ *Broadcast Design*).

It should be noted that the definitions of the various terms above vary to some extent from country to country based on the degree to which production functions are specialized. For example, in the United States, set designers work in collaboration with a team of other designers including projection, costume, light, and sound designers. This is not the case in other countries, particularly in Europe, where a single designer is often responsible for all of the technical or physical aspects of the production.

It is important to understand that the design of the set is not simply functional; it creates an atmosphere that gives the audience a visual feel of the environment of the event. Each craft brings an essential element to the production. The choice of backdrop, light, sound, props, costume, and, increasingly, projected media impacts the viewer's experience of the production. In choosing these elements, the set designer's task is defined by a multiplicity of factors. The general requirements of a set are usually predetermined in the form of a written play, screenplay, or script that specifies the time period, number of performers, number of scenes, types of locations, characters' movements, and the action that takes place. Even if the performance is entirely improvised, the designer still usually has to work within constraints posed by the director's concept, limited funding, and the physical attributes of the space.

In contemporary theater, the creation of a set is usually approached in one of three distinct ways: as the imitation of reality created to evoke a "suspension of disbelief" in the audience, as a physical and psychological barrier between performer and audience, or as a space in which performer and audience collide. These approaches can be traced back to seminal movements in the history of theater that broadly altered our conceptions regarding what constitutes "the stage."

The conceptualization of the stage as an imitation of reality was popularized during the Renaissance, and was the overwhelming norm until relatively recently. Set designers working within this realist or naturalist approach go to great lengths in order to create sets that mimic the natural world as closely as possible—this may involve backdrops painted to imply depth, historically accurate costumes and props, and so on. The primary purpose of these efforts is ostensibly to "suspend disbelief"—that is, to induce a willingness in the audience to accept the performance as believable.

The second conceptualization of the stage attempts to keep the audience at an emotional distance from the performed action— a complete departure from the the suspended disbelief sought after by those working within a realist framework. This idea was popularized in the twentieth century, when experimental or avant-garde playwrights (like Samuel Beckett and Bertolt Brecht) responded to the realist tradition critically by ushering in a new kind of theater that featured a focus on subjectivity, critical discourse, and nonlinear or illogical depictions of time, place, movement, and plot. The influence of late modern and postmodernist theater is still apparent today, in spare, minimalist stagings that treat the set as a constructed (nonrealistic) site (→ *Modernity, Postmodernism*).

The final approach to set design is one that reconsiders the stage as the space in which performers and audience members interact. In contemporary productions like participatory theater, performance art, and street theater, the physical stage no longer exists in any traditional sense because the distinctions between performer and audience are essentially dissolved. The set designer in this context articulates the environment in which the performer/audience interaction takes place, whether it be a street, a subway platform, or traditional theater. These recent forms of contemporary theater therefore have drastically different motivations from the realist, modernist, and postmodernist forms that preceded it. RLU |

→ *Audiovisual Design, Event Design, Lighting Design, Performance, Sound Design*

SHOP DESIGN

→ *Retail Design*

SIGNATURE DESIGN

→ *Auteur Design*

SIMPLICITY

Simplicity is complex. Complexity is simple. There is no answer to this relationship between simplicity and complexity. Because it exists as a question.

Due to the advances in technology that have brought us the Internet, Blackberries, and two-hundred-plus channels of cable TV entertainment, we live in a world of more knowledge, more e-mails, and more ways to waste our time. Technology continues to give us more for less effort and money. There is no need to complain in this utopian land of digital plentifulness. Like the baby bird in the nest with its beak open wide, waiting for mother bird to place food in its mouth, our brains are open wide for neural nutrition.

But wait. Mother bird continues to deliver food. I think to myself, "I am full, mother."

"Here's some more e-mails darling," she says to me. I try to thank her but before I can speak a word, she pops web pages and digital music into my mouth. Mmmmmmph. I cannot cry out, only chew and swallow quickly to avoid choking. We consume and consume and consume.

Perhaps I reveal my own loss of youthfulness? "More cookies? Why, of course!" "More chicken? Yes, thank you, it's delicious." I remember in my youth being ravenous—the proverbial empty pit at the dinner table that could eat continuously. Today I find it hard to want to eat. It is a sign of getting older, I am told. Your body's metabolism slows down; a biological switch in your cells is flicked to the "die" setting. More than all the money you could amass in the world, TIME suddenly becomes the most precious quantity you have left in your wallet.

The third Law of Simplicity, of which I have ten such Laws, is just that: TIME. "Savings in time feel like simplicity." Whenever you save a few seconds in line at the post office or any other task that involves waiting, you breathe a sigh of relief. "My, that was simpler than I expected." The younger generation loves mobile phones and other gadgets that consume hours upon hours to learn how to use; older people generally sit bewildered by such devices—not born of inferior intelligence of course, but of the realization that time is not to be wasted. Time should be spent on relaxation and enjoyment instead of meaningless button-pressing calisthenics. For those sixty-plus gadget "freaks" that read this text, I apologize if I offend your favorite pastime.

My dear friend Michael Erlhoff wishes me to write more on this topic of simplicity than this, I am certain. Yet who am I to break my own Laws of Simplicity. I have espoused on one Law, and the rest are visible on the Web or in my appropriately named book, *The Laws of Simplicity*. It makes little sense to review them here if they are already elsewhere, as I must now tend to my family of five children who get extremely little TIME from me.

To conclude, simplicity is about when less can be good, and more can be bad. Simplicity itself can be undesirable. Imagine a life with less friends? This would be sad. I need Michael Erlhoff around to make me write things. Having more (instead of less) family makes life infinitely complex. But friends and family are complexities that we all enjoy. So I say, f*ck simplicity. But read my book or visit my web site to learn more about simplicity if you so deign. JM |

→ *Complexity, Usability, Use*

Maeda, J. 2006. *The laws of simplicity: Design, technology, business, life*. Cambridge, MA: MIT Press.

SKETCH

The term "sketch," derived from the Italian *schizzo* (splash, spatter), refers in design to a quick rough drawing or outline by hand in simple strokes. Its purpose is to give an idea of something or to illustrate a process. The focus is not on capturing the precise details of the thing depicted, but rather on schematically recording its essential (formal) features.

The sketch is considered the quickest but also the simplest form of visual expression in design. It is therefore an elementary medium in the design process and is used above all for preliminary studies and quick and direct visual communication. Frequently used media include pencil, marker or ink pen, charcoal, and chalk. MKU |

→ *Rendering, Visualization*

SKILLS

The controversial term "skills" can be traced back to the Old Norse word *skil*, meaning distinction or discernment. In order to arrive at a clear definition of the term, it is first necessary to compare it to "ability," which comes from the Latin *habilitas*, meaning aptitude. Although both terms can be broadly defined as "the capability of doing something," there are some distinctions between the two. "Skills" implies gaining a proficiency that enables one to do something, whereas "ability" refers to both congenital capabilities, such as sight, hearing, or smell, and acquired knowledge such as reading, writing, or riding a bicycle.

The German word for skill, *Fertigkeit*, is etymologically derived from *Fahrt* (meaning "journey" in English), and *fertig* (meaning "completed"). This implies that skills are the end result of a process—in this case, a learning process. In the context of design, however, the question arises as to whether such an end state is ever possible or even desirable. Today, the "hard skills" listed under position requirements in job advertisements (like the mastery of current layout programs) become quickly outdated and, hence, must be continually updated and expanded upon. In addition, such skills often only apply to specific professional groups, for whom an end to the learning process would be fatal.

There are learnable skills and abilities (soft skills) that are essential in all areas of design aside from the specific craft-based ones. These include keen observation, empathy, diplomacy, a high level of tolerance for frustration, and proficiency in writing and communication in order to present ideas in an effective and lucrative manner. DPO |

→ *Craft, Design Competence*

SLOW DESIGN

Slow design goes far beyond the act of designing. It is an approach that encourages a slower, more considered, and reflective process, with the goal of positive well-being for individuals, societies, environments, and economies. Slow design positions itself again the "fast design" of the current industrial paradigm, which is governed by unsustainable cycles of fashion and overconsumption, business ethics, and an anthropology that defines everyone as customers. The use of "slow" as an adjective, or instructive adverb, deliberately introduces ambiguity in this context; it implies that time is implicit in all facets of (the) design, and that the purpose is to slow down the process, the outcome, and the effects of the outcome.

The anthropocentric and eco-efficient tenets of slow design have many antecedents, from the late-nineteenth-century British and American (→) Arts & Crafts movements to the present day. The anthropocentric root can be traced back to the post-1950s design movements that contested the profligate production and (→) consumption model of the developed West. Design for Need, spearheaded by Victor Papanek and championed by the Royal College of Art in the United Kingdom during the mid-1960s, was one of the most important movements in this vein. Design for Need later transmuted into (→) universal design, and, more recently, inclusive design, user-centered design, (→) participatory design and (→) collaborative design. The eco-efficient root can be traced back to the environmental and ecological design of the 1970s, the green consumerism of the 1980s, and green design of the early 1990s, as well as the more sophisticated approaches of Design for the Environment, eco-design and sustainable design that have since emerged (→ *Environmental Design, Sustainability*). Slow design grows from these two roots and recognizes them as parts of a synergistic system where man and nature redefine their acquaintance (→ *Synergy*).

More recently, alternative socioeconomic models and systems are becoming an important third root for slow design, as observed in the convergence of new (→) social groupings and technology, eco-entrepreneurialism, social enterprise, and ways of living (Manzini & Jegou). Various forms of slow activism such as the Italian Slow Food and Slow Cities movements, as well as the establishment of Eternally Yours (van Hinte), a Dutch foundation that encourages more physically and emotionally enduring (→) artifacts, were also significant stimuli for the emergence of slow design.

The first formal publication of a "slow design manifesto" in 2003 (Fuad-Luke) called for repositioning the focus of design on a triad of individual, sociocultural, and environmental well-being, and posited eight overlapping themes: ritual, tradition, experiential, evolved, slowness, eco-efficiency, open source knowledge, and (slow) technology. New York's slowLab (Strauss et al.) defines slow design in terms of creative activism: "A way of thinking, designing, making and doing that focuses on, and beyond, the materialized artifact or environment in order to raise fresh perspectives, encourage reflection, challenge intentions, and deepen life's experiences." SlowLab's Strauss and Fuad-Luke posit slow design as a space, both real and imagined, which designers and users alike are incited to occupy under the rubric of the following six principles:

1. Reveal: Slow design reveals spaces and experiences in everyday life that are often missed or forgotten, including the materials and processes that are can easily be overlooked in an artifact's existence or creation.

2. Expand: Slow design considers the real and potential "expressions" of artifacts and environments beyond their per-

ceived functionality, physical attributes and life spans (→ *Affordance*).

3. Reflect: Slowly designed artifacts and environments induce contemplation and "reflective consumption."

4. Engage: Slow design processes are "open source" and collaborative, relying on sharing, cooperation, and transparency of information so that designs may continue to evolve into the future.

5. Participate: Slow design encourages users to become active participants in the design process, embracing ideas of conviviality and exchange to foster social accountability and enhance communities.

6. Evolve: Slow design recognizes that richer experiences can emerge from the dynamic maturation of artifacts and environments over time. Looking beyond the needs and circumstances of the present day, slow design artifacts become (behavioral) change agents.

The ethos of slow design is to encourage human flourishing (*eudaimonia*, Greek) within a metaparadigm of a socially equitable world, a regenerative environment, and renewed visions of living and enterprise. AFL |

→ *Ethics, Intuition, Need, Redesign, Usability*

Fuad-Luke, A. 2003. Slow. www.slowdesign.org. March 2003 to present.
Manzini, E., and F. Jégou. 2003. *Sustainable everyday: Scenarios of urban life*. Milan: Edizioni Ambiente.
Strauss, C. et al. 2003–6. SlowLab. www.slowlab.net. 2003 to present.
Van Hinte, E. 2004. *Eternally yours: Time in design*. Rotterdam: 010 Publishers.

SMART MATERIALS

Smart materials represent a new and expanding class of materials that bring a dynamic component into the processes as well as the products of design. Developed primarily for engineering applications, these materials are a radical shift away from the static materials that are typically used in the various design fields. Rather than selecting a material based on its appearance or properties, the designer instead foregrounds phenomena and thereby chooses a "smart material" based on its phenomenological behavior.

Specifically, the term "smart materials" refers to materials, or material systems, that behave thermodynamically rather than mechanically. As thermodynamic (→) materials, they take an active role when submitted to an energy stimulus—either undergoing a transformation or producing a transformation. The behavior of all materials, conventional as well as smart, in response to an energy stimulus, can be described by the following conceptual relationship:

energy transfer ∞ material property $\times$ change in state

The state refers to the unique thermodynamic state of any material system as determined by its temperature, pressure, density, and internal energy. For conventional materials, the material property is a constant, and it only scales the relationship between the energy transferred into the system and the resulting state of the system. Whereas the traditional material is passive in that it is acted upon, the smart material is dynamic in that it is the actor. As an example, the production of a predictable amount of strain under a given stress scaled according to Hooke's Law is representative of the performance of conventional material. Smart materials are no longer scalar, and they can directly influence the relationship between the variables and properties. This influence can be classified into four different relationships for smart materials as follows:

1. Change in state produces a change in a material property. For example, a change in temperature will alter the spectral reflectivity of a thermochromic material, causing it to reflect a different color.

2. Energy transfer produces a change in a material property. An applied current will alter the transmissivity of an electrochromic material, causing it to transmit a different quantity or quality of light.

3. Energy transfer results in a transformation of the energy type from one form to another. Photovoltaics are a well known example of this in which radiant energy is converted into electrical energy.

4. Energy transfer results in a change of the internal state of a material which in turn changes the external state. In shape memory alloys, an energy input will cause the molecular structure of the material to shift resulting in motion.

In addition to these thermodynamic relationships, smart materials also exhibit two characteristics that further distinguish them from conventional materials. The first is that their discrete size allows for direct location without secondary components and with minimum infrastructure. The "intelligence" that is more typically associated with supporting networks and control systems is instead integral to the material. The second unique characteristic is their reversibility upon removal of the stimulus. As a result, smart materials offer the ability to controllably and predictably produce at least two distinct behaviors, essentially providing the opportunity to optimize material performance under differing conditions. These active behaviors produce functional types of material behavior rather than the more common nomitive categories based on material composition. Instead of categories such as "glass" or "plastic," smart materials can be organized according to the predominant results of their actions. Regardless, then, of how the behavior was generated, the following "types" broadly encompass the range of material responses currently applicable for design uses: color changing, light emitting, heat absorbing, energy producing, energy absorbing, and shape changing.

Color changing is one of the largest classes of smart materials, as many different mechanisms give rise to a wide variety of color conditions. Translucent materials may change their total transmissivity, whether from opaque to transparent (thermotropics, suspended particle, electrochromic, photochromic) or selectively change the color that is being transmitted (liquid crystal, chemochromic). Opaque materials may change their reflectivity, from one color to another (also photochromic and chemochromic) or through several colors depending on the environmental state (thermochromic).

Light-emitting materials are based on wholly different mechanisms from the conventional means for producing light which generally depend upon inefficiency in energy exchange: incandescent light is produced when a current meets resistance in a wire (thereby producing infrared radiation), and fluorescent devices depend upon the resistance of a gas (thereby producing ultraviolet radiation). Light emission from smart materials results from the photons released whenever the material undergoes a molecular or micro-structural change in its composition. This direct production of light is not only more efficient than conventional means, but also more divisible and controllable. Light can be produced of any color (electro-luminescent, light-emitting diodes), of any size, intensity, or shape (light-emitting capacitor, electro-luminescent). Light can be produced in direct response to the environmental state (chemo-luminescent, photo-luminescent) and light can also be stored and re-released at a later time (photo-luminescent). Of this type, solid-state lighting (organic and inorganic light-emitting diodes and polymers) are the largest and fastest-growing segment.

Heat-absorbing materials convert heat into internal energy (which involves a molecular or microstructure change). Thermal energy can be absorbed and inertial swings dampened by material property changes (phase change materials, polymer gels, thermotropics).

Energy-producing materials are further distinguished from other energy-exchanging materials, all of which output some form of energy, by the purpose of that energy. The materials in this category are those that we can consider as "generators"— they directly produce useful energy. The energy can be in many forms: generated electricity (photovoltaic and thermo-photovoltaic), heat pump or engine (thermoelectric) as well as elastic energy (piezoelectric).

Energy-absorbing materials, in contrast to the energy-producing materials whose focus is the form of the output energy, are materials that focus on the form of the input energy. More precisely, the intention of energy-absorbing materials is to dissipate or counteract the input energy. Vibrations can be dissipated by conversion to electricity (piezoelectric) or dampened by absorption produced by a material property change (magnetorheological, electrorheological, shape memory alloy). Column buckling can be counteracted by an applied strain (piezoelectric) and other types of deformations can also be counteracted by selectively applied strains (electrostrictive, magnetostrictive, shape memory alloys).

Shape changing tends to be defined to a much smaller scale than color changing, which can take place over a large area of material. This is due to inherent limitations in the scaling of dynamic forces. Nevertheless, even though all materials undergo some form of shape change from an energy input (the elongation of a metal rod under tension, the swelling of wood when saturated with water), the shape-changing smart materials are differentiated by not only their ability to be reversible, but also by the relative magnitude of the shape change. For example, smart polymer gels (chemotropic, thermotropic, electrotropic) can swell or shrink volume by a factor of 1000. Most shape-changing materials move from one position to another—the movement may be produced by a strain, or it may be due to a microstructural change—but the result is a spatial displacement. A material may bend or straighten (shape memory alloys, electrostrictive, piezoelectric), or twist and untwist (shape memory alloys), or constrict and loosen (magnetostrictive), or swell and shrink (polymer gels).

The opportunities posed by smart materials are not so much about the actual materials or products themselves as objects, but about the results produced from their behavior. Designers must be fully aware of the results they wish to produce before selecting a material, as a multitude of behaviors from a multitude of materials can often produce a similar result. For example, the desire for a surface to be selectively transparent or transmissive can be achieved by manipulating any of the optical characteristics of refraction, reflection, and/or absorption, and most of the color-changing materials, as well as many of the energy-absorbing materials are capable of altering those characteristics. This is an inversion of the more normative design process in which the choice of material often precedes the identification of specific characteristics. MA |

→ *Bionics, Engineering Design, High Tech, Materials, Mechatronic Design*

Addington, M., and D. S. Schodek. 2005. *Smart materials and technologies for the architecture and design professions.* Oxford, United Kingdom: Architectural Press.
Brownell, B., ed. 2006. *Transmaterial.* New York: Princeton Architectural Press.
Mori, T., ed. 2002. *Immaterial/ultramaterial.* New York: George Braziller.

SOCIAL

Society influences designers, design processes and designed objects and establishes the context that repeatedly stimulates changes in design's direction. Only when these social parameters have been grasped can (→) theory, science and (→) practice employ highly deliberate planning and design not only to interpret and comment on society but also to influence it—in the best sense.

Design reflects society in all its facets and forms. Designers take positions on the mental states, including anxiety, indifference and euphoria, problems, and desires of social groups. They plan and work out interpretations of society in the form of trivial or ingenious (→) products, media and systems by giving them (→) functions and meanings. Designers do not act autonomously in that process but as part of a society, subject to its influences.

Designed objects are social messages. The unique variety of products today speaks to societies that are increasingly organized for individuality and (→) consumption, and filled with contradictory ideologies and social antinomies. Light, transportable, and highly technical everyday objects that facilitate contact and allow access to globally networked communication technologies at the touch of a button testify to the mobile rapidity of modern, media-dependent (→) lifestyles. Furnishing components suited to quick assembly and disassembly simplify transient living and working situations. Products are made up of modules so that they can always seem fresh and individually customizable. Comfortable, cozy worlds for living and health respond to living circumstances that are perceived as transitory, mechanized, and raw. Order becomes increasingly significant in the face of (→) complexity. What, how and where to store stuff—the solutions to such problems fill entire trade fairgrounds. Urban public spaces are increasingly impoverished and satisfy few social (→) needs apart from those of consumption. Open spaces give way to shopping malls; vending machines and flat screens entice us to spend quickly. Human services are replaced by multilingual avatars—customers are asked to serve themselves and have fun doing it.

Design can be viewed from two sides in this context. On the one hand, it seems that designers work in order to arouse new desires, to generate (→) trends, and thus ultimately serve a society that is understood and accepted as highly focused on consumption. On the other hand, design is in a position to do much more than arouse and satisfy consumer demand, because design can also be understood as a planned process (→ Design Process) that responds to social questions and injustices with logic, reason and clarity. By focusing its energies on production and sales while neglecting to address the need for a solid socio-theoretical substructure, design as a discipline has been stuck for years in a crisis of positioning and meaning. In order to regain social relevance, there has to be an effort to establish a design theory that addresses economic, social and cultural considerations and also identifies and addresses the weaknesses and failures of design in those contexts.

The concept of a social order is based on social categorizations on the basis of certain identifications like age, gender, class, ethnic origin and sexual orientation. The hierarchies inherent to such classifications are evident in the ways in which designs are created, marketed, and consumed by and for the communities that comprise them. For example, in Western societies, where life expectancies are getting longer, designs that capitalize on the widespread obsession with youth have become increasingly desirable. Likewise, products are almost always gendered, whether consciously or unconsciously, through the use of coded forms, colors, sizes, materials and so on. The use of "feminized" products by those ranked higher in the social hierarchy (men) is, generally speaking, associated with a loss of social respect (→ Gender Design).

Precisely because these markers of identity are to a large extent socially constructed, designers must necessarily consider the implications that their decisions will have on the perpetuation or reversal of these cultural stereotypes. Design for men, design for women, design for young people and design for old people—such designations can only be accurate if there are genuinely different needs that should be taken into account in the design process, independent of purely symbolic assessments. Designs can have powerful social repercussions, both positive and negative, but this is not yet well established in the awareness of many designers. One reason for this is the legitimizing of social orders by (→) value systems such as religion, culture, ethnocentrism, and government that normalize the hierarchical social structures of communities. The given models of thinking about themes like the distribution of power, hygiene, beauty, family, or sexuality essentially determine which designed objects are acceptable, what they can look like, who will use them, and how.

Questioning learned normalities is a fundamental technique in design, but it does not always enable us to surpass the limitations of our own socialized perceptions. Compensating for this very human deficit is reason enough to develop the emerging discipline of design science, and to encourage an awareness of the varied relationships between designers, their objects and the use of those objects that would be useful for the development of both theory and practice.

The process of design has always been dependent on value-laden decisions; every designer needs to constantly revisit and address the ways in which their personal ideologies are compatible with prevailing social circumstances, whether they are artistically, economically, or sociopolitically motivated. Some designers choose to reinforce the existing social order by adopting a strictly market-oriented approach, while others take it to the other extreme through methods like (→) protest design and (→) critical design. Yet others focus their attention on improving accessibility for disadvantaged social groups, like those with disabilities (→ *Universal Design*).

Thus, socially responsible designs simultaneously take account of the contexts in which they are created, and draw notice to the fact that the majority of design processes overlook or discount the needs of underserved communities. Numerous organizations have emerged that attempt to rectify or alleviate social inequities, often with innovative and far-reaching results. *One Laptop per Child*, a project designed to develop and distribute cheap functional laptops for children in developing nations, was effective in highlighting the need for better global educational resources, to be sure—but on top of that, it

Kirkham, P., ed. *The gendered object.* Manchester: Manchester Univ. Press.
Schepers, W., and P. Schmitt, eds. *Das Jahrhundert des Design: Geschichte und Zukunft der Dinge.* Cologne: VG Bild-Kunst.
Schneider, B. 2005. *Design: Eine Einführung; Entwurf im sozialen, kulturellen und wissenschaftlichen Kontext.* Basel: Birkhäuser.
Sturm, H. 1998. *Geste und Gewissen im Design.* Cologne: DuMont.

was also an exciting (→) innovation in technology, with ramifications that extended far beyond the original contexts of use. As a result of this project, manufacturers in developed and industrial nations have also begun investigating the possibilities inherent in the creation of simple, functional, high-performance laptops with power supplies that work independently of electrical networks. Those designers who are socially aware perceive the world critically, imagine how it can be, and point the way to the future of design. SH |

→ *Design and Politics, Ethics, Not-for-Profit*

SOFTWARE

The term "software" is used to refer to all of the nonphysical components of a computer—that is, its operating system, programs, and games. It represents the preprogrammed instructions for running the computer's (→) hardware (that is, its physical processors, monitors, and controllers). Examples include the computer's operating system, programs, and games. Software programs can come in a variety of forms (most often CDs), and may require downloading. Software and hardware work together to form a functioning unit that allows the user to operate the computer. TK |

SOUND DESIGN

For quite some time, sound has been acknowledged as an important element in the creation and reception of design. This is not only the case in the context of sound effects and musical scores for films, television and web design, but also, and more significantly, with respect to the designs of our everyday artifacts, systems, brands, services, and public spaces.

For far too many years, both designers and users have judged designed artifacts almost exclusively in terms of their visual— and occasionally (→) haptic—qualities. The design's functional and perceptual qualities are generally limited to the senses of sight and touch, to the exclusion of the other senses. This attitude corresponds with the centrality of vision particularly within most western cultures, and assumes a hierarchy of sensory significance that privileges sight over the more visceral "near senses" of smell, taste, and touch, which are downplayed as baser animal perceptions.

This hierarchy of the senses has had a powerful impact on design. While designers have been experimenting with acoustics since the early days of the field, it took many decades before the idea of consciously employing sound as an essential element of design became widely accepted. Gradually, sound came to be increasingly appreciated, not only as an important and often subliminal signifier of particular qualities, but also as a critical dimension of instructional and (→) information design.

While working in the United States during the 1950s, the French-born Raymond Loewy (→ *Streamline Design*) designed the iconic Frigidaire refrigerator. He designed the acoustics of the closing mechanism so that it made a sound analogous to that of a closing Cadillac door. A great number of sound checks were conducted to achieve the intended result, which was to produce acoustic image transfer that would lend the fridge, through its acoustic qualities, the aura and prestige of a (→) luxury car.

The automobile industry played a leading role in the development of sound design. In 1970, the German car manufacturer Porsche released a recording of various "Porsche sounds," promoting these distinctively exciting and attractive sounds as explicit (→) brand attributes. It was not for another two decades, however, that car manufacturers began to incorporate sound design as an integral dimension of the overall design process. This shift was apparent when a Japanese brand produced a car model that sounded quiet on the outside while on the inside, via hidden loudspeakers, it conveyed the acoustic impression of a racing car. Nowadays, all of the major car manufactures invest significantly in their sound-design departments, and each car model is designed to have its own specific acoustic identity. Careful consideration is given to each component: the starting of the ignition, the shutting of the doors, the running of the motor, and so on—even down to such details as the sound of the indicators. No longer controlled by mechanical switch relays, indicators can now produce any sound but are designed to sound like the original familiar mechanical relay sounds played through loudspeakers.

The shift from mechanical to electronic systems of production, and the increased capacity for miniaturization that resulted, has meant that one's sensual interaction with a product is no longer as dependent on its analog functions and construction. Consequently, there is greater attention paid to the design of touch and sound in particular, as a suggestive and subliminal dimension of a product.

Sound design is also important in the context of design the interfaces and navigational systems we use in our day to day lives. As another example, studies have shown that pedestrians who are hearing-impaired are often at greater risk in road traffic than those who are visually impaired, as we typically register dangers aurally before we register them visually. Consequently, many municipalities and companies are now supplying traffic lights with acoustic signals in order to improve both safety and mobility for the visually impaired.

Design studios are becoming increasingly aware of the importance of our acoustic environment, as well. The products of poor sound design are all around us: from the awful noise that vacuum cleaners and hair driers make—the kind of noise that drives you out of bed and makes it impossible to think straight—to the disappointingly hollow clinks made by poor-quality wine glasses when people enthusiastically gather to drink a toast. Of course, this is inevitable since nearly everything makes a sound: spoons clatter, clothes rustle, water babbles, plastic bottles crack, ovens mumble, tables squeak, doors click, and so on. What we consider to be the "ambience" of any particular environment is largely the product of its various sounds. When Starbucks set out to establish a "European" coffee culture, they paid very careful attention to sound—the company's style guide even makes reference to the hiss of the steam, the click of the ceramics, and so on. And then there is the multiplicity of sounds made by customary audio devices like radios, televisions, and mobile telephones. Acoustic design is urgently needed to coordinate the cacophony of everyday life.

This is particularly evident in the field of (→) web design, where there is now a much greater awareness of the informational richness and navigational capabilities made possible through the use of acoustics. Audible instructions (cf. new guidance systems) are recognized more rapidly and easily than ever before.

Sound design also has an important role in (→) branding with companies like Honda producing jingles and other short musical compositions to represent their brands as far back as the 1960s. However, it would take many years before companies fully realized just how powerfully acoustics could affect our memory and powers of recognition. In the mid-1990s, designers began cooperating with music experts to develop distinctive acoustic (→) logos and signatures for brands, companies, and products in order to enhance their overall recall value. This practice has now developed to a point where particular sounds (like the tapping of a spoon on a can of cat food) can be registered as acoustic (→) trademarks, giving them the same legal status as graphic logos.

Finally, a word must be said about the relevance of sound design in the context of the film and television industries. Since the advent of the very first "talkies," people have been aware of the profound effects that music can have on our experiences and interpretations of film to the point where sound can profoundly change our perception of images. Nowadays, of course, sound effects are used far more extensively in media to powerfully manipulate our responses to visual images—for instance, a car chase can appear faster than it is with acoustic manipulation, sounds can announce scenes and entrances, and sometimes sound is even used to psychologically signify the presence of an unseen object, event, or character. Film sound design has progressed to the point where the stars of major films now may have their own distinctive acoustic identities, as sound can accelerate the process of viewer identification.

Sound has become a key method of design and, as a result, has become established as an independent and integral dimension of the field. ME |

→ *Audiovisual Design, Automobile Design, Broadcast Design, Olfactory Design, Synesthetic*

STAGE DESIGN

→ *Set Design*

ST. MORITZ DESIGN SUMMIT

Seven times between 2000 and 2006, thirty internationally renowned design experts met for the St. Moritz Design Summit, an unusual event held at the ski resort of St. Moritz, Switzerland. The name was chosen as an ironic allusion to the economics summit in Davos. With no fixed agenda, no lectures—and above all no audience—the designers would spend three days discussing the sociopolitical and intercultural role of design, its positive and negative ties to economic and global processes, and opportunities for critical intervention. Particular attention was paid to specific and very different conditions of design in various cultures—a concern that was also reflected in the composition of the design group. The participants came from a number of European countries, the United States, Japan, China, South Africa, Lebanon, South America, and elsewhere. Although the meetings were not meant to be result-oriented, participants formulated two statements known as "declarations" that were publicized worldwide. The first critically examined the question of design within the context of (→) globalization; the second turned against the co-optation of design as a dubious machine for innovations and called for time to reflect and meditate. In addition, in an open letter to the president of the United States, the summit demanded the "return" of the phrase "intelligent design," which has been monopolized in the United States by opponents of Darwin's theory of evolution. The St. Moritz Design Summit was supported by the Raymond Loewy Foundation International. UB |

Raymond Loewy Foundation International, ed. 2002. *St. Moritz Design Summit.* Stuttgart: Arnoldsche.
Raymond Loewy Foundation International, ed. 2005. *St. Moritz Design Summit & International Design Action Day.* Cologne: Walther König.

STORYBOARD

The storyboard is the central visual planning instrument in the development process of a film or video production. During the storyboarding process, every production setting is precisely planned in advance and visualized using drawings or computer-generated images. In terms of quality, these designs range from simple black-and-white drawings to elaborate color productions that reproduce every scene in great detail or serve as a basis for planning in the art department.

Fundamentally, one can distinguish between four different types of storyboards:

- Film/video storyboard (sequential presentation as groundwork for direction and camera)
- Key frames (elaborate visualization of important frames in a production—especially in the context of production design)
- Production drawings (serve above all as a draft for the film architects/stage designer)
- Advertising storyboard/style frames (supports the "sale" of a concept to the customer)

The concept and technique of the storyboard are also used to visualize sequences for the development of noncinematic media products (CD-ROMs, web sites, and so on). Nowadays, so-called "previz" systems are increasingly employed: interactive (→) animation software programs that permit whole sequences of a planned production to be simulated on a computer. BB |

→ Illustration, Presentation, Visualization, Time-based Design

STRATEGIC DESIGN

The term "strategy," originally used in military contexts to refer to the art of winning a battle, has come to mean any long-term guideline, tool, or plan intended to accomplish a competitive task. As such, the term is currently widely used in a variety of fields such as politics, economy, and management. Recently, many have pointed out the importance of "strategic design" in the context of both internally and externally focused management approaches.

Because the term "strategy" implies the existence of a competing body, strategic design is intended to promote the performance and efficiency of a company in the eyes of its designers, consumers, and competitors alike. Toward this end, strategic design is based on the articulation of both internally and externally oriented business practices. Internally oriented strategies typically focus on how well an organization promotes inter-organizational communication, knowledge, and understanding. Externally oriented strategies, on the other hand, are often market driven, and focus on how effectively the design reaches the target market, promotes a consistent (→) brand identity, and gives the company its competitive edge. Naturally, internally and externally oriented design strategies are closely related, and dependent upon one another to succeed.

Business objectives related to design almost always emphasize (→) innovation as a primary factor in determining a company's success. There is no single proven strategy to ensure successful design; the (→) design process is a strongly (→) heuristic one, and therefore difficult to direct or even to articulate. As such, strategic design is not a set course of action, but characterized by broad, long-term design initiatives that constantly undergo adjustments and revisions in order to better meet business objectives. In this capacity, strategic design is also distinct from (→) design management, which connotes the day-to-day oversight over design related operations.

There are a number of theories that incorporate differing roles for design in relation to management practices. "Core competence management," introduced by Gary Hamel and C. K. Prahalad, entails the strategic management of specialized expertise. A core competence may be any process, skill, attitude, or approach that is unique or difficult to imitate, provides consumer benefits, and can be applied to a number of different markets. Making good use of core competencies enables any given company to differentiate itself and maintain its competitive advantage. A related management strategy, (→) "knowledge management," comprises practices that utilize the identification, organization, distribution, and application of knowledge in an effective manner. According to Ikujiro Nonaka, knowledge may be categorized as either tacit knowledge or explicit knowledge. Tacit knowledge is usually learned through personal experience and thus not verbalized, whereas explicit knowledge is usually codified in some manner and thus easily communicable. Effective management strategies integrate, transform, and expand both forms of knowledge in order to apply them across the organization.

In both core competence and knowledge management theories, design plays a pivotal role in the strategic (→) visualization and codification of (→) information. Core competencies and tacit knowledge are, of course, often subconscious and therefore difficult to identify much less manage. At the same time, core competencies and tacit knowledge related to design processes are especially important to recognize, communicate, and understand when innovation is a primary objective.

Of course, design strategies must also consider the demands and characteristics of the market in order to achieve business objectives, especially as related to growth. Ansoff's matrix, proposed by H. Igor Ansoff, is intended to provide corporate management with a strategic framework for future growth. The matrix presents four main options for managers to select from: market penetration, market development, product development, and diversification. Penetration strategies involve marketing existing products to existing markets; market development strategies involve marketing existing products to new markets; new product development strategies involve marketing new products to existing markets, and diversification strategies involve marketing new products to new markets. Each category has a different level of risk involved, and uses differing design practices in order to achieve growth objectives. For instance, penetration strategies would most likely concentrate on finessing product (→) styling and advertising as opposed to (→) product development strategies that require the design of completely new or modified products.

Another strategic design theorist, Michael Porter, proposed the "five forces framework" in his competitive strategy theory.

Combined with the SWOT analysis (using a matrix with Strength and Weakness on the horizontal axis and Opportunity and Threat on the vertical axis) developed by Harvard Business School, this framework became popular as an analysis method for companies seeking a competitive advantage. Porter identified five forces that determined competitive status in an industry: competitive rivalry, supplier power, buyer power, threat of substitution, and threat of new entry. The analysis of these five forces enable analysts to predict success in any given market situation. Porter also presented strategies for building on this analysis: "cost leadership," "differentiation," and "focus." In terms of the role of design, the "cost leadership" strategy would require a highly cost-effective product design. Under the "differentiation" strategy, design is expected to help add unique product value. And under the "focus" strategy, companies provide a small segment of users with an optimal design.

As demonstrated in the examples above, strategic design almost always has the business objectives of achieving competitive advantage and increasing profit as end goals. However, this need not always be the case—for example, strategic design can occur outside the framework of a corporate entity, in any design process that involves a careful, self-reflexive, and long-term approach to design planning. Strategic design therefore addresses not only the optimized relationship between managers and designers, but the possibility that all designers are managers and vice versa.

In a sense then, all design can be said to be inherently strategic, and all strategy can be said to be inherently designed. The act of naming these kinds of design activities as explicitly "strategic" is useful, however, in that it emphasizes the importance of long-term planning in the design process. The same can be said for other design considerations that are tacitly understood to be part of the typical design process, yet benefit from the act of naming: for instance, most designers typically try to derive maximum effects from minimal resources when designing a project, and try to keep the broadest audience in mind during every stage of development. These are not new considerations in the design process; they have been practiced for centuries on end. However, as environmental problems and an aged society in developed nations become increasingly important matters of public concern, codifying the phrases "sustainable design" (→ Sustainability) and (→) "universal design" has helped draw attention to, and thus theorize and refine, these inherent aspects of the design process. This is true for strategic design as well.

Ansoff, H. I. 1965. *Corporate strategy*. New York: McGraw-Hill.

Hamel, G., and C. K. Prahalad. 1994. *Competing for the future*. Boston: Harvard Business School Press.

Nonaka, I., and H. Takeuchi. 1995. *The knowledge-creating company: How Japanese companies create the dynamics of innovation*. New York: Oxford Univ. Press.

Porter, M. E. 1985. *Competitive advantage: Creating and sustaining superior performance*. New York: Free Press.

STREAMLINE DESIGN

The term "streamlining" in the scientific sense is used for bodies that have little resistance or "drag" when put into motion through an external medium—usually air or water. In the design context, streamline design refers to an important stylistic movement as well as a more general description of aerodynamic forms.

As the network society comes to maturity and a broad range of (→) values emerge that go beyond traditional corporate purposes of surviving in the market and earning profits, there are increasingly various levels of strategic design that may require a wider framework of understanding. What we need now is the "strategy" that takes account of the sustainable development of a society and a wider range of relationships that extend beyond the pursuit of traditional corporate objectives to a way to coexistence. MI |

→ *Branding, Corporate Identity, Design Planning, Design and Politics, Product Development*

One quantitative measure of a streamlined form is "drag coefficient," also known as c_d value. The lower the c_d value, the more streamlined the body. c_d was once measured through (→) aerodynamic experiments in wind tunnels that quite literally observed the course of stream "lines" in the external medium; today, modern technologies have made it possible to access this information through computer simulations.

Such studies lent their name to Streamline Design, one of the most important stylistic movements in twentieth-century design, with its heyday during the 1930s and 1940s. Because streamlined forms remain influential today as models for design, however, the phrase "streamline design" can be understood more broadly to refer to objects designed to be streamlined.

The basic laws of aerodynamics and the behavior of fluids were already being explored in the early decades of the twentieth century. In design, this research was applied first to building cars, airplanes, and ships, where minimizing drag both reduces fuel consumption and makes higher speeds possible. One of the earliest attempts to create a low-drag design was a bodywork by Pierre Selmersheim (1895). Among the most famous examples of streamlined forms in the decades that followed were the cigar-shaped locomotive, the German construction series 03.10 and 05, and the aptly named Tropfenwagen (Teardrop car) by Edmund Rumpler (1921), one of the first and most famous examples of streamlined forms. The Tropfenwagen's fairing was based on the knowledge that the teardrop form is one of the most streamlined possible, and indeed the design had an outstanding c_d value of 0.28. In its wake, streamlined fairings in the automobile sector grew more significant, as Ferdinand Porsche's precursor to the VW Bug (1938) demonstrates.

For many designers and architects of the 1920s, the speed, progress, and (→) mobility suggested by streamlined forms embodied "a genuine liberation from the constraints we have till now been subjected to" (Le Corbusier 1927, trans. Frederick Etchells). By the late 1920s, the enthusiasm for streamlined design led to its establishment, alongside the strictly rectangular ideal of the (→) Bauhaus, as a model for style. Streamline Design was quickly embraced by those working in fields outside of the transportation sector as well, and its impact was soon evident in the design of everything from roof terraces to building facades to tubular steel furniture.

The stylistic movement achieved its real breakthrough during the 1930s in the United States, evolving from an avant-garde aesthetic to a mass phenomenon. In the wake of price regulating in 1932, intended as a measure against the Depression, a product's "look" and effective advertising became crucial factors in determining its economic success. In turn, designers began to pay more attention to aesthetic surfaces, creating everyday objects with attractive designs. Among the first famous advocates of this new understanding of design were the "Big Four"—Raymond Loewy, Henry Dreyfuss, Walter Dorwin Teague, and Norman Bel Geddes. Embracing slogans like "never leave well enough alone" (Raymond Loewy), these designers used streamlining not only to improve the (→) ergonomic qualities of industrial products, but also to stimulate consumption and appeal to new markets (such as female consumers) through the use of exciting new forms.

Streamlined forms were made possible in no small measure by technical (→) innovations in metal and woodworking that made it easier to produce curved three-dimensional forms. The movement became associated with technological progress, and became the epitome of a (→) futuristic design aesthetic that also appealed to the masses. Initially used in the design of American cars like the Harley Earl and Chrysler models of the 1930s and 1940s, streamlined designs quickly moved on to influence the design of household appliances like Raymond Loewy's 1932 Coldspot refrigerator. The aesthetic eventually became symbolic of the American way of life, dominated by colorful paints, chrome fixtures, curved forms, and dynamic printed letters. American influence on European consumer behavior in the postwar period brought Streamline Design back to Europe, and in the 1950s it became one of the first global design (→) trends.

Despite the worldwide popularity of the movement, Streamline Design had its share of critics (including Edgar Kaufmann Jr. of the Museum of Modern Art in New York). In particular, it was criticized as a superficial formal aesthetic, and was often regarded as synonymous with (→) "styling"—the design of attractive surfaces to encourage sales. By the end of the 1950s it had largely become a purely aesthetic gesture with at times absurd results. With the rise of new plastics and the organic design of the 1960s, the significance of the movement waned—though its influence continued to be apparent in work of designers such as Luigi Colani and Olivier Mourgue among others.

Since the 1990s, streamlined forms have gained in currency again. This is the result of, on the one hand, a revival of Streamline Design as part of retro fashion (→ *Retro Design*) and, on the other, new scientific discoveries in aerodynamics. In particular, (→) bionics has identified new streamlined forms and surfaces based on natural models, and breakthroughs in computer simulation have considerably simplified the analysis of fluid behavior. Contemporary examples such as Chris Bangle's (→) redesign of the BMW model series or designs for athletic shoes illustrate how streamlined designs can still be used to appeal to buyers who value speed and mobility. The continuing significance of reducing fuel consumption that low air resistance can provide ensures that streamlined forms will remain very important in design and will be continually refined especially in the case of sports cars and airplanes. ^{MKR} |

→ *Art Deco, Automobile Design*

Boissière, O. 1987. *Streamline: Le design américain des annés '30–'40*. Paris: Éditions Rivages.
Kaufmann, E. 1950. *What is modern design?* New York: Museum of Modern Art.
Weingartner, F. 1986. *Streamlining America*. Dearborn, MI: Henry Ford Museum & Greenfield Village.

STYLE

Style is a strangely aristocratic-sounding category: either you have it or you don't. In contrast to manners, which can or should be learned, style refers to something you were born with. That changed, however, in Europe at the end of the nineteenth century, when dandies rebelled against the established Biedermeier of the nouveau riche bourgeoisie (which had partly tried to imitate the aristocratic style, in conflict with its own interests, but actually achieved its own style in Biedermeier), shocking the Biedermeier by countering style with manners. They did this with clear awareness that the style they manifested was artificial—both quotation and transformation.

Consequently they developed requisite routines for how to dress, began wearing tuxedos and tails again, decked themselves out as men and sought sensation, respect, protest, and identity in (→) "styling." This certainly called for stylistic confidence—that is to say, incarnating the established rules.

The German writer and theorist Johann Wolfgang von Goethe expressed himself quite differently in his essay "Einfache Nachahmung der Natur, Manier, Stil" (Simple Imitation of Nature, Manner, Style): his sublime position of style viewed manners as merely the ability to grasp the whole of appearances, beyond a simple imitation of detail, and to compare and depict it. In Goethe's view, style, by contrast, is the expression of insight, beyond any sensory (→) perception, into the essential features of (→) objects and hence their design.

It is all the more strange, given such stylistic guidelines, that in design (and notoriously so in German design) style is generally ignored as a category and as a form and dismissed as (→) "styling"—that is to say, as merely decorative and specific. The time has come to seriously discuss style again in design. ^{BL} |

→ *Aesthetics, Beauty*

STYLING

By the middle of the twentieth century, American (→) product design with regard to theory and practice differed greatly from the European. While Europe's population (especially after the Second World War) suffered from a lack of industrial commodities, Americans were enjoying a rich range of products. The increasing oversaturation of the American domestic market and the resulting pressure of competition among companies made design an important marketing factor along with advertising. Changing the appearance of the product in short cycles was to stabilize or even increase sales. This caused many American designers to focus their design objectives solely on the object's shell.

The word "styling" defines this application of the discipline. It describes the pure aesthetic surface design of products, which reveals design's departure from technical or (→) ergonomic considerations.

This sometimes created a wide gap between the external appearance of the object and its (→) function, as well as formal arbitrariness. Styling characteristically applies existing styles and formal elements from other areas, without developing the relevant object in its own essential formal language, or without optimizing it with regards to function or production. A typical example here is the "dream cars" of the 1950s. The various car models differ very little or not at all from their predecessors, either functionally or technically. Yet they were donned with a new metal suit every year, since variation in form and product shell were supposed to stimulate customer interest. The aim was to place the products in a fashion context, to have them look old as soon as possible in order to arouse the desire for the new shape, and in this way, boost product (→) consumption.

Under Raymond Loewy (1893–1986), the streamline form, a symbol for dynamics, progress, and freedom, became an icon of American styling, particularly in the 1950s (→ *Streamline Design*). Applied in aircraft construction because of its (→) aerodynamic qualities, it was next transferred onto other mobile objects (cars and locomotives), and then onto household and office appliances (like toasters or pencil sharpeners) to connote speed and therefore modernity. Styling was very successful at

Aicher, O. 1991. *Kritik am Auto: Schwierige Verteidigung des Autos gegen seine Anbeter.* 2nd ed. Berlin: Ernst & Sohn.
Loewy, R. 1951. *Never leave well enough alone.* New York: Simon and Schuster.
Petsch, J. 1982. *Geschichte des Auto Designs.* Cologne: DuMont.
Pulos, A. J. 1986. *American design ethic: A history of industrial design to 1940.* Cambridge, MA: MIT Press.

SUSTAINABILITY

Sustainability is a measure of the resilience of a system, the capacity of a system (and all its components) to repair itself when damaged.

this time in fulfilling its job in encouraging sales via the cosmetic styling of shells and surfaces.

It was not until the 1960s that manipulating consumers with product aesthetics attracted heavy criticism. The accusation being that design had been directing its focus purely on corporate profit and superficial gimmickry (→ *Gimmick*) while neglecting its sociocultural responsibilities. This changed the meaning of styling from a once positively associated term to a disparaging word for simple formalism. MKU |

→ *Aesthetics, Coating, Redesign, Style*

Awareness has been growing over the last thirty years that the design of modern built environments and the (→) lifestyles they support and promote appear to be fundamentally unsustainable. The construction and operation of those environments destroy resources at a faster rate than natural systems can create them, particularly when those natural systems are also hampered by a range of pollutants. The extent to which the designing behind modern societies has failed to deliver ongoing resource efficiency, durability, and flexibility is leading some to believe that "sustainable design," if not an oxymoron, is insufficient for the problem.

The most commonly cited definition of sustainability is the one put forward in relation to the term "sustainable development" in the 1987 Bruntland Report *Our Common Future:* meeting the needs of the present without harming the ability of the future generations to meet their needs. This formulation of intergenerational equity is not practicable because it merely raises further questions about the needs of the present, the future, and the nature of "harm."

Clarification of the meaning of the term sustainability is best found in the relatively modern discourse of ecology. The term was coined in the middle of the nineteenth century by Ernst von Haeckel, a promoter and advancer of Darwinism. Haeckel coined the term to capture the "fit" of species and their habitats. Haeckel argued that all the living things in particular niches were interdependent; if one species changed then all the species in that environment would be under evolutionary pressure to change in response.

At the time, nature was considered to be in eternal harmonious balance. Modern ecologists now argue that areas of wilderness are not as they have always been, but instead experience violent booms and crashes in the populations of certain species, with resulting exoduses and invasions that lead to constantly changing environments. In fenced-off national parks, where migration is not possible, the balance between interdependent species can only be maintained through occasional human intervention, such as culls.

In this context, the sustainability of a species refers to its resilience to changes in its environment and the other species that comprise its environment. In other words, sustainability is the measure of the capacity of a system, whether this be a particular species, or the whole ecosystem of which it is a part, to reproduce itself in the changing circumstances upon which it depends. Importantly, the sustainability of a system is not just its ability to stay the same, but rather its ability to flourish, which may involve changing, moving location for example, or evolving in (→) form and (→) function over time. It also means that there is no final state of sustainability, just moments of dynamic equilibrium.

Human civilizations have long experienced the extent to which natural systems can be damaged through resource extraction before the ability of such systems to recover from damage is exceeded: for example, rates of logging. Human beings have also long been aware of the fact that damaging the sustainability of one species can in turn lead to the damage of other species and entire ecosystems; for example, hunting predators leads to destructive booms in the population of their prey.

Modern civilizations have started to damage ecologies in less explicit ways. Contemporary ecological politics is often thought to have begun with the publication of Rachel Carson's *Silent Spring*. After noting the absence of birdsong on a walk through the forest, Carson discovered the way in which pesticides bioaccumulated, that is, built up in concentration along ecological food chains. This drew attention to the fact that species could lose their regenerative capacity not only through direct exploitation, but also as a result of relatively small amounts of pollutants moving through the interdependencies that make up ecosystems.

After Carson, who was both a scientist and an activist, ecological sustainability centered on the protection of natural ecosystems from the risk of damage beyond repair. There is much argument in the philosophical field of "environmental ethics" (→ Ethics) as to why natural ecosystems should be protected from damage: anthropocentric arguments emphasize the dependence of humans on natural ecosystems (for example, the Amazon rainforest as the "lungs of the earth" as well as prospective source for cancer cures); biocentric arguments emphasize the intrinsic value of nonhuman species.

Ecological sustainability throughout the early 1990s was primarily concerned with minimizing qualitative ecological impacts. These are particular pollutants that can damage ecosystems almost in any quantity: heavy metals, acid rain causing gases, persistent chlorinated compounds. Manufacturers, mostly as a result of imposed regulations, pursued "cleaner production" or the minimized use of proscribed chemicals.

Toward the end of the 1990s, the scope of sustainable production increased to also take account of quantitative ecological impacts. These are pollutants that are less toxic in themselves, but become damaging when present in larger quantities: for example, global climate-changing carbon dioxide emissions ("greenhouse gases"). Manufacturers attempted to reduce the amount of these emissions through "eco-efficiency" initiatives. These were often undertaken voluntarily because of their "win-win" nature: improving the efficiency of industry, so that it needs less resource input and has less waste output, saves businesses in on-going costs, as well as "saving the environment." Investment in eco-efficient reforms were judged in terms of "pay-back" periods, that is, how long before the cost of the reforms were recouped by ongoing savings to the business in its operating costs. Unfortunately, most of the reductions in ecological impact accomplished by cleaner production and eco-efficiency in the late 1990s are being eroded by the "rebound effect." This is where the cost savings from one initiative are reinvested in increased net production/consumption. If a business is saving money by not being fined for pollution by a government environment agency, it will have more cash to expand its operations. The rebound effect also applies to domestic (→) consumption. If a household is convinced to buy a more efficient air-conditioner, that household will save money on its electricity bills that over time it will probably respend on extensions to the house, creating whole new spaces to be filled with furnishings and cooled/heated by air conditioners.

In recognition of the fact that "per product" efficiencies can be outstripped by increasing numbers of products being purchased and used, the focus of current sustainability research and policy also includes sustainable consumption. This refers not just to informing customers about the qualitative ecological impacts associated with products on offer in order to encourage "buying green," but also persuading consumers to consume less—sufficiency rather than efficiency.

Ecodesign refers to the role designers played in facilitating eco-efficient cleaner production. Throughout the 1990s many guides were developed to help expand the process of designing products and environments to include consideration of ecological impacts. Design for the Environment was to be given equal weighting alongside all the other concurrent "Design for"s (that is, cost minimization, ease of manufacture, durability, usability, safety, marketability, and so on). Unfortunately, many of these guides were not easily integrated into the creative processes of designers, and gave no guidance on how to handle conflicts between the various "Design for"s.

Some of the more sophisticated guides developed to help designers select less eco-impacting materials or operational designs were Life Cycle Assessments. These are decision-making tools that attempted: firstly, to identify all the ecological impacts associated with a particular product configuration over its life span, from raw material through manufacture and use to disposal; and secondly, to compare different types of ecological impacts, for example, ozone depletion versus groundwater contamination versus endangered species habitat destruction. The aim was to quantify all the impacts, each weighted in terms of unsustainability, to give figures that could be used to calculate the least unsustainable design option. A crucial factor in Life Cycle Assessments is the "functional unit." Comparing the ecological impacts of one 1 liter glass milk bottle with one 1 liter liquid paper-board milk carton will miss that glass milk bottles are washed and reused, so the LCA's functional unit needs to be perhaps the packaging associated with one hundred liters of milk. Comparing one cloth nappy with one disposable nappy will miss that disposable nappies are designed to "take the wetness away" from the baby's skin allowing the baby to be changed less frequently before crying, so the LCA's functional unit needs to be twenty-four hours worth of nappies.

Life Cycle Assessments have proved problematic decision making tools for sustainable design. They are time-consuming and expensive to do comprehensively. And despite seeking objective measures of sustainability, they always depend on contestable decisions, most notably in the weightings given to distinct types of ecological impacts, but also in determining where the boundaries of these impacts lie. For instance, the transport energy used to ferry miners to remote locations could be counted as part of the embodied energy of the final product made with those minerals. So too could the energy associated with the food that sustains the workers. A final questionable area of Life Cycle Assessments is the predicted ecological impacts associated with average use-life. Use is usually one of the most impacting periods in the life span of a product, whether it be a toaster or a building; but it is also the aspect of a product's ecological impact profile most open to variation, depending on whether the user is, or is able to be, diligent or negligent.

Taking up these last complications have been new attempts to calculate whole-of-system ecological impacts, such as those associated with cities, bioregions, or nations, rather than those that can be attributed to this or that product, or even industry. In keeping with what was discussed earlier, these are measures of quantitative ecological impact only; they assume that a good indicator of the unsustainability of modern societies is the amount of stuff it takes to sustain a set of people. The best known of these is the "ecological footprint" which converts quantities of goods consumed over a given period into the amount of land nominally needed to produce those goods. Generally, if everyone in the world was to live as most people do in developed urban centers, the land area needed would be the equivalent of three to seven earths. A more detailed measure comes from Material Flows Analysis, which calculates the total weight of material in (standing stock), and passing through (throughput), a place over a given period of time.

A related measure that has proved useful for design is Materials Intensity per unit Service, also known as "ecological rucksacks." This latter was developed by the Factor 10 Club, a group of sustainability researchers and policy makers who argue that a good target for a more sustainable future would be for developed nations to service their lifestyles using one tenth of the amount of materials currently required. This figure is not based on any measure of the carrying capacity of the earth's ecosystems, but rather global equity given that one fifth of the world (the developed nations) at the moment consumes four fifths of the world's resources. Attaining this target is unlikely to be achieved soon enough, and without rebound effects, through lightweighting or energy-efficiency breakthrough technologies. Factor 10 is therefore best achieved by households having less stuff (sufficiency), having what stuff they have for longer, getting more use out of it (increasing service intensity), and spending more of their time on activities that do not require as much stuff (also known as dematerialization).

Designers committed to developing more sustainable futures in the last decades have tended to arrive at (→) heuristics similar to those of the Factor 10 Club as a way of steering through the complexity of Life Cycle Assessment. Exemplary is the designer Ezio Manzini's typology of product life spans: for some product categories, those with strong symbolic ties to their users, or those subject to little technological innovation, it is appropriate to prioritize very longlife designs; for most products, subject to changing fashion or technological improvement, priority should be given to making the product disassemblable, for repair, upgrade, or component and material recovery; for all products with necessarily short use-lives, priority should be given to making the products from single or separable biodegradable materials. Crucial to this version of design for sustainability is not confusing material and product use-life; for example, using near-eternal plastics for disposable products, or fusing moving parts liable to wear and tear to longer life casings.

The strategies Manzini identified for midlevel longevity products are now being institutionalized through Extended Producer Responsibility regulations. These primarily European Union initiatives force or persuade manufacturers to take their products back from consumers at the end of their use-lives. As a result, manufacturers are beginning to design products in anticipation of their return, so that their components and materials can be more easily removed and reused.

The "closed loop" nature of product take-back by manufacturers represents a fundamental shift from the current mostly linear nature of capitalist economies. (It is noteworthy that a strong current sustainability initiative in China goes by the name "The Circular Economy.") For example, one of the easiest ways of ensuring the return of products to manufacturers is to not transfer the ownership of the product to the consumer in the first place, but instead lease the products. By selling the use of the product rather than the product itself, businesses are in a position to influence the use-phase of products, allowing integrated strategies for sustainable production and consumption. By retaining ownership of the product, businesses have an incentive to invest in more efficient, more durable, but also more easily serviceable and parts-recoverable products. Where conventional product-sales companies concerned about sustainability suffer from "split incentives"—the need to sell more product for profit, but sell less product for sustainability—"functional sales" companies internalize environmental costs and profit from being more sustainable. While there are political concerns for the autonomy of the household for example (families outsourcing their appliances to profit-driven companies), these sorts of "product-service systems" seem to suggest business opportunities that would lead to significant leaps toward much reduced societal materials intensity. This is a very different game to the current management discourse of "triple bottom line," where companies report on the competing objectives of economic, ecological, and social sustainability. (Social sustainability in this sense refers to investments in fostering the resilience of people, by enhancing their know-how and know-who for example.)

Other non-market-driven initiatives toward reduced materials intense lifestyles have been identified in a series of recent research projects initiated again by Ezio Manzini. "Creative communities" in both developed and developing nations are groups of people who establish systems for the shared-use of products (carpooling for instance) òr for the procurement of less ecologically impacting goods, such as locally produced, organic, and/or fair trade (the Slow Food movement for instance). For Manzini, sustainable design then becomes the project of finding these attempts by people to create new systems of provision not currently offered by mainstream markets, and (→) redesign them so that they are more sustainable, and more desirable to other people less ideologically committed than those who initiated them. Again, this role, as a facilitator of (→) participatory design, is a new set of skills for conventionally product-oriented sustainable designers (→ *Service Design*).

To conclude, Ulrich Beck has argued that ecological politics is a form of reflexive modernization. By this he means that issues of ecological risk put lay people in a very ambivalent position. Ecological impacts, such as the toxicity first identified by Rachel Carson, are not discernible except with the assistance of technical experts, the very technical experts who caused the problem in the first place—hence public ambivalence toward modern institutions like science and engineering. Much ecological politics is therefore about people reasserting some control over their future. Sustainability is less a scientifically determinable state than the state of being able to be involved in forming the future (and not just being informed about the choices experts are making). The aim of sustainable design is therefore to avoid what Tony Fry has called the "defuturing" that characterized twentieth century design, that is, designing in ways that close off alternative futures, restricting future options. It is to create what Manzini has called "error-friendly" design, designs that remain open to being redesigned for other futures. CT |

→ *Environmental Design, Materials, Slow Design*

Beck, U. 1997. *Ecological politics in the age of risk*. Oxford, United Kingdom: Polity.
Fry, T. 1999. *A new design philosophy: An introduction to defuturing*. Sydney: University of New South Wales Press.
Manzini, E., and F. Jegou. 2003. *Sustainable everyday: Scenarios of everyday life*. Milan: Edizioni Ambiente.

SYMBOL

A symbol is an object, design, property, text, or other marker representing something other than itself, often an abstract idea or set of relationships.

According to Charles Sanders Peirce's definition of (→) semiotics, a symbol is a sign without any connection to what it represents. Unlike other forms of signs, which may look, sound, smell, feel, or taste like what they represent, symbols are arbitrary and stand for what they represent solely by (→) convention. Therefore, unlike other forms of signs, symbols necessitate agreement amongst a community of interpreters in order to have meaning. Symbols can be signs invented for the purpose of representation (language), or existing objects that have had symbolic properties conferred upon them (the designation of the lily as a symbol of purity in Christian iconography).

In more general usage, however, the relationship between the symbol and the (→) object or idea it represents is not always as purely arbitrary as Peircean semiotics suggests. Indeed, the terms sign, icon, and symbol are often used interchangeably to denote any marker that evokes another object or idea, whether arbitrarily or by means of resemblance, metaphor, or association. For example, objects can take on symbolic meaning because of their material characteristics: a snail might be used as a symbol of slowness in general. Likewise, the fleur-de-lis symbol represents a type of lily not because of an arbitrary designation, but because it works as a (→) pictogram, a visual representation, however highly stylized, of the shape of the flower's petals. Many user (→) interface designs employ pictogram symbols (called "icons" in this context) to represent a device's functions by means of analogy or metaphor. Style can also become symbolic because of its historical or cultural associations. A chair in the neo-Gothic style might evoke ecclesiastical functions, whereas a (→) Bauhaus-style chair might be used by an interior designer as a symbol of corporate efficiency. Even if a symbol is not arbitrary, its meaning is largely defined by a community of interpreters; it can have different meanings, or no meaning at all, to people in different places or in different eras.

Symbols can also evoke other symbols, thus representing by forming a chain of associations. For example, the fleur-de-lis symbol, having been chosen by the French king Clovis I as a sign of his purification through baptism, comes to symbolize the entire French monarchy, and, by extension, both France itself as well as the concept of royalty. The same graphic mark can have a host of other symbolic meanings depending on the community of interpreters. The same fleur-de-lis symbol can represent Scouting organizations, for example, based on a set of symbolic associations quite independent of its history as a representation of France or of royalty.

Designers have often turned to the symbol to be the basis of a universally comprehensible representational system. For example, Otto Neurath developed a set of stylized pictograms called isotypes as a way of describing facts more precisely than possible with the arbitrary codes of verbal language. A graphic symbol that represents an idea rather than a word can also be called an ideogram. Many designers have aspired to develop universally legible symbols, signs whose comprehension is not dependent upon a community of interpreters, but is rather grounded in common experience. Most symbol systems do, however, ultimately require familiarity with particular visual conventions to be understood.

The symbol can also be used to describe an approach to design modeling. As differentiated from iconic modeling, which uses

Goodman, N. 1968. *Languages of Art: An approach to a theory of symbols.* Indianapolis: Bobbs-Merrill.
Kampen, M. 1962. Signs and symbols in graphic communication. *Design Quarterly* 62:3–31.
Liungman, C. G. 1991. *Dictionary of Symbols.* Santa Barbara, CA: ABC-CLIO.

representations that share characteristics—proportions, shape, and so on—of the objects or procedures represented, and analogue modeling, which represents certain characteristics of the object or process with equivalent terms or qualities, symbolic modeling represents the object or process wholly abstractly, for example though a series of mathematical equations. ER |

→ *Corporate Identity, Logo, Trademark, Semantics, Visual Communication*

SYNERGY

"Synergy" is most commonly used to describe the process whereby two or more people or organizations with complementary skills, resources, and knowledge are able to achieve more through collaboration than the simple addition of their efforts working individually would have suggested. Thus, synergy best describes the goal of the collaborative processes (→ *Collaborative Design*) used by design teams—be they teams of designers or of designers and non-designers.

The (→) design process itself is often described as being "synergistic" for two reasons. First, the design process aims to achieve a synergy from the contributions of team members and, second, design itself attempts to synthesize (→ *Synthesis*) and optimize the potentially competing, and sometimes contradictory, economic, social, technological, cultural, and environmental realities that all influence the design process and outcome (→ *Discipline*).

A separate yet related use of the term refers to certain cross-marketing strategies that have gained popularity in recent decades. For instance, the release of many blockbuster films today are accompanied by a variety of licensing agreements or "tie-ins" ranging from soundtracks to games to tableware that increase the film's profitability and vice versa. TM |

→ *Coordination, Crossover, Gestaltung, Integration, Strategic Design*

SYNESTHETIC

The word "synesthetic" refers to the act of conflating particular impressions from the five main senses of sight, hearing, touch, smell, and taste. Given that the day-to-day perceptions of these senses are clearly linked (smell and appearance give contours to taste, hearing can shape sight and so on), visual artists, writers, musicians and designers have attempted to trace and design an inner logic to this "mixing" of senses. This was popular in the last decade of the nineteenth century to a certain extent as a reaction against the categorization and stark division of human skills and labor brought on by industrialization. In line with the era's theoretical insights into the category of experience (for example, by Ernst Mach or Sigmund Freud), many artists in the mid- to late nineteenth century worked with these synesthetic processes. They designed multi-sensory works such as "color keyboards," "color symphonies," and the beginnings of "visual poetry." These artists enhanced the (→) haptic through optical or acoustic impressions, or devised ways to formulate and experience these senses as actively tangible in their own right.

It has since been clarified that sound and color waves have nothing physically in common (except that both are conveyed in wave form). Physiology has also revealed that synesthesia exists as a rare neurological disease that compulsively mixes usually two senses of (→) perception—so that certain numbers, for example, unavoidably associate with particular colors or vice versa. In a sense, synesthesia is merely an integrative construction of the brain. Yet there remains a constant challenge for any design approach that reflects on and consciously designs the relationship between the human senses—because every product, sign, and service operates in a multisensory context. Vacuum cleaners for example have an appearance, they make a sound, they are touched, and often even give off a scent. Books are not only looked at, but also make sounds, have a smell, and are held. The process of understanding and designing the sensory experience is made even more complex by the idea that all of these configurations are preceded by learned notions of harmony that establish the connections between individual sensory impressions as desired or feared.

Any design has to find its way within this network, has to integrate "harmonious" design into this system or unexpectedly contradict it. ME |

→ *Food Design, Olfactory Design, Sound Design, Visualization*

Cytowic, R. E. 2002. *Synesthesia: A Union of the Senses.* 2nd ed. Cambridge, MA: MIT Press.
Emrich, H. M., U. Schneider, and M. Zedler. 2002. *Welche Farbe hat der Montag? Synästhesie: Das Leben mit verknüpften Sinnen.* Stuttgart: Hirzel.

SYNTHESIS

For many designers, synthesis describes the (→) design process itself. Its literal meaning is the combination of a variety of objects, ideas, and/or intentions to produce a new complex whole. The process of design described in the entry for (→) discipline describes design's unique quality of negotiating a range of specialist knowledge and techniques in order to reconcile these into a coherent design artifact. This understanding of design suggests that it is a "synthetic practice." In Hegelian philosophy, synthesis suggests a dialectical process rather than a rhetorical one. Hegel used the term to indicate a process of ideation whereby one idea (thesis) is proposed, then another idea (antithesis) negates the first idea, and then a third resolves the conflict between the first two and transcends them (synthesis). This synthesis becomes a new thesis that generates a new antithesis and so on.

The design process is not unlike the one that Hegel developed, though it is usually directed toward a particular rather than an abstract end. Donald Schön described this process in his observations of the teaching of design—ideas are proposed and then new proposals developed in response to the "talkback" generated by the first idea and a process of synthesis is achieved as the complex dynamics of the reality are better understood.

For instance, a graphic designer will have technical issues to consider—the paper stock and the printing quality that can be afforded, the number of inks required, and the means of distribution of the printed material. Then the client's intention has to be considered as well as the age, demographic, and educational characteristics of the likely consumer. The sociocultural implications of color choice and graphic iconography need to be accounted for and, increasingly, the ability to design for multiple languages is necessary. The environmental impacts of the materials and processes used needs to be determined and strategies deployed to negate or minimize these by a variety of behavioral and technical means.

So even in a relatively simple design print project the designer has to be able to synthesize a variety of issues, concerns, ambitions, and ideologies into a technically constrained final "whole." As designers engage in increasingly complex scenarios, the ability to synthesize seemingly irreconcilable issues of growing complexity in the final "resolved" design piece becomes ever more important. Indeed the importance of synthesis is implicit in the fact that "unresolved" must be one of the most common negative criticisms of a design proposal. Synthesis is this resolution. TM |

→ *Complexity, Coordination, Convergence, Gestaltung, Integration, Organization, Understanding*

Hegel, G. W. F. 1969. *Hegel's science of logic.* Trans. A. V. Miller. London: George Allen and Unwin.
Schön, D. A. 1987. *Educating the reflective practitioner.* San Francisco: Jossey Bass.

SYSTEM

System (from the Greek word *systema* meaning a whole compounded of parts) refers to a combination of related parts organized into a complex whole, such as the cosmos, organisms, political or social bodies, or even cognitive constructions such as a theory or philosophy. The behavior of the whole cannot be derived by a reduction to its parts (emergence). In addition to the concept of element-relation, the distinction between system and environment has become increasingly important: allopoietic systems, or systems that produce something other than themselves (like an assembly line), are determined externally in terms of their objectives and limits. Autopoietic systems produce and reproduce themselves and determine their limits autonomously. They can be disturbed, but not controlled, from outside and as such they are described as being informationally closed. Biological, thought (psychological), and social (commu-

Jonas, W. 1994. *Design, System, Theorie: Überlegungen zu einem systemtheoretischen Modell von Designtheorie.* Essen: Verlag Die Blaue Eule.

nicative) systems can be described as separate autopoietic systems (Niklas Luhmann).

The aversion many traditional designers have to the concept of a system is based on a misunderstood ideological association with control, mechanism, rationality, and so on. In contrast to technology, however, system design always deals with conglomerates of artifacts (allopoietic), organisms, consciousnesses, and communications (autopoietic), which can never be completely controlled, planned for or designed. System design describes the competency of dealing with ignorance. WJ |

→ *Components, Constructivism, Gestaltung, Organization, Networking*

T

TARGET GROUP

A target group is a set of people to whom a producer aims to advertise and sell a product or service. The concept of target group, originally target audience, emerged from psychological research and marketing studies, particularly those conducted by sociologist Paul Lazarsfeld. Lazarsfeld found that people formed judgments of services (such as radio programs) primarily through interactions with others; communications with consumers should therefore be held with an understanding of their (→) social environments.

Companies initially worked with market segmentations, based on socio-demographic variables such as age, sex, and income, to design and sell consumer products. Some went on to use Maslow's hierarchy of human (→) needs to argue that the increase of affluence and security created post-materialist milieus in the Western world. This development led to greater subtlety in market segmentation with research into niches, (→) lifestyles, and consumer needs. Another development, the digitalization of production, prompted the emergence of user-centered design and design-oriented research with in-depth, ethnographic studies into consumers' lives and user profiles using devices such as (→) personas and (→) scenario planning. Driven by mass (→) customization, attention to the niche, and the emergence of Web 2.0, current participatory approaches place an even greater emphasis on consumer input, involving users at the outset of the production process instead of at the end. Design research on the potential of usage-led design is being conducted using methods such as co-design. [SB]

→ *Market Research, Needs Assessment, Participatory Design, Product, Product Development, Research, Usability*

TEAMWORK

→ *Collaborative Design*

TEASER

The term "teaser" in film is used to describe a short sequence of scenes to advertise an upcoming feature. The teaser is generally shorter in length and appears much earlier than the separate (→) "trailer," which is typically produced closer to the release date. In online journalism, especially on news portals, the home page often consists of a collection of different teasers that point to the content of articles, usually in the form of headlines on which the readers are encouraged to click. [TK]

→ *Advertisement, Audiovisual Design, Broadcast Design*

TEMPLATE

A template is anything that serves as a guide or (→) pattern (such as a stencil or mold) from which other similar things can be made and, by extension, can refer to systems or protocols that can be followed in non-manufacturing situations. Templates are a very important form for designers. They are used in a wide array of design processes and are a means to set up a design for future use and adaptation by users without returning to the designer. A template might be used to establish a graphic style for documents and forms, to determine consistent page (→) layouts and formats for desktop publishing, make mold forms used in manufacturing processes, or to develop source code in software development and so on. TM |
→ *Model, Prototype*

TESTING

Almost all designed (→) artifacts and services have to be tested in some way or other. This is to determine if the design performs as originally conceived and intended or to identify unexpected consequences prior to a design going into final production and distribution, or implementation. The method of testing varies greatly according to the type of design being undertaken and the intended (→) use. Design testing ranges from relatively informal methods of observation to assess simple (→) usability, to complex technical testing to determine (→) ergonomic, material, and mechanical viability through to highly structured and rigorous "blind" testing methods that remove all biases and instruction by the designer so as to determine potential usage problems. The more complex areas such as (→) software development have very lengthy testing periods—known as beta testing—to attempt to fine-tune the product through extensive periods of use. TM |
→ *Evaluation, Design Process, Needs Assessment, Product Development*

TEXTILE DESIGN

A textile is a cloth or fabric made from a network of natural or artificial fibers. It can be woven or knitted, crocheted, felted, or knotted. Textiles can satisfy an enormous range of requirements from the strictly utilitarian to purely decorative, they can be extremely strong and durable or delicate and fragile. The cultural significance of textile designs, as well as the techniques used tp produce them, can be traced back thousands of years. The twentieth and twenty-first centuries have introduced fundamental changes to the produc-

The design of textile surfaces that have been woven, knitted, felted, and so on, has a history that dates back many centuries. The production of weaving (which has been dated to the early Stone Age based on impressions left in fragments of clay) went hand in hand with a desire for (→) ornamentation by means of patterns (an individual motif repeated).

The possibilities for applying a design to a textile surface are diverse: printing (woodblock, wax resist, roller, silkscreen, tie-dye), embroidery (including beads and sequins), and appliqué (from fabric to feathers), to name a few of the most common processes. The process of weaving also offers design possibilities. There are three basic types of weave: plain or tabby weave (one over, one under—calico, organza, canvas, taffeta); twill (two or more over, one or more under with a steplike offset making a diagonal pattern—denim, gabardine, tweed, chino); and satin or atlas (a warp-dominated weave four or more over, one under and a two to eight thread offset, yielding a slippery, smooth fabric with a shiny and a dull side). Each has a different surface structure resulting from right-angled intersections of warp (the lengthwise threads in the loom) and weft (the threads inserted crosswise to the warp). By combining and varying these three basic types and their derivations, it is possible to produce a large number of structures, both one after the other and next to one another. Velvet, plush, and terry are among the weaves that introduce a third dimension: the upright tuft.

Using warp threads of different colors or inserting colored warp threads results in lengthwise and crosswise stripes, respectively; single warp or weft threads of a different color can produce other geometrical patterns, including checks. Figurative patterns (which date back to about 2000 BC) were made possible by an elaborate process: a dobby loom, for which the "draw boy" raised/pulled the warp threads according to a specific system.

All of the hand processes for producing textiles have been mechanized over the past three centuries. Industrialization began in the mid-eighteenth century (the first spinning machine, the Spinning Jenny, appeared in 1767 and the first mechanical loom in 1787). The invention of the Jacquard loom, named after its designer, Joseph-Marie Jacquard, made it possible to produce colorfully patterned and figurative weaves mechanically.

In the industrial era, patterns ceased to be the unique assets of a weaver or printer but were created by specially trained (→) pattern designers. There continued to be artists who produced patterns for textile products (not just fabrics but embroidery, carpets, and tapestries), but for a long time they were not identified by name. The first training center for pattern designers was established in the silk factory in Lyons in the early nineteenth century.

In the mid-nineteenth century, the suitable and contemporary form of a pattern began to be discussed. William Morris (→ *Arts & Crafts*) and Christopher Dresser made use of medieval motifs for their designs of decorative fabrics, tapestries, and carpets, and translated the old formal idiom into a contemporary form that took into account the two-dimensional principles of textiles.

On the European continent, in studios and workshops like the Wiener Werkstätte (Viennese Workshops 1903) and (→) Deutscher Werkbund, the idea of the *Gesamtkunstwerk*, or total work of art, was pursued, and textiles (both household textiles and clothing fabrics) were incorporated into this. Until that time, artists (such as Raoul Dufy and Sonia Delauney) or architects (Henry van de Velde and Josef Hoffmann) had provided the designs for patterns, but the (→) Bauhaus in Weimar and later Dessau trained the first industrial textile designers (including Gunta Stölzl, Anni Albers, and Hajo Rose). The Bauhaus also experimented with especially tightly woven yarns (known as *Eisengarn,* literally, iron yarn) and other synthetic materials like cellophane.

At the Bauhaus, there were no pattern designs for printed fabrics (printed patterns were considered ornamentation additional to weaving); weaving and using colored weft threads were the only methods used to create patterns for the surface design. That was not the case in Russia, where artists such as Ludmilla Popova created special printed patterns (which were particularly inexpensive) with political messages and images of tractors and airplanes for the masses.

In Krefeld in the mid-1930s (1932–38), the Höhere Fachschule für textile Flächenkunst (Advanced Technical School for Two-Dimensional Textile Arts) was established, with Johannes Itten as its director. In 1938 it was turned into a master class directed by Georg Muche, having been absorbed by the Textilingenieurschule Krefeld (now the Hochschule Niederrhein). There, as at the Bauhaus, weaving patterns were created based on weaves and colored weft threads, but they also produced new types of printed fabrics with painted surfaces and glow-in-the-dark pigments.

Not only artificial dyes but also the first artificial yarns had appeared by the end of the nineteenth century. Until then, all fibers had been naturally occurring, derived from plants (flax had been made into linen, cotton used for voiles, cambric and calico) or animals (wool from sheep for serge, suiting and tweed as well as rarer or more precious fibers such as camelhair, cashmere, angora from rabbits, mohair from goats, silk from silkworm larvae and alpaca). Artificial silk (viscose) was one of the main attractions at the World's Fair in Paris in 1889. Viscose (cellulose extracted from wood by means of sodium hydroxide) was the first synthetic fabric (1884) and it was followed by man-made threads produced from synthetic materials: nylon, the first commercially successful synthetic polymer (1935), polyester (1941), acrylic (1942), and spandex or elastane (1959). Synthetic fibers did not have the same properties as natural ones, such as the ability to absorb moisture, be permeable to air and so on, but they had different features, including being tear-resistant or wrinkle-free. In contrast to natural fibers, they could be produced directly without extensive preparatory phases, and were considerably cheaper and more versatile in terms of use.

Meanwhile, the productivity of weaving was increased by further mechanizing the weaving process (inserting the weft thread by means of a jet of water or, later, air). The rising demand for textiles could be met in this way from the mid-twentieth century onward, and this accelerated fashion trends (→ Fashion Design, Trend) in the clothing sector. Colors and patterns changed every season, reflective of an increasing preference for printed fabrics. The technical preparations were not as elaborate as for woven patterns, but here too technical innovations accelerated the production process (screen printing was patented in the United States in 1907 and rotary screen printing was introduced in the 1960s).

In 1940s London, Zika and Lida Ascher brought together experimental techniques with artistic design, screen printing designs by Henry Moore, Matisse, and Jean Cocteau to produce collections of high-quality silk scarves. The surfaces were distinguished by elaborate weaving structures and pastose, together with the flexible application of color.

After the Second World War, working with designers became more popular in the case of household textiles, as well. Textile designers trained at the Arts & Crafts schools of the prewar period shaped the corporate image or founded their own companies: Tulipan of Tea Ernst in Germany, Marimekko (1951) in Finland, Lucienne and Robin Day in England, Fritz Hansen and Alvar Aalto in Denmark, and Florence Knoll in the United States. The (→) Deutscher Werkbund experimented with a *Wohnstudio* (living studio) in Berlin to create models for contemporary living that responded to the frequently changing textile trends, as people wanted to be fashionable in their homes as well as in their dress. Whereas up until the 1950s textile designers had typically followed the centuries-old tradition of creating floral patterns, they increasingly began to take their lead from contemporary art, creating emphatically linear, geometric, and psychedelic designs inspired by artists such as Paul Klee, Joan Miró, and Victor Vasarely.

The oil crisis of 1972–73 and the general growth of environmental awareness triggered a transformation that was felt in all aspects of daily life. The sense that there had been a loss of (→) quality due to mass production led to a return to the crafts and to individuality. Several exhibitions (for example, *De main de maître*, in Paris in 1988) addressed the cultural legacy of textiles and their associated techniques. Old (→) craft techniques were increasingly employed during this period; small quantities of fabric were produced on hand looms, yarn was dyed and patterns printed with natural colors, bleaching was done by traditional methods. The British designer Georgina von Etzdorf worked for a full year to produce her hand-printed fabrics featuring rich colors, abstract patterns, and natural fibers such as velvet, chiffon, and silk.

This return to traditional methods also led to an increased awareness of the tactile and other sensory qualities of weaving. Natural fibers began to be preferred and new structures were produced. In Japan, Makiko Minagawa experimented with simulating the character of handwoven fabrics by computer. His compatriot Junichi Arai (who worked for Issey Miyake, among others) used unusually strong yarn to give his woven fabrics an extremely stretched structure to lively effect.

The computerization of the textile industry that had begun in the late 1970s was increasingly exploited by designers: new and old pattern elements were digitalized to produce new composite patterns, as found, for example, in the work of the French designer Nathalie du Pasquier. The use of plotters made it possible to apply different elements and groups of patterns in quick succession to the fabric. The American Jack Lenor Larsen, by contrast, worked primarily with woven patterns and found inspiration in non-European motifs produced in new colors. The computerization of the Jacquard loom, which had already produced a revolution in patterning two centuries earlier, concluded this development by making digital weaving a possibility.

In recent years, the areas in which textiles are employed have increased: in addition to traditional areas such as clothing (athletic attire and sportswear have made particularly innovative use of synthetic and functional fabrics) and household products (featuring transparency or luster, and easy-care properties), exciting new developments in textile design have arisen in the fields of architecture (inflatable halls) and in medicine (antibacterial fabrics and woven materials for heart transplants).

Many of the most important elements of textile design cannot be perceived through sight alone, and much is embedded invisibly within the fibers of a given fabric. Some aspects can be perceived by touch, such as laminated surfaces, bubbled structures alongside delicately worked velvety areas, or applications of flexible paint. Some characteristics can only be appreciated when wearing a garment: protection from cold or heat; wind- and rainproof materials that are nonetheless permeable to skin moisture; protection from ultraviolet radiation; or blocking perspiration odor while releasing perfumes (tiny molecules in swollen fibers). Even while taking these aspects into account, textile designs must simultaneously continue to fulfill aesthetic expectations. KT |

→ *Fashion Design, Haptics, Materials, Texture*

Colchester, C. 1991. *The new textiles: Trends and traditions*. London: Thames & Hudson.
Schoeser, M. 1995. *International textile design*. London: Calmann & King.
Wichmann, H. 1990. *Von Morris bis Memphis: Textilien der Neuen Sammlung Ende 19. bis Ende 20. Jahrhundert*. Basel: Birkhäuser.

TEXTURE

Among the Latin words related to *texere* (to weave) are the nouns *textus, textum,* and *textura* (fabric, web, context, structure; makeup, style) which were applied to the context of the spoken and written word very early on. Texture is considered a fundamental element of design, like (→) form or color. There is no surface without a texture, even if it is as smooth as glass. In design, texture is used, on the one hand, as an immediate, tactile (3-D) or visual (2-D) surface quality and, on the other, in a metaphorical sense, as a stylistic expression or syntactic chain of signs, writing, images, or actions. The entire surface of the world can be read as a web of signs if one follows a structuralist understanding of textuality.

The question as to whether textures are representations of deep structures and hidden truths or simply phenomena perceived by the senses is one raised by all designed surfaces. Many modern debates in the history of design (from Semper's principle of *Bekleidung* [cladding, dressing] to the appropriateness of materials or the prohibition on ornament) can be considered from this perspective. With the advent of (→) postmodernism, the design of the surfaces of products, also known as (→) styling, became an essential factor in designing products that appealed to individuals in specific (→) target groups and to represent the spirit of the times. Textures take on the same communicative functions as the objects they are applied to: the functions of retextured clothes, wristwatches, mobile phones, tennis shoes, and furniture can be perceived entirely differently once their surfaces have been altered, even if their essential forms remain the same. The dichotomy of shell and core continues in the twenty-first century, if perhaps less marked by moralistic claims to truth—though the core is becoming increasingly dematerialized and the shell is becoming increasingly autonomous. Newly developed textiles take on the function of technical interfaces; haptic displays organize communications or give "force feedbacks" in which resistance is perceived as a material quality. In digital parallel universes (at Google Earth, for example) and virtual game realities, by contrast, the focus is on the illusionistic function of texture. In order to simulate materiality in CAD models (→ *CAD/CAM/CIM/CNC*), material surfaces—so-called pattern textures—from preexisting texture libraries for designers and architects (much like nineteenth-century pattern books) are mapped onto renderings of volumes. Whether tangible or not, textures offer stimuli to (→) perception and remain—with varying degrees of semantic transparency (or intelligence)—communicative interfaces between people and things. RM |

→ *Coating, Haptics, Materials, Ornament, Textile Design*

THEORY

Design exists both as practice and as theoretical reflection. As a consequence, the questions repeatedly arise as to whether, and in what ways, the (→) practice of design is dependent on, reflects on, and develops theory. The variety of theoretical forms and modes of reflection that designers engage in is itself a strong indicator that theory is essential to design practice in a number of ways. Recognizing this diversity and the related opportunities, the (→) design process that repeatedly links practice and theory in new ways represents persistent challenges for the designer. This text is an attempt to extend this variety on the basis of examining different factors and using a range of examples that can expand designers' possibilities.

From a phenomenological perspective, it is striking that designers have developed and referred to heterogeneous and contradictory forms of theory and modes of reflection for very different reasons and with a wide variety of objectives. A few representative functions of theory in design, which can occur alone or in combination, include:

· Theory as reflection: design repeatedly arrives at a point at which reflecting on its own actions, results, and processes becomes essential when deciding between diverse design possibilities, positioning one's own ideas, analyzing specific questions in the design process, and locating one's own action in the context of other design perspectives, attitudes, and so on.

· Theory as contextualization: design does not happen in isolation but rather, refers to the various social, cultural, and intellectual perspectives on design, to the possibilities of the medium, and to the history or present-day state of one's own field of action. This contextualization provides design with a well-grounded orientation and with the opportunity to find its way within a system of reference and establish its own identity.

· Theory as generalization: to develop an attitude and perspective on the context of design, it is essential to generalize aspects of it so the theory becomes independent of problem-specific questions and solutions and can become a reference and orienting framework for the process and contextualization of a design.

· Theory as communication: the design process often requires the discussion and exchange of results, information and developments with others who are directly or indirectly involved. Intelligible documentation and analysis of the design context, concept, and process are critical to providing the foundation necessary for this communication to take place.

· Theory as justification: theoretical reflection and the persuasive presentation of key results, decisions, and opportunities in the design process are important prerequisites to the critical consideration and justification of one's own working methods—particularly in response to the questions, proposals, and conflicts from various perspectives on the design proposition.

· Theory as critique: the reflective and analytical justification of one's own design practice (and those of others) will lead back to critiquing one's own (and others') opinions. Critical debate and analysis is essential to shaping perspectives on design: what it is, what is taken for granted, what could be, what should be developed and so on.

· Theory as (→) evaluation: the design process can involve evaluations and assessments of strategies, questions, perspectives, and solutions. Theories are relevant to this process as they can explain or criticize these evaluations, localize or question them, justify or challenge them, establish them as self-evident or expose them as problematic—thereby making renegotiation possible.

The objectives of different theories vary according to their stages of development. It is essential to understand whether a way of thinking or a perspective is to be understood explicitly as a theory, understanding that a theory's claim to be scientific frequently plays a central role in this determination. The question of what should or should not be considered "scientific" in relation to design theory and practice is controversial for a number of reasons.

· Science-based theories on design may justify their claim to science by selecting the method of reflection that explicitly formulates and justifies their own premises and central statements. Due to the controversies about what constitutes empirical evidence, it is important to reflect on one's own definition and to consider the assumptions behind a "universal understanding of science."

· The experience of observing, feeling, and acting enables us to develop our own (everyday) theorems to describe, explain, and relate important everyday phenomena and events and their context. These "everyday theories" can be formed from individual experiences or collective traditions. The transition from "everyday theories" to typologies, overgeneralizations, prejudices, and faith is, however, fluid.

· Theories of implicit understanding, developed by sociologists of knowledge, argue that "everyday theories," unlike scientific theories, are typically not formulated and formalized explicitly but formed implicitly from situated experiences and then updated and depicted in actions, stories, and examples. Implicit theory is therefore most often conveyed through the performance of everyday actions, and are appropriated, embodied, updated, and refined in specific situations and contexts.

· Practice-based theories are typically not about explanations and justifications ("knowing why"), but rather about establishing facts ("knowing what") and instructions for action ("knowing how"). Consequently, theories of (→) practice are focused primarily on action and effectiveness rather than reflection. The goal is to support, accompany, and standardize everyday actions and practice and generate and communicate practical information.

· Practitioner theories raise the question of the theoretician themselves. The role of the theorist is not limited to scientifically based (→) research; any active subject has this capacity including the designer—for example, when working with (→) sketches, (→) prototypes, and solutions as part of designing and referencing them, reflecting on them, making them explicit, and communicating them. The visual, linguistic, textual, and media-based statements that designers make can be regarded and discussed as an autonomous form of developing theory in design.

· "As if" theories are highly relevant to designers who frequently deal playfully and subversively with common-sense expectations of (scientific) theories by reinterpreting, revaluing, shifting, and transforming them.

The relationship of theory to practice should be considered on the basis of the distinction between theory and practice presumed in these reflections. Some sociologists of knowledge argue that the primary concern in this context is to describe more precisely the possible relationships and mechanisms of transition between theory and practice, while others take the position that the very distinction between theory and practice must be called into question using the following arguments.

· The dependence of language and observation on theory: a variety of debates have pointed out that every verbal utterance and, under some circumstances every observation, is already tied to theoretical premises and general concepts and either explicitly or implicitly presume abstract ideas and idealizing typologies (→ Observational Research). Specifically, this means that any statement is always dependent on theory and implicitly expresses a theoretical perspective.

· Practice as a form of reflection: it seems plausible that assertions about design can be reflected on visually, tested by media, and communicated and discussed through artifacts. This makes it difficult to distinguish sharply between design theory and design practice since such a distinction does not take into account the essential, integrative quality of action and reflection in design.

· The sociology of knowledge: certain sociologists have pointed out that no objectively binding and irreproachable method can make conclusive decisions about a theory's correctness and validity. It is the scientific community of researchers and practitioners who, at a given point in time, determine by their specific actions a theory's validity and relevance, its significance and weight, and its appropriate application to and translation into practice. They do so by deciding during the specific design process and situation which theories they want to refer to and how they will do so.

· Historicity and openness: in the design process it is essential that the historical and temporal dimension of theoretical developments be taken seriously. Theoretical perspectives that are at one point widely dismissed as dissident or problematic by a majority of those involved can, at another point in time, be reintroduced as innovative, and have a significant impact on questioning or displacing established positions. The contentious interplay of competing theoretical perspectives together with current questions of design is constantly defining, forming, and restructuring itself. It can best be understood as an open process of searching, discussing, exploring, and researching, in which designers can take part by reflecting and doing. Theoretical developments are also subject to the cycles of fashion.

Circulating references: recent studies of science have concluded that theory and practice are not antithetical or even clearly different but rather mark two abstract, inaccessible points of extremity, between which the specific practice of research, of daily life, and consequently of design oscillate in an effort either to continue unquestioned and thus stabilize established abstractions and approaches, or assert and affirm new connections.

In conclusion, the particular characteristics of design suggest that a great variety of theoretical approaches and modes of reflection are deployed in the design process; a heterogeneity of structural and formal dimensions of theory are systematically postulated and discussed; design's theories are formed with different objectives in mind; and the question of the relationship between theory and practice is controversial and independent of the specific conceptions of practice or theory being advocated. Designers always have to orient and locate themselves in a variety of contexts and situations within this field of possibilities. SG |

→ *Design Methods, Design Process, Practice, Rhetoric*

Heiz, A. V. 2003. *Design—ein Zwischenfall: Annäherung an Theorie und Praxis.* Zurich: ITH.
Jollant-Kneebone, F. 2003. *La critique en design.* Nîmes: Éditions Jacqueline Chambon.
Margolin, V., ed. 1989. *Design discourse: History, theory, criticism.* Chicago: Univ. of Chicago Press.
Meier, C. 2001. *Designtheorie: Beiträge zu einer Disziplin.* Frankfurt am Main: Anabas-Verlag.

TIME-BASED DESIGN

Time-based design refers to the use of measured time intervals for sequences of images and/or sounds in either real time or recreated (→) performances. The designer generally begins by using notation methods such as screenplays, time lines, musical scores, Labanotation, (→) storyboards, and animation exposure sheets to shape the use of time. The performed event is often (but not always) recorded onto a time-based medium such as videotape, digital storage media, or film and then reproduced by means of projection onto a screen or broadcasting technology. Some of the most readily recognizable examples of time-based design include (→) audiovisual design, cinematographic design, title design, motion graphics, (→) animation, and interactive media such as (→) game design and (→) virtual reality. However, because of the ubiquity of time in human experience, the term can also apply to the design of dance, sound, music, systems, data, kinetic sculpture, architecture, electronics—even the production process itself. AS |

→ *Broadcast Design, Continuity, Screen Design, Virtuality*

TITLE DESIGN

→ *Broadcast Design*

TOOLS

Broadly speaking, a tool is any course of action, occurrence, thought, or (→) object that assists, facilitates, or makes possible another course of action, occurrence, thought, or object. In design, tools are generally used in the construction of hand-crafted or manufactured objects through manual or mechanical activity, the generation and organization of (→) information, or the accomplishment of design-related tasks. Often they take the (→) form of a physical object (that is a hand-held device or machine) that is used to accomplish a particular action requiring certain properties—that is, strength, skills, dexterity, stamina—that the user does not possess or only accesses with difficulty. Other times, they refer to systems, protocols, programs—even individual people. Tools are therefore defined by the context of their (→) use. For instance, in the context of computing, a tool has two distinct definitions: a program used to create, change, or analyze other programs, or an aspect of a program used to shortcut a process or accomplish a task. TWH |
→ *Affordance, Function, Product*

TRADEMARK

"Trademark" is the generic term for (→) symbols that identify a (→) brand, a company, or a service. In a somewhat less specific form, trademarks have existed since the time of the Romans or earlier, and were used by fourteenth-century artisans as a sales tool to indicate the origin and quality of their products. Today, trademarks can be registered and officially protected at a national, multinational, or global patent office.

Some trademarks are purely text-based and merely indicate the name of a company or product. Visual trademarks, by contrast, utilize appropriate graphic symbols. A combination of graphic and textual elements is usually called a (→) logo.

In today's global economy with its complex structures and rapid cycles of (→) innovation, it is increasingly important to offer a means of orientation and differentiation. Largely as a result of the Internet's rise and the growing availability of multimedia networks, the traditionally two-dimensional world of the trademark has expanded to include the incorporation of sounds and smells as well as animated and three-dimensional trademarks (→ *Olfactory Design, Sound Design*). There are also so-called flexible trademarks, which are based on the design concept of constantly changing the form and color. KSP |
→ *Copyright, Corporate Identity, Intellectual Property*

TRAILER

The term "trailer" is commonly used in the film industry to describe a brief sequence of scenes intended to arouse the viewer's curiosity about a particular film. They may also be used to advertise the launch of a new television show, computer or video game. Typically shown before feature films or on television alongside other (→) advertisements, trailers have evolved typical design forms—certain gestures, cuts, and perspectives—in order to effectively convey (→) information and draw attention to the film, show, or game in a time-efficient way. TG |

→ *Audiovisual Design, Broadcast Design, Teaser*

TRANSDISCIPLINARY

→ *Discipline*

TRANSFORMATION

Transformation describes very well a core competency in design: namely, the ability to take one thing (materials, views, experiences, processes, and so on) and turn it into another. The word derives from the Latin and means "reshaping." Transformation indicates in general a change of shape, (→) form, or structure without loss of substance. The most important method of transformation is variation. In principle, it involves two different substances that need to be defined: transformations of material (form versus material) and of content (form versus content).

The concept of transformation is increasingly applied in the (→) design process to parameters relevant to technology, production, and reception. Transformation in the realm of digital design occupies a unique position. The use of databases, games, and Internet sites such as blogs, and so on, always leads to transformation. The substance of this transformation is an invisible and variable data record (→ *Software*), so that one could say that such a transformation is one of substance. Traditionally, however, this would only be said of the physical substance of the computer (→ *Hardware*). ESC |

→ *Design Competence, Gestaltung, Materials*

TRANSPORTATION DESIGN

Transportation design is a concept that covers the design of all means of transportation, traffic networks, routes, and the services connected to them. The term is most often used in context with vehicle design, and sometimes in the English-speaking world it is used as an alternative to (→) automobile design. There is a recognizable trend toward increasing the role of design in all forms of modern-day popular means of transportation, from the plane to the boat, from the automobile to the truck and the train, from the bicycle to the motorcycle. Individual (→) components are assembled under a skin made of metal or plastic that offers functional and technical advantages, and that becomes another arena for design advantage and differentiation (→ *Coating, Styling*). Technology that relies on electronics has produced new functions and opportunities for comfort that have in turn been integrated into the design. At the same time, manufacturing using modular constructions has gained acceptance and this now permits manufacturers of streetcars, for example, to distribute their products worldwide while making regional adaptations for local markets.

The process of integration, electronic control, and modularization in the construction of vehicles make them more complex. Transportation design today is expected to integrate a vehicle's exterior and interior design as completely as possible while simultaneously contributing to (→) brand identity. Transportation design has had to meet higher physical demands, such as rapid acceleration and abrupt braking. Quickly changing temperatures and weather conditions place additional limitations on the use of (→) materials and their design, as do the many safety requirements (→ *Safety Design*) that have led to a dramatic decrease in the number of fatal accidents despite a considerable increase in automobile use.

Budgets for developing various means of transportation can vary considerably. The introduction of industrial automobile manufacturing has resulted in different sets of rules for infrastructure and marketing and hence the attention paid to design (→) quality and execution has varied considerably.

The attention devoted to the automobile as a means of individual transport in developed industrial nations has increased constantly since the mid-1950s. Indeed, it could be claimed that the individual (→) customization of innumerable industrial products started with the automobile. Public transportation such as trains and buses, on the other hand, have been neglected for a long time, including from the design perspective. Nevertheless, a renaissance of train design and manufacture occurred in France, Spain, and Germany in the mid-1980s, beginning with the construction of new high-speed railway links that soon expanded to include trains, stations, waiting rooms, and signs. Initially, there was no attempt to call on the experience of other nations, such as Japan, for example. Railway companies were thinking very much in national terms and largely renounced such transfer of proficiency. One of the aims was to make trains desirable as a premium means of transportation for business travelers and to develop an attractive alternative to the airplane for midrange journeys. Correspondingly, aspects of airplane design influenced the design of trains.

This process of renewal is very instructive when considering transportation design. In the Netherlands, for example, new railway lines are developed in collaboration with designers, while in Germany high-speed routes correspond to the design ideals of the railroad engineers who devised them. The design of the

German high-speed train ICE (Inter City Express) was a political issue from the outset, in which the contractor (Deutsche Bahn—German Railways) struggled with the manufacturing companies as well as various design offices for supremacy.

The comfort of the passengers could be markedly improved by using new materials and production methods. However, the integrated design approach found in automobile design, that results in a consistently improved experience for the user and that affects every detail, still remains the exception rather than the rule. As the airplane evolved from an elite means of transportation for special occasions (as it was in the 1950s) to the relatively inexpensive mass transport machines of today, it was not just the technology and construction of airplanes that changed, but also—and importantly for passengers—the formal design of the cabins. Their modular standard equipment and furnishings can, according to the airline and the class, correspond to the very simplest or the most luxurious design standards. Whereas the tubular steel furniture of the 1920s was first used on airships, today's reclining armchairs and beds in first-class transatlantic airplanes look like cheap, tired copies of styles of domestic furniture.

The situation is much the same in the design of passenger ships whose interior details often seem to be taken from a stylebook of international mainstream hotel design. Individual means of transportation have certainly established something akin to design standards (as questionable as this may seem in practice), yet the links between transportation design and transportation architecture appear quite tentative. For example, intelligent design is rarely found when automobiles have to be integrated with airports or railway stations, or even when passengers have to transfer from one flight to another.

At a time of increasing concern about the reality of climate change, strategic transportation design also has to develop ways to avoid excess traffic while maintaining (→) mobility. Nevertheless, the concrete tasks of transportation design remain seriously fragmented. It remains rare to find realistic and robust links between different transportation systems, despite intense creative efforts in the field of transportation design and attention to detail. TE |

Bodack, K.-D. 2005. *InterRegio: Die abenteuerliche Biografie eines deutschen Zugsystems*. Freiburg: EK-Verlag.
Erlhoff, M., ed. 1992. *ICE: Der Zug ist abgefahren*. Göttingen: Steidl.
Form Spezial 2. 1998. "Alles, was Menschen bewegt." Special issue on transportation design.
Kries, M., ed. 1999. *Automobility: Was uns bewegt*. Weil am Rhein: Design Museum Weil.

TREND

A trend is a relatively durable direction, (→) style, or preference in consumer behavior that results in a prolonged market movement in one general direction. Although trends are most often associated with fashion (→ *Fashion Design*), they play an important role in the conception, design, marketing, and (→) consumption of all consumer goods and services. Trends often start as fads (and a fad may be the resurgence of a once-fashionable style), but the two should not be confused. A fad is a style of short duration that could be represented by an inverted "U" on a graph. A trend, however, is tracked on a graph by a typical "S" curve. Rather than sinking into quick oblivion, a trend is sustained upon reaching saturation.

Trends may be initiated or driven by prominent or respected figures—that is trendsetters—that give them a certain cachet. The development of trends is also influenced by changes in technology, politics, consumer (→) needs, economics, and other factors in popular culture and world events; as a result, trends often reflect the shifting (→) values of the societies in which they take place. For example, in *The Language of Fashion* (1993), Roland Barthes shows that the movement toward standardization of masculine clothing was produced by the French Revolution, which resulted in men's clothing that was democratic, practical, dignified, and austere. In contrast, the hip-hop clothing trends of today are derived from the romanticization of prison styles and are an extension of the adolescent "rebel" trend of the late 1950s (popularized by Elvis Presley in "Jailhouse Rock"). By emulating qualities of masculinity associated with prisoners (such as toughness, strength), the wearers of these looks simultaneously identify themselves as a group and position themselves in opposition to the established attire associated with success (suit and tie). The evolution of this trend can be read as a kind of visual and material code, revealing the shifting identifications of power within gender conventions across time.

A fashion trend that has been reinvented several times over is denim. Originally invented in the 1850s by Levi Strauss as sturdy trousers for gold-rush workers, blue jeans have been popular since the post-Second World War era when they were introduced to the world by American soldiers. In the 1950s, they were popularized for children and became a fad for rebellious teens (famously worn by James Dean in *Rebel without a Cause*), and again during the counterculture years of the 1960s. It wasn't until the 1970s, however, when they were expressly made to fit women, that blue jeans became a bona fide international trend. And in the twenty-first century, the trend has been reinvented yet again as the "luxury jean," a status symbol that demonstrates the power of the brand in the current marketplace and provides a marked distinction from its humble origins.

Identifying, understanding, and predicting trends is important for a number of industries, particularly fashion, and trend spotting and trend forecasting have themselves become a trend in advertising, marketing, and retail. Trend spotting and trend forecasting are conducted using techniques and processes from

Barthes, R. 1993. *Le système de la mode.* In *Œuvres complètes, 1962–1967*. Paris: Éditions du Seuil. English trans. by A. Stafford as *The language of fashion*. Oxford: Berg, 2006.
Popcorn, F. 1996. *Clicking.* New York: HarperCollins.

TV DESIGN

TYPOGRAPHY

psychology, the social sciences, and (→) intuition (and perhaps a bit of smoke and mirrors), in order to tap into sustained currents of thinking, feeling, and behavior. As these techniques are further developed, companies are increasingly able to not only capitalize on the shifting of styles and tastes across time, but also direct them. PK |

→ *Semiotics, Social, Symbol*

→ *Broadcast Design*

Marshall McLuhan, in his ground-breaking book of 1967, *The Medium Is the Massage*, said: "The goose quill put an end to talk. It abolished mystery; it gave architecture and towns; it brought roads and armies, bureaucracy. It was the basic metaphor with which the cycle of civilization began, the step from the dark into the light of the mind. The hand that filled the parchment page built a city."

The invention of movable type was the next major leap in human social development. What up until then an individual had to write once by hand, or even chisel in stone, could now be repeated anywhere and everywhere. The separation of action and function was the condition for most of the developments of the modern age: individualism, democracy, Protestantism, capitalism, and nationalism. The technology of printing and typesetting fundamentally altered our habits of (→) perception.

The general term "typography" refers to the functions of typeface design and the arrangement of type and other elements on a page. This page can also be a computer screen or the wall of a building. Up until the introduction of mechanized typesetting, compositors were the only typographers and, as such, they were also responsible for designing the pages. The history of typography is both a history of technology and of culture. Each technical development left its trace in typographic design and (→) layout. The classification of typefaces employs the same descriptions as those used for stylistic periods in architecture.

It was the goldsmith Johannes Gutenberg (ca. 1398–1468) who first had the idea of cutting single letters as steel punches. These were stamped into metal to make molds, which, in turn, were filled with a soft metal. Working in Mainz around 1450, Gutenberg also developed the tools for type founding, which remained in use almost unchanged until the mid-nineteenth century. The first printing press consisted of a screw press, like those used to press grapes. The thin liquid inks that had been used to print from wooden panels were unsuitable for printing from lead characters. Gutenberg formulated an emulsion using linseed oil and soot that was sufficiently thick and dried quickly.

Each sheet of paper had to be inserted and removed by hand. It was 1814 before the *Times* became the first newspaper in the world to be printed on a steam-powered press made by Koenig & Bauer, a German company, allowing the production of up to 1,100 copies per hour. Twenty years later the industrial manufacture of type using casting machines would also become a practical reality.

The punchcutters in Italy of the late fifteenth century, such as Nicolas Jenson (1420–1480) or Aldus Manutius (1449–1515), based the design of their lowercase characters on the cursive humanistic minuscule writing. Due to their geographic and historical origin these are classified as Venetian Renaissance Antiqua. As it still is to this day, the uppercase was modeled on the unrivalled Roman Capitalis, as represented on the Trajan column in Rome. Named after a cardinal, Bembo (ca. 1495) by Aldus Manutius and his punchcutter Francesco Griffo (1449–1518) marks the end of this development and is the prototype for Renaissance Antiqua. It took several centuries for the cursive forms to be integrated into complete typeface families. To this day they are known in English as italics, acknowledging their Italian origins.

The most famous representative of the French Renaissance Antiqua was the Parisian punchcutter Claude Garamond (ca. 1499–1561). He and his contemporary Robert Granjon (1513–1589) are the originators of the typeface known as Garamond, which became the most common typeface for books around 1600. The large Garamond family of typefaces still remains among the most commonly used today.

At the beginning of the seventeenth century the Netherlands became the center for type founding. The typefaces at the height of the Baroque period are more casual, more robust and therefore more functional than the Renaissance typefaces. The typefaces of the Englishman William Caslon (1692–1766) represent the peak of this development. His designs may not be particularly innovative or original but were pragmatic in the British tradition and soon spread successfully. Britain's expansion as a colonial power certainly helped in this and it became very popular in America leading to the Declaration of Independence of the United States of America actually being set in Caslon.

Classicism in typography, as in architecture, was never very inclined toward luxurious adornment. The ideals of the Enlightenment also required typography to suggest clarity and generosity. Symmetry and reduction were the overriding principles of design. As it became possible to print larger forms with greater precision, books increased in size (the first all-iron Stanhope press was built in 1800). Technology allowed serifs to be designed very delicately and for a lot of detail to be expressed in the characters. Constructing letters with the precision of a compass and ruler may have led to the desired ideal shapes, but the typefaces were actually harder to read than their Renaissance and Baroque predecessors.

Giovanni Battista ("Giambattista") Bodoni (1740–1813) was called the King of Printers and Printer of Kings. Bodoni devised and cut 270 different alphabets, for which he had to engrave some 55,000 steel punches by hand.

The beginning of the industrial revolution in the early nineteenth century led to different production requirements, and with that came a proliferation of manufactured goods. Typefaces from previous centuries were neither technically nor formally suitable for the large-format printing of product and services advertisements. Now headlines had to scream and ruthlessly use up what little space there was. Fast steam-powered printing machines like the press for the *Times* (1814) enabled large editions to be printed quickly, but were rather harsh on the printing materials. The high-speed platen presses in particular, first introduced by Isaak Adam in Boston in 1830, really damaged the fine lines of classical typefaces with their delicate, tapered serifs and subtle details.

If serifs are not there they cannot break off, while bold serifs withstand the rigors of printing better. Sans serif typefaces also take up less space while slab serif letters appear loud and impressive. The first sans serif typeface appeared in 1816 in a catalog from the Caslon type foundry, and was unaccountably called Egyptian.

Actually that term describes slab serif typefaces, while Vincent Figgins (1766–1844) still called a serif an Antique.

Typography soon changed to fit the new (→) advertisement typefaces. Simple pure (→) beauty, as stipulated by Bodoni a few years before, was no longer in demand. Volume, size, and variety were instead the order of the day. White space became expensive, sheets had to be crammed with print right up to the edges. Newspapers had narrow columns in order to squeeze many different topics onto one page, so narrower, more robust typefaces were cut for that purpose. Technology kept up with the increasingly diverse contents of printed material. Around 1829 Firmin Didot in Paris introduced the stereotype, a process of producing letterpress plates by making a mold for a complete page and then casting it in an alloy. The use of several casts made larger print runs possible and meant less wear on the original fonts. In 1838 Moritz Hermann von Jacobi invented galvanizing, with which artwork such as woodcuts could be "lifted" and then copied to make a durable block. Typographers could now integrate illustrations into their pages because text and image were easily printable in one form. The invention of the process block in 1840 made it possible to insert handwritten typefaces or company (→) logos into the page for printing and, around the end of the century, the invention of the halftone screen by Meisenbach meant that photographs could also be reproduced.

Typography toward the end of the nineteenth century could politely be called eclectic. Everything was technically possible, so everything that could be done was done.

Manufacturing techniques around this time determined both the design and production of type. In the United States in 1886 Ottmar Mergenthaler (1854–1899) introduced the Linotype, a line-casting machine principally intended for newspaper setting. Just one year later the Lanston Monotype hit the market, invented by Tolbert Lanston. It cast single letters and was operated by a keyboard. Typographic design was thus subject to the changing parameters of typesetting machines. New typefaces had to be designed that could match the technical requirements of the new machines as well as the prevailing fashions, which changed ever more regularly due to the increasingly short periods between the design and production of type.

The first machine for engraving steel punches was patented by Lynn Boyd Benton (1844–1932) in 1885, enabling the development of the typefaces demanded by the market at this time. Monotype and Linotype were responsible for many reissues of classic typefaces that later served as drafts for the phototypesetting of the 1960s and the first generation of digital typesetting machines in the 1980s. Times New Roman, the most famous of all Antiquas, was designed by Stanley Morison (1889–1967) and Victor Lardent in 1932 at Monotype in England. It was based on Plantin, which F. H. Pierpont had already designed for Monotype in 1913 and which in turn drew on Dutch Baroque typefaces of the seventeenth century.

There was a new form of type being used at the start of the twentieth century, although it still played a minor role. To get a taste of how unusual and alien this new type seemed at the time, contemplate the title of Grotesque given to these typefaces on their first appearance in the early nineteenth century. In the United States the sans serif typefaces were deemed equally strange, earning them the name "Gothic." In Germany, Akzidenz Grotesk, first released in a single weight in Berlin in 1896, is regarded as the mother of its genre.

Sans serif typefaces such as Akzidenz Grotesk and Franklin Gothic trace their origins back to the classical ideal. Univers by Adrian Frutiger (born 1928), the first typeface to be systematically constructed and named as a family, also adheres to this model. The sans serif styles from England also conform to the Renaissance model, the best known being Gill Sans (1928) by Eric Gill (1882–1940).

The design of sans serif typefaces can also be defined by their pure geometric form. In the 1920s every major type foundry in Germany had a form of Grotesque on offer. The most successful of these typefaces was Futura by Paul Renner (1878–1956), released by Bauer in 1928. Although Futura was an exact fit for the kind of typeface espoused for the modern age by the Bauhaus representatives of Elementary Typography, it came out too late to be used for the school's typesetting.

In the 1920s typography became an important (→) discipline because it merged (→) communication and expression. Dadaists like Kurt Schwitters did not set their work in cumbersome lead type, but made montages of prints, photos, and words on shreds of paper. On the other hand De Stijl in the Netherlands and Moholy-Nagy, Joost Schmidt, and Herbert Bayer of the Bauhaus used typefaces, colors and halftone images for book pages, catalogs, and posters. The artist El Lissitzky (1890–1941) was the Soviet cultural delegate in Weimar. There he developed his form of expression, the "typophoto," and strongly influenced his (→) Bauhaus colleagues and De Stijl. In 1925 a young Jan Tschichold (1902–1974) published an essay (using the first name of Iwan) in a special edition of *Typographische Mitteilungen* (Typographic News) under the title "Elementary Typography," his manifesto for a New Typography.

After the Second World War, Swiss graphic design became the prevailing trendsetter, first spreading from Zurich to Germany and then throughout the world. The search for a rational and straightforward typeface led most graphic designers to Akzidenz Grotesk, cast and sold by Berthold in Berlin. The Haas'sche type foundry in Münchenstein had its Haas Grotesk on offer, which could be traced back to Scheltersche Grotesk by Schelter & Giesecke in Leipzig. Scheltersche was the font which lay in the cases at the Bauhaus workshops and in which much of the material was set that represented the eponymous style. It nevertheless didn't quite match the expectations of designers who were looking for a typeface free of historical ballast and which served its function without becoming a feature itself.

The success of Akzidenz Grotesk prompted Eduard Hofmann, business director at Haas, to commission his Swiss colleague Miedinger to finalize sketches for a typeface that would compete in the same market. The Haas'sche type foundry belonged to D. Stempel AG in Frankfurt, which in turn was owned by Linotype. It was Stempel who suggested they find a popular name to help sell the new typeface. It was released as Helvetica (derived from the Latin name for Switzerland) in 1957, the year of the Treaty of Rome and the Citroën DS.

This cool, plain typeface became world famous in the mid-1960s, particularly as American businesses sought to lend themselves a cosmopolitan air of modernity by adopting it as their company typeface. It was no surprise then that it was an American who determined that Helvetica would become the standard typeface for the new tool of the graphic industry. In 1984 Steve Jobs selected the thirteen fonts to be installed on the first Apple laser printer. Among them was Helvetica, the neutral, objective business font, with which one could not go wrong. (Ironically, most computers do not have the original Helvetica typeface installed but make do with a fake. In order to save license fees, Microsoft installed a clone in 1990 that has the same character widths as Helvetica and—like all imitations—is formally inferior. But it can be found under the name Arial in all font menus and it has thus become the most used word processor font.)

The type foundries had already reworked the classic typefaces for new typesetting systems. They had to do so again in the late 1960s, when the first phototypesetting machines came on the market. The designs were no longer cut in steel and cast in lead, but drawn and transferred photographically onto carriers from which each letter was projected onto film. As the new material was not subject to any mechanical limitations, typeface designers were free from creative restrictions. Many of the 1970s typefaces can now be compared with the exuberant typography that appeared toward the end of the nineteenth century. The International Typeface Corporation (ITC) in New York not only released many typefaces that reflected the spirit of advertising on Madison Avenue, they also had a new distribution model. Until then all manufacturers of typesetting systems had their own type formats that could not be used on their competitors' machines. This gave graphic designers and typographers an incentive to favor a particular system because each offered exclusive access to certain fonts. At the same time it allowed many companies to prosper by either copying typefaces and selling poor imitations cheaply or altering them slightly and releasing them under different names. The ITC now delivered artwork to all manufacturers who paid license fees, and consequently these ITC-registered typefaces were the only fonts that were available on all machines.

Phototypesetting fonts could be made to any size and placed in any position on a page by paper or film makeup. The right angle was no longer all-important for the layout. For the hippie design practitioners of the flower power era this was excellent news. The end of the design process always required a piece of film from which the printing plate was produced. Apart from a type-setter, this process requires a reproduction photographer who was required to capture the images on film, a lithographer or finished artist to copy and combine type and images for each individual color, and graphic designers to have the ideas and specify layouts.

This mode of production became outdated virtually overnight in the mid-1980s with the invention of Adobe's page description language PostScript by John Warnock and Chuck Geschke. This computer language allows every point on a page to be defined and marked to within a thousandth of a millimeter. Everything, including images, graphic elements, or type, is composed of tiny pixels that are transferred to paper, film or printing plate by laser beam or ink jet.

The appearance of the Apple Macintosh along with the first laser typesetter by Linotype established desktop publishing (DTP). The job description of typesetters became that of a digital media designer. In addition to the visualization of ideas, graphic de-signers today are responsible for the layout of the entire page, which typically goes to press without the need for film exposure of any other visual manifestation. The end of the division of la-bor meant that there was a loss of expertise and new generations of designers needed to learn the rules all over again. A phase of deconstruction ensued in the mid-1990s, when many of the old rules were discarded although there was a lack of new ones with which to replace them.

Along with the liberation of page design from most mechanical constraints, the possibility of manipulating any of the fonts available in Postscript format became a reality. Now anyone can become a type designer, providing they can pay for one of the programs with which letters can be drawn and fonts produced.

As in all previous phases of typographic history, after these devel-opments it takes a while for new rules to be developed (which surprisingly often yields results that are identical to the time-honored ones) and for the readers and users of visuall commu-nications to become again the focus of design activities. Well-established designers like Adrian Frutiger and Hermann Zapf oversaw the digitalization of their old typefaces, while masters like Matthew Carter designed fonts for the computer screen us-ing that medium. Carter's Georgia is not only perfectly legible on screen but can also be compared favorably with the classics as a proper text face. In 1990, Erik Spiekermann's FF Meta heralded the arrival of a new kind of sans serif that anticipated the design trends of that decade.

Huge font families, some with more than 144 members, offer every kind of possible use, even for complex printing tasks. The

Bringhurst, R. 1992. *The elements of typographic style*. Washington: Hartley and Marks.

Forssmann, F., and R. de Jong. 2002. *Detail-Typografie*. Mainz: Hermann Schmidt Verlag.

Lupton, E. 2004. *Thinking with type*. New York: Princeton Architectural Press.

Spiekermann, E. 2004. *ÜberSchrift*. Mainz: Hermann Schmidt Verlag.

first of these families was Thesis by Lucas de Groot, which was released by FontShop International in 1994. Newspapers and magazines can have special typefaces designed for them that not only reinforce their (→) brands but can also be specifically tailored to suit production requirements such as particular papers or printing machines, and even be compatible with their readers' habits and expectations.

At the start of the twenty-first century there are better tools than ever for the design of printed matter and other media. The differences between traditional book typography, functional design concepts and sophisticated, colorful advertisements are no longer the guiding parameters, but rather contemporary typographical design relies on the synthesis of these varying strands. Different typefaces may be combined, justified type exists alongside ragged type, freeform page layout alongside strict grid systems. And for headlines, packaging, flyers, and other forms of disposable printed matter, web sites and videos, there are more than 50,000 typefaces that are sold or given away as fonts. And if it is illegible, it only serves to boost the expressive creativity of its originators.

Designers have great choices: there have never been such useful tools for creating good typography—nor so few excuses for doing the task badly. ES |

→ *Communications, Graphic Design, Visual Communication*

U

ULM SCHOOL OF DESIGN

From 1952 until its politically motivated closing in 1968 the Hochschule für Gestaltung in Ulm (hfg Ulm/Ulm School of Design) pursued a new, democratically inspired project whose concept for education policy, pedagogy, and design was unique in the world.

The history of the Hochschule für Gestaltung in Ulm (hfg Ulm, or Ulm School of Design) was closely tied to the struggle to create democratic structures after the National Socialist era. Immediately after the end of the Second World War, Inge Scholl—the surviving sibling of Sophie and Hans Scholl, who had been murdered by the National Socialists in 1943 for high treason because of their membership in the Weisse Rose (White Rose) resistance movement—created the Geschwister-Scholl-Stiftung (Scholl Siblings Foundation) and championed the founding of a free university for democratic education. After a great deal of effort and many political controversies, she succeeded, with the help of her friends Otl Aicher, Max Bill, and Hans Werner Richter, in persuading the American High Commissioner at the time, John McCloy, to support her idea. The resolution to create the Hochschule für Gestaltung was finally made in 1952, and in 1953 construction was begun, with a design by the Swiss architect and artist Max Bill. It was opened in 1955, and Walter Gropius gave the opening speech.

They had created a university whose concept for education policy, pedagogy, and design differed utterly from all such institutions. A small group of teachers and students lived and worked on the Kuhberg and strove to create a well-designed social environment. Functional products were to be as important as theoretical and empirical analyses on urbanism, technology, industry, and transforming human living and working conditions.

The hfg was originally divided into four departments: (→) Product Design, (→) Visual Communication, Information, and Industrial Architecture. In 1961, the Institute for Film Design was added. One important component was the internationality of both teachers and students, as a reaction to the racist nationalism of the Third Reich. Studies lasted four years, though the first year was a basic course that had to be completed as a prerequisite to being accepted into one of the departments.

Viewed from outside, the hfg seemed very self-contained, unified, influential in style, and almost harmonious for a long time. From the beginning, however, there had been intense internal conflicts over the concept, education, and its direction. Six phases can be identified. From 1947 to 1953, the period of Scholl, Aicher, Bill, and Zeischegg, the school endured struggles developing its concept, institutionalizing its structures, and above all financing the project (a constant problem that only grew worse over time). The period from 1953 to 1956 was marked by the consolidation under Max Bill, the first rector, who saw the hfg as clearly following in the (→) Bauhaus tradition. From 1956 to 1958 the conflicts between the older supporters of the Bauhaus and the younger teachers, who called for independent training based on science and theory, began to come out into the open. In 1957 Bill left the university in protest. In the phase between 1958 and 1962, positivist ideas of a strictly mathematical methodology as a supposedly scientifically neutral value began to proliferate. Finally, from 1962 onward Aicher, Gugelot, Zeischegg, and Maldonado pursued a pragmatic rebellion and pushed through a change to the university's constitution, under pressure from the state government of Baden-Württemberg. The first ideas of design theory were formulated and the character of the profession was oriented more strategically around the interests of industry. By now the impending financial disaster was inevitable: the Geschwister-Scholl-Stiftung was deeply in debt, teachers had to be dismissed and teaching activities reduced. From 1967 on the hfg was in its death throes. Because of increasing political controversies with the federal and state governments, public subsidies were massively reduced once again. The state government called for the hfg to be merged with the engineering school and subjected to the state laws for universities. Teachers and students argued over strategies for resistance. In October 1968 the teachers refused to teach because circumstances had become personally and financially untenable. In November the conservative government of Baden-Württemberg closed the Hochschule für Gestaltung in Ulm.

The hfg failed for at least three reasons: financial difficulties (undoubtedly made worse by incompetent handling of funds), the discrepancy between its ambitions and their realization, and finally, and quite banally, because of the vanity and self-interest of various teachers. Most of the famous teachers had already abandoned the sinking ship or had prospects of new contracts elsewhere. Nevertheless, the hfg in Ulm established a concept of design that went far beyond its time and national borders, changing and modernizing everyday life, communication, and the visual world once and for all. UB |

→ Bauhaus, Education

Krampen, M., and G. Hörmann. 2003. *Die Hochschule für Gestaltung Ulm: Anfänge eines Projekts der unnachgiebigen Moderne / The Ulm School of Design: Beginnings of a Project of Unyielding Modernity.* Berlin: Ernst & Sohn.
Lindinger, H., ed. 1987. *Hochschule für Gestaltung Ulm: Die Moral der Gegenstände.* Berlin: Ernst & Sohn.
Rübenach, B. 1987. *Der rechte Winkel von Ulm.* Darmstadt: Verlag der Georg Büchner Buchhandlung.
Spitz, R. 2002. *hfg ulm: Der blick hinter den vordergrund.* Stuttgart: Axel Menges.

UNDERSTANDING

Even today it is still frequently assumed that understanding can be achieved by the simple and precise transfer of (→) information. That, in turn, presumes that there is a relationship of reflection that exists between the world and subject, sender and receiver, consciousness and communication. We have known since Schleiermacher's time, however, that acts of understanding are determined by mental manifestations that have to be thought of separately from the external world. The cognitive apparatus is connected to each individual life and its experiences and selects from the complexity of events according to internally recognized and selected (→) patterns of meaning.

Because it is so difficult to understand the individual world of a human being, a text, or a complex artifact, we have to abandon the simple metaphor of transfer and instead approach the object of cognition in hermeneutic circles, in circular, perpendicular, spiral, or lateral movements. We must abandon the simple metaphor for the transfer of information as bilateral and linear and instead conceive of it as possibly multilateral, circular, and three-dimensional.

Anyone who wishes to understand has to be able to construct (or reconstruct) contexts of significance from empirical sources; they have to learn to see and conceptualize items in the material world, each in its specific context.

Whereas artists seek through their works to evoke and retain a certain openness to interpretation in order to enrich the recipient's reference to reality by offering alternatives, designers have to use a methodology that goes beyond that and attempt to focus on acts of understanding and communication. Designers have to compress the possible space for different views according to the principles of (→) simplicity and affectation, so that the quasi-transfer of the offering is successful. Thus way-finding guidance and information systems, whether at an airport or on a web site, have to be clearly comprehensible, but can never be completely unambiguous because of the separation between the signifier and the signified. The impossibility of transferring identical meaning impels designers to liberate their work from unnecessary and excessive elements such as ornament, decoration or superfluity. SA |

→ *Communications, Construction, Constructivism, Perception, Semiotics*

Frank, Manfred, ed. *Hermeneutik und Kritik, mit einem Anhang sprachphiloso-phischer Texte Schleichermachers*. Frankfurt am Main: Suhrkamp.
Luhmann, N. 1995. Was ist Kommunikation. In idem, ed. *Soziologische Aufklärung*. Opladen: Westdeutscher Verlag. English trans. by S. Holmes and C. Larmore as *The differentiation of society*. New York: Columbia University Press, 1982.

UNIVERSAL DESIGN

The term "universal design" was first coined by architect Ronald L. Mace in 1985. Universal design is also known as design for accessibility, design for all, transgenerational design, and inclusive design. Despite the terminological and sometimes normative differences, the ethical principles are analogous across countries and regions.

Universal design is not a specialized field of design practice but an approach to design, an attitude, a mindset conducive to the idea that designed objects, systems, environments, and services should be equally accessible and simultaneously experienced by the largest number of people possible.

Although the term would not appear until much later, the ideas behind universal design stand in the tradition established by scientists, researchers, engineers, and designers of the 1940s, who worked together in military-sponsored research units to provide design solutions for many of the engineering problems the Second World War had brought to light. Toward the early

1950s, these reflections on the Second World War experience had prompted several large research universities in Europe and the United States to conduct scientific studies on human performance and the man-machine relationship. During this period, Alexander Kira conducted well-known studies of lavatory use and sanitary equipment for the United States military, closely observing sanitary attitudes and corresponding behavior patterns of army personnel. Similar studies of office workers in task-specific environments were conducted across the world, particularly in the United Kingdom and Sweden.

By the mid-1950s, the "systems approach" to design had brought together researchers in the areas of (→) human factors and engineering factors into the field of human engineering (also known as human factors engineering or (→) ergonomics), with the aim of creating optimal configurations of human and physical aspects of the man-made world in order to improve accessibility for people of all ages and across physical and mental abilities. The emerging term in common use at that time was "barrier-free design," which usually meant modifying existing designs to allow for more appropriate and comfortable use by people with disabilities.

Throughout the 1960s and 1970s, government research centers and national organizations in Sweden, Denmark, France, the United States, the United Kingdom, and Japan conducted environmental studies and developed standards for (→) environmental design aimed at reaching a desirable balance between human performance and corresponding task environments, the so-called "environmental fit" or "good fit." In 1977, Michael Bednar proposed that in order to achieve a desirable environmental fit for all users, all potential physical barriers had to be removed from the environment in the early stages of the (→) design process. One way of accomplishing that goal was to methodically involve endusers in the process of design. In the 1970s, Henry Sanoff initiated the Environmental Design Reseach Association, an organization that performed evaluative studies of architecture and environmental planning, and began developing (→) participatory design methods that involved a range of stakeholders in the early stages of designing.

In the mid-1980s, Ronald Mace and his collaborators at the University of North Carolina began arguing for more inclusive practices of environmental design that made both social and economic sense. A major milestone in this effort was the Americans with Disabilities Act of 1990, which renders illegal any discrimination based on physical or mental impairment that "substantially limits" human performance. In 1995, the analogous Disability Discrimination Act was passed in the

United Kingdom. These acts changed the discourse on disability from one based on building codes and regulations to one based on civil rights and equal opportunities for all citizens. They also had a deep impact on the design industry; designers were expected and encouraged to integrate universal design as a mode of thinking into all stages of the design and production process, rather than a set of technical or normative requirements to be satisfied at the end. This mode of thinking extended beyond building design to the design of everyday objects and services traditionally covered by the (→) industrial design profession. A whole new market opened up for products such as OXO Good Grip potato peelers or public buses with floating floors and wheelchair access.

In 1997, Mace and a group of researchers at the Center for Universal Design, State University of North Carolina at Raleigh, developed seven principles of universal design:

· Equitable Use: the design is useful and marketable to people of diverse abilities.

· Flexibility in Use: the design accommodates a wide range of individual preferences and abilities.

· Simple and Intuitive Use: use of the design is easy to understand, regardless of the user's experience, knowledge, language skills, or current concentration level.

· Perceptible Information: the design communicates necessary information effectively to the user, regardless of ambient conditions or the user's sensory abilities.

· Tolerance for Error: the design minimizes hazards and the adverse consequences of accidental or unintended actions.

· Low Physical Effort: the design can be used efficiently and comfortably, and with a minimum of fatigue.

· Size and Space for Approach and Use: appropriate size and space is provided for approach, reach, manipulation, and use, regardless of the user's body size, posture, or mobility.

Today, with the growing life expectancy and aging demographics across the world, with an increasingly globalized economy, growing purchasing power and the emergence of consumer economies in the world's most populated regions, universal design is gaining in significance. In 2001, the World Health Organization (WHO) established the International Classification of Functioning, Disability and Health (ICF). Rather than diagnosing people with stable disability conditions, this classification describes limited ability as a function of the capacity to perform specific environmental tasks. ICF views both disability and functioning as outcomes of the interactions between "health conditions" and "contextual factors." These contextual factors include external environmental factors (social attitudes, material environment, legal and social structures, climate, landscape) and internal personal factors (demographic profile, past and current experiences, natural predispositions). Two important qualifiers regulate the essential information about disability and health: the "performance qualifier" describes what an individual does in his environment, and the "capacity qualifier" describes an individual's ability to execute a specific environmental task. The "gap" between capacity and performance points to the misfit between human beings and their environment: if, for example, capacity is greater than performance, then some aspect of the environment de facto disables optimal performance outputs.

As with the anti-discrimination acts of the 1950s, ICF is indicative of a shift in the way the world understands and defines disability today. The contemporary understanding is based on the belief that everyone at some point in their lives experiences reduced functionality; aging, farsightedness, back problems, and immobility can all contribute to a misfit with the surrounding environment. Disability, therefore, is a universal human experience that depends on the context, time, and circumstances of social and professional practices. In that respect, the role of universal design is, as Ronald Mace wrote, to promote the "design of products and environments to be useable by all people, to the greatest extent possible, without the need for adaptation or specialized design." MM |

→ *Need, Needs Assessment, Usability, Use*

Center for Universal Design (CUD). About universal design. http://www.design.nc-su.edu/cud/index.htm. Accessed November 1, 2006.
International Association for Universal Design. http://www.iaud.net/en/. Accessed November 1, 2006.
Mace, R., G. Hardie, and J. Plaice. 1991. Accessible environments: Toward universal design. In W. Preiser et al, eds. *Design Interventions: Toward a More Humane Architecture*. New York: Van Nostrand Reinhold.
World Health Organization (WHO). 2002. *Towards a common language for functioning, disability and health: The international classification of functioning, disability and health (ICF)*. Geneva: WHO.

URBAN DESIGN

Urban design enables society to create settings relevant to its current paradigm, respectful of past worldviews and adaptable to future uncertainties and potential. Although urban design can be described generically as the act of shaping human environment patterns, paradigmatic shifts in contemporary culture have precluded a single definition of the term. Having first appeared in the 1950s as a reaction to modernist urban planning, urban design as an academic and professional field is currently enjoying a newfound interest in public and educational institutions, where the trend is toward multidimensional, cross-disciplinary courses.

In its most generic definition, urban design is the act of shaping human settlements. Historically, urban design has involved a more or less direct translation of contemporary belief systems (worldviews and paradigms) into the physical layout of buildings and temples in relation to the natural and manmade environments. Belief systems have evolved over centuries from superstition and philosophy to religion, to ideology, and science. The longest-lasting imprints on cities and people from ancient Mesopotamia to modernist new towns have been made by whoever controlled the urban design decisions, whether a pharaoh, priest, king, politician, architect, or even abstract planning system.

In that generic sense then, urban design actions have included the construction of gigantic pyramids, of city-wide street grids, of cathedrals and temples and defense walls, as well as the destruction of historic settlements and their replacement with more "planned" ones in the name of civilization and utopia (the colonization of the Indian Territories in America, Hausmann's boulevards in Paris, garden cities, modernist *villes radieuses,* the Regeneration projects of the mid-twentieth century, the Zionist settlement movement in Palestine, and so on).

Beyond the generic sense, urban design has been formalized as an academic field and a profession since the actual term began to circulate in the mid-1950s. Harvard University's Graduate School of Design organized the first urban design conference (1956) and university course (1960). The instigator, José Luis Sert, defined it as "the part of planning concerned with the physical form of the city," an unfortunate definition that eventually came to handicap the profession by excluding "nonphysical"— but just as influential—concerns from its scope.

The concept gained momentum, spearheaded namely by the ideas of Kevin Lynch and Jane Jacobs, and urban design courses appeared in many major American and European universities in the 1960s and 1970s. This formalization was partly a reaction to the Modern Movement's disastrous effect on the quality of urban space (→ Modernity). It aimed to overcome the perceived loss of the sense of place and identity caused by general zoning and planning rules, generic architectural expression, and a disregard for the intermediate scale where the human user interfaces with her environment.

Christopher Alexander, Leon and Rob Krier, and Robert Venturi, amongst others, developed their definitions of urban design in the 1970s and 1980s. As a reactionary solution, the postmodern 1980s (→ Postmodernism) saw a large section of mainstream urban design education and practice become dominated by new dogmas such as the New Urbanism movement. In turn, New Urbanism has been criticized for naivety and (→) nostalgia because of its insistence on neo-classical form and morphologies and its failure to deal with more complex urbanization.

By 1995, it was almost impossible to find any unified definition of what urban design actually was, and even public institutions agreed that it was not for governments to dictate what constitutes good urban design.

Traditionally, one of the most popular definitions had been that urban design is the mediator between (→) urban planning and architecture (→ Architectural Design). The latter directly tackles the physical built form in unitary particles, while planning manages more "abstract" notions such as zoning, functions, transport networks, and economy. Even so, most actors and players in the planning process still perceive urban design as little more than "big architecture," limiting its effectiveness in most real-life scenarios.

Beyond planning and architecture, other seemingly independent disciplines play equally crucial roles in the study and creation of cities: landscape architecture, topography, communication and transport engineering, and many of the "soft" disciplines—sociology, economy, ecology, group and individual psychology, and behavioral studies, art, and the humanities—are some of the poles that together shape the urban environment and give it its inherent subjective qualities. These have unfortunately been left out of most formal urban design courses, but the current attitude is toward cross-disciplinary courses integrating urban design with sociology, economics, politics, and so on.

Since the mid-1990s counterreactions have been calling for less formal attitudes that would take into consideration the major shifts in technologies, lifestyles, and worldviews. The highly influential Dutch architect Rem Koolhaas was one of the first to call for a new form of urbanism as a "way of thought" and as "the staging of uncertainty" in his *S, M, L, XL*.

In reaction to the inadequacy of urban design education's current formalism in addressing chaotic, ultra-dense, non-western cities, the 2002 book *Quantum City* developed the conceptual language to deal with such a paradigm shift from formal to relational. It extended the definition of design beyond the shaping of mere physical form to the shaping of virtual (→ *Virtuality*) and mental spaces in a society-space-time continuum, bringing back both the *urbs* (city) and the *civitas* (culture) into the realm of urban design (→ *Environmental Design, Event Design*). A redefined role of urban design thus emerges:

Urban design is the multidimensional interdisciplinary interface responsible for managing and transforming the interactions of the different aspects of urban life into a physical and/or usable environment.

And since a setting is only "real-ized" once activated by its end-users, then the definition of "urban designers" crosses the boundaries of disciplines and professions to include all actual anonymous citizens in their daily interaction with one another and their environments.

Urban design enables society to create settings relevant to its current paradigm, respectful of past worldviews, and adaptable to future uncertainties and potential.

Urban design is slowly shifting away from top-down approaches based on fixed master plans to more flexible and error-tolerant, long-term strategic plans involving end users (→ *Participatory Design*) and multiple scenario development (→ *Scenario Planning*). AA |

→ *Anonymous Design, Complexity, Discipline, Landscape Design, Sustainability*

Arida, A. 2002. *Quantum city*. Oxford, United Kingdom: Architectural Press.
Hasic, T., ed. forthcoming 2008. *New urbanism and beyond*. New York: Rizzoli.
Koolhaas, R., and B. Mau. 1995. *S, M, L, XL*. New York: Monacelli Press.
LeGates, R., and F. Stout, eds. 1999. *The City Reader*. 2nd ed. London: Routledge.

URBAN PLANNING

Urban planning is a professional and administrative discipline concerned with the laws and policies that organize the development of the built environment. Generally the domain of governments and municipalities, it is involved with the design and managed growth of towns and cities at the medium and large scale of detail. Urban planning teams can involve many backgrounds, in particular civil and traffic engineers, geographers, economists, (→) landscape designers, and so on. Urban planning is considered a highly politicized activity since it is one of the major influences affecting economic and social development, and is largely responsible for the distribution of resources across the territory.

Urban planning in general sets rules of development that regulate the production of (→) urban design and architecture (→ *Architectural Design*). The difference between urban planning and urban design education is sometimes blurry in the US, while in Europe, and in particular in the United Kingdom, these are two very distinct expertises. AA |

USABILITY

Usability refers to the functional relationships between people and the products and systems they use. The concept is relatively straightforward: if something is able to fulfill its purported function (if it is "usable"), then it exhibits "usability."

Over the last several decades, the definition of usability has undergone a steady transition in meaning. The term initially emerged from the study of (→) ergonomics, where it was strongly linked to the quantitative analysis of the machine interface. A number of factors have contributed to a significant shift in the way designers define, predict, analyze, and optimize usability in the twenty-first century, however. The proliferation of new technologies has of course been influential; in a field where (→) innovation is of paramount importance, and in an effort to differentiate their offerings from competitors, designers are increasingly conceptualizing designs that are burdened by technological excess. Furthermore, in the economies of the developed world, designing things to be more usable has evolved to the staging of experiences where the product may play a relatively minor role in the exchange of daily life—in a sense, manufactured products have been replaced by serviced experiences (→ *Service Design*). Usable products still play a role in the staging of an experience, but the service is an elaborate structure whose existence is first prefigured visually, and then structured to fulfill desires that have none of the clear signs that mere "usability," as a principle, could understand or attempt to control by deploying traditional methods.

Current uses of the term usability have thus expanded the scope of the definition to include all interactions that take place between human beings and the designed world they live in; everything from industrial products to screen interfaces to services and experiences can be discussed in terms of usability today. Regardless of the different forms these interactions might take, it is clear is that designers have been increasingly required in almost every professional design practice to continually consider (and reconsider) user perspectives, needs, desires, expectations, behaviors, and aptitudes throughout the entire design process.

In the pursuit of usability, the phrase "user-centered design" has become popular in recent years, particularly in the realm of (→) Industrial Design. Simply put, this design philosophy aims to improve usability by keeping the experiences of end users in mind at every stage in the design cycle. Without a doubt, user-centered design is often successful in identifying and tracking those characteristics that make products more or less intuitive, efficient, and safer to use. User-centered design has made significant contributions to the field of design research in particular, by developing techniques to manage and analyze findings systematically. The specific methods used to collect and analyze data about usability typically include interviews, questionnaires, focus group discussions, (→) prototype evaluations and (→) testing.

Despite these benefits, however, the phrase "user-centered design" can be said to be vague at best and misleading at worst. The term "user" is in and of itself complex and poorly defined— not only is it difficult to define what characterizes a "user" in design, but the term is also often loaded with pejorative connotations related to consumption and the manipulation of circumstances. Furthermore, the practice of user-centered design can be somewhat misleading in that it indicates a degree of user agency that may or may not be present in actual practice.

Take for example the two primary research methods used to measure usability criteria: direct observation (studying how users interact with products) and (→) semantic analysis (studying how users read and thereby understand how to use products). Both types of (→) research are usually conducted by someone who remains outside the interaction, but translates all their findings to the rest of the design team. They take place within the prescribed limits of the product or product type and, like all research conducted in a semiempirical manner, are often self-fulfilling with their prophesies (for example, issues identified at earlier stages in the research process may be presented to users in the form of survey questions, and are subsequently "solved" for later design development). Along the same lines, usability testing results are frequently misleading, particularly if the tests do not take place in the environments in which the designed product will ultimately be used. In short, many activities that are purportedly "user-centered" are not so different from the ways in which designers have historically conducted (→) market research and testing–they still differentiate the "designer" from the "user," and the end product is still largely identified, framed, and enacted by the former role.

It is also easy to cast doubt over the method. The motorcar for instance has been the subject of the most research in user-centered design in history—yet, fundamental questions about the product's usage abound. It would be fair to ask the question of motorcar design—if it is so well understood from the point of view of usability, then why are there so many fatal car accidents? Invariably, the answer is to point to a fault by the user that is called "driver error." That drivers can transform the highly developed usability of the motorcar from transport to tragedy, despite the best intentions of design, opens up the possibility that the user might have their own intentions for the usability of a product. That is, by exerting their individual will, people use the manufactured world to suit their intentions and may not be using it as designed.

What emerges from these scenarios is a situation where usability describes the intentions of two distinct and sometimes conflicting projects: the design project and user project.

Until recently, the people who use designed products and systems have been characterized as passive consumers as opposed to active users. The act of consulting potential end users systematically throughout the various steps in the design process is not a new phenomenon—producers, marketers, and designers have traditionally spent considerable amounts of time and effort attempting to predict the circumstances that compel groups of people to consume more. Despite the attention paid to the meticulous tracing of "consumer attitudes" and trends, however, those same groups of people have typically had little to no agency in the design of the products and systems that they use in their everyday lives.

A growing awareness of the divergence between the different projects of the designer and user has led to the creation of new branches of usability research like (→) participatory design and inclusive design. In participatory design practices, the user is regarded not as a consultant or test subject—a passive receptor of predetermined messages—but as an active and integral member of the design team. By giving the user actual production potential, the ability to assemble experiences according to his or her own (→) needs and desires, participatory design ostensibly breaks down the boundaries between those characteristics that differentiate "designers" from "users." In very simple terms, this is design *with* people not simple *for* them. The aim of participatory design is to give people something to do in the design process, some agency beyond being surveyed and studied, and not leave the user with something they are given. Inclusive design is aimed at optimizing usability for the largest number of people possible, and seems to have the strongest trajectory in design for the aging (→ *Universal Design*).

The concern by design for usability has not only added universal and participatory design, but spawned another development known as "design and emotion" (Delft University). This branch of usability is concerned with how it feels to be living in a designed or artificial world that requires the development of purely qualitative research methods. It has expanded usability to encompass not only products and services, but also scenarios of living. Just as usability assumed the role of sustaining the historic notion that better use might equate to a better world, design and emotion presumes that we can design better experiences and hence a better world.

Regardless of the way you look at usability, in order to develop an understanding of it, you need to engage in observation, and to do so designers are turning increasingly to ethnology for methods (→ *Observational Research*). But what suits anthropologists does not necessarily fit design, and when designers are required to gather information or document what they see, it has proven very hard to present as engaging evidence without lengthy explanation. Having found "relevant" information, documented it in numerous ways, transformed it into new images, and illustrated the findings, observational design struggles to explain why the subject and object should matter.

This line of inquiry is worth pursuing because clues to the utility of observation as a primary method of research into usability do exist courtesy of the study of "material culture" (Miller 1998)—a recent offshoot of ethnographic research into everyday life. Heavily influenced by the French school of sociology (Certeau 1984), material culture is pursuing the meaning of causal links between what is observed and its eventual interpretation. But while design has never expressed a strong interest in meaning, how meaning might be constructed through observation has given designers the potential to transfigure the here-and-now into what-might-become. This is useful for considering a more usable and hence better world.

However, as a framework for design thought and action, and as a notion lending legitimacy to design outcomes, usability runs into one major problem—it doesn't account for fashion. The world of fashion is certainly the most volatile battleground for the contest between the different projects of the user and designer, but instead of this tussle causing usability to be omitted from fashion theory, as an unrelated subject, the phenomenon of fashion in fact points to new possibilities for the study of usability where people might craft their own personalized and customized world (secondlife.com). CBR |

→ *Intuition, Simplicity, Understanding, Use*

Certeau, M. de. 1984. *The practice of everyday life*. Trans. Steven Rendall. Berkeley: Univ. of California Press.
Design and Emotion Society. http://www.designandemotion.org. Accessed November 17, 2007.
Miller, D., ed. 1998. *Material cultures: Why some things matter*. London: UCL Press.
Second Life. http://secondlife.com. Accessed November 17, 2007.

USE

Designers create objects that are used by people or, in other words, are simply needed. (When you need a streetcar ticket to visit a friend, you use a vending machine to purchase it). Use has both an inner motivational aspect (→ Need) and an external one when it comes to practical applications. When something can be described as being in use it can also mean that one normally uses it or completes it, when in the context of a form of practical activity.

The purpose of design is to produce an (→) object or (→) system to be used by a user. This applies to both product and communication design. The designer can create or encode (to use a semiotic term) objects with regard to one or more uses. This can be called monofunctional or polyfunctional design, and can be illustrated by using interior space as an example.

A student's room is a typical example of polyfunctional design. Work, recreation, sleep, dressing, personal hygiene, cooking, eating, and so on, all take place in the one room. At the other extreme would be an English country house built in the second half of the nineteenth century. It was common at that time to assign a single (→) function to each room, and then to furnish it optimally for this one function. So the dressing room was separate from the bedroom; there was a smoking room, a library, and a salon in which to receive guests with a separate dining room for most meals as well as a separate breakfast room. Each child had their own bedroom, playroom, and a room for private instruction and homework. This division by function continued in the garden: you could enter the rose garden or park from the salon and there was a kitchen garden with herbs that belonged to the domestic wing.

Forgetting for a moment that only this very small group, the aristocracy, and a small number of the newly wealthy bourgeoisie, could afford such a country house, which would have been impossible to manage without a large and diverse staff, examples like this marked the birth of the monofunctional design doctrine, that is that "form follows function." In the twentieth century, Le Corbusier applied this model, which at first only involved a room's functions, to the architectural components of an entire house, and then to (→) urban planning. Subsequently, an internal house wall supported by a steel frame no longer had the function of supporting the ceiling or the weight of the upper stories. According to Le Corbusier, its massive quality should not even pretend to perform this function, and it did not even have to extend to the ceiling. This wall has one function only, that is, to separate rooms (and hence, the rooms' separate functions).

Monofunctional design's fundamental rule, that is to separate functions, was often ignored. Yet, without this, the aphorism "form follows function" makes no sense. Le Corbusier's urban planning philosophy illustrates precisely how breaking down functions can lead to problems.

Le Corbusier was an advocate of the rigid separation of functions—residential, work, recreational, and traffic. The first three functions were each allocated its own city zone, which was then equipped to fulfill that area's functional requirements as well as possible. The traffic system had the task of connecting the above three zones. Many cities in postwar Germany and elsewhere were restructured according to these criteria. What Le Corbusier intended to be humane, civilized and democratic soon turned into the desolate high-rise ghettoes on the edges of the city, to which residents only traveled at the end of the day to sleep. Work was shifted to industrial areas, the bleak local recreation areas with jogging paths were vacant, and inner cities were reduced to shopping malls and offices which, after closing time, became ghost towns. The quality of urban life deteriorated as the resultant commuter society led to traffic jams and noise pollution that greatly deteriorated the quality of urban life.

When architects and designers talk today about the need to reclaim cities, to repopulate and energize them, they are advocating a strategy to correct monofunctional urban planning schemes by reallocating more functions to different urban areas. This discourse, around the issues of reurbanization, was initiated in the 1960s by Jane Jacobs (1916–2006) in New York. Designers, of course, have to analyze the particular circumstances of a project before deciding on whether a monofunctional or polyfunctional design will be appropriate.

Although, by definition, the term use belongs to the user, the focus up until now has been on the aspect of design, that is, on product design. It is interesting that when actually using a designed object, users often develop a different use than that originally intended by the designer (→ Non Intentional Design), whether the designer's initial intention was monofunctional or polyfunctional. Jimi Hendrix played his guitar with his mouth, particularly his teeth and tongue, and then smashed it—presumably not the original, intended use of the stringed instrument.

Examples of unplanned uses of designed objects include chairs used as hangers for clothing, newspapers used to chase away annoying mosquitoes, books used to prop up projectors, and Galileo using the tower at Pisa for physics experiments. The reception of or, semiotically speaking, the decoding of design products allows the user to contribute creatively to the actual use of a designed object. In principle, the handling of an object is always available for new uses. Uta Brandes and Michael Erlhoff called this phenomenon "non intentional design."

This also applies to forms of secondhand use and recycling. The use of secondhand products also addresses the issue of conservation, because it keeps design objects in circulation and use for longer. A growing market for used goods is available for those who cannot afford or do not wish to buy new products. Not only are flea markets flourishing but eBay is also responsible for a huge and continuing growth in this market sector.

Objects are often kept precisely because they can be reused. Art historians and archaeologists use the term "spoils" (from the Latin, *spoliare*, meaning to plunder) for the remains of old or dilapidated buildings that are used to construct new buildings. Some Roman gravestones survived because they were used to build Romanesque churches in the Middle Ages. The industrial Ruhr area of Germany provides a more contemporary example of conservation through reuse. After the decline of coal mining and steel manufacturing, many old, dilapidated buildings survived because they were converted into new museums, government offices, and other public buildings.

The use of objects leaves traces, which can have a fetishizing or defetishizing effect (→ *Patina*). If you own an original, 1925 Wassily chair by Marcel Breuer, and use it regularly, the evident signs of use will have a defetishizing effect. The chair will no longer be an almost sacred design icon, an object to be revered when it is placed on view. It is secularized through use. However, if you had one of Marcel Breuer's own chairs, one he owned and used throughout his life, the chair would gain immense value in the eyes of the viewer precisely because of the signs of use, because they are Marcel Breuer's, that is, it would be esteemed as The Master's Chair.

Living means leaving traces, wrote the German Marxist literary critic and philosopher, Walter Benjamin (1892–1940), who pointed out the practical difficulty of inhabiting modern interiors made of smooth, hard materials. He considered it the painful but unavoidable price to be paid for the progress and disenchantment that led the bourgeoisie to abandon the years of Bismarck and Kaiser Wilhem I, 1871–1914 (the *Gründerzeit*—literally the foundation years) with its dark upholstered caves, for the bright and shining "machines for living" (Le Corbusier's phrase) of modernism and their rational "respectable austerity." Today's return from aura to anti-aura design might suggest that the process of disenchantment has stalled. TF |

→ *Need, Function, Functionalism, Interface Design, Modernity, Usability*

Benjamin, W. 1980. Erfahrung und Armut. In R. Tiedemann and H. Schweppenhäuser, eds. *Gesammelte Schriften*. Vol. II. 1. Frankfurt am Main: Suhrkamp.
Brandes, U., and M. Erlhoff. 2006. *Non Intentional Design*. Cologne: daab.
Fiske, J. 1999. Politik: Die Linke und der Populismus. In R. Bromely, U. Göttlich, and C. Winter, eds. *Cultural Studies: Grundlagentexte zur Einführung*. Lüneburg: Verlag zu Klampen.
Hall, S. 1999. Kodieren/Dekodieren. In R. Bromley, U. Göttlich, and C. Winter, eds. *Cultural Studies: Grundlagentexte zur Einführung*. Lüneburg: Verlag zu Kampen.

USP

"Unique Selling Proposition," abbreviated USP, refers to the outstanding feature of a product or (→) brand that distinguishes it clearly from the competition's offerings. Rosser Reeves introduced the concept to marketing theory and practice in the 1940s. This feature can be associated with virtually any characteristic of a product: form, service, interface, cost, a previously unavailable function, a new concept for use, and so on. All these factors can be influenced in crucial ways during the design process, so design has the task of making the USP objectively evi-

Reeves, R. 1961. *Reality in advertising*. New York: Knopf.

dent to the user. This is often a decisive argument in hiring a designer: the USP is the focus of a company's advertising in order to achieve high sales or increase profits. AD |

→ *Added Value, Advertisement, Branding, Strategic Design*

V

VALUE

Value refers to the relative worth or utility of something. Many of the terms defined in this dictionary address, directly or indirectly, the concept of value. Indeed design can be understood as being a value-adding and value-negotiating process.

Value is a very basic and broad concept. It relates to the worth that we humans ascribe to anything and for almost any reason. If you were to think of any reason that some thing, someone, some feeling, some experience might be of some worth, importance, or significance then you have placed a value on it. Value is most commonly understood to represent the amount of money (or other "in-kind" currency) that it takes to complete an exchange—to buy, to rent, to employ, and so on. The relative amount that one must exchange is the value of the thing exchanged. The precedence usually given to quantitative valuation has led to attempts to quantify the less tangible qualitative aspects related to design.

Design credits objects with value and the success or failure of a design can be understood in large part by how much additional value design imparts to the designed ($\rightarrow$) artifact. Predictably, the process for determining the success or failure of a design in terms of adding value to the "base" is through ($\rightarrow$) evaluation. (The difference between evaluation and ($\rightarrow$) testing is the key to understanding the idea of value in relation to design.) The relative value of the things in our life is derived from a combination of how they make us feel (non-substantive assessments) and how well the artifact works in relation to the design criteria (substantive assessments).

There is a greater demand on designers to be able to articulate the substantive value of design to clients and, at the same time, a growing appreciation in business circles that ($\rightarrow$) innovation will rarely result from strictly quantitative and efficiency-based processes. Consequently there is a growing awareness of other value systems for all those involved in the commissioning, manufacture, and distribution of designed objects and systems. The combination of a heavy reliance on metrics-based accounting and the increased appreciation of the importance of qualitative values for business has resulted in what is known as "triple-bottom line accounting." This is an attempt to quantify on the balance sheet the social and environmental impact of a business operation and this in turn influences design decisions (see entry on $\rightarrow$ *Sustainability* for a critique of this approach).

Qualitative values are critical to design: a newly designed object that reduces waste will encourage a buyer who is concerned about the environment to assign civic value to it; if it embodies a technical innovation, the financial backer gains status value; and, if it is bought as a gift implicit with emotional understanding and intimacy, then the recipient attributes an emotional value to it. The designer or design team make choices at every point in the design process and most of these are value laden. Every decision at each "choice point" will give priority to certain values over others. TM |

→ *Added Value, Design Process, Ethics, Quality, Social, USP*

VIRTUALITY

Virtuality describes a general condition (for example, of a historical period), a localized state (of a social environment), or a peculiar status (of a network, system, or object) of being virtual, that is, characterized mainly by immateriality.

The term "virtuality" is rare, and typically occurs in theoretical efforts to adapt technical uses of the more common adjective "virtual" (which in computer science is used interchangeably with "logical" as opposed to "physical") into a philosophical status. In these discussions, the process by which objects, functions, systems, and situations take digital form (through very ill-defined mechanisms) has been called "virtualization" by thinkers heavily invested in new technologies (such as Howard Rheingold). These discussions of virtuality typically rely on historical determinism, the belief that technological development is the determining factor in social, cultural, and political change. Those who do not share these views rarely devote many words to rebutting a concept as baroque as virtuality (Arthur Kroker, Michael A. Weinstein, and Michael Heim are notable exceptions); as a result, "virtuality" and "virtualization" often carry strong connotations of advocacy.

In the English language, the term "virtuality" is venerable but marginal. It first appears in a 1483 translation of the hagiographic *Golden Legend,* published by William Caxton, the first Englishman to introduce a printing press into, and to retail books in, his native land. For centuries after its introduction, the term mainly appeared in religious contexts as a way to describe the potential of material (→) objects to express, perpetuate, or elaborate the cosmos. Thus, for example, in *Pseudodoxia epidemica* (1646) Sir Thomas Browne observed that in "one graine of corne ... there lyeth dormant the virtuality of many other, and from thence sometimes proceed an hundred eares." Scientific thought has since illuminated in mechanistic terms the numerous processes that contribute to how this "virtuality" is realized; yet mechanistic explanations are hard-pressed to address the sense of wonder that such processes can sometimes inspire. This tension, between mechanism and eruptive potential, is a central to the dynamics that have made ideas about things virtual so popular.

In its modern form, virtuality is generally associated with the rise of computer networks, in particular the Internet (→ *Networking*). Like several terms that became popular on a global scale in this context (for example, "digital," "information," and so on), it is difficult to arrive at any precise definition: the proliferation of terms via these networks across wildly different cultural and disciplinary contexts ensures that there is no clear, unified framework within which to define the term. Yet this phenomenon is recent, so it remains to be seen whether such a transcultural condition might itself come to be seen as a unified context for understanding the meanings of these terms in new ways. If it does, the resulting polyvalence may be a (or even the) defining characteristic of ideas such as virtuality; for now, their defining characteristic is ambiguity.

For recent or contemporary thinkers heavily invested in ideas of or about virtuality, the potential of something "virtual" is often thought to be inversely proportional to its materiality: the less something takes material (→) form (runs the argument), the less limited it is by that form, ergo the greater its potential. In primarily technical contexts, this approach makes sense. The use of "virtual" techniques in computation allow many different types of procedures to be performed by software running on general-purpose devices such as PCs, as opposed a few processes running on single-purpose devices; the benefits—in terms of economies of scale in hardware and flexibility in software development and maintenance—are profound.

However, when applied in nontechnical contexts (for example, in theories of subjectivity, class, or governance), notions of virtuality quickly become problematic. Arguments of this kind—proposals, in essence, that substantial parts of human experience can somehow be translated into "virtual" form—have been, if not common, remarkably influential. For example, John Perry Barlow's "Declaration of Cyberspace Independence" (1996) posited two utterly separate worlds and pitted a collective "mind," rooted in "cyberspace" and equated with the future and potential, against the political structures of the material world, which were equated with the past, industrialism, and physical being. This manifesto struck many as extremely bombastic at the time (as indeed it was intended to); but his argument was substantially similar to widely popular beliefs—about the limitless possibilities of virtual compared to "bricks and mortar" businesses, the inability of governments to enforce laws or impose taxes on virtual commerce and communities, and so on.

The roots of these polemical claims about the potential of "virtuality" are extremely complex. On the one hand, the fundamental discourses about Turing machines—in essence, machines capable of simulating any other machine—derive directly from the work of first-generation cyberneticians such as Norbert Wiener and John von Neumann, whose milieu was professedly secular, materialistic, technocratic, and apolitical (or at least hostile to "leftist" concerns associated with communism in the post-Second World War period). On the other hand, mature converts to Christianity, such as legendary media theorist Marshall McLuhan and the *Wired* magazine founding editor, Kevin Kelly, made critical contributions by promoting organicist, communitarian, and above all utopian visions of collective human thought and action. At the same time, theories about virtuality also bear strong traces of the optimistic futurism (for example, in "extropians") with a profound mistrust of materiality (seen by some as a resurgent form of Neoplatonism). This eclecticism itself has many sources and contributing factors, ranging from the dominance of American thinkers (for whom systematic or pure philosophical inquiry is rare) in articulating these theories, to the applied context that drove these theories (that is, the rise of digital computers and networks).

Curiously, the two most influential twentieth-century thinkers who devoted sustained effort to analyzing "virtuality" seem to have almost no influence in technology-oriented uses of the concept: Henri Bergson, who applied the concept in describing the process by which a material object becomes or spawns a representation through (→) perception; and, later in the postmodern period, Jean Baudrillard whose analyses of the arbitrary operations of metaphysical thought drew heavily on the pre-absurdist French writer Alfred Jarry and his creation "pataphysics." Instead, the importance of ideas about "virtuality" in technological contexts can be attributed to two maverick American thinkers, Ted Nelson and Jaron Lanier.

Nelson, an iconoclastic technologist (credited with, among other things, having coined the term (→) "hypertext" in the mid-1960s), gave the term a decisively modern meaning and application when he used the term "virtual" to describe "conceptual structure and feel" and as "the opposite of reality." More specifically, he understood virtuality as the range of possible functions that (→) software, whether in a specific or in general, is capable of prior to the reductive expression of those capabilities in the tangible form of an interface (including logical and physical interfaces, not just human or graphical interfaces) (→ *Interface Design*). Nelson's ideals centered mainly on texts and intertextuality, which conceived in terms of what he called a "docuverse." The quixotic nature of his vision of the first hypertext project, Xanadu (beginning in 1960 and running, in fits and starts, for almost four decades), can be surmised from his criticism of the web and its "ever-breaking links, links going outward only, quotes you can't follow to their origins, no version management, no rights management." At the same time, though, Nelson was uncompromising in his critique of "the computer as a paper simulator" and denounced the two-dimensional understandings of digital (→) artifacts as a "four-walled [i.e., four-sided] prison." In essence, Nelson envisioned a technical system capable of preserving all the perceived limitations of material documents as options rather than inevitabilities: for example, users would have access to every stage of a digital artifact's development as well as to every possible connection or association (formal, temporal, semantic, and so on) that artifact might share with any other artifact. In this sense, then, Nelson's vision of the "virtual" can be seen as a technical realization of the marvelous potential implied in centuries-old uses of the term "virtuality."

It was largely on the basis of Nelson's theories and activities, on the one hand, and the phrase "artificial reality," which had achieved some popularity in experimental computing circles in the early 1970s, on the other, that Jaron Lanier is credited with having coined the term (→) "virtual reality" in the early 1980s to describe three-dimensional, purportedly "immersive" environments. Lanier's efforts took much more practical, functional form than Nelson's—for example, quasi-3-D environments that users could explore and manipulate through experimental input (for example, haptic) and output (for example, "heads-up") devices. Like Nelson's work, though, the technical (→) complexity and computational intensity of Lanier's efforts far outstripped commonly available computing resources, with the result that his work, too, remained beyond the means of all but the wealthiest institutions and therefore marginal.

Ultimately, it was the confluence of Nelson's and Lanier's respective efforts—and, of course, that of many others across myriad aspects of research, development, and use—that "virtuality" came to become an all-purpose (and consequently vague) term used to describe the immateriality of things digital. This popularization, which largely coincided with the rise of the internet, led to the popular use of the term "virtual" to refer to phenomena ranging from descriptive and/or depictive environments (for example, MUDs [multiuser dungeons], MOOs [MUD Object-Oriented], and RPGs [role-playing games]), "communities" such as mailing lists web sites that rely heavily on users' contributions, and so on. However, as these forms of media and exchange become more normal, the terms "virtual" and "virtuality" will almost certainly lose their last shreds of historical specificity and become obsolete, and perhaps even camp. TBY |

→ *Form, Information, Materials*

Heim, M. 1993. *The metaphysics of virtual reality*. New York: Oxford Univ. Press.
Heims, S. J. 1991. *The cybernetics group*. Cambridge, MA: MIT Press.
Kroker, A., and M. A. Weinstein. 1994. *Data trash: The theory of the virtual class*. New York: St. Martin's.

VIRTUAL REALITY

These days, the phrase "virtual reality" (abbreviated VR) describes the technology that enables users to interact with computer-generated, three-dimensional environments that have been designed primarily through optic depictions to appear as realistic as possible. The stated aim of this technology is the production of a "total display" that purposefully activates the senses, allowing the perceptual apparatus to construct a virtual environment that is perceived as just as "real" as reality. Virtual reality is also variously referred to as artificial reality, cyberspace or 3-D simulations.

The term "virtual reality" was coined in 1989 by Jaron Lanier, an early computer visionary. Although the concept has been around for quite a few years, the forms and the degree of immersion that recent technologies has now achieved are, however, of such a quality that they can scarcely be compared to earlier forms.

A milestone in the systemic depiction of realistic environments was achieved through the invention of perspective rendering in the medium of painting. Other advances were made through the introduction of photography, film, and their successors. The abilities of these systems to enhance the illusion of reality are measured on the degree to which they effect a sensory or emotional "immersion" in the simulation. For example, the moving image of cinema has a higher degree of immersion than photography, which in turn has a higher degree of immersion than a painted picture. Similarly, one can trace this development in other areas of the senses. For instance, the use of Stereo and DHX hi-fi systems in films far surpasses the use of a phonograph in terms of its immersive capabilities. By making it possible for the filmgoer to not only hear the sound of a lurking danger, but even to perceive the direction from which it is coming, these systems have a great effect on enhancing the illusion of reality.

Today's gaming world of consoles and PCs, with their three-dimensional adventure worlds and highly developed graphic and acoustic representations, offer a strong sense of immersion. The possibilities of interacting with these "alternate realities" particularly increase the feeling of being present in person. Data gloves that detect movements of individual fingers on a hand enable the user to engage with their virtual surroundings manually. In addition to the optically traceable effect, systems with force feedback enable the simultaneous activation of (→) haptic perception. We not only see how we clutch something, we can also feel how soft or heavy the virtual object is. The simulation of this complex control loop represents a particular technical challenge, because the haptic sense, in contrast to the optic or the acoustic, is always dependent on how we clutch an object—we thus determine the manner and strength of the sensations.

In addition to the simulation of entirely virtual environments, the development of "augmented realities" through the use of virtual objects is becoming increasingly significant. Semitransparent glasses do not impede our views into the world, but enable a depiction of individual objects in the user's field of vision. Visors for jet pilots project important flight data on their interior rims, so that crosshairs and distances are directly reflected in the pilots' fields of vision. In civilian vehicles, there have already been experiments with projecting speed, rpm, and navigation information onto windshields.

All advancements in virtual reality technology are based not only on technical possibilities, but also on advancements in human self-awareness. Only when we comprehend the principles and exact sequences of our perceptual and cognitive processes will we be able to activate and use them selectively. STS |

→ *Visual Effects, Virtuality*

Dery, M. 1996. *Escape velocity: Cyberculture at the end of the century.* New York: Grove Press.
Flusser, V. 2000. *Ins Universum der technischen Bilder.* 6th ed. Göttingen: European Photography.
Gibson, W. 1984. *Neuromancer.* New York: Ace.
Rheingold, H. 1991: *Virtual reality.* New York: Summit Books.

VIRTUAL SET

In television, "virtual set" refers to the generation of virtual backdrops in real-time (→) animation. The actors are filmed in a blue- or green-box studio—a room painted a monochrome blue or green—which is later replaced using electronic or digital keying techniques with whichever virtual background image is required. Using both a real and a virtual camera results in a perspectively correct, moving, three-dimensional background image, which together with the actor, creates the impression of a real space.

Despite high initial investments in (→) production technology, the virtual studio set is above all a cost-effective alternative to real studio set productions. When faced with time-consuming rebuilding, there is often almost no alternative. In addition to these economic aspects, the virtual studio makes it possible to create structures that would not be physically possible. The size of the studio does not determine the scale of the virtual architecture. Animated elements can also be integrated into the virtual scenography, thus expanding the range of special effects possibilities even further. BB |

→ *Audiovisual Design, Broadcast Design, Set Design, Visual Effects, Virtuality*

VISUAL COMMUNICATION

Visual communication is an artificial phrase intended to describe the combination of textual, figurative, formal, and/or time-based elements to convey meanings greater than the sum of the parts—that is, not merely to convey ideas but to do so with heightened effect.

The phrase "Visual Communication" arose in European and American higher educational circles in the 1980s and 1990s to supersede the phrase "communication design;" communication design had been adopted in the same milieu in the early 1970s to supersede W. A. Dwiggins's phrase (→) "graphic design" (coined in 1922, but popularized after the Second World War). The dynamics that drove these two renamings were very different; but neither phrase ever came into sufficiently widespread use outside of the academy to supplant graphic design.

Communication design was adopted in the context of newly popularized theories of media associated with theorists such as Marshall McLuhan and Quentin Fiore. The phrase was more aspirational than accurate: it reflected the optimism with which graphic-design techniques were being applied on larger scales in many senses. On the one hand, advertising (→ *Advertisement*) was becoming increasingly systematic in its aim of projecting unified identities and ideas across nations using all available media; on the other hand, efforts to project institutional identities onto and into quasi-public spaces (for example, theme parks and events such as the Olympics or the World Fair) provided compelling examples of an intuitive and accessible internationalism.

These expanding possibilities did not result from fundamental changes in the practice of visual design. Instead, they reflected changes outside the field—notably the growing interest in a wide range of "communication"-related practices by sponsors, mainly in the commercial sector. This rising prestige was crucial for visually oriented practices, which had often been relegated to secondary status alongside other more "authorial," verbally oriented practices; but it was in no way limited to them. Interest extended across numerous fields, from electrical engineering to sociology. Not surprisingly, then, "communication"-related specialties and entities proliferated across the academy. This proliferation gradually led to administrative confusion within the academy.

It was against this backdrop, decades later, that the phrase visual communication was nominated as an alternative to communication design. Only so much precision can be attributed to any two-word phrase, of course, but the thrust of the new phrase was to prevent confusion by limiting the scope of the practice to visual fields. In doing so, it implicitly distinguished vocationally oriented programs centered on visual (→) practice from professionally oriented social-scientific programs centered on scholarship, research, and policy. Given these inward-looking, administrative motives for introducing the phrase, it is hardly surprising that it has not come into popular use. Outside of the academy, it mainly serves as a self-consciously broad category that encompasses the creation and appreciation of entire swaths of visual culture, from the intentionally professional and to the naively vernacular.

Even within the academy, the introduction of the phrase visual communication has been a step backward in some respects. Historically, it coincided with the rapid adoption of digital computers as the predominant tool in virtually every aspect of creative processes, from the development of component media (writing, image, form, collage) through entire cycles of production and distribution. Yet rapid increases in the capability, sophistication, and integration of these devices have also driven more complex forms of hybrid media: in terms of production, by enabling visual designers to explore time-based, interactive, and audio forms and integrate it into their practice; and, in terms of reception, by enabling audiences to do the same, thereby fueling demand for hybrid media. In this regard, it is unfortunate that the phrase visual communication was introduced just when technical advances enabling mass hybrid media made the possibilities implicit in the communication design more accessible.

Yet it is also true that academic and institutional graphic-design culture showed little interest in the emergence of early interactive and time-based media (→ *Interface Design, Time-based Design*). There were pragmatic reasons for this. Traditionally, the field had been animated by a craft-oriented (→ *Craft*) attention to subtlety, precision, and fidelity in (→) typography, image, color, and abstract form; but early computers (whether time-sharing systems or, later, personal computers) were unable to attain anything close to the accustomed finish or quality of "analog" techniques. For example, early digital typesetting was a poor approximation compared to its optically generated counterparts; and digital color quality and consistency was crude compared with the flexibility of pigment-based systems. (A notable exception was digital image processing, which was widely embraced by professionals and amateurs alike.)

However, digital technologies developed much more rapidly and systematically than specialized fields of practice such as graphic design were able to absorb. As a result, these specialist fields of practice adopted only very limited aspects of these new technical capabilities. Thus, while the practice of graphic design struggled, to good and bad effect, with what came to be called "desktop publishing" (in essence, digitized page layout and image-processing), it failed to respond organically to other crucial developments such as the sudden rise of the Internet. In that sense, then, the unrealized promise of the ambitious name communication design—exemplified in the communitarian, organicist, and utopian thinking of McLuhan—made the older name something of a misnomer. In this regard, visual communication has the virtue of being more accurate.

This complex dialog between the field and its rapidly changing technical circumstances was neither simply a myopic failure to adapt nor a valiant stewardship of tradition. Instead, the continuity of concern stems mainly from the peculiar understanding of (→) "communication" that dominates the field. Unlike two-way systems such as telephony, for example, which assume a free-form, negotiative understanding of communication, visual communication is a "one-way" activity oriented toward the transmission of ideas, associations, and feelings. This admittedly reductive understanding can be traced to the origins of graphic design per se, namely, the mass production of print materials using techniques derived from lithography and/or photography. (Of course, component or contributing disciplines such as typography and (→) illustration claim older histories and mythologies.) Though very flexible in their capacity to integrate a wide variety of textual, figurative, and abstract media and forms, the ultimate goal of these techniques is to fix constituent elements into more or less static forms; the resulting artifacts serve as the vehicles of standardized visual communication.

Yet with the seemingly inexorable spread of digital devices, which typically rely on ever more complex or detailed manual interaction (as distinct from the conceptual or cognitive interaction that a book, for example, relies on to "work"), traditional assumptions about "static" or "standardized" forms are becoming increasingly problematic. In many contexts where print and other fixed formats have been dominant, the iterative, real-time creation and consumption of communicative activity and artifacts is becoming common. Despite the bombast of successive waves of futuristic rhetoric (predicting the "death of the book," denigrating paper as "dead trees," and so on), these innovations are integrated in every way and at every stage with the traditions of visual communication, whatever it is called.

What is changing very decisively, though, is the reductive, one-way (→) understanding of communication. Interactions that previously might have taken the form of marginal notes or heavily thumbed sections of a book are now giving way to feedback-oriented systems (for example, through the use of browser cookies and digital rights management authorization techniques) that give authors, designers, publishers, and/or distributors more detailed access to how their audiences, individually and collectively, interact with aspects of their artifacts and systems. While markedly different from the free-form, negotiative understanding of communication of telephony, these forms of feedback nevertheless tend to promote an increasingly bivalent understanding of communication. In doing so, they are likely to undermine some of the most basic assumptions that have shaped visual communications—while, at the same time, continuing to affirm its coequal status alongside other, more verbally oriented authorial practices. TBY |

→ *Communications, Discipline, Visualization, Web Design*

VISUAL EFFECTS

"Visual effects" refers to the artificial generation and manipulation of visual components in film and video. These manipulations of frames, nowadays often done in conjunction with (→) compositing, range from unspectacular touch-ups to the addition and subtraction of entire components within a scene. The production of artificial matte paintings also has an important role here. The effects this process produces can be generated by hand as well as through the use of digital 2-D and 3-D imagery. People working in visual effects concentrate on creating frames that are difficult to realize using live action means, either because of budgetary reasons or simply because of the laws of physics (impossibly large buildings, alien landscapes, crowd scenes, simulated physical effects).

The history of visual effects is as old as the history of film itself. As early as 1902, the Lumière brothers used techniques to simulate nonexistent objects in their film *Le voyage dans la lune*. Early techniques included multiple exposures, rear projections, and the integration of analog (→) animation elements. Nowadays, thanks to the development of powerful computer and robotic technologies, almost every concept is realizable through visual effects; the realistic simulation of humans represents one of the last visual effects hurdles.

The distinctions between the terms "visual effects" and "special effects" (SFX or FX) have largely disappeared. BB |
→ *Audiovisual Design, Broadcast Design, Virtual Set, Virtuality*

VISUALIZATION

The term visualization has two distinct yet related definitions. The first entails the (→) perception of visual (→) information, and is somewhat synonymous with the act of "seeing." The second entails the process and end products of communicating visual information, and is related to the act of designing. In both cases, visualization is a complex process that requires filtering and abstraction in order to be interpreted.

Visualizations as applied to the act of "seeing" are not simply a matter of acquiring sensory information. Indeed, the term often applies to the formation of mental images in the absence of external stimuli (as in a daydream or representation of an abstract theory or concept). Even in the purely physiological process of perceiving light information, filtering and abstraction occur at various hierarchical stages along the visual pathway—at the retina, the thalamus, and at multiple regions of the visual cortex devoted to motion, color, object identification, and other mental processes. "Top-down" cognition in turn affects perception and memory, which further reframe our visual experience.

A similar process occurs in the other application of the term, that is the purposeful communication of visual information. In design, the visualization process is determined by the agenda of the communicator (intent), the viewer's disposition (interpretation), and the environment in which the entire process takes place (context).

In applied visualization, the communicator's intent is often to persuade or to assist willing users. In the very broadest sense, graphic visualizations can be divided into four realms. These include: visualizations that in some manner represent real or abstracted images associated with the way humans see the world, such as photographs or illustrations; visualizations that utilize quantitative methods to convey time, number, or other factors, as commonly used in scientific and financial fields; visualizations that are composed of symbols, as used in text documents or road navigation; and (increasingly more commonly) visualizations that convey more complex structured relationships, such as "node-and-link" diagrams or tables. Most visualizations are hybrids of the above, employing different degrees of emphasis and accuracy for any particular realm.

Once the purpose of the visualization is determined, it is then created in anticipation of the viewer's reaction. The degree to which visual information is conveyed well is influenced by how carefully that information is filtered and abstracted in recognition of the viewers' perceptual and cognitive tendencies and capabilities (→ Heuristics), as well as the environment in which the communications takes place. As such, designers need to situate their visualizations within a canon of (→) convention or (→) innovation, as well as the larger social contexts in which they are perceived. There are some domains of visualization, such as the deep and well-established history of applied (→) typography, that provide immeasurably rich sources of predetermined visualization styles and methods which are constantly reapplied and adapted for new requirements. The most effective visualizations often come as the result of a careful interplay between standard and nonstandard approaches; overly conventional visualizations run the risk of losing the viewer's attention, while overly innovative ones may fail to be comprehended entirely. A visualization's form and effectiveness is therefore dependent on the viewer's interpretation of the designer's intent in a specific environment. AK + WB |

→ *Communications, Design Process, Graphic Design, Information Design, Visual Communication, Visual Effects, Understanding*

W

WEB DESIGN

Web design is concerned with the conception, design, and structure of web sites and the navigation, user guidance, and (→) interface design of information services and applications on the World Wide Web (WWW).

One peculiarity of web design is the fact that designers have only conditional formal control over the products and applications they design. Only contingently can they determine how the various elements of their design will appear on a user's screen, particularly with regard to sizes, positions, font sizes, and colors. This is primarily a result of the different technologies that users employ (computers, displays, operating systems, browsers), though it is also linked to the fact that the foundational structures for the WWW are written in the page description language HTML (Hypertext Markup Language), which necessitates that formal data is always defined variably, depending on the structured marking of information.

The World Wide Web, created by Tim Berners-Lee and Robert Cailliau at the Center for European Nuclear Research in 1989, was originally intended to facilitate the rapid exchange of text-based documents communicating scientific results across international networks. Hypertext Transfer Protocol, or HTTP, was specifically created for this purpose. As web sites developed, however, the division of content, on the one hand, from layout or formal design, on the other, created additional possibilities for personalized presentations (colors, hierarchies, fonts, sizes, etc.). This compelled designers to think systematically so as to create a consistent and comprehensible presentation of content. Subsequently, technological developments and the increasing (→) complexity of the information supply have led to a growing emphasis on user-friendly designs that work from the user's point of view. Only content and information that come across quickly and comprehensibly have a chance to get noticed amidst the vast resources of (→) information available.

Legal structures have been significantly expanded in recent years to eliminate barriers to information resources for users with limited perceptual abilities, thus giving them access to participation in Internet communication. As part of this effort, a series of standardizations has been issued to optimize the (→) usability and accessibility of web sites. One disadvantage is that this has sharply restricted the development of what might be a wholly new medial language unique to the Internet. Jacob Nielsen, who has made particular use of cognitive psychological research to make web sites simpler and more intuitive, deserves particular mention as one of the pioneers of usability in web design.

In recent years, HTML-independent software technologies like Flash have given designers more control over the formal presentation of their designs, as well as opening up new (→) animation, (→) audiovisual and interactive possibilities. With all of the tools at hand, designers should keep in mind, however, that simple solutions are often best, as demonstrated by the success of the relatively minimal search engine interface for Google.

The next generation of the Internet, Web 2.0 (Social Web), meets the new needs of web design, particularly those regarding the strategic integration of users. It is increasingly the case that users not only view web sites, but also interact with them through the use of comments and links. This represents a fundamental change in the paradigm of (→) "use" in information services, since users can increasingly influence or even directly build the content of the sites they use. Among the best-known examples of this development are Wikipedia and the book reviews on Amazon. What is more, the evaluation of pages and information services in connection with dynamic information architectures generates a structure determined by usage. Frequently searched or highly rated data are positioned at a higher hierarchical level, thus making them potentially easier to find. For designers, this means designing not only the interface level, but taking on an expanded role in the structuring and strategic conception of information services themselves. Systematic design leads to the development of intelligent interfaces, with designers defining rules for the appearance, procedures, and interconnectedness of the elements. Here, too, designers must anticipate use, since this determines the form of presentation and renders the system's structures, to the extent necessary, transparent and comprehensible (→ Information Design).

The (→) convergence of such media as print, television, the Internet, and mobile communications into a transmedially networked system demands a formal language that will be consistent for users, a comprehensible interaction concept, and an editorial and formal design of content that conforms to the respective media (and their most likely usage situations). It is therefore important that all of the different media be taken into consideration when developing information services for the Internet. Designers play a decisive role in this process as expert mediators between the participating (→) disciplines. Their strengths lie in the evaluation of user behavior, the development of dynamic information architectures and concepts of interaction, the design of accessible and recognizable layouts, and the anticipation of future forms of use through (→) personas and scenarios. [PH]

→ Hypertext, Screen Design, Virtuality

Khazaeli, C. D. 2005. *Systemisches Design*. Reinbek: Rowohlt.
Skopec, D. 2004. *Digital layout for the Internet and other media*. Reinbek: Rowohlt.
Studio 7.5. 2002. *Navigation for the Internet and other digital media*. Reinbek: Rowohlt.

WICKED PROBLEMS

"Wicked problems" is a phrase first coined by Horst Rittel and Melvin Webber, theorists of design and social planning respectively, at the University of California, Berkeley, in 1973.

A wicked problem defies any standard attempt to find a solution because it is a symptom or result of multiple, contingent, and conflicting issues. Environmental degradation, social and economic inequity, and terrorism are some of the classic wicked problems that we face in the twenty-first century. Designers often work on particular problems that comprise or contribute to a complex "wicked problem." However, an isolated design solution (or that of any discipline) arrived at through an established process will almost by definition make the problem worse.

Due to their (→) complexity, wicked problems require the work of collaborative teams of people with a range of expertise over space and time. A process designed to address a wicked problem typically has no definitive solution, but, can, at best, achieve incremental improvements to the situation. In this context, the trans-disciplinary qualities of the (→) design process can be and are used to enable and facilitate a range of disciplinary and professional experts (including designers) to work on the wicked problem together with the relevant public (→ *Participatory Design*).

The term has also more recently been adopted in interaction and (→) software design to describe complex programming problems where a solution to one problem compromises other desired features of the software. TM |

→ *Collaborative Design, Discipline, Heuristics*

Rittel, H., and M. M. Webber. 1973. Dilemmas in a general theory of planning. *Policy Sciences* 4:155–69. (Reprinted in N. Cross, ed. *Developments in design methodology,* pp. 135–44. Chichester: J. Wiley & Sons, 1984).

The Editors

Michael Erlhoff

Michael Erlhoff earned his Ph.D. (Dr. phil.) in German Literature and Sociology, was member of the board of documenta 8, CEO of the Rat für Formgebung/ German Design Council, Founding President of the Raymond Loewy Foundation, Founding Dean of the Köln International School of Design, among others guest professor in Hong Kong, Tokyo, Taipei, editor of the Kurt Schwitters-Almanach and author of numerous books on design, art, and culture. He is professor at KISD, author, and design consultant. He lives in Cologne.

Tim Marshall

Tim Marshall is Dean of Parsons The New School for Design in New York. Marshall was formerly director of Academic and International Programs and Chair of the School of Design at the University of Western Sydney and has an extensive professional-photography background. He has written and lectured internationally on academic topics related to design research and education and for professional design journals. Marshall received his education at the University of South Wales and the City Art Institute in Australia. He lives in New York.

The Authors

AA | Ayssar Arida

Urban designer, architect, writer, entrepreneur, and director of cross-disciplinary consultancy Q-DAR (www.q-dar.com); author of *Quantum City* (2002), a work influencing urban design education and practice across Europe; co-founder of the Centre for the Spatial Realm (theCSR.com). Previously taught at the American University of Beirut. He lives in London.

AAP | Arjun Appadurai

John Dewey Professor in the Social Sciences at The New School; author of *Modernity at Large: Cultural Dimensions of Globalization* (University of Minnesota Press, 1996); editor of *Globalization* (Duke University Press, 2001). His most recent book is *Fear of Small Numbers: An Essay on the Geography of Anger* (Duke University Press, 2006). He lives in New York.

AAU | Astrid Auwera

Freelance graphic designer; conducts research and develops projects relating to service design; conducts trend research for BASF Coatings in Munster. She lives in Cologne.

AD | Annette Diefenthaler

Designer; projects include the International Furniture Trade Fair in Cologne 2004; assistant to the advisory board of the International Design Forum in Ulm. She lives in Cologne.

AFL | Alastair Fuad-Luke

Sustainable design facilitator, lecturer, writer, and maker; Senior Lecturer at University College for the Creative Arts, Farnham, UK; author of *The Eco-Design Handbook*, 2002, 2005, an international bestseller; facilitator/consultant for clients in Denmark, France, USA, and the UK. Author and originator of SLow (www.slowdesign.org); board member of *SlowLab* (www.slowlab.org); member of the Advisory Board for the 10th & 11th Towards Sustainable Product Development conference, the *Centre for Sustainable Design* (www.cfsd.org). He lives in Devon, UK.

AK | Arno Klein

Information Synthesis Theorist at the Parsons Institute for Information Mapping (PIIM). Conducted research in display holograms, image processing software for brain imaging, and methods to visualize data; current research includes the creation of web applications related to visualization. He lives in New York.

ANT | Annette Tietenberg

Professor of Art Theory with a focus on contemporary art at the University of Art in Braunschweig; journalist, art and design critic, curator of numerous exhibitions. She lives in Heppenheim.

AR | Anna Rabinowicz

Associate Professor in the Product Design department at Parsons The New School for Design; founder of RabLabs, a company that creates designs for the home that are sold around the world; worked with Design Continuum and IDEO Product Development to examine the human needs and frameworks that result in design opportunities; designed products for Logitech, General Motors, and devices for cardiac surgery. She lives in New York.

AS | Anezka Sebek

Director of the MFA in Design and Technology at Parsons The New School for Design; film-industry credits range from documentary filmmaking to feature-film production; collaborated to create a pilot animation workshop for UNESCO entitled *Africa Animated!*; juror for the *Computer Animation Festival in 2003* and Animation Theater Director for *Siggraph 2004*. She lives in New York.

AT | Axel Thallemer

Director of the industrial design program at the Kunstuniversitaet Linz; guest professor in the USA and China; appointed member of the Royal Society of Arts; has been awarded numerous national and international design prizes. He lives in Munich.

BB | Björn Bartholdy

Professor of Audiovisual Media at the Cologne International School of Design (KISD); founder of "cutup" agency for audio visual design; member of the board of Eyes and Ears of Europe. He lives in Cologne.

BF | Barbara Friedrich

Editor-in-chief of the living, architecture, and lifestyle magazines *Architektur & Wohnen* and *Country,* published in Hamburg by Jahreszeiten publishing house; initiator and co-author of the *Euro Design Guide* published in 1992 by Heyne Verlag, Munich; jury member for the German Federal Design Prize. She lives in Hamburg.

BK | Barry Katz

Professor of Humanities and Design at the California College of the Arts; Consulting Professor of Mechanical Engineering at Stanford University; Fellow at IDEO, Inc.; author of numerous books on cultural history and the history of technology. Served as Executive Editor of the *Design Book Review*; currently researching the history of Silicon Valley design. He lives in Palo Alto and works throughout the San Francisco Bay Area.

BL | Benjamin Lieke

Published a novel (under a pseudonym), exhibition curator, he works mainly as an author and consultant for design and texts. He lives in Montpellier.

BM | Birgit Mager

Independent consultant specializing in the service industry; established the department of service design at the Cologne International School of Design (KISD); founding member of the International Service Design Network; Pro-Dean of the Department of Art Theory at the University of Applied Arts in Cologne. She lives in Cologne.

CB | Craig Bernecker

Founder of The Lighting Education Institute; faculty in the MFA Lighting Program at Parsons The New School for Design; published widely on research and education in lighting design. Formerly Director of the lighting program in the Department of Architectural Engineering at Penn State University; Senior Vice-President and President (2003–2005) of the Illuminating Engineering Society of North America (IESNA). He lives in New York.

CBR | Craig Bremner

Professor of Design and head of the School of Design and Architecture at Canberra University; specialist in user-experience; organizer, Canberra Architecture and Design Biennial. Developed new research practices that led to changes in housing-design criteria in Scotland. He lives in Sydney and works in Canberra.

CH | Claudia Herling

Designer; founder of digital frische, a design and illustration studio; translator and author of *index logo* (Bonn, MITP 2005); teaches Design Theory in the department of Media Design at the University of Applied Sciences. She lives in Cologne.

CM | Colleen Macklin

Chair of the Department of Communication Design and Technology at Parsons The New School for Design; fellow at the India China Institute at the New School. Collaborative research projects focus on open source and grassroots media. Worked as an interaction designer at several design firms and a technology-based installation artist with exhibitions and events in New York and Asia. She lives in New York.

CN | Claudia Neumann

Co-owner of Neumann + Luz in Cologne, an agency specializing in culture and design communication; member of the Deutsche Gesellschaft für Designtheorie and -forschung (DGTF) (German society of design theory and research); author; journalist; published the *Handbuch Design International* (Cologne, DuMont 2004) together with B. Polster and M. Schuler. She lives in Cologne.

CT | Cameron Tonkinwise

Director of Design Studies at the University of Technology, Sydney; Director of Change Design, an independent think-tank developing more sustainable lifestyles by design; teaches service design and researches philosophies of design and product sharing; previously worked with the EcoDesign Foundation. He lives in Sydney.

CTE | Carlos Teixeira

Faculty member in the Department of Design and Management at Parsons The New School for Design. His expertise is revealing the operational logics that guide design practice; at Parsons, his work centers on the application of such logics to processes of research and development. He lives in New York.

DB | David Brody

Assistant Professor of Design Studies at Parsons The New School for Design. His current book project is titled *Visualizing Empire: Orientalism and American Imperialism in the Philippines*. He has published chapters of this forthcoming book in *Prospects* and the *Journal of Asian American Studies*. He is also working on a design-studies reader. He lives in New York.

DGC | Denise Gonzales Crisp

Graphic designer, SúperStové!; author; and Associate Professor in the College of Design at the North Carolina University. Visual and written investigations into the "DecoRational" sensibility constitute ongoing design research. "Design Criticism" editorial board member; co-organizer, Schools of Thoughts Design Educators Conferences; author of a textbook on typography, Thames Hudson publishers, due 2008. She lives in Los Angeles and Raleigh.

DL | David Ling

Founder of David Ling Architects; teaches at Parsons The New School for Design and at the University of Nuremberg; has received awards including Best Retail Design (2001) and Best Office Design (1995) by *Interior* Magazine and Best Exhibition Design (2001) by ICFF. He lives in New York.

DN | Dan Nadel

Owner of PictureBox, Inc. (www.pictureboxinc.com), a Grammy Award-winning New York-based packaging and publishing company; editor of *The Ganzfeld* (www.theganzfeld.com), an annual book of visual culture; author of *Art Out of Time: Unknown Comic Visionaries 1900–1969*; Assistant Professor of Illustration at Parsons The New School for Design; published in *The Washington Post, Print, Eye,* and *The Economist.* He lives in New York.

DP | Derek Porter

Director of the MFA Lighting Program at Parsons The New School for Design; lighting designer; and owner of Derek Porter Studio. He has worked in interior, furniture, and product design as well as fine arts, is recognized for dozens of international lighting design awards, and is published in numerous lighting and architecture journals. He lives and works in both New York and Kansas City.

DPO | Dirk Porten

Designer, consultant, author, and model builder; employee at be design; founding member and online editor of the Deutsche Gesellschaft für Designtheorie and -forschung (DGTF) (German society for design theory and research). He lives in Cologne.

EG | Elke Karoline Gaugele

Empirical Cultural Theorist and Professor of Fashion at the Vienna University of the Arts. Formally scientific assistant at the Institute for the Arts and Art Theory at the University of Cologne, and Research Fellow at Goldsmiths College/Department for Visual Arts in London. Publishes on fashion and new technologies as well as on visual cultures. She lives in Cologne and Vienna.

EPV | Eva Perez de Vega

Architect, designer, and founder of EPdVS Studio (epdvs.com), a multidisciplinary architecture practice also involved in product design, interiors, set design, and choreography; currently teaches at Parsons The New School for Design. Recent work investigates dynamic systems and generative techniques that incorporate movement, flow, and ecology. Originally from Rome, Italy, she lives in New York.

ER | Ethan Robey

Assistant Director of the M.A. Program in the History of Decorative Arts and Design at Parsons The New School for Design and The Cooper-Hewitt National Design Museum, Smithsonian Institution; has taught at Binghamton University, Columbia University, Hunter College, The City College of New York, and Pace University. Publishes on consumerism, class, taste, exhibition theory, and other aspects of material culture in the nineteenth and twentieth centuries. He lives in New York.

ES | Erik Spiekermann	Designer, typographer (FF Meta, ITC Officina, FF Info, FF Unit, Nokia, Bosch, Deutsche Bahn, et al.) and author; founder of MetaDesign (1979), Germany's largest design company, as well as FontShop (1988); currently manages Spiekermann Partners with offices in Berlin, San Francisco, and London. He lives in Berlin and San Francisco.
ESC | Erik Schmid	Professor of Design Theory and Dean of the design program at the Niederrhein University of Applied Sciences in Krefeld; freelance pianist, theater and film musician and composer; music teacher; freelance journalist and author of *Form–Funktion–Produktion–Rezeption: Design* (Freiburg, Orange Press 2007). He lives in Krefeld.
ET | Earl Tai	Associate Professor and Associate Chair of Art and Design Studies at Parsons The New School for Design, where he works in the area of design studies, design pedagogy, and design writing; recipient of academic and design awards including first prize in the national American Institute of Architects Prestressed Concrete Design Competition, a Fulbright Fellowship, a Harvard thesis award, a Columbia President's Fellowship, a U.S. Department of Education Grant, and a Taiwan Ministry of Education Grant. He lives in New York.
FD | Fred Dust	Leads IDEO's Smart Space practice, which helps clients with their strategic and innovation goals around space and real estate by putting multidisciplinary teams into the field to translate consumer insight into design concepts for a broad range of industries. Co-author of a book on space design titled *Extra Spatial;* taught at California College of the Arts and the University of California at Berkeley; and holds numerous guest professorships. He lives in San Francisco.
FR | Fiona Raby	Partner at Dunne & Raby London, a company that specializes in projects collaborating with groups in the fields of industrial research, universities, and cultural institutions; founding member of CRD Research Studio at the Royal College of Art in London; runs furniture and architecture departments. She lives in London.
GB | Gerda Breuer	Professor of Art and Design History at the University of Wuppertal; Chair of the academic advisory board of the Bauhaus Dessau Foundation since 2005. International exhibition experience and the former head of three different museums. Has taught in the USA, the Netherlands, and Germany, and published works on art, architecture, photography, and design history. She lives in Wuppertal.
GJ | Gitte Jonsdatter	Design researcher with the Smart Space group at IDEO Chicago. Her specialty is doing contextual research to understand the social, emotional, cognitive, and physical issues that surround services and environments, and in synthesizing research insights into actionable design criteria. Prior to IDEO, she planned and designed experiences for special events and exhibits with clients including Time Warner, Deutsche Bank, IBM, and DaimlerChrysler. She lives in Chicago.

GJO | Gesche Joost — Senior Research Scientist at the Deutsche Telekom Laboratories in Berlin in the field of usability and interaction design. Has worked as an interface designer in Cologne, Vienna, and Tokyo, 2003–2004; taught Design Theory and Media Rhetoric at the Cologne International School of Design (KISD); member of the board of the Deutsche Gesellschaft für Designtheorie und -Forschung (DGTF) (German society of design theory and research). She lives in Berlin.

HS | Henriette Schwarz — Designer and author; has published many texts on design; is a founding member of U.S. Anti-Design and Guerilla Gardening groups. She lives in Palo Alto.

HW | Heico Wesselius — Assistant Professor in the Design and Management Department at Parsons The New School for Design; industry experience with IBM Business Consulting Services in Amsterdam, Tokyo, and New York. He currently has his own consulting firm specializing in managing business complexity; formerly worked as an investment banker in the global institutions group and for several other strategy consulting firms. He lives in New York.

JH | Jürgen Häusler — CEO of Interbrand Zintzmeyer & Lux, provides numerous companies with strategic marketing consultancy, including the Deutsche Telekom for over ten years. Honorary Professor of Strategic Business Communication at Leipzig University; author on the subject of marketing. He lives in Zurich.

JHU | Jamer Hunt — Teaches at The University of the Arts in Philadelphia, where he is Director of the Graduate Program in Industrial Design; has lectured internationally and consulted and worked at design practices such as Smart Design, frogdesign, WRT, and Virtual Beauty. His written work engages with the poetics and politics of the built environment and has been published in various books, journals, and magazines. He lives in Philadelphia.

JM | John Maeda — Graphic designer, visual artist, computer scientist, and Associate Director of the research department at MIT Media Lab in Boston. A leading advocate of simplicity in the digital age, he publishes and exhibits widely and is the recipient of numerous awards and honors. He lives in Lexington, Mass.

JR | Jen Rhee — Assistant Director for Academic Communication at Parsons The New School for Design; sculptor, illustrator. Previously worked at Minetta Brook and the New Museum of Contemporary Art. Sculpture and research projects involve investigations into light perception, Newtonian optics, and physics. She lives in New York.

JS | Jörg Stürzebecher — Journalist and exhibition curator. Publications include works on Max Burchartz (1993), Hans Leistikow (1996), Richard Paul Lohse (1999), and Anton Stankowski (2006); works for *design report*. He lives in Frankfurt am Main.

JT | Joel Towers	Director of the Tishman Environment and Design Center at The New School and the Associate Provost for Environmental Studies; Associate Professor of Architecture at Parsons The New School for Design where he was also the first Director of Sustainable Design and Urban Ecology. Previously on the faculty at Columbia University; founding partner of SR+T Architects. His focus is on ecological issues and their relationship to both design conceptualization and construction methodology. He lives in New York.
KF | Kevin Finn	Joint Creative Director of Saatchi Design, Sydney (part of the Saatchi & Saatchi network); founder, editor, and designer of *Open manifesto,* currently Australia's only journal of graphic design writing (www.openmanifesto.net). Previously worked at a number of leading design studios in Dublin, Wellington, and Sydney; recipient of numerous national and international awards including a D&AD Silver in typography and a Type Directors Club Judges Choice award, among others. He lives in Sydney.
KK | Kent Kleinman	Professor and Chair of the Department of Architecture, Interior Design and Lighting at Parsons The New School for Design. His scholarly focus is twentieth-century European Modernism, and his publications include *Villa Müller: A Work of Adolf Loos*, *Rudolf Arnheim: Revealing Vision*, *The Krefeld Villas: Mies's Haus Lange and Esters*. He has taught at international architecture schools in Austria, Germany, and Switzerland. He lives in New York.
KS | Katie Salen	Associate Professor in the Design and Technology program, Parsons The New School for Design; co-author of *Rules of Play: Game Design Fundamentals* and *The Game Design Reader*; core team member of Gamelab; editor of *The Ecology of Games.* She writes extensively on game design, interactivity, and game culture, including some of the first dispatches from the previously hidden world of machinima. She lives in New York.
KSP | Kathrin Spohr	Freelance design author and assistant professor at the University of Applied Sciences in Düsseldorf; guest professor at the Art Center College of Design, Pasadena; developed the first furniture series for David Lynch, worked at *form* magazine and at frogdesign. She lives in Cologne.
KT | Karin Thönnissen	Research Assistant in the department for design at Bauhaus University in Weimar; diverse exhibitions and publications on the cultural history of textiles, fashion design, and art of the twentieth century. She lives in Weimar.
KW | Katrin Wellmann	Graduate industrial designer and managing owner of:echtform–Industriedesign & Beratung; lectures and publications as well as publications in trade literature. She lives in Rösrath.
KWE | Katalin Weiß	Designer specializing in interior design, product design, and food design, with a focus on sweets and pastries. She lives in Berlin.

LS | Loretta Staples

Has over twenty years of experience in graphic, exhibit, and interface design. Her work has included specialized applications, conceptual models, and prototypes for emerging technologies. She has lectured widely on digital design and currently teaches in the Department of Design & Management at Parsons The New School for Design. She lives in New York.

LW | Lois Weinthal

Director of the BFA Interior Design Program at Parsons The New School for Design; licensed interior designer; previously Associate Professor in the School of Architecture at The University of Texas where she co-developed the Interior Design Program. Her primary area of interest is in the relationships between architecture, interiors, and objects, which includes the design of furniture and clothing. Her design and research projects have been published nationally and internationally. She lives in New York.

MA | Michelle Addington

Associate Professor of Architecture at Yale University; teaches courses in Energy/environmental Systems, Advanced Technology, and Smart Materials. Previously worked as a research engineer with NASA and in the chemical industry with Dupont; taught at Harvard University for ten years. Her writing on energy, fluid mechanics, lighting, and smart materials has appeared in several journals, books, and reference volumes, and she recently co-authored a book titled *Smart Materials and Technologies for the Architecture and Design Professions*. She lives in New Haven.

MB | Michelle Bogre

Associate Professor and Chairperson of the Photography Department at Parsons The New School for Design; intellectual property lawyer; active photographer whose work has been featured most recently in a group show titled *The Way We Work* at the Lawrence F. O'Brien gallery in the National Archives building in Washington, D.C. Teaches copyright and writes legal columns for American Photo On Campus. She lives in Pennsylvania.

MBO | Marcus Botsch

Industrial designer working in the fields of furniture and accessories, exhibition design and public design; Editor-in-chief of *Design Revue*; founding dean of the Dr. Stahl Institute, patron of the Designinitiative des deutschen Humors (DDH) (German humor design initiative); freelance work for *form* and *design report*. He lives in Berlin.

MDR | Michael D. Rabin

Associate Professor in the Department of Design and Management at Parsons the New School for Design; expert in human-computer interaction; founder and head of a consultancy specializing in user experience; patentee in voice-driven application design; recipient of the Jerome H. Ely Award for best article published in *Human Factors Journal* (1995). Published academic articles on the influences of memory on perceptual/sensory systems with emphasis on fragrance perception; current research interests are in the area of sensory design. He lives in New York.

ME | Michael Erlhoff

Is the editor of this book.

MF | Michaela Finkenzeller	Designer, research in Shanghai, project realization for designaffairs/Siemens Mobile in Seoul, developed car paint for BASF Coatings Munster. She lives in Munster and Cologne.
MG | Marion Godau	Co-initiator and board member of DESIGNMAI, Berlin's international design festival; member of the Deutscher Werkbund (German work federation). In addition to publishing in numerous publications, she teaches design, design theory and history at the University of Vechta. She lives in Kleinmachnow.
MI | Minako Ikeda	Associate Professor of contemporary design and design journalism at the design department at Kyushu University; co-founder of the Institute for Information Design Japan (IIDj); author of several books. She lives in Tokyo and Fukuoka.
MK | Martina Kohler	Architect; teaches architecture as an Assistant Professor at the Technical University in Berlin and was a Visiting Assistant Professor at the Pratt Institute in New York. She has worked in offices in Munich, Berlin, and New York for eight years and holds an independent practice since 2000. She lives in New York.
MKR | Mateo Kries	Associate Director of the Vitra Design Museum in Weil am Rhein; curator of numerous international traveling exhibitions; co-founder of DESIGNMAI, the international design festival held in Berlin; lecturer on design theory at the Humboldt University and the University of the Arts in Berlin; author of many books on design. He lives in Basel.
MKU | Melanie Kurz	Designer at BMW Design. Formerly worked with Alexander Neumeister in Munich. Research projects have been awarded several prizes. She lives in Munich.
MM | Miodrag Mitrasinovic	Architect; Associate Professor at Parsons The New School for Design; author of *Total Landscape, Theme Parks, Public Space* (Ashgate 2006); co-editor of *Travel, Space, Architecture* (with J. Traganou, Ashgate, 2007). Both books are recipients of the Graham Foundation grant. Published in professional and academic journals in Europe, Japan, and the Unites States; has taught and lectured internationally. He lives in New York.
MR | Mark Roxburgh	Senior Lecturer at the School of Design, University of Technology Sydney (UTS); co-managing editor of the peer-reviewed journal *Visual Design Scholarship*. Previously Director of the Visual Communication Program at UTS; has worked extensively in editorial publication as a photomedia image-maker. He lives in Sydney.

MS | Michael Schober

Dean and Professor of Psychology at The New School for Social Research; editor of *Discourse Processes*; co-editor of *Envisioning the Survey Interview of the Future*. His research focuses on collaborative processes, with papers on the dynamics of interviewing, chamber musicians coordinating, perspective-taking in conversation, and mediated communication appearing in *Public Opinion Quarterly, Cognition, Applied Cognitive Psychology*, and *Virtual Reality*, among others. He lives in New York.

MSI | Marco Siebertz

Owner and Editor-in-Chief of the design magazine *ROGER;* freelance author for the Deutsche Welle and other media; recipient of German National Academic Foundation scholarship; active in the field of design research. He lives in Cologne.

MV | Detlev Meyer-Voggenreiter

Exhibitions, structures for trade fairs, museums, and collections, discourses and concepts on and for public urban space; co-founder of the design groups Pentagon and Casino Container; member of the founding board of the Deutsche Gesellschaft für Designtheorie und -Forschung (DGTF) (German society for design theory and research) and the sponsoring committee of the European Kunsthalle. He lives in Cologne.

NS | Nancy Salvati

Adjunct Professor at Parsons The New School for Design; new business and marketing consultant in the New York metropolitan area. Clients range from Dow Jones and AT&T to the broadcast community—CBS, CNN, and RAI. She has published several articles for technology periodicals such as *Satellite Communications* and *Communications Technology*. She lives in New York.

PE | Petra Eisele

Author; Professor of Design History, Design Theory, and Media Theory at the Technical University of Mainz; work on the research project bauhaus medial at Trier University, numerous publications on design history and design theory. She lives in Trier.

PH | Philipp Heidkamp

Professor of Interface Design and head of the European Design MA program at the Cologne International School of Design (KISD); Dean of the Department of Cultural Studies; co-founder of syntax design in Cologne; numerous publications and lectures on interface design. He lives in Cologne.

PK | Pamela Trought Klein

Associate Professor and Founding Chair of the Associate in Applied Science Degree Department (AAS) at Parsons the New School for Design; design educator, painter, and architectural and interior design color consultant. Her work has been exhibited at Neill Gallery, AS Van Dam, ABC No Rio and AIR Invitational, and included in publications including *New York Magazine, Town & Country*, and the *New York Times*. She lives in New York.

PS | Peter Friedrich Stephan

Author, designer, producer, and consultant on media productions relating to business communication; Professor of Cognitive Design at the Academy of Media Arts in Cologne; research in the field of knowledge design, digital marketing, and design theory; co-founder and business manager of the Forum for Knowledge Media Design. He lives in Berlin.

PT | Paolo Tumminelli	Founder and managing director of Goodbrands business consultants; Professor of Design Concepts at the Cologne International School of Design (KISD); columnist for the *Handelsblatt;* author of *Traffic Design* (Cologne, Daab 2006). Main fields of research include the history and development of automobile culture. He lives in Cologne.
RL | Robert Langhorn	Professor of Industrial Design at the Pratt Institute in New York. Prior to moving to the United States, he was a Senior Lecturer in Three Dimensional Design at The Arts Institute of Bournemouth in the United Kingdom. He lives in New York.
RLU | Robert LuPone	Director of The New School for Drama; President of the Board of Alliance of Resident Theaters/New York; Artistic Director of MCC Theater. Recent Broadway credits include *True West, A Thousand Clowns,* and *A View from the Bridge.* Nominated twice for a Tony Award; received an Emmy nomination; won a Joseph Jefferson Award, a Screen Actors Guild Award, and The Actors Studio Award. He lives in New York.
RM | Renate Menzi	Assistant Professor for Design and Design Theory at the Zurich University of Applied Arts and Sciences (ZHGK); member of the board of the Deutschen Gesellschaft für Designtheorie und -Forschung (DGTF) (German society for design theory and research). She writes about design for a number of newspapers and trade magazines and is currently working on a research project dealing with the cultural significance of branding. She lives in Zurich.
RO | Rosemary O'Neill	Associate Professor of Art History and Assistant Dean for Faculty at Parsons The New School for Design. Writing and curatorial interests include modern and contemporary art and visual culture in the Americas, Europe, and Korea; currently working on a study of the arts and visual culture of the post-war Riviera. Her work has been published by Yale University Press, College Art Association, and the Corcoran Museum. She lives in New York.
RR | Raoul Rickenberg	Specialist in information architecture, interface design, and how these practices can be used to articulate the interaction of social and technical systems; faculty at Parsons The New School for Design, where his research and teaching focus on the relationships between communication technology and organizational behavior; Director of MAPstudios, a firm that develops a broad range of digital and material interfaces. He lives in New York.
RS | René Spitz	Managing partner of rendel & spitz, business consultants for strategic product management; chairperson of the advisory board of International Design Forum (IFG) in Ulm; responsible for the realignment of IFG activities and for the proposal of the politics of design program. He lives in Cologne.
SA | Stefan Asmus	Professor of Interactive Systems and Dean of the Design Department at the Düsseldorf University of Applied Sciences; communication designer specializing in the development and design of complex digital knowledge systems as well as cross-medial formats. He lives in Düsseldorf und Wuppertal.

SAB | Sven-Anwar Bibi	Designer; teaches product design as a guest professor at the Free University in Bolzano, Italy; his main focus is in the field of industrial design; he designs exhibition concepts and works as an author and journalist. He lives in Bad Tölz and Bolzano.
SB | Stella Böß	Assistant Professor in the field of user research at the Delft Technical University; previously taught at Staffordshire University; consults businesses on product design and user research. She lives in Rotterdam.
SBA | Stuart Bailey	Graphic designer, editor, writer, and co-founder of the journal *Dot Dot Dot;* has worked on a broad range of projects including theater and performance, as well as a publishing imprint workshop intended to model a "Just-In-Time" economy of print production. He lives and works in New York and Los Angeles.
SG | Simon Grand	Economist and entrepreneur; founder and academic director of RISE Management Research at the University of St. Gallen; academic staff member at the Institute for Research in Design and Art at the Academy of Art and Design University of Applied Sciences Northwest Switzerland in Basel. Works in the fields of management and organization theory, free enterprises and innovation, corporate identity and strategic design. He lives near Zurich.
SGU | Steven Guarnaccia	Chair of the Illustration Department at Parsons The New School for Design; author and illustrator of numerous books including *Black and White;* regular contributor to *BLAB!.* Previously art director of the "Op-Ed" page of the *New York Times.* Has illustrated for major magazines including *Abitare,* the *New York Times Magazine,* and *Rolling Stone,* and created artwork for clients including Disney Cruise Lines and the Museum of Modern Art. He lives in New York.
SH | Susanne Haslinger	Freelance information designer; has worked for over ten years for book publishers in Austria and Germany. Lectures and holds workshops on gender-sensitive design and marketing and social design at design academies and universities. She lives in Berlin.
SIB | Silke Becker	PR consultant in the fields of design, art, and architecture; in collaboration with Judith Mair published *Fake for Real—Über die private und politische Taktik des So-tun-als-ob* (Fake for Real—on the private and political tactics of faking it) (Frankfurt/Main, Campus 2005); writes for *Kunstzeitung* and other publications. She lives in Cologne.
SP | Scott Pobiner	Assistant Professor in the Department of Design and Management at Parsons The New School for Design. Research interests include the development and implementation of new applications for interactive media, the effects of the introduction of new media on interpersonal communication and interaction, and the integration of display and interaction technologies in learning environments. He lives in New York.

STS | Stefan Stocker

Graduate industrial designer and managing co-owner of :echtform—Industrie-design & Beratung; oversees and realizes diverse design productions; recipient of several design prizes and patents; lectures and publishes widely. He lives in Rösrath.

SY | Susan Yelavich

Assistant Professor in the Art and Design Studies Department at Parsons The New School for Design; independent curator and writer; regular columnist for *I.D. Magazine;* contributing editor to *Patek Philippe International Magazine.* Publications include *Pentagram/Profile, Inside Design Now, Design for Life, The Edge of the Millennium, Product and Communication Design*, and the forthcoming *Contemporary World Interiors*. Specializes in twentieth-century and contemporary design and architecture. She lives in New York.

TB | Tevfik Balcioglu

Founding Dean of the Department of Fine Arts and Design at Izmir University of Economics in Turkey; teaches at the Middle East Technical University, Goldsmith College, and at Kent Institute of Art and Design; founder of the Turkish Design History Society; member of the Institute for Learning Technologies and the European Academy of Design. He lives in Izmir.

TBY | Ted Byfield

Associate Chair of Communication Design and Technology at Parsons the New School for Design; co-moderator of "nettime" mailing list; co-editor of ICANN Watch; co-edited README! (Autonomedia, 1999) and NKPVI (MGLC, 2001). He lives in New York.

TE | Thomas Edelmann

Staff member at *Architektur & Wohnen* as well as at the magazine *form;* freelance journalist; member of the board of the Deutsche Gesellschaft für Designtheorie und -forschung (DGTF) (German society of design theory and research); author of *Tara—Armatur und Archetypus* (Basel, Birkhäuser 2003). He lives in Hamburg.

TF | Thomas Friedrich

Professor of Design Theory and Philosophy; head of the Institute for Design in the design department at Mannheim University of Applied Sciences; founding member of the Deutsche Gesellschaft für Designtheorie und -forschung (DGTF) (German society of design theory and research); appointed member of the Freie Akademie der Künste (Free academy of the arts) Mannheim; head of the design section of the German Society of Semiotics; editor of the *Zeitschrift für kritische Theorie.* He lives in Mannheim und Würzburg.

TG | Tanja Godlewsky

Designer; co-founder of FRAM; has worked on several award-winning projects (reddot, coredesign, ADC). She lives in Cologne.

TK | Tobias Kuhn

Works in Cologne, Zurich, and Basel as a freelance designer in the field of interiors and graphics; author of *Das Zippo* (The zippo) (Frankfurt am Main, from 1999); developer of book concepts. He lives in Cologne and Winterthur.

TM | Tim Marshall

Is the editor of this book.

TR | Terry Rosenberg	Head of Design at Goldsmiths; practicing artist and design theorist. His research centers on the "representation of ideas" and "ideation through representation." Lectures at a number of institutions including the Architectural Association and The Royal College of Art. Recently completed a research project involving networked technology situated in the urban fabric; currently working on an interactive co-innovation environment and a series of scopic objects. He lives near London.
TW | Thomas Wagner	Author, philosopher, Honorary Professor of Art History and Art Criticism at the Academy of Visual Arts in Nuremberg; editor of visual arts and design section of the *Frankfurter Allgemeine Zeitung*. He lives in Heppenheim.
TWH | Tony Whitfield	Furniture designer and writer; chair of the Product Design Department at Parsons New School for Design; president and principle designer, Red Wing & Chambers; published in *Interiors, Essence, Interior Magazine*, Metropolis, and the *New York Times*, among others. His works have been exhibited at the International Contemporary Furniture Fair and other exhibitions. He lives in New York.
TWM | Timothy de Waal Malefyt	Vice President, Director of Cultural Discoveries at BBDO advertising; Adjunct Professor at Parsons The New School for Design; co-editor of *Advertising Cultures* (2003) from Berg publishers. Recipient of Fulbright and National Science Foundation Research Grants to study flamenco in Spain; widely quoted in *Business Week,* the *New York Times,* and *USA Today.* He lives in New York.
UB | Uta Brandes	Professor of Gender and Design as well as of Qualitative Design Research at the Cologne International School of Design (KISD; chairperson of the Deutschen Gesellschaft für Designtheorie und -forschung (DGTF) (German society of design theory and research); author of numerous books including (with S. Stich and M. Wender): *Die verwandelten Dinge* (The changing things) (Basel, Birkhäuser 2008). She lives in Cologne.
VA | Volker Albus	Professor of Product Design at the Karlsruhe School of Design; architect and designer; curator of exhibitions held at various museums and galleries including the Centre Georges Pompidou in Paris and the Louisiana Museum of Modern Art in Denmark; author, publisher, and editor of numerous books and texts. He lives in Frankfurt am Main.
VM | Victoria Marshall	Landscape architect and urban designer; founder of TILL (tilldesign.com), a Hoboken-based landscape-architecture practice dealing with permanent and temporary public open space, water management, and green roof systems. Taught at the University of Pennsylvania School of Design, Harvard GSD, Columbia GSAPP, and The University of Toronto ALD. Her research on Patch Dynamics informs her practice and is part of a forthcoming book and atlas. She lives in Hoboken, N.J.

VR | Vyjayanthi Rao

Assistant Professor of Anthropology at The New School for Social Research; research associate and co-director of Partners for Urban Knowledge, Action, and Research (PUKAR), based in Mumbai, India. She studies anthropology and ethnography of South Asia; forced migration, displacement, and citizenship in postcolonial societies; trauma, catastrophe, and memory; and urban change through extended fieldwork in Mumbai. She lives in New York.

WB | William Bevington

Executive Director of PIIM (Parsons Institute for Information Mapping), an independent research lab of The New School. He has taught Typography, Information Design, and multiple courses dealing with 2D and 3D design for over twenty-five years at such colleges as The Cooper Union, Parsons The New School for Design, and Columbia University. He lives in New York.

WJ | Wolfgang Jonas

Professor of System Design at University of Kassel. Publications on design include *Design—System—Theorie: Überlegungen zu einem systemtheoretischen Modell von Designtheorie* (Design—System—Theory: Reflections on a system theoretical model of design theory) (Essen, Die blaue Eule 1994) and *Mind the gap!—on knowing and not-knowing in Design* (Bremen, Hauschild 2004). He lives in Kassel and Berlin.

The cover design was realised using effect pigment
Iriodin® 123 Bright Luster Satin produced by Merck KGaA.

Design Concept BIRD: Christian Riis Ruggaber, Formal
Satz: Bertschi & Messmer AG, Basel
Typefaces: Akkurat, Arnhem

Editorial assistance: Angela Marshall, Jen Rhee
Copy editing: Ingrid Bell
Translation from German into English:
Laura Bruce, Steven Lindberg

Library of Congress Control Number: 2007939897

Bibliographic information published
by the Deutsche Nationalbibliothek
The Deutsche Nationalbibliothek lists this publication in
the Deutsche Nationalbibliografie; detailed bibliographic
data are available on the Internet at http://dnb.ddb.de.

© 2008 Birkhäuser Verlag AG
Basel · Boston · Berlin
P.O. Box 133, CH-4010 Basel, Switzerland
Part of Springer Science+Business Media

Also available:
German edition (ISBN: 978-3-7643-7738-0)

Printed on acid-free paper produced from chlorine-free pulp.
TCF ∞

Printed in Germany

ISBN: 978-3-7643-7739-7

987654321

www.birkhauser.ch

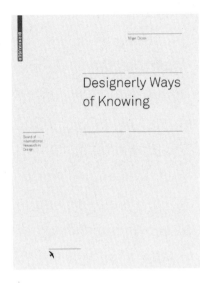

Designerly Ways of Knowing

The concept 'designerly ways of knowing' emerged in the late 1970s alongside new approaches in design education. Professor Nigel Cross, a respected design researcher, first articulated this idea in his paper 'Designerly Ways of Knowing' published in 1982. This book is a unique insight into an expanding discipline area with important implications for design research, education and practice.

This book traces the development of a research interest in articulating and understanding the idea that designers have and use 'designerly' ways of knowing and thinking. The following topics are covered: nature and nurture of design ability; creative cognition in design; natural intelligence of design; design discipline versus design science; expertise in design.

As a timeline of scholarship and research and a resource for understanding how designers think and work, this book will interest researchers, teachers and students of industrial and product design, design practitioners, and design managers.

Nigel Cross
In cooperation with the Board of
International Research in Design, BIRD
141 pp. 32 b/w ills.
16.8 x 22.4 cm
Softcover
ISBN 978-3-7643-8484-5